# BENCH AND BAR

OF

# WEST VIRGINIA

EDITED BY

GEO. W. ATKINSON, LL.B., LL.D.

Of the West Virginia Bar

---

"I hold every man a debtor to his profession; from the which as men of course do seek to receive countenance and profit, so ought they of duty to endeavor themselves by way of amends to be a help and ornament thereunto."—*Lord Bacon*

---

THE LAWBOOK EXCHANGE, LTD.

Clark, New Jersey

2008

ISBN-13: 978-1-58477-898-1
ISBN-10: 1-58477-898-9

*The quality of this reprint is equivalent to the quality of the original work.*

**THE LAWBOOK EXCHANGE, LTD.**
33 Terminal Avenue
Clark, New Jersey 07066-1321

*Please see our website for a selection of our other publications and fine facsimile reprints of classic works of legal history:*
www.lawbookexchange.com

**Library of Congress Cataloging-in-Publication Data**

Bench and bar of West Virginia / edited by Geo. W. Atkinson.
p. cm.
Originally published: Charleston, W.V. : Virginia Law Book Co.,1919.
ISBN-13: 978-1-58477-898-1 (cloth : alk. paper)
ISBN-10: 1-58477-898-9 (cloth : alk. paper)
1. Lawyers--West Virginia. 2. West Virginia--Biography. I. Atkinson, Geo. W. (George Wesley), 1845-1925.
KF354.W4A7 2008
349.754092'2--dc22
[B] 2008009282

*Printed in the United States of America on acid-free paper*

# BENCH AND BAR

OF

# WEST VIRGINIA

EDITED BY

GEO. W. ATKINSON, LL.B., LL.D.

Of the West Virginia Bar

---

"I hold every man a debtor to his profession; from the which as men of course do seek to receive countenance and profit, so ought they of duty to endeavor themselves by way of amends to be a help and ornament thereunto."—*Lord Bacon*

---

1919

VIRGINIAN LAW BOOK COMPANY

Charleston, W. Va.

Printing and Binding by
J. B. LYON COMPANY
Albany, N. Y.

# PREFACE.

For several years past, the State Bar Association has had in mind the publication of one or more volumes of Biographical Sketches of the distinguished deceased members of the profession in the State of West Virginia.

Preliminary to entering upon the undertaking, however, the Secretary of the Association in 1914 was directed to communicate with the members of the same in the different Counties of the State, to secure, as nearly as possible, their wishes as to the availability of the enterprise. Only a comparatively few responses were received to his inquiry, which, to say the least, was anything but encouraging. At the 1915 annual meeting of the Association it was decided to continue the Special Committee on "Bench and Bar" with instructions to proceed with the work, provided a sufficient number of subscribers for the proposed volume were secured, in advance, to meet the expenses of the publication. This test was made by the Committee, and not being satisfied with the results of its investigations, in compliance with both the letter and spirit of the resolution of the Association, it was deemed best to abondon the enterprise.

It is apparent, therefore, that the living members of a profession care but little for those *"who have crossed the divide"*; consequently the editor herein decided to publish this volume principally of members of the profession *who are still in the flesh,* wholly upon his own individual responsibility. However, he desires it explicitly to be understood that this is, in no respect, an advertising scheme where space in this volume can be secured at a certain amount of cash *per page.* It is, therefore, a publication upon a legitimate basis, and no member of the profession has received mention herein, unless he was believed to be worthy of such recognition. The editor, therefore, presents this volume of THE BENCH AND BAR of West Virginia with the firm belief that it will be favorably received by the members of the profession throughout the State.

We feel that our State Association acted wisely in inspiring a publication of this character, because each passing year renders it more difficult to procure the facts from which to prepare biographies, even of living members of the profession. Lamartine says, "History is neither more nor less than biography on a large scale," and Carlyle adds that "Biography is the only true history."

A great writer has said that biography and geography are the eyes of history. Biography is by nature the most universally profitable, universally pleasant of all things, especially biography of distinguished men, because the biographer finds his inspiration in a really worthy subject; and the reader is entertained as well as profited by studying the personal histories of distinguished individuals. Two thousand years ago Julius Caesar wrote his autobiography in his Commentaries. A thousand years before, Homer gave to the world the biographies of Achilles and Ulysses in the Iliad and Odyssey. At a period still more remote by several centuries, Moses sketched the lives of Adam and Noah and Abraham and Tubal Cain. Ever since the Book of Genesis was composed by the great Hebrew leader and law-giver, biography has constituted an essential part of history. Thomas Carlyle said: "For, as I take it, universal history, the history of what man has accomplished in this world, is at bottom the history of great men who have worked here." Macaulay asserts that biography is properly a department of history, and that it should not be a history of the kings solely, but of the common people also.

The difficulties in the way of achieving eminence in any calling are commensurate with its character. The law is no exception, and, as a prefession, ranks among the noblest. Law has to do with all the varied relations of man. It has been aptly said: "How noble the work, how great the responsibility, how sacred the trust committed to the lawyers! His it is rightly to comprehend, fairly to adjust and justly to administer that which secures man in the enjoyment of life, liberty and the pursuit of happiness; but only when thus considered is there thrown around the profession of the law that dignity, infused into it that moral force, which alone can inspire with an adequate and just conception of his duties and responsibilities of the one who aspires to a place in its rank. The true lawyer, therefore, sees in his profession a noble science, worthy of his manliest effort, and he it is, who, bringing to it a mind cultured and richly stored with profound and varied learning, can be to it an ornament, and in his life reflect that honor which to the true lawyer it cannot fail to impart. To attain the highest excellence, the lawyer must possess the most varied and ofttimes opposite qualities. With understanding there must be combined discernment. Learned in the subtleties of legal lore, he must also know men, and have tact to deal with them. He must be a student, and at the same time be able to leave the solitude of study to adapt himself to the everyday doings of men; and he must also be able to command the respect of superiors at all times and upon all occasions."

The men who have distinguished the West Virginia Bar, and added to the fame of a commanding State, are men of steadfast purpose and undaunted courage, whose precept and example will serve as an inspiration for succeeding generations.

The leading aim in the preparation of these sketches has been to sum up the legal lifework of the best known and most prominent members of the Bar of West Virginia, into such compass as to give only main features, and avoiding all flattery, adulation and comparison of one with another, or of any one against the rest. Such as have achieved fame do not need special mention here to record that fact. By their own works alone shall they be known. By no other standard can one's real worth be properly gauged.

In preparing this volume the editor has sought faithfully to represent a fair proportion of the members of the legal fraternity of the State of West Virginia. The *data* have been secured by personally interviewing, as far as it was possible so to do, their immediate friends, and also by consulting public records. That the editors' work is faultless he does not assume; that it will meet with unqualified approval he dares not hope. He has, however, conscientiously performed his task, and with that knowledge, submits this volume to the intelligent judgment of a fair-minded, liberal and generous-hearted profession. If there be undervaluation or overvaluation of any lawyer or judge, it is attributable solely to want of information or to misinformation. On the whole, however, it is believed that the publication will prove acceptable to the members of that noble profession which has contributed so much to the honor and dignity of this great Commonwealth.

This volume, therefore, is respectfully submitted in the confidence that the careers of the members of the legal profession of West Virginia, herein described, will prove a potent factor in cheering and inspiring the efforts of coming generations. If this volume is generously received a second volume will be published, so that all worthy members of the profession may be properly represented.

We have deemed it important to include in this volume a brief history of the Origin and Growth of the Jurisprudence of Virginia, which we believe will be read with interest and, it is hoped with profit, by the members of the profession throughout the Commonwealth.

This book is incomplete, for the reason that it does not contain sketches of a considerable number of distinguished, successful lawyers in different sections of the State. Some of them regarded it as an advertising scheme, and frankly refused to furnish data from which a personal sketch could be prepared, whilst others, who were favorable to the enterprise waited for a convenient time to fill the blanks and return them to the editor, which "more convenient season" seemingly never came, although they were urged by personal letters that quick action was absolutely necessary to properly complete the enterprise, and thus make the book, what it was intended to be, a complete roster of the notable members of the Bench and Bar of West Virginia. We append a list of gentlemen, who deserve a place in the volume, because of merit and achievement in the profession, to whom several letters were written by the editor, urging favorable action on their part, and in addition many of them were also personally called upon for the purpose. In only an occasional instance was a direct refusal given to appear in the book but simply further time in which to furnish data for a sketch was asked by them, which data, however, was never sent in.

We, however, only mention a few of those left out, either from neglect or choice on their part: V. B. Archer, Judge J. M. Addleman, John P. Arbenz, John W. Arbuckle, J. Robert Anderson, Col. George C. Baker, J. F. Barron, A. M. Belcher, Louis Bennett, Jackson V. Blair, Judge Henry K. Black, Judge Linn Brannon, A. N. Breckenridge, George M. Beltzhoover, S. O. Boyce, B. H. Butcher, Harry P. Camden, John J. Coniff, Frank W. Clark, Judge Charles S. Dice, Thomas Ray Dille, M. K. Duty, E. B. Dyer, E. C. Eagle, G. R. E. Gilchrist, W. B. Gribble, Henry Gilmer, Judge W. S. Haymond, W. H. Hearne, John A. Howard, Nelson C. Hubbard, A. G. Hughes, W. T. Ice, W. W. Jackson, J. W. Kennedy, R. F. Kidd, John F. Laird, James R. Marcum, W. Scott Meredith, O. S. Marshall, Lace Marcum, J. W. McIntire, W. H. McGinnis, George J. McComas, Judge Frank Nesbitt, Elliott Northcott, Judge P. H. Napier, J. M. Payne, W. Dallas Payne, Walter Pendleton, T. N. Read, M. G. Sperry, Judge M. F. Stiles, Judge George C. Sturgiss, O. E. Swartz, E. L. Stone, James H. Strickling, William W. Scott, H. Roy Waugh, Stuart W. Walker, C. C. Watts, Judge John B. Wilkinson, and others.

THE EDITOR.

Charleston, West Virginia,
June, 1919.

# INTRODUCTION.

The biographies of the members of the Bar of the various States present in clear outline the political history of the country. The lives of the leading lawyers of America include the careers of twenty-one of the twenty-eight Presidents, at least seventy-five per cent of all the cabinet officers from Washington's administration to the present time, and the majority of the governors of the various states. This wide-reaching influence of the Bar makes a book, such as the one here presented, very truly a record of the achievement and progress of the State.

Political and personal liberty and a strong Bar go together. In America, England and France the leadership of the Bar is recognized. In the Anglo-Saxon nations the lawyers have always been the leaders in promoting freedom and democracy. Here again the lives of the lawyers of West Virginia are typical in containing the history of the growth of human and political liberty in the State from the time of its admission into the Union.

Few, if any, are as well qualified to prepare this book as is Judge Atkinson. Probably no living man has a wider acquaintance with the members of the West Virginia Bar, or has had greater opportunity or ability to judge accurately the work and influence of each of its members. His memory more than spans the life of the State, and his personal efforts and achievements have made a deep impress upon its history and development as well as upon its jurisprudence. A well-earned confidence in Judge Atkinson, and the belief that a record of the leaders of the Bar of West Virginia should be preserved, are expressed by the financial support and official approval of the project by the West Virginia Bar Association. The generosity, public spirit, and professional interest shown him in editing this volume are worthy of the unqualified gratitude and commendation of the Bench and Bar of the State.

HENRY CRAIG JONES,
*President West Virginia Bar Association.*

MORGANTOWN, June 1, 1919.

# LIST OF BIOGRAPHIES

# THE ORIGIN AND GROWTH OF THE JURISPRUDENCE OF THE TWO VIRGINIAS.

In the preparation of this article we claim no special originality for what we shall herein offer, because the work we have done is in the line of a compiler only. The books we have found most helpful are "Bruce's Institutional History of Virginia in the Seventeenth Century," "Minor's Institutes," Vol. IV, 3d Edition, "Henning's Statutes" and the records of some of the early counties, or shires, of the Jamestown Colony, which have materially aided us in our investigations.

The Cavaliers, who formed a settlement at Jamestown in 1607, brought with them from England its system of laws, social customs and religious doctrines. Their aim was to maintain, as far as possible, not only the spirit, but also the letter of the English laws. The edict of the King issued to them, after the formation of the Colony, was to adhere as closely as they could "to the common law of England, and the equity thereof." As early as 1631 the oath which each Colonial Justice of the Peace and Judge was required to take commanded him "to do justice as near as may be to the English laws;" and we find Governor Berkeley, in 1662, declaring that justice was administered in Virginia according to "the laws of England as far as we are able to understand them." He stated further that "all things of fact were tried by jury," and *Magna Carta,* the Petition of Right, and the Writ of Habeas Corpus also formed a part of the fundamental ordinances of the Virginia Colony.

Bruce in his Virginia History of the Seventeenth Century states that, inasmuch as all the acts of the General Assembly had to receive the King's assent before they finally became laws, that assent made valid even those acts which were repugnant to the ordinances of England; therefore, the conclusive test was whether this assent had or had not been given. When, in the commissions of the Governors and the judges of the county courts it was declared that they were to perform the duties of their respective offices in harmony with the "known laws of England and the laws and customs of Virginia," it was simply intended, so far as the laws, as distinguished from the customs of Virginia were involved, to enforce only such enactments as had received the royal approval; and if that approval had been refused it was a ground of no concern whether or not these enactments were in conflict with the English statutory or common law. The continual usage, however, up to 1684, was according to the laws and usages of Virginia, and all the precedents in the several courts, both civil and criminal, whereof there are many precedents.* The successive Kings seem to have respected strictly even mere custom unless supposed to be inimical to the royal prerogative; in which case custom was overridden.

Six different courts constituted the judicial system, viz., the Magistrate's Court, the Parish Court, the County Court, the General Court, the General Assembly and the Court of Admiralty. Also a Court of Chancery was maintained for a few years, but was abolished by the English Government as unnecessary. Bruce further states that there was no place to be found in which justice more speedy or at a smaller charge was to be obtained than in Virginia at this time; and what was true of this peroid was also true of every other after the meeting of the first General Assembly in 1619, the time from which the colony's history as a free and practically self-governing community really dates. The lowest and least important of these courts was the Magistrate's Court, the highest and most important was the General Court. In 1642 there was passed an act of Assembly authorizing the justices of the peace to try every case involving an amount not exceeding twenty shillings, or two hun-

* Letters of William Fitzhugh, June 10, 1684.

dred pounds of tobacco. The object this law had in view was twofold — first, to avoid the expense which, by a suit in the monthly court, would have been entailed on both parties by having to go a great distance and to lose much valuable time attending its sessions; and, secondly, to discourage unnecessary litigations in that court, where a dispute over twenty shillings would have absorbed as many hours and required the presence of as many costly witnesses as a dispute over a thousand pounds.

The Magistrate's Court was not confined exclusively to civil controversies, but also had jurisdiction over criminal acts. As early as 1656 a justice of the peace possessed the power to arrest and bind over any inveterate law-breaker.

But one Parish Court was in operation in the Colony which was created by an act of the Assembly in 1656, for Henrico and Charles City Counties only. It had concurrent jurisdiction with the County Courts and was established for the convenience of the residents of the two counties named, but it was discontinued before the end of the century, as it was found to be unnecessary.

The most important of these early courts to the people at large was the Monthly or County Court. It was created by an act of the General Assembly in 1618, and was the people's own court, as it was for nearly three hundred years thereafter, for the adjustment of petty legal disputes between citizens. The establishment of this legal tribunal, therefore, was in strict conformity with one of the most important rights guaranteed to all Englishmen by *Magna Carta* at Runnymede. The members of the court were chosen from "the most able, honest and judicious citizens" of the different counties. In the beginning the court did not exceed four members, but in 1628 the number was increased to eight and still later to ten justices of the peace. The office of a justice was looked upon as being so purely honorable that, following the English precedent, it carried no salary in the strict sense of the term; nor were there any perquisites growing out of the position approaching in importance those which made the office of councillor so valuable from a pecuniary point of view. The only remuneration at any time bestowed on the judges of the county bench by an act of the General Assembly was the thirty pounds of tobacco ordered under the provisions of a statute passed in 1681, to be paid towards the maintenance of these judges by every litigant in their respective courts who should fail to win his suit.*

These County Courts were extremely dignified tribunals, which insisted on maintaining strict decorum on the part of litigants and bystanders who attended them. They convened early in the mornings and continued their sessions until late in the afternoons and frequently into the nights. The justices were a plain county folk, who showed no respect for limited hours of toil and deliberation.

When these courts were established in 1619, their jurisdiction was confined to small or petty matters; but in the Act of 1623 their powers were extended to controversies not exceeding the value of one hundred pounds of tobacco, it being the common or basic currency of the realm. Five years later the limitation of their jurisdiction by a second act of the Assembly expressly prohibited them from deciding any question that placed either life or limb in jeopardy.† They were empowered to enter final judgment in all suits not exceeding five pounds sterling in value. They were also directed to inquire into petty crimes, to insure the safety of the people and to maintain peace.

The General Assembly in 1634 adopted ten pounds sterling as the general amount of the court's jurisdiction. Under this limitation if the suit decided involved more than ten pounds sterling the defeated litigant should be dissatisfied with the manner in which the judgment had been rendered, possessed the right to take an appeal to the General Court; but if the sum fell below that amount the judgment was to be conclusive. They were, first, to enforce the acts for the preservation of good government, and to punish everyone guilty of violating them; secondly,

* Henning's Statutes, Vol. I., 66.
† Henning's Statutes, Vol. I., 132.

to arrest all persons who threatened or actually assaulted any of the King's subjects; thirdly, to impanel juries who were to inquire into all manner of felonies, witchcraft, extortions and the like; fourthly, to examine witnesses, take depositions and decide suits between party litigants; fifthly, to carry out all orders of the General Court and proclamations of the Governor and Council, and to punish any one who disregarded them; and, finally, to require their clerk to make a permanent record in all matters of general controversy already determined.* In a general way, the County Court's jurisdiction resembled the combined jurisdictions of the principal courts of England, viz., the Chancery, King's Bench, Common Pleas, Exchequer, Admiralty and Ecclesiastical. The readiness of their response to every appeal made to them by the poor was one of the most remarkable and commendable of their many characteristics as a judicial body.

This court also sat as a Court of Probate, and the act of Assembly of 1645 provided that letters of administration should be granted by this court. Wills, however, had been approved in the County Courts prior to this act, as also had been the probating of wills by the General Court alone. One of the County Court's most original features was that it was a court of record for all kinds of land conveyances. All conveyances of real estate were required to be recorded at the county seat of each of the counties or shires, as a means of affording the people at large the fullest information as to the basis of title to all land situated in their respective counties. Mortgages were to be regarded as fraudulent unless they were recorded in the books of either the County or General Court.

Bruce, after citing Henning, Vol. I, 303, states that by the terms of an act passed in 1645 either party to a suit in a county court, no matter how large or how small the sum or values involved might be, possessed the right to call for the settlement of the controversy by the verdict

* Northampton County Records, 1689–98, p. 99.

of a jury. If, before the case came to an actual hearing the defendant should demand relief in equity, the case was to be stayed until the issue of the appeal to the Chancery Division of the Court was known; and should that issue be unfavorable to the defendant's side, the trial by jury was to be begun and pressed to a conclusion. If, on the other hand, the issue was favorable, the justices could enter a decree at once and dismiss the jury.* It would appear that, even after the jury had delivered its verdict, an appeal could be made to the chancery side of the Court. The General Court, which at the present time is the Supreme Court of Appeals of Virginia, was the first and highest tribunal for the administration of justice established by the English inhabitants of North America. Its pre-eminence, therefore, is increased by the fact that its membership, then as now, was composed of men who were the foremost of their times in ability, character, social rank, political standing and influence among their fellow citizens. Bruce states that the history of this court can be appropriately divided into two distinct periods — first, its history previous to 1619, when the Colony was held under established rule and was in an unsettled condition which extended its influence to the action of the court; and, second, its history after 1619, when the Colony had become a self-governing community and its affairs were regulated by its own acts of Assembly and the laws of England, a fact in its turn also reflected in the action of the court. During the first period the jurisdiction of the General Court was entirely original; during the second it was original and appellate. "When the government was first organized for Virginia the President and Council were invested with judicial as well as with political powers. They were particularly authorized to punish with death all persons convicted of rebellion, conspiracy, mutiny, sedition, murder, manslaughter, rape and adultery, but the grounds of the original accusation first had to be investigated by twelve impartial, sworn jurymen. There are

* Henning's Statutes, Vol. I., 303.

numerous instances of the exercise of these judicial powers in criminal cases at the very threshold of the Colony's history."*

Its sessions were usually held at Jamestown, the capital of the Colony, but it frequently met elsewhere, notably at Williamsburg. Its terms ordinarily continued through a single week, and its members consisted of the Governor and the entire body of men belonging to his Council. At first three composed a quorum, which was subsequently increased to five, and in 1631 a fine of forty shillings was levied against every member who failed to attend the sessions of the Court unless reasonable excuses were shown. However, it nowhere appears that any of the judges was ever fined for the neglect of duty.

As we have already stated, the jurisdiction of the General Court was both original and appellate, and its most important feature was its exclusive right to try all original cases for loss of life and limb. An early statute required that every criminal should be tried in the county wherein the offense was committed. In a very few years, however, this law, which was adopted for the immediate relief of the people, was repealed and the General Court was thereafter given exclusive jurisdiction of all extreme cases of crime.

An appeal to this tribunal from the County Courts was allowable when it was clearly shown that an unjust decision had been rendered and public justice had miscarried. However, by an act of the Assembly adopted in 1647 no appeal was allowable in civil cases unless the sum in dispute was equal in value to sixteen hundred pounds of tobacco, or its equivalent, which, at that time, was ten pounds sterling. In 1659 this limitation was removed in all the counties except Northampton, and at the same time it was provided that in case the appeal was overruled by the high court the appellant was required, in addition to the cost of the appeal, to pay to the appellee a sum in the way of damages equal to one-half of the amount in controversy. The Act

* Bruce's History, Vol. I., 647.

of 1661 removed the restriction on the right to appeal when a small amount or an object of small value was involved, on the ground that there "might be as great error in judgment of matters of small value as of the greatest." The appellant in such a case, however, was still required to give security that he would prosecute the cause; and also that, if cast in the suit in the General Court, he would, in the form of damages alone, pay the appellee fifty per cent of the sum in dispute.* A few years afterwards it was decided that an unconditional appeal would be allowed only in those cases involving values exceeding sixteen hundred pounds of tobacco, or ten pounds sterling.†

The principal officers of the Appellate Court were its clerk and Attorney-General. The latter was the chief legal adviser of the Governor and Council as well as the highest public prosecutor for the Crown in the Colony. His salary was twenty pounds sterling annually, in addition to the fees required to be paid to him by the litigants in appeal cases.

Under an act of the General Assembly adopted in 1642, an appeal might be taken to the General Assembly from the County Courts, and also from the General Court, should it be clearly shown that the Court in trying the same had failed to promote equity, or in cases where the Governor had sat as a judge on the circuit.‡ There, however, was seemingly no inhibition on the right of any citizen to appeal to the General Assembly touching any matter involving a general right. But later on this right was taken away by the action of the English Government, and the Burgesses never fully reconciled themselves to the change, because they regarded it as an encroachment upon their rights as members of the legislative body of the Crown in the Colony.

Bruce in his history of the Seventeenth Century, in discussing the Admiralty and Chancery Courts, says that

* Henning's Statutes, Vol. II, 65.
† Bruce's History, Vol. I, 683, 685.
‡ Henning's Statutes, Vol. I, 345.

" during the greater part of the seventeenth century all cases involving questions of admiralty were tried, not by a single court which possessed the exclusive right of inquiry in that field, but by both the County Court and the General Court. It would appear that the latter, in conformity with the character of its most important original jurisdiction, decided all admiralty causes in which the punishment to be inflicted consisted of the loss of life or limb. Such causes were principally those in which persons were brought up before it for having committed murder or a like offense on the high seas." Governor Berkeley in 1671 declared that there was no need of an admiralty court, " since not a single prize in the course of twenty-eight years had been brought into the waters of the Colony."* But in 1697 such a court was established in the Colony as a permanent part of its judicial system. Its officers consisted of judge, register, marshal and advocate, who, upon the recommendation of the Governor, were appointed by the Lord High Admiral of England. All of these officers were men of high standing and were citizens of the Colony.

The jurisdiction of this court " embraced not only all cases of piracy, privateering and violations of the navigation acts, but also all cases of unlawful conduct on the collectors' part in performing their duties; or of unlawful conduct which these collectors had detected on the part of other persons in relation to the taxes on exports. It also determined all controversies arising between master and mariner, whatever might be the subject of the dispute."

The only other court created in Virginia during the seventeenth century was the Court of Chancery, which, owing to the usurpations of its High Chancellor (Governor Howard) had existed only a short time and played but a small part in the judicial history of the period of its existence, when it was abolished by the General Assembly.

At various times it was suggested that a separate Court of Exchequer should be established in the Colony; but

---

* Bruce's History, Vol I, 396.

inasmuch as the duties of such a tribunal were fully embraced in the jurisdiction of the General Court it was never created.

From the foregoing statements it appears that Virginia is the mother of the Common Law Practice and Procedure in the New World, from which has spread into the different States of the Republic — except Louisiana — the *Lex Non Scripta,* which, in a restricted form, in conjunction with State statutory enactments, will ever remain the law for the government of the various Commonwealths of our common country. From *Magna Carta* to the present time the methods of enacting law and the succession of great exponents and expounders of the law are established and well known: Glanvill in the twelfth century and Bracton in the thirteenth were followed by Littleton in the fifteenth, by Coke in the seventeenth, by Blackstone in the eighteenth and by Kent in the nineteenth century.

The first Constitution of Virginia was adopted in May, 1776, and from that time the powers of the Convention ceased. Patrick Henry was elected the first Governor of the State June 29 of that year — the same day the Constitution was adopted. He was succeeded in 1779 by Thomas Jefferson, who resigned in June, 1781, and was succeeded by Thomas Nelson, junior, who resigned the same year and was succeeded by Benjamin Harrison, who continued in office until November 29, 1784, when Patrick Henry was again elected Chief Executive of the State. The Colonial Courts were thereafter continued, although changes from time to time were made by Constitutional conventions and by legislative enactments, yet for a long period of time the English system was not materially altered. The Convention of 1849 required members of the County Court to be chosen by popular election, and the Convention of 1869 changed the system so the court ceased

In the History of North America, published by Barrie at Philadelphia, Vol. 3, p. 90, speaking of the Virginia courts, he says the Spanish Ambassador, Gondomar, warned James II that the Virginia courts were a "seminary for a seditious parliament."

to be held by Justices of the Peace, and in all of the counties the court was presided over by a County Judge, who was chosen from the legal profession. This tribunal, therefore, for more than two centuries was a peculiar feature in the distribution of the judicial power in Virginia; and until 1870 it maintained a prominent place in the domestic polity of the Commonwealth.

From 1776 down to 1831 the administration of the jurisdictions of law and equity were wholly separate in Virginia, except in the County and Corporation Courts; the tribunals with that exception being as entirely distinct as they were in England. These two courts were at once courts of law and equity, yet the two jurisdictions were by no means blended, nor in any wise counfounded. At first, in the imitation of the English system, there existed but one Superior Court of Chancery in the State, which held its sessions in Richmond, and was known as the High Court of Chancery. In 1802 the State was divided into three districts, and a chancery court was provided for each district to hold sessions at Richmond, Williamsburg and Staunton. Subsequently the number was increased to nine, and courts were held, in addition to the three places above designated, at Norfolk, Fredericksburg, Lynchburg, Wytheville, Winchester and Clarksburg. Later on Lewisburg was added to the list. This system continued until 1831, when it yielded to that which has ever since been in force.*

In 1809 Superior Courts of Law were held by a single judge twice a year in every county and corporation; and in 1831 this system was followed substantially by the present organization, which commits common law and equity jurisdiction to the same judge, just as has long been practiced in the County and Corporation Courts, keeping separate jurisdictions, however, as distinct as if they had been administered by different judges. These courts were required to be held twice a year in every individual county

* Minor's Institutes, Vol. IV, 3d Ed., 271.

and corporation. In 1851 the name, but not the jurisdictions of these courts, was changed to Circuit Courts, and as such they are now held throughout the State.

Under the Constitution of 1904 the following courts only are now in existence, viz.:

Magistrates' courts, with jurisdiction in all misdemeanors, with right of appeal to the Circuit Courts, and civil jurisdiction up to $100, with similar right of appeal. Recently the Legislature increased the amount to $300.

Circuit Courts, which have general jurisdiction in all civil and criminal matters, law and equity, and which are held for the various counties in the State by a judge elected by the Legislature. There are now 31 Circuit Courts in the Commonwealth of Virginia.

Corporation Courts, which have the same jurisdiction as the Circuit Courts, except they are confined to the larger cities. There are, at this time, 18 such courts in Virginia.

The cities of Norfolk, Richmond and Roanoke each has a Court of Chancery, presided over by a judge elected, as all other judges are in the State, by the Legislature. And finally, the court of last resort — the Supreme Court of Appeals — of five judges, which, as its name implies, has state-wide jurisdiction over all appeal cases.

When West Virginia became a separate State in 1863 the judicial and legal system of Virginia was practically adopted by the new State, except the County Court for the trial of civil and criminal causes, which tribunal gave way to township Boards of Supervisors, whose jurisdiction was limited solely to the management of the fiscal affairs of the different counties; but under the Constitution of 1872 the supervisor system was changed back to the old plan of County Courts, which are still in vogue. These courts, however, are limited in their jurisdiction to the appointment of administrators and executors, the probating of wills, the recording of deeds, etc., and the management of the fiscal affairs of the various counties. In some of the counties, however, county business is controlled by Boards of Commissioners and not by County Courts, except in name and in the manner above stated. We still retain the office of Justice of the Peace, who has jurisdiction in criminal procedure, and also in civil causes in amounts not exceeding $300, with the right of appeal to the Intermediate and Circuit Courts. We have Circuit Courts throughout the State with identically the same jurisdiction as those in Virginia. In a few of the counties Criminal Courts have been created by the Legislature to hear and dispose of criminal cases only. In Kanawha and Marion Counties Intermediate Courts were established to relieve the Circuit Courts of those counties from the congestion brought about mainly by the numerous appeals to them from Magisterial Courts. In 1914 the Common Pleas Court of Kanawha County was created by an act of the Legislature, whose jurisdiction is substantially concurrent with the Circuit Court of that county. And finally, West Virginia, the same as the Mother State, has its Supreme Court of Appeals, composed of five judges, although there were only three when the State was created, which number was increased to four by the Constitution of 1872. The amendment providing for a fifth judge was adopted in 1902. As its name implies, this court is the final arbiter in both law and equity in all appeals from the Circuit Courts.

We have, therefore, in Virginia and West Virginia today practically the same system of jurisprudence that was in existence three hundred years ago. Whilst law is now a more exact science than it was in the seventeenth century, yet its basic principles, now as then, are the same, and will doubtless so continue to be through the coming centuries.

# BIOGRAPHIES

## Hon. John J. Davis

Among the many able, representative lawyers of the West Virginia Bar, the subject of this sketch, for more than a half century, stood forth as a tall cedar on a mountain crest. Tall in stature, he was also tall in his profession, and in everything that goes to distinguish one as a man of mark among his fellowmen. Although he lived to pass his eightieth milestone, it can be truthfully said of him, that he wronged no man, living or dead, and his personal character was as spotless as a maiden's, and as unsullied as a ray of light. He was a man of positive convictions on all important questions, but he was so fair and reasonable in all his contentions that no fair-minded man could be offended over his utterances. On the other hand, he invariably conceded the right of all adversaries to defend their convictions of right and duty. His language was as chaste as violets, as was his long life of a little more than four score years. No one ever heard an unchaste expression fall from his lips on any occasion, or at any time. He was ever and at all times a gentleman, and more than that, a Christian in the truest sense of the word. His entire life was one of unpretentious gentleness, and as modestly as he had lived through a long and successful life, his sun went down calmly, and "he fell on sleep."

Mr. Davis was born in Harrison County, Virginia, May 5, 1835, and died March 19, 1916, in the City of Clarksburg, near the spot where he first saw the light, where his entire life was spent. He received his preparatory education at the old Northwestern Virginia Academy in Clarksburg. His professional training was obtained at the law school of Judge John W. Brockenbrough, which afterwards became the law department of Washington & Lee University at Lexington, Virginia. He never sought a public office and those filled by him were practically forced upon him. His public services consisted of membership in the Virginia House of Delegates, to which he was elected in 1861; member of the Second West Virginia Convention, which met in 1861, and which was instrumental in organizing the State of West Virginia; member of the West Virginia Legislature, to which he was elected in 1870; member of the Forty-second and Forty-third Congresses of the United States; Presidential Elector in 1865 and again in 1885; member of the Board of Visitors of the West Point Military Academy; Regent of the State University of West Virginia, and director of the Hospital for the Insane at Weston.

Possessing an incisive intellect and a profoundly logical mind, Mr. Davis speedily won and for more than a half century held a position of pre-eminence as a lawyer. He did not specialize in any particular branch of the law or line of practice, but possessed a wide general knowledge and thorough grasp of the fundamentals of the profession, and was always a safe counsellor. As an advocate he attained and held a position of pre-eminence at the Bar and in the forum of West Virginia, freely recognized by all of his compeers.

He was not only prominent in the law and in religious activities, but he held a high position in the Masonic Order, and was honored and loved by his brethren throughout the State. While, as we have already stated, he was not only a really eminent lawyer, his fame as a man and a citizen will outlive that achieved in his professional capacity. His literary attainments were marvelous. Books were his constant and loved companions, and in spite of the labors of a busy life, he found time to read and study works on literature, history, science and every branch of human knowledge, and indeed in his old age reading was with him an abiding passion. He was a man of deep convictions and possessed a profound knowledge of the political and governmental questions which had to be met and settled by the government of the United States, the duration of which antedates by less than half a century the date of his birth. He never for a moment surrendered or compromised a conviction, on the many and multifarious matters which came before the public during his long career. He exerted a great influence upon his fellow men in those affairs, which influence widened as the years went by, and which is destined to make for righteousness in public affairs for many years to come. He felt deeply the obligations resting upon him as a man and a citizen, and his life was a continuous manifestation of his sincere convictions; and we may truthfully say of him what the Regent Merton said over the grave of John Knox, "He never feared the face of mortal man."

## Judge David McComas

Among the early distinguished Judges of what was then known as the Kanawha Circuit, which consisted of more than a dozen counties, extending from Wythe County, Virginia, to Wood County, West Virginia, was the subject of this brief notice. He was the son of General Elisha McComas, and was born in Wythe County, Virginia, in 1795, and after a brilliant career as a lawyer and jurist he died in Giles County, Virginia, in 1864. He was a Whig, although he never had much to do with politics. He, however, served one term in the Senate of Virginia from the Kanawha Senatorial District. While a Circuit Judge, his home was on Virginia Street, in Charleston, not far from where the office of the "Charleston Daily Mail" is now published.

Judge McComas married a Miss French, but they were never blessed with any offspring. The Judge is remembered by many of the older citizens of Charleston as an erudite lawyer, and a jurist of great ability. He was also a man of high grade integrity, and was the soul of honor; and is still referred to as one of the able jurists, who was an honor to the judiciary of the Western portion of Virginia, more than sixty years ago.

HON. JOHN J. DAVIS

## Hon. Charles James Faulkner

The subject of this brief memorial was one of the great lawyers and most distinguished statesmen of the States of Virginia and West Virginia. He was born at Martinsburg, Virginia, in 1806, and died in the city of his nativity, November 1, 1884. He was a man of great learning and broad views, covering all branches of literature, science, history, law and statesmanship. For a half century or more, he was considered generally by the people of Virginia, as one of the greatest lawyers of the entire South. He was originally a member of the Whig Party, but in 1852 he felt that his party had abandoned its principles, and he became a Democrat and supported Franklin Pierce for the Presidency of the Republic. For eight years prior to the Civil War he represented what is now known in West Virginia as the " Eastern Pan-handle " of the State, in the Congress of the United States. However, before he entered politics he studied law, was admitted to the Bar and had made himself a distinguished member of the legal profession, and was heralded as such, not only throughout Virginia, but in many other portions of the South. In Congress he took an active part in the public debates on important questions that arose in legislation, and became generally known as a Representative far above the average statesmen of that period. When James Buchanan became President, he selected Mr. Faulkner, toward the end of his term, as the Ambassador of the United States to Paris, France. He entered upon the duties of this exalted station March 4, 1860, and discharged its onerous duties with discretion and statesmanlike ability, until the change of administration when he was recalled, and consequently returned to his native country. Many political charges were preferred against Mr. Faulkner, but none of them affecting his integrity and honor was sustained, and he emerged from all the attacks absolutely unsullied and unstained.

He was a man of the highest conceptions of honor, dignity and character during his entire life, and exerted a wide influence for the higher conceptions of life and duty among all the people who had the honor of his acquaintance.

After his stay of something more than a year in France, he returned to his native State, and remained in comparative retirement until the close of the Civil War, studying national and international questions at the home of his daughter in Appomattox County. When all of the storm-clouds of war had blown away, he returned to his home at Martinsburg, Berkeley County, and resumed the practice of law. The people, however, would not allow him to remain in retirement, and he accordingly was elected a member of the State Constitutional Convention of 1872 to frame a new Constitution for West Virginia, and was its temporary president. He was elected a member of Congress from the Second Congressional District, and served two years from March 4, 1875, to March 4, 1877, and declined a re-election. This was his last public office. He had a large estate; was President of the Agricultural Association of Berkeley County, and President of the Martinsburg and Potomac Railroad Company up to the time of his death. He had a very large law practice, chiefly in the Supreme Court of the United States, the Supreme Court of Appeals of West Virginia, and the Judicial Circuit in which he resided.

He was one of the most courteous, knightly gentlemen the writer ever knew, and bore the confidence and respect of every person who knew him personally. He had a family of several children — two of his sons were distinguished Circuit Court Judges of the State, and one of them, Charles James Faulkner, Jr., was twelve years a Senator in Congress from West Virginia, and has a large corporation practice in the City of Washington, D. C., and is eminent in the profession.

## Hon. Charles James Faulkner, Jr., LL.B.

The name of Faulkner is inseparably interwoven with the history of the two Virginias, from Major James Faulkner, who was prominent as a brave officer in the War of 1812, down to the present generation. The elder Charles James Faulkner, who is sketched in another part of this volume, was a noted lawyer and statesman in his day, and his son, the subject of this sketch, the namesake of his distinguished father, who also bears a high rank as a lawyer, jurist and statesman in his native State. He was born in Berkeley County, Virginia (now West Virginia), September 21, 1847, and during the time his father was Ambassador to France, he attended the best schools of France and Switzerland. On his return to the United States in August, 1861, he entered the Virginia Military Institute at Lexington to round out his education. In 1862 he, with other students of that noted school, volunteered in the Confederate Army, and remained until the close of the War in 1865. His record as a soldier is an enviable one, to which his friends "point with pride," as he had participated in a number of hotly contested battles. After the close of hostilities between the States, he returned to his home at Martinsburg, began the study of law under the direction of his father; later he entered the law department of the University of Virginia at Charlottesville, and graduated therefrom as a Bachelor of Laws, in the class of 1868, and was admitted to the Bar in September of that year. Being thoroughly educated in the fundamental principles of the law, and possessing many natural gifts, especially in public speaking, he soon took front rank among the able lawyers of the Berkeley County Bar.

In 1880, he was elected Judge of the Thirteenth Judicial Circuit, and was serving ably and satisfactorily in that responsible position, when he was elected to the United States Senate by the Legislature of West Virginia, without being a candidate. He entered upon the duties of that exalted position March 4, 1887. After serving the full term of six years, he was re-elected for a second term. During his twelve years in the National Legislature his record was both honorable and able. After retiring from the

Senate, Judge Faulkner resumed the practice of his profession, with offices at Martinsburg, West Virginia, and Washington, D. C. He has specialized in corporation laws, and is, at this time, Attorney for a large number of railroads and other large corporations of different sections of the United States.

Senator Faulkner has been twice married, and resides, during the summer seasons, at the old Faulkner homestead in the City of Martinsburg, and the winter months are spent in the City of Washington. He is a thorough lawyer, and possesses superior natural abilities. He has applied himself to the study of his profession with all the vigor and assiduity which a love for the law inspires, and his success is the sure reward of ability and merit.

Senator Faulkner is a member of the Protestant Episcopal Church, and is also a prominent Freemason, having served a term as Grand Master of the Most Worshipful Grand Lodge of West Virginia.

## Judge Mathew Dunbar

We very much regret that the immediate relatives of this eminent lawyer and jurist (Judge Dunbar) have, themselves, passed into the great beyond, which places it beyond our power to give the merest outline of his distinguished career. He was born in Monroe County, Virginia, in 1781. It is said he was well educated, and came to Kanawha County, when he was a young man, and read law in the office of James Wilson, who was a prominent member of the Charleston Bar, in the early part of the nineteenth century. He was known as a great student, and was not long in mastering the legal text books upon which he had to be examined. He was admitted to the Charleston Bar in 1818. He was not long, because of his studious habits and close attention to business, in attaining a high rank as a lawyer, among his associates. He is still by the older citizens of Kanawha County, kindly remembered, both as a lawyer and a judge of sterling integrity and honor.

He was elected a member of the Virginia Legislature, first, in 1823, and again in 1829–30. He was elected Prosecuting Attorney of Kanawha County in 1853, and afterwards served a term as Circuit Judge. To all of these offices he gave his strict attention, and acquitted himself with honor and ability. He was a member of the Presbyterian Church, and died in 1859.

## Judge Thomas C. Green

Judge John W. Green, father of the subject of this brief memoir, entered upon his duties of Judge of the Supreme Court of Appeals of Virginia, October 11, 1822, when his son Thomas was two years of age, who was born at Fredericksburg, November 5, 1820. Shortly, thereafter, the family moved to Culpeper County, where the son grew to manhood and was carefully and

JUDGE THOMAS C. GREEN

thoroughly educated. He read law under the direction of his father, and in 1843 was admitted to the Virginia Bar, and located in Charlestown in Jefferson County, where he remained the greater part of his life. In 1861 he joined the Confederate army as a private soldier, serving two years in General Thomas J. (Stonewall) Jackson's brigade. He was then appointed Chief Collector of Virginia War Taxes, remaining in that position until the end of the war. At the close of hostilities he returned to Charlestown and entered, with great earnestness, upon the practice of his profession, in which he took a leading position. While in the Confederate army he served two terms in the Virginia Legislature. In 1876 he was appointed by Governor John J. Jacob a Justice on the Supreme Court of Appeals of West Virginia to fill the unexpired term of Judge James Paull, deceased, and in 1880 he was elected for the full term of twelve years as a member of that tribunal. He departed this life December 4, 1889, after having served most ably for fourteen years.

Judge Green was universally regarded as one of the most erudite, broad-minded lawyers and jurists of his generation. No judge on any bench ever gave to the important questions submitted to him more complete and exhaustive research and consideration. He traced the law, step by step, through the various windings, down to the date of his opinions, considering and referring to the numerous authorities, English and American, pro and con, bearing thereon. His opinions are in volumes 9 to 33, inclusive, of the West Virginia Reports. The writer never heard but one criticism made on Judge Green's work as a judge, and that was his opinions were too lengthy and too exhaustive. He seemingly could not stop without minutely considering every point in the case. Two cases deserve special attention, Radford v. Carwile, 13 W. Va. 572, on the rights of married women under West Virginia statutes, and Pegram v. Stortz, 31 W. Va. 222, on the question of damages. This is the longest opinion he ever wrote and covers 107 printed pages, and is quoted almost entire in the American and English Encyclopedia of Law. His opinions are widely quoted in the text books and reports of other States.

In the discharge of his official duties his industry was patient and indefatigable. He loved pure mathematics, which is plainly displayed in all his processes of reasoning. He knew nothing of the parties to any controversy that came before him for decision. Plaintiffs and defendants were to him as impersonal as the letters of an equation, and he applied himself to the solutions of the questions presented as if he were searching for an unknown quantity. Truth was ever the object of his search, and he followed it with an unerring judgment. When engaged in the investigation of a judicial question, he would become so completely absorbed in the train of his thoughts as to cause him to forget the demands of physical comforts and bodily health, and this, no doubt, shortened his days.

Judge Green could always be relied on with absolute confidence in those exigencies which require firmness and ability. No public clamor or fear of personal popularity could influence his conduct. Undemonstrative and apparently indifferent for the regard of others, he was nevertheless kind hearted and fond of conversation and the society of his friends. His nature was simplicity itself; confiding and loyal in his friendships, but firm and uncompromising in his convictions and duties.

Judge Green married Miss Agnes McDonald, a daughter of Colonel Angus McDonald, of Charlestown, shortly before the beginning of the war between the States, where he subsequently spent the greater portion of his life. They were both held in the highest esteem by the residents of that charming section of the "Mountain State."

Judge Green was a Democrat in his political affiliations, but was so constantly absorbed in the business of his profession that he took only a passing interest in the political affairs of the State and Nation.

## Judge James Henry Brown

One of the distinguished lawyers, statesmen and jurists of Virginia, before the State was divided, is the subject of this brief biographical sketch. He is of English ancestry, and was the son of Benjamin Brown, a native of Virginia; was born in Cabell County, Virginia, December 25, 1818. His mother was a native of North Carolina, and was the daughter of Major Nathaniel Scales. He was educated at Marietta College, Ohio, and Augusta College, Kentucky, and from the latter well known institution he graduated in the class of 1840. In person he was tall (a little more than six feet) and was always, even in later life, as erect as an Indian. He was also sinewy and active. Up almost to the period of his last illness his step was as elastic as a man of forty, or even less.

He read law under the direction of John Laidley, a prominent attorney of Cabell County, and in 1842, after two years of careful study of legal text books, he was admitted to membership of the Cabell County Bar, and promptly began the practice of his chosen profession. He was a natural orator, and it was not long until he took a leading rank as a superior advocate, and a forceful and effective trial lawyer. Desirous of a wider field of operations and better opportunities for development of his talents, he located at Charleston, Kanawha County, in 1848, where he spent the major portion of his life in the ardent practice of his profession. He was always regarded as a man of the highest sense of honor and probity; was thoroughly reliable in all his statements and dealings; was a hard student, and was a careful and honorable counselor. It is no wonder, therefore, that his clientele soon grew to large proportions. His practice was in both State and National courts, and covered all the branches of the law, and extended into all of the surrounding counties. He was universally regarded as an all round, able and successful lawyer.

Judge Brown, though a Democrat, took an active stand for the Union in 1860 and '61, and was one of the leaders in the formation of the new

Commonwealth of West Virginia; was a member of all the conventions looking to the building of the State; was elected a member of the Legislature of the Restored Government of Virginia, May 23, 1861, from Kanawha County, amid the turmoil of a divided county, and addressed many meetings when his hearers were armed for personal protection. He was an eloquent stump speaker and a fearless defender of his political faith. He became an ardent Republican and was a member of the Convention that framed the first Constitution of the State of West Virginia. In the winter of 1861 and '62 he was elected and commissioned Judge of the Eighteenth Judicial Circuit of Virginia. While acting in this capacity the records of his courts in several of the counties of his circuit, as fast as they were made, were captured and destroyed, and on several occasions he narrowly escaped the repeated efforts that were made to capture the Court. It is claimed, and we believe correctly, that no appeal from any of his decisions was ever taken to a higher court. As a judge he was courteous, firm and fearless.

May 28, 1863, he was elected an Associate Judge of the Supreme Court of Appeals of the new State of West Virginia. On this court he exhibited the same firm and wise qualities as revealed by him on the bench of the *nisi prius* court. He served with great acceptability until the close of his term. He was by nature and education fitted for the law. He carried to a high degree the power of convincing statement. His opinions are models of good English. His supreme desire was to be just, and nothing could swerve him from doing right, as he was able to see the right. When he retired from the bench he returned to active practice, and kept it up until a short time before his death, which occurred at his home in Charleston, October 28, 1900.

Judge Brown was twice a candidate for Congress, but his Congressional District, being strongly Democratic at that time, he was both times defeated, but he ran ahead of his ticket on both occasions. In 1882 he was elected a member of the Legislature of West Virginia, and took an active part in shaping the legislation of that session.

In 1844 he married Miss Louise Beuhring and reared a large family. One of his sons — James F. Brown — is one of the ablest lawyers of the entire State. Judge Brown was an ardent member of the Presbyterian Church, and for about half a century was a ruling elder of that denomination. However, in matters of religion, he favored the largest liberty of conscience. He at all times had the implicit confidence of all people who knew him, and he was for a-half century one of the best known men of the Great Kanawha Valley.

Judge Brown late in life, and many years after the death of his first wife, married the widow of the late Fayette A. Lovell, who was in life a member of the Kanawha County Bar, and she survived him several years. They had no offspring. She too passed into the "Great Beyond" a few years subsequent to his demise.

JUDGE JAMES H. BROWN

## Hon. John Harper Riley

The subject of this sketch, son of Robert and Elizabeth (Cleek) Riley, was born and reared on a farm in Jackson County, Virginia; as to the date, he informed the writer, that "He is advised he should not think himself old, nor tell his age, but just to keep on keepin' on," and this he is doing splendidly, because although he is past seventy he could readily pass for fifty-five or sixty. His father was a Whig, but at the demise of that party he became a Republican, and our subject followed in his footsteps, and has always been a Republican, but has never been an office-seeker. The father was a prominent man in his community; was County Assessor for a number of years and held other county offices of trust. John's elder brother was Clerk of the Circuit Court of Jackson County for a term of years, and our subject was a Deputy for him and also for his father. His education was limited to county and subscription schools, but he was ambitious and aspiring and consequently kept on reading and studying, thus storing his mind with the kind of knowledge that would be useful in after years. While employed in the Clerk's office he was advised by the Circuit Court Judge — R. S. Brown — to take up the study of law, which he did with earnestness and vigor, and while thus engaged he filled the offices of County Treasurer, and Justice of the Peace, the latter being in the direct line of his contemplated profession. In about two years he was able to stand an examination for admission to the Bar. After receiving his license as an attorney, which was signed by Judges Brown, Loomis and Hoge, he was admitted as a member of the Jackson County Bar in 1869. He formed a partnership with U. S. Flesher, who was at that time Prosecuting Attorney of the county, and thus became his Assistant. Mr. Flesher died the following August and Mr. Riley was appointed to fill the unexpired term. He was then elected Prosecuting Attorney for a full term and served with great acceptability and success. While discharging the functions of this office he became generally known in Jackson and adjoining counties as one of the best known attorneys in that section of the State, and his reputation was therefore fixed for the future.

Mr. Riley was elected to the West Virginia Legislature in 1876 and again in 1880, and served with distinction and efficiency. During the latter year he was chosen one of the two delegates at large from West Virginia to the National Republican Convention, which nominated James A. Garfield for President of the United States. He married Miss Melissa J. Harpold, of Jackson County, and they had four children — two sons and two daughters — three of whom are living and one son is deceased. In October, 1882, he removed his residence to Marietta, Ohio, mainly for the purpose of educating his children at Marietta College. In 1892 he was sent as a delegate to the Republican National Convention that renominated Benjamin Harrison for the Presidency. In 1896 he was elected a member of the State Senate of Ohio, and in 1911 he was elected a member of the Fourth Constitutional Convention of the State of Ohio. In these positions he served ably and honorably and to the entire satisfaction of his constituents.

For many years Mr. Riley has been an active and progressive member of the Masonic Fraternity, and before he moved to Marietta he received the highest honor the craft could confer upon him — that of Grand Master — and he never fails to attend its annual communications and actively participate in its deliberations. Since locating in Ohio he has engaged in agriculture, grazing and fruit raising, and has made quite a reputation as a real "granger" as well as a lawyer. He possesses large property holdings and through a long and useful life not a stain of dishonor has ever soiled his spotless character.

## Hon. Charles Wells Russell

Hon. Charles W. Russell was a distinguished man in Northwestern Virginia prior to the rebellion. He was a man of unusual brilliancy as well as the possessor of solid parts and great learning. He was distinguished both in law and in politics, and possessed almost unlimited influence among the people of his section of the State. He died just as his sun had reached its noon, and left an untarnished name as a heritage to his devoted family.

Mr. Russell was born at Sistersville, Tyler County, Virginia, July 19, 1818. During his earlier years he received a common school education, and as he was growing into manhood he went to Wheeling and became a student at Linsly Institute, and later finished his general education by graduating from Jefferson College at Cannonsburgh, Pennsylvania. He subsequently studied law in the office of the late Z. Jacob at Wheeling; and after being admitted to the bar practiced his profession in Wheeling, with unusual success, until the breaking out of the war in 1861. He then went South and served two, if not three, terms in the Virginia Legislature. He was also a member of the House of Representatives in both the "Provisional" and the "Permanent" Congress of the Southern Confederacy. In these Legislative and forensic bodies, as well as at the bar, his great powers as an orator and debator were demonstrated. In these particulars but few of the great Virginians of his time were his equal.

At the end of the war he went to Canada, where he remained until the Spring of 1866, when he settled in Baltimore, and resumed the practice of law. He was becoming well established as a leading attorney at that distinguished bar when he died, November 22, 1867, leaving a widow and three sons.

He married Margaret, daughter of the late Henry Moore of Wheeling, and had three sons, two of whom — Henry Moore Russell — who practiced law in the city of Wheeling, and became one of the leading lawyers of that section, and, as a matter of fact, of the entire State of West Virginia, who died before reaching the age of sixty, in the midst of his usefulness and success. The other son, Charles W. Russell, Jr., who spent many years as an attorney in the Judiciary Department at Washington, and for several years ably filled the office as an Assistant Attorney-General of the United States. He was also several years Minister of the United States at the capitol of Persia, and is at this time a resident of Washington, D. C. Henry M. Russell, Jr., son of the late Henry M. Russell, is now a successful lawyer in the city of Wheeling.

## Hon. John S. Carlile

Mr. Carlile was born at Winchester, Virginia, December 16, 1817. He was educated by his mother, who was a woman of high culture, until he was fourteen years of age. He then entered a dry goods store as salesman and clerk, remaining till his seventeenth year, when he commenced business for himself. At an early age, having a decided taste for the profession, he began the study of law, was admitted to the bar in 1840, settled at Beverly, Randolph County, and began practice. He was elected to the Senate of Virginia in 1847, and served until 1851. His associates were not long in finding in Mr. Carlile a man of untiring energy, a close student, a diligent legislator, and a ready and forceful debater. He took a leading rank in the Senate, which was filled with the ablest men of Virginia. In 1850 he was elected a delegate from Randolph County to the Constitutional Convention to revise the Constitution of the State. In this body of learned and distinguished Virginians Mr. Carlile's splendid natural abilities, added to his experience of four years in the Senate, made him influential, and placed him along side of the ablest men in that body. The people by this time recognized Mr. Carlile's commanding abilities, and in 1855 nominated him as a candidate for Congress and elected him in one of the most spirited campaigns peculiar to that day. He served one term and returned to the practice of his profession, which had become large and lucrative.

To secure better opportunities for the display of his superior legal attainments Mr. Carlile removed his residence to Clarksburg, Harrison County. He was employed in all the important cases in litigation in County, Circuit, Federal and Supreme Courts in that portion of the State, and accordingly achieved great distinction as a member of the bar. At the breaking out of the war he was an avowed Unionist, and threw all of his great powers on the side of the Government. He was a member of the Wheeling Convention that established the Restored Government of Virginia, and was one of the leading spirits in all of its councils. He was elected to the Thirty-seventh Congress from the Wheeling District in 1861, and remained a member until his promotion to the Senate of the United

States, the latter part of that year, from the Restored Government of Virginia. While in the Senate he served as a member of the Committee on Public Lands and Territories. His Senatorial term expired in 1865, when he retired to private life at Clarksburg and resumed the practice of his profession.

As an orator Mr. Carlile had but few, if any, superiors in Virginia. He died at his home in Clarksburg in 1878. While it is true that Senator Carlile is regarded most as a statesman, yet he was universally esteemed as an eminent and successful lawyer, and was an honor to the profession in and outside of the "Mountain State." He was unusually talented, and maintained a high rank both as a lawyer and a statesman.

## Judge William A. Harrison

Judge Harrison, the senior member of the first Supreme Court of Appeals of the State of West Virginia, was born in Prince William County, Virginia, August 27, 1795. His education was obtained in the schools of that section. He, however, was ambitious and was an earnest seeker after knowledge, and consequently used every facility within his reach to store his mind with such knowledge as would be of value to him in after life. At an early age he chose the law for his profession, and all the books he read, and really mastered, were in that direction. In this way he pieced out what, in that day, was considered a fairly good education for even a professional man. He, therefore, may be classed as a self-educated and self-made man. He read law under the guidance of his brother-in-law, Obed Waits, of Winchester, Virginia, one of his most valued friends and helpers in time of need. In 1819 he was sufficiently informed in the fundamental principles of the profession to enable him to pass a creditable examination for admission to the Winchester Bar. Shortly after his admission he came to Parkersburg, Wood County, on the Ohio River, and entered upon the practice of his chosen profession. The first circuit in which he practiced was presided over by Judge Daniel Smith, which was composed of the Counties of Rockingham, Pendleton, Preston, Monongalia, Brooke, Ohio, Tyler, Wood, Lewis and Harrison. This circuit embraced all the territory between the Pennsylvania line and the Little Kanawha River. The custom of that period was for the aspiring attorneys to travel with the judge and attend all of the courts embraced in the Judicial Circuit twice a year. In this way lawyers of ability and industry managed to secure a paying practice, and young Harrison, who possessed many natural gifts, succeeded in picking up more than his share of the cases disposed of on these various swings around the circuit.

In 1821 he moved to Clarksburg, Harrison County, and thereafter made that town his permanent home, and remained there up to the time of his death, which occurred December 31, 1870. In 1823 he was appointed

Assistant United States District Attorney for the Western District of Virginia, which office he filled acceptably and ably, traveling on horseback twice a year to Wytheville to attend upon the sessions of the court. After the establishment of the Court of Appeals of Virginia at Lewisburg in Greenbrier County, he practiced regularly at its bar until the breaking out of the Civil War in 1861. His practice, during a long, successful life, was one of immense labor, requiring great research and profound investigation. He appeared, during his career, before seven Federal Judges, fifteen Circuit Judges, and twelve judges of the Supreme Court of Appeals of Virginia. He was elected a member of the Supreme Court of Appeals of West Virginia after the formation of the State in 1863, and served with great ability.

Judge Harrison was a Union man and a Republican, but was never a politician. He preferred the calm and dignified contests of the bar to the more animated scenes incident to partisan warfare. He, however, represented Harrison County three terms in the Legislature of Virginia in *ante bellum* days. He was also United States Attorney for the Western District, and Prosecuting Attorney of Harrison County, one term in each office. When the Civil War came on in 1861 he took a firm stand for the Union, and was one of the leaders in the erection of the new Commonwealth of West Virginia. The Circuit Judge of the Harrison County District was vacated by its judge going with the South, and Judge Harrison was elected that year (1861) to fill out his term, which position he occupied until elected a member of the Supreme Court of Appeals of the new State in 1863.

He was an able and a just judge, and ranked among the leading lawyers of his time. He was of large stature and commanding presence; in religious convictions he was a Presbyterian; was married and left a large family of honored citizens; one of his sons, Thomas W. Harrison, became a prominent citizen and was one of Harrison County's distinguished Circuit Court Judges. No better people can be found anywhere than the immediate descendants of William A. Harrison.

---

## Hon. James A. Brown

James A. Brown, one of the able attorneys of Kingwood, Preston County, and son of Thomas Brown, was born June 11, 1836. He was educated liberally, graduated at Washington College, Pennsylvania, and subsequently attended the University of Virginia. He read law with his father and the Hon. John A. Dille, and was admitted to the Bar in 1859; was elected Prosecuting Attorney of Preston County, and filled the office with general satisfaction from 1861 to 1863. In 1880 he was chosen as the Republican candidate for Judge of the Third Circuit, receiving a flattering majority in his own, but was defeated by the Democratic majorities of the other counties. He was a man of irreproachable personal character and was a successful practitioner.

JUDGE WILLIAM A. HARRISON

## Judge Edwin S. Duncan

Judge Duncan, of Clarksburg, is remembered by the older people of that city as one of the ablest lawyers and jurists of the first half of the last century. He was born in Shenandoah County, Virginia, in 1790, and was educated in the schools of that section. He came to Randolph County, in the western part of the State, where he read law and was admitted to the bar at Beverly, the seat of justice of that county, about the year of 1812. He was a man of large natural endowments, and in a very short time became an attorney of distinction. He served for a short time as chief of staff in Col. Booth's Virginia regiment during the second war with Great Britain, shortly after his admission to the bar in 1812. After the close of the war he returned to Beverly and resumed his practice; but being desirous to secure a broader field of operations for a young lawyer of high ambitions, he removed his law office to Clarksburg in Harrison County in 1816 and began to practice there. He also opened an office at Weston in Lewis County, twenty-six miles distant, and had but little trouble in finding clients there as well as at Clarksburg. His residence, however, was in the latter town. He was elected Prosecuting Attorney for Lewis County in the fall of 1816, and in 1820 he was elected to the State Senate of Virginia from the district of which Harrison and Lewis were a part; was appointed United States District Attorney for the Western District of Virginia in 1824, and served four years; was elected a member of the Constitutional Convention of 1829–30; was later elected a Judge of the General Court of Virginia and of the Eighteenth Circuit in 1831; was appointed by the Governor to represent Virginia at the World's Fair in London, England, in 1851, and after his return from this service he retired to private life at Clarksburg. He departed this life February 4, 1858, and is still referred to as one of the eminent lawyers and judges of that prosperous city.

Judge Duncan lived an upright, honorable life, and left his impress for good and exalted citizenship in that portion of the State where he spent a long and useful life. He never devoted any of his energies to politics, but preferred to spend all of his time in the profession which he made a special life work. He was truly a learned lawyer and an incorruptible judge. His prominent characteristics were a strong will, sound judgment, a large fund of humor, a keen knowledge of human nature, rigid devotion to what he believed to be right, and an integrity of character that riches dared not attempt to bribe and could not corrupt. His character was beautiful in simplicity and gentleness.

A number of his descendants are residents of Clarksburg and Harrison County. He was a man of medium stature and carried an air of greatness as he moved among the people. He was, in every respect, a truly representative citizen and stood for the highest ideals in life and character.

## Judge John J. Allen

Judge Allen for many years was one of the most distinguished lawyers and jurists of Western Virginia. He was born at Woodstock, Shenandoah County, Virginia, September 25, 1797. His father, Judge James Allen, was also an able lawyer and jurist and was eminent in his day and generation. The subject of this brief sketch was educated at Washington College, Lexington, Virginia, and Dickinson College, Carlisle, Pennsylvania. He read law under the guidance of his father and was admitted to the practice in the courts of the Valley of Virginia. In 1819 he located at Clarksburg in the western part of the State and began the practice of his profession in Harrison and adjoining counties. Being thoroughly equipped he was not long in forging to the front and securing employment in important litigations of those early days. Indeed by ability and learning he very soon found employment on one side or the other in most big law suits in the three or four counties in which he practiced. Late in the twenties he formed a partnership with Gideon D. Camden, also a lawyer of prominence at Clarksburg, which continued for eight or ten years, until Mr. Allen in 1836 was appointed a Judge of the Circuit Court of Virginia, when he retired from the firm.

In 1827 Judge Allen was elected to the State Senate, and while a member of that body he introduced a bill, which afterwards became a law, for the settlement of land titles, in trans-Allegheny, Virginia. In 1834 he was elected Commonwealth's Attorney for the counties of Harrison, Lewis and Preston. At the same time he was a member of the 23d Congress, serving from 1833 to 1835. In all of the public positions he held he was faithful, honorable and able. He married in 1824. Although he was extremely reserved while in public life, he was gentle, affectionate and communicative in his social relations with his family and friends, and was firm and sincere in his religious convictions. He was appointed a Circuit Judge in 1836, and removed his residence to Botetourt County, and was promoted to the Supreme Court of Appeals in December, 1840. He died at Fincastle in 1871. He was an ardent secessionist at the beginning of the war, and retired from active life in 1865. He was a member of the Supreme Court for a quarter of a century, and his opinions show him to be a man of vast erudition. He was, beyond question, an able and just Judge, and his private and public life were above reproach.

## Judge George Hay Lee

Judge Lee was one of the eminent lawyers and jurists of Western Virginia. He was born at Winchester in the Shenandoah Valley in 1807, and was educated at the University of Virginia, and graduated about 1830, and soon thereafter was admitted to the bar. In 1831 he located at

Clarksburg, Harrison County, in the western part of the State, and practiced his profession with great success until the time of his death, which occurred November 20, 1873. He was learned in the law, and for nearly a half century maintained a high rank among the members of the profession prior to and after the division of the State. For a number of years he and the late Judge Mathew Edmiston, of Weston, Lewis County, were partners in the practice, with offices at Clarksburg, Weston and Parkersburg. Both of them being men of unusual ability, the firm was employed on one side or the other, of most, if not all, of the important causes in all of the courts in the half dozen or more counties of the interior section of what is now the State of West Virginia. Judge Lee is remembered as one of the ablest of office lawyers or pleaders of his day, while Judge Edmiston was noted as a trial lawyer or advocate, thus giving the firm unusual prominence, and rendering them almost invincible as trial lawyers in all classes of cases.

Judge Lee was twice elected a member of the Legislature of Virginia from Harrison County while he was comparatively a young man, and was also Prosecuting Attorney of Harrison County for one or more terms. Later he served a full term as United States District Attorney for the Western District of Virginia, and was an able and faithful official. He was next appointed a Circuit Judge by the Legislature, where he developed superior qualities as a jurist. His decisions were clear, pointed and strong, and clearly showed that he possessed, in a marked degree, the judicial temperament. In 1850 the Constitution of Virginia was amended so as to require the election of all judges by the people, and Judge Lee was elected one of the judges of the Supreme Court of Appeals of the State. In this appellate position he served with great acceptability until the close of his term. He returned to Clarksburg and resumed the practice of his profession, which he kept up, in important causes, until the time of his death, as stated above in 1873. He was tall of stature, wore a long beard, and was a commanding figure in any gathering of men. He was also a man of exalted character, and commanding influence in both of the Virginias. His integrity was absolutely above reproach. Rarely is there found in the ranks of men one so symmetrical in mind and character, one so sound in judgment, so unerring in moral perception, so faithful to every duty, and so loyal to the right, as he, through his entire career. His life as a lawyer and a jurist, whether judged by reference to labor performed, pecuniary gain or fame, he stood in the forefront of his profession.

He was twice married and had six children, three daughters and three sons, all of whom but one are now deceased. He lived in a palatial home on Lee Street in the city of Clarksburg, where forty-two years of his life were spent.

## Hon. Waitman T. Willey, LL.D.

Mr. Willey, although for many years an able and successful lawyer, is best known as a public official and a statesman of prominence and worth. He was for many years, prior to his death, regarded by the public generally as one of the really great characters to whom West Virginians, without regard to political affiliations, pointed with pride. He was born on Buffalo Creek, Monongalia County, Virginia, October 18, 1811. He was reared on a farm until he reached the age of seventeen, when he entered Madison College, now Alleghany College, Meadville, Pennsylvania, from which he graduated, *cum laude*, in June, 1831. At college he was rated as a hard working student, but was noted most for his gifts of oratory. He was recognized not only as the towering orator of his class, but of the entire college as well. All through his long and useful life he ranked as one of the very greatest public speakers of both Virginias. This wonderful gift made him almost invincible as an advocate and court house trial lawyer. He read law for two years in the office of the distinguished Philip Doddridge, at Wellsburg, Brooke County, who was one of the greatest lawyers of his generation, and was admitted to the Bar of Monongalia County in September, 1833; he immediately opened a law office and began to practice. He was not long in getting his share, and more of the law business of the community. He was well known, not only as a well educated and eloquent man, but his standing among the people was that of one who was thoroughly upright, conscientious and reliable. From his boyhood up, there was not a blot upon his moral character, and his veracity was absolutely unimpeachable, and this sort of a reputation and character were continuously and constantly the same until the end of his great career. A lawyer of that sort, will never be required to hunt clients, or drum up supporters or followers among the people. The truth is, Mr. Willey was so often sought after by the people, to fill highly important public positions that he scarcely was allowed the necessary time to attend to his own private affairs.

In 1840, he was an elector on the Harrison and Tyler ticket, and was required to stump the entire Western part of the state for the Whig party. He was the Clerk of both the County and Circuit Courts of Law and Chanchery of Monongalia County, from 1841 to 1852; was a member of the State Constitutional Convention in 1850–'51; was the Whig candidate for Congress for his District in 1852; was the Whig candidate for Lieutenant-Governor of Virginia in 1859; he was a delegate to the National Convention in 1860 that nominated Bell and Everett for President and Vice-President; was a member of the Virginia Convention of 1861, and voted against the Ordinance of Secession; he ably aided in organizing the Restored Government of Virginia at the City of Wheeling; was elected United States Senator by said Restored Government; was a member of the Convention that framed the first Constitution of West Virginia; was elected one of the two United States Senators, and drew the short term of two years. At the expiration of said term, he was re-elected to the Senate for the full term of six years, which expired March 4, 1871. How could one practice law very extensively with all these public duties loaded upon him? And yet a good part of the time, he maintained a large practice.

In 1834 Senator Willey married Miss Elizabeth Ray, of the City of Wheeling. He was an active and faithtful member of the Methodist Episcopal Church; was always a leader on the moral side of every important question that came before the people during his entire life. Allegheny College and the West Virginia University each conferred upon him the honorary degree of Doctor of Laws. After his retirement from the Senate, he was Clerk of the Circuit Court of Monongalia County, which furnished him all the necessary comforts of life. He died at his home in Morgantown when he was nearly ninety years of age, and was mourned by all classes of the citizens of the city. He was six feet three and a-half inches tall, and was one of the most powerful athletes of his generation.

## Hon. Arthur I. Boreman

Among the distinguished men of West Virginia who were leaders, not only in the legal profession but figured prominently in the organization of the State, was the subject of this sketch. He was born in Waynesburg, Pennsylvania, July 24, 1823. In boyhood he came to Virginia, and after receiving a common school education, he read law with his elder brother, William I. Boreman, at Middlebourn, Tyler County, and was admitted to the Bar in May, 1843. In November of that year, he located at Parkersburg, where he continued to reside, until the day of his death, when he was about eighty years of age. For many years he was a Whig in his political convictions, but became a Republican at the organization of that party, and remained in that political party the remainder of his life. He was a tireless worker, a man of unlimited energy, of sleepless industry, of absolute courage and during his entire life there was never an aspersion, or an attack of any sort on his moral character. His long public and private life were noted for integrity, uprightness and usefulness. He was successful as a lawyer, and was thoroughly honorable in all of his dealings with his fellow men. He was a man of positive convictions, and was, during all of his mature years, sought by the people for counsel and advice.

In 1855 he was elected from Wood County a member of the Virginia Legislature, and was successively re-elected until 1860, and was a member of that distinguished body in 1861 when the question of secession was discussed, and his opposition to that movement was conspicuous. During that year he presided over the Wheeling Convention that organized the Restored Government of Virginia. In October, 1861, he was elected a Circuit Judge of the Parkersburg Circuit, and discharged the functions of that office ably, until his election in 1863 as the first Governor of the new State of West Virginia. Two years later he was re-elected to the same high office, serving both terms honorably and ably. In 1868 he was elected to the United States Senate, and was regarded as a faithful and able Senator. After retiring from a six-year term as a Senator he returned to Parkersburg, reopened his law office, and was re-establishing a profitable practice; without the asking on his part, he was elected Judge of the Circuit Court over which he had presided a quarter of a century before. As a lawyer he was able, and as a Judge he was fair and just, and was absolutely incorruptible. He ended his days on the Bench he had highly honored in his early and later life. He was for many years, a leading member of the Methodist Episcopal Church and was a delegate to its General Conference in 1888. He married Mrs. Lauraine Bullock, November 30, 1864, but left no direct descendants.

## General James S. Wheat

General Wheat came to Wheeling from Washington, D. C. in 1830, and was admitted as a member of the Ohio County Bar shortly after his arrival. He at once became prominent as an attorney. He was a man of culture and refinement, and courtly and faultness in his manner; consequently he was not long in taking a front rank among his associate attorneys. While he was not considered as profound and learned in the profession as some of his compeers, he was nevertheless one of the best equipped attorneys of his day. He was a ready and fluent speaker, and on all important public occasions, he was much in demand as a public speaker. Being an orator, his special power was as an advocate and trial lawyer. He was so fluent and ready in speech, it was difficult to take him by surprise, or in any way to discomfit him. He was self-asserting, self-reliant and courageous, and generally was able to extricate himself from any temporary embarrassment thrust upon him by opposing counsel in any important court trial. He was a ready and effective debater, and was a Lord Chesterfield in courteousness and suavity. He was popular with his associates at the Bar, and was particularly strong in arguing jury cases. He was not a native of Virginia, but was highly educated on general subjects and was well read in the law.

He came to West Virginia about the time of the breaking out of the war, and being an intense Union man, he promptly fell in with the Union people of Western Virginia to prevent Virginia from seceeding from the General Government. He, therefore, became a leader in the movement of that period to organize what was termed the Restored Government of Virginia at Wheeling. He was a delegate to the Convention, and was an important factor in establishing said Government, which ultimately resulted in bringing West Virginia into the Great Sisterhood of States in June, 1863. He was elected Attorney-General of the Restored Government of Virginia, and served as such, until the new State of West Virginia was brought into existence by the Congress of the United States. General Wheat was one of the minute men of that trying period, whose eminent services will not soon be forgotten. In 1872, he was a delegate from Ohio County, to the Convention at Charleston which framed a second Constitution for West Virginia, and was an important factor in that body of distinguished men.

General Wheat was never an office seeker. He, doubtless, would have been kept in office constantly, if his consent could have been secured. He was a man of great popularity. The people rallied around him continuously. He, however, preferred the law to politics, and, therefore, stuck closely to his calling. His business was large and profitable. He was a man of a high sense of honor and integrity. The people trusted him implicity, and he never deceived them. He was public spirited and delighted in the prosperity and progress of his city, county and state. He was industrious, and kept his working harness on until the final call reached him, thus ending a useful, successful and honorable career.

## Judge John Brannon

Among the really great lawyers and jurists of West Virginia, now deceased, the subject of this brief sketch must be classed. He was born at Winchester, Virginia, October 19, 1822. His ancestors on both his paternal and maternal sides were engaged in the Revoluntionary War for American Independence. His Grandfather Brannon was a native of Ireland, and his father was a thrifty farmer in the valley of Virginia, where he was recognized as a man of sterling integrity and of high moral character in the citizenship of that highly cultured community. Mr. Brannon received a thorough academic training in the Winchester Academy, a well-known, high grade classical school of that section of Virginia, where a large number of the prominent, influential men of " The Mother State " received their educational training. Shortly after his graduation from this educational institution, the Brannon family moved their residence to Lewis County, now West Virginia, and established a home in Weston, the county seat of that very rich and prosperous county. Our subject before he left Winchester had already begun the study of law, and was pursuing it diligently, which he continued at Weston, and after passing a creditable examination, was admitted to the Bar in 1847. He rapidly acquired a leading, profitable practice. He was a solid, sedate, honorable man in all of his dealings, and possessed the implicit confidence of the general public, who entrusted their business to his management and supervision. It was not long, therefore, until he stood at the head of that able, progressive Bar.

He was in politics a Whig, and was elected to the Legislature of Virginia, serving therein ably from 1853 to 1857. He was then promoted by an appreciative constituency to the State Senate from 1857 to 1865. In both branches of the State Legislature he was regarded as an able and careful legislator. After the close of the Civil War he allied himself with the

Democratic Party, and in 1872 he was elected a Circuit Judge, serving the full term of eight years. Being thoroughly informed in all branches of the law, and being absolutely honest and just, he proved to be satisfactory to both lawyers and litigants. He was urged to accept a second term, but courteously declined and returned to the practice of the law at Weston. In 1884 and 1886 he was the nominee of the Democratic Party for a seat in the American Congress, but was both times defeated by Gen. Nathan Goff, the Republican candidate, by a majority each time of a little more than two hundred. The Legislature came within two or three votes of electing him to the Senate of the United States.

He married a Miss Bland of Weston, and was a member of the Protestant Episcopal Church. He departed this life at about eighty years of age. No man in Lewis County was more highly respected than he.

## Hon. William G. Brown

The ancestry of this branch of the Brown family was Scotch. From Edinburgh, James Brown came to Virginia, in 1790, and located in Monongalia County. William G., his fourth son, was born September 25, 1800. He studied law with Oliver Phelps and J. H. Samuels, of Parkersburg, Virginia; was admitted to the Bar of Preston County, Virginia, in 1828; served as Prosecuting Attorney of Preston County for several terms, until 1832; supported Andrew Jackson for the Presidency every time he was a candidate; was a member of the Legislature of Virginia in 1832, 1840–1–2–3; was elected a member of Congress in 1845, and was re-elected in 1847; was a member of the Constitutional Convention of Virginia in 1850; was a delegate to the Richmond Convention of 1861, which adopted the Ordinance of Secession, but he voted against its adoption. He participated in the Wheeling Convention that organized " The Restored Government Virginia," and saved Western Virginia to the Union, and was elected to the 37th Congress as a Representative of the Restored Government of Virginia, and was the first Representative from the 2d Congressional District of West Virginia, after she was admitted to statehood. He was a member of the Convention of 1872 that framed the second Constitution for West Virginia. He was also elected to the Legislature of 1872–3. He was a man of the highest character, and always had the implicit confidence of all his fellow citizens. He was also known and recognized as one of the ablest and most successful lawyers of his period.

Mr. Brown died at Kingwood at an advanced age, and left a widow and one son William G. Brown, Jr.— who was also a very successful lawyer and a resident of Preston County all of his life. He was serving his third term in Congress, from his father's old district, when in 1916, death took him in his prime of strength, usefulness and success in life.

Both of them were Democrats of the strictest sect, although the elder Brown, who was a staunch Union man, acted with the Republicans until after the close of the Civil War, when he returned to his first love — the Democratic Party. "Junior" Brown, as he was always called, from his boyhood, adhered to the Democratic party. Both of them were men of wealth, as well as of influence and high standing in the State.

## Hon. James Morrow, Jr.

Few citizens of the State have made greater impress upon the community in which Providence placed them than the subject of this brief sketch. He was born in Brooke County, Virginia, May 26, 1837. His boyhood was passed upon his father's farm, and in the neighborhood schools. Ohio and Pennsylvania both contributed to a classic education of later years; he studied law as opportunity occurred for several years, and in 1862 was admitted to the Bar of Illinois. In 1865 he began practice in Fairmount, West Virginia. Marion county electors chose him to represent their interests in the Legislature in 1871, and again in 1881. In the House he was popular and influential in shaping the legislation of those years, serving on the important Committee of the Judiciary. He was one of the Special Court in the contest case of Harrison against Lewis for Judge of the Second Circuit, and voiced the opinion of the majority of the Court; and was counsel for Auditor Bennett and Treasurer Burdett in their attempted impeachment before the West Virginia Senate in 1875–6. Urbane in manners, strict in integrity, Democratic, but conservative, in politics, and properly ambitious for exalted responsibilities, however difficult or laborious, yet modest in urging his own preferment, he was peculiarly sensitive of unfair criticism and neglect. At the State Convention of his party at Huntington, in 1888, he was a formidable candidate for the gubernatorial nomination. He held many appointments from the Governor upon State Boards and was elected to numerous county positions of trust.

After severe mental afflictions, November 19, 1888, he passed into the Great Beyond. He was one of the most erudite lawyers the State of West Virginia has produced.

## Hon. William A. Quarrier

Mr. Quarrier, son of Alexander W. Quarrier, who was for a generation, Clerk of the County Court, and Circuit Superior Court of Law and Chancery of Kanawha County. William A. was born in Charleston, Virginia, in 1828, where he attended the schools of the town, ending with a full course at Mercer Academy, and finally completed his studies at the University of Virginia, where he graduated in the Law Department, and promptly entered upon an illustrious career as a member of the Kanawha Bar. He enlisted in the Confederate Army in 1861 and remained therein until the close of hostilities in 1865, when he returned to Charleston, and resumed the practice of law. He married Miss Cora Greenhow, by whom he had six children, one of whom — Russell G.— is now a prominent attorney of the Kanawha Bar. Mr. Quarrier never was a politician, but was twice sent to the West Virginia Legislature against his will. He was originally a Whig, but after the Civil War, he aligned himself with the Democratic Party. He loved his profession, and devoted his life to its study.

Mr. Quarrier was one of the ablest lawyers of the West Virginia Bar. It has been said of him that he was the best lawyer in a bad case that ever practiced at the Kanawha Bar, and his practice was large and important, and he was almost invariably employed, on one side or the other, of practically every important case tried in the courts of Kanawha and adjoining counties. He was also a leader in the civic development of his section of the State.

He was a member of the Episcopal Church, and was a leader therein. He was a tall and commanding man, and was courteous and urbane in all of his movements. He died September 10, 1888, and the entire community mourned his loss.

## Hon. Nathan Goff, LL.D.

The subject of this sketch has had a distinguished and illustrious career. He was born in Harrison County, Virginia, February 9, 1842; was educated in the Clarksburg Northwestern Academy, Georgetown University, Washington, D. C., and took the law course at the University of New York at the close of the Civil War. In the Spring of 1861, while a student at Georgetown University, young Goff was among the first to enlist as a volunteer in the service of the United States Government as a private soldier. Soon after, he was elected by the members of his company as a Lieutenant; was soon thereafter promoted to Captain, and finally was made a Major of his regiment. He participated in a number of severe battles, including Second Bull Run and Antietam. He was captured by the Confederates at Moorefield, West Virginia, January 20, 1864, and was confined in Libby Prison for a number of months. At the close of the war he was given the brevet rank of brigadier general of volunteers for bravery and valor on the field of battle, although he was then only 23 years of age.

His first political office was membership in the West Virginia Legislature from Harrison County in 1868; was appointed United States District Attorney for the State of West Virginia in 1869, which office he ably filled for thirteen years. He was Secretary of the Navy in President Harrison's Cabinet from January 6, 1880, until the close of the administration, when he was reappointed United States Attorney for West Virginia. He was a member of Congress for three consecutive terms from 1883 to 1889. In 1876 and 1888 he was the Republican candidate for Governor of the Commonwealth, but he was defeated in both campaigns. However, he was elected in 1888 on the face of the returns by a majority of 110 votes, but upon a recount by the Legislature his opponent was given the office. He was appointed a United States Circuit Judge by President Harrison in 1890, and filled that office with great acceptability until 1913, when he was elected by the West Virginia Legislature a Senator in the Congress of the United States, which office he held for six years.

In 1888 Georgetown University conferred upon him its highest honorary degree — Doctor of Laws.

Senator Goff is married, has two sons, lives within gun-shot distance of where he was born in the City of Clarksburg, is a man of large means, and has always been an uncompromising Republican in politics. The State has never produced an abler or more popular man.

His wife, who was Miss Laura Despard, died October 29, 1918.

## James McNeil Stephenson

Mr. Stephenson, one of West Virginia's most learned lawyers, late of the city of Parkersburg, was born November 4, 1796, in Greene County, Pennsylvania. He received his education in the log school houses of the pioneer, which did not extend beyond the three R's of that early period, and for which he had to labor, early and late. He possessed more than an average intellect and an innate ambition to make a record in life. He was large of stature, and was physically able to endure the severest of hardships, and possessed the industry and energy to read and carefully digest all of the books that he could buy or borrow. His reading and study increased his ambitions. Unsatisfied with existing conditions, and thirsting for a higher grade of knowledge, he decided to become a lawyer. Whilst learning the trade of a tanner, all of his spare time was devoted to a careful study of legal text books. Many times he was found currying leather with his text books open before him. By these means, and the unsparing use of the "tallow dip," he became qualified for, and was admitted to the Bar, and commenced practicing law at Wheeling, Virginia, but shortly thereafter he located at Middlebourne, the county seat of Tyler County. Here he practiced his profession for several years, and by close attention to his law office, and by judicious investments in real estate, he prospered beyond many of the favored of fortune. Looking for a wider field of labor he moved to Parkersburg, Wood County, and opened a more pretentious law office, and largely increased his business as an attorney.

When thirty-three years of age he married Miss Agnes M. Boreman, a member of a noted family of Wood County. They reared a family of six children, three boys and three girls. He was very fond of his family, and his home-life was beautiful and exemplary. When the Civil War broke out in 1861 he stood strenuously by the Union, notwithstanding the fact that he had a son in the Confederate Army. He was a slave-holder, or rather his slaves owned him. He bought a number, but never sold one. Notwithstanding the fact he never went to college, he was in many ways a learned man. As a lawyer, perhaps, he had no superior in West Virginia. He was remarkably successful in handling his cases. He accumulated a large estate, mainly by his efforts at the Bar. He was noted for his unswerving honesty and integrity. He was learned in all the branches of the law, but specialized in land laws and suits in ejectment.

He was a whig in politics, but was never a politician, nor an office-seeker. He represented Tyler County three terms in the Legislature of Virginia in 1838, '39 and '40. Subsequently he represented Wood County, a number of terms in the State Legislature. He was also a man of large public spirit. To his exertions more than to any other man or men, the construction of the railroad from Grafton to Parkersburg is due. He also organized two banks, and was also a leader in a number of other public improvements. He was foremost in his day, in every movement that was for the betterment of the community in which he lived and adorned.

He died April 12, 1877, and carried to his grave the respect of all the people with whom he associated in life. He was a benevolent man, giving much money for the good of mankind. He was a devout Christian. His death was universally mourned by the citizens of Parkersburg.

## Hon. Andrew Edmiston, LL.B.

Mr. Edmiston son of Judge Mathew Edmiston, is a native of Weston, Lewis County, Virginia, where he was born in September, 1849. He had three brothers, all of whom were successful physicians, and three sisters, all of whom remained citizens of Lewis County. The subject of this sketch received his primary education in the Weston schools. Later he was a student at Marietta (Ohio) College in 1867 and '68; he was one year at the University of Virginia, and took the law course at Washington and Lee University at Lexington, Virginia, graduating with the degree of Bachelor of Laws in the class of 1872; he returned to Weston and was admitted to the Lewis County Bar in the summer of that year, and has since been admitted as a practitioner in all the courts of West Virginia, both State and Federal, his office, all the while, being at Weston, although his practice extended into the surrounding counties, and became large and profitable. He possessed a thorough knowledge of the law, and became a noted attorney in the central portion of the State. He is energetic, studious and fearless, and has been unusually successful in the trial of important causes. He maintains a high rank as an advocate, a gift possessed, in a high degree, by his distinguished father. His clientele has always been large and profitable, notwithstanding the fact, that for several years past, he has been trying to restrict his clientage, rather than increase it. He is a man of upright character, and has always been trustworthy in every respect.

He was born a Democrat and has never wavered in his allegiance to that faith; still, he cannot be classed, in any respect, as an office-seeker or a politician, *per se*. Nevertheless, he was, for many years, active in politics, simply to see his party succeed. He was elected a member of the West Virginia Legislature in 1881, and served ably for two years; he was again elected to the same honorable position in 1894. He was elected Prosecuting Attorney of Lewis County in 1872, and rendered such efficient service in enforcing the law, that he was re-elected in 1876, serving eight years in that office. He was nominated by the Democrats as their candidate for Circuit Judge in 1904, and although not elected, he ran ahead of his ticket in the counties composing the circuit, nearly 1,800 votes. President Roosevelt carried the two counties by nearly 2,700 of a majority, while Mr. Edmiston lost them by less than 900 votes. Mr. Roosevelt carried Lewis (Mr. Edmiston's native county) by 525 majority, while Mr. Edmiston carried it the same day by 327 of a majority. This shows his standing and popularity at home, the best of all places to test one's real merits and standing.

Mr. Edmiston has never married, and is a member of the Protestant Episcopal Church, and the order of Knights of Pythias. He was Chairman of the Democratic State Executive Committee for four years, and was a Delegate to the Democratic National Convention, in 1912, which nominated Woodrow Wilson for President of the United States.

## Judge Daniel Polsley

Daniel Polsley, Congressman, Judge, Lieutenant-Governor, was born at Palatine, Marion County, Virginia, November 3, 1803. His father was of German descent, and his mother a sister of the grandfather of Judge Alpheus F. Haymond, formerly a Judge of the Supreme Court of West Virginia. His early education was obtained while assisting in clearing and improving the farm. He studied law, and attended the lectures of Judge Tucker, in Winchester, Virginia. After his father's death, he removed to Wellsburg, in Brooke County, and soon gained an enviable reputation at the Bar. In 1827, he wedded Eliza V. Brown, niece of the celebrated Philip Doddridge, and granddaughter of Captain Oliver Brown, an officer in the Revolutionary War. In connection with his profession, in 1833, he edited and published the "Western Transcript," a Whig paper. This he continued until 1845, when he retired from law practice, sold out his printing office, and moved to a 1,200-acre farm on the Ohio river, opposite Racine, Ohio, engaging in agriculture, as more congenial to his unpretentious nature. In the turbulent days of 1861, he was not allowed to longer remain in quiet life, and was elected a member from Mason County of the Wheeling Convention to Restore the State Government. Upon its restoration, he was made Lieutenant-Governor. In 1862, he was chosen Judge of the Seventh Circuit of Virginia, and over the same counties in West Virginia afterwards, ably presiding until 1866, when he was elected to the Fortieth Congress from the Third District. At the end of his term, he located at Point Pleasant, where he died October 14, 1877. Unostentatious, yet able, honest, and active, he was a force in the early days of our Statehood.

HON. ANDREW EDMISTON

## Hon. Allen Taylor Caperton

Among the distinguished lawyers and statesmen of southeastern West Virginia, we find the name of the subject of this sketch. He was born near Union, Monroe County, Virginia, November 21, 1810, and died at the National Capital, July 26, 1876, at the beginning of a promising term as a Senator in the American Congress. His paternal ancestors were English, and his maternal were Scotch. He was educated at the Huntsville, Alabama Academy, the Lewisburg, Virginia, Academy; graduated A. B. from Yale University in 1832; spent a short time at the Virginia University at Charlottsville; and graduated in law from Judge Briscoe G. Baldwin's Law School at Staunton, Virginia. Immediately thereafter he was licensed to practice as a member of the Monroe County Bar, and was not long in becoming its acknowledged leader. He was a superior public speaker, and early established himself as one of the foremost trial lawyers in Virginia.

He was elected as a Whig from Monroe County in April, 1841, a Delegate to the General Assembly of Virginia. In 1844 he was elected a State Senator from the district in which Monroe County was a part, and served ably for the term of four years. He was a member of the Constitutional Convention of Virginia, 1850, and was a member of the Committee to adjust the question of the White and Mixed basis of Taxation between the eastern and western counties of the State, then a subject of bitter contention. Because of his ability as a stump speaker he was twice a Whig Elector on the Presidential ticket. In 1859–'61 he was again a leading member of the General Assembly of Virginia. While thus serving, he was chosen a delegate to the Richmond Convention, which passed the Ordinance of Secession. In 1862 he was elected by the Legislature a United States Senator of the Confederate Congress, to fill the vacancy occasioned by the death of the Honorable William Ballard Preston, in which position he served until the close of the war between the States in 1865. He then returned to his home, and resumed the practice of the law, which very soon grew to large proportions. He inherited his father's popularity, as well as his estate; and in 1875, the Legislature of the new State of West Virginia elected him to a seat in the Senate of the United States. From this, his last earthly duty, after serving less than a year, he was suddenly called to the realms where Christian faith ends in fruition. Gentle in manner, honored by those who knew him well, and admired by a large circle of friends, he will long be remembered as one of the old school, lawyer gentlemen of his native State.

In the 22d year of his life he was united in marriage with Miss Harriet Echols, a lady of refinement and culture, with residence at the homestead in Union, the county seat of Monroe County, who survived him for a number of years. He became a Democrat at the close of the rebellion.

## Hon. John Bassel

Mr. Bassel, who, in life, was one of the most eminent lawyers that the Virginias have produced, was born, reared and died in the County of Harrison, born June 9, 1840, and died in the City of Clarksburg, December 28, 1914. He was educated at Moore's Academy at Morgantown, Virginia, where he spent two years; later he entered Washington and Jefferson College, Washington, Pennsylvania, from which he graduated with honor; read law in the office of the late John J. Davis for one year; later he was a student in law in the Cincinnati College of Law, from which he graduated and was admitted to practice in the Courts of Harrison County, January 8, 1864. He was noted for his diligence, mental acuteness, and power of analysis; hence it was not long until he received recognition as an attorney, and his success was, therefore, early assured. He ranked among the able lawyers of his day, always conducting his cases with admirable effectiveness and superior judgment. He had a comprehensive and accurate knowledge of the law, and never failed to exalt his profession in which it was his ambition to excel, and lamented the tendency, in later years, to lower its ideals. He never failed to keep in mind the advice of Lord Coke, that, "He that knoweth not the reason of the law, knoweth not the law." At the trial of causes he was alert, adroit and untiring. In the argument of cases he reasoned well and convincingly. He was a dangerous opponent in debate, but was never spectacular nor offensive. He possessed a remarkably retentive memory and could cite cases with marvelous precision. He was always a student, and remembered what he read, and his mind was accordingly stored and enriched not only by a knowledge of the law itself, but by the history of events culled from the classics and from profane and sacred writers as well, which he often used with telling effect in his arguments before courts and juries.

Mr. Bassel was twice married, first to Miss Martha Lewis, by whom he had six children, and second to Miss Mary Bean, who survived him and is still a resident of Clarksburg. She is a woman of marked ability, and was a valuable assistant to her husband in aiding him in the management of his large volume of business which was a burden to him in his declining years.

Mr. Bassel was a Democrat, but devoted very little time and thought to politics. The first and only office, to which he was ever elected by the people, was a member of the State Convention that prepared the Constitution of the State in 1872, under which we are still living. In that body of distinguished men, he took high rank, because of his thorough knowledge of the law.

He was for many years counsel for the Baltimore and Ohio Railroad Company, and gave to its affairs the most careful and assiduous attention.

He was a member of the Presbyterian Church, was domestic in his tastes and habits, enjoyed associations with his friends, and in his intercourse with members of the Bar, he was ever courteous, kind and considerate. He was president of the State Bar Association in 1901, and was a faithful attendant upon its annual meetings. The association was in session at Parkersburg the day of his demise, and twenty of its members, as a mark of respect, were appointed to attend his funeral.

## Judge Samuel Woods, A.M., LL.D.

Hon. Samuel Woods, deceased, a former judge of the Supreme Court of West Virginia, was born in East Canada, September 19, 1822. When he was but a boy, his father moved to Meadville, Pennsylvania, where he learned the plasterer's trade. He, however, in the meantime became a student at Allegheny College, and by energy and perseverance, working at his trade during the summer seasons, and attending college the remainder of the years, when twenty years of age, he completed the required classical course, and received the diploma of Bachelor of Arts. He studied law with Fox Alden, an able attorney of Pittsburg, Pennsylvania, and in the meantime he was one of the teachers in the well-known academy at Morgantown, Virginia. After his admission to the Bar, he located at Philippi, Barbour County, Virginia, where he spent the remainder of his life, having attained the standing of one of the greatest lawyers of the State.

Judge Woods was large in brain and stature. He was a little more than six feet tall, weighed over two hundred pounds, was round-faced and handsome, and was commanding in appearance. He was as well rounded morally as physically. He possessed strong religious convictions, and his personal character was as spotless as a maiden's, and as unsullied as a ray of light. At every period in his long and useful career, he was always found on the moral side of every question that came before him. He never apologized for his faith, but always showed his faith by his works. By his superior mental training, fidelity to his clients, and his highly honorable methods, he achieved success in the practice of his profession. Being a natural orator, he was almost irresistible as an advocate in a court trial. He made the most careful preparation of his cases, and was so well grounded in the law and so eloquent and convincing as a speaker that he seldom, if ever, lost a deserving case. He was free from the use of spirits and narcotics that often dwarf the body, deaden the intellect and poison the soul of brilliant men. He was also a man of fine literary tastes and habits, and was devoted to his family and to his home. In 1844 he married at Meadville, Pennsylvania, Miss Isabelle Neeson, and has reared an interesting family, three sons being successful lawyers, two of whom reside in Philippi, Barbour County, the place of their birth, the elder of the three being deceased.

He was a member of the Virginia Convention that passed the Ordinance of Secession, and when the Civil War came on he went with the South, was a member of the celebrated "Stonewall Brigade," and there remained

JUDGE SAMUEL WOODS

until the close of hostilities, when he returned to his Philippi home and resumed his law practice. He was a Democrat in his political convictions, and in 1871 he was elected a member of the State Convention that produced the State Constitution of 1872, which is still the organic law of West Virginia. In 1883 he was appointed a member of the Supreme Court of Appeals of the State to fill the vacancy occasioned by the resignation of the late Judge A. F. Haymond, and in 1884 he was elected by the people to that important position. At the expiration of his term of service in 1888 he retired from public life to manage his large private interests. In that year Allegheny College conferred upon him its highest honorary degree, that of Doctor of Laws, an honor most worthily bestowed.

Judge Woods was an ardent member of the Methodist Episcopal Church, and was a leader in its councils. He was one of the founders of West Virginia Weslyan College at Buckhannon, and was president of its Board of Trustees from the origin of the same until the time of his death. He was also a prominent member of the Masonic Fraternity. He died suddenly at his Philippi home February 17, 1897. Thus passed from the throng of the living one of our States ablest lawyers, a learned and conscientious jurist, an honest, upright citizen, and above all a faithful Christian gentleman.

## Judge Daniel B. Lucas, LL.D.

Judge Lucas was one of the most distinguished lawyers, jurists and literateures that this State has produced. He was born in Charlestown, Jefferson County, Virginia, March 16, 1836, and was known as "the poet of the Shenandoah Valley." He came of distinguished ancestry, who for generations have been prominent in the wars and the public affairs of Virginia, even prior to the Revolution. He possessed a poetic temperament, and was an orator of power and force. He was a graduate of the University of Virginia, and was the valedictorian of his class. After his graduation he entered the law school of Judge Brockenbrough at Lexington, Virginia, and graduated therefrom in the class of 1859. Early in 1860 he removed to Richmond, and at the opening of the Civil War cast his fortunes with the South, and became a member of the staff of General Henry A. Wise. He had many experiences and narrow escapes, but emerged from the conflict unscathed and unharmed. During that period he wrote several poems that rendered him famous, one of which was "The land where we were Dreaming," also "The Wealth of Eglantine," "The Maid of Northumberland." A volume of poems, "Ballads and Madrigals," etc.

He returned to his home in Charlestown, and in 1870 formed a partnership with Thomas C. Green, who subsequently became one of the ablest lawyers and most distinguished jurists of the Commonwealth, and by his ability, training and skill young Lucas took high rank in the profession. He had a large practice in the State and Federal Courts, and especially

JUDGE DANIEL B. LUCAS

in the Supreme Court of the State, many of his cases being of great importance, which he managed with signal success. While devoting himself assiduously to his profession and many spare hours to poetic compositions, he yet found time to deliver numerous platform lectures on literary subjects. Among his most notable lectures were those on Daniel O'Connel, John Brown, John Randolph and Henry Clay.

He always took a high position on, and maintained a strong adherence to, the Democracy of the fathers of that party, against the alleged departure from the faith and doctrines of Jefferson, Madison and Monroe, and was instrumental in the defeat of the Hon. Johnson N. Camden, the Democratic nominee, for a seat in the United States Senate in 1887, because of that alleged departure. The Legislature failed to elect a Senator, and after its adjournment Governor Wilson appointed Mr. Lucas to that position during the *interim*. But a special session of the Legislature was held the following April and Judge C. J. Faulkner was elected to the existing vacancy, and thus that controversy was ended.

Mr. Lucas was a Regent of the West Virginia University for eight years and showed an active interest in the educational affairs of the State; and in July, 1876, he was tendered the Deanship of its Law Department, an honor which his large law practice compelled him to decline. For the same reason he declined to accept the position of a Circuit Court Judge which was tendered to him to fill the vacancy occasioned by the resignation of Judge John Blair Hoge. He was elected a member of the West Virginia Legislature in 1884, and was re-elected in 1886. His opposition to sumptuary laws and the coeducation of the sexes in the State University were very marked. He also vigorously favored a system of high license and equalization of taxation of all property, whether real or personal, corporate or individual, maintaining that inequality of taxation had been the bane of all Republics. Taking him all in all he proved to be a legislator of great influence and ability.

On the death of Judge Thomas C. Green, a member of the Supreme Court of Appeals of the State, his former law partner, Mr. Lucas was, in 1889, appointed to fill that vacancy, and in 1890 he was elected to fill Judge Green's unexpired term, which he ably did until January 1, 1893. His opinions are marked by careful thought and a full knowledge of the law, and are expressed in correct language and with the grace that bears the touch and taste of an accomplished scholar. Rarely is there found in the ranks of men one so symmetrical in mind and character, one so sound in judgment, so unering in moral perception, and so faithful to duty as the subject of this brief memoir. He was by no means a robust man, and yet he was capable of almost unlimited labor and application. He was married in 1869 to Miss Lena Brooks, of Richmond, Virginia. They had an only child — a daughter. He departed this life aged above three score and ten.

In 1844 the West Virginia University conferred upon Judge Lucas the honorary degree of Doctor of Laws, which was, in every respect, a well merited compliment and fully deserved.

## Judge John W. English, B.A.

The Hon. John Warth English, the subject of this brief memoir, was the son of Job English, one of the early salt manufacturers of the Great Kanawha Valley, was born in Jackson County, Virginia, January 31, 1831. When he was four years of age his father moved to Malden, Kanawha County, where the son attended the common and select schools of that locality until he was sixteen years of age, when he was sent to Illinois College at Jacksonville, Illinois, where he took the complete academic course, graduating with honors when he was twenty years of age with the degree of Bachelor of Arts. When he returned home he assisted his father in his store at the salt furnace for two or three years, while he was reading law under the tutelage of his uncle, John A. Warth, and Judge George W. Summers, of Charleston. After becoming qualified he passed the required examination, and in 1855 he was admitted to the Kanawha County Bar. A short time thereafter he located at Point Pleasant in Mason County, formed a partnership with Henry J. Fisher, the leading lawyer of that locality, and one of the best known attorneys in that section of the State. The firm of Fisher and English carried on a very large legal business not only in Mason County, but in all of the surrounding counties, until the beginning of the Civil War, when Mr. Fisher went South and remained until the close of hostilities. Mr. English, however, remained at home and carried on an extensive practice in Mason and the adjoining counties, in which he established a reputation as one of the leading lawyers of Western Virginia. In his practice he was honest in his convictions, honest with the courts before whom he appeared, and honest with his adversaries. He was an upright man and was four-square in all of his acts and purposes. Such men are always successful in their undertakings. Such was his character and reputation during the many years he was engaged in active practice.

In 1888 he was nominated by the Democratic party for a seat on the Supreme Court of Appeals of West Virginia, and was elected by a large majority over the opposing candidate, and served twelve years with great acceptability to both suitors and attorneys. He was a man of quiet and retiring disposition and was exceedingly modest in his demeanor. He engaged but little in the political controversies of the State, preferring to devote his time and energies to the practice of his profession. His literary education and studious habits fitted him especially for the position of a judge. He was honest, industrious and painstaking in all the cases that came before him during the twelve years he served on the Appellate Court. Through his entire life his reputation for integrity was never questioned.

Judge English was a man of marked personal appearance. He was six feet tall, wore long whiskers, had strong features, a kindly disposition, and would command attention in any audience. His career as a lawyer and judge was a record of manliness, complete in every detail.

May 6, 1862, he was united in marriage with Miss Fannie Lewis, a descendant of General Andrew and Colonel Charles C. Lewis of the Continental Army, who commanded the American troops in the historic battle of Point Pleasant against the Indians in 1774. At this now prosperous town, at the confluence of the Great Kanawha with the Ohio River, Judge English spent the greater portion of his honorable and distinguished career, and where on the 18th of July, 1916, in the quietude of a delightful home, respected by all the people, he disappeared into the "Great Beyond." No cleaner and purer man ever donned the judicial ermine in this or any other State. He was a faithful member of the Protestant Episcopal Church.

## Wesley Mollohan

One of the most illustrious legal products of West Virginia was the subject of this sketch. He was a man of simple habits; was courteous and dignified in his general deportment; attended to his duties promptly and faithfully; was more inclined to listen than to speak; was kind hearted, frank, straight forward, and independent; was conscientious and upright, and was a philosopher and a thinker. In fact he knew something of most everything; could reason from cause to effect on most every branch of human knowledge, and could give a logical reason for every principle he chose to present. He was apparently always thinking about something worth while wherever and whenever one might chance to meet him. He had pronounced convictions practically on everything beneath the sun, except politics. Whilst he always claimed to be a Democrat, yet on election day he generally split his ticket. He was eccentric. That much cannot be denied. He was peculiar. He at times was abstracted. Like Cassius, "he thought too much." But no one can say that he did not always stand "four square" every day in the week and every week in the year.

Mr. Mollohan was the son of the Reverend Charles Mollohan, and was born in Braxton County, Virginia, January 31, 1841, and died while visiting in Kansas, September 25, 1911. His early education was obtained from the public schools of Gallia County, Ohio, and later at Gallipolis, Ohio, Academy. He possessed an aspiration for knowledge which no circumstances of his youth could suppress, and an ambition to achieve a name and place among men undaunted by any prospect which the future could present to his view. When he quit the Academy he read law under the direction of the late Judge Simeon Nash at Gallipolis, one of the eminent lawyers and text writers of Southern Ohio. In less than two years he was thoroughly prepared for examination. He was critically examined, passed with a high grade, received his license and was admitted to the Gallipolis Bar. He, along with James Henry Nash (son of Judge Nash), a brilliant, brainy young attorney, came to Charleston, West Virginia, in 1865, opened a law office and began a business which was lucrative from the day they hung

JUDGE JOHN W. ENGLISH

out their " shingle." Mr. Nash died in about ten years after his arrival and location at Charleston. Later George W. McClintic and William Gordon Mathews became partners with Mr. Mollohan and were members of the firm at the time of his demise.

Mr. Mollohan's practice embraced a period of nearly a half century and extended through the State and Federal Courts to the Supreme Court of the United States, and he appeared in many important cases involving a large number of land titles, tax sales, forfeitures and kindred subjects in many of the different counties of the entire State, he being recognized as one of the foremost, if not the best equipped and strongest land lawyer West Virginia has thus far presented to the profession. He was also a specialist upon all matters involving the construction of all constitutional questions. Indeed he seemed ready and at ease in the discussion of all cases, and especially appeals to the higher courts, involving intricate questions of law. In all cases where he appeared he rarely failed to show that he was generally well fortified behind impregnable breastworks. His successes were the fruits of his unceasing efforts, of vigorous, systematic application, a rectitude of purpose and a determination which nothing short of the achievement of the highest and noblest ends could satisfy. He commanded success and he deserved it.

He was a marked man in another respect. He never was a candidate for an office, never held an office, and never wanted one. He was distinctively a lawyer, and allowed nothing outside of his profession to draw his attention from it.

He married Miss Mary E. Donnally of Warren, Ohio, in 1872, who passed away in the early part of January, 1918. They left five daughters surviving them. Mr. Mollohan never connected himself with any religious organization, nor any secret society. He was an active member of the State Bar Association, and was president of the Association in 1902. He was a marked man, and must be classed among the great lawyers of his generation.

## Judge Charles Page Thomas Moore, M.A.

The Supreme Court Bench has had upon it few, if any, more gifted and popular wearers of the judicial ermine than the one whose kindly eyes face this brief biographical sketch. Since the early days of the State's existence, when party lines were sponged out by the overshadowing issue of National preservation, has any party candidate been more generally indorsed by the people than Judge Moore.

He was the youngest of three children from the marriage of Thomas Moore and Augusta Delphia Page, both of Shenandoah Valley, Virginia. His parents died when he was young. He was born February 8, 1831, and was adopted by his uncle, George Moore, and was taken to Mason County, on the Ohio River, who gave him a broad and liberal education. He first

JUDGE C. P. T. MOORE

attended Marshall College, Cabell County, Virginia; then at Jefferson College, Pennsylvania, and at Union College, New York, graduating from the latter in July, 1853, with the degree of Bachelor of Arts. He afterwards took the prescribed law course at the University of Virginia, and in 1856 he was admitted to the Bar of Mason County Circuit Court. In 1858 he was elected Prosecuting Attorney of that county, serving in that capacity until the beginning of the Civil War. He vigorously opposed secession, although he was a Democrat in his political affiliations. In 1868 he was a candidate for Congress, but failed of election.

In 1870 he was elected on the Democratic ticket as one of the judges of the Supreme Court of Appeals of West Virginia for the term of twelve years, but by the adoption of the State Constitution of 1872 his term was made to expire December 31, 1872. He was nominated for the same office at the following general election, and was overwhelmingly re-elected by the people. In the allotment provided by the Constitution of 1872, he drew the full term of twelve years. In 1881, owing to failing health, and after having rendered most faithful and efficient service for about ten years, he resigned from that high position, and thereafter adopted the more quiet and congenial life of the farm left to him by his uncle near Elwell, Mason County, in the splendid Ohio Valley, where he remained until his death.

Judge Moore wedded Miss Urilla K., daughter of Jacob A. Kline of Mason County, by whom he had four daughters. He loved the people and they revere his memory. No taint ever rested upon his private or public life. He was one of the most genial and generous of men, and was a man of marked personal appearance.

## Judge Alpheus F. Haymond

Judge Haymond, son of Col. Thomas S. and Harriet A. Haymond, was born on a farm near Fairmont, Marion County, Virginia, December 15, 1823. His early life was uneventful, but even in his youth he showed the vigor of thought and bold independence characteristic of subsequent years. Until the age of thirteen he attended school near his home, then went to Morgantown, Monongalia County Academy, where he remained two years, then to William and Mary College, Williamstown, Virginia, where he remained for a few terms. He read law with Edgar E. Wilson, of Morgantown, and was admitted to the Bar in 1842 when only nineteen years of age. He soon became recognized as an able lawyer, and had secured a paying practice before the Civil War. In early life he revealed a liking for politics. In 1853, and again in 1857, he was elected a member of the Legislature of Virginia from Marion County, and in 1861 he was a member of the Virginia Convention, and opposed Secession; but after the State seceded he entered the Confederate Army and remained therein until after the surrender of General Lee at Appomattox, when he returned to his home at Fairmont and resumed his law practice, which rapidly grew to large proportions.

JUDGE ALPHEUS F. HAYMOND

Being a strong lawyer he was appropriately chosen a member of the Constitutional Convention of 1872 to frame a new Constitution for the State of West Virginia, in which he figured conspicuously and ably. At the first election under that revised Constitution he was elected a member of the Supreme Court of Appeals of the State; served ably thereon until 1876, when he was re-elected to the same position for the full term of twelve years. He was a just and able judge. He wrote many opinions, all of which reveal honesty of purpose and determination to deal out justice without fear or favor. He was most careful in the preparation of his opinions, because he knew that hasty, ill-considered decisions by Appellate Courts are unprofitable to the public, unreliable as precedents and authority for the legal profession or the citizen, and discreditable to the court that makes them. Consequently he labored zealously to get at the facts, merits and law of every case he passed upon, or was decided by any of his associates on the Appellate Bench during his membership of the Court. He was necessarily an untiring worker, so much so that he found his health giving way under the necessary strain of the daily grind, and he decided to abandon his work upon the bench; consequently he resigned the position January 1, 1883, which he had so ably filled for ten years, and retired to private life.

Judge Haymond was a Democrat, a man of medium height, heavy build, face of a round contour, of agreeable and graceful manners, and of even temper. In his later years his practice was confined exclusively to the Supreme Court. He departed this life December 15, 1893, thus ending a distinguished and useful career.

He was a married man and had an interesting family. One of his sons is now judge of the Circuit Court of Marion County, and is a lawyer of acknowledged ability, and a safe and reliable jurist.

## Hon. Sherrard Clemens

Mr. Clemens was the son of Dr. James W. Clemens, and was born in Wheeling, Virginia, April 28, 1826. He received a thorough home training in the rudimentary principles of an English education, and was sent to Washington College, Pennsylvania, from which he graduated A.B. in the class of 1840. He studied law in Wheeling and was admitted to the bar in 1843. He became eminent as an advocate and was a successful practitioner. He entered politics and was elected to the Congress of the United States as a Democrat in 1852, and was re-elected in 1857. He was a man of brilliant parts; was a great debater, and was one of the most attractive and entertaining public speakers of his time. He was seriously wounded in a duel with O. Jennings Wise, the eldest son of Governor Henry A. Wise, of Virginia. He moved to Missouri and died at St. Louis in 1874. He was regarded as an eminent lawyer while he resided in Virginia.

## Major Isaac Noyes Smith

Major Smith, son of Col. Benjamin H. and Roxalana Noyes Smith, was born in Charleston, Kanawha county, Virginia, in April, 1832. He was educated at Washington and Lee University, Lexington, Virginia, from which he graduated with high honors in both the academic and law departments. After completing his college studies, he returned to his home at Charleston, entered the law office of his father, and very soon became an active member of the Kanawha County Bar.

In 1860 he was elected a delegate from his native county to the Virginia Legislature at Richmond, but when the Civil War broke out in 1861, he volunteered in the Confederate Army as a private soldier, and was shortly thereafter promoted to Major of his regiment. When the war was ended, he was honorably discharged, returned to Charleston, and vigorously resumed the practice of the law in which he was remarkably successful. When his father, who was eminent in the profession, retired from active practice, Major Smith took his place as the senior member of the law firm of Smith & Knight, in which he continued as an active member until his untimely death, which occurred at his residence in Charleston, October 6, 1883. He came of an ancestry marked by strong, able and brave men, and his distinction at the Bar was only less than that of his illustrious father, who survived him.

Major Smith was united in marriage with Miss Caroline S. Quarrier in November, 1860, daughter of Hon. Alexander W. Quarrier, a prominent citizen for many years of Charleston. Major Smith was an official member of the Presbyterian Church, and was noted for uprightness, integrity and honor, as well as a successful lawyer. Several members of his family are still living in the city of Charleston. One of his sons — Harrison Brooks Smith — is a member of the long and well-established law firm of Price, Smith, Spilman & Clay of Charleston, that maintain a state-wide reputation as attorneys and counselors.

## Hon. Edward Boardman Knight, M.A.

Edward B. Knight, one of the really eminent lawyers of West Virginia, prior to the days of modern-help text books and encyclopædia compilations for quick reference, when lawyers had to carry the law in their heads and not merely in their libraries, where they could turn to a cyclopædia and find what they wanted in a few minutes, in order to succeed in their practice and become eminent as barristers. Mr. Knight was of the kind who was erudite and learned in every branch of the profession, and was unusually apt in knowing how to apply his vast learing in an emergency, so as to prove most effective in a court trial. The writer has heard him in the trial of a considerable number of important causes in our high courts, and without disparaging other distinguished members of the Bar, he is clearly of the opinion that Mr. Knight had but few equals as a trial lawyer in this or any other State. He was self-poised, of free and forceful speech, incisive in delivery, and rarely failed to impress a court and jury of the justness of his contentions. He possessed a large fund of knowledge outside of his profession, which he often used with telling force in his court trials. He carried a serious bearing, and yet he had a remarkable vein of wit and humor when occasion called for an expression of this natural feature of his make up. He seemed to possess on all occasions all of the elements of an all round able and successful lawyer, who possessed the confidence of his brothers of the profession and the respect of all the people who knew him personally.

Mr. Knight was a native of New Hampshire; was born August 22, 1834; graduated from Dartmouth College in the class of 1861; was admitted to the bar in 1863 and practiced for a short time in his native town of New London, and also in Dover, N. H. In the spring of 1863 he located permanently in Charleston, West Virginia, and became a partner of the late Colonel Benjamin H. Smith, who was known all over the State as one of its greatest lawyers, who was a specialist in land titles and land litigations generally. A short time after Mr. Knight became a member of the firm of Smith and Knight, Colonel Smith, who was advanced in years, retired and his place was taken by his son, Major Isaac N. Smith, who was also a lawyer of erudition, the firm name remaining as before. Major Smith died in 1883, when Mr. Knight and Mr. George S. Couch entered into partnership under the firm name of Knight and Couch, which continued until Mr. Knight retired from practice January 1, 1892.

Mr. Knight was a man of large stature, of even temper and kindly disposition. He had a host of friends, and lived a clean, moral and upright life. He was fond of out-door living, and usually spent his summer vacations in the beautiful hill country around Sunipee Lake, New Hampshire, in fishing and other out-door sports, among his relatives and friends of early life. He was twice married. By his first wife he had two sons and one daughter. One of the sons is a noted lawyer of Charleston, who is mentioned in another place in this volume, the other son, Harold Warren Knight, a successful business man of Charleston, now deceased, and the daughter, Mary Ethel, who is the wife of Hon. George W. McClintic, another prominent lawyer of Charleston, who is also mentioned in this volume.

Mr. Knight was a Democrat in politics, but was in no sense a politician, never having sought an office of any kind. He, however, was Solicitor of the City of Charleston for a number of years, and was a member of the State Constitutional Convention of 1872. In both of these positions he rendered able and efficient service.

After spending a long, useful and successful life, he quietly passed into the unseen, December 16, 1897, sadly mourned by a host of admiring friends, leaving a record of a private and professional life equaled by few and difficult to surpass.

## Hon. Daniel Peck

Mr. Peck was born in Woodstock, Vermont, in 1798, and starting at the bottom reached the top, through trials and tribulations, which at times seemed insurmountable, but being endowed by nature with a remarkable intellect and an uncommon amount of pluck, he came out a conqueror, leaving his impress indelibly upon the times in which he lived. We put it mildly when we state that he was one of the greatest natural lawyers who ever adorned the State. His father died when Daniel was a mere lad, leaving a wife and six small children, Daniel being the eldest, and leaving no means for their support; consequently it was left for the subject of this sketch to earn a livelihood for all of them. He was fifteen before he started to school, and had to walk a distance of four and a half miles. Before his death his father moved his family to Eastern Ohio in a road wagon, stopping for a time at Washington, Pennsylvania, and Wheeling, West Virginia, the father being stricken with paralysis the entire support of the family depended upon Daniel, which he did bravely by working at anything he could get to do. Being a natural musician, he learned that art through a shoemaker at Wheeling, and in a short time became a teacher himself. He was stricken with smallpox which so disfigured his face that he was tabooed by society wherever he went; but he was not daunted. He kept on, though at times he was sad at heart. The family remained in Wheeling for a year or two on their way to Ohio, our subject working at house painting in day time and teaching music at night. The family finally settled at St. Clairsville, Ohio, where our subject studied law and began practice. Business came to him slowly, but he was so successful in handling his cases that in a very few years he was classed among the able attorneys of Eastern Ohio.

Mr. Peck at the same time had a large clientage also in Wheeling, but for many years maintained a palatial residence at St. Clairsville, only ten miles from Wheeling. He resided there for thirty-four years. In February, 1863, he purchased a lot of ground on the southeast corner of Chapline and Fourteenth Streets in the city of Wheeling, built a handsome residence and a large law office adjoining it, where he spent the remainder of his life. He was a sound and thorough lawyer and a wise counselor, and earned a large estate wholly from his law practice. He practiced in all the courts of Ohio and West Virginia for full sixty years. He was a man about six feet tall and weighed about two hundred pounds, and was extremely homely, but was gentle, generous and kind. His home life was simply beautiful, and his integrity was above reproach.

He married Miss Olivia Jones, of St. Clairsville, in 1843, and reared an interesting family. He died November 5, 1885, in the eighty-seventh year of his age.

Although he never was in college he was a man of great learning and industry. He was a Republican in politics and a Christian in whom there was no guile. The only office he ever held was a member of the Constitutional Convention of Ohio in 1850. He never sought an office of any kind. He was first a Whig and finally became a Republican in politics.

## Hon. John J. Jacob, A.M.

The subject of this sketch was the son of a local Methodist minister, and was born at Romney, Hampshire County, Virginia, December 9, 1829. He received his education at the High Grade Academy at Romney, known as the Romney Classical Institute, where he took a complete course in all of the higher branches of a classical education. He at once entered Dickinson College at Carlisle, Pennsylvania, where he remained until 1859, graduating in the class of that year with the degree of Bachelor of Arts. He thereafter became a professor in the University of Missouri. In the meantime he began the study of law, which he vigilantly pursued while a member of the faculty of the University. In 1865 he resigned from the University, returned to his former home at Romney, passed a creditable examination, was admitted as a member of the Hampshire County Bar, and began practicing as the junior member of the law firm of White and Jacob in the summer of 1865. Both members of the firm were well grounded in all branches of the law, and it was, therefore, but a short time until they became the leading lawyers of Hampshire and surrounding counties. Their practice was of a general character, and extended into all the State and Federal Courts. Both of them were known, not only as strong members of the profession, but were regarded as men of integrity and of high moral character, which greatly increased their volume of business. Both of them were Democrats, and that political party was largely in the ascendancy in that part of the State, which was helpful to them in business and added greatly to their popularity as attorneys.

In 1869 Mr. Jacob was elected a member of the State Legislature from Hampshire County, and therein was brought into such general notice and popularity throughout the State that, in 1870, he was elected Governor of the Commonwealth. While he was holding the office of Chief Executive a Constitutional Convention to frame a new Constitution for the State was held, which, among other things, fixed the term of Governor at four years, instead of two, as it had been formerly, and Governor Jacob became a candidate for re-election. The Democratic party, of which he was a member, nominated Hon J. N. Camden as the candidate of the party for the office. Governor Jacob became an independant candidate, the Republicans being in the minority, declined to nominate a candidate, indorsed Governor Jacob, and he was elected, thus enabling him to serve six years as Chief Executive, a longer term than was ever held by any other candidate since the organization of the State, in 1863. At that time the capital of the State was at the city of Wheeling.

At the expiration of his term he located in Wheeling in the practice of his profession, and became one of the leaders of that eminent Bar. He was thoroughly posted in all branches of the law, and in a brief period he secured a profitable share of the business of that thrifty city. In 1879 he was elected a member of the State Legislature, and in 1881 Governor Jackson appointed him Judge of the First Circuit to fill the vacancy caused by the resignation of Judge Thayer Melvin. In 1882 he was elected by the people to that responsible position.

He was a learned lawyer and was an exceptionally able judge. No taint of any sort was ever attached to his name or to any of his public acts. He returned again to his law practice and was remarkably prosperous, when he was stricken with apoplexy, and died within a few minutes. He was honorable and upright in all of his public and private dealings. His death occurred at Wheeling when he was but little above the age of sixty.

## Captain Alexander M. Poundstone

Among the well known, long established and successful lawyers of the central portion of the State was the subject of this sketch. He was born in Fayette County, Pennsylvania, February 26, 1835, and after a long and useful life of nearly eighty-three years, died at Buckhannon, West Virginia, April 14, 1917, where he had practiced law successfully for upwards of half a century. He was educated at Dunlap's Creek Academy and Green Academy, at Carmichael's Pennsylvania, and at Alleghany College, Meadeville, also in Pennsylvania. After completing the junior year he answered the call of the colors, enlisting in the Federal Army and serving until the close of the war. His fighting rank was that of Captain, but at the end of hostilities he was given a Major's Commission by brevet. He, however, always went by the title of Captain. During the war he participated in a large number of hotly contested battles. After peace was declared he began the study of law under the direction of an uncle who resided at New Lexington, Ohio.

Though a native of Pennsylvania, he removed to Buckhannon, West Virginia, went through his work of preparation, and entered at once upon the duties of his chosen profession, serving Upshur County fourteen years as its prosecuting attorney. He was frequently called upon to sit as Special Judge, presiding there with both dignity and accuracy. He soon won his way into a successful practice; indeed, he was one of the leaders of the Bar in the series of counties of the central section of the Commonwealth. In 1872, and again in 1879, he was elected a member of the West Virginia Legislature. As a lawmaker, as in everything else, he was painstaking in everything that came before him. He was a loyal member of the Republican Party and was a life-long member of the Methodist Episcopal Church, serving many years as an official member thereof. He was a member of the military order of the Loyal Legion and of the local Grand Army Post. He died firm in the Christian faith, loyal to his country and faithful to kindred and friends.

He appreciated the worth of the highest education, declaring to the writer that the regret of his life had been that he did not return to college and complete the course and receive the instruction of the senior year. He excelled in language, being ready in Latin and such a master in the use of English that inaccuracies therein were little less than painful to his trained ear.

He was made a trustee of Wesleyan College, Buckhannon, when the school was first established as a seminary, and continued in that relation to the end of his useful life, having been vice-president of its board of trustees for many years.

Captain Poundstone married a daughter of James McCormick, of Fayette County, Pennsylvania, by whom he had three children, two daughters and a son, Homer C., who is now a Lieutenant Commander of the United States Navy.

## Judge James Brewer Sommerville

Mr. Sommerville was born in Brooke County, Virginia, June 5, 1852. He was reared on a farm, and knows the ins and outs of hard labor "from sun-up to sun-down." He graduated from the State Normal School at West Liberty, Ohio County, West Virginia, a high grade academy, in 1872. He subsequently attended Bethany College at Bethany, Brooke County, where he rounded out a college education. For five years thereafter he taught in the public schools of his native locality, during which time all of his leisure moments were devoted to the study of legal text books. In 1878 he found himself sufficiently equipped to pass the required examination; in September of that year he was licensed to practice, and was admitted as a member of the Brooke County Bar, from which point as an office centre, he, in an unusually short period of time, found himself in the possession of a very profitable business. Seeking a wider field of labor, however, and feeling his ability as a lawyer, to take care of a larger business, he moved his office to Wheeling, where he has since resided, and where he is regarded one of the leading lawyers of that able and progressive Bar. He conducts a general practice in all State and Federal Courts, but for several years past, he has specialized in corporation matters, in which he has been unusually successful, and has a profitable clientele. He is a man of the highest honor and integrity, and has the confidence of the people generally, and particularly those members of the profession with whom he transacts business. He is one of the most genial of gentlemen and has an air of sociability about him most difficult to rival.

He is a Democrat, and has mixed considerably in politics, but never to the injury or detriment of his practice as a lawyer. He was a member of

JUDGE J. B. SOMMERVILLE

the West Virginia House of Delegates in 1877, and was promoted to the State Senate in 1885, where he served with marked ability for four years. He is a forceful trial lawyer, and his superior debating qualities served him well as a legislator. In one of the legislative sessions he only lacked a very few votes to elect him to the United States Senate, although he was not seeking the position.

He has always manifested a deep interest in education, and was for a number of years an active member of the Board of Regents of the State Normal Schools, the State University, and the Deaf, Dumb and Blind Schools. He married Miss Aggie G. Hosie, of Brooke County, May 13, 1879. He is an active member of the State Bar Association, and takes a deep interest in the civic development of his county and State. He is attorney for several large corporations in his section of West Virginia.

In September, 1918, he was appointed by Governor Cornwell Judge of the First Judicial Circuit, to fill out the term of Judge H. C. Hervey, deceased. His appointment was agreed to by the Republican attorneys of the circuit, as well as the Democrats, as a wise and proper selection, because he is a well-equipped lawyer, and possesses the judicial temperament. He declined to accept until he was assured of the united support of the lawyers of all classes and all political parties. He will no doubt prove to be an able and just judge, and will continue to wear " the judicial ermine " the rest of his days, unless he decrees otherwise.

## Hon. Daniel Lamb

Mr. Lamb was one of the most distinguished and able members of the Ohio County Bar. He was born in Connellsville, Pennsylvania, January 22, 1810, and died at Wheeling, West Virginia, when nearly eighty years of age. In April, 1823, his parents moved to Wheeling, Virginia. Having acquired a good scholastic training Mr. Lamb chose the law as his vocation in life. He read law under Morgan Nelson, a distinguished Wheeling attorney, and was admitted to practice in the Wheeling Courts in 1837, and soon took a leading position by virtue of his energy and ability. Whilst his success at the Bar seemed to be determined, and certainly could not have been more promising, yet in 1848 he accepted the position of cashier of the old Northwestern Bank of Virginia in Wheeling, and remained as such until the bank was merged into another institution in 1863. He, however, again promptly resumed his law practice, and kept it up to the day of his death. In knowledge of the law as a science, and in character and personal influence with his associates at the Wheeling Bar, no man, in his day, stood higher. He was one of the wisest and safest of counselors. In draughting intricate and difficult papers of any sort he was an expert, and was always sought after and relied upon. In codifying laws he had no superior in this State, and very few, if any, equals.

He was one of the strong men, after Virginia seceded from the Union, that organized the Restored Government of Virginia at Wheeling, in May, 1861, which ultimately resulted in bringing West Virginia into the Union as a sovereign State. He was a member of the Convention that prepared West Virginia's first Constitution, and was its chief draughtsman. He was also a prominent member of the first Legislature of West Virginia, and to his wise counsel and great power as a legal draughtsman may be attributed, in a large degree, the success of the new State. He was kept in the Legislature, from Ohio County, continuously up to and including 1867. He was often urged to enter politics, but declined. He was also urged to become a candidate for a position on the Supreme Court of Appeals of the State, but he declined, because he preferred the practice to a place in the judiciary. As a lawyer he was noted for the thorough preparation of his cases, as having a sound legal mind, and a perfect knowledge of the law he sought to present. He was a poor advocate, but was always strong before a court.

Mr. Lamb was originally a Whig, but was a Republican until 1870, when he became a "Conservative," and in his later years acted with the Democrats. He married in early life, and had one son, Gibson Lamb, who was a prominent banker of Wheeling for many years, but died when comparatively a young man. Mr. Lamb's people were Quakers, but he was an Episcopalian. The people who knew him were all his friends. He is often referred to as one of the wisest and best of men.

## Col. Joseph H. Pendleton

One of the very best natural lawyers the writer ever knew was the subject of this brief sketch. He was a native of Louisa County, Virginia, where he grew to manhood. He came to the western part of the State, and entered Bethany College in Brooke County in 1844. Four years later he graduated with high honors. Immediately thereafter he went to Staunton, Augusta County, and entered Judge Thompson's Law School in that town. After completing the prescribed course of study in that school he returned to Brooke County and opened a law office in Wellsburg, the seat of justice of that county. He remained there until August, 1851, when he located in the city of Wheeling, where he soon became one of the leading lawyers of that city. When the Civil War came on, he entered the Confederate Army as Major of the 23d Regiment of Virginia Volunteers and remained in that service until the close of the war, when he returned to Wheeling and resumed the practice of his profession. As we have stated above, he was by intuition a lawyer, although he was never a hard student of the law, but as an advocate he had but few equals, and as such he ranked among the most brilliant of his contemporaries.

While he was in the Confederate Army he was chosen, in 1863–4 and 5, a member of the Virginia Legislature, which convened in the City of Richmond, holding his commission at the same time in the Confederate Army. He died in the City of Wheeling, at an advanced age, where he spent the larger portion of his life.

## Judge Ralph L. Berkshire

R. L. Berkshire was born in Bedford County, Pennsylvania, April 8, 1816. From there he moved with his father, William Berkshire, a farmer, the following year, to Monongalia County, Virginia. He worked on the farm with his father until he reached his " teens ", when he learned the carpenter trade, which he followed for a time and in which he became proficient. When he reached his majority he began the study of law under the direction of Guy R. C. Allen, in 1838, one of the eminent lawyers of the Morgantown Bar. In 1841 he was licensed to practice, and gave all his time to reading and study that he could spare from the limited practice that came his way. He had a retentive memory and a strong intellect, which, coupled with honesty and industry, enabled him to command the attention of the people of the community, and aided him to earn a respectable support. In 1847 he was appointed Prosecuting Attorney of Monongalia County, and in 1852 he was elected by the people to the same office. He made a strong prosecutor and was thoroughly honorable and trustworthy. In 1860 he was the Whig candidate for Circuit Court Judge, but was defeated by the candidate of the Democrats.

He took an active part in the formation of the State of West Virginia; was a member of the Wheeling Convention, and his loyalty and fidelity to the Union made him one of the strong supports of the loyalists in the early days of the State. Judge Thompson, who was elected Circuit Judge in 1860, joined the Confederate cause in 1861, and Mr. Berkshire was appointed in his stead, and served efficiently until 1863, when he was elected one of the three first Supreme Court Judges of the State. Before Judge Berkshire was elected to any office, except that of Prosecuting Attorney, he was an unusually successful practicing attorney. He was strong of body and mind, and his industry and attentiveness to his business were almost without limit, and with the exception of the six years he was on the Bench, he devoted all of his mature life to the active practice of his profession.

Judge Berkshire, in a large degree, possessed the judicial temperament. He had strong common sense and could see the strong point in a case, and his unflinching integrity guided him to a proper conclusion in every case. His prominent characteristics were a strong will, unerring judgment, a large fund of humor, a keen knowledge of human nature, rigid devotion to what he believed to be right, and an integrity of character that riches dared not attempt to bribe and could not corrupt. In short, his personal character was beautiful in simplicity and gentleness.

JUDGE RALPH L. BERKSHIRE

He was a life-long member of the Methodist Episcopal Church, and till the day of his death he had the confidence and respect of all the people who knew him. He was social in his make-up, was devoted to his family and friends, and was at all times a Christian gentleman. He was an honor to the Bench and Bar of the Commonwealth.

## Hon. John Edward Kenna

John E. Kenna, the son of Edward and Marjory (Lewis) Kenna, was born in Kanawha County, Virginia, April 10, 1848. When he was ten years of age his parents moved to Missouri, where he grew to manhood, working on a farm, and attending common schools, thus obtaining the best rudimentary education within his reach. When he was but sixteen years of age he volunteered in the Confederate Army as a private soldier and remained therein until the Civil War closed. He possessed a marvelously retentive memory, and by associations with men of intelligence during that period his mind was developed in a remarkable manner. He participated in a number of hard fought battles, in one of which he was badly wounded in one of his shoulders, but he never left his command. He, however, was confined in a hospital with typhoid fever for six weeks while on duty in Arkansas. In June, 1865, he was captured when his command was surrendered at Shreveport, Louisiana. His parents, in the meantime, had returned to their Virginia home, whither he came, and where he spent the remainder of his life. He was employed at a salt furnace until 1866, when, realizing the importance of a more thorough education, he entered St. Vincent's Academy at Wheeling, where he remained two years in faithful study. His father was an able lawyer, and in early life the son decided to adopt that profession, so he returned to Kanawha County, and entered the law office of Miller and Quarrier, where he began a systematic course of study, and pursued it diligently until June 20, 1870, when he was admitted as a member of the Kanawha Bar.

He was energetic, self-assertive and self-reliant, and very soon after his admission as an attorney the fact was revealed that he possessed unusual ability and was a young man of great promise; consequently in the Fall of 1872 he was nominated and elected Prosecuting Attorney of Kanawha County, in which office he served efficiently and with great acceptability. In 1874 he was a candidate for Congress, and came within a few votes of winning the nomination. The cause of his defeat was his youthfulness. However, in 1876 he secured the nomination and was elected a member of the American Congress. Being a ready debater, and a hard worker, he proved to be a useful member, and the result was he was three times re-elected, making in all four terms. He however, served only a part of his fourth term, because of the fact he was elected a United States Senator in the Winter of 1883, and was re-elected six years later to a second term in the Senate. He was a natural leader of men. His power over men of all classes was wonderful. He was tall and well-proportioned, was a magnetic speaker and was genial and social, and was courageous in the extreme. No sort of opposition daunted him. He met all comers without fear or favor. Like Spartacus he never lowered his arm. He was firm in his convictions, and stood unalterably by what he considered right and in the line of duty. It cannot be denied that he possessed many elements of greatness. His marble statue stands in the Hall of Fame in the Capitol of the United States at Washington. He was always a consistent adherent to the Democratic Party, and "never deserted the faith." No other West Virginian ever commanded a larger following of personal friends.

Senator Kenna was also an able lawyer. Notwithstanding the fact that much of his time was spent in public life, he, at the same time, conducted a large and profitable law business, and participated in the trial of a large number of important cases. Had he devoted all of his time and energies to the practice of his profession his rank, as a lawyer, would have been very high. His great natural ability would have unquestionably placed him in the front rank. As it was, he, nevertheless, stood high in the legal profession of West Virginia.

Senator Kenna was twice married and had one daughter by his first wife, and five sons and one daughter by his second wife. All of his sons, except one who died in infancy, are big, strong, brainy men. One of them (Edward B.) died in young manhood. One of the three who are living is a very promising young lawyer of Charleston, who is making good as a member of the Kanawha Bar. The other two are engaged in business pursuits.

Senator Kenna departed this life before his sun had reached its noon, January 11, 1893, while serving his second term as a Senator in the Congress of the United States, and his remains were buried in the City Cemetery at Charleston amid a great throng of his admiring fellow citizens. He died as he had lived, a faithful adherent of the Roman Catholic religion, as did his father before him.

## Hon. Aretas Brooks Fleming, LL.D.

Our subject is the son of Benjamin F. and Rhoda B. Fleming, all of whom are natives of Marion County, Virginia, now West Virginia. He was educated in the common schools, and at the University of Virginia at Charlottesville, from which he graduated in the law department, then conducted by that able and distinguished lawyer and teacher Dr. John B. Minor, who never issued a diploma to a student who was not, in all respects, competent to receive it. He was admitted to the Marion County Bar in 1860, where he is still practicing. He is of medium height, of stocky build, and although long since past the meridian of life, carries the appearance of one much younger in years. His practice, extending over many years, embraced cases in all the State and Federal Courts, in which he has been unusually successful. By industry, honorable conduct, and proper methods of living, he has accumulated a large estate, which he carefully supervises and thoroughly enjoys. He is known and respected as an upright man, and honest in both thought and purpose, which in a large degree, account for his success in life. In the beginning of his career, he saw and believed that the ability to earn, power to learn, and the faculty of looking forward are the three capacities requisite to success in his profession, and he followed them to the letter, and has succeeded grandly.

Judge Fleming was a member of the West Virginia Legislature for two terms, and served successfully eleven years as a judge of the Circuit Court. In 1888, he was the nominee of the Democratic Party and was elected and served faithfully until the end of a four-year term as Governor of the Commonwealth. In all of his official acts he was both courteous and conservative, and with his modesty and urbanity went no shadow of weakness or lack of decision, but on the contrary, the " fortiter in re " was an essential part of his nature, necessary to his own self respect and commanding the respect of others.

After his term of Governor expired, he returned to Fairmont and resumed his law practice, which was large and profitable, and although his health has not been good for the last two or three years, he has several attorneys in his office, who carry the greater part of the burden of his large volume of business, but it is all supervised and directed by himself. For several years past he has confined all of his energies to the business of large corporations, and is known to be one of the State's ablest attorneys in that branch of the law.

Governor Fleming married in early life, has five children, and resides in the City of Fairmont, in the county where he was born, with several grandchildren gathered about him, who are a pleasure and comfort to him in his declining years.

## Judge John S. Hoffman

The subject of this sketch was born at Weston, Lewis County, Virginia, June 25, 1821, and received his education in the common and select schools of that section of the State. He was a young man of industrious habits, and of excellent character. His purpose in early life was to become a lawyer, and his reading of books was in that direction. He was of large stature and possessed a rugged intellect. He read law under the direction of his uncle, Gideon D. Camden, a distinguished lawyer and jurist of that period, and was admitted to the Lewis County Bar soon after he reached his majority. During his mature life he was an industrious, methodical student. From the beginning of his career he was imbued with the deter-

JUDGE JOHN S. HOFFMAN

mination to become a successful lawyer, and he, therefore, lived a life of labor and self denial in order that he might make good his early determination. He not only succeeded, but he succeeded grandly.

Whilst he was well informed in all the branches of the law, he specialized in land titles and land litigations, in which he made a distinguished reputation. There have been but few, if indeed any, lawyers in Virginia and West Virginia who surpassed him in his legal knowledge of all questions affecting land titles. In this branch of the profession he amassed a large fortune, which he distributed wisely prior to his death.

He was an ardent Whig in politics, and possessed a genial and friendly disposition, which made him popular with the people, but he rarely took part in political campaigns. However, he was elected a member of the Legislature of Virginia in the campaign of 1858, wherein he served with distinction. The only additional office he ever held was an Associate Judge of the Supreme Court of Appeals of West Virginia, to which he was elected in 1872. His opinions, whilst a member of that distinguished tribunal, were marked by thoughtful care and an accurate knowledge of the law.

At the breaking out of the Civil War he went with the South, entered the Confederate Army, and lost a leg in the defense of his convictions. He never fully recovered from the wound, which robbed him of much of his former energy and vigor. In his later years he identified himself with the Democratic Party. At no time did he ever deviate from the paths of rectitude and virtue in his methods of living. His devotion to his profession and his success therein is a worthy example to young men in all callings of the present day. His health while he was on the Supreme Bench of the State gradually weakened, until in 1876 he was compelled to resign and cease labor of all kinds; and on November 18, 1877, at the City of Clarksburg, where he had resided for a number of years, he surrendered his trust and quietly "fell on sleep."

Judge Hoffman never took unto himself a wife. His remains lie buried in the Odd Fellows Cemetery at Clarksburg, and the spot is marked by a plain, but imposing monument inscribed to his memory, and that of his uncle, the late Judge G. D. Camden.

## Judge Henry Brannon, A.B.

Judge Henry Brannon, of the Lewis County Bar, departed this life on the 24th day of November, 1914, at his home in the City of Weston, aged 77 years.

Judge Brannon was born November 26, 1837, at Winchester, Virginia. He was graduated from the University of Virginia in the year 1857 with the degree of A. B. He was married to Miss Hetta J. Arnold, of Weston, in 1858, and was admitted to the Bar in 1859 and soon became a lawyer of distinction. He was prosecuting attorney of Lewis County from 1860 to

JUDGE HENRY BRANNON

1865. He served two terms in the Legislature, in 1870 and 1871. He was elected Judge of the Eleventh District and served as a Judge of the Circuit Court for eight years, and was a Judge of the Supreme Court of Appeals for twenty-four years, when he voluntarily retired.

Judge Brannon retained his mental faculties until the last. On the day that death came to him suddenly he had argued a case in court.

Thus passed one of the greatest lawyers and perhaps the greatest jurist that West Virginia has ever brought forth. He was a natural born lawyer and he possessed an analytical mind and could express himself with a clearness that has been rarely equalled. His decisions lay down the law in such a comprehensive and convincing manner that his opinions are greatly relied upon in all the States of the Union. He so dignified the subjects upon which he exercised the powers of logical deduction that his cases are leading cases on the topics discussed therein. He had the wisdom of the historian; the wit of the poet; subtlety of the mathematician; and the logic and rhetoric of the eminent lawyer.

He found pleasure and peace in literature, and in conversation was one of the most entertaining of men. He was a pleasing writer. He was the author of a treatise on the Rights and Privileges under the Fourteenth Amendment to the United States Constitution, which is a standard authority upon the questions arising thereunder.

No man had a greater part in forming and fixing the laws of West Virginia than Judge Brannon. He was the interpreter of the law of a new State, and thoroughly identified with the formation and progress of West Virginia. As Cicero said: "For as the law is set over the magistrate, even so are the magistrates set over the people. And therefore it may be truly said, that the magistrate is a speaking law, and the law is a silent magistrate." As great as West Virginia has become by reason of its fixed and comprehensive laws and rules of conduct, a large part is due to the work, ability, and comprehension of Judge Brannon, performed during the long years of his service to the people of the State.

Whilst a practitioner at the Bar, he was regarded as one of the ablest and most successful lawyers of the entire State. He was careful, methodical and painstaking in the preparation of his cases. As an advocate he was logical and eloquent, and usually won, by his superior skill and thorough knowledge of the law, many hotly contested cases in the courts. He was a man of marked personal appearance; was about six feet tall and weighed, perhaps, 190 pounds; his features were strong and his whole appearance presented an aspect of force. Through his entire career he was an untiring student. His learning was varied and extensive. Rarely is there found in the ranks of men one so symmetrical in mind and character, one so sound in judgment, so unerring in moral perception, so faithful to every duty and so loyal to the right. In private life he was pure and without a cloud or a stain. He was a devoted husband and a loving father. What he believed he felt, and what he felt he spoke, and acted promptly, vigorously and with conscientious candor, and withal, he had a charming and winning personality. In manners he was at all times suave and courteous, and was a genial companion of both the young and the old, and always demeaned himself as a thorough gentleman. His like, in all respects, will be difficult to find. He was universally respected by all who knew him.

## Hon. Samuel A. Miller

One of the able lawyers of the Kanawha Bar, of a generation recently passed, is the subject of this sketch. He was born in Shenandoah County, Virginia, in 1818, and in 1842, when he was a young man, in the bloom of youth, he migrated to Kanawha County, and made up his mind to locate there permanently. He had received an ordinary English education, and before leaving the Valley of Virginia, he decided to read law. After a careful study of the required legal text books, he successfully passed the necessary examination, was licensed as an attorney, and became a member of the Kanawha County Bar. He had a clear legal mind, and being naturally studious, he was not long in taking a fair rank with the leading lawyers of that period. He found the land laws in this portion of Virginia in an unsettled and unsatisfactory condition, so he decided to make the settlement of land titles a specialty, although he was well posted in the different branches of the profession; and in the course of a few years, he built up a reputation as a prominent "land lawyer." He also became deeply interested in the manufacture of salt, which at, that time, was the chief industry of the Great Kanawha Valley. For a few years, he was president of the Kanawha Salt Company, a corporation that controlled the price of salt for many of the states to the West and South of the place of its manufacture. He, however, did not, during this period, give up his large law practice, or any part of it.

The war came on, and he volunteered in the Confederate Army, remaining therein until the close of hostilities, and retiring therefrom with the rank of Major. He returned to Charleston, resumed his law practice, and became one of the leading lawyers of that section of the State. During the pendency of the war, he was a Representative of the Southern portion of Western Virginia in the Confederate States Congress. He married the daughter of A. W. Quarrier, by whom he had five children. He continued to reside in Charleston, until the time of his death, which took place in October, 1890. He was a close student of the law, and is remembered as a genial man of gentle nature, who was honored and beloved by those who came in contact with him.

## Judge Adam C. Snyder

Judge Snyder was born in Highland County, Virginia, March 26, 1834. In 1852–53 he attended Mossy Creek Academy, Augusta County, Virginia, and in 1854–55 Tuscarora Academy, Pennsylvania, for a year (1856) he was a student at Dickinson College, Pennsylvania, and from there he went to Washington College, Lexington, Virginia, where he remained through 1857 and '58, and then entered the celebrated law school of Judge John W. Brockenbough, of Lexington, Virginia, where he remained through the college year of 1859. In the Fall of that year he was admitted to membership of the Greenbrier County Bar, where he practiced his profession until the time of his death, July 24, 1896.

Judge Snyder was an apt student, strong of both body and mind, and what he learned was not by memory or rote. His ideas became a part of his life, like the sap of a tree, enlarging and strengthening him, year by year, by real growth and vitalizing force. His thoughts therefore, were clear cut, exact and easily understood.

In 1861 he volunteered in the Confederate Army and was an Adjutant in the "Stonewall Brigade"; was captured by the Federals in 1863 and was held as a prisoner of war until 1864, when he returned to his command, and remained until the close of the war. He then resumed his practice at Lewisburg. In 1869 he married Miss Henrietta H. Carey, of Lewisburg. Five children resulted from this marriage.

In the meantime he became one of the noted lawyers of his section of the State, and in 1882 he was appointed a member of the Supreme Court of Appeals of the State to fill the unexpired term of Judge J. F. Patton, deceased. In 1884 he was elected to the same position for the full term of twelve years. He served ably until 1890, when he resigned and returned to the practice of his profession. His opinions which are published in several volumes of our West Virginia Reports (20 to 36 inclusive), are models. They generally give but one reason for the point decided and that the best one which is sustained by citation of the most pertinent authorities. He was a most conscientious judge. His whole desire was to decide a case according to law, without regard to consequence. Nothing but strong reason and authority, having the force of *stare decisis*, could force him from a position he had taken, after he had given it due consideration. As long as jurisprudence shall command the admiration of lawyers and judges, and have the respect of the people, the value of Judge Snyder's strong and convincing opinions will never fade, but will increase as the years go by.

Judge Snyder was a Democrat in his political convictions, but was never narrow or hide-bound. He was at all times a broad, liberal, brainy man. He was tall, rawboned, with clean cut features, wore whiskers closely trimmed, was round shouldered, even stooped as if the weight of years of wisdom might have taxed his frame. He died in the prime of life, esteemed by all his fellow citizens, whose pleasure it was to know him.

JUDGE ADAM C. SNYDER

## Judge James Paull

Hon. James Paull, an Associate Judge of the Supreme Court of Appeals of West Virginia, and an eminent member of the Ohio County Bar, son of George and Elizabeth Paull, was born near St. Clairsville, Bellmont County, Ohio, July 6, 1818. He began his studies in the Ohio public schools; subsequently he matriculated as a student at Washington College, Pennsylvania, from which he graduated in the class of 1835. After reading law for a time in the office of Zachariah Jacob, of Wheeling, one of the eminent attorneys of that city, he finished his law studies at the University of Virginia. For a year or more he taught some of the higher branches at Linsly Institute, a high grade academy at Wheeling, and then began the practice of the law in partnership with his former instructor, Z. Jacob, under the firm name of Jacob and Paull, and was successful almost from the day he began to practice.

In 1855 and '56 he represented Ohio County in the Legislature of Virginia at Richmond, as a Whig. With this exception he never held a political office, and never aspired to any. The only other public office he ever held was an Associate Judge of the Supreme Court of Appeals of the State, to which he was nominated and elected as a Democrat in 1872. With the exception of his two years' service in the Virginia Legislature, he devoted himself wholly to the law, in which he became eminent before he passed his fortieth milestone. He was of frail build, and was an inveterate worker. The duties of the Supreme Bench were both trying and exacting, which overtaxed his strength, and rather than shirk his duties or fail to do his full share of the work of the court, his strength gave way, and he died in the harness at his home in Brooke County, May 11, 1875, at the age of fifty-seven years. His decisions were clear, able, exhaustive, honest. He left a lofty record as an Appellate Judge, and as a citizen he was universally regarded as an honest man. As a lawyer and judge no other man ever left a cleaner or nobler record as a heritage to his family and his friends. He had no other aim or desire in life than to be right and to do right. His own and not the public sense was his rule of action as a citizen, a lawyer and a judge. There were never any ins or outs in his private or public life. He paid little court to the people, and practiced no artifices and employed no gratitudes to enlist them in his interests or purposes. He influenced men not so much by the sublimity of his sentiments as he inspired confidence and admiration of the dignity of his manners, and clearness of his understanding and the purity of his life. In taste, culture, information and sound judgment he occupied a high place among men. His home life was beautiful. He was not a negative, but was an active Christian. For the greater part of his life he was an active, useful member of the Presbyterian Church, eighteen years of which he was a Ruling Elder of the same. He was constant in good words and works, and left an abiding influence for good on the times in which he lived.

JUDGE JAMES PAULL

Judge Paull was twice married. The greater part of his life was spent in the city of Wheeling, but some eighteen months before he died he purchased a beautiful residence on high ground at Wellsburg, Brooke County, which is still occupied by one or more members of his family.

Judge Paull is a name that adorns the historic page of both Church and State, whose talents were used for the good of his fellow men, and whose name will be cherished for what he was and did, even after the marble slab that marks his last resting place shall have crumbled into dust.

## Hon. John William Davis, A.B., LL.B., LL.D.

The subject of this brief sketch, son of the late Hon. John J. and Anna Kennedy Davis, of Clarksburg, West Virginia, was born in that city April 13, 1873; was educated in the schools of his native city, and at Washington and Lee University, Virginia, from which he graduated in the classical course in 1892 with the degree of Bachelor of Arts. In 1895 he completed the required law course, and was awarded the degree of Bachelor of Laws. In 1915, his alma mater conferred upon him the degree of Doctor of Laws. For a short time after his graduation, he was a member of the faculty of the law department of the university, and proved himself to be a teacher of remarkable qualifications. At the urgent request of his father, who was an eminent lawyer, our subject returned to his native city, and in September, 1895, was admitted to the Bar of Harrison County and associated himself with his father in the practice of law under the firm name of Davis & Davis. From the very beginning of his practice, he revealed an unusual aptitude for his chosen profession, and so marked was his success that it soon became evident that he was destined to reach the highest place in the legal profession.

Being a young man of unusually attractive personality, he soon had a host of admiring friends, many of whom urged him to enter politics, which he persistently declined to do. However, in 1899, he was prevailed upon to become a candidate for the House of Delegates, and notwithstanding the fact that he was a pronounced Democrat and his county was strongly Republican, he was elected by a decisive majority. He was made Chairman of the Judiciary Committee of the House; served with zeal and efficiency, and acquitted himself with credit and honor. His friends soon learned that he possessed the elements of leadership, and accordingly began to urge that he should stand for further political preferment. He persistently declined to enter politics, but the nomination to the 62d Congress from the First West Virginia District was practically forced upon him, and, although the district had a large Republican majority, he was elected, and two years later he was re-elected a member of the 63d Congress. In the House of Representatives, he showed unusual adaptability for legislative service, and distinguished himself as a member of the Judiciary Committee.

HON. JOHN W. DAVIS

Because of his well-known legal attainments, he was selected as one of the managers on the part of the House in the impeachment of Judge Robert W. Archbold, a Judge of the Circuit Court of the United States. His argument at the trial of the impeachment made a profound impression upon the Senate of the United States. It overwhelmed the contentions of the eminent and learned counsel for the accused. It was unanswerable.

While serving his second term in Congress, Mr. Davis was tendered the office of Solicitor General of the United States by President Wilson. In this great office, where his legal attainments have been thoroughly tested in many noted causes before the Supreme Court of the United States, he has made a nation-wide reputation as a lawyer of pre-eminent ability. He has not only the respect, but the admiration of that great court, every member of which would, as is well known, welcome him with open arms to fellow-membership.

Mr. Davis was president of the West Virginia Bar Association in 1906, and in 1909 was a member of the West Virginia Commission on Uniform Laws.

With all the honors that have come to the Solicitor General, he is a very modest man, genial, courteous, kindly and ever and always considerate of others. Above all, he is a princely gentleman.

It may be truly said of him that he never wore "an undeserved dignity," and that his great honors have been "purchased by the merit of the wearer."

He was recently appointed by President Wilson, Ambassador of the United States to the Court of St. James, London, England. Although young in years, his friends are confident he possesses the qualifications to fill the same with credit to himself and honor to his country.

## Judge Marmaduke H. Dent, A.M.

The subject of this short memorial, son of Marshall M. and Mary C. Dent, was born in Monongalia County, Virginia, April 18, 1849. From both sides of his family he inherited strong qualities of mind. His grandfather, Dr. D. W. Roberts, was an original Republican, a man of prominence in his day, and a delegate to the Republican Convention at Chicago that nominated Abraham Lincoln for President of the United States in 1860. Judge Dent, however, was always a Democrat.

Judge Dent's life was spent in his native county. He graduated, in the classical course, at the West Virginia University in the class of 1870, receiving the degree of Bachelor of Arts. After his graduation he spent several years as a teacher in the public schools. Having decided in early life to become a lawyer, while teaching school, he began a systematic reading of legal text books, and in 1875 was admitted to the Taylor County Bar at Grafton, where he was engaged in active practice for

JUDGE MARMADUKE H. DENT

nearly twenty years, up to 1892, when he was elected to membership of the Supreme Court of Appeals of the State.

He was a successful practitioner before he became a Judge of the Appellate Court. He was handsome and distinguished in appearance, dignified and peaceful and affable in manner, and withal he was modest and unassuming, with ready sympathies, a keen sense of humor, and a refined and cultivated taste in literature. He was solidly grounded in his profession, and showed legal ability in important cases. On the whole, as a practitioner he made a record worthy of emulation, and one to be envied. He was an eloquent and logical speaker, and had the capacity for hard, persistent work. In a large degree he possessed the judicial temperament, and gave to the causes submitted to him an intelligent mind carefully trained. His opinions, therefore, are marked by the most careful research and are supported by ample authorities. It was not unusual for him to support his judgments with a line of unanswerable citations of authorities on points deemed only secondary by counsel, and yet, after reading the opinions of Judge Dent, they readily observed their weight and correctness.

Judge Dent was always conscientious and of a profoundly religious character. He was a member of the Presbyterian Church, and never neglected his Christian duties. He was invariably found on the moral side of every question that arose in civic matters. In his judicial opinions, he was sometimes facetious and novel in his utterances, for example, I quote a paragraph from *Atkinson* v. *Plumb*, 50 W. Va. 104, which was a controversy between two members of the same church: "But while it was the hand of Esau, it was the voice of Jacob. His confidence was abused under the guise of friendship, which blinded his eyes and he was despoiled by those of his own household: and with the earnest plea for retribution he seeks justice against his despoilers. What we have we freely give unto him,— the suit appears to be a contest over a bag of wind."

Judge Dent was of a most genial disposition, agreeable and gentle in his bearing, positive in his convictions, fearless in their expression, all which amply fitted him for the judicial ermine. He was absolutely incorruptible. Whilst he was extremely affable, he was extremely candid. He was always essentially just. His ability was unusual. His life and achievements stamped him both as a lawyer and a jurist of the highest types. He loved the masses and they revere his memory. He was tender, affectionate and thoughtful of the wants of those in his home-life and in his associations with the people generally. There was no blot or stain on his private or public career. He will ever be regarded as a clean lawyer, a just judge, a true and faithful husband and father, and a man whose life and character were enriched with noble qualities of head and heart.

He died at the city of Grafton, September 11, 1909, honored, respected and highly revered by all the people who knew and loved him.

## Hon. Jacob Beeson Jackson

From a family whose collateral branches extend into many States of the Southland, and whose name is not only historic but renowned and influential, destiny determined this member of the Jackson progeny to become a noted West Virginia lawyer and politician. His ancestors, on both maternal and paternal sides, were among the pioneers of Wood County, along the majestic Ohio river whose beautiful waves sweep noiselessly through Mississippi's currents to the Gulf and farther on to the sea. Upon his father's side are generals, lawyers, jurists, statesmen; and upon his mother's — the Beesons — who were among the early settlers of the splendid Ohio valley, who possessed firmness, probity, amiability and mental and physical vigor. Mr. Jackson was born in Wood County, Virginia, April 6, 1828. His early education was obtained in select and private schools, especially the one in Parkersburg conducted by the Rev. Festus Hanks, whose every effort was to inspire in the boys oratorical taste and a desire to equip themselves for high positions in life. In early manhood our subject determined to take law for a profession, and began the study of legal text books, under the tutelage of his father, which he studiously pursued until he was able to pass the required examination for admission to the Bar, which occurred in 1852. Departing from the county of his nativity, and the assisting influences of home, he began practice at St. Marys in the adjoining County of Pleasants. Genial and accommodating he soon became popular with the voters, who elected him Prosecuting Attorney of the county, which office he successfully filled for eleven years.

Desiring a wider field of opportunity, in 1864, he located in the city of Parkersburg, where his clientele largely increased. By this time he was classed among the leading lawyers of that section of the State. In 1870 he was elected Prosecuting Attorney of Wood County, holding the office six years. Near the close of his term he was elected, in 1875, a member of the West Virginia Legislature, and was Chairman of the Judiciary Committee, becoming one of the floor leaders of the House. In 1879 he was elected Mayor of the city of Parkersburg, and his friends still insist that the city never had a better ruler. He was a generous, sociable and enjoyable gentleman, and had many strong friends throughout the entire State, so he announcel himself as a candidate for the nomination of the Democratic Party for Governor of the Commonwealth. Accordingly he was nominated, and was elected to that high office and served the four-year term with great acceptability, from March 4, 1881, to March 4, 1885. After retiring from the Governor's office, he resumed the practice of law in all of the State and Federal Courts, which he kept up until his death, which occurred at Parkersburg at a ripe old age.

Governor Jackson was a member of the Protestant Episcopal Church. In June, 1855, he was united in marriage with Miss Maria Willard, of Pleasants County, an amiable and accomplished young lady. They had one son, who resides in the old home at Parkersburg, who is a successful attorney.

## Judge Okey Johnson, A.M., LL.B.

The subject of this brief memoir was born in Tyler County, Virginia, March 24, 1834, and was one of a family of fifteen children, all of whom were brought up on a farm. He worked on his father's farm in the summer and attended the country schools in the winter. In 1856 he graduated from Marietta High School: he studied law at Harvard University, graduating therefrom in 1858 with the degree of LL.B., and in July of that year he was admitted to the Virginia Bar. He located at Parkersburg in Wood County; opened a law office and entered upon the practice in that and adjoining counties. In 1874 Marietta College, Ohio, conferred upon him the degree of Master of Arts, *honoris causa.* He had a liking for politics, and was a presidential candidate in 1864 on the McClellan ticket, and in 1872 on the Greeley ticket. He was an orator of great attainments, and was popular with the people. In 1870 he was elected, as a Democrat, a member of the State Senate, and in 1872 he was chosen as a member of the West Virginia Constitutional Convention. In both of these bodies he took an active and influential part. He was a superior debater, which gave him leadership on most all occasions. In the campaign of 1872 he was nominated and elected by a large majority of the voters an Associate Judge of the Supreme Court of Appeals of West Virginia, and served the full term of twelve years, with great acceptability to both litigants and attorneys. He wrote upwards of 300 opinions, which appear in volumes 10 to 31 inclusive of the State Reports. His opinions took a wide range, and are marked by profound learning. He aided in no small way in building up a system of jurisprudence in West Virginia, and lived to see our Supreme Court brought into prominence by text book writers and by the courts of last resort of other and older states. He set his face against fraud of all kinds, and did not fail to hit it wherever and whenever it raised its hydra head. In all of his opinons he sought to be just and fair to all litigants, and when parties came before him, and came with clean hands, they could rely implicitly on receiving a fair deal. No jurist ever left behind him a cleaner record.

Judge Johnson was a man of very large stature, standing more than six feet and weighing more than 250 pounds. His voice was loud and sonorous, so much so that an audience, however large, had no trouble in hearing all of his utterances. He was a life-long member of the Baptist Church, and was a leader in its ranks. He was often chosen to preside at the Associations and Councils of that denomination.

After his retirement from the Bench of the Supreme Court, January 1, 1887, he located at Charleston and resumed the practice of his profession. The benefit of his long and severe training on the Bench showed itself in the number of important cases that came to him. However in June, 1895, the position of Dean in the Law Department of the West Virginia University was created, and Judge Johnson was elected to fill it. He accepted

JUDGE OKEY JOHNSON

and moved his residence to Morgantown, the seat of the University, and assumed the role of a teacher, which he enjoyed, and to which he devoted his energies, his great learning and natural gifts to the end of his life, which occurred June 16, 1903.

In early manhood Judge Johnson married the daughter of Hon. J. M. Stephenson, an eminent lawyer of the Parkersburg Bar, and some of his heirs survive him.

## Judge Warren Miller

The subject of this sketch was born in Meigs County, Ohio, and was educated in the public schools of his native State and the Ohio University at Athens, Ohio. Later he became a resident of Ripley, Jackson County, West Virginia, where he became a student of law, reading the legal text books systematically and thoughtfully. Being well educated and, therefore, possessing a trained mind, he was not long in acquiring a thorough knowledge of the fundamental principles of the great science of jurisprudence. After passing a creditable examination, he was admitted as a member of the Jackson County Bar, and began an active practice. He was studious and gave all of his time to his law office, and consequently was not long in building up a profitable clientele. In 1881 he was nominated by the Republican party as a candidate for Prosecuting Attorney of Jackson, County, and was elected thereto by the people. He discharged the duties of the office so ably and efficiently that four years later he was re-elected to a second term. He acquitted himself so creditably the people rallied to his support, and it was not long until he was recognized as probably the best and safest attorney of the Jackson County Bar.

Like most young attorneys, he exhibited a taste for the school of politics, and was early quite active in that direction. In 1884 he was sent as one of the Delegates at Large to the Republican National Convention at Chicago. In 1891 he was elected a member of the lower house of the West Virginia Legislature, and proved to be a law maker of ability and distinction. In 1894 he was elected a member of the Congress of the United States, and was re-elected two years later. In this high position he showed an aptitude for legislation and was an efficient member. In 1900 he was appointed a Circuit Judge by Governor G. W. Atkinson to fill a vacancy occasioned by the resignation of Judge Reese Blizzard. This position he filled satisfactorily and successfully. In 1903 he was appointed by Governor A. B. White to fill a vacancy on the Supreme Court of Appeals of the State. In this high position, as in the *nisi prius* Court, he served ably and satisfactorily to attorneys and litigants. He is well grounded in the law, and possesses, in a large degree, the judicial temperament, consequently it was not a difficult matter for him to fill this Appellate Court position in a most satisfactory manner. In 1911 he was again elected to the lower branch of the West Virginia Legislature, and in 1914 he was

JUDGE WARREN MILLER

elected to membership in the State Senate. In these positions he proved to be an active, intelligent, safe and sane maker of State laws.

He is a broad, thorough, conscientious lawyer, devoted to his profession in which he early took a leading place. As we have shown, he held many public offices, in every one of which he did his duty well. As a Judge he was faithful, upright and absolutely incorruptible. He possesses a strong will, sound judgment, a rigid devotion to what he believes to be right, and an integrity of character that no one dares encroach upon.

Moreover, he possesses unusual business ability. He invested wisely, and has accumulated a large estate, which includes two or three big farms on the Ohio River, to the cultivation of which, these later years, he devotes much of his time and careful attention.

Judge Miller is a bachelor, and makes his home at a leading hotel at Ripley, the seat of justice of Jackson County, where he has a large following of warm personal friends. He is but little taller than was the first Napoleon, but has a strong and well developed frame, and on the whole is rather a handsome man.

## Judge James F. Patton

Judge Patton, son of Hon. John M. Patton, one of the leaders of the Bar of Virginia for many years, was born September 19, 1842, at Richmond, Virginia, and died at Wheeling, West Virginia, March 30, 1882. He was educated in the private schools of his native city, and in 1858 he was graduated from Hanover Academy, one of the then well known educational institutions of Virginia. In 1859 Mr. Patton, with his mother, moved to their country seat in Culpeper County, Virginia. When the Civil War broke out young Patton entered the Confederate Army, and remained therein until the close of hostilities. On several occasions he distinguished himself for bravery on the field of battle, for which he received promotion, he having entered the service as a private soldier. He promptly entered the law office of his brother-in-law, John Gilmer, of Pittsylvania County, and under his tutelage read law, and in due time passed the necessary examination and was admitted to the Bar of that county. He possessed a fertile brain, and it was not long until he was recognized as a lawyer of distinction.

In April, 1869, he married the accomplished daughter of Hon. Allen T. Caperton, a Senator in Congress from West Virginia. Within a year after his marriage he became a partner of his distinguished father-in-law, who resided at Union, Monroe County, where he came rapidly into prominence as a lawyer and citizen. In 1872 he was nominated by the Democratic party as a candidate for Prosecuting Attorney of Monroe County, and was elected, which office he filled with marked ability for four years. He declined a renomination, finding it necessary to devote all of his time to his already large and growing practice. At the early age of 37 he was

JUDGE JAMES FRENCH PATTON

appointed, June 1, 1881, by Governor Jackson, to fill a vacancy on the Supreme Court of West Virginia, occasioned by the resignation of Judge C. P. T. Moore. He promptly entered upon the duties of that high judicial office. Being strong, both mentally and physically, he threw all of his energies into the discharge of his official duties. At the Spring term of the Court of 1882 he delivered four able opinions, when his life and his labors were at once ended by sudden death. In this brief period, however, he had won for himself the respect and esteem of his brethren of the Bench and Bar, as also the admiration and affection of all the lawyers who had appeared before him. It was generally conceded that Judge Patton had before him a brilliant future. He was naturally kind and gentlemanly, and yet, at the same time, he was firm and unwavering. He possessed a well balanced judicial mind, and was both just and honorable. He possessed not only the ability to discern the legal rights of a litigant, but he had the moral stamina, indispensable in an upright judge, to decide according to the law and the right against all influences of every kind whatever. His untimely death was universally mourned. His home-life was devotion personified, and every one who knew him personally was his friend. His sun set before it had even reached its noon.

## Judge John W. Mason

The subject of this sketch will doubtless ever be known and remembered as one of the rugged and able lawyers and jurists of West Virginia. He was born on a farm in Monongalia County, Virginia, January 13, 1842, and departed this life in the adjoining county of Marion, April 23, 1917. Although his opportunities for schooling were somewhat meager, he was far from being uneducated. He attended the public schools of his neighborhood for a number of years, and later graduated from the Monongalia Academy at Morgantown, which subsequently became the foundation of the West Virginia University, in which, for a short time, he was a teacher. Being an earnest seeker for an education, he acquired, by the careful and systematic reading of good books, a varied and substantial learning, and thus became master of a clear, terse and vigorous style, both in writing and in speaking.

He early decided upon the law as a profession, and began the reading of legal text books. However the Civil War came on, and at the age of seventeen he entered the military service of the United States as a private soldier, and after attaining the rank of a non-commissioned officer, and had engaged in a number of hotly contested battles, he returned to his native county, and took up the study of the law, which he earnestly pursued by reading the required text books, until he was able to pass the necessary examination as a licensed attorney in 1867. He often stated that his four years of army experience was most helpful to him in after years. He was a Republican, and for a time was quite active in the politics of the State

JUDGE JOHN W. MASON

and Nation, although he was never an office seeker. He was once nominated for a seat in Congress, and was only defeated by ten votes. He was four years Chairman of the Republican State Executive Committee, and for twelve years he was a member of the National Executive Committee of that party. He was not only a good organizer, but ranked high as a platform speaker during political campaigns. But at no time did he allow politics to interfere with his large and ever increasing law practice, and repeatedly refused to accept nominations for Governor, Supreme Court Judge and Federal appointments. In 1889, he, however, accepted the position of Commissioner of Internal Revenue at Washington, D. C., which was tendered to him by President Harrison, and he filled that great office in a most acceptable manner for four years.

For thirteen years he served as Circuit Court Judge of the Fourteenth Circuit, and it was universally conceded that he was one of the foremost judges in ability and acceptability in the entire State. Shortly after his voluntary retirement from the Bench he was made a member of the Virginia State Debt Commission, in which capacity he rendered invaluable service to the State. In the summer of 1915 a vacancy occurred on the Supreme Court of the State, and Judge Mason was appointed to that important office November 1st of that year to fill said vacancy, and until January 1, 1917, he made the same high record as an Appellate Court Justice that he maintained as a *nisi prius* judge. After leaving the Supreme Court Bench he retired to private life in his splendid home in the city of Fairmont.

Judge Mason was happily married to Miss Rebecca E. Wallace, of Morgantown, in 1870, to them only one son was born, John William Mason, Jr., who is a young lawyer of great promise at Fairmont, and who, like his father, offered his services as a volunteer in defence of his country, and is now at the front in the terrible war now prevailing in Europe.

Judge Mason was a Ruling Elder in the Presbyterian Church for many years prior to his death. He was also a member of the Masonic Fraternity, and he is remembered as an able lawyer, a just judge, a true and faithful husband and father, and a man whose life and character was enriched with noble qualities of head and heart.

## Judge Mathew Edmiston

Judge Edmiston in his day was one of the ablest lawyers and jurists in the State of West Virginia. He was born in Little Levels, Pocahontas County, Virginia, September 9, 1814, and died at Weston, West Virginia, June 29, 1887. He was educated in the public and private schools of the early part of the nineteenth century, and by the systematic reading of historical and biographical books that came within his reach. In this way, mainly, he stored his mind with information and facts which were valuable and helpful through a long, useful and successful professional life. He read law in the office of a friend and relative at Fincastle, Botetourt

JUDGE MATHEW EDMISTON

County, Virginia. He possessed an inquiring mind and a remarkably retentive memory, and was at all times able to use readily what he had read and digested. In less than a year's study of legal text books he was able to pass a creditable examination, and was admitted to the Fincastle Bar in 1839. He returned to Pocahontas County that year, subsequently located permanently at Weston in Lewis County, where he remained as a lawyer and judge until his death. He and Judge George H. Lee, of Clarksburg, formed a partnership in the practice, and maintained offices at Parkersburg, Clarksburg and Weston for upwards of ten years. Both of them being men of unusual ability they were not long in securing employment in a large number of important causes in the towns named. Later both of them became Judges of the Supreme Court, and both of them were regarded eminent jurists.

Judge Edmiston represented Lewis County in both branches of the Virginia Legislature prior to the Civil War. In 1852 he was appointed a Judge of the Circuit Court and served ably as such until 1860, when he returned to the regular practice at Weston. In 1886 he was appointed a Justice of the Supreme Court of Appeals of the State to fill the vacancy caused by the death of Judge Hoffman, and served ably until his death, one year later. He exhibited marked ability as a judge as well as a counselor. His opinions as an Appellate Judge are in the Ninth West Virginia Reports. His mind was bright and his analytical faculties were of a high order. He had an inate love for justice. His power of condensation was conspicuous. His perception was keen and incisive. He was, while a practicing attorney, an illustrious advocate, who strove to do his full duty to his clients, and was a just, able and upright judge. His mind possessed sturdy characteristics. He was elected a member of the Constitutional Convention of 1872, but was physically unable to serve even a single day, and soon thereafter passed away forever. He said prior to his demise, that "death had no sting for him, nor had the grave a victory."

Judge Edmiston married Miss Minerva Bland, of Weston, in February, 1840. They had four sons and three daughters. Three of the sons were physicians and one son, Hon. Andrew Edmiston, mentioned elsewhere in this volume, is a successful lawyer at Weston.

In his political convictions Judge Edmiston was a Democrat, as were all the members of his family. He was also a man of the highest order of integrity and personal character.

## Col. Alexander Monroe

Col. Monroe, the Jeffersonian Democrat, who fairly presided over the House of Delegates of West Virginia in the session of 1875, is from Hampshire County, and was born December 29, 1817. At the early age of eighteen he was left an orphan, with four younger brothers and two sisters to rear and educate. He taught school in winter and worked on the farm in season to accomplish this. He read law with A. P. White at Romney; was admitted to the Bar in 1858, and was made Prosecuting Attorney of the county the next year. In 1861 he went into the Confederate service as Colonel of Militia, and held the oldest commission in the State. After the Conscript Bill passed he raised a battalion of cavalry and continued in service till Lee's surrender. He was a member of the General Assembly of Virginia in 1849–'50, and from 1862 to 1865 serving in each session during the war, but returning after the Assembly adjourned to military duty. He was elected in 1872 to the Convention to revise the State Constitution of West Virginia, and in 1875 became a member of the House of Delegates from Hampshire County and therein was elected Speaker. He was also a member in 1879–'81–'82, serving upon the Revisory Committee to amend the Statutes in 1881. He was regarded as an able lawyer, who specialized in Land Law.

## Hon. Caleb Boggess

The Judiciary of our State never lost a more honored or more honorable jurist, nor its Bar a more able attorney, than when Caleb Boggess died, April 14, 1889. Congestion of the lungs caused his sudden demise at his home in Clarksburg that night. One daughter, Genevieve, was all that was left to mourn her double bereavement — the mother preceding the father to a better rest only two months.

Caleb, son of Caleb Boggess, was born April 29, 1822, in Lumberport, Harrison County, Virginia, where he resided in early life. His father came from Fredericktown, Maryland, to Monongalia County, Virginia, in 1800, and soon after settled in Harrison County. Young Caleb received all the advantages his father could secure for him in the common schools of that day, preparatory to entering him at the Virginia Military Institute at Lexington, whence he graduated in 1845, with honor and great promise. He studied law under Judge E. S. Duncan; was admitted to the Bar in 1847 at Clarksburg, Virginia, and continued to practice law through life. For twenty years, up to the time of his death, he was chief counsel in this State for the Baltimore and Ohio Railroad Company. His views made him averse to partisan office holding, only once allowing a departure, when he served his people in the Virginia Constitutional Convention of 1861.

In 1848 Mr. Boggess married Miss Eliza A., daughter of Judge G. D. Camden, and located for the practice of his profession in Weston shortly afterward. He soon took a leading position at the Bar. He was elected as a Union candidate to represent Lewis County in the Convention at Richmond, which passed the ordinance of secession, defeating Dr. Bland, who was the secession candidate. He served his constituents faithfully in that Convention. He was one of the West Virginia delegates who returned home before the adjournment of the Convention. While at Richmond his residence in Weston was destroyed by fire. When the Convention adjourned he located at Clarksburg and resided there until his death.

When Judge Lee died Mr. Boggess was retained as chief counsel for West Virginia for the Baltimore and Ohio Railroad Company, and was still so employed at the time of his decease.

Mr. Boggess possessed a rare legal and mathematical mind. He took delight in investigating intricate legal questions, and when he undertook a case he always mastered it thoroughly. He had a large practice in the Supreme Court of Appeals of the State, and argued a number of important cases in the Supreme Court of the United States. He was employed on one side or the other of most all of the leading cases in the Clarksburg Court for more than a quarter of a century prior to his death.

## Judge Joseph M. Sanders

Our subject is a graduate of no college and, therefore, carries no scholastic degrees, but he is a graduate of that world wide school of experience and every day practice, and carries with him the diploma of success, and we may add, wonderful success, both as a lawyer and a jurist. He was born in Wythe County, Virginia, August 26, 1866, and is yet only in the prime of life, with the promise of greater results in the future. His parents moved to Tazewell County in 1870, where our subject attended the common schools as an earnest seeker after an education, which he knew well was essential to success in any calling in which he might engage for a life work in future years. In the meantime he was a careful reader of books, which, with his rudimentary studies that occupied his spare moments, furnished him a varied and substantial learning, and in this way he became master of a clear, terse and vigorous style, both in writing and in speaking. Having decided in early life to become a lawyer, he early began the reading of legal text books, which occupied every hour of time that he was able to devote to study and research until 1888, when he was only twenty-two years of age, he passed the required examination for an attorney-at-law, and was admitted to the Tazewell County Bar. Divining the rapid development of Southern West Virginia he chose Bluefield for a permanent residence, and there he began the practice of his profession. Devoting all of his energies and time to his business he soon developed into a successful practitioner. His legal attainments were so apparent and pronounced that in 1896 he was nominated by the Republicans for Judge of the Circuit Court of the Ninth Circuit and was elected by a large majority of the voters of the circuit.

Judge Sanders served the full term of eight years with entire satisfaction to the Bar of the counties in the circuit. He was unanimously renominated and the Democrats agreed not to nominate an opponent, so that he would be accorded the compliment of a unanimous election. At

JUDGE JOSEPH M. SANDERS

the Republican State Convention of 1904, however, he received the nomination for Judge of the Supreme Court of Appeals to succeed Judge Warren Miller, so he resigned the circuit judicial nomination and was elected a member of the highest court in the State. His service on the Appellate Court was most satisfactory, and his opinions were terse and able. He, however, preferred the practice at the Bar to the judiciary, and accordingly at the expiration of three years of active, successful service on the Supreme Court, tendered his resignation as a Judge and again resumed his membership of the Bar of Practitioners of Mercer County, where he resides and conducts a very profitable legal business. He has, therefore, shown himself twice to be not only an able and efficient Judge, but has twice proved himself to be a successful attorney in the courts of the State.

Judge Sanders was in 1888 united in marriage with Miss Mamie Crockett, of Tazewell, Virginia, by whom he is rearing an interesting family in their home at Bluefield. A son, Joseph M., junior, is a student at the West Virginia University, who is following in the footsteps of his father, and later on expects to join him as the firm of Sanders and Sanders, attorneys-at-law, Bluefield, West Virginia. It is hoped that he may be equally successful in his chosen life work as his distinguished forebear. If he learns well in early life that there is always room at the top in all important undertakings, he will most surely reach the goal of his ambition.

Judge Sanders, in 1916, was elected president of the West Virginia Bar Association, of which he has been for years past, an attentive and efficient member. He was elected a member of the State Senate in 1918.

## Judge Ira Ellsworth Robinson

Judge Robinson descended from a family of pioneers who at an early period settled in the Tygart's Valley portion of Western Virginia, and opened up and developed that rich and attractive stretch of country. His parents were William and Mary (Sayre) Robinson, whose home was in Taylor County, West Virginia, not far from Grafton, its seat of justice. There the distinguished son first saw the light, September 16, 1869. In youth he rendered industrious service on the farm, which is greatly to his credit. His early years were spent in the common schools of that section. Later he entered the State Normal School at Fairmont, where he received a thorough academic training, and graduated with honors in the class of 1889. Having made up his mind to become a lawyer, he at once entered upon preparation for the profession, and spared no pains to make his training thorough. In 1890 he was a student under the eminent John B. Minor at the University of Virginia. He was admitted to the Bar in 1891 and promptly entered upon the practice, at Grafton, with that earnestness and vigor peculiar to his subsequent years of earnest, active service

JUDGE IRA E. ROBINSON

as a lawyer and a judge. From the very beginning he started in to win, and it cannot be questioned that he won out grandly. He was a student and an untiring worker, and never failed to go down to the bottom of all his important cases. These habits enabled him to forge to the front of the Bars in the counties where he engaged in the profession of a lawyer.

Although he was never, *per se*, a politician, he, as a Republican, for four years held the office of Prosecuting Attorney of Taylor County, and was a good one. There was no compromise or half-way business in his make up; every violator had to come into court and answer. Not even a drop of timid or swash-buckler blood ever coursed through his veins. This is one of the main reasons why he steadily reached towards the top of his profession with sure and steady steps.

Later on he was chosen as a candidate for State Senator, was elected, and served with distinguished ability, satisfying his associates in the Senate, and the people at large, that he was an able legislator. His footprints are noticable in the legislation of that period.

In October, 1907, one of the justices of the Supreme Court of Appeals of West Virginia having retired, Judge Robinson was appointed to fill the vacancy, because of his marked qualities in the law and his possession of a singular judicial turn of mind. At the general election in 1908 he was elected by the people of the State to continue in the place to which he had been appointed. Although only thirty-eight years of age when he assumed the Bench, he soon demonstrated the wisdom of the Governor in selecting him for that high honor. His first written opinion exemplified a correct conception of justice, as well as a fine literary style. His rhetoric has not been surpassed by any of our justices in the history of the court. He developed an unconscious judicial fitness, and possessed the judicial temperament in a high degree, and was just and conscientious in all his judicial acts. His every act showed him to be incorruptible. In all relations, in his family-life, at the Bar, and in his friendships, he has been loyal and true.

He is an active member of the Methodist Episcopal Church, and has twice been elected to its General Conference, in which great deliberative body he wielded large influence. He married Miss Ada Sinsel, of Grafton, in 1892, and to her he has always given credit for inspiration leading him to success.

October 26, 1915, after eight years of devoted service on the Bench, Judge Robinson resigned his seat on the Supreme Court. In 1916 he was nominated by the Republican Party as its candidate for Governor of West Virginia, but in the November election of that year went down to defeat with the candidacy of another able man from the Bench, Mr. Justice Hughes. He immediately returned to his profession and has exhibited again his old time qualities as a lawyer, matured by judicial experience.

Judge Robinson is a real devotee of the law. He is a lecturer in the College of Law of the West Virginia University, lending great leadership to the young man in his preparation. He is widely known by his contributions to legal periodicals.

## Judge James H. Ferguson

The subject of this brief memoir was born in Montgomery County, Virginia, April 14, 1817; was entirely self-educated, and was self-made. He possessed a massive intellect, and was almost a giant in stature. By application and industry he became one of the great lawyers, jurists and legislators, the State of Virginia ever produced. He showed greatness in everything he undertook. He was learned in the law and towered above most men in knowledge as well as in physical stature. He left his impress upon the times in which he lived, and was recognized by the people who knew him personally as a man who possessed the elements of true greatness. He was regarded, not only as an erudite lawyer; but as a law-maker, in which, he had but few equals, and probably no superiors. He was admitted to the Bar in 1840, and settled in Logan County, now West Virginia, and in a very short period of time, became the leading lawyer of that entire section. In politics he was a Whig. He was elected Prosecuting Attorney of Logan County, which office he held and ably filled until 1848, when he was elected to the Virginia Legislature from the counties of Logan and Boone, and was re-elected to the same office each year until 1851. In 1850, he was elected a member of the Constitutional Convention of Virginia of 1850 and '51, while he was a member of the Legislature of the State, and was one of the leaders of both bodies. He was formidable in all of the debates on all of the important questions that arose. He opposed everything that pointed toward a dissolution of the Union, and opposed the pernicious doctrine of secession from the commencement to the close of the Civil War.

In 1864, he became a citizen of Cabell County, and in the Fall of that year he was elected a member of the Legislature of the new State of West Virginia, and was re-elected to the same position every year to and including 1871. In all of these bodies he was Chairman of the Judiciary Committee, and was the controlling factor in practically all of the legislation that was enacted at those several sessions. In 1868 he was chairman of the Joint Commission on the revision of the West Virginia Code. He did most of the work, and by direction of the Legislature prepared and indexed the Code of 1868 for publication. During the autumn of that year, he was elected Judge of the Circuit Court of Cabell, Boone, Logan, Wayne and Lincoln Counties; and after about two years of pronouncedly able service on the Bench, he resigned, opened a law office in Charleston, became chief counsel for the Chesapeake and Ohio Railroad, where he remained until his death. He was elected to the Legislature from Kanawha County in 1876. He was able in all branches of the law, but was perhaps strongest in land litigation. There were but few equals to him in all branches of the law pertaining to the adjustment of controverted land titles. He was also a specialist in corporation controversies. As a matter of fact, he was an all-around lawyer: and as a law maker, he had no superior in West Virginia.

He was twice married, and was a devout member of the Baptist Church. He died at his residence in Charleston at the advanced age of 86 years.

At the close of the Civil War, Judge Ferguson identified himself with the Democratic Party, but never was a pronounced partisan.

## Judge John G. Jackson

The Jackson family of West Virginia includes some of the most illustrious citizens the Commonwealth of Virginia, from its origin, has produced. Many of them were distinguished lawyers, several of them were able jurists, and one of them, Thomas J. (Stonewall), was one of the greatest military chieftains, the entire Republic has ever produced.

The subject of this brief sketch was one of the very prominent lawyers and jurists of Western Virginia, for a great many years before the division of the State. He died in 1828, and we have found it difficult to collect but a few facts pertaining to his distinguished career. He was born in Harrison County, in 1774, and died, as we have stated, in 1828. He married Miss Payne, in the White House, in Washington, D. C., a sister of President James Madison's wife. After her death, he married a daughter of the late Gen. Return Jonathan Meigs, who at that time was the first Governor of the Territory of Ohio. At the time of his second marriage Mr. Jackson was the Surveyor General of the United States under General Meigs for the State of Ohio. He was a member of Congress of the Wheeling District of Western Virginia from 1795 to 1797, and again from 1799 to 1810, and still again from 1813 to 1817. When the United States District Court for the Western District of Virginia was created in 1822, he was appointed its first Judge, and held that important office until the time of his death in 1828. It is claimed that he was a distinguished lawyer and a Judge of marked ability and fairness. He was a man of great force of character, and weilded a powerful political and social influence throughout the territory which comprises what is now the State of West Virginia.

His politics was that of the Whigs. He erected what, at that time, was termed a fine frame residence in the town of Clarksburg, which was recently razed for the purpose of erecting a better and more modern building. He has no immediate relative residing in that locality; hence our failure to furnish more details of his prominent career.

## General John Jay Jackson

General Jackson was born in Wood County, Virginia, February 13, 1800, and for two or three years when a boy was tutored by Dr. David Creel in the rudimentary branches of education. At fourteen years of age he entered Washington College, Washington, Pennsylvania, and at the expiration of one year, he was appointed a cadet to West Point Military Academy.

March 8, 1815. In less than four years, having completed the required course of study, he graduated high in his class July 24, 1818, in the nineteenth year of his age. He served for about two years in the Seminole War in Florida in the Engineers Department. Later he was promoted to Adjutant, and during 1821 and 1822, he served on the staff of Gen. Andrew Jackson in Alabama and Florida. In 1822, while on a furlough at his home in Parkersburg, he resigned from the United States Army and at once took up the study of law. Having a strong and thoroughly cultured mind, he made rapid headway, and the 28th of April, 1823, he became a member of the Wood County Bar. By studious application and force of character, he soon took position in the front rank of his profession, and was recognized as one of the leading lawyers of the Commonwealth, which position he successfully maintained through his long and useful life.

In 1826 he became Prosecuting Attorney of Wood County, which office he held until 1852. He also filled the same office in the adjoining County of Ritchie from 1842 to 1852. It is said of him that he was a terror to the wicked ones in those counties. He guarded well the interests of those counties and the State, whose official he was, with the utmost care. He was a Whig in politics, and was elected to the Legislature of Virginia, several times, his first term being in 1825 and his last in 1844. Here, too, he displayed his accustomed energy, and showed himself to be a wise and discreet legislator.

In 1842 he was elected by the Legislature, General of the Twenty-third Brigade of the militia of Virginia, and remained such until 1861, when the State seceded from the Union, and the peaceful avocations of the people were changed for the active duties of tent and field, in our late and deplorable fratricidal war. General Jackson was a member of the historic Convention of 1861 held at Richmond, and ably and earnestly opposed the heresy of secession. He stood firmly by the Union then and throughout the Civil War.

General Jackson was not only at the forefront as a lawyer, but was a leader also in the civic development of the section of the State in which he resided, and was easily its foremost citizen for a-half century or more. He was a member of the Protestant Episcopal Church. After the close of the Civil War, he identified himself with the Democratic Party, and remained an adherent of the same until his death, which occurred at his home in Parkersburg, January 1, 1877. He was twice married, and left several children by both unions, three of his sons, by his first wife, became eminent lawyers, sketches of each of them appear elsewhere in this volume.

General Jackson's fame rests upon his legal ability and erudition, his patriotic and wise deeds and counsel, his benevolent and Christian career, and his illustrious example of fortitude, integrity, industry and success in all of his laudable undertakings.

## Judge John Jay Jackson

Judge Jackson was the eldest son of the late Gen. John Jay Jackson, of Parkersburg, West Virginia. He is a native of Parkersburg, Virginia, as was his father, and was born August 4, 1824. He was educated at private schools and at Princeton University, graduating in the class of 1845; studied law under the direction of his father, whose personal sketch appears in this volume, and also under Judge John J. Allen, a member of the Supreme Court of Appeals of Virginia; was admitted to the Wood County, Virginia Bar in 1846, and practiced successfully until he was appointed, in August, 1861, Judge of the United States District Court for the Western District of Virginia, which office he held and ably filled for the unprecedented period of forty-three years. During the rebellion he opposed the fallacy of secession, and stood out boldly for the perpetuation of the Union. On this great question he never wavered. Before his appointment as Federal Judge, he was a remarkably successful lawyer. He was a natural orator, and hence was an able advocate. He served several terms as Prosecuting Attorney of Wirt and Ritchie Counties, and was an unusually successful prosecutor. Law breakers dreaded to come before him, because they knew that he was able, firm and courageous, and had no sympathy for law-breakers of any kind.

Like his eminent father, he was an ardent supporter of the Whig party, but became an Independent Democrat after the Civil War, yet at no time was he a partisan. His strong mind, was at all times, given over to settlements and dispositions of the many towering law problems that were brought almost continuously before him on subjects which grew out of the Civil War.

During his lengthy service on the Bench he had to consider and decide some of the most important legal questions that have ever been brought before the courts of any country. He was required to pass upon abstruse and difficult law and chancery suits, involving land titles, bankrupt cases, admiralty causes, corporation cases and criminal cases, of all varieties. His decisioins in most cases, when appealed, have generally been affirmed by the Appellate Courts. He was noted for firmness in his make up, and when convinced that he was right, he was as unchangeable as the sun. For many years, he was called the "Iron Judge." He was emphatic in his rulings, and many lawyers and litigants regarded him as austere. This was not true. Naturally he was as kind, gentle and sympathetic as a woman. The writer knew him intimately and well, and can testify to his sympathetic and unusually gentle nature. He was generous even to a fault, and often showed it in a large degree, when compelled to sentence men to penitentiaries, thus causing pain and breaking up of homes and destroying the pleasures of home-life. He wore the judicial ermine longer than any other judge of any court in both Virginia's, and wore it honorably, ably and well. He was an erudite lawyer, and an honest and upright judge.

We failed to note that he was a member of the Virginia Legislature in 1852, and was re-elected in 1853. He took an active part in the discussions of questions of internal improvements, and the questions growing out of the basis of representation. He was a Whig elector in the campaigns of 1852, '56 and '60, and made a reputation as a powerful stump speaker.

He was a member of the Episcopal Church; was married; had a son and a daughter; kept up a beautiful home in the city of Parkersburg, and departed this life shortly after retiring from the Bench, after serving upwards of forty-three years. He was 83 at the time of his death.

## Judge James Monroe Jackson

James Monroe Jackson was born in Parkersburg, Virginia, December 3, 1825. He had a careful preparation for college, and in early life entered that celebrated institution of learning, Princeton College, from which he graduated in his twentieth year. Like his father, elder and younger brother, he chose the profession of law, and after two years study, under the direction of his father, was admitted to the Wood County Bar in 1847. By his natural talents and constant application, he rose rapidly to an enviable position in his profession. In May, 1856, he was elected prosecuting attorney of Wood County, and was re-elected at the close of his term. He was elected to and served as a member of the House of Delegates of West Virginia in 1870, in the proceedings of which body he took an active and a leading part. He was re-elected, and served in the legislative session of 1871, after the removal of the State capital to Charleston. He was a member of the Convention that sat at Charleston in 1872 and framed the second Constitution for the State of West Virginia. Being an able lawyer, he was a valuable member of that distinguished assembly. In October, 1872, he was elected to the office of Judge of the Fifth Judicial Circuit, in which he served, for the term of eight years, and was re-elected to the same position in 1880. His careful legal training, coupled with his strong common sense, fitted him for the judicial office, and it was not long after his first election until he made for himself the reputation of being among the very best judges in the State, and accordingly gave satisfaction to all with whom he had official dealings.

Though not *per se* a politician, yet at times he took a lively interest in public affairs. On many occasions he was urged to become a candidate for political preferment, notably for Congress; and in 1888 he was nominated by the Democratic Party — with which he had acted since the death of the old Whig organization — for a seat in the Fifty-first Congress. The campaign of that year was a spirited one, and the result in all of the four districts of the State was so close that it took the official vote to decide who had been victorious. Judge Jackson was awarded the certificate of election, but his seat was contested by his competitor, the Hon. Charles B. Smith, who was given the seat by Congress.

Judge Jackson was a man of scholarly attainments which specially equipped him for public service.

He was originally an " Old Line Whig," but became a Democrat at the beginning of the Civil War. He was twice married.

He closed his career by serving two terms as Criminal Judge of Wood County, and departed this life at his home in the city of Parkersburg when nearly eighty years of age.

---

## Samuel Sprigg

One of the most brilliant lawyers who practiced at the Ohio County Bar for many years, and who is still often referred to by the older citizens of the city of Wheeling, is the subject of this brief sketch. He was admitted to the practice early in 1800. We fail to find anything of his early history, such as the date of his birth and where born, his educational advantages, etc. He was appointed attorney for the Commonwealth in 1814, and remained in that office for nearly sixteen years, which proves that he was an efficient prosecutor, and performed his official duties satisfactorily to the people of Ohio County. Sixteen years is almost an unprecedented period for an attorney to continuously fill an office of that character; and to do so, is evidence of a high grade of ability and integrity. His professional career was one of unusual activity and brilliancy, his name appearing more frequently on the dockets of the courts than that of any of his contemporaries, perhaps barring one — that of Zachariah Jacob, and there is some doubt among the older members of the profession at Wheeling as to the correctnes of that statement. There is no doubt, however, that they were the acknowledged leaders of the Wheeling Bar, when they were in their prime. Both of them were learned lawyers, but were different types of men. Mr. Sprigg was the more brilliant, and showed to a better advantage in a court house trial of an important cause, whilst the other, perhaps, was more of the calmer sort, and prepared his cases with more deliberation, and would, probably, win more cases at the round up. Any way, it is generally conceded that they were the " top-notchers " of the Wheeling Bar in their day and generation.

Probably, no better estimate of Mr. Sprigg's professional character and ability can be obtained at this time, than that found in the record of a meeting of the Wheeling Bar at the time of his death, which occurred in 1843. At that meeting Zachariah Jacob presided. The following testimonal was presented by General James S. Wheat, who was also a lawyer of prominence: "Death has come among us and has stricken down our brightest ornament, Samuel Sprigg. While we bow with submission to the force that has terminated a life of honor and usefulness, we would with fond regret dwell upon his virtues and remember his merits. With talents peculiarly adapted to his profession, exalted and strengthened by an ardent temperament and generous ambition, he was an advocate of unrivaled favor, whenever the oppressed needed vindication and support, or the vicious exposure or punishment. He gained the highest honors of his profession and wore them with the modesty peculiar to his merit. A long and intimate association with him left upon our memory nothing to lessen our admiration and affectionate regard. As a man we all loved him, as a citizen he was the able and untiring advocate of every public interest.''

## Col. Benjamin Harrison Smith, A.M.

The subject of this brief memoir, for more than a half century was one of the ablest of all the prominent lawyers of the Kanawha Bar. He was born in Rockingham County, Virginia, October 31, 1797, and died at Charleston, West Virginia, December 10, 1887. In 1810 his father sold his Virginia possessions and moved to Fairfield County, Ohio, where our subject grew to manhood. He attended the public schools, and was graduated from the Ohio University, at Athens, in 1819, with the classical degree of Bachelor of Arts. He studied law in the office of the Hon. Thomas Ewing, senior, one of Ohio's most distinguished lawyers, and was admitted to practice in the Ohio courts in 1821. He had a longing for the hills of his nativity, and he came to Kanawha the next year and located permanently at Charleston, and there spent the remainder of his long and useful life in a most active and successful practice of his profession. He was learned in every branch of the law, and was a student and a worker. He was a student especially of the Virginia land laws, and did, perhaps, more than any other man to make land titles more certain and less complicated. He was, therefore, classed, for more than a generation, West Virginia's foremost land lawyer. He was tall, massive in build and courteous in manner, not eloquent or polished, but able, massive, powerful, irresistible.

He was a Whig in politics until after the close of the Civil War, when he became a Democrat. He, however, was an uncompromising Union man throughout the war. In 1833 he was elected a member of the Virginia Senate, and served as such for six years. In 1849 he was appointed United States District Attorney for the Western District of Virginia, which office he held for four years. He represented Kanawha County in the General Assembly of Virginia in 1855; he had been an active member of the Convention of 1850, which framed a new Constitution for the State. In 1861 President Lincoln appointed him United States District Attorney for the Western District of Virginia, in which office he served under the old and new State until 1868, when he resigned. He was also a member of the Convention that framed the first Constitution of West Virginia. He was the Democratic candidate for Governor of West Virginia in 1866, but was defeated by Governor Arthur I. Boreman, and in 1870 he represented Kanawha County in the Legislature of West Virginia.

Colonel Smith never connected himself with any Church, but always claimed to be a Methodist in principle and doctrine. His family, however, were Presbyterians. He reared a large family, and several of his descendents are still residents of the city of Charleston. His son, Isaac Noyes

Smith, deceased, was a prominent attorney for many years, and his grandson, Harrison Brooks Smith, is at this time, one of the successful members of the Charleston Bar.

Colonel Smith was strictly honorable in all his dealings, and wielded an almost unlimited influence over the citizens of the Great Kanawha Valley, where he was known and highly honored.

## Hon. Benjamin Wilson

Mr. Wilson was born in Harrison County, Virginia, April 30, 1825; educated at the Northwestern Academy, at Clarksburg; attended law school at Staunton, Virginia; was admitted to the Bar in 1848; served as Commonwealth's Attorney for Harrison County from 1852 to 1860; member of the Constitutional Convention of Virginia in 1861; was Presidential Elector-at-Large on the Democratic ticket of 1868; a member of the West Virginia Constitutional Convention that met at Charleston in 1872; was made a delegate-at-large to the National Democratic Convention at Baltimore in 1872 that nominated Horace Greeley for President; elected as Representative to the Forty-fourth Congress from the First Congressional District; re-elected to the Forty-fifth Congress, serving from December 4, 1875; was again re-elected to Congress in 1880, defeating John A. Hutchinson, the Republican candidate; was appointed Assistant United States Attorney in the Department of Justice at Washington by Grover Cleveland till superseded in 1889.

Colonel Wilson served his constituents in Congress in a most efficient manner. He was constantly at his post of duty, and was attentive, courteous and polite to all with whom he came in contact in the discharge of his public and private duties as a citizen and Representative. He was a lawyer of high grade, and was a man of unusual popularity. He was in the employment of the Government at Washington in settling the French Spoliation Claims when stricken with a fatal illness. He died at the ripe old age of a little more than eighty years.

## Judge Homer A. Holt

Judge Holt, son of Jonathan and Eliza (Wilson) Holt, was born at Parkersburg, Virginia, April 27, 1831. His ancestors came from England in Colonial days, and settled near Norfolk, Virginia, where his grandfather, John Holt, was born, and who later moved to and settled in the Monongahela Valley. Our subject was educated in the select and private schools of that period. Later he was, in 1850 and '51, a student at the University of Virginia. The method of instruction given at that great institution, is by different schools, a diploma being issued in each department. During the first year Mr. Holt received diplomas in five different

JUDGE HOMER A. HOLT

schools, and at the end of the second year he passed the required examinations in four other different schools, thus making a record that but few, if any, have equaled or surpassed. After leaving this historic school of learning, he taught school two years, and then read law in the office of his brother-in-law, the late Hon. Benjamin W. Byrne, at Sutton, in Braxton County, after which he was admitted to the Braxton County Bar, in which, and the adjoining counties, he practiced successfully for a number of years.

When the war between the States came on in 1861 Mr. Holt went with the South, and in 1862 was captured by the Federals and was confined in Camp Chase, at Columbus, Ohio, where he remained for about a year. After his liberation he joined Gen. Albert G. Jenkins' Cavalry Brigade, at Salem, Virginia. Subsequently he was transferred to General McCausland's command, where he served until the close of the war.

He was a man of medium height, his head was large with prominent forehead, and he was of a studious and thoughtful turn of mind. Both the imaginative and practical elements predominated in his character; from the one he was able to foresee the future material development of the natural resources of the State, and by the reason of the other, he invested extensively in the then cheap mineral and timber lands, from which he subsequently acquired a considerable estate. He was, therefore, not only an able lawyer, but he was a successful business man as well.

He had but few equals as a trial lawyer in the entire State. His thorough knowledge of the law, coupled with his untiring industry peculiar to him from his school days to the time of his death, made him a dangerous adversary in the trial of a lawsuit. It is said of him that even in the later years of his life he kept up his academic studies, in which he was, at all times proficient. He delved deeply into Latin, French, history and mathematics. During his one year's imprisonment at Camp Chase he utilized practically all of his time reviewing his school text books. One of his prison associates was a Frenchman, from whom he learned the French language so he could speak and read it fluently and correctly. In this way he relieved himself almost entirely of the monotony of his prison life.

He was a Democrat, and took rather a lively interest in politics. He was a member of the Constitutional Convention of 1871–2, and discharged his duties with fidelity and marked ability. He served sixteen years as a Circuit Judge in two separate circuits of the State, satisfying, in a marked degree, both suitors and lawyers. November 8, 1890, he was appointed one of the Judges of the Supreme Court of the State for the unexpired term of Judge A. C. Snyder, resigned, and in 1892 he was elected by the people to said positiion, making six years that he served upon said court.

As a judge he ranked among the best of his day. He possessed a mind of unusual grasp and accuracy, and a heart capable of the tenderest sympathies and affections. In private life he was pure and without a stain.

As a Judge he was honorable, upright and just, and was a devoted husband and father. No higher encomium could be passed upon any public man.

At Sutton, Braxton County, January 27, 1857, he married Miss Mary A., daughter of Mr. John Byrne. Their son, the Hon. John H. Holt, of Huntington, is one of the most distinguished lawyers the State of West Virginia has ever produced. The father was a great man, but the son was still greater. This, however, is only as it should be, as the son has the advantage of standing on the shoulders of the father, and necessarily should be able to see farther in the future, if he properly applies himself, which he has done most successfully.

In 1874, Judge Holt removed to Lewisburg, Greenbrier County, to give his attention to his large land holdings in that section of the State, and on January 7, 1898, he surrendered his trusts after a long, honorable, well spent life.

## Hon. William H. Travers

The subject of this brief memoir was one of the very able lawyers of the "Eastern Pan Handle" of this State, and stood at the head of the West Virginia Bar for a generation or more. He was born in Dorchester County, Maryland, November 2, 1833, and was educated at St. Mary's College, Baltimore, from which he graduated in 1848. He studied law and was admitted to practice in that city in 1851. He settled permanently at Charlestown, Jefferson County, Virginia, when a young man, and began the practice of his profession. Being a man of far more than ordinary ability and attainments, he was not long in taking a leading rank at the Jefferson County Bar, and in building up a very profitable clientele, which continued to increase up to the period of his final illness and demise.

Mr. Travers was always a Democrat, but was in no sense a politician; nevertheless he was elected a member of the House of Delegates of Virginia from his adopted county of Jefferson in 1856–7, and was chosen Speaker of that distinguished body, in which he served with ability and fairness, and with honor to his State and her citizens. In 1872 he was elected to membership in the Constitutional Convention which framed the Constitution of West Virginia and ranked among the ablest members of that distinguished body of statesmen. In that Convention he was Chairman of the Finance, Education and Corporation Committees. He was a Presidential Elector at large from West Virginia in the campaigns of 1876 and 1888.

Mr. Travers faithfully and ably served the people of his adopted State in all of the public positions to which the people elected him. He was a learned lawyer and was thoroughly upright, and commanded the confidence and respect of all the people who had the honor of his acquaintance. When he surrendered his trust the people universally mourned his loss. He was truly a representative citizen and lawyer of pronounced ability and success.

## Judge Thayer Melvin

There have been, and are yet, natural lawyers and jurists as there are natural musicians and natural artists. Judge Melvin was a natural born jurist. He was born at Fairview, Hancock County, Virginia, in 1837, and received a fair English education in the common and high schools of his native and adjoining counties to begin with, and later by study and careful reading of good books he became a really accomplished scholar and litterateur, and a man of broad and general knowledge.

At the age of seventeen years he began the systematic study of the law in his home town, which was the seat of justice of the county at that time, and was furnished books and was counseled by the lawyers of the town. He had a strong, clear mind, and was remarkably industrious. Later he went to New Lisbon, Ohio, where he remained for something like a year, and was tutored by a friend who took a special interest in his advancement, so that in 1853, at the age of eighteen, he passed the required examination, and was admitted to the Bar of Hancock County. During his minority, in 1855, he was elected Prosecuting Attorney of Hancock County. Our present statute prohibits one from receiving license as an attorney at law until he is twenty-one years of age, and it is also mandatory that no man is eligible to hold an office of any kind until he is full twenty-one. We believe these prohibitions existed at that time. If they did it is apparent that no one paid any attention to them, and consequently Judge Melvin was allowed to begin, what turned out to be, a distinguished professional career at least three years ahead of time. Any way "he made good," but it could not be "put over" in these times. In 1856 and in 1860 he was elected and re-elected to the same offie, notwithstanding the fact that in 1857 he had moved his residence to Wheeling, Ohio County, where he had associated himself in the practice of the law with Joseph H. Pendleton, a prominent lawyer of that period.

The Civil War came on about this time and young Melvin promptly volunteered to defend the flag as a private soldier in Company F, 1st Regiment, West Virginia Volunteer Infantry. In a very short time he was commissioned an Assistant Adjutant-General of Volunteers, and served in that capacity until the close of the war, when he was honorably discharged. He located in Wellsburg, Brooke County, and resumed the practice of his profession. In 1866 he was again elected Prosecuting Attorney of Hancock County. He was Attorney-General of West Virginia from January 1, 1867, to July 1, 1869, when he resigned to accept the office of Circuit Judge of the First Judicial District of the State, to which he had been appointed by the Governor to fill the vacancy caused by the death of Judge E. H. Caldwell. This was the beginning of the career of one or the ablest and most upright Judges the State of West Virginia has ever produced. Tiring of the "wool sack," however, he resigned from the Bench after serving ably for years, in November, 1881, and returned to the practice in the City

JUDGE THAYER MELVIN

of Wheeling until the death of Judge Joseph R. Paull, when he was appointed by Governor Atkinson to fill the unexpired term of the deceased Judge. When his term expired he was elected for another term of eight years without opposition, and died from apoplexy before the term expired. He was a Whig prior to the Civil War, but after the " cruel war was over " he became a Republican, and remained such until his death, but was never a strenuous partisan. In the discharge of his judicial duties he knew no party or creed. He sought only to be just and fair, and rarely, if ever, failed in deciding right. It was a rare occurrence for one of his decisions to be reversed by the Appellate Court. Furthermore he was one of the most courteous, urbane of men, and was at all times absolutely honest and sincere. He died in the City of Wheeling where he had spent the greater part of a long and useful life, mourned by all the people who admired his manly and noble character.

He never married.

## Hon. William E. Chilton

Hon. William E. Chilton was born in St. Albans, Virginia, March 17, 1858. He received his education in the public schools and at Shelton College, in his native town. He studied law while engaged in teaching common schools in Kanawha and Lincoln Counties, and had no trouble in passing the required examination for admission to the Kanawha County Bar very soon after arriving at his majority. Shortly thereafter he formed a partnership with the late United States Senator John E. Kenna, which continued until the death of the latter in 1893. From the very beginning he showed a natural aptitude for the legal profession, and not long after being licensed as an attorney he began to attract the attention of the leading members of the Kanawha Bar, which then, as now, was one of the ablest bodies of lawyers in the State. Indeed it was not long until he himself was classed among the best of them, which position he still maintains. He was a member of the well known firm of Chilton, MacCorkle and Chilton, of Charleston, the other members of the firm being his senior brother, Major Joseph E. Chilton, and Ex-Governor William A. MacCorkle. Their business is so extensive that the firm includes also Mr. T. S. Clark and William G. MacCorkle.

He withdrew from this firm, however, in 1918, and is conducting a business on his own account in large and important cases only.

Among West Virginia's native sons now living the most commanding figure, from a national point of view, is the subject of this sketch. Going to the United States Senate at a time when many momentous questions were at issue in Congress, he at once took his place among the leaders on the Democratic side, and his voice was potent and his influence great in their consideration and disposition. The reasons for this are plain. He carried to the Senate a mind naturally strongly analytical, well versed

HON. WILLIAM E. CHILTON

in the law and thoroughly trained by hard study and deep thought to engage in the solution of big problems, coupled with a strong natural bent for political affairs and an unconquerable ambition to succeed in all his undertakings, it was no wonder that he took high rank in that most exalted deliberative body of statesmen in the civilized world. . He was Vice Chairman of the Democratic Caucus of the Senate (his political party being in the majority), and being second on the Judiciary Committee, and inasmuch as the Floor Leader or Caucus Chairman was in extremely poor health and the Chairman of the Judiciary Committee was in ill health also, Senator Chilton, who was nearly always present when the Senate was in session, necessarily became his party leader of the body. Being quick of perception, an able speaker, affable and courteous, he was looked to as the main man of the Senate, and was pushed to the front as its active leader, and in reality, perhaps, as its most influential member. The writer hereof was a resident of Washington during Senator Chilton's Senatorial term and, therefore, knows whereof he speaks, and it is only fair that this statement should be here made a matter of public record. He was also an efficient member of several other important Senate Committees and was a regular attendant upon all of them. These facts, among others that could be mentioned, show why Senator Chilton's Senatorial career was among the most conspicuous perhaps, of any of his predecessors in that delegated body of statesmen and patriots.

Mr. Chilton was Prosecuting Attorney of Kanawha County for the period of about two years; was a candidate for State Senate in 1884, but was defeated, and was Secretary of State for the term of four years. He has a wife and four children and occupies a charming home at the capital of the State.

## Hon. William L. Wilson, LL.B., LL.D.

Our subject was one of the illustrious sons of West Virginia. He was a lawyer, a scholar, an educator, a statesman and an ideal, honored citizen of the Commonwealth. He was born in Jefferson County, Virginia, May 3, 1843, and was primarily educated at the Charlestown Academy, where he was noted for his quick mind and studious habits. At the age of fifteen he had read more Latin, Greek and French than is required of college graduates, although mathematics was his favorite study. He then entered the junior class of Columbian University at Washington, D. C., and graduated in 1860 at the age of seventeen. From there he entered the University of Virginia, but on account of the breaking out of the Civil War he remained but a short time, and entered the Confederate Army as a private soldier, and remained until its close, retiring with the rank of sergeant-major.

In June, 1865, he was made Assistant Professor of Ancient Languages in the faculty of his *Alma Mater* (Columbian University), and while thus engaged he took the required course of study in the Law Department, and graduated *cum laude* in the class of 1867. He was promoted to a full professorship of the Latin Language and Literature, and remained in that position until 1871, when he resigned and began the practice of law at Charlestown, West Virginia, as junior partner in the firm of Baylor and Wilson, and had almost from the start a full practice, being not only prominent as an advocate, but also largely entrusted with chancery business. After an active and successful practice of eleven years, in June, 1882, he was chosen by unanimous vote of the Regents as President of the West Virginia University, which he reluctantly accepted, entering upon his duties September 20 of that year. In the fall of the same year he was nominated and was elected a member of the American Congress, and was thereafter three times re-elected to the same position. He served as President of the State University until the end of the college year of 1883 without salary, when he resigned. During that short period he won great popularity at the State University.

From the beginning of his term in Congress he stepped to the front rank as a legislator, and was placed on the Ways and Means Committee, and was the principal framer and patron of what was known as the Wilson Tariff Bill of that session of Congress. At the next election he was defeated for the fifth term to which he had been renominated.

As a lawyer he ranked high. He was not only versed in legal principles, but he had the ability to present them effectively. As a public speaker and representative he joined the wisdom of the schools to practical experience, and ably carried out the courage of his convictions. As well as a pleasant public speaker he was a fluent and classic writer. Under President Cleveland's second administration he ably filled the position of Postmaster-General in his Cabinet. At the close of his term in that exalted position he was elected President of Washington and Lee University, of Virginia, in which position he was succeeding grandly when his health gave way, and he departed this life in the midst of his usefulness while yet a comparatively young man. He was truly a great and good man. He was naturally genial, kindly and courteous.

## Professor William P. Willey, M.A.

One of the " land marks " in the Law Department of the West Virginia University at Morgantown is the subject of this sketch. He is known to the older members of the Bar as a practitioner of the law when he was a young man, and to many of the younger members of the profession in the State as their teacher, running back for more than thirty years. He is also personally known to the members of the State Bar Association as one of its founders and one of its Presidents and as editor of its monthly publication called " The Bar " for nearly a generation, which he recently abandoned and turned over to younger hands. He is the son of the late United States Senator Waitman T. Willey, who was a distinguished lawyer and statesman in the early history of this Commonwealth.

Professor Willey was born at Morgantown, Virginia, in May, 1840, and had the advantages in his boyhood of the excellent schools in that section. When a young man he entered Dickinson College, Carlisle, Pennsylvania, and graduated in the classical course of study in the class of 1862. He read law under the direction of his father and was admitted to the Morgantown Bar in 1864. In 1866 he was elected Prosecuting Attorney of his native county and discharged his official duties with great acceptability. In 1868 he was nominated as the Democratic candidate for Attorney-General of the State, but was defeated. He located in the City of Baltimore in 1873, where he remained for five years in general practice, and was succeeding admirably.

He, however, had a liking for politics, and was induced in 1878 to move to Wheeling in his native State and become editor-in-chief of the Wheeling Daily Register, the leading Democratic newspaper of West Virginia. With industry, tact and ability he conducted the editorial interests of that paper until 1883, when he was elected to membership in the Law Faculty of the State University at Morgantown, where he remained until about two years ago when, on account of impaired health, he retired from active work, and is living in quietude in the City of Morgantown, where he was born over three-quarters of a century ago.

Professor Willey is a member of the Methodist Episcopal Church, and his life has been an example of wisdom, learning, integrity and fidelity to principle and an unsullied conscience. He married Miss Lida Allen, of Morgantown, a daughter of Guy R. C. Allen, a distinguished lawyer of that town. They reared a family of worthy children, who are mostly residents of the State. Mrs. Willey died a few years ago.

## Hon. Benjamin Franklin Keller, B.S., LL.B., LL.D.

Judge Benjamin F. Keller, son of Henry and Margaret Keller, was born at Boalsburg, Pennsylvania, April 21, 1857, and graduated from Pennsylvania State College in the class of 1876 with the degree of Bachelor of Science. He taught school for three years; decided to become a lawyer; accepted a clerical position in the Interior Department at the City of Washington for a short time; took the course of study prescribed in the Law Department of Columbian University, now George Washington University of that city, and graduated in the class of 1882 and was given the degree of Bachelor of Laws. He came to West Virginia in 1891; settled at Bramwell, Mercer County; opened a law office in conjunction with the late Judge Henrietze, under the firm name of Henrietze and Keller. Both of them being good lawyers, their business was prosperous. Later Judge Keller became a member of the extensive law firm of Rucker, Keller and Hamill, with their principal office in Welch in the adjoining county of McDowell, where he remained in the active practice until he was appointed Judge of the United States District Court for the Southern District of

JUDGE BENJ'N F. KELLER

West Virginia in April, 1901, wherein since that time he has been ably and faithfully serving. His residence is at Charleston, the capital of West Virginia.

Judge Keller's career has been able and exemplary, both as an attorney and a judge. He possesses the absolute confidence of the public, and especially those who have business in his court. He is conscientious and is absolutely incorruptable. Nature seems to have especially designed him to be an arbiter of the affairs of men. He possesses great candor and a stern and abiding integrity. An acute and penetrating discernment, a nice discrimination, a clear perception and a sound judgment are predominating faculties of his mind; and the pursuit and attainment of justice afford him the highest gratification. He is tireless in the evolution of legal principles and always seeks an equitable adjustment of the most complicated circumstances. His powers of analysis and amplification are peculiarly adapted to the elimination and development of the varied issues of law, equity and fact, often presented by the pleadings under the system which obtains in our West Virginia Courts. His conclusions are never arbitrary nor sententious; but are combinations of truth, justice and fairness as far as the technicalities of law will allow him to go along clear and logical paths of common fairness in the decision of a case. His nearly twenty years on the Bench cannot suggest an instance wherein he has not decided every case that came before him strictly according to the law and the evidence as he understood both to be. To sum up in a word, his career on the Bench is that of an able and just Judge, who bears the confidence and respect of all the people who know him personally or have had business dealings with him. Judge Keller is a communicant of the Protestant Episcopal Church; is a member of all the branches of Freemasonry; is of large stature and of commanding personal appearance. He married Miss Mercy J. Baldy, October 25, 1887, but has no children. The home office of his court is at Charleston, the capital of the State. He became a member of the West Virginia Bar Association in 1900 and was its President in 1912.

Columbian University conferred the degree of LL.D. upon him in June, 1902. An honor worthily bestowed.

## Judge Francis A. Guthrie, LL.B.

Judge Guthrie was born in Tyler County, Virginia, April 12, 1840. He was attending Allegheny College at Meadville, Pennsylvania, when in September, 1861, he enlisted as a private soldier in the Union Army. He was steadily promoted until he was made captain of Company E, 111th Pennsylvania Volunteer Infantry. After the close of the war he entered the Law Department of Michigan University at Ann Arbor, and graduated therefrom with the degree of LL.B. He located at Point Pleasant, Mason County, shortly after his graduation, and began the practice of law. Having thoroughly mastered all of the fundamental principles of the profession

JUDGE F. A. GUTHRIE

it was but a very short time until he found himself in possession of a large and profitable clientele. He was courteous, polite and affable, and was a strong advocate, which enabled him, in a short period of time, to rank among the leaders of that Bar. In 1870 he was elected Prosecuting Attorney of Mason County. This office he filled ably. In 1880 he was the nominee of the Republican party for the office of Circuit Judge for the Counties of Mason, Putnam and Kanawha, and was elected for the term of eight years. He filled the office so ably and satisfactorily to lawyers, suitors and the people generally that he was twice re-elected. He was so deeply grounded in the law, and having naturally the judicial temperament, he was rarely reversed by the higher courts. Moreover he was thoroughly honest and sincere and had the confidence and respect of all the people who came in contact with him, either personally or officially. He was an erudite lawyer and a just and able jurist. He died August 16, 1904, a short time before the expiration of his third term as Circuit Judge, after nearly twenty-four years of continuous service on the Bench. Every one who knew him was his friend.

He married Miss Clara Van Gilder, April 30, 1866, by whom he had one son, Dr. Lewis V. Guthrie, an eminent physician, who has, for going on a quarter of a century, been at the head of two of the Insane Hospitals of West Virginia, and has become an eminent specialist on diseases of the mind.

## Hon. John A. Hutchinson

Mr. Hutchinson was born in the City of Parkersburg, Wood County, Virginia, in 1840, and for a generation was one of the leaders of the strong Bar of that city. As a court house trial lawyer he had but few equals in the entire State of West Virginia. He was admitted as an attorney in 1861 after having read law with his father-in-law, James M. Stephenson, who was an eminent member of the profession. He was elected Prosecuting Attorney of the adjoining County of Pleasants in 1862, and served as such for nine consecutive years. In 1863 he was elected to the same office in Wood County and served in that capacity until 1870. He was also elected Prosecuting Attorney of Wirt and Ritchie Counties and served from 1866 to 1869, inclusive. He was a noted criminal lawyer and was a successful and powerful prosecutor. He was elected a member of the West Virginia Legislature of 1875–6 and was the Republican floor leader of that body. He was a ready and indeed powerful debater, and was practically irrepressible. He was the candidate of the Republican party in 1876 and also in 1884 for the office of Attorney-General of the State, and was defeated both times. He was likewise defeated in 1880 as a candidate for Congress in the old First Congressional District, but he ran considerably ahead of his ticket in all of these elections. In 1886 he was defeated by his Democratic opponent as a candiate for Congress in the Fourth Congressional

District. While he dabbled considerably in politics yet for years he was regarded as one of the ablest lawyers in the entire State, and for a long time had the largest practice of any of the strong Parkersburg lawyers.

Mr. Hutchinson's forte was trial practice; the examination and cross-examination of witnesses always being entrusted to him by his associates. While he was noted specially as a great criminal lawyer he was equally strong in civil practice, and had a large clientage in all State and Federal Courts. For many years he was Chief Counsel in West Virginia for the Baltimore and Ohio Railroad Company. He was not a college man, and yet he was an omniverous reader and possessed an almost unlimited fund of general knowledge, which he used with telling effect in his court trials. He was a tall, commanding man in appearance, and was genial and agreeable with his associates. He was a learned lawyer and was unusually gifted in successfully presenting his cases to a court and jury.

Mr. Hutchinson was the author of two valuable works on law, viz.: "Law Titles in Virginia and West Virginia," and an "Official Form Book." These publications added greatly to his reputation as a lawyer. He died at Parkersburg, West Virginia, while in his prime mentally and physically, and was mourned by a large concourse of admiring friends.

## Judge George Loomis

The first Judge of the Sixth Circuit under the new State and afterwards presiding over the ninth continuously to January 1, 1873, when the revised Constitution cut short the term, was the above named attorney from Parkersburg. He was born at Little Falls, New York, April, 1824. In 1840 he removed to Fairfax County, Virginia, taught school, completed academic studies with Professor Burnley, of Culpeper, located in Fayette in 1848, and was County Surveyor, studied law and was admitted to practice in 1851; fixed his residence in Parkersburg in 1852, and served as Prosecuting Attorney for Jackson and Roane Counties in 1860. He was elected Judge of the Circuit in 1862 'ere West Virginia was created, and ably served on the Bench for ten years. He took an active part in establishing free schools in the State, in extending the elective franchise, in organizing West Virginia, and advocating its advancement and substantial development. He was Mayor of Parkersburg in an exciting period; was State Senator from 1875 to 1877; contested unsuccessfully the election of Judge J. Monroe Jackson for the eight years' term, beginning January 1, 1873, as Judge of the Circuit; was made the candidate of the Republican party for Congress in the Fourth District, but failed of election, though he made a vigorous and prudent campaign. Judge Loomis had a large practice in State and Federal Courts. He passed into the Great Beyond when about eighty years of age.

## Hon. Joseph Moreland, A.B.

Mr. Moreland, who departed this life December 2, 1913, was one of the prominent and successful lawyers of the Monongalia County Bar for more than forty years. He was the son of John and Priscilla (Rogers) Moreland, and was born May 26, 1842, at Connellsville, Pennsylvania. When he was a lad his parents migrated to Morgantown, Monongalia County, Virginia, where our subject was reared and received his early education in the Monongalia Academy, conducted by President Moore, who was a second Arnold of Rugby — one of the most noted educators within the limits of the entire State of Virginia. He was also a student at the Dunlap's Creek Academy at Merrittstown, Pennsylvania, and finally entered Washington and Jefferson College, Washington, Pennsylvania, and was an honored graduate in the complete classical course, with the degree of Bachelor of Arts, in the class of 1866. At that period but few men had the advantages of as thorough an education as Mr. Moreland, which in part accounted for his eminence at the Bar and as a leader among men.

He was always a Democrat in politics, but was never a zealous partisan, nor was he at any time an office-seeker. The only offices he ever held came to him without the asking. He was Mayor of Morgantown many times; was appointed a Commissioner by the Governor of West Virginia to assess the railroad property within the State in 1874; was a delegate to the National Democratic Convention at St. Louis in 1888, and was a local Regent of the West Virginia University from 1882 to 1896. In all of these public positions he discharged his duties with efficiency and fidelity. He was at all times honorable, reliable and trustworthy. There was no period in his mature life that he did not have the absolute confidence and respect of the people in the community where more than half a century of his life was spent. He was tender, affectionate and thoughtful of the wants of others in his home and community life, and his history as a man and an attorney is a record of manliness complete in every detail. He was a man of marked personal appearance — tall, rugged, strong features, and his whole aspect full of force. His practice extended into all the branches of the profession in all the courts of the State and Federal Governments. He was a hard student of the law and always kept up with the decisions and text books, and dignified the profession by exhibiting in the practice the highest types of integrity, fidelity, learning and wisdom.

Mr. Moreland married Miss Mary Ellen Brown, October 26, 1875, by whom he had one daughter and one son. The son is mentioned in another part of this volume, and is a successful member of the Morgantown Bar. The senior Moreland was an active member of the Presbyterian Church; was an Odd Fellow, and a member of the Delta Tau Delta College Fraternity. He was also a son of the American Revolution. His death, which occurred December 2, 1913, was universally mourned by the people of Morgantown.

HON. JOSEPH MORELAND

## Judges Lewis and George W. Summers

These two brothers were among the most distinguished lawyers and jurists of Western Virginia, who, taken together, covered a period in public life of more than a half century. They were sons of Col. George Summers of Fairfax County, Virginia. Lewis, the elder of the two brothers, was born in Fairfax County, November 7, 1778, and died in Kanawha County, August 27, 1843. George W., who was the youngest of the family of ten, was born March 4, 1804, and also died in Kanawha County, July 23, 1868. Lewis was liberally educated at Alexandria, Virginia, and "read law" before coming to Kanawha. George W., who was twenty-six years younger, attended the Ohio University at Athens, Ohio, and graduated in the classical course, with the degree of Bachelor of Arts. He subsequently read law under the direction of his elder brother, Lewis. Both of them became members of the Kanawha Bar and became eminent as practitioners as well as able and learned judges. Lewis, perhaps, possessed more of the judicial temperament, while George W. was more distinguished as an advocate or trial lawyer. It cannot be controverted that the younger Summers was far and away the most powerful orator who ever inhabited the Western portion of Virginia. In the trial of important causes before juries he was practically invincible. His brother Lewis on the other hand possessed no such gift, and never aspired to anything of that sort. He was, perhaps, more deeply grounded in legal principles and more erudite in the law, as a science, than his younger brother, but lacked in a marked degree his brilliancy and force; and while he stood in the front rank with his contemporaries as a jurist, he never achieved the reputation in the profession that clustered around the younger brother. This, however, may be accounted for in the fact that the senior never intermeddled with politics, while the junior had a strong penchant in that direction. Anyway, they were both great lawyers and jurists, and both of them were men of the highest order of honor and integrity. In politics both of them were Whigs, and in religion both of them were ardent Episcopalians. Both of them were men of large stature, though not overly tall, and were commanding in appearance. Their very presence indicated towering ability. Judge Lewis never married. Judge George W. married Miss Amacetta Laidley, of Cabell County, and had several children, one of whom, Lewis Summers, is a resident of Charleston.

Lewis Summers was appointed by the Legislature, in February, 1819, one of the judges of the General Court and Judge of the Kanawha Judicial Circuit. As a judge he was painstaking, laborious and of inflexible integrity. His learning eminently qualified him for the Bench, and he had the confidence of lawyers and people. He died while in office, having served faithfully for twenty-four years.

George W. Summers had a vast practice in Kanawha and adjoining counties, but now and then he took time for a dash in politics. He was a member of the Virginia Legislature in 1830 and '31, and again in 1834 and '35. He was elected to Congress in 1841, and again in 1843, and was a member of the Virginia Convention of 1850, and was ranked among the ablest debaters of that body of distinguished men. He was elected Judge of the Kanawha Circuit Court in 1852, and resigned after serving ably the greater part of the term. He was the Whig candidate for Governor of Virginia in 1851 and was defeated by the Democrats. In 1861 he was sent to the Peace Conference at Washington and opposed secession, standing firmly for the Union. He, however, took no part in the organization of the Restored Government of Virginia at Wheeling.

He and his brother Lewis were both buried on the Summers farm, which is still in the possession of the family, at Walnut Grove on the Great Kanawha River, about twenty miles below Charleston.

## Zachariah Jacob

Mr. Jacob for many years stood at the head of the Ohio County Bar of the City of Wheeling. He was a native of Ohio County, Virginia. We regret that we cannot find the exact date of his birth, but it must have been in the latter part of the seventeenth century, because he was admitted to practice along about the year of 1820 to 1823 or '24. His long life of usefulness as a lawyer and a citizen of that section of the State was never tainted by even a suspicion of dishonesty or wrongdoing of any sort whatever. The men who were contemporaneous with him in the profession have themselves all passed away, and there only remains the general impression of him that he was the foremost lawyer of the section in which he flourished during a long, useful and successful life as a member of the Wheeling Bar. The records of the courts show that his practice for a half century or more was not only very large, but was of a general character, which shows that he was informed and well informed on all branches of the law. It is safe, therefore, to class him among the learned members of the profession of his generation. It is generally agreed that he did not excel as an advocate; that his strength did not lie particularly in oratory. On the contrary he was a man of unusual force of character; he possessed a logical mind and argued his cases in such a manner as to convince both judge and jury of the true merits of what he claimed. He was sincere in all of his utterances; consequently he lost no cases that he ought to have won. He was not, *per se*, a great trial lawyer, as that term is generally understood by the profession, but his arguments were invariably logical, reasonable and convincing. He knew the law and knew how to apply it with convincing force, and never allowed himself to be forced from his true bearings, or to be confused or thrown off his feet. We do not mean to say that he was not a strong attorney in a court trial, but rather that he was not a brilliant advocate and did not attempt to win a case by tawdry gum flowers of rhetoric or oratory alone. From what we can learn of him he never tried to win a case by a camouflage of any sort. He tried his cases like an erudite lawyer should have tried them, wholly upon the law and the facts, and tried them ably and fairly.

Mr. Jacob meddled but little with politics, but at the same time he was a man of deep convictions on all important subjects. He simply preferred his law office to any other business and he thus lived out his days. He was a useful citizen and it is said he was always in the lead in whatever promised to promote the interests of the community in which he was born and spent a long and useful life. He died late in the sixties much lamented by all the people. He was unquestionably a great, good and useful lawyer and citizen. If he ever held an office we have no record of it.

## Hon. Samuel Price

Senator Price was eminent both in law and in statesmanship. He was born in Fanquier County, Virginia, July 28, 1805. His early education was quite meager, and was confined to common school branches. He, however, in later years, by studious habits, became well informed upon most every possible subject, which constitute real learning, real education. He moved, in early life, from Fanquier to Preston County in the western part of the State, but remained there only a short time. From there he moved into Nicholas County, and in 1830 he took the United States Census of that county. While there he began the study of legal textbooks, which he vigorously pursued. He passed a creditable examination and was admitted to the Bar of that county in 1832. Before he was admitted to practice he was chosen Clerk of the County Court of Nicholas County in 1831. In 1833 he was elected Prosecuting Attorney of the county. In 1834 he was elected to membership in the Virginia Legislature as a delegate from Nicholas and Fayette Counties, and was re-elected in 1835 and '36. He also was elected a delegate to the Legislature from Braxton County in 1837, an adjoining county to Nicholas, where he attended the regular terms of court and was known as a young lawyer of noble character and great promise. In fact, his practice extended into all of the adjoining counties, and he felt almost as much at home in them as in his own adopted county of Nicholas. Braxton County continued to send him to the Legislature as its delegate up to and including 1850. In 1838 he removed his residence to Lewisburg in Greenbrier County, where the possibilities for a rising young lawyer were much greater than in the interior counties, and was sent to the Legislature from that county continuously from 1837 to 1852, except one year. He represented Greenbrier County in the Virginia Constitutional Convention of 1850–'51, and again he represented that county in the Convention of 1860–'61; and still again, he was called upon to represent that county in the Constitutional Convention of 1871–'72 of West Virginia, after the formation of the new State, and was President of it.

In politics he was a Whig, but in 1861, when Virginia seceded from the Union, he cast his lot with the South and became a Democrat. During the Civil War, in 1863, he was elected Lieutenant-Governor of Virginia. After the close of hostilities he returned to Greenbrier County and resumed the practice of law, and was elected a Circuit Judge, but declined to qualify. He was appointed a United States Senator from West Virginia to fill the vacancy occasioned by the death of Hon. Allen T. Caperton and served as such from December 4, 1876, to January 31, 1877. He was able in all branches of the law, but specialized in the settlement of land titles, in which he had a State-wide reputation. He was a man of honor and of the highest integrity, and, during his entire life, he had the implicit confidence of the people who knew him.

He married Miss Jane Stuart of Greenbrier County and as a result of their union nine children were born to them. He was a member of the Presbyterian Church and was a Ruling Elder therein for the greater part of his mature life. He died at Lewisburg, February 25, 1884, and was mourned by many people.

## Judge Moses C. Good

Judge Good is remembered by the people of Ohio County as one of the early, able and distinguished lawyers of the Northern "Pan Handle" of Virginia; but there is a dearth of the printed history of those times of the prominent men of the section, and we find it next to an impossibility to secure the details of even the prominent men of that period. There are plenty of men now living in the city of Wheeling who remember Judge Good, but they can furnish no detailed facts of his early life, such as the date of his birth, his educational advantages, his family history, etc. They simply remember him as one of the prominet lawyers, whose career at the Wheeling Bar covered a period of nearly three-quarters of a century of past history.

Mr. Good seems to be best remembered for his zeal and ability as Prosecuting Attorney of Ohio County that he always brought to the discharge of his official duties during the many years he filled that office. It is still said of him that he knew neither friend nor foe. He was a terror to evil doers, and in the discharge of his official obligations he was a most vigorous prosecutor. If one violated the statutes of the State he had to be punished for his folly, and he knew it when he was brought before the court. He was well versed in the law, and in the trial of causes he was the peer of any member of the Bar, especially if he was prosecuting. He was a plain but forcible speaker and was a strong and, indeed, powerful advocate, and never failed to hold the strict attention of his auditors. He was distinctively a jury lawyer, and handled his cases with unusual skill and judgment. He began the practice in Wheeling in 1826 and kept going practically all the time until his death, which occurred in 1873. He was never an office-seeker, but devoted his undivided attention to the practice of his profession. He never held but one political office and that was Mayor of Wheeling, and one year in that position was all that he could endure, and positively refused to accept a second term; and he also declined to accept a salary for the year (1846) he served as such.

In May, 1865, he was elected Judge of the Municipal Court of Wheeling, which had been created by an act of the State Legislature, which position he ably filled for nearly eight years and was holding when death called him. He was a man of exalted moral character, was a conscientious legal adviser, an incorruptible judge and had the absolute confidence of the people generally. He is still referred to as one of the strong, ideal lawyers and citizens of the times in which he flourished. He was, during his entire mature life, deeply interested in the progress and development of the resources of Wheeling, and devoted all his energies to that laudable purpose.

## Judge Charles S. Lewis

Judge Lewis was born in Clarksburg, Virginia, February 26, 1821. He received a liberal education in his county, then a preparatory course in the Ohio University, at Athens, and was graduated in 1844 from Augusta College, Kentucky, and admitted to the Bar in Harrison County, September 15, 1846. He held many influential official positions and in all discharged his duties well. He was a member of the General Assembly of Virginia from 1849 to 1852, and a member of Congress in 1854–55; elected to the House of Delegates of West Virginia, session of 1871; was State Superintendent of Free Schools and ex-officio Adjutant-General from March 4, 1871, to December 31, 1872, when he resigned to enter upon the duties of Judge of the Second Circuit, composed of the counties of Wetzel, Marion, Monongalia, Taylor, Doddridge and Harrison. His term of office would have expired December 31, 1880. He died January 22, 1878, esteemed for his upright life, his social qualities and impartial official career. His home was in the city of Clarksburg.

## Judge Joseph L. Fry

Judge Fry was an eminent lawyer of his day and served from 1831 to 1852 as judge of the Circuit Court of the First Judicial District of Virginia, known as the Wheeling Circuit. He was also a learned Judge and honored the judicial ermine. He was born in Culpeper County, Virginia, February 2, 1805, and died at Lewisburg, Greenbrier County, Virginia, June 10, 1865. He combined the highest legal talent with scrupulous integrity in the discharge of his official duties. He possessed a vigorous, cultivated mind, was of untiring devotion to the profession of his choice and rapidly rose to distinction. His prominence as a jurist was acknowledged by his associates on the Bench who constituted the General Court of Virginia. His profound knowledge of the law, his scrupulous impartiality, his spotless integrity won and claimed the highest respect of the Bar; while his official urbanity secured their warm personal regard. Whilst he was thoroughly honest and fair in his rulings as a Judge, he possessed an air of austerity that made him unpopular with the masses. It was this peculiarity that caused his defeat by Judge G. W. Thompson when Judge Fry was a candidate for re-election to the office of Judge of the Wheeling Circuit and caused his retirement from judicial service and from public life. Nevertheless he was distinguished for great soundness of knowledge in all of its various departments and for the culture of a pure literary taste.

Judge Fry spent the declining years of his life among his near relatives at Lewisburg, Greenbrier County. He was twice married, and had four children by the first and eight by the second wife. The majority of them are still living.

## Judge Gideon Draper Camden

Judge Camden, son of the Rev. Henry Camden, was born in Anne Arundel County, Maryland. While yet quite a youth he came to West Virginia with his father and settled on the West Fork River, about fifteen miles south of Weston in Lewis County. Here young Camden attended the common schools of that locality, and in 1822, at the instance of Col. John G. Stringer, who was Clerk of the Superior Court of Lewis County, employed Mr. Camden as a deputy. He remained in this position for a number of years, studied law, and in 1827 attended, for about one year, the Law School at Wytheville, Virginia, conducted by General Alexander Smyth. After leaving this school he was given a license to practice by Judges Johnston, Taylor and Allen, all men of high standing in the profession of that period. Near the close of 1827 he returned to Weston and commenced the practice of law, with great energy, in Lewis and adjoining counties. His experience in the Clerk's office had familiarized him with court forms and methods of procedure, which were very helpful to him as an attorney. In a very short time he became a prominent and well-known lawyer of that section of the State.

In 1850 Mr. Camden was elected as a Whig to the Constitutional Convention of that year to amend the State Constitution. This Convention changed and reformed the State government by giving the right of suffrage to all male citizens of the State, who were twenty-one years of age, and provided for the election by the people of the Governor, Judges and all other State and county officials. It also provided for a system of public schools. Mr. Camden took an active part in the proceedings of the Convention, advocating and sustaining most of the reforms that were adopted. In May, 1852, Mr. Camden was elected Judge of the Twenty-first Circuit. He gave entire satisfaction as a Judge and was re-elected for a second term of eight years. Prior to his election as Judge he moved his residence to Clarksburg and was very successful as an attorney.

He went with the South during the Civil War, although he voted against secession, and remained until its close. In 1872 he was elected a member of the State Senate, serving the full term of four years. He was an able lawyer and a just Judge. He was twice married; by his first wife he had a large family. He was successful in the management of his business affairs and left a large estate. He possessed, in a large degree, the confidence of his fellow citizens. He lived to the ripe old age of eighty-six.

He acted with the Democratic party after the Civil War.

## Judge Edwin Maxwell

Judge Maxwell was born in the town of Weston, Lewis County, Virginia, July 16, 1825. He was reared on a farm until he was twenty-one years of age. His educational advantages, therefore, were limited. He, however, was studious and industrious and spared no opportunity to attain all the knowledge by careful courses of reading and study within his reach. He never attended a college of any kind, but by the time he had reached twenty-five years of age he had acquired, by the thoughful reading and study of valuable books, a large amount of useful knowledge and had become master of a clear, terse and vigorous style both in writing and speaking. What a man makes of himself, and not what he is made by the aid and influence of friends and family, is the most patent and prominent thought that arrests the attention and deepens the convictions of his fellow men. President Eliot, of Harvard University, once said, "Ability to earn, power to learn, and the faculty of looking forward, are the three capacities requisite for success in any undertaking, and constitute a definition of education." If this is true, and we believe it is largely so, Judge Maxwell must be classed as an educated man, although he never rubbed his back against a college wall.

Judge Maxwell read law, under the direction of a legal friend, passed the required examination and was admitted to practice at the West Union, Doddridge County, Bar in 1852. From the start it was apparent that he possessed the elements of success. He was honest, industrious, conscientious and fair, and soon won the confidence of the people of that locality. He was a safe counselor, and consequently was careful in giving his opinions on law. His business grew, and in order to reach a field of wider opportunities he moved to Clarksburg in 1857 and formed a law partnership with Col. Burton Despard, a successful lawyer of that town. In 1865 Gen. Nathan Goff, Jr., a brilliant young lawyer, who subsequently became a Member of Congress, a United States Circuit Judge and a United States Senator, was taken into the firm, which continued until 1867 when Mr. Maxwell was chosen an Associate Judge of the Supreme Court of Appeals of the State. He served ably in that capacity until December 31, 1872.

JUDGE EDWIN MAXWELL

Judge Maxwell was a Republican and always had a strong liking for politics. He took a leading part in forming the State of West Virginia. From 1863 to 1866 he was a member of the State Senate, and as Chairman of the Judiciary Committee had much to do with the formation of the early legislation of the new State. In 1866 he was also Attorney-General of the State. In 1884 he was the Republican candidate for Governor and was defeated along with the balance of the ticket. In 1888 he was again elected a member of the State Senate, in which body he was an active and able member. Later on he was elected a member of the lower branch of the West Virginia Legislature. He was honest and efficient in every public office he ever held and acquitted himself invariably with credit. He died at his home in Clarksburg, where he resided the larger part of his life, February 5, 1903.

Judge Maxwell was an able lawyer and jurist. He was absolutely incorruptible and was severely candid and just. His life and achievements stamped him as a man of integrity and an uncompromising patriot. He married Miss Laura Shuttlesworth when he was about forty years of age and left two sons, one of whom became a lawyer of note and is now serving, with great acceptability, as Circuit Judge of the Harrison and Lewis Circuit, a sketch of whom will be found on another page of this volume.

## Judge George W. Thompson

This eminent lawyer, jurist and publicist was born in Wheeling, or near there, in Ohio County, Virginia, May 14, 1806. He was graduated from Jefferson College, Cannonsburg, Pennsylvania, in the class of 1824. He read law in the office of W. B. Hubbard at St. Clairsville, Ohio, and was admitted to the Bar in 1826. Thereafter he spent about two years with his uncle, W. P. Thompson, at Richmond, Virginia, where he entered upon a wider and more comprehensive study of the law; and in 1828 returned to St. Clairsville, Ohio, opened a law office and soon achieved a large and lucrative practice. He also entered, with great earnestness, into the political campaigns of that day, having espoused the Democratic side in politics. In 1832 he married the daughter of Daniel Steenrod, a wealthy citizen of Wheeling, Virginia. In 1837 he moved to Wheeling and continued the practice of his profession, which soon became large and profitable. In the meantime he was appointed Postmaster of that city by President Van Buren, in 1838, which at that time was the most important post office in the West. In 1844 he was appointed United States Attorney for the Western District of Virginia, by President Polk, in which position he remained until 1848, achieving unusual distinction in the discharge of his official duties.

In 1851, whilst he was serving his first term in Congress with much distinction and advantage to his constituents, he was nominated and elected

Judge of the Circuit Court of Wheeling District, defeating Hon. Joseph L. Fry (who is sketched in another part of this volume), an eminent lawyer of great erudition, who had been Judge of that Circuit for a number of years and was serving acceptably. In 1860 he was re-elected to the same office, which he filled ably until July, 1861, when he was removed because he refused to take the required oath to support the Restored Government of Virginia, which was established after the State of Virginia had seceded from the Union, his sympathies being with the South in the great conflict from 1861 to 1865. At the close of the Civil War he retired from active participation in politics and from the practice of the law, living in dignified retirement on his farm, which was on Wheeling Creek in the outskirts of the city of Wheeling, finding agreeable occupation in literary work until his death, which occurred February 24, 1888.

In 1866 he published a book entitled "The Living Forces." He followed this publication with another volume in 1870, which was a further discussion of the same subject, entitled "Deus Semper"; and still another volume entitled "The Administration of Good and Evil," or what may be termed a summary of his previous philosophical works, embodying an immense field of ideas in condensed form. His wide range of knowledge made him one of the most companionable of men. In this manner he closed his distinguished career as a lawyer, jurist, scholar and statesman.

## Hon. Philip Doddridge

This great man was a native of Bedford County, Pennsylvania, where he was born May 17, 1772. When seventeen years of age he was placed in school at Wellsburg, Virginia, under the tutelage of an educator by the name of Johnson. Here he remained for several years, devoting himself principally to the study of the Latin language. In those days educational facilities were very meager; but the determination of young Doddridge to become a scholar made up in a large degree for the lack of college advantages. It was said he was so apt that his vigorous mind drank in knowledge with the rapidity of thought, as a dry sponge absorbs water. It was a habit with him, while in school, as a memory exercise, to change the conversation around him into the idiom of his studies; and following his father in his morning and evening devotions, he soon learned to render his prayers into very good Latin and to converse fluently with his teacher in that dead language, He never attended college, but he was nevertheless an educated man. The lack of a regular college training in early life made it all the more difficult in after years to reach a fair rank in scholarship; but close application all through life enabled him to sustain himself upon all occasions as a man of vast erudition. It is not claiming too much to say that he possessed great acquirements.

In the study of law he was his own teacher; and May 23, 1797, he was admitted to the Bar at Wellsburg. He pursued practice with but little intermission until 1815; and by this time he was the acknowledged best lawyer in northwestern Virginia. Those who knew him well say he probably was never excelled by any Virginian lawyer, if he has been equaled, in his discrimination in fathoming the depths of an intricate case, or in his powerful and logical reasoning in unfolding it.

The first important official position filled by Mr. Doddridge was that of a member of the Legislature of Virginia for the years 1815–16. It was at this session that he commenced his opposition to the arbitrary principles of the then existing Constitution of Virginia, which he never relaxed until the Convention of 1829–30 crowned his efforts in behalf of popular rights with partial success. He was again a member of the Legislature of 1822–23. During this session he manifested a lively interest in the promotion of education, both in the University of Virginia and in the private schools. All through life he was the earnest friend of education. He was a leading member of the Constitutional Convention of 1829–30, and was perhaps the ablest debater in it. The great men of the Eastern part of the State found in him an adversary worthy of their steel. He was a candidate for Congress, from the Wheeling district, in 1823, and was defeated by the Hon. Joseph Johnson, of Harrison County, the Democratic candidate. Again, in 1825, Mr. Johnson defeated him for the same position. In 1829 they were again competitors, and this time Mr. Doddridge was successful. His reputation had preceded him to Washington; and he at once occupied an intellectual rank equal to that of his eminent colleagues and hardly second to any member of the House. Especially was this true upon all matters involving the discussion of legal and constitutional questions. His faculty as a draughtsman was remarkable. He had a wonderful power of condensation. The appropriate words, like well-drilled battalions, fell harmoniously into their proper places; and there were neither too many nor too few of them. Daniel Webster once said of Mr. Doddridge, that he would give all he possessed if it would secure him this talent in the same degree of perfection. He also stated on a public occasion that Philip Doddridge was the only man he really feared in debate.

Mr. Doddridge continued a member of Congress up to the time of his death, which occurred in 1832, in the maturity and full vigor of his wonderful intellect, just at the time when his eminent abilities and distinction in the chief council chamber of the Nation had so attracted and commanded the public attention as to presage for him a higher and still more illustrious career. All of his contemporaries are now dead, but the late United States Senator Charles Sumner, himself a distinguished member of the legal profession, stated that he regarded Mr. Doddridge as one of the most erudite lawyers he ever knew. The county of Doddridge, of this State, was named in his honor. Our information is, his father was the Rev. Dr. Joseph Doddridge, who was the author of a volume entitled "Doddridge's Notes on Virginia."

## Hon. Spencer Dayton

Spencer Dayton was a native of Litchfield County, Connecticut, born January 22, 1820. He had the benefit of about one-half the course of the Connecticut common schools. After laboring on a farm until he was sixteen years of age he learned the trade of a millwright. In 1837 the panic, and consequent hard times, destroyed the business of a millwright, so he learned the carpenter and joiner's trade, at which he continued to work until 1843. Having studied Latin and Greek under a private instructor, in the fall of 1843, he began the study of law in the office of Nelson Brewster, a noted attorney of Litchfield County. In 1846 he was admitted to the Bar, and practiced in the courts of that section until June, 1847, when he moved to Barbour County, Virginia, where he resided and constantly kept up the practice of his profession until his final illness and death. He served one term in the State Senate of West Virginia, having been elected to that office in the Spring of 1869. He filled the office of Prosecuting Attorney for Barbour, Randolph, Taylor and Tucker Counties. He was a thorough lawyer in all the branches of the law and was remarkably successful as a practitioner. He was the father of Judge Alston G. Dayton, of the United States District Court for the Northern District of West Virginia. He died at his home at Philippi, at a ripe old age, where he spent the greater part of his life.

## Judge Robert Wood Dailey

Judge Dailey is a son of Robert W. Dailey, Sr., and Rebecca H. (Taylor) Dailey, and was born April 18, 1849, at Romney, Hampshire County, Virginia. He was educated in private schools at Cumberland, Maryland, and Winchester, Virginia. He read law privately, passed the required legal examination and was admitted to the Hampshire County Bar in 1870, and later to the Bars of the adjoining counties of Hardy, Mineral and Grant. He was elected Prosecuting Attorney of his native county and faithfully served in said capacity from January 1, 1871, to April 21, 1892, when he was appointed Judge of the Circuit Court of the Thirteenth Circuit. After filling out the vacancy to which he was appointed by the Governor, he was elected by the people to the same office. The boundaries of the Circuits were changed by the Legislature, and his Circuit or District became the Seventeenth, and he was again re-elected by the people for another term and is still serving in the same highly honorable and responsible office, which makes his term of service, to the present time, upwards of twenty-six years. No man can serve that length of time in the same judicial position when the statutory term is only eight years, unless he is particularly qualified for such position.

As a lawyer Judge Dailey was thorough, accurate and well informed. The accuracy of his pleadings, his uniform urbanity and simplicity of manner, his fidelity to his clients and the force and character which he brought to bear upon a cause, all contributed to his popularity and success. He was a good lawyer and for more than a quarter of a century he has been an honor to the Bench, and his upright character and professional qualifications are exemplary and elevating to both the Bar and Bench. His decisions manifest an earnest search for truth and a conscientious dispensation of justice. He is firm in his convictions, yet tolerant of the opinions of others, and never obtrudes or urges the reception of his views as a condition of his courtesy and regard. He is courteous and kind to lawyers, suitors and witnesses and is remarkably popular with the people of his circuit.

He is a Democrat in politics and a Presbyterian in his religious convictions and for many years has been a Ruling Elder. He married Miss Louisa Booker and has six children — three boys and three girls.

## Judge Harold A. Ritz

The subject of this sketch, son of James M. and Catherine Ritz, was born in the city of Wheeling, West Virginia, July 25, 1873, and received a liberal education in the public schools of his native city and at Marshall College, Huntington, West Virginia. He moved to Bluefield, West Virginia, where he vigorously pursued the study of the law. After reading and rereading the required textbooks he passed a creditable examination and was admitted to the Bluefield, Mercer County, Bar in 1894, shortly after reaching his majority; he promptly entered upon his duties as an attorney-at-law. Being endowed with a powerful physical body, a rugged intellect and unlimited energy, he very soon took an enviable rank among the leading lawyers of that rapidly developing section of the Commonwealth. He speedily gained strength in his calling by practice and experience, and from the beginning he was careful and thoughtful in giving his opinions and advice to clients who sought his counsel on questions of law, and early made a reputation for being honest in his convictions, honest with the courts in which he practiced and with his adversaries also. In this manner he never failed to acquit himself with credit in all of the cases he was called upon to manage.

His first public office was that of Judge of the Circuit Court of Mercer and the surrounding counties, where he gave satisfaction to suitors and their attorneys. His next office was United States District Attorney for the Southern District of West Virginia, to which he was appointed by President William H. Taft, in which he served faithfully and ably for the full term of four years. In 1916 he was nominated by the Republican party as a candidate for the highest judicial office in the gift of the voters of the

JUDGE HAROLD A. RITZ

State, that of membership on the Supreme Court of Appeals of West Virginia, and was elected by a handsome majority. As a member of said tribunal he has rendered intelligent, able and satisfactory service to both litigants and attorneys. He has proved to be a man of broad vision, thoroughly grounded in the fundamentals of the law, and above all a just and upright judge. His marked judicial temperament and his large experience as a trained lawyer qualified him for the discharge of his appellate duties with a high order of merit. The Supreme Bench, therefore, has been greatly strengthened by the acquisition of his vigorous and pronounced judicial powers.

Whilst he was engaged in teaching in the public schools of Wayne County, West Virginia, for the period of one year, he employed all of his spare time reading legal textbooks, thus laying the foundation for his chosen profession.

He was united in marriage with Mrs. Helen Ruffner Jackson, during his term as District Attorney, and maintained a delightful home in the city of Bluefield; but since his elevation to the Supreme Court Bench he has become a resident of the city of Charleston, where the Supreme Court holds its sessions.

## Judge Alston Gordon Dayton, A.M.

Judge Dayton is a scion of the illustrious family of Daytons who figured conspicuously in the early history of the United States. His great-grandfather was a captain in the Revolutionary War. One of this family of Daytons was Jonathan, Speaker of the House of Representatives of the Fourth Congress, and another, William L., was the candidate for Vice-President on the first Republican ticket, headed by Fremont in 1856, and was a strong competitor of Lincoln's for the Presidential nomination in 1860, and was sent as Minister to France by Mr. Lincoln. The father of the Judge, the late Hon. Spencer Dayton, a lawyer of eminence, came to the central part of this State in the early forties, and located in Barbour County. He was a man of strong convictions, stood by the Union cause in the early sixties and was one of the founders and builders of the State of West Virginia.

Judge Dayton was born at Philippi, October 18, 1857, and has resided there all his life. He attended the public schools until he was sixteen years of age, when he entered the State University at Morgantown, from which he graduated in the classical course in the class of 1878, receiving the degree of Bachelor of Arts. During his last two years in college he began to read law, and on his twenty-first birthday he passed a creditable examination and was admitted to the Barbour County Circuit Court Bar. He formed a partnership with his father and immediately entered upon vigorous practice. It was not long until he took high rank at the Bars of Barbour and the surrounding counties of Upshur, Tucker, Taylor and Randolph, and had more or less connection with the important litigations

JUDGE ALSTON G. DAYTON

arising in those counties in a period of over twenty-five years. During this period, until his death, he was in partnership with his father, Spencer Dayton, under the firm name of Dayton and Dayton. The Supreme Court of Appeals Reports for this State for this period disclose his connection with a large number of cases — too many to enumerate here.

In 1879 Mr. Dayton was appointed Prosecuting Attorney for Upshur County, served two years and was a faithful official. In 1884 he was elected Prosecuting Attorney for his native county and the county never had a more active and efficient prosecutor. In 1894 he was the Republican nominee for Congress and was elected by an unexpectedly large majority over the late Hon. William L. Wilson, a man of great learning and ability. He was re-elected four successive terms, making ten years' service in the American Congress. His record as one of our national law makers was of a very high order. He was a hard working member and had the confidence and esteem of all his fellow members. West Virginia never had a more faithful, painstaking member in that great legislative body of men. He was appointed Judge of the United States District Court for the Northern District of West Virginia in March, 1905, where he is now serving with credit and honor. Since going on the Bench he has, in addition to his regular work, by designation, held court in the Southern District of the State, in Pittsburg, New York and at least on an average each year of one term has sat on the Circuit Court of Appeals for this Circuit. During these eleven years, besides routine trial work, he has filed more than 150 written opinions, published in the Federal Reporter, and has sat in more than 75 cases with other Judges on the Circuit Court of Appeals wherein written opinions have been filed by such other Judges.

Judge Dayton is a man of unquestioned ability, of spotless personal character and of unsullied integrity. He has been nearly forty years a Ruling Elder in the Presbyterian Church, a Freemason, a Knight of Pythias and an Odd Fellow. In 1893 he was Grand Master of the latter for the State of West Virginia. He is married and has one son, who is one of the rising young lawyers of West Virginia.

---

## Professor St. George Tucker Brooke, LL.B., LL.D.

Dr. Brooke was a member of the Tucker family of Virginia, who were seemingly a family of "born lawyers," running through two or three generations. His father was Henry Laurence Brooke and his mother was Virginia Tucker, and he was born in Albemarle County, Virginia, July 22, 1844. His early schooling was received at Winchester and Ashland, Virginia, up to and including 1860, when he became a midshipman in the Confederate Navy, serving through 1861 and '62. He continued in the service of the Confederate Army until its close, and the historian of his regiment classes him as among "the bravest of the brave." From the latter part of 1862 he was a member of Company "B," 2d Virginia

PROFESSOR ST. GEORGE TUCKER BROOKE

Cavalry; was thrice wounded in battle and was awarded the Confederate Cross of Honor for bravery in action. He evidently was a man of undaunted courage and bravery. After the close of the Civil War he took the law course at the University of Virginia, graduating in the class of 1869. The year he left the University he was admitted to practice as a member of the Craig County Bar, of Virginia. He only remained in that county a short time, and after a brief stay in Southwestern Virginia, he finally located permanently at Charlestown, Jefferson County, now West Virginia, where he conducted a profitable practice in the Virginia and West Virginia courts until 1878, when he was elected to the chair of Law and Equity of the West Virginia University at Morgantown, where he remained until 1909, when he retired under the Carnegie Foundation, having served ably and efficiently for upwards of thirty-one years. He was not only a learned lawyer, but he was gifted as a teacher, and was a most entertaining instructor. His retirement on account of failing health was a matter of general regret by the Board of Regents of the State University and by the people at large throughout the State, especially the hundreds of young lawyers who had received instructions in his recitation room. It has been often said, and perhaps correctly, that "teachers are born, not made," and this was true of Professor Brooke. He was not only an erudite lawyer, but he knew how to impart his knowledge to others.

He was in 1896 the author of a "Text Book on Common Law Practice and Pleading," which was not only helpful to students of law, but was popular with those already engaged in regular practice. He also wrote a large number of legal, historical and geneological articles which were published in law journals and magazines in the different States. He was president of the West Virginia Bar Association in 1907–8, and was one of its founders, and for nearly a generation a regular attendant up to the time of his retirement from the University. Wake Forrest College honored itself as well as Professor Brooke by conferring upon him the degree of Doctor of Laws, and the same may be said of the West Virginia University for conferring upon him the degree of Master of Arts *honoris causa.*

Dr. Brooke was a member of the Protestant Episcopal Church; was a Democrat in politics; was admitted as a member of the Bars of the different courts of the State, but never practiced after he entered the faculty of the West Virginia University.

He was united in marriage with Miss Mary Harrison Brown, August 15, 1882. Four children were the result of this union — two sons and two daughters, one of the daughters is deceased, the other three heirs are still in the flesh. Dr. Brooke was a member of the Delta Psi Greek letter fraternity. After he retired from the faculty of the University he returned to his old home at Charles Town in Jefferson County, where he spent the remaining five years in literary work, principally preparing an autobiography of his successful and useful life, which will be published later. He quietly surrendered his trust and passed into the Great Beyond, May 16, 1914, mourned by his many relatives and friends scattered over the two Virginias. He knew the law, and knew how to apply it.

## Judge H. C. Hervey

Judge Hervey was the son of Hon. James Hervey, who, in his day, was a prominent lawyer of Brooke County. The Judge was born in the city of Wellsburg, in September, 1861, and was educated in the public schools of that city. He studied law under the supervision of his father, and was admitted as an attorney of the Brooke County Bar just after he reached his majority. He had not practiced law very long until he entered the political field and was twice elected Prosecuting Attorney of Brooke County on the Republican ticket by handsome majorities, and proved to be a strong prosecutor.

Keen of mind and perspicuity Mr. Hervey was thought to be ideal timber for Judge of the Circuit Court; he was persuaded to run and was elected in 1894. At the next election of Circuit Judge, Judge Hervey was endorsed by the Democratic party and was elected, having no opposition. At the two succeeding elections no opposition appeared and he had the distinction of filling his exalted office as the choice of both political parties by whom he was loved and admired.

He never married, but preferred home life with his two sisters in their beautiful old home at Wellsburg, where his spare hours were spent with his books. He was a great reader and student. These tendencies were inherited from his grandfather, the Reverend David Hervey, and his father, both omniverous readers of the highest grades of literature.

His religious faith was Presbyterian, of which church he was a devout member and regularly attended the church in Wellsburg, where he taught a Bible class and also a teachers' class. He was liberal in church and charities and will be missed by the needy of his native town.

When not on the Bench in his professional duties he was always at his home, for his love for home life amounted almost to idolatry.

Judge Hervey was a born jurist, "fitted by nature and by learning taught," to weigh carefully and to value accurately questions of law and fact. A profound student, gifted with the ability to go quickly to the bottom of a subject, to analyze facts, and to give to them their proper value, he had also the calm judicial mind. He was never swayed by prejudice nor by preconvinced opinions. He was never influenced by public clamor, nor by the itching for popular applause. The law was his guide; and justice was his aim.

In private life he was an admirable character. The strict attention that he gave to his work prevented him from taking much part in social affairs; but the friends whom he knew and loved he grappled to himself with bonds of steel. While never practicing nor permitting undue familiarity he was gentle and courteous in all his personal associations.

Death unexpectedly called him September 4, 1918, just after his sun had reached its noon, and thus passed one among the ablest jurists West Virginia has thus far produced.

## Judge Joseph T. Hoke, A.M., LL.B., LL.D.

Our subject was born in Berkeley County, Virginia, February 6, 1835. He was educated at Rock River Seminary, Illinois, Oberlin College, Ohio, and Hillsdale College, Michigan, graduating A.B. from the latter in 1860. He decided upon the law as a profession, and accordingly entered the Law Department of Michigan University at Ann Arbor, graduating LL.B. in March, 1864. In the summer of that year he was admitted as a member of the Berkeley County Bar and began to practice. In 1864 he was elected Prosecuting Attorney of his native county, serving the Statutory Term in an efficient and satisfactory manner. He was a superior public speaker and, therefore, was a successful trial lawyer. For a time he was engaged in publishing a weekly newspaper at Martinsburg called The Berkeley Union. In 1866 he was elected to the State Senate of West Virginia, and was a valuable member, and in 1868 he was re-elected to the same office and served as Chairman of the Judiciary Committee. In 1869 he was appointed Judge of the Fifth Judicial Circuit to fill an unexpired term of six years. He was a faithful, efficient and conscientious Judge. In this high position he served until January 1, 1873, when the newly adopted Constitution of the State became effective and terminated his official career.

He was a Republican in politics, and was three times elected a delegate to the National Convention of his party (1868, 1872 and 1880). In 1880 he was the candidate of the Republican party for a seat in Congress from the Second Congressional District, but was defeated. In 1886 he was elected to the West Virginia Legislature from Preston County, and was one of the most influential members of that body. In 1888 he was elected a Circuit Judge of the Third Judicial Circuit, and ably served for the full term of eight years. He then retired from the profession and was appointed United States Consul at St. John's, New Brunswick, where he ended his useful career.

Judge Hoke was never classed as a great lawyer, but he was well grounded in legal principles. He was a success in the practice and was an honorable and upright Judge. His tastes ran to literature rather than to law. He was a master of pure English and delved no little in poetry. He wrote much for magazines, both in prose and poetry, and was regarded as a man of high literary merit, and was a profound scholar as well. His personal and public acts were spotless, and he was respected by all the people who knew him. Hillsdale College conferred upon him in 1870 the honorary degree of LL.D., an honor worthily bestowed.

His remains were interred in the cemetery at Kingwood in the presence of a throng of admiring friends.

## Hon. Fredrick O. Blue

Our subject, son of George F. and Mary Lee Blue, was born at Grafton, Taylor County, West Virginia, November 25, 1872, and received his early educational training in the public schools of Taylor County and later in the Grafton High School. This, however, was only the merest beginning of the education he afterwards secured by studious habits and persistent application to a systematic course of reading and study under his own direction. He never attended a college, but he acquired a splendid literary style, became a close logical reasoner, a sound thinker, and a superior public speaker. He is a master of a choice style of English, and argues propositions in a forceful, pleasing and fascinating manner. But few men are his equal as a trial lawyer or an all round advocate. He is kind and fair to every one concerned in a court trial, and yet at the same time he is so earnest and zealous in behalf of his own clients he becomes a dangerous competitor in any important court trial in which he is engaged; and yet but few lawyers adhere as strictly as he to all the rules of legal ethics. He is absolutely sincere, upright and trustworthy. He has for many years past been found on the moral side of every important question that has been brought before the people. Indeed this has been true of him from his early manhood. Such men are rare in any profession or calling.

In private life Senator Blue is amiable and refined. Like Lord Chesterfield he considers politeness the lubricator of society and to smooth the pathways of those he recognizes as the prime duty of man. He is a fond husband, a doting father, a devoted friend, and the golden chain is linked with the jewels of domestic felicity. He married Miss Margaret J. Ice, of Barbour County, November 26, 1905. They had two sons, one a prattling little boy who, a year or so ago, on account of a fatal illness, drew his chubby, little hand out of his father's palm and flew away to the summerland of song — the other, a young man, now completing his college work.

Mr. Blue read law in the office of Judge A. G. Dayton at Philippi in Barbour County, where he was not only an apt, but a diligent student. When twenty-one years of age he passed a satisfactory examination and was admitted to the Bar of the Supreme Court of Appeals of the State at Charleston, in December, 1893. Immediately, thereafter, he opened an office at Philippi, the capital of Barbour County, and began an active and successful career as a practicing attorney. He has always been a Republican in his political affiliations, and was elected a member of the West Virginia Senate, serving in that position from 1906 to 1910. In this position he revealed marked usefulness in legislative service. He was Chairman of two committees and was a member of six others. He was very active during sessions of the Legislature as well as very useful.

Senator Blue was appointed State Tax Commissioner by Governor Dawson, March 1, 1911, and held the office for six consecutive years. This is a position requiring a high grade of executive ability, and Mr. Blue filled it with remarkable acceptability. Being a strong lawyer he personally represented the State's interests in hundreds of court trials in almost every portion of the State. When the voters threw West Virginia out of the "wet column" he was designated by the Legislature to enforce the "dry" law, and he devoted his best energies to that important service. But few of our people know how zealously he labored to enforce the Prohibition Law and the amount of energy and toil he put into it. He, however, never faltered, but did his full duty faithfully and heroically. He has written a book entitled, "When a State Goes Dry," which is well worth any one's time to read and ponder over. Since he has retired from public life Senator Blue located at Charleston, has opened a law office in conjunction with Mr. Robert E. McCabe, a thorough-going young lawyer, a sketch of whom will be found on another page of this book, the firm name being Blue and McCabe, a busy and successful combination of enterprising attorneys.

Mr. Blue is a vigilant member of the Baptist Church and is a Free Mason of deserving high rank, and strives to live true to the ideals of that order. He is a forward-thinking man, broad and liberal in his views and thoroughly democratic in spirit. Though of a positive nature he disagrees with his opponents without rancor. He is devoted to his home and loves the evening communion of the family circle. He is an upright citizen, keenly devoted to the social welfare and the betterment of the human mass. It is by no means out of place to class him as an ideal lawyer and a true representative citizen.

## Judge Frank Cox, LL.B.

The subject of this sketch, son of Henry L. and Elizabeth M. (Boydston) Cox, of Monongalia County, West Virginia, is one of the distinguished lawyers and jurists of the State. He is a native of Monongalia County and was born June 18, 1862, and is, therefore, in the prime of physical and mental manhood. He received a liberal education in the public schools of his native county and at the West Virginia University, from which latter institution he graduated in the Law Department in the class of 1883. Almost immediately thereafter he was admitted as an attorney in the Circuit Court of Monongalia County, where he has since continuously practiced. Barring the two years that he served as an Associate Justice of the Supreme Court of Appeals of the State. From the outset his practice was successful. He is an advocate of unusual force and effectiveness and, therefore, ranks high as a trial lawyer.

In 1888 he was elected Prosecuting Attorney of his native county, and served four years in that responsible position, in which he acquitted himself with credit as an able and faithful public servant. During his term as County Prosecutor he formed a law partnership with George C. Baker, who subsequently succeeded him in the office of Prosecuting Attorney of the

JUDGE FRANK COX

county, by whom he was appointed as his (Mr. Baker's) Deputy, and as such he served another four years' term.

In 1904 Mr. Cox was elected by the Republicans a member of the Supreme Court of Appeals of West Virginia, in which exalted judicial office he rendered faithful and satisfactory service for two years. Although he enjoyed the work of an Appellate Judge he had a longing to return to the Bar as an attorney, where the opportunities were, in a monetary sense, far greater than in a judicial office; consequently he resigned from the Court, returned to his home at Morgantown and re-established the law firm of Cox and Baker, which firm is still conducting a large and prosperous business in the State and Federal Courts.

Judge Cox is not only a lawyer of merit and distinction, but he is also engaged in a number of local business enterprises and is a public spirited citizen, and is active in the development of the resources and interests of the prosperous city in which he resides. He is a vigorous member of the Board of Trade of Morgantown; is a large owner of real estate; takes great interest in the educational development of the section where he resides, and was an active member of the Morgantown School Board for many years; served as Judge Advocate General during the administration ot Governor Atkinson; declined to accept the office of Circuit Court Judge to fill a vacancy, which was tendered to him by Governor Atkinson; was a member of the World's Fair Commission in 1904; is a member of the Methodist Episcopal Church, and is also a Mason and an Odd Fellow.

He is a man of upright and blameless character and has acquitted himself honorably in all of the public positions he ever held. In all relations—in his family, at the Bar, in his friendships, and in his home community, he has ever been loyal, true, generous, charitable and considerate. He married Miss Mattie J. Weaver March 8, 1885, and they have been blessed with two children, a son and a daughter, and no happier home than theirs can anywhere be found.

---

## Judge Charles W. Lynch, A.M., LL.D.

Charles W. Lynch is a native of Harrison County, West Virginia, and was born March 11, 1851. He was classically educated at the West Virginia University, graduating therefrom in the class of 1874, with the degree of Bachelor of Arts. He engaged in school teaching for a few years, being Superintendent of the Public Schools at Burning Springs, Wirt County, and at Clarksburg in his native county. In 1877 his *alma mater* conferred upon him the degree of Master of Arts, *pro merito*. Meanwhile he read law, and in 1882 was admitted to membership in the Harrison County Bar. In politics he is a Republican, and was quite active in that organization for a number of years. He was elected to the House of Delegates from Harrison County in 1882 and again in 1890, and served the people faithfully. He was eight years Prosecuting Attorney of that county,

JUDGE CHARLES W. LYNCH, LL. D.

from 1885 to 1889 and 1893 to 1897, and discharged the duties of the office with ability and efficiency. Being a man of upright and blameless character he never swerved from the line of duty nor showed fear or favor in any of his public acts, and consequently acquitted himself honorably in all the public positions he ever held.

After a number of years in active practice at the Bars of his native and adjoining counties, and after establishing himself as a lawyer of pronounced experience and ability, he was elected Judge of the Judicial Circuit in which he resided, and ably filled the same for the full term of eight years. No predecessor in that responsible position ever filled the same more satisfactorily than he, and it was generally expected that he would be nominated and elected for a second term as Circuit Judge; but before the Convention was held, unknown to and undesired by him, the State Judicial Convention assembled and nominated him as a candidate for an Associate Justice of the Supreme Court of Appeals of the State, to which exalted position he was elected by the people for a term of twelve years. His many years of practice in the various State and Federal Courts, embracing all branches of the law, and his eight years experience on the Bench of the Circuit Court, thoroughly equipped him for the arduous duties of his present position, in which he is making an enviable record as an Appellate Judge. He is incorruptible. He is severely candid and is essentially just. His ability is unusual, and his life and achievements stamp him as a lawyer, jurist and a patriot of the highest grades.

Judge Lynch is happily married and has one son, who is a graduate of three universities, and is ready to enter upon the practice of the profession which his distinguished father has so highly honored.

The Judge is a member of the Methodist Episcopal Church; is a Free Mason of high rank, and has been honored therein by being elected Grand Master of the State. He is President of the Board of Trustees of West Virginia Wesleyan College, from which institution he received in 1915 the honorary degree of Doctor of Laws. He is a man of the people and is highly respected by all who know him.

## Judge George Poffenbarger

Our subject is one of the very able jurists West Virginia has produced. He is strong in both body and intellect and has proved himself capable of work almost unlimited. No Supreme Court Judge of this State has piled up a longer series of decisions that have stood the test of close scrutiny and gone farther towards clarifying and settling the laws of West Virginia than Judge Poffenbarger, who is now serving his second term as one of the five Supreme Court Justices of this State. He is a born jurist, and has made, and is still making, a record which all well-meaning lawyers can and will point to with pride.

JUDGE GEORGE POFFENBARGER

He is a native of Mason County, Virginia, and was born November 24, 1861. He was brought up on a farm and attended the common schools; being naturally studious and industrious he acquired a fairly good common school education, which he supplemented by teaching for a period of seven years in the public schools, and by continuous study in the privacy of his home. He subsequently took a course of study in Rio Grande College, Ohio, but did not graduate. For several years while a school teacher he devoted all his spare time to the study of legal text books, under the direction of Judge John W. English, of Point Pleasant, and in 1887 he was licensed as an attorney in the courts of Mason County.

From early manhood Judge Poffenbarger showed a strong inclination towards politics, and in 1888 he was elected Sheriff of Mason County, which office he creditably filled for the term of four years. He is a forceful public speaker, and also established a reputation as a political organizer of unusual capacity and strength. In the campaign of 1900 he was nominated by the Republican party for a place on the Supreme Court of Appeals and was elected by the people to a twelve years' term in the highest judicial position in the State; when his term expired he was renominated and re-elected without serious opposition to a second twelve years' term, in which office he is still ably serving.

From the beginning of his judicial career Judge Poffenbarger has been a persistent originator and advocate of reforms in Appellate Court procedure. In 1903 the Court adopted the preliminary conference of judges upon every case submitted in advance of the preparation of the opinion at his suggestion, and it has been rigidly adhered to ever since. There is, therefore, no longer any possibility of a one judge decision in the court of last resort. Not long afterwards he urged a reduction of the time allowed for oral argument, from two hours and a half to one hour and a quarter. The rule was accordingly amended, but later rescinded. In 1913, however, it was again so amended and is now in force. In the same year, acting upon a suggestion made by him and previously considered in consultation with all the members of the court and several prominent members of the Kanawha County Bar, the Legislature amended and re-enacted section 20 of chapter 135 of the Code, so as to give the court complete control of its docket and enable it to regulate the submission of cases in accordance with its ability to decide them. This alteration of the statute, the reduction of the time for oral argument, and the abolition of the Wheeling and Charles Town terms of the court, enabled that body to dispose of a vast accumulation of delayed business, and now enables it to keep entirely up with its business. He also suggested, drafted and contributed largely to the revision and amendment of sections 1, 5, 6 and 26 of chapter 135 of the Code, by virtue of which questions of process and pleading may be reviewed and settled by the Supreme Court of Appeals in the progress of litigation as they arise and before final judgment on certificates from the trial courts; applications for appeals and writs of error may be made on the original papers, transcripts obtained when needed at greatly reduced cost, and plain cases affirmed or reversed on motions made by leave of the court. All of these measures greatly facilitate the disposition of business and effect large reductions in costs.

Judge Poffenbarger married Miss Livia Nye Simpson, of Point Pleasant, West Virginia, a woman of great ability and wonderful intellectual endowments and of exalted personal character. They have two sons, Nathan Simpson Poffenbarger and Perry Simpson Poffenbarger. They have a pleasant home at Point Pleasant, where they are respected and held in high esteem by the entire community.

## Hon. Benjamin Stanton

Mr. Stanton was not only a lawyer of ability and prominence, but was a statesman and a leader in politics as well. His parents were Quakers. He was born at Mount Pleasant, Ohio, June 4, 1809, and died at Wheeling, West Virginia, June 2, 1872. He was reared on a farm and had the advantages only of the public schools to receive an early educational training. His real education was procured by the reading and study of books after the school period with him had ended. Like a large number of other distinguished men he dug out an education after he attained manhood by constant study, application and persevering energy. Although he never attended a college or even an academy, no man can say that Benjamin Stanton was not a highly cultured man. He read law in the office of Stokely and Morris at Steubenville, Ohio, and was admitted to the Jefferson County, Ohio Bar, in the fall of 1833. In April, 1834, he removed his residence to Bellefontaine, Ohio, where he began active practice, and where he remained until 1866, when he became a resident of Wheeling, West Virginia. He became a leading lawyer and had a large practice for a quarter of a century while a resident of Ohio.

In 1841 he was elected to the State Senate of Ohio, but prior to that he had served as Prosecuting Attorney of his county. In politics, before the Civil War, he was a Whig, but later he became an active Republican. He was re-elected to the Senate in 1842. In 1851 he formed a partnership at Bellefontaine with C. W. B. Allison, who was an able lawyer, under the firm name of Stanton & Allison, which firm continued in existence at Bellefontaine for fifteen years, and in 1866 they opened a law office at Wheeling, West Virginia, where they conducted a large business until Mr. Stanton's death in 1872. In 1850 he was a member of the Constitutional Convention of Ohio. He was later elected a member of the Thirty-second Congress. He was not a member of the next Congress, but was re-elected in 1854, and served in Congress by successive re-elections until March 4, 1861. He was a forceful and eloquent public speaker and took an active part in legislative debates. He was elected Lieutenant Governor of Ohio in 1862 on the ticket with Governor David Tod, serving two years. A considerable number of Wheeling lawyers had participated in the Rebellion and were thereby inhibited from practicing, so Governor Stanton and his partner, Mr. Allison, in 1866, transferred their residence to Wheeling, and from the start had a very large practice.

For native ability and power in debate Governor Stanton has rarely been excelled either in Ohio or West Virginia. He was a great trial lawyer, which was his specialty. His private character was above reproach, and in all the social relations of life, he enjoyed the warm friendship of all the people who knew him. He was kind hearted and generous, affable and courteous, and had hosts of friends, and was admired no less for his brilliant talents than for his estimable qualities as a man.

## Judge Joseph Marcellus McWhorter

Joseph Marcellus McWhorter was born at what was then known as McWhorter's Mills (Virginia), near what is now Jane Lew, Lewis County, West Virginia, April 30, 1828, and died at his home in Lewisburg, West Virginia, August 18, 1913. He was the eldest son of Fields and Margaret Kester McWhorter, and brother of Henry C. McWhorter, late Judge of the Supreme Court of Appeals of West Virginia. In addition to the training received at the public schools he was a persistent and untiring reader of the best literature and acquired a good knowledge of the English branches of learning. He also taught school in his neighborhood during the winter season when he could be spared from the farm.

Judge McWhorter was always greatly interested in public affairs. In politics he was a Whig before the Civil War and later a staunch Republican. In 1856 when Roane County was organized he was appointed County Clerk of that county, also acting as Circuit Clerk, and was later twice elected to the same office. On the formation of the State of West Virginia he was elected a member of the first Legislature from Roane County. After the adjournment of the Legislature the Governor appointed him Superintendent of the Penitentiary, but he soon resigned from this office. In 1864 he was nominated by the Republican party and elected State Auditor, and was again elected to the same office in 1866. He was elected Secretary of the West Virginia Insurance Company in 1869 and served until 1870, when Governor Stevenson appointed him Circuit Judge to fill the vacancy caused by the resignation of Judge Nathaniel Harrison. The Circuit was composed of Greenbrier, Monroe, Pocahontas and Nicholas Counties, and Judge McWhorter moved from Wheeling to Lewisburg, where he resided until his death. His term as Judge expired December 31, 1872. After his retirement from the Bench he practiced his profession in Greenbrier and adjoining counties, and merited the respect and admiration of all the people. He was elected Mayor of Lewisburg in 1887, was County Superintendent of Schools of Greenbrier County one term, and also served four years as Postmaster. In 1892 he was nominated by his party for Judge of the Supreme Court of Appeals, but with the rest of the ticket went

JUDGE J. M. McWHORTER

down to defeat. He was elected in 1896 as Judge of the Tenth Judicial Circuit and served the full term of eight years. From 1905 until his death he was actively engaged in the practice of law at Lewisburg.

Judge McWhorter was twice married. His first wife was Julia A. Stalnaker of Harrison County, who died August 26, 1869. To them ten children were born, three of whom died in infancy. Those living are: Alessandro G., of Charleston; Artemus W., of Norfolk, Va.; Louis E., practicing attorney in Charleston; William B., of Charleston; Mrs. Margaret E. Lewis, of Charleston; Joseph C., of St. Louis, Mo.; and Deccie, wife of C. L. Carr, of Lewisburg. On October 26, 1870, he married Julia A. Kinsley, daughter of Rev. Hiram and Elsie L. Kinsley, of Geneva, Ohio, and to them were born four children: Emma L., wife of R. B. Holt, of Lewisburg; Jennie P., deceased wife of J. Scott McWhorter, of Lewisburg; Kinsley F., died in infancy; and Charles N., of Charleston.

Judge McWhorter's reputation as a Christian gentleman was enviable. He was a member of the Methodist Episcopal Church, South, at Lewisburg, and had religious convictions deep and abiding. As an honest, consistent Christian he walked uprightly, lived at peace with all men, and died at peace with his God.

---

A tribute by L. E. McWhorter to his father, J. M. McWhorter, and his uncle, H. C. McWhorter.

With the passing of Judge Joseph M. McWhorter and Judge Henry C. McWhorter the State of West Virginia lost two of its most valuable citizens. Reared in the old school of honesty and integrity both were model men of their generation. Their ideals being high were maintained throughout the more than three score years and ten allotted to them, and their characters and influence for good are indelibly stamped upon the communities in which they lived. The name of each was a synonym for honesty and righteousness. Their deeds of charity, kindness and benevolence are legion, and all through busy lives they always had time to listen and heed the call of distress. Men of their type are benedictions to the State, the family and the Church, and fortunate are those who can claim the heritage from such ancestors.

---

## Judge William N. Miller, A.M.

Our subject is a native of the State of Ohio, where he was born at Uniopolis, October 18, 1855. His parents were Charles W. and Sarah Ellen (Niswonger) Miller. He attended the public schools of his native State and later was graduated from Otterbein University in the class of 1879, receiving the classical degree of Bachelor of Arts, and in 1881 the higher degree of Master of Arts, *pro merito*. Shortly thereafter he moved to Parkersburg, West Virginia, and became a law student in the office of Wyman L. Cole, an able and successful lawyer of that city. After studying

JUDGE WILLIAM N. MILLER

legal text books, under the tutelage of Mr. Cole for nearly two years, he passed a creditable examination and was in 1882 admitted to the Wood County Bar. It was not long until Mr. Cole, who saw great promise in his young law student, invited him to become his partner in the practice of his profession, which he accepted, and the firm of Cole & Miller took high rank among the noted law firms of that distinguished Bar. He continued as the junior member of the firm for several years, until Mr. Cole moved to Washington, D. C., to join his brother, Charles C. Cole, in a larger field of opportunities than was then attainable in West Virginia. Mr. Miller, however, remained in the State, and being a young man of liberal education, of studious habits, and of upright life and character, forged forward, until he had gathered about him a large and profitable clientele, which kept on expanding until he was called by Governor Dawson, January 28, 1907, to the position of an Associate Judge of the Supreme Court of Appeals of West Virginia, to fill the vacancy created by the resignation of Judge Frank Cox, of Morgantown; and the following year his services on the highest court of the State being eminently satisfactory, he was nominated by the Republican party, of which he had been all his life an active member, as a candidate to fill out the unexpired term of Judge Cox, and he was thereto triumphantly elected by the people. After serving eight years in this exalted position, in 1916 he was again placed in nomination by his political party by acclamation, and was elected by the people to the same position for the full term of twelve years, where he is now serving with great acceptability to both suitors and attorneys.

During the ten or more years Judge Miller has been a member of this high court, he has demonstrated his splendid qualifications for the position. He is not only a just Judge, but he possesses, in a high degree, the judicial temperament. His opinions are clear, terse and logical, and he gives to every case careful and painstaking consideration. He married Miss Anna A. Bright, of Westerville, Ohio, September 3, 1883, and has one daughter. Judge Miller was appointed Judge Advocate General of the West Virginia National Guard by both Governor White and Governor Dawson. For fifteen years he was Treasurer of the West Virginia Bar Association. He is a member of the American Bar Association, the B. P. O. Elks, and of the Protestant Episcopal Church, is a public spirited citizen, and has the confidence and respect of all the people with whom he associates.

## Judge Francis Marion Reynolds

Judge Reynolds' grandfather, Cornelius Reynolds, emigrated from Loudon County, Virginia, and was a pioneer settler near Pruntytown then in Harrison County. When his grandfather moved to that section, it was practically a wilderness and he had to clear the spot where he erected his first home.

Judge Reynolds was born September 18, 1843, on the old homestead. After remaining on the farm with his father until 1862, and in the mean-

JUDGE F. M. REYNOLDS

time attending during the winter months such schools as were then in that vicinity, he became a student at the old Monongalia Academy in Morgantown in the fall of 1862 and continued there until the summer of 1864, when he commenced the study of law in the office of Judge Edward C. Bunker at Morgantown, and was admitted to the bar in 1865. He commenced the practice of his profession at New Creek, then Hampshire County, now Mineral County, West Virginia, although he resided for a short time at Romney, the county seat of Hampshire County before the county of Mineral was established. He was married to Belle R. Hennen, eldest daughter of Washington and Justina Hennen, at Morgantown, in October, 1866. He has two sons and one daughter still living.

His political support was given to the Republican Party from the time he cast his first vote, which was for Abraham Lincoln as President in 1864. He was elected to the office of Prosecuting Attorney for Mineral County and served two terms of four years each. He also was, at the same time, Prosecuting Attorney of Mineral County; was elected Prosecuting Attorney of Grant County and continued to hold the latter office for three consecutive terms of four years each and was afterwards assistant to his law partner, L. J. Forman, as Prosecuting Attorney for three terms of four years each. He also served three terms as a member of the legislature of West Virginia, 1895–96, 1901–02 and 1903–04, including the extra session of July, 1904, when the new tax system for West Virginia was adopted. During all of these terms he served at each session as Chairman of the Finance Committee and was a member of the Judiciary Committee and also other committees; was chosen Republican nominee for Congress to represent the Second District of West Virginia in 1884, having William L. Wilson as his opponent, who was elected. In 1896 he was chosen as a delegate at large to the Republican National Convention, which met at St. Louis, and served on the Committee on Platform, and was one of a few members who at that time voted to put in the platform an unqualified declaration in favor of the single gold standard, which was shortly thereafter adopted by Congress. In 1890 he was the nominee of the Republican State Convention for Judge of the Supreme Court of Appeals against Daniel B. Lucas, and was defeated. He was chosen Mayor of the town of Keyser and filled this office efficiently; was also a member of the Common Council of the town, and a member of the Board of Education; was appointed a member of the Board of Regents for the Deaf and Blind Schools at Romney, and was elected President of that Board in 1897, and continued in that position until elected Judge of the Sixteenth Judicial Circuit at the election of 1904, and he was again re-elected in 1912 to serve a second term of eight years and continues in that service at the present time.

Among the financial institutions and other business corporations with which Judge Reynolds is connected was the Keyser bank, of which he was elected President in 1887, and continued to hold that position until the bank was succeeded by the First National Bank of Keyser, and he was then elected President of the latter, and still continues to hold that position. He has been President of the Keyser Electric Light Company ever since it commenced business in 1894, is President of the Piedmont Grocery Company, and a Director in the Potomac Milling & Ice Company and the Siever Hardware Company.

He became a member of the Methodist Episcopal Church in 1871, and has been an official member of that organization ever since; was chosen Superintendent of the Sunday School the same year, and has been re-elected to that position ever since, holding the office for forty-eight years.

He is an able lawyer and a just and upright Judge. Through a long, useful and successful life, no stain of dishonor was ever connected with his name.

## Hon. Jonathan McCally Bennett

The County of Lewis, the Town of Weston, and the State of West Virginia lost a friend and valuable citizen when the Honorable J. M. Bennett died October 28, 1887. He was born October 4, 1816, on the farm in Lewis County that had belonged to the family a century, and which he owned at his death. He was the youngest child of William and Rebecca (McCally) Bennett. The grandfather, Joseph Bennett, came from Scotland to Augusta County, Virginia, before the Revolutionary War; his son, William, moved to Lewis County in 1800, where he resided on his valuable tract of land and died in 1857.

Jonathan M. Bennett married Margaret Elizabeth Jackson, daughter of Captain George W. Jackson, a soldier of 1812; she was a cousin of "Stonewall" Jackson, who was a lifelong intimate friend and protege of the subject of this sketch.

Mr. Bennett was deservedly popular with his people and bore a distinguished reputation throughout the old Commonwealth as well as in the new. Before the State was separated he was Deputy Sheriff of Lewis County, 1836–38, when he was appointed Deputy Clerk of both the County and Circuit Courts, holding the position several years. In 1843 he was admitted to the Bar, and practiced as partner of Gideon D. Camden until the latter was elevated to the Bench in 1852. Mr. Bennett was the first Commonwealth's Attorney for Gilmer County, and the first Mayor of Weston, in 1846. After filling various county commissions, in 1852–3 he was a member of the Virginia General Assembly from Lewis County; in 1853 was President of the Exchange Bank of Virginia at Weston; was First Auditor of Virginia from 1857 to 1865; he was before the Democratic Convention for the Congressional nomination in 1858, but Albert G. Jenkins was nominated on a close vote.

Mr. Bennett went with his State in its secession, and during the war filled important positions at Richmond. When peace came, he resumed his law practice at Weston. He was in the West Virginia Senate from 1872 to 1876, and was Chairman of the Committee on Finance. He was also one of the three Commissioners to adjust with Virginia the proportions of the State debt due by each State. He filled minor positions for the new State, always with satisfaction and credit. A hard student, a painstaking official, a business man of strict integrity, a zealous, public-spirited citizen, a kind neighbor, a loving husband and father — such acknowledged characteristics are blocks in his monument "more enduring than brass." Mr. Bennett was made an Odd Fellow in 1850. He was a Democrat in politics, and for many years was recognized as among the strongest lawyers in the central portion of West Virginia.

## Hon. James Dallas Ewing

Our subject was well known to the present generation of lawyers in the "Northern Pan Handle" of West Virginia; he was a son of William Ewing, of Marshall County, Virginia, and was born September 19, 1832, on the farm known as "Fairhill," which had been the Ewing family homestead since 1795. He remained there, working on the farm and teaching school, until he reached his majority. He possessed a strong and rugged intellect, and desired better things than farming and teaching school; so he determined to be a lawyer. His education had been meager, but he concluded that he, by hard study, application, energy and grit, could overcome that embarrassment, and so he went at it, "hammer and tongs," and stayed "on the job" until he succeeded grandly. He took up the study of law under Wylie H. Oldham, a leading lawyer of Marshall County, and worked at it heroically until 1858, when he was licensed, and was admitted to the Moundsville Bar. Being practically compelled to suspend practice for a time on account of the War of the Rebellion, he engaged in mercantile pursuits for a couple of years, and then opened a law office in Moundsville. Business came to him better than he had thought, or had even dreamed of. He had all the legal work he could attend to, and more. He also practiced in the adjoining county of Wetzel, where he had a considerable volume of business. He rapidly gained confidence in his abilities as a lawyer, so he transferred his residence to Wheeling, twelve miles distant, where the opportunities for an ambitious lawyer were better and the field was broader. His business increased rapidly, and he possessed the knowledge and ability to handle it successfully. He kept on growing as a lawyer and his business grew likewise. Ability and business moved *pari passu*. They always do.

He practiced alone for several years, but his clientage justified it, and so he associated General T. S. Riley with him, under the firm name of Ewing and Riley. Business kept on increasing, and Judge Thayer Melvin was added, under the firm name of Ewing, Melvin and Riley, all of them able lawyers. The firm, therefore, became one of the strongest in the northern part of the State, and carried on a vast business. Their business embraced every branch of the law in all the State and Federal courts.

JAMES DALLAS EWING

Mr. Ewing was not endowed with the highest gifts of eloquence, but at the same time he was a superior trial lawyer. He was eloquent in the depths of his convictions, in the earnestness of his manner, in the logical train of his thoughts, in the force and power of his language and in the moral makeup of the man. His arguments were always clear, logical and concise; his oratory was more like the blows of a sledge-hammer than that Ciceronian gentleness which glides upon the waves of conciliation. He depended upon the rod of reason rather than upon the wand of suasion. He possessed a keen sense of humor and was open and generous in all his dealings, punctilious in the discharge of his duties to his clients, resolute in the prosecution of every undertaking and was all that Horace meant by his *justus et tenax propositi vir*. He walked through the world in the path of duty and conscious rectitude, and in the faith of piety, down to the brink of the valley, and when he stepped forth into its shadows, he, no doubt, caught the promised visions which flash from the blessings of the faithful servant in a well spent life.

Mr. Ewing was a Democrat, but never a politician. He never sought an office, and only a time or so did he allow himself to be drafted as a candidate. He married Miss Emma Anderson, of New Martinsville, West Virginia, by whom he had ten children, one of them — James W. Ewing — who is a distinguished member of the Wheeling Bar, who is treated in another portion of this volume. He passed to the unseen, August 30, 1898, at his home in the city of Wheeling, and was mourned by a large circle of admiring friends.

## Hon. William Pallister Hubbard, A.M.

The Hubbard family of Wheeling is one of the oldest and most distinguished families in the State of West Virginia. Dana Hubbard, the pioneer manufacturer of Ohio County, came from Connecticut in 1819 and settled in Wheeling. He erected a saw and grist mill and engaged in the lumber business. He died in 1852. He had five children, three of whom became business men of prominence and large means and influence, viz.: Chester D., Henry B. and John R. Hubbard. Chester D. Hubbard, the father of our subject, for more than fifty years was one of the most influential, progressive business men of Ohio County, and at the same time he was a leader in the civic development of that section of the State. He was also prominent in the political, educational and religious growth of the entire State. He was a leader in the formation of West Virginia; was twice elected a Member of Congress; was one of the builders of the Methodist Episcopal Church in West Virginia and was twice elected a Delegate to its General Conference. He died full of honors in 1891.

The subject of this sketch was the eldest son of Hon. Chester D. Hubbard, who was born in the city of Wheeling, December 24, 1843. He was educated in the schools of his native county and at Linsly Institute, a high grade

HON. WILLIAM P. HUBBARD

academy of the city of Wheeling. Later he matriculated as a student of Wesleyan University, Middletown, Connecticut, and in 1863 was one of its honored graduates, as had been his father, and afterwards was his son, Nelson C. Hubbard, who is a prominent lawyer in the city of Wheeling. After completing his college work, W. P. Hubbard returned to his native city, read law and was admitted to the Ohio County Bar in 1864. During the year 1865 he served in the Third West Virginia Cavalry until the close of the Civil War, volunteering as a private and being honorably discharged as first lieutenant. Immediately thereafter he opened a law office in Wheeling and entered upon one of the most honorable and noted careers as a practitioner of the law that the State of West Virginia has ever produced. His practice extended into all the West Virginia courts, the courts of Western Pennsylvania and Eastern Ohio, and also the Supreme Court of the United States. His force of will, self-reliance and courage are much more than common. In whatever duty he enters he throws his strong personality and he never fails when he ought to succeed. He fears no antagonist and was unfaithful to no client. He declined judicial honors because he thought himself better fitted for the Bar, and there found work more to his taste and liking, just as honorable as that on the Bench, not to say more profitable. Personally he has a side of geniality and sociability, which on some occasions has to be discovered, but when found is stimulating and refreshing. As an advocate he is gifted with unusual logical powers and a faculty of expression remarkably lucid. His diction is of a kind such as to present to the minds of his hearers the argument as clearly as he sees it in his own mind. As an all round lawyer he is thorough and accurate and has a wide grasp of legal principles.

From 1866 to 1870 Mr. Hubbard was Clerk of the West Virginia House of Delegates, and the State never had a more efficient one; in 1881–2 he represented Ohio County in the West Virginia Legislature; in 1888 he was a Delegate to the Republican National Convention; that year he was his party's nominee for Attorney-General of the State and was defeated along with the other candidates of his party; in 1890 he was the unsuccessful Republican candidate for Congress from the Wheeling district; in 1902–3 he rendered valuable service as Chairman of the commission to revise the tax laws of West Virginia; in 1906 he was nominated and elected a Member of Congress from the Wheeling district, and was re-elected two years later. He declined to be a candidate for a third term, and again resumed the practice of the law with his son, Nelson C. Hubbard, as junior member of the firm of Hubbard and Hubbard, one of the ablest law firms of the entire State. In 1912 he was again a delegate-at-large to the Republican National Convention.

Mr. Hubbard married Miss Anna E. Chamberlin, of Louisiana, May 21, 1868. Five children were born to them — Julia P., who married W. I. Kelly; Nelson C., who, as before stated, is an attorney in partnership with his father; Alma R.; Louise P., who married Rev. W. E. Hudson; and Sarah

P., who died in infancy. The wife and mother departed this life in 1901. The family home is on the old National Pike, east of Wheeling, just outside the city limits.

Mr. Hubbard was one of the organizers of the West Virginia Bar Association, is one of its most faithful members and was its President in 1895. During the last few years the large business of the firm has been handled almost entirely by the junior member of the partnership, although the senior member is in robust health and is in the full possession of all his powerful faculties.

## Col. William H. Hogeman

Colonel Hogeman was born in the city of New York, December 20, 1845, and after receiving a liberal English education, studied law and was admitted to the Bar by the New York Supreme Court, December 16, 1867, soon after attaining his majority. A short time previous to his admission to the Bar he made a business trip to the Kanawha Valley of West Virginia, and being pleased with the people and country, settled in Charleston and began the practice of law. He was eminently successful, and soon acquired a State reputation as a lawyer and a man of general business ability. He took an active interest in all the political movements in the State, though never holding and never seeking political office. Governor John J. Jacob made him one of his aides-de-camp with the rank of Colonel, which honor was contined by Governors Mathews and Jackson.

In 1870 Colonel Hogeman was appointed general counsel for the Chesapeake and Ohio Railroad Company, and was so continued until his death, which occurred at his home in Charleston, after a short illness, on the 5th day of January, 1885. The fatal illness, it was supposed, was superinduced by his labors and exposure by travel on necessary railroad duties. He was small of stature but compactly built, giving promise of a long and useful life. He was not only a sound and thoroughly equipped lawyer in the science of pleading, but an accomplished and successful advocate. In social life it was remarked of him that few men coming from a distant and distinctly different State more thoroughly and quickly became identified with a new people in their sympathies and interests than he did.

Colonel Hogeman married Miss Anastein Ruffner of Charleston, daughter of the late Colonel James Ruffner, and sister of Andrew and Meredith Ruffner, distinguished merchants of that city. She with two children were left to mourn their bereavement. But few men in West Virginia achieved a more distinguished legal reputation than did Colonel William H. Hogeman.

## Judge Henry Clay McWhorter, LL.D.

The writer knew Judge McWhorter intimately for more than a generation, and is therefore competent to pass upon his merits and qualifications as a citizen, a lawyer and a jurist. He was the son of Fields and Margaret M. (Kester) McWhorter, and was born in Marion County, Ohio, February 20, 1836, and came with his parents to Roane County, Virginia, in early life. He lived on a farm until he was eighteen years of age; was a clerk in a drug store for a short time and was afterwards appointed Deputy Clerk of the County and Circuit Courts of Roane County, which office he held until the breaking out of the Civil War, when he volunteered as a private soldier in the 9th West Virginia infantry. He was later promoted to First Lieutenant and finally he became Captain of his company. On account of a severe gunshot wound in his right leg, received in battle in 1863, he was transferred to the Provost Marshal's Department, where he remained until the close of the war.

He then located at Charleston and took up the study of law, and after his admission to the Kanawha County Bar he was nominated by the Republican party in 1870 and was elected by the people to the office of Prosecuting Attorney of Kanawha County, in which office he served faithfully and efficiently for a term of four years. He was a member of the Legislature of the State in 1865, '66, '67 and '68, in which latter year he was Speaker of the House of Delegates, fulfilling its onerous and intricate duties in a satisfactory manner. Again, he served as a member of the Legislature from Kanawha County from 1885 to 1887. In 1888 he was the candidate of the Republican party for Judge of the Supreme Court of Appeals and was defeated along with all the other candidates of his party.

He was a useful member of the Methodist Episcopal Church for practically his entire life; was twice a member of the General Conference of that Church; was a member of the Masonic Fraternity and Grand Army of the Republic and Loyal Legion; was a member of the Board of Education and also of the City Council of Charleston; was President of the Board of Trustees of West Virginia Wesleyan College for many years prior to and at the time of his death; was Postmaster of the city of Charleston for three years and was elected an Associate Justice of the Supreme Court of Appeals of West Virginia and served faithfully and efficiently for a full term of twelve years, and declined to be a candidate for re-election. He was happily married four times, and no one enjoyed home life more than he.

Judge McWhorter was affable in manner, modest and unassuming, with ready sympathies, a keen sense of humor and refined and cultured taste in literature. In all relations, in his family, at the Bar, on the Bench, in his friendships, he was loyal, upright and generous, and above all he was not only a just Judge, but in all his dealings he was a man of blameless life and unblemished personal character.

A few years before his death the West Virginia Wesleyan College conferred upon him the honorary degree of Doctor of Laws, an honor most

JUDGE HENRY C. McWHORTER

deserved and most generously bestowed. In 1905 Judge McWhorter was one of the Electors of the Hall of Fame, Syracuse University.

In the dawning of the morning of the 15th day of April, 1913, and before the sun had fairly risen, God's finger touched him and he slept. He is missed in his home life, missed by his family and friends, missed by the State at large, as an honorable and useful citizen.

## Hon. George Warwick McClintic, A.B., LL.B.

George W. McClintic, son of William H. and Mary Mathews McClintic, was born in Pocahontas County, West Virginia, January 14, 1866. He was graduated from Roanoke College at Salem, Virginia, in 1883, receiving the classical degree of Bachelor of Arts. He then entered the law department of the University of Virginia at Charlottesville, and was graduated therefrom in the class of 1886 with the degree of Bachelor of Laws. He returned to his native county and in the early part of the next year (1887) was admitted to the Bar of the Circuit Court of Pocahontas County. October 1, 1888, he located at Charleston, Kanawha County, and enterd upon the practice of the law as the junior member of the firm of Mollohan and McClintic,— Wesley Mollahan, an able and well-known attorney, being the senior member of the partnership. In 1900 William Gordon Mathews was added to the firm. In 1911 Mr. Mollohan died, and later the firm became McClintic, Mathews and Campbell, Mr. John Edgar Campbell being the junior member of the partnership as it now stands. Mr. McClintic, therefore, is now the senior member of one of the most noted law firms within the entire Commonwealth. His firm has specialized in land litigations, corporations and constitutional controversies, and at the same time practices in all the varied branches of the law in all the State and Federal courts within the State and also in the Supreme Court of the United States; and we may add, handles a large volume of important legal business.

Mr. McClintic owes his success at the Bar largely to his laborious preparation of his cases. He is thoroughly grounded in the fundamental principles of the law, and by indefatigable industry avails himself of his knowledge and resources. The accuracy of his pleadings, his uniform urbanity and simplicity of manners, his fidelity to his clients and the force of character which he brings to bear upon his causes, all contribute to his popularity and success. He possesses promptness, energy and decision, which coupled with love of justice and fair dealing, have placed him among the high grade members of the profession in the State. His rank as a member of the Bar of the State, therefore, is firmly established.

He was united in marriage with Miss Ethel Knight, of Charleston, daughter of the late Hon. Edward B. Knight, an eminent member of the Kanawha Bar, October 17, 1907. They have one child, Elizabeth Knight McClintic. Their home life is ideal, and among their friends they are always social, joyous and happy. They are Presbyterians in faith, and enjoy the confidence and respect of a large circle of admiring friends.

Mr. McClintic is "high up" in the Masonic Fraternity, having filled, with distinction, the exalted position of Most Worshipful Grand Master of the Grand Loage of West Virginia in 1905–6, whose annual sessions he never fails to attend, unless something of unusual importance intervenes to prevent.

He is a Republican in politics, but has never sought an office of any kind; except he was Solicitor of the city of Charleston for a full term and was a valuable official. Said office, however, is in the line of his profession. He was made the candidate of his party for membership in the West Virginia Legislature in June, 1918, without his seeking, and was elected by an unusual majority by the voters of his county.

## Hon. David Edwin French

Senator French, son of Henley Chapman and Harriet (Easley) French, was born in Giles County, Virginia, July 26, 1871, and was educated in the public schools and at the Pearisburg Academy, an institution of high grade at the seat of justice of Giles County, where he took a complete course. Its curriculum was equal to the average second grade colleges of that period in the Southern States. Early in life Mr. French exhibited an aptitude for study in acquiring knowledge, which he has kept up to this day. He is a constant reader of books, not only pertaining to the law, but on general subjects also, which make up the full and well-rounded mind of a successful lawyer. Of all the varied characters of men there is no one whose traits are wrought to a higher standard of excellence than that of a truly learned member of the legal profession. An attorney who thoroughly understands legal principles and knows how to correctly apply them is not only sure of success, if he adhere closely to his calling, but he is helpful to the courts in enforcing the law correctly and in raising the standard of other practitioners to a higher and a broader conception of the duties of members of the profession with whom he is associated. Strong Bars never fail to make strong Judges, and strong Judges invariably raise the standard of the Bars over which they preside. Learning and integrity in any calling reflect their light upon society, penetrate the dark confines of depravity, which is constantly showing its varied forms in the criminal side of our court trials, and present a guidance and a light, so to speak, of rectitude for the future. Law, as we understand it, is right, and the lawyer, as well as the just Judge will see to it that the right shall and must prevail in every court trial. Hence the necessity of thorough training on the part of every member of the legal fraternity in this and in all other countries.

We have offered these general remarks for the purpose of stating that Senator French is a lawyer of fine ability and thoroughly acquainted with the history and character of our Virginia jurisprudence, and is never at a loss for the proper methods of reaching the true issues in a controversy and rarely errs in the selection of his legal standpoints. He is, therefore, a safe counselor and possesses the confidence of both Bench and Bar. Necessarily he does not lack a paying and profitable clientage. Souna lawyers, who are upright and just never are short of business, we think, may be stated as a truism.

Senator French is a Democrat, and, so far as the writer knows, has always been of that faith. He was admitted to the Giles County, Virginia, Bar in May, 1895, and has devoted the greater part of his time to his profession. Soon after his admission as an attorney he located at Welch, in McDowell County, West Virginia, and moved to Bluefield, Mercer County, in 1905, where he now resides and has gathered about him a large body of admiring and profitable clients. His practice is general and extends to the adjoining counties and in all the State and Federal courts. He was City Attorney of Bluefield from 1908 to 1915, and was elected to the State Senate of West Virginia as a representative of the 7th District in 1910, and served with dignity and ability the full term of four years, taking an active part in all the legislatve debates.

November 15, 1899, he was united in marriage with Miss Minnie Reid of Athens, West Virginia. Five children resulted from this marriage. Their home is in the city of Bluefield, the metropolis of the extreme southern border of the State.

## Hon Fred. Lee Fox, LL.B.

One of the well-known and very successful law firms in the central part of West Virginia is composed of Hon. William Edgar Haymond and the subject of this sketch. Both of them are natives of Braxton County, and their practice extends into all the surrounding counties. Mr. Fox, the junior member of the firm, was born October 24, 1876, and is the son of Camden and Caroline McMorrow Fox, who resided at the mouth of Birch River. His primary education was received in the schools of Braxton County and later at the West Virginia University, from which he graduated in 1899 with the degree of LL.B. Immediately after his graduation he was admitted as an attorney of the Braxton County Bar and later became a member of the firm of Dulin and Fox, remaining therein for three years. In 1904 he became an associate of the Hon. William E. Haymond, and as stated above, is still a member of said energetic and successful firm of practitioners. Their practice embraces all general and civic lines of the law in both State and United States Courts in Braxton and adjoining counties, including the Supreme Court of Appeals of West Virginia, and it is but just to say that they have a large and profitable clientage, which is increasing as the years roll by.

For a number of years our subject has been quite active in politics. For ten or more years he acted as Chairman of the Democratic Executive Committee of Braxton County, in which position he proved to be a successful leader and organizer. His first political office was that of State Senator, to which he was elected by the people in 1912, and was re-elected in 1916, in

HON. FRED L. FOX

which highly honorable and important position he is now serving with distinction and great acceptability to his constituents. Almost from his entry in the Senate his ability and tact made him the acknowledged floor leader of his party in that legislative body. He is a superior public speaker, a ready debater and a safe and sane leader. It is entirely safe for us to predict that there are higher honors in store for him in the future, if his life should be spared, and it is to be hoped that it will.

Mr. Fox married Miss Annie Lee Frame, of Sutton, the seat of justice of Braxton County, and they are the parents of five children. He is a member of the Sutton Masonic Lodge, Chapter and Commandery and is also a member of the Nobles of the Mystic Shrine of the city of Charleston. He is of medium stature, of agreeable and pleasant disposition and is popular with the people. He possesses not only the elements of a successful lawyer, but a winner in politics as well. The writer is impressed with the belief that our subject, as a State Senator, is cutting the grooves that will carry him to higher political advancement in the future.

## Judge Reese Blizzard

Judge Blizzard, one of West Virginia's noted attorneys and jurists, who has been a resident of the city of Parkersburg for a great many years, engaged in active and successful practice, is a native of Nicholas County, West Virginia, where he was born October 17, 1865. His parents were James and Elizabeth Blizzard of that county, who subsequently moved to Gilmer County, where the subject of this sketch attended the public schools and was later graduated from the Glenville State Normal School. After graduation he engaged in teaching in the public schools of Gilmer and Calhoun counties in which he was quite successful. After following this profession for several years he took up the study of law in the office of Linn and Withers at Glenville and was admitted to the Bar of that county. He subsequently located at Grantsville, Calhoun County, where he opened an office and began what soon turned out to be a very lucrative practice. He possessed, in a large degree, energy, force of will and tenacity of purpose to win. He was found in his law office early and late, went to the bed-rocks of his cases, and when he appeared in court he knew the law and tried them successfully, in most instances; consequently, in a remarkably short time he made a reputation as an unusually successful young lawyer. In the meantime his business kept on expanding.

The Republican party, to which he belongs, nominated him for Judge of the Circuit Court in a Democratic district and he was elected, after a heated contest, and filled the position creditably and ably. At the end of four years he resigned and opened an office in the city of Parkersburg, where he, in a short time, built up a large practice. Shortly after he located at Parkersburg he was appointed United States District Attorney for the Northern District of West Virginia, which office he ably filled for ten years.

His force of will, self-reliance and courage are more than common. From the beginning he had no assistance and really wanted none. In whatever duty he entered he threw his strong personality. He likes everybody and is owned by none. If there is such a personage as a "self-made man" Judge Blizzard is that one. He mapped out his own career and won out grandly. He is not only an able lawyer, but he is a leader in civic matters. He is a farmer and stock raiser, specially of fine bred horses, and for a number of years he has been president of a successful banking institution in the city of Parkersburg. He has been twice married and has seven children. He has always been a Republican in politics. He helps every one who needs help and seeks for himself the help of none. Hs is one man who "paddles his own canoe."

## Judge Samuel C. Burdett

Judge Burdett was born September 23, 1848, in Scioto County, Ohio, and was moved by his parents to Ironton, Ohio, when he was an infant. He received a fair English education in that city, which he supplemented by the study and reading of proper books through all the years that followed. He was at all times an untiring student, and in this manner he pieced out an education above the average lawyer of his day. He learned the art of a decorator and painter under his father and became an expert in that business. He was, however, ambitious for other things in life, and from early youth he was determined, some day, to become a lawyer, and finally began a systemmatic course of reading legal textbooks, until he was able to pass the statutory examination for license to practice. Having located at Charleston, West Virginia, he was admitted to the Kanawha County Bar in 1870. His rapid advancement followed, as he soon demonstrated his ability, especially in the criminal practice, and as such, for many years, he has been regarded as one of the ablest and most successful criminal lawyers in the entire State. As a natural orator and advocate but few attorneys are comparable with him.

In 1884 he was first elected Prosecuting Attorney of Kanawha County, and was subsequently re-elected and served until 1889.

He was Assistant United States District Attorney under two Presidents. His private business had grown to such proportions that he resigned and devoted all his time to his private practice. He was elected Judge of the Circuit Court of Kanawha and Clay Counties and served ably and satisfactorily for the full term of eight years. As Circuit Judge his clear and practical decisions are proofs of his legal attainments, and his sound judgments as a jurist. After retiring from the judiciary he resumed practice at the Kanawha County Bar. His health, however, for several years past has been quite feeble, which has materially hampered him in his professional work.

Judge Burdett has been twice married and has several sons and daughters who are residents of Charleston. He is a very prominent factor in Republican politics and has no superior as a campaign orator in the entire State — Republican or Democrat. As a man of unusual brilliancy his rank is high among his contemporaries.

## Judge John L. Whitten, LL.M.

Judge Whitten was born on a farm in Mason County, Virginia, February 5, 1861, and is a son of John W. and Melinda A. Whitten; was educated in the common schools and attended normal school at Point Pleasant, West Virginia, and Lebanon, Ohio; received his legal education at Georgetown University, Washington, D. C., from which school he graduated in 1891, receiving the degree of Master of Laws. He was admitted to the Bar in 1883 at Point Pleasant, West Virginia, but did not begin active practice until after his graduation in 1891. He has had an extensive and general practice in the State and Federal courts.

His first public office was that of County Superintendent of Free Schools of Mason County, to which office he was elected in 1883 and re-elected in 1885; was elected Prosecuting Attorney of Mason County in 1896 and re-elected in 1900, being the only Prosecutor who has ever succeeded himself in Mason County; resigned that office to accept the appointment of Judge of the Circuit Court of the old Seventh Circuit, composed of the counties of Mason, Putnam and Kanawha, succeeding the late Judge F. A. Guthrie; Referee in Bankruptcy of the counties of Mason, Jackson, Putnam and Roane for ten years and resigned that office upon moving to Huntington, West Virginia, in November, 1916.

He was a Republican candidate for the nomination for the office of Attorney-General in 1916, but was defeated. Since that time he has been actively and successfully engaged in the practice of his profession in the city of Huntington, West Virginia.

He belongs to the Knights of Pythias and I. O. O. F. societies and is a member of the Baptist Church.

While Judge of the Circuit Court he tried many important cases, a number of which were appealed to the Supreme Court of this State, but he was not reversed in any of them, all of his decisions being affirmed; neither were any appeals taken from his rulings while Referee in Bankruptcy.

He married Mary R. Gwinn, a daughter of Henry Gwinn, a large farmer of Mason County, on the 18th of April, 1888. To this union five children were born, namely: Major R. G. Whitten, now located in Washington, D. C.; Ann Whitten Vogel, residing at Boston, Massachusetts; John Lamar Whitten, Jr., a student at the Naval Academy, Annapolis, Maryland; Lynda Whitten and Othniel Edward Whitten, who reside with their parents at 524 Fifth Street, Huntington, West Virginia.

Judge Whitten's career as lawyer, Judge and citizen is difficult to parallel or surpass. Better than all, he has always lived a moral, upright life.

JUDGE JOHN L. WHITTEN

## Judge James Henry Miller

But few, if any, men in the southern portion of West Virginia are better known or have had a more successful and varied career than the subject of this sketch. He was born at Green Sulphur Springs, Greenbrier County, Virginia, December 29, 1856. His parents' names were William Erskine and Sarah Barbara Miller. He worked on his father's farm until he was twenty-one years of age and was inured to hard labor, by which he equipped himself with whip-cord muscles that served him well in later years. He attended the neighborhood public schools in the winter seasons until he was seventeen, when he entered the Concord State Normal School, from which he graduated in the class of 1879; taught in the public schools for five years; studied medicine for a year or more, but abandoned it for law, and read law under the direction of W. W. Adams, an able lawyer of Hinton, Summers County; took a course in law at the University of Virginia, but before entering the University he was elected to and served a term as Superintendent of the Public Schools of Summers County; was admitted to the Bar at Hinton in 1882; two years later he was elected Prosecuting Attorney of Summers County and served in that office so ably, successfully and acceptably that he was thrice re-elected, making his term of service sixteen years, something rarely, if ever, duplicated in this or any other State. His service in that responsible position is a record of vigor, efficiency and manliness in every detail. As a lawyer he is thorough and accurate and has a firm grasp of legal principles, and this is one of the reasons he got on so well in the world.

In early life he exhibited a strong leaning towards politics. Being a pronounced Democrat, and always ready for strenuous party service, he was placed on various committees of his party, serving four years as Chairman of the Democratic State Committee, in which position he exhibited unusual skill and judgment as an organizer. In 1890 he was the nominee of the Democratic party for State Auditor, but was defeated along with the balance of his party candidates. Two years later he was his party's candidate for Congress, and as his party was in the minority, he was again aefeated. Still, in both of these races, he showed a pronounced popularity with the people. Being a lover of the "hook and line," he served a term as District Fish Commissioner and was alert in enforcing the law. He also served under two Governors as a member of the Board of Regents of the State Normal Schools and was always found at his post of duty. He was for a time captain of a company in the State Military Guards and was a delegate to the Democratic National Convention in 1896.

In the campaign of 1904 he was elected Judge of the Circuit Courts of Summers, Raleigh and Wyoming counties, and after serving a full term of eight years he was re-elected to the same high position, after a slight change of the boundaries of the circuit. He has been a hard student all through life, has kept abreast of the decisions and textbooks and has dignified the

JUDGE JAMES H. MILLER

Bench by exhibiting the highest types of integrity, fidelity, learning and wisdom.

A few years ago he wrote a complete "History of Summers County," which shows industry, research and a fine literary style. He is married and is the father of four interesting children. His home is at Hinton, the seat of justice of Summers County, where he is highly respected by the people generally.

## Judge Luther Judson Williams

Our subject, the son of Albert G. and Nancy (Donnally) Williams, who were descendants of the early settlers of Greenbrier County, Virginia, was born near Williamsburg in that county, October 18, 1856. He attended the local schools of his county and subsequently entered the West Virginia University, where he took an academic course, and later at the University of Virginia, where he received his training in law. He was reared on a farm and was inured to manual labor, which caused him to develop a strong, muscular physique that served him well through life. The natural transition of the young men in those years was from the bench in the schoolroom to the teacher's chair, and young Williams followed the custom strenuously for a few years, which experience gave him his first serious ideas of the importance of study and the value of an education. While teaching he acquired, by the careful reading and study of good books, a varied and substantial learning supplementary to his college studies.

Mr. Williams was admitted to the Greenbrier County Bar at Lewisburg in June, 1888, which was then, and before, recognized as one of the strong and learned Bars of the State, and practiced in Greenbrier and adjoining counties until his elevation to membership on the Supreme Court of Appeals of West Virginia, January 1, 1909, to which exalted body he was elected as a Republican in the campaign of 1908 for the regular term of twelve years. His prior practice included all of the courts of the State and also the Federal courts as well. As an attorney he was careful and thoughtful in giving his opinions to clients on questions of law and was honest in his convictions, honest with the court and with his adversaries in the trial of causes in a courtroom. Naturally, therefore, his practice at the Bar was successful and profitable.

Judge Williams has intermeddled with politics only in a limited way and consequently has held but few official positions. He was a member of the State Tax Commission, which rendered great service to the people in equalizing and readjusting the taxable property of the State, and from 1903 to 1908, inclusive, he served efficiently as a member of the Board of Regents of the West Virginia University. Neither of these was a partisan position, but, of course, they were, in a sense, political and highly responsible offices.

As we have already stated, Judge Williams became a Justice of the Supreme Court of Appeals of West Virginia January 1, 1909, and is

JUDGE L. JUDSON WILLIAMS

regarded as a just Judge, an upright man, honest in thought and purpose, and is rendering efficient and satisfactory service to the people. He is a member of the Methodist Episcopal Church, South; is a thirty-second degree member of the Masonic Fraternity; has been twice married, and has two sons, the younger of whom was a volunteer in the marine service of the United States government in the war with Germany and Austria-Hungary and was killed in action near the "Hindenburg Line" in July, 1918.

## Hon. William Gustavus Conley, LL.B., LL.D.

Abraham Lincoln once said: "No men living are more worthy to be trusted than those who toil up from poverty; none less inclined to take or touch aught which they have not honestly earned." To this class of honest toilers our subject belongs. He worked on the farm for several years and later drove mules on railroad construction work, dug coal, drew coke, worked in the stone quarries, on the sawmills and whatever honest labor he could find to do to help support a widowed mother and sisters and to obtain an education. Those earlier years of Mr. Conley's life stand as a splendid monument to his energy and pluck.

William G. Conley is a grandson of John Conley, an industrious farmer who resided near Tunnelton and died there in the year 1852 at the advanced age of over eighty years. He had a large family of sons and daughters. One of these sons was Major William Conley, the father of William G., a highly educated man in his day and a successful educator. Major Conley's early life was spent on a farm and in teaching school. He was principal of the Kingwood Academy for fourteen years. He was also a contractor for a number of years and was one of the builders of the Northwestern Turnpike and the Morgantown and Kingwood Turnpike.

Our subject was born near Kingwood, Preston County, West Virginia, January 8, 1866. He attended the district schools, the summer normals and subsequently the West Virginia University, from which he graduated in June, 1893, with the degree of LL.B. His honorary degree of LL.D. was conferred upon him by the Nashville College of Law in April, 1903. After performing manual labor, mentioned above, he taught school five terms and was Superintendent of Schools of Preston County one term, beginning July 1, 1891. Upon graduation at the West Virginia University he began the practice of the law at Parsons, West Virginia, and was soon elected a member of the town council and later Mayor. His legal attainments were soon recognized and he was nominated and elected Prosecuting Attorney of Tucker County in 1896 and was re-elected in 1900. He moved to Kingwood in March, 1903, and served as Councilman and Mayor of that town. On May 9, 1908, he was appointed Attorney-General of West Virginia, and the following July was nominated by the State Republican Convention for both the short and the long terms and at the general election that fall was elected by the largest plurality of any candidate on

HON. WILLIAM G. CONLEY

the State ticket. His term as Attorney-General expired March 4, 1913, when he again resumed the general practice of the law.

Attorney-General Conley is considered one of the strong men of West Virginia. In the numerous important matters submitted to and determined by him and the many grave constitutional questions raised in and out of court upon which he was called to pass during the five years he served as the Attorney-General of the State he exercised a judgment seldom equaled and rarely excelled. His name will be favorably linked for all time to come with the jurisprudence of his State as the Official Reporter of the Supreme Court of Appeals and because of the number and importance of the litigation in the State and Federal courts in which he participated as counsel for the State.

General Conley was not a candidate for renomination, but in the Republican primary of June, 1912, he was nominated for Congress in the Second District of West Virginia without opposition and in the general election that fall came within fourteen votes of election, notwithstanding the Republican party was badly disorganized and his Democratic opponent was the most popular and one of the wealthiest men in the district and at the election preceding had been elected by a plurality of 4,492.

On July 14, 1892, he married Miss Bertie Ison Martin, of Preston County.

General Conley is a member of the Presbyterian Church, Knights of Pythias, Odd Fellows, Modern Woodmen of America, Freemasons Chapter, Commandery, Consistory and Shriners, the American Academy of Political and Social Science and the Southern Sociological Congress. As a lawyer he has been remarkably successful.

## Harrison M. Calhoun

Among the well-known and successful lawyers of a rather remote, but really attractive, portion of West Virginia is the subject of this sketch. He is the son of Francis M. and Phoebe C. Calhoun and was born in Pendleton County, West Virginia, where the hills are highest, the sky is bluest, the grass grows more luxuriantly, the birds sing sweeter, the air is purer and the sun shines brighter than in any other portion of the Commonwealth. Among those charming surroundings, and in that splendid region, he first saw the light September 18, 1866, and there he has spent his life thus far and doubtless there he will end it. His early education was obtained from the public schools of the county; and if one is industrious, ambitious and painstaking such training as is there given out often is more useful than can anywhere else be obtained. A strong country lad, with an open mind, under the direction of a sensible, industrious instructor, can completely master the rudimentary elements of an English education, which can be augmented by subsequent college training, or if that is not available, by the systematic reading and study of books that can be obtained most

H. M. CALHOUN

anywhere. After all, in this manner, the most valuable educations are often secured. Our subject possessed an aspiration for knowledge which no circumstances of his youth could suppress, and an ambition to secure a name and a place among men undaunted by any prospect which the future could present to his view. In early life he decided to become a lawyer, and under the instruction and direction of Judge Okey Johnson, of the West Virginia Supreme Court of Appeals, he read law at his home while he was County Superintendent of Public Schools of his home county, which office he held from January 1, 1895, to December 31, 1898. Having thus prepared himself for the practice of law, he attended the short term in the law department of the West Virginia University and there passed a creditable examination for admission to the Bar; and in August, 1898 he was added to the roll of Attorneys of the Pendleton County Bar, where he has since practiced. His career as an attorney has presented more remunerative rewards than he had ever hoped for or expected. He has found from experience that work wins, and that the lawyer who is square in his acts and sticks closely to his business never fails to succeed.

In addition to a four-year term as County Superintendent of Public Schools, to which we have already referred, he was nominated and elected by the Democratic party, to which he belongs, to two terms of four years each as Prosecuting Attorney of Pendleton County, from 1901 to 1908, inclusive. The fact that he was re-elected is proof of his efficiency as a prosecutor of violators of the laws of the State. As another evidence of his popularity and faithfulness as an official he was nominated and elected, in 1912, to a two-year term in the lower branch of the West Virginia Legislature, wherein he served with credit to himself and honor to the people who had elected him.

Mr. Calhoun married Miss Virginia Mullanax, of Highland County, Virginia, May 28, 1889. Seven children are the result of this union. Their home is at Franklin, the seat of justice of Pendleton County. They are Methodists in their Church relations, and Mr. Calhoun is also a member of the Independent Order of Odd Fellows.

## Robert Linn, LL.B.

The subject of this sketch, son of Robert G. Linn, and a junior member of the strong law firm of Linn and Byrne, of Charleston, West Virginia, was born July 25, 1882, at Glenville, Gilmer County, West Virginia, and was educated in the public schools of his native county and the State Normal at Glenville, where he took a thorough academic course. Later he entered the law department of the West Virginia University at Morgantown and graduated with the degree of Bachelor of Laws in the class of 1906. He was admitted to the Kanawha Bar, a few weeks after leaving college, and has since practiced as a member of his father's firm. He has a strong legal mind, has broad and clear conceptions of legal principles and is thoroughly grounded in the law. He is a strong pleader, and while he handles his cases well, his strongest hold is that of an office lawyer, especially in the preparation of briefs in appellate cases.

Mr. Linn is of large stature and commanding presence. He is of a retiring disposition and is modest and unassuming. He never intrudes himself upon others and is always gentlemanly and urbane, and is well up in all branches of the law. He practices in all the State and Federal courts within the limits of West Virginia. He has never married, and makes his home with his parents in the city of Charleston. He is a Democrat in his political affiliations, but has never sought nor held a political office. His undivided time and energies are devoted to his profession.

## Hon. William E. Arnold

Among the law makers of the Old Commonwealth who became legislators in the new was the Hon. William E. Arnold, a native of Culpeper County, Virginia, born April 10, 1819. After receiving a classical education he attended law school and then settled in Weston, Lewis County, where he resided up to the time of his death; admitted to the Bar in 1846, he continued in the profession, except when serving his people in State offices. Elected to the Virginia Legislature in 1857, he was active in the passage of the law locating the Hospital for the Insane at Weston. He remained in the Legislature by re-election until 1861, serving during the time on the Committees of Courts of Justice and Lunatic Asylums. A Union Democrat, believing that secession meant civil war, he espoused the cause of the whole Union and supported the Government. As a member of the West Virginia Legislature in 1877 he served on the Judiciary Committee, on Claims and Grievances, and on Roads and Internal Navigation. He introduced a measure to raise by State aid ''An Internal Improvement Fund to build Roads throughout the Commonwealth.'' Retiring from official work, he devoted his attention to law practice, banking, farming and grazing, by which he amassed a fortune which he enjoyed with his family. He was a prominent and highly respected lawyer and was well informed on all general subjects of history and literature. He died at his home at Weston more than a quarter of a century ago.

## Hon. Braxton Davenport Gibson

Mr. Gibson was born in Jefferson County, Virginia, August 13, 1856, and received a liberal education at Shepherdstown and Charlestown Academies and at the University of Virginia. During 1880 and 1881 he was a member of the faculty of the Charlestown Academy, where he proved to be a very successful teacher. He was employed by the Shenandoah Railroad Company during 1882 and '83. In the meantime he was a law student, and in 1884 was admitted to practice in the courts of Jefferson County and later on in the higher courts of the State. He is a man of the highest personal character, and was not long in building up a lucrative practice. He is of a modest disposition and is rather retiring in his make-up, but he is a man of positive convictions and is firm in his determinations, and belongs to that class of men "who would rather be right than to be President." He is a strong lawyer and a safe counselor and has hosts of friends wherever he is known.

He was elected a member of the West Virginia Legislature, as a Democrat, in 1889, and was a faithful and efficient legislator and was always found at his post of duty. He was re-elected to the same office for a second term, which is proof of his efficiency and popularity.

He is one of the best known Freemasons of the State, having acceptably filled many of the highest offices of that great fraternity, including its highest honor, that of Grand Master; also Past Grand High Priest of the Royal Arch Chapter of West Virginia. He is, therefore, well and favorably known by the thousands of that great Order in the State.

He was happily married and resides near the place where he was born in the historic "Valley of Virginia" in the enjoyment of the full faculties of mental and physical manhood and surrounded by hosts of admiring friends.

He was a member of the West Virginia National Guard and was an Aid-de-Camp on the staff of Governor Flemming of West Virginia, with the rank of Colonel. He also served as a member of the Board of Directors of the State Hospital for the Insane at Weston for a number of years and was faithful and efficient in the discharge of his public duties.

Colonel Gibson is a Protestant Episcopalian in his religious connections and has always voted with the Democrats.

## Judge David E. Johnston

Judge Johnston was one of the strong characters, for many years, in the extreme southern portion of West Virginia. He was born in Giles County, Virginia, in 1845. His educational advantages were limited, but he managed to secure a sufficient knowledge of the primary branches to enable him to teach in the public schools for a short time. In 1870 he came to West Virginia, read law with James H. French, a relative of his mother, was admitted to the Mercer County Bar and became one of the distinguished lawyers of the State. He, however, before leaving Virginia, had been engaged in the practice in his native county of Giles and had succeeded in impressing the people of that section that he was one of the coming young lawyers of Virginia.

When the war came on, Mr. Johnston went with his State and the people of that section into the Southern Confederacy and remained until the close of the war, and was in many a hard fought battle. He was with Pickett's brigade in the "stone fence" charge at Gettysburg, which, perhaps, was the greatest charge in all history. He was as brave a soldier as ever shouldered a musket or unsheathed a sword. When peace came Mr. Johnston

JUDGE DAVID E. JOHNSTON

returned to his home, prepared himself for the legal profession, became a lawyer, and a good one; came to West Virginia, as we have already stated, and was not long in forging to the front of a Bar of able attorneys. He made some wise investments in coal lands, and being a natural developer. it was not very long until he became a wealthy man and a leading citizen.

He was a Democrat and was elected Prosecuting Attorney of Mercer County, and was an unusually vigorous one. He was a sincere man himself and a thoroughly honest one, and if men refused to obey the law, he made them do it, and he was right. The people saw that he was a full-sized man and a courageous one, and they elected him a Circuit Judge in 1880, and he served eight years ably and honorably. In 1898 they sent him to Congress and "he made good" as a National legislator. The section in which he lived turned Republican, or doubtless he would have been kept in Congress permanently. He was an able Representative, and was honest from hat to heels.

In the fall of 1893 he moved his residence from Princeton to Bluefield, and while he was an all round lawyer, he began to specialize in corporation law. He had a number of big clients and was engaged in big enterprises, such as banking, coal mining, projecting railroads and the like. If the facts were all told we believe it would appear that Judge Johnston, more than any other man, was the real projector of the Norfolk and Western Railroad, perhaps the foremost coal road in all the world. It was big things that Judge Johnston devoted his time to. He was a big man.

Judge Johnston married Miss Sarah E. Pearis, of Pearisburg, Giles County, Virginia. Four children were the result of their marriage. The Judge is to be most commended for his devotion to and service in the Baptist Church. He spent practically all of his mature life in the cause of religion, and left a lasting impression upon all the people with whom he associated. A few years ago he sold out all of his large holdings in West Virginia, pulled up all the roots he had planted here, went to Portland, Oregon, planted them there in that sunny clime, was living honestly and happily in the enjoyment of his large possessions, when on the 7th of July, 1917, he was summoned to a higher and nobler sphere. Like the Prince he always was, he swept through the gates of the New Jerusalem. He answered the call like a hero. He was no more, and many people mourned.

Peace to his ashes,
Rest to his soul.

## Hon. George Edmund Price

Mr. Price is of Welsh descent and was born near Moorefield, Hardy County, Virginia, November 9, 1848, and was educated in the schools at Moorefield in all the rudimentary branches. Later he entered Georgetown University, District of Columbia, where he was an honor student, standing high in his classes and from which he graduated *cum laude* in 1869. He then went to Frederick, Maryland, and read law with his great uncle, General James M. Coale, for two years, and in December, 1871, he was admitted to the Frederick County Bar, where he began the active practice of his profession, remaining until 1875, when he removed to Keyser, Mineral County, West Virginia. Here he continued in the practice until 1890 when he located in Charleston, Kanawha County, where he has since resided. Here he formed a partnership with Hon. S. L. Flournoy, a lawyer of pronounced ability, which continued until the death of Mr. Flournoy. He is at this time the senior member of the able and well known law firm of Price, Smith, Spilman and Clay, of Charleston, which firm is carrying on an immense business in all the varied branches of the law with a leaning toward specializing in the directions of corporation and commercial practice.

Mr. Price, although in no sense a politician, became interested in politics and political economy in early manhood, and his friends recognized his unsolicited claims to party recognition, in 1882, by electing him to the West Virginia Senate, and through re-election he served in that dignified position for eight consecutive years with great distinction and usefulness to the people of the State. During the sessions of 1885, '87 and '89 he was the presiding officer of that body, which made him *ex officio*, Lieutenant-Governor of the Commonwealth. He presided with dignity and absolute fairness, and at the same time he was one of the most active and efficient members of the body, being the patron of several bills which were of State-wide importance. Whilst he was a safe and sane legislator, his strong hold was then, as now, his erudite knowledge of the law, which served him well upon all occasions and at all times.

As a lawyer Mr. Price is careful, clear-headed, systematic, vigilant and thorough in his work. In argument he addresses the reason and the practical judgment of a court and jury. He is clear-sighted and wide awake in respect of motives and ulterior influences. He is always thoughtful of the wants and feelings of others, and in the trial of his cases he is always fair and just. He has no enemies. Every one who knows him well is his friend. His learning is varied and extensive, and his life as a lawyer, whether judged with reference to the extent of labor performed, pecuniary gain or fame, it must be admitted that he stands in the forefront of the profession. As a trial lawyer it would be difficult to find his superior. His prominent characteristics are a strong will, sound judgment, a keen knowledge of human nature, rigid devotion to what he believes to be right, and his character is beautified by simplicity and gentleness. No taint has ever rested upon his private or public life.

Senator Price has handled so many important cases in State and National courts that we will not attempt to mention them here. We will, however, state the fact that he was appointed years ago by Governor Fleming to represent West Virginia in the boundary suit between it and Maryland in the Supreme Court of the United States, involving certain lines between said States. He prepared the pleadings, wrote the brief and argued the case orally before the court, and finally won the decision in West Virginia's favor. This has become one of the leading cases of its kind in the entire country, and Senator Price is entitled to great credit for the able manner in which it was handled by him.

He is also a business man of tact and enterprise; is Vice President and Director of the Kanawha Banking and Trust Company, one of the largest banking institutions of the State, and is also connected with other important developments in the southern portion of West Virginia.

In June, 1878, he was united in marriage with Miss Sallie A. Dorsey, of Harvard County, Maryland. They have reared a large family, two sons living, being at this time resident lawyers of Charleston.

He is a member of the Presbyterian Church, in which denomination he has for years been a Ruling Elder.

He is of medium stature, firmly built, loves home-life and enjoys associations with his legion of friends. Although he is nearing his three score and ten station in the journey of life he is vigorous and active, and is at all proper times at work either at his desk or in a court room, where he is "at home" in the broadest meaning of that term.

## Hon. James F. Brown, M.A.

The subject of this sketch, son of Judge James H. Brown, who was eminent both as lawyer and jurist, was born in Charleston, Virginia, March 7, 1852. After completing a preparatory course at the "Charleston Institute," the then leading educational institution in the Kanawha Valley, he entered the West Virginia University, from which he graduated, receiving his A.B. in 1873, and later the degree of A.M. On leaving college he took up the study of law under the tutelage of his father, and in 1875 was admitted to the Bar. He rapidly advanced in his profession; his practice soon extending beyond the courts of the State and to the highest courts of the country. He is not only learned in law, but is an able advocate, skilled in court practice and maintains a high rank, with but few equals, and perhaps no superior, among the members of the West Virginia Bar.

For nearly thirty years he has been senior member of the law firm of Brown, Jackson and Knight, the oldest and one of the best known law firms in the State of West Virginia.

Mr. Brown, though devoted to his profession and always yielding to it his first allegiance, was not unmindful of the duties of the citizen, and from the first shared in all movements looking to the public good. He was especially interested in what made for the welfare of his native town and the Kanawha Valley, given unstintingly of his time, energies and means to the advancement of both toward the worthy position they now occupy commercially and industrially, being from the beginning identified with most of the solid institutions which distinguish Charleston and the Valley as the most promising and prosperous section of the State.

HON. JAMES F. BROWN

Early in his business life he was chosen to the City Council, and for nearly twenty years continued an active and useful member of that body — prominent in inaugurating and influential in carrying to successful realization all movements to transform the modest town to the progressive and prosperous city.

In 1883–4 he represented his County in the Legislature of the State, serving on the Judiciary, Finance and other important Committees; and for years under successive Governors of different politics was appointed and reappointed a member of the Board of Regents of the State University. In these positions, as well as in the many others of confidence and trust, public and private, to which he has been called from time to time, the results demonstrated his character, his sound judgment and broad acquaintance with business and of public affairs, have made his counsel and services widely sought for beyond the strict lines of his profession.

Mr. Brown may well be designated one of the "oldest inhabitants," having for more than two-thirds of a century resided at the old family home, "The Elms," a relic of the early days of Charleston, which has withstood the onrush of a progressive community, a beautiful spot in the heart of the city which has grown up around it, the ample grounds still intact and the great elms which adorn them are unique among the tall business blocks now on every hand. His grandchildren are the fifth generation to live there; and the "home" still the gathering place of a wide family connection has lost none of the old-time hospitality which characterized it in the *ante-bellum* days.

Mr. Brown, among his many activities, has for years been Vice President of the Kanawha Valley Bank, the oldest and the leading financial institution of the Southern half of the State; Vice President of the George Washington Life Insurance Company; charter member of and actively identified with the Central Trust Company; the Cabin Creek Consolidated Coal Company; West Charleston Improvement Company; the Charleston Window Glass Company, and many other undertakings helping to the development of the material interests of the Kanawha Valley all prosperous, and in the organization and management of which he has had an active part.

He is a trustee of the City Hospital, the Masonic Temple, the Kanawha Presbyterian Church, and had much to do with the planning and direction of the handsome buildings occupied by each of these institutions. He is also identified with the Y. M. C. A., the Edgewood Country Club, and other like local institutions. While a tireless worker Mr. Brown has none the less found time for the home life and for culture along liberal lines; has been a broad reader and has traveled widely in this country and abroad.

In 1877 he married Miss Jennie Woodbridge, of Marietta, Ohio, and has six children, all living in the home town and close about him, except his son Benjamin B., who after graduating at Princeton and Harvard, is, at the age of twenty-four now an officer at the front in France, participating in the great world war.

## Benjamin Mason Ambler

One among the ablest and best known law firms in West Virginia is that of Van Winkle and Ambler, of Parkersburg. The subject of this sketch is the junior member of this successful combination. He is a native of Winchester in the Valley of Virginia, which has been very appropriately termed " The Garden Spot of the World," and is the son of the Reverend John and Anna Mason Ambler. He was liberally educated in private schools in Richmond, Virginia, and at the University of Virginia at Charlottesville; but perhaps his broadest education was obtained by the systematic reading of good books in all of the various branches of literature, history, etc. He always has on hand a large fund of valuable information from which to draw on any occasion and in any emergency. No man in our acquaintance is his superior in the presentation of an intricate and difficult problem in law, or for that matter on any sort of a subject. His mind at all times is as clear as a bell. Any one can see what he is driving at, and he possesses the art of making one see a proposition as clearly as he himself sees and understands it. He, therefore, is an advocate of great force, and rarely loses a case that he ought to win. There are in the profession more magnetic lawyers than he, but we know none his superior in the plain presentation of a cause to a court or jury.

Mr. Ambler is naturally as well as by education and training fitted for the work of a lawyer. A thorough, close and logical reasoner, as we have already stated, his early absorption of the underlying principles of jurisprudence was a solid foundation for the study, observation and experience of an active and successful practitioner. He always carries to a high degree the power of convincing statement. In his preparation for trials he is thorough and tactful, and is masterful in the examinations of witnesses. In the play of humor he is dry and grim, as well as artful and witty; and as a counselor he is wise and judicious. He always carries an abundance of force of will and self-reliance, which in a large measure account for his success as a lawyer. He is optomistic and cheerful in his make up, and the effect of associations with him are always reassuring. He is accurate in all his transactions and his integrity is equal to his accuracy. Taking him all in all he must be classified among the very strong, able lawyers of the State. He could have been in the judiciary years ago, but he preferred to remain in the regular practice, because it is more congenial and perhaps more remunerative.

Mr. Ambler was admitted to practice in July, 1874, at Parkersburg, West Virginia. Since then he has been admitted to the Bars of all the State and Federal Courts, including the Supreme Court of the United States, in which latter tribunal he has had a number of important cases. In politics he is a Democrat, but never would consent to be a candidate for any office, and consequently never held an office, except City Attorney of Parkersburg. He preferred to devote all his time and energies to his profession and this, perhaps, is one of the reasons why he has reached the top rungs of the legal ladder in his adopted State. He is married and has three children, one of them (a son) is a member of the Parkersburg Bar, and is a young man of unusual promise.

Mr. Ambler has been one of the leaders of the West Virginia Bar Association from its organization to the present time, and was its efficient President in 1888. He is also a member of the Protestant Episcopal Church at Parkersburg and is one of its Vestrymen. He is likewise a leader among the developers of the City of Parkersburg in all of its civic betterments. In every way he is entitled to be classed among the prominent and useful citizens of the Commonwealth.

## Hon. Alfred Caldwell

Mr. Caldwell was born in the City of Wheeling, July 14, 1847. He was educated at Harding's Academy, Wheeling, Va., West Liberty Academy, Oahu College, Punahon, Hawaiian Islands, where his father for several years was engaged in the United States Consular Service, and in 1867 he graduated as a Batchelor of Philosophy from Yale University. He studied the text books of the law under the direction of his father, who for many years was one of the able barristers of the City of Wheeling, and was admitted to practice in the courts of that city in 1868 when he had barely reached his majority. He possessed a brilliant intellect, and being gifted as a public speaker it was not long before he reached an enviable position among the many noted lawyers of his native city.

General Caldwell is a strong trial lawyer. He is gifted in speech, with satirical tendencies which drifts into humor, and never fails to secure the closest attention of both court and jury. Opposing counsel soon learn he has a master to deal with in the trial of important causes. The firm of Caldwell & Caldwell, composed of his senior brother, George B. Caldwell, and himself, for a generation or more was one of the leading law firms of the City of Wheeling. George B. died about two or three years ago and his place was taken in the firm by the General's son, William G., who is a young man of industry and ability, and thus is continued the well known law firm of Caldwell & Caldwell, attorneys and counselors at law.

The subject of this sketch early in life became interested in politics. He served in both branches of the Wheeling City Council; was City Solicitor one term, and was a member of the State Senate from 1875 to 1879. He was eight years Attorney-General of the State, from 1885 to 1893, and filled that high office with great acceptability. He was a Democrat in politics until 1896, when he abandoned his party on account of its advocacy of the free and unlimited coinage of silver as the basis of our national currency, and has, since that time, aligned himself with the Republicans. He is admitted to be one of the most effective campaign speakers the State has ever produced, and also stands at the top of his profession as a lawyer.

HON. ALFRED CALDWELL

He is a master of satire and sarcasm, and is really a great orator and advocate.

General Caldwell married a daughter of Mr. Wm. S. Goshorn, of Wheeling, and has reared an interesting family of eight children, all of whom, except two, that are deceased, and two married daughters, still reside in the city of their nativity. He is a learned lawyer, and has the confidence and respect not only of the people of the City of Wheeling, but of the entire State as well. But few, if any, men in West Virginia are better known or more highly respected than he.

## Judge John A. Campbell, A.M.

Judge Campbell is one of the distinguished and best known lawyers and retired Circuit Judges of the northern portion of the State. He was born in Columbiana County, Ohio, and came to Hancock County with his father, Alexander Campbell, when he was thirteen years of age, and became a citizen of New Cumberland, where he has since resided. He received his education in the public schools of Ohio, and was graduated, *magnum cum laude*, from Washington College, Pennsylvania, in 1867, with the degree of Bachelor of Arts. For a time he thought of making teaching his profession, and was tendered the chair of Mathematics in Hiram College, Ohio, the year of his graduation, which he declined. A short time thereafter, however, he became Professor of English, logic and literature, in the Normal College at Hopedale, Ohio, where he remained for four years. In 1871, on account of impaired health, he resigned his professorship and returned to West Virginia; read law, passed the required examination, and was admitted to the Hancock County Bar in 1872. Being a natural orator of unusual force he very soon developed into a trial lawyer of renown, and took high rank in the Hancock and surrounding county Bars, and was not long in securing a profitable clientele. In early life he exhibited a taste for politics. Without solicitation on his part in 1871 he was nominated by the Republicans and elected a member of the lower branch of the State Legislature, and subsequently was twice re-elected to the same position. While in college he had devoted much study to parliamentary laws, and was very soon recognized by his colleagues as the best parliamentarian in the Legislature. Being a superior debater, coupled with his knowledge of parliamentary tactics, made him a leader of that body. In 1880 he was tendered the nomination of his party for a seat in the American Congress, but declined; later he was mentioned in connection with a like nomination, and in 1888 he was actively in the field for that position, but was defeated. He is a master of the English language, and is one of the cleanest cut and most eloquent stump speakers in the entire State. He has, therefore, in many political campaigns rendered efficient service to his party in every section of West Virginia. In 1888 he was nominated and elected a Circuit

JUDGE JOHN A. CAMPBELL

Court Judge for the First Judicial Circuit, and served faithfully and efficiently for the full term of eight years. He proved to be one of the fairest, painstaking judges that ever wore the judicial ermine in this or any other State.

Judge Campbell's entire life is an example of wisdom, learning, fidelity, forceful presentation, and above all absolute fairness, and scrupulous cultivation of the best elements of the profession and stainless observance of its best traditions the writer has ever known. He has ever worn above him the white flower of a blameless life. He was fewer times reversed by the Supreme Court than any other judge of his day. He is an intense American. He believes in the equality of the human race and the just rights of all men before the law. While he is a pronounced partisan in politics he is not narrow in his views, but believes in the doctrine of allowing the greatest liberty to every citizen. He is a member of the Disciples Church, yet he is liberal in his religious convictions. For the past few years he has devoted a large part of his time to the banking business at New Cumberland, where he has spent the larger part of his life. It can be truly said of him that he has the confidence and respect of every one who knows him personally.

He was married rather late in life, and is a model in his home life and surroundings.

## Hon. John D. Alderson

Hon. John D. Alderson was born in Nicholas County, then Virginia, November 29, 1854, and died at Richwood in that county on the 2d day of December, 1910. Even while a mere boy, and before he attained his majority, he was an active participant in the Democratic politics of his State, and his interest therein continued throughout his entire life. At about the age of eighteen years he was appointed a page in the West Virginia Constitutional Convention of 1872, which framed the present Constitution of this State, and for nearly twenty years thereafter he was connected in some capacity with the State Legislature, being door keeper of the Senate at the session of 1872–3; sergeant-at-arms of the Senate at the session of 1875, 1877, 1879 and 1889, and Clerk of the Senate at its sessions of 1883, 1885 and 1887. Having studied law and prepared for the Bar he was admitted to practice and opened an office at Summersville, Nicholas County, January 1, 1876, and in April of that year was appointed Prosecuting Attorney of Nicholas and Webster Counties, and was elected to the same office in the fall of 1876 and re-elected in 1880 and 1884, thus serving for twelve years.

In 1888 Mr. Alderson received from his party the nomination for Congress from the Third Congressional District and made an active and vigorous campaign, and was elected by a small majority over his opponent, Hon. James H. McGinnis, to the Fifty-first Congress. He was nominated

HON. JOHN D. ALDERSON

and re-elected to the Fifty-second and Fifty-third Congresses and was renominated in 1894, but was defeated by the Hon. James H. Huling, the complexion of the West Virginia delegation being completely changed at the election in the fall of 1894 from a solidly Democratic to a solidly Republican representation.

After his service in the National House of Representatives Mr. Alderson resumed the active practice of his profession at Summersville, at first having as his partner Mr. A. J. Horan, under the firm name of Alderson & Horan, and later Mr. Alex N. Breckenridge and his son, Fleming N. Alderson, under the firm name of Alderson, Breckenridge & Alderson. As a trial lawyer he was exceedingly vigorous and effective, and he enjoyed the largest practice in his section of the State, extending to many counties beyond the home county of Nicholas. After his service in Congress he maintained a most active interest in the politics of his State, being a delegate to the Democratic National Conventions of 1900, 1904 and 1908, and in the year 1900 he accepted the Democratic nomination for the House of Delegates of West Virginia from Nicholas County and was elected and served in that body, being the leader of the minority in the House of Delegates and participating in all debates of that session.

Mr. Alderson was a man of strong natural ability and intellect, cultivated by industry and research, and as a public speaker and advocate was thoroughly able to sustain himself; and his natural abilities, experience and knowledge of human nature rendered him at all times a most dangerous opponent in the trial of causes. He was of a frank and impetuous disposition, but of such generous and genial manner and heart that his contests never engendered bitterness, either to himself or in his opponents. His long practice and public service rendered him one of the best known and most popular lawyers in the State, and his death was mourned as a real loss among all classes and conditions of his friends and adherents.

## Hon. Samuel V. Woods, A.B.

The subject of this sketch is one of the able and well known lawyers of West Virginia. He is a son of the late Hon. Samuel Woods, who served with distinction for a term of years as a Judge of the Supreme Court of Appeals of the State, a sketch of whom will also be found in this volume. The son was born in Barbour County, West Virginia, August 31, 1856. He took the academic course at the West Virginia University, graduating with honor. He studied law under the tutelage of his father and was admitted to the Bar by the Supreme Court of Appeals of the State in 1881, and has been engaged in active practice at Philippi, the seat of justice of Barbour County, since that time in which he has been unusually successful in every sense of the word. Honored in his profession he is equally esteemed as a citizen of the community in which he was born, and thus far where his professional life has been spent, and with all the interests with which he

HON. SAMUEL V. WOODS

has been identified. His serenity of disposition, his unfailing courtesy to all men, his ready response to every call of charity or duty, endeared him to all who came in contact with him. In his court work he has always been distinguished for the thoroughness of his preparation, the tact of his examination of witnesses, his accurate knowledge of all the details of pleading and practice, and a coolness, self-poise, never shaken manner, he exhibits under circumstances the most adverse and trying.

As an advocate he is gifted with logical powers and a faculty of expression remarkably simple and lucid. His diction is clear and correct and his language is forceful and pointed. He always speaks directly to the point at issue and to the minds of his hearers. In short, he is a high grade public speaker and debater, and better still, he is moral, honorable, upright and reliable, which add greatly to his influence as a trial lawyer. He looks carefully into the facts of a case before he advises the sort of action to be taken. In this way he keeps clients out of trouble, instead of getting them into it — a wise course for every lawyer to pursue.

From early manhood Mr. Woods has shown a liking for politics. He has always been an earnest Democrat and a loyal partisan. Unfortunately he lives in a Republican locality, and because of this and also because he would never "trim" or make false promises or deceive, he has several times failed of an election, when he could otherwise have won. He was two terms Mayor of Philippi; was four years a State Senator and President of that body, which made him *ex officio* Lieutenant-Governor of the State; he was twice a candidate for Congress; was a Delegate in 1890 to the National Democratic Convention; and has several times served acceptably as Special Judge of Taylor and Upshur Counties Circuit Courts.

Senator Woods is a prominent and useful member of the Methodist Episcopal Church, which has honored him with a seat in its highest law-making body — its General Conference, which meets quadrennially. He has been for a number of years a Trustee of the West Virginia Wesleyan College at Buckhannon. He is also an efficient official member of his home church at Philippi. During his entire mature life he has been on the moral side of every public question that has come before the people. He is also a member of the Masonic Fraternity and the Knights of Pythias, and is influential in both of them. He is married and lives in the town where he was born, a little more than sixty years ago, and has the confidence of all the people who know him. He is large of stature, commanding in appearance and genial in disposition.

## John Hopkins Woods

The Woods family of Barbour County, West Virginia, embraces a body of distinguished lawyers. The father, the Hon. Samuel Woods, was for many years an able lawyer and jurist, who is considered in another part of this volume, had three sons who also became noted members of the profession. Frank, the eldest son, was a classical graduate of the West

J. HOP. WOODS

Virginia University and also an *alumnus* of its Law Department, practiced for a few years at Grafton, West Virginia, as a member of the strong law firm of Martin and Woods; finally located at Baltimore and attained a high rank as a member of that great Bar of illustrious lawyers, and died just as his sun had reached its noon, mourned by many friends, because of his unusual ability and worth. Another of this distinguished legal household is the subject of this sketch, who has also reached an enviable rank in the profession, who is still in the flesh and commands a large clientele in the City of Philippi, Barbour County, where he was born November 23, 1853, and where he has spent an active and successful professional life, thus reversing the Scriptural rule " that a prophet is not without honor, save in his own country." He is known personally to, most likely, every man of any importance in his native county, and has a State-wide standing among the legal fraternity. He is distinguished in person, dignified and graceful in manner, and withal modest and unassuming. Solidly grounded in his profession, upright in character, and reveals marked legal ability in important cases, of which he has at all times many. Measuring his life work in all of its bearings he has made a record worthy to be envied and followed as well as to be admired by his fellow citizens. He is a broad, thorough and conscientious lawyer, and an exemplary citizen who has the absolute confidence and respect of all his fellow citizens who know him personally.

Mr. Woods was educated in the public schools of his native county, the West Virginia University, and spent one year (1875) as a cadet at West Point Military Academy; studied law under the tutelage of his father and at the State University at Morgantown. He has always been a consistent Democrat, but was never a candidate for an elective office, except Mayor of the City of Philippi, when he was elected without opposition in 1903, and proved an efficient and painstaking official. He, however, served from 1889 to 1895 as a member of the Board of Directors of the Boys' State Reform School, and gave particular attention to its careful management. He is a superior public speaker and has shown unusual aptitude and fondness for the law and the forum. He, therefore, excels as an advocate and trial lawyer. He was admitted to the Bar in 1878 and carries on a general practice in all the courts of West Virginia, both State and Federal.

He was united in marriage with Miss Jennie Canter June 22, 1898. They have one son, Nelson Canter Woods, who is now a cadet at the Staunton (Virginia) Military Academy. Mr. Woods is an active member of the Methodist Episcopal Church, and is a member of the Masonic Fraternity. He is also a member of the West Virginia Bar Association and was its President in 1907, and was President of the Local Draft Board of his county in the war with Germany.

## Hon. Charles Edgar Hogg, LL.D.

Dr. Hogg, son of James A. Hogg, was born in Mason County, Virginia, December 21, 1852, and was educated in the common schools of his native county and at Carleton Academy in Meigs County, Ohio. When but little above fifteen years of age he taught his first school. Later on he graduated from Oldham and Howe's Business College. In 1871 he was employed as bookkeeper for the Valley City Salt Company, where he remained for a year or more. During these early years he was a diligent student of history and English under the direction of his uncle, Dr. A. L. Knight, who was a noted linguist and a well known student of science and history. He was also tutored by Professor D. P. Guthrie, a graduate of the Ohio University, and a high school teacher of Mason County, West Virginia, and Meigs County, Ohio. Under Professor Guthrie's direction and tutelage young Hogg vigilantly studied Latin, Greek, German and the higher branches of mathematics, which included algebra, geometry and astronomy. He also took lessons in physiology and physics. In all of these branches of learning he was an apt and industrious student, and in this way he pieced out the equipment of an average college education of that period. During all this time he was determined to end up as a lawyer, and his thoughts were continuously in that direction. So he began the regular study of legal text books in 1874 in the office of Judge C. P. T. Moore and Hon. Henry J. Fisher at Point Pleasant, two of the ablest lawyers of the Mason County Bar, which he steadfastly pursued for five years. During this period, however, he was twice elected Superintendent of Public Schools of his native county, and in this position he rendered faithful and satisfactory service for four years. He was admitted as a member of the Mason County Bar, and began life as a lawyer during his first term as Superintendent of the public schools of that county, with the exception of the seven years he was Dean of the law department of the West Virginia University, he has since been engaged in active practice. He was admitted to the Bar of the Supreme Court of the United States in 1888 and has, at intervals, been practicing in that court ever since. He appeared in the Supreme Court of West Virginia for the first time in January, 1875, and has practiced in that court ever since, and has also practiced in the courts of Pennsylvania, Ohio and Indiana. His life, therefore, as a lawyer, a law teacher or a law writer, whether judged with reference to labor performed, pecuniary gain or fame, he stands to-day in the forefront of the legal profession in his native State.

He was selected as Dean of the law faculty of the West Virginia University in 1906, and in that position he proved equal to every emergency. In the meantime he raised the standard of his department until it ranked among the foremost law schools in the country. In this position he remained seven consecutive years. It was agreed when he accepted the position of Dean that he was to be allowed to appear in important cases in the Supreme Court of Appeals of West Virginia and the Supreme Court of the United States, which he frequently did. For more than a generation he has been a close, hard student of the law, and he has dignified the profession by exhibiting in his practice the highest types of integrity, fidelity, learning and wisdom.

In 1907 Temple University, of Philadelphia, conferred upon Dean Hogg, in recognition of his attainments as a lawyer, teacher and publicist, its highest honorary degree,— that of Doctor of Laws.

Dr. Hogg has not only proved his ability as a practicing attorney and teacher, but he is recognized as the foremost writer and publicist of legal authority that the State of West Virginia has ever produced. He is the author of "Hogg's Pleading and Forms," "Equity Principles," "Equity Procedure," in two volumes, and "Treatise and Forms." The first of these works is now in its third edition with the fourth in course of preparation, and a second edition of "Treatise and Forms" is now being prepared. He is also the author of the following subjects in the "Encyclopedia of Evidence": Conclusive Evidence, Vol. 3; Documentary Evidence, Vol. 4; Judgments, Vol. 7; Variance and Admissibility of Evidence as Depending upon the Pleadings, Vol. 13; and is also the author of Accounts and Accounting, in Vol. 1, "Standard Encyclopedia of Procedure," and is one of the consulting editors of "American and English Encyclopedia of Law and Practice."

He now has in course of preparation the following works: "The Physician as an Expert"; "Rights and Duties of School Teachers under the Law"; "Form Book with special reference to Virginia and West Virginia"; "Law Procedure in the Virginias," and some other books which he has in contemplation.

He was a Democrat in politics until 1896 when he left that party on account of its free coinage of silver advocacy, and has since acted with the Republicans. He is a Presbyterian and a Freemason. He is a genial companion, always cheerful and the effect of his society is reassuring. As a hard worker he cannot be surpassed. He is a living example of the proverb that "Work Wins." As a public speaker his rank is high and as an all-round lawyer he is difficult to equal or surpass. He served with credit to his constituency as a Member of the Fiftieth Congress of the United States, from 1887 to 1889, inclusive. At the expiration of his two-year term he retired, and since that time has declined to be a candidate for, or to accept, public office.

## Judge Homer B. Woods

The Woods family, from which the subject of this sketch descended, originally came from Wales. His parents were Philip A. and Salina (Wells) Woods. Homer B. was born near Harrisville, Ritchie County, West Virginia, July 16, 1869, and received his primary education in the public schools of his native county. While only sixteen years of age he began to teach in the public schools of Ritchie County, which he followed for four or five years. However, feeling the need of a higher grade education, he attended Marietta (Ohio) College and remained for several years, studying the higher branches. He returned to his native State and was principal of the Harrisville High School, and during that time he served two terms as County Superintendent of Public Schools of Ritchie County. Deciding to become a lawyer he took the law course at the West Virginia University, and was admitted as a member of the Ritchie County Bar in 1892, and immediately entered upon the practice of his profession in which he rapidly rose to an enviable rank. He was known as a young man who bore an irreproachable personal character and could be trusted in all that he said and did; consequently he never lacked in having a profitable clientele. Twice he was elected Prosecuting Attorney of his home county, and on the second occasion he received the largest majority that had theretofore ever been given to any other candidate for any office in Ritchie County, which was proof of the fact that he was an able and honest prosecutor of violators of the State laws. His motto was "Let no guilty man escape," and he enforced it "without fear or favor."

In 1904 he was nominated by the Republicans and was elected Judge of the Third Judicial Circuit of West Virginia. Eight years later he was re-elected to the same high and responsible office and is still serving with great acceptability. He, therefore, holds a high rank among the Circuit Judges of the State. Having been an earnest and faithful student of the law for many years, and being absolutely sincere and honest, he could not fail to be an honor to the judiciary department of his native State. He is widely and favorably known and is highly esteemed as a man of honor and integrity. He has the confidence and respect of all the people who know him.

Judge Woods is a useful member of the Baptist Church at Harrisville where he resides. He was united in marriage September 10, 1892, with Miss Winifred Davis, of Harrisville. They have a large family and maintain a pleasant home in the town of their nativity. Judge Woods is devoted to his home and loves the evening communion of the family circle. He is of medium stature and his picture shows him to be an extremely sociable and an all round agreeable gentleman. He is not only a sound lawyer and a just judge, but he is in every respect an ideal citizen.

## Judge Samuel D. Littlepage

Samuel D. Littlepage, son of Adam and Rebecca Littlepage, was born in the two-story stone dwelling known as the Old Stone Mansion in the western limits of Charleston, West Virginia, February 14, 1856, owned and occupied by him at the time of his death, which took place August 18, 1917, at Atlantic City, New Jersey, where he had been for several months in search of health. His education was limited to the schools of Charleston and to a course in the law department of Washington and Lee University. Being a young man of high ambitions and unlimited energies and industry he did not falter, but kept on perservering until he obtained, through every possible channel, what may be termed a liberal education. His law school training afforded a thorough knowledge of the technique of the profession, which was strengthened by experience in the practice as the years went by. He was received as a member of the Kanawha County Bar in 1886, and his practice very soon widened so as to include all the State and United States courts. Almost from the beginning his practice in all the courts was large and profitable.

He was a hard student of law and kept abreast of the decisions and the textbooks, thus dignifying the profession by exhibiting in the practice the highest types of integrity and fidelity in his calling. One of his able associates of the Kanawha Bar, after his demise, thus spoke of him: "No obituary of Judge Littlepage can be fully appreciated unless it be read in the light of full knowledge of his remarkable personality. One must know of his struggles as a boy, his devotion to his mother who died several years ago; his originality, resourcefulness and dynamic energy; his exuberance of spirits and genuine, while unique, social qualities; and last, but not least, one must have crossed the threshold of his hospitable home, and have felt the warmth of greeting and imbibed the spirit of family accord at his fireside, to understand fully what we have in mind to say. His father was killed during the Civil War. His mother was left with the property at the mouth of Kanawha Two Mile as the only means of supporting a family of five husky boys and two girls. The mother did her part well. She kept the family together; organized the forces of all and developed in her sons her own remarkable powers. Till her death she was not only the beloved mother and companion of all, but their acknowledged leader."

In politics, as in law, he was whole-hearted and thorough. He was the Democratic candidate for Circuit Clerk in 1884 and, while defeated, ran ahead of his ticket. He was the Democratic nominee for Circuit Judge in 1912 and was elected for the term ending January 1, 1921. As a Judge he was untiring, courteous, prompt and fair. He seemed to strive to find the truth in every controversy and then to work for the nearest approximation to justice. He was respected and loved by the members of the Bar, and there is no question that, among the masses of the people, he was probably the most popular man in this section of the State.

The office of Circuit Judge in the Kanawha Circuit is no sinecure. It requires a strong constitution to hold up under the work and strain demanded by a faithful and successful discharge of its duties. Judge Littlepage needed a long rest when he entered upon its duties, but he worked harder on the Bench than he did in the practice of law. He gave about twelve to fifteen hours a day to official duties and the terrible strain began to show upon him two years before his death. Against the advice of friends and the pleadings of his family he clung to his task till he was compelled to give up, and at last "he fell asleep."

Judge Littlepage's force of will, self-reliance and courage were more than common. Into whatever duty he entered he threw his strong personality, and he never failed when he ought to have succeeded. He feared no antagonist and was unfaithful to no client. As a Judge he sought only to be just. He was always cheerful and optimistic and the effect of his associations were always reassuring.

He was united in marriage with Miss Mollie Kemp in 1887. Three children resulted from their marriage — B. Kemp Littlepage, who is the present Prosecuting Attorney of Kanawha County, Mrs. George R. Wood and Miss Charlie Littlepage, all of whom are residents of Charleston.

## Hon. Joseph H. Gaines, A.B., A.M.

Mr. Gaines was born in the city of Washington, D. C., September 3, 1864, and is the son of Theophilus Gaines, who was a Major of United States Volunteers in the late Civil War between the States. Major Gaines settled in Fayette County, West Virginia, in 1867, and engaged in the practice of the law, where our subject attended the public schools and later became a student at the West Virginia University, and still later he entered Princeton University, from which institution he graduated with the degree of Bachelor of Arts. Subsequently the degree of Master of Arts, *pro merito*, was conferred upon him by his *alma mater*. Thereafter he read law under the direction of his father, passed the required examination and was admitted to the Bar of Fayette County in 1887. Being thoroughly equipped from an educational point of view, and being gifted as a public speaker, he very soon took high rank both as a lawyer and an advocate, and became a well known and highly esteemed lawyer in Fayette and the surrounding counties. Being desirous of a wider field of usefulness, and broader opportunities, he became a resident of Charleston, the capital of the State, where he has since resided and is still practicing his profession.

He is a Republican in his political affiliations and was appointed by President McKinley United States District Attorney for the State of West Virginia in 1897, wherein he proved to be a lawyer of superior attainments and consequently filled that high and responsible office with great acceptability. He resigned the same in June, 1901, to accept a seat in the American Congress, to which he had been elected in the campaign of 1900, and was subsequently re-elected to that high position for four consecutive terms, which made ten years of service in the Congress of the United States from the Third District of the State.

While Mr. Gaines is known and accepted as a lawyer of splendid attainments, yet he is best known as a Congressman of pre-eminent standing and ability. During his ten years' service in the Congress he was a member of several important committees, including Ways and Means, the most important of all the committees of the House of Representatives. On these committees, and the floor of the House, he made for himself a national reputation as an able, judicious and wise legislator. He devoted much time to the careful study of all political questions and became an authority upon all branches of political economy, and was and is sought after by the political committees of a number of the States to discuss such measures before the people during political campaigns.

Mr. Gaines is a man of upright and blameless personal character and has acquitted himself well in all of the public positions he has ever held. He is absolutely incorruptible, is severely candid, is essentially just, and his ability is unusual. He was defeated in his sixth campaign for a seat in Congress, and although he has many times since been pressed to re-enter political life he has persistently declined to do so, as he prefers the practice of his profession, in which he holds a high rank, to the turmoils and the ups and downs of political life. He has a wife and five children. His home life is ideal. Naturally hopeful and happy, his hours with his friends are the oases in a strenuous life. Among his friends he is always social, joyous and happy, and he has a remarkably strong hold upon the people at large.

In the political campaign of 1916 Mr. Gaines was Chairman of the Republican State Executive Committee of West Virginia, which office he still holds.

Since writing the above, he was induced by his many friends to enter a State-wide primary campaign of the Republican party of West Virginia for the nomination as its candidate for a seat in the United States Senate. Whilst it was generally conceded that he was splendidly equipped for the position, he was late in entering the contest and was defeated.

## Major Joseph E. Chilton

Major Chilton, one of the ablest and best known West Virginia lawyers and politicians in the Great Kanawha Valley, head of the well-known, State-wide law firm of Chilton, MacCorkle and Chilton, of Charleston, was born at Coalsmouth, Kanawha County, Virginia, December 6, 1855, and received his education in the common schools and at Shelton College in his native county. He read law textbooks in a law office and mastered fundamental principles by close application and unremitting toil. He read with a purpose and read to fully comprehend what he knew he must possess to become an erudite lawyer. With this single purpose in view he toiled on until he was able to pass a creditable examination, and in January, 1877, he was admitted to membership in the Kanawha County Bar. He began practicing in Boone, Lincoln and Logan counties, and was not long in taking a high rank as an attorney in those counties. He was elected Prosecuting Attorney of Lincoln and Boone counties in 1884 and was re-elected for a second term in both counties. Although a young man he proved to be a vigorous and fair prosecutor. His motto was "Let no guilty man escape." On one occasion he went before a Grand Jury and upon his own testimony indicted himself for a technical violation of a State statute. When he called the docket he plead guilty and paid the fine and costs. We believe there is no

MAJOR JOSEPH E. CHILTON

similar case to this on record. These are the only public offices ever held by Major Chilton. Although he delighted to mix in politics he was never a candidate himself except as stated above; his ambitions were satisfied in supporting his friends. He is an excellent organizer and a high grade platform speaker. Indeed, we know none superior to him, at least in the southern part of the State.

In November, 1887, Major Chilton began the practice of law in Charleston, as a partner of the late Judge James H. Ferguson, who was chief counsel of the Chesapeake and Ohio Railroad Company, and remained with him until the firm of Chilton, MacCorkle and Chilton was organized some twenty odd years ago, which consisted of himself, former Governor MacCorkle, and his brother, William E. Chilton, ex-United States Senator for this State,— a firm of State-wide reputation, known for the strength and standing of its members. Their business embraces all branches of the law, but they specialize in large corporation enterprises.

Major Chilton is large of stature, as well as of brain; at times he is full of humor; is thoughtful of the interests of others; is kindly disposed in the trial of his causes; is particularly strong as a trial lawyer, being always full of resources, and under the pressure of emergencies in a court trial his work is often brilliant. He is a most genial companion, a hard worker and when interested in a subject he considers no labor too great to devote to it. His life as a lawyer, whether judged with reference to labor performed or pecuniary gain, he stands in the front rank of his profession. He is optimistic and cheerful and associations with him are always pleasant.

Major Chilton was a Regent of the West Virginia University during the administration of Governor Jackson, is a bachelor and resides with his mother in a splendid residence erected by him in the capital city of the State. One of the characteristics of the Chilton brothers is their devotion to their mother, a sweet-spirited old lady who has passed the octogenarian milestone.

He received his military title by being an officer on the staff of the late Governor Jacob B. Jackson. No man has done more to develop the great natural resources of the southern portion of West Virginia than he.

## Elbert Lee Nuckolls, LL.B.

Mr. Nuckolls is a native of Gambetta, Virginia, where he was born August 2, 1868. His parents were Thomas and Jestin Nuckolls, who were also Virginians. He was educated at Wood Lawn Normal School and at Washington and Lee University, from which latter institution he received the degree of Bachelor of Laws. He was admitted to the Bar at Hillsville, Virginia in 1893. Shortly thereafter he came to West Virginia and located at Fayetteville, the county seat of Fayette County, where he now resides, and is a member of the well-established law firm of Dillon and Nuckolls, who has a leading practice in all State and Federal Courts of the southern

E. L. NUCKOLLS

part of West Virginia. They are both lawyers of distinction and they have a large and profitable clientele.

Our subject has been, since his admission to the Bar, giving all his time and energy to the single object of making himself a leader in his profession. While he is a Democrat in politics, he has never sought political favors of any kind, but has toiled early and late in his law office, giving his best efforts to all the branches of the law common to his locality, until he has attained a prominent standing among the leading lawyers of the southern part of West Virginia. This is one of the reasons for his high attainments in his profession. He is of strong physique and possesses good health, splendid social qualities and great powers of endurance. He is one of the kind of men who rarely, if ever, fail to bring honor and success to one's calling in life. Later on when he becomes more fully established in the law, it is possible he may heed the many calls of his friends, as Theodore Roosevelt expressed it, to "cast his hat" in the political arena and become a candidate for some high office in the power and possession of the people.

His professional traits are fashioned in the mold of law, his morale in the cast of rectitude. The simplicity of his virtues as a lawyer and a citizen admit no vanity or affectation and he enjoys with modesty the standing he has attained in his profession and the respect of the people with whom he associates. His personal character is above reproach and his integrity is unimpeachable. He is a safe and sane counselor and his advice on any legal question is worthy of the most serious consideration. He commanded success and he deserved it.

Mr. Nuckolls and his law partner, Mr. C. W. Dillon, published a flexible bound copy of the Code of West Virginia a few years ago, which, as a pocket edition, was almost universally used by West Virginia lawyers and proved to be a helpful companion in everyday practice.

He has a wife and two children and is living happily at Fayetteville among the foot-hills of the Allegheny Mountains, which span the State from its northern to its southern boundaries.

He is an active member of the Masonic Fraternity, from the Blue Lodge to the Shrine, and is one of the most useful members of the State Bar Association, being at present a member of the Executive Council, and has not, for years, failed to attend its annual sessions.

## Hon. William Rootes Thompson

Mr. Thompson is the son of Benjamin S. and Elizabeth Lewis Thompson, well-known residents of West Virginia. He was born at Coals Mouth (now St. Albans), Kanawha County, Virginia, in 1856. He received his primary education in private and public schools of his native county. Later he attended the West Virginia University, at Morgantown, from which he became an honor graduate. He was admitted to the Bar of Summers County, at Hinton, its seat of justice, in 1880. He was then a young man of striking appearance, of medium height, graceful and erect. He was, therefore, not long in finding his way into public life. He possessed a delicacy of sentiment which characterized his conduct at all times; also a quietness of demeanor, an utter absence of display or of harshness and a suavity and gentleness to an extent that no act of his offended even the humblest citizen. His dominant characteristic is his integrity. He never allowed himself to compromise a principle, always holding that principle is indivisible. To him justice is a supreme principle and he never allows himself to waiver from it even for a cherished friend or kinsman. He possesses a fertile brain and his diction is unusual. He has an acute discrimination and a relish for the ludicrous, which make him one of the most genial of companions. No one who knows him well will deny that his proper place as a lawyer is among the foremost men in that calling in the entire Commonwealth. And better than all, he can be fully trusted.

From early manhood he revealed a somewhat natural taste for politics; and yet he never allowed it, to any considerable degree, to interfere with his success as a lawyer. With him, it has always been his determination to keep the law first and foremost, making politics take second place, for the reason that politics with him is a recreation and not a business. The only offices he ever held were strictly in the line of his profession. He was Prosecuting Attorney of Summers County from 1880 to 1885, to which he was elected as a Democrat. As a matter of fact he never was anything but a Democrat, and he proved himself to be an able and just prosecutor. During President Cleveland's first administration he served as Assistant District Attorney for the State of West Virginia. Here, again, he showed himself to be a strong and just official. Later on he was the nominee by acclimation of his party for Governor of the Commonwealth, but was defeated along with his entire ticket, notwithstanding the fact that he received several thousand more votes than any other candidate on his ticket.

For many years he has resided in the city of Huntington, West Virginia, where his law firm, composed of the Hon. Z. T. Vinson and himself, have conducted a large and profitable law business in all the courts of West Virginia, the United States District Court and Circuit Court of Appeals for the Fourth Judicial Circuit and the Supreme Court of the United States. His practice includes all branches of the law, but both his partner and himself specialize in corporation practice, which has been large, profitable and successful.

Mr. Thompson married Miss Salie H. Huie in 1899 and they have one son. He is a member of the Protestant Episcopal Church and the Freemasons and Odd Fellows societies. He takes a deep interest in the progress and welfare of his native State. He is modest and retiring and has the confidence of the people generally.

## Judge Jonathan T. Graham

Judge Graham is one of the prominent members of the West Virginia Bench and Bar. He was born at Oil City, Pennsylvania, December 11, 1865, and is a son of William T. and Lucy Ann Graham, of the Keystone State. The son came to West Virginia in 1892 and settled at Wayne, Wayne County, and entered upon the practice of the law. He was educated in the public and normal schools of western Pennsylvania and New York. After leaving school he read law and was admitted to the Bar of Venango County, Pennsylvania in the summer of 1892. Having previously decided to remove his residence to West Virginia, he located in Wayne County and was received as a member of the Bar in September, 1892, and at once entered upon the active practice of his profession. His diligence, energy and fidelity to the interests of his clients soon won for him deserved success and remunerative pecuniary rewards. Although he has always been a pronounced Republican, he was elected Prosecuting Attorney of his newly adopted county, which had a large Democratic majority, and served to the satisfaction of all the people. By this time he had become, from experience and application, a very successful counselor and attorney; and being thoroughly upright and reliable in all of his business transactions, he had become very popular with the people. His business kept on increasing until he decided to seek a wider field, so he moved his office to the city of Huntington, which was in an adjoining county to Wayne and where his business in all of the courts rapidly increased, and where he took a high rank at that very able Bar.

In the campaign of 1913 he was the nominee of the Republican party for Judge of the Sixth Judicial Circuit, composed of the counties of Cabell, Putnam and Lincoln, was elected, and for the past five years he has worn the judicial ermine with both dignity and ability. He is a most genial companion, of splendid address and naturally attracts men to him. He is a hard worker, and when concerned in a subject he considers no labor too arduous to devote to it. As a lawyer he was gifted with unusual logical powers and a faculty of remarkably lucid expression, and his integrity was equal to his accuracy. As a Judge he is absolutely sincere and just and is giving satisfaction to the lawyers and litigants of his circuit.

Judge Graham married Miss Mary L. Chapman in 1895. They have but one child — a son now seventeen years of age.

The Judge is a member of the Orders of Masons and Elks and his permanent home is in the city of Huntington, the second largest city in the State.

Judge Graham's friends all know he goes by the name of "John," when in fact his correct name is "Jonathan." He feels that this mistake should be corrected and that he owes it to his beloved mother to use the name given to him by her; and we beg to add that we feel the same way.

## Zachary Taylor Vinson, B.S.

One of the foremost and best known of West Virginia lawyers is the subject of this brief sketch. He is the son of Hon. Samuel S. and Mary Vinson, and was born in Wayne County, Virginia, December 22, 1857. After attending the public schools of his native county for several years he entered Bethany College in Brooke County, Virginia (now West Virginia), and graduated B.S. in the class of 1878. He then entered the law department of the University of Virginia, where he remained one year, and being desirous to become familiar with Northern methods of practice, he went to Boston University and finished his course in law. This division of schools prevented him from receiving a degree, which, however, he had fully earned. He returned to West Virginia and was admitted to the Bar of Cabell County in 1885, where he has since practiced with a remarkable degree of success. For a number of years past he has been the senior member of the distinguished and well-known law firm of Vinson and Thompson, of Huntington. He is a thoroughly educated lawyer, and ever since he entered the profession he has been a hard worker. He is strong in both body and intellect and possesses unusual powers. When he undertakes the management of a case he goes to the bottom of it, and when it comes on for trial he is ready for any question that can be raised. While he is always kindly disposed, he is, at the same time, self-reliant and self-asserting and is unyielding in any matter wherein he believes he is right. He is a great trial lawyer, and when one has contested an important cause with him he finds he has found an opponent worthy of his steel. He is remarkable for antipodal elements of character. That is to say, the active and passive features are so set over against each other as to give him a unique standing among his fellows. While he is a formidable contestant in debate, he is just and generous, and according to others, he is not slow in demanding the same in return. He is noteworthy for quietness of force and reservation of power. With a branch of vision above the ordinary and remarkable insightedness and absolute calmness in his poise, and never disturbed by the clash or clamor of contest, he metes out his strength in proportion to the demands of the occasion which elicited it, and leaves the impression that abundant power is held in reserve for whatever emergency might arise. We believe that such an one is entitled to be classed high as a courthouse trial lawyer.

Mr. Vinson has practiced in all State and Federal Courts and has many times appeared in the Supreme Court of the United States. He is also "at home," so to speak, in all branches of the profession, but he has specialized no little in corporation practice, where he seems to feel still more "at home." We will mention but one particular case, out of the many in which he has appeared as counsel, because he made some *new* law, revising an old, apparently well-settled principle in the courts of England, which had been followed by the Supreme Courts of a large number of our American States, relating to subjacent and lateral support of the surface of land by removing the coal thereunder. The decisions of the courts formerly required the coal operator to leave unmined a sufficiency of columns of coal to prevent the sinking or caving in of the surface, otherwise he would be held liable for damages caused by injury to the surface. The West Virginia Court, with one Judge dissenting, held that "where a deed conveys the coal under a tract of land, together with the right to enter upon and under said land and to mine, excavate and remove all of it, there is no implied reservation in such an instrument that the grantee must leave enough coal to support the surface in its original position."

This new view of this most important subject has been sustained by some Federal authorities, notably the Court of Appeals of the Fourth Judicial Circuit, and is most likely to become the settled law of the land, because when one purchases the coal under a parcel of real estate, and no reservations are made in the deed, the presumption is he buys all of it, and therefore has the right to remove what he purchases and pays for, without reference to damage to the surface of the land from which the coal has been taken. Anyway, it is the law in West Virginia, and we congratulate Mr. Vinson on having a leading part in so important a cause.

Mr. Vinson is a Republican in politics, but never held a public office. Practically his entire life has been devoted to the study and practice of the law. He is a member of the Christian Church and the Odd Fellows and the Elks Benevolent Orders. He is a member of the Delta Tau Delta College Fraternity, which was organized at the college of which he is an *alumnus*. He married Miss Mary Chaffin in 1901 and has one child. He is a public spirited citizen and is one of the developers of the city of Huntington, where he has resided the greater part of his life.

## Robert George Linn, LL.B.

Mr. Linn, one of the leading lawyers of the Kanawha Bar, son of Robert Linn, who was also a lawyer of prominence, was born at Glenville, Gilmer County, Virginia, April 6, 1849, received his education at Witherspoon Institute, Butler, Pennsylvania, and the Cincinnati Law School, from which well known College of Law he graduated in April 1870, receiving the degree of Bachelor of Laws; the same year he was licensed to practice at the Gilmer County Bar; was elected Prosecuting Attorney of that county in October 1870 and served two years; was attentive to his public duties and served efficiently for the full term. In 1872 he was elected Prosecuting Attorney of the adjoining county of Calhoun; became a resident of Grantsville, Calhoun County, and remained there until March 1, 1884, when he returned to Gilmer County, where he continued to reside until 1900, when he located permanently in Charleston, the capital of the State. He married Miss Mary Hamilton, of Weston, Lewis County, June 12, 1876. Eight children resulted from this marriage, two of whom are deceased. A son, Robert, who graduated from

HON. R. G. LINN

the law department of the West Virginia University in the class of 1906, is a member of his father's present law firm.

Mr. Linn from early manhood has been an untiring worker, and his practice has been of a general character and has been spread out over several contiguous counties. He had several branch law firms; for example, the one in Braxton County, for several years was Linn and Byrne; in Gilmer County the firm for eleven years was Linn and Withers; in Lewis County, Linn and Brannon; in Calhoun, Linn and Hamilton; and in Charleston since 1889 the law firm is Linn and Byrne. In the earlier years of his practice it was his custom to attend the terms of court in several counties wherein he maintained partnerships and assist in the trial of important causes, but since his location at Charleston the business of his present firm has become so extensive that he seldom attends court sessions in any of the counties wherein he formerly had an extensive practice He is an able, ingenuous trial lawyer and handles his cases skilfully, and generally successfully; consequently he maintains a large clientage. He is never short of business, and he may be found in his office at all reasonable hours, except when engaged in court sessions.

Moreover, he is careful, clear-headed and thorough in his work. He is thoroughly grounded in the law and devotes special care to the preparation of his pleadings. He is a man of marked courage, and yet is fair and courteous. His force of will and self-reliance are far above the average and his integrity is equal to his accuracy. He asks no favors and fears no adversary. He is strong in body and mind. In politics he is a Democrat, but he is much more of a lawyer than a politician. He never aspired to any office, except positions strictly in the line of his profession. As we have stated above, he was six years Prosecuting Attorney of two different counties, and in 1916 he was vigorously pressed as a candidate for Circuit Judge of the Kanawha Circuit, a place he was well qualified to fill, but failed to secure the nomination. Had he been chosen he would have honored both the Bench and the Bar.

Mr. Linn is a member of the Presbyterian Church. He is both upright and reliable in all of his dealings. Since writing the above Mr. Linn died, May 13, 1919.

## Hon. Romeo H. Freer

Mr. Freer was a native of Ohio and was born in Trumbull County, of that State, November 8, 1845. He grew up on a farm, attended the public schools and spent one term at Oberlin College, Ohio, which was the extent of his schooling. At sixteen, in 1861, he entered the United States Volunteer Army and served until the close of the Civil War; at its close he settled in Charleston; taught school for two years, read law in the office of Smith and Cracraft, and in 1868 was admitted to the Charleston Bar. Being gifted in public speaking, and possessing almost unlimited energy and ambition, he soon forged to the front as an attorney, especially in criminal cases; in 1877 he formed a partnership with Captain H. C. McWhorter, who subsequently was elected a member of the Supreme Court of Appeals of the State. The firm controlled a large business in all the courts of the State and the Federal courts as well. The firm of McWhorter and Freer continued until 1872, when Mr. Freer was appointed by President Grant United States Consul to Nicaragua, C. A., where he remained for four years.

In the meantime, however, before entering the consular service, he served as Prosecuting Attorney for the counties of Fayette and Boone and also as Assistant Prosecutor for Kanawha County, and later he was elected Prosecuting Attorney for his adopted county. He was regarded as an able and successful prosecutor. He moved his residence to Harrisville, in Ritchie County, in 1882, and in 1890 he was elected to the West Virginia Legislature from that county. For a number of years he was an active and leading member of the National Guard of West Virginia and worked his way from private to the rank of Brigadier-General. He was also a very efficient member of the Grand Army of the Republic, having filled all of its official positions in this State.

He was a Republican in politics and participated in every State and National campaign for more than forty years. He was inimitable as a public speaker and possessed unusual popularity. In fact, he was an idol of the masses. In 1890 he was elected Attorney-General of the State. He was later elected Judge of the Circuit Court of the circuit in which he resided and proved to be a successful jurist. While holding that office he was elected to the Congress of the United States, retiring of his own volition at the end of one term. The last of his public service was as Postmaster of the town of Harrisville, which he held to the time of his death, which occurred before he had quite reached his seventieth milestone.

Judge Freer was thrice married: first to Miss Lillie Fuller, of Warren, Ohio, by whom he had one child who died in infancy; second, to Miss Effie Brace, of Charleston, by whom he had a son, R. H. Freer, Jr.; and third, to Miss Iams, of Ritchie County, by whom he had no children.

Judge Freer was a member of the Presbyterian Church and will ever be remembered by the people of West Virginia as one of the State's most brilliant citizens.

## Judge John M. Woods, LL.B.

The subject of this brief sketch is a native of Stafford County, Virginia. and is the son of F. M. and Julia M. Woods. He was born November 1, 1869, and was carefully taught for one year by his father; attended a private school in Martinsburg for two or three years and the High School of that city three years; had two years' training at Pantops Academy, near Charlottesville, Virginia; spent the Freshman year at Washington and Jefferson College at Washington, Pennsylvania; taught a private school in

Martinsburg the next year and later took his law course at Washington and Lee University at Lexington, Virginia, from which he graduated in 1892 with the degree of Bachelor of Laws. He received an offer to teach two hours a day at the Potomac Academy in Romney, West Virginia, and taught at that institution for two years, from 1892 to 1894, and was admitted to the Bar in Romney, West Virginia, while there in August, 1892. On the 1st day of March, 1893, he formed a partnership with the late Col. Robt. W. Monroe in that town and remained in partnership with him until March, 1896, when he returned to Martinsburg and opened a law office there. He was in partnership with the late J. Nelson Wisner under the firm name of Wisner and Woods from January 1, 1897, to January 1, 1898, when the partnership was dissolved. April 1, 1899, he formed a partnership with Senator Charles J. Faulkner and Hon. S. W. Walker under the firm name of Faulkner, Walker and Woods, which continued until he went on the Bench of the Circuit Court the 1st of January, 1913. He was a successful practitioner and an able trial lawyer.

In April, 1902, upon the death of the late U. S. G. Pitzer, Prosecuting Attorney of Berkeley County, he was appointed by Judge E. Boyd Faulkner to fill the vacancy caused by his death until the following November, when the late Ward B. Lindsay was elected to fill the vacancy for the residue of Mr. Pitzer's term. He was vigorous in seeing to it that all infractors of the laws of the State in Berkeley County were properly punished. He was thoroughly conscientious and just in the discharge of his official duties.

He was elected Judge of the 18th Judicial Circuit, composed of the counties of Berkeley, Jefferson and Morgan, in November, 1912, and entered upon his duties on the 1st day of January following. He is still serving most satisfactorily in that high and responsible position.

He was married the 16th day of October, 1901, to Miss Eleanor Tabb. They have two children, a daughter and a son. Their home is in the beautiful and prosperous city of Martinsburg.

Judge Woods is well grounded in the fundamental principles of the law and is an able, upright, conscientious Judge.

## Hon. William W. Brannon

The subject of this sketch is one of the noted family of Brannon lawyers who first came to this State from Winchester, Virginia, upwards of a half century ago and settled at Weston, Lewis County, in what is now West Virginia. He is the son of Stewart J. and Mary (Carper) Brannon, and was born in Winchester in the Valley of Virginia, November 13, 1853. For a time he attended a private school at Winchester, where he received a fairly good rudimentary education; and after coming to Lewis County he pieced out a still more complete English education than he had already received in the mother Commonwealth. Being of an ambitious turn of mind, and being naturally industrious, he was a constant companion of books and, therefore, allowed no opportunity to pass him unimproved to store his mind with all the valuable knowledge and information within his reach. While it is true Mr. Brannon never attended a college, yet it is also true that through perseverance and unabated energy he never ceased his efforts until he secured a passable English education, which has served him well through life. He has a good vocabulary, is fluent in speech, forceful in expression, uses the best of language and argues a case with fluency and zeal. Indeed, it would be difficult to find a better trial lawyer at any Bar of any State than William W. Brannon.

He began the study of law under the direction of his two eminent uncles, John and Henry Brannon, both of whom, in later years honored the judiciary of West Virginia, and the nephew proved to be an apt student. In due time he was able to pass a creditable examination and was admitted to the Weston Bar in 1881, where he has since practiced with unremitting zeal and with abundant success; and it is safe to say that W. W. Brannon is now one of the leading lawyers in the central portion of West Virginia. He possessed a vigor, perseverance and inquisitiveness of mind which permitted nothing to pass from under his observation without his thorough comprehension of its character; and to this trained habit of sensation and perception was added a well-regulated judgment. Whilst these qualities will assert their superiority in whatever sphere they may be exercised, they are, of all others, the most important qualifications for success at the Bar.

Mr. Brannon is methodical and laborious in the preparation of his cases and is always well armed with precedent and authority; hence there is a fixed precision attending the positions he takes which skill or sophistry cannot shake. His judgment is initiative and his logical powers spontaneous. He rarely indulges in the lofty strains of rhetoric and never in impassioned challenges of applause. He readily perceives the main points of a question and addresses himself to the gist of the controversy — a rule which commends itself and would greatly enhance the expedition of the courts and the attainment of justice, while it would often lift a heavy burden from the patience of both courts and juries. Another feature which adds greatly to Mr. Brannon's success as a lawyer is his uniform placidity and good nature; and still another, that of probity and integrity. He is thoroughly trustworthy and dependable.

He is a reliable Democrat, but outside of being Mayor of the city of Weston from 1886 to 1890 he never held any political office, except one term as a member of the West Virginia Legislature, and he proved to be a very able and useful member. We find we are mistaken. He was four years a member of the West Virginia Board of Pardons. Being a good lawyer, and knowing the weight of evidence, he was extremely useful in that capacity.

He married Miss Addie Alkire in 1884 and has two children, and no one enjoys home life more than he. He is a Knight of Pythias and an Odd Fellow. During Governor Atkinson's administration he was a valuable member of the State Pardon Board.

## Hon. John H. Holt, LL.B., LL.M.

The subject of this sketch is known, and is generally regarded by the people of West Virginia, as one of the ablest and among the most distinguished lawyers the State of West Virginia has ever produced. He is, to say the least, a very remarkable man. He is a born lawyer — a natural lawyer. He is the best lawyer in a bad case the writer ever knew. He can get from under a court decision against him with a mildness and suavity that surprises an opponent. We do not believe he ever lost a case he ought to have won. Only a first grade attorney can accomplish that feat. Mr. Holt has done it many times. He has lost many hotly contested big causes, but it was not through any fault or neglect of his. Good lawyers often lose cases and they ought to. The ablest lawyers are generally the ones who are employed in the worst cases, and Mr. Holt no doubt gets his share of them. He is an orator of great power, and is so self-poised and affable, and so ready and forceful in rejoinder it is difficult to force him from any position he takes. He is so even and equable in temper and manner that he is never disconcerted or disturbed when taken unawares by opposing counsel in any cause. He appears to be ready for whatever may come, and therein is one of his greatest points, and another is he knows the law and knows how to apply it. Is there any wonder that he has succeeded and succeeded grandly?

Mr. Holt is the son of Judge Homer A. Holt, who was a distinguished lawyer and jurist in his generation, and from him, doubtless, our subject inherited much of the power and ability he possesses as a lawyer and an advocate. He was born in Braxton County, West Virginia, August 10, 1860, and was educated at Randolph-Macon College, Virginia, the University of Virginia, Georgetown (D. C.) University, and a post graduate course in law at Yale University. In these great schools he studied the classics, literature and law, taking the degrees of Bachelor of Science, Bachelor of Laws and Master of Laws. Thus receiving as thorough training as could be imparted to an ambitious young man in this or any other country. He, therefore, started in his life work "with a sharp scythe." But few young men, before or since, had so thorough a training and equipment. It is, therefore, no wonder that he has proved successful. After these courses of study in four different colleges and universities he located for practice in the City of Wheeling, with M. T. Frame as a partner, in 1887. In 1890 he moved to Huntington, Cabell County, and has since remained there, where he has a most lucrative practice in the courts of the State and United States, including the Supreme Court of Appeals of West Virginia, the United States Circuit Court of Appeals of the Fourth Judicial Circuit, and the Supreme Court of the United States, where he has tried a large number of important causes. He has specialized in corporation laws; but, as a matter of fact, he is about as successful in one branch of the law as another, and is remarkably successful in all of them. He, therefore, should be classed as an able "all-round lawyer."

HON. JOHN H. HOLT

In politics he has always been a Democrat and enjoys the excitement "of the political game." He is not an office-seeker, but has allowed himself to be drafted by his party for important political positions. In 1896 he was his party's candidate for Judge of the Supreme Court of Appeals of the State to succeed his father, who retired from that highly honorable office, but was defeated by his Republican opponent, although he received about 2,000 more votes than any other candidate on his party ticket. In 1890 he was nominated by his party for the office of Governor of the Commonwealth and was again defeated, this time also running ahead of his ticket. He is a brilliant campaign speaker. He has no superior in the State as a platform stump-speaker, and but few, if any, equals. His thorough college training and his broad knowledge of the English language and English literature, coupled with natural gifts in oratory, have placed him in a class of public speakers and advocates difficult to excel. Chivalrous and magnanimous in his disposition, he abhors the methods of artifice, and spurns that which he believes to be unjust. These well known features of his character engage universal confidence in him as a lawyer and the highest respect for him as a man.

In 1886 he married Miss Effie Ewing, a daughter of J. Dallas Ewing, of Wheeling, a prominent lawyer of that city, by whom he had four children, one of them — Homer — is practicing law with his father in the City of Huntington. His wife recently departed this life.

## Judge Marsh Haymond Willis

The subject of this sketch is one of the brilliant, able and successful lawyers and jurists of this Commonwealth. He was born in Ritchie County, Virginia, January 31, 1862; is the son of N. G. and Louisa Martin Willis. His earlier years were spent upon his father's farm, where he obtained a whipcord muscle and a physical development that have served him well as he advanced in life. He is of medium stature, is compactly built, and is attractive in appearance, having a full suit of hair which was quite gray before he was twenty years of age. He was an industrious student in the school of his neighborhood. He became a teacher in the common schools at the early age of sixteen, and for several years thereafter his time was given principally to that occupation. At the same time he was industriously engaged in the acquirement of knowledge and the development of his own vigorous and receptive intellect. For a time he was a student at the West Virginia University at Morgantown. Later he entered Valparaiso (Indiana) University, from which he graduated *cum laude*, in 1886, being the Valedictorian of his class of seventy-six members. For a short time he engaged in school teaching in Dakota, Wisconsin and West Virginia, while at the same time he was engaged in reading law. In 1890 he was granted a license to practice in the Circuit Court of Doddridge County, where he resided for a number of years and built up a profitable

JUDGE M. H. WILLIS

clientage. His career is a splendid illustration of the sure triumph that perseverance and grit will bring to a young man endowed with genuine merit in his make up, and a firm determination to leave his impress upon the times in which he lived. In 1900 he was named without opposition in Convention as the Republican candidate for Judge of the Fourth Judicial Circuit to fill the unexpired term of Hon. Romeo H. Freer, who had resigned to accept a seat in Congress. He was elected and immediately entered upon the duties of his office. All of the counties of this Circuit were in the oil belt and the work was very heavy. The Legislature of 1903 rearranged the Judicial Circuits, and in so doing took off Ritchie County, leaving Doddridge, Tyler and Wetzel together, and called the new Circuit the Second instead of the Fourth. His work on the Bench was so satisfactory to the Bar and the people generally that he was renominated without opposition, and was re-elected for the full term of eight years.

He is naturally, as well as by education, fitted for the law, a thorough, close and logical reasoner, his early absorption of the underlying principles of jurisprudence was a solid foundation for the study, observations and experience for an active practitioner and an able judge. He possesses in a high degree the powers of convincing statement, and above all is honorable and upright in all of his acts. He is a good lawyer, a just judge and an ideal citizen.

In 1887 he was united in marriage with Anita Magness, of Waterloo, Iowa. To them one child, Frances Louise, was born January 21, 1892, and she departed this life September 15, 1901.

While serving as a Circuit Judge he moved his residence to New Martinsville, Wetzel County, where he is now engaged in the active practice of his profession.

## Judge Thomas Perry Jacobs, A.M.

The subject of this sketch, who is a descendant of sturdy stock, long identified with American institutions, was born in Allegheny County, Maryland, January 27, 1852. Shortly thereafter his parents moved to Preston County, Virginia, and after residing there a short time they finally settled permanently at Morgantown, the seat of justice of Monongalia County, Virginia, where our subject grew to manhood. He received his education in the Preston Academy, and later graduated from the West Virginia University in 1874, carrying off the honors of his class. During his collegiate course he became a student of law, and after graduating from the Department of Liberal Arts of the State University he vigorously pursued his law studies in the law offices of Berkshire and Sturgiss at Morgantown, where he became proficient in the legal text books required of students of law. In 1875 he located at New Martinsville, Wetzel County, West Virginia, and in that year was admitted to practice, where he has ever since resided.

JUDGE THOMAS P. JACOBS

As a lawyer he has long ranked among the most able and distinguished in West Virginia. On the civil side his practice has been extensive and varied, covering many counties of the State, and he has occasionally appeared with success in important criminal proceedings. He has specialized in the law relating to mining and operating for oil and gas. Many important principles now universally held, having been established in cases with which he was connected as counsel or during his term as a Circuit Judge, to which position he was elected in 1888, which he ably filled for eight years, proving himself to be not only a learned lawyer, but a sound, painstaking judge. During his term on the Bench in 1890 he conducted the Summer Law School of the West Virginia University, and was so successful as a teacher that the Board of Regents tendered him the Deanship of that institution, which, however, he declined.

Judge Jacobs has been a regular attendant upon and a leader of the West Virginia Bar Association for more than a quarter of a century, and was its President in 1895.

In politics he has always been a Republican. He served five terms as Mayor of New Martinsville. In 1884 he was a member of the National Convention which nominated James G. Blaine for President. On the stump he has ever been a sound and convincing speaker.

He is an official member of the Methodist Episcopal Church, and has as a Lay Delegate represented his Conference in the General Conference of that Church. He is a Freemason of high rank, and during 1913–1914 served as Most Worshipful Grand Master of the Grand Lodge of West Virginia, and is held in high esteem by the members of that great Fraternity throughout the State.

He resides at New Martinsville and commands a large and profitable law business.

Since writing the above we are pained to announce the death of Judge Jacobs, which occurred at his home October 29, 1918.

## Hon. Uriah Barnes

Uriah Barnes was born in Jackson County, West Virginia, thirty-five years ago, where he spent his early life in arduous toil on the farm. He was educated in the public schools and the State University. At the age of sixteen, he taught the first of two successive terms in the common schools.

He left the farm with a powerful physique, a vast repository of dynamic power. With this he combines an equally powerful intellect, exemplifying in a high degree the ideal of the Latin maxim, *Mens sana in corpore sano.* Thus equipped he early entered upon life in Charleston, where he began to expand his intellectual horizon by reading widely along lines carefully marked out. Outside of his regular employment, he found time to prescribe a rigid course of self-imposed discipline, which he followed with an iron will and a fixity of purpose rarely, if ever, excelled, until he had

HON. URIAH BARNES

covered a wide field, similar to that embraced in the college courses. He absorbed knowledge easily, and read with a profound understanding. These qualities, coupled with a retentive memory and a habit of mastering every subject or task he took in hand, soon showed very marked and substantial results, so that properly it may be said he had won a place among highly educated men before he entered upon his university training.

For four years he was law instructor in the College of Law of West Virginia University. He also acted for a year as Secretary of the College of Agriculture and the Agricultural Experiment Station at the University.

For many years he was engaged in work with the Supreme Court of Appeals, and in the exhaustive investigation of cases pending therein. He has done much important work as a law writer and editor on legal text books and on special articles for legal encyclopedias. He recently compiled and edited the ordinances of the City of Charleston. He was the editor of the *West Virginia Code of 1916*, in the preparation of which he made a careful and exhaustive study of all the state statutes. This book is now the hand book of the laws.

He conceived the idea of publishing all the Federal Laws in one handy volume. This had never been accomplished, and it was an undertaking requiring an enormous amount of labor and great editorial skill. The task was finally completed early in 1919, when *Barnes' Federal Code* appeared. He brought to bear in this work a comprehensive knowledge, a sound and discriminating judgment, a genius for editorial detail that have combined to bring him universal recognition as a master in his field. The remarkable sale of the *Federal Code* in every State in the Union and abroad, and the unsolicited encomiums upon it, coming from bench and bar and from eminent scholars and educators throughout the country, attest its rank as a masterpiece of compilation.

Mr. Barnes is a member of the local, State and American Bar Associations, and the American Institute of Criminal Law and Criminology.

He married Miss Lena Belle Ice, and has two children. He is a Methodist, and has participated very largely in the civic and social life of the community. He is intensely interested in the best in literature, and especially in history, sociology, economics and political science. He resides at Charleston, where he enjoys the full confidence and respect of all who know him, and where his honorable life and fair dealing are universally recognized.

## Judge Elisha Boyd Faulkner

Hon. Elisha Boyd Faulkner, one of the able lawyers and jurists of West Virginia, son of Hon. Charles James and Mary W. (Boyd) Faulkner, was born near Martinsburg, in what is now West Virginia, July 24, 1841. There he passed his early youth attending private schools and studying under private tutors. He was also a student at the Winchester (Va.) Academy. Later he entered Georgetown, D. C., College, and the University of Virginia; he next attended lectures on Constitutional Law in Paris, France, where he was attached to the Legation of the United States, his father being Ambassador of the United States at the Court of St. Cloud. He has made law his life work in which he attained eminence. From 1867 to 1872 he lived in Kentucky, leaving Virginia on account of the "Test Oath" required to be taken at that date. March 3, 1869, the Legislature of West Virginia passed an Act relieving him of taking the test oath, but that was not taken advantage of by him. In 1872 he returned to Martinsburg for the practice of law. In granting him his certificate preceding his license to practice, Judge Balsh added in the certificate: " . . . that he is a man of honest demeanor, unless the fact that he has been an officer in the Rebel Army may be regarded as affecting his demeanor." He was elected to the House of Delegates of West Virginia in 1876; to the State Senate in 1878, declining the Presidency of that body; appointed a member of the Revisory Committee by the Legislature to revise the laws of the State; was defeated for the Democratic nomination for Governor at Wheeling in 1884 by a very small vote in an exciting convention; during President Cleveland's administration he was tendered the office of Consul General and Agent to Cairo in 1885, also Minister to Persia, both being declined. He was appointed Judge of the Thirteenth Judicial District, and was three times re-elected to that office with little opposition. He has served in all more than twenty-one years on the Bench, declining in 1912 to be re-elected. At the time of his appointment as Judge he was attorney for the Baltimore and Ohio and the Cumberland Valley Railroads; for all the numerous banking institutions of Martinsburg and for other large corporations. He was Trustee of the Berkeley Springs Corporation. Politically he is a Democrat. Judge Faulkner's war record is as follows: At the outbreak of the war he entered the Wise Artillery, later joining the Rockbridge Artillery; he was then appointed on the staff of Governor Letcher; and afterwards was made a Captain in the Provisional Army of the Confederacy. He was captured at the battle of Piedmont in June, 1864, when Gen. W. R. Jones was killed, and was confined as a prisoner on Johnson's Island for a year. At the first battle of Manassas he received wounds in the ear from a bursting shell. He was in many hard fought engagements, including those of Manassas and Cedar Creek. He fought as he believed was right, and was a brave soldier in the greatest civil conflict of the world's history.

February 11, 1868, he married Susan Campbell, of Hopkinsville, Ky., daughter of John P. Campbell, of Scotch descent, who died in Hopkinsville at the age of 73 years, leaving surviving him his widow, Mary (Buckner) Campbell, and eight children, all of whom have now passed away except Judge Faulkner's wife.

The Judge and his wife have had two children: Mary Buckner, unmarried; and Nannie Holmes, who died in 1883. In all of his relations at the Bar, on the Bench, in his home life, and in his community relations generally, Judge Faulkner has always been loyal, true and upright.

## Hon. William George Bennett, LL.B.

This eminent lawyer, judge and distinguished citizen, son of the late Hon. Jonathan M. Bennett, died suddenly of heart disease at his home in the City of Weston, November 8, 1915, aged sixty-nine years. His untimely death proved a shock to his thousands of friends and admirers throughout the entire State. He was a native of Lewis County and was well and favorably known all over the State of West Virginia. He received his early education under private tutors principally in the City of Richmond, and in 1866 he graduated from the Virginia Military Institute at Lexington. In 1869 he graduated, LL.B., from the Law Department of the University of Virginia, and shortly thereafter opened a law office in his native town of Weston. He possessed a legal mind and being thoroughly grounded in the principles of the law, his success from the beginning was almost phenomenal. He was elected a Circuit Court Judge in 1898, and filled that responsible office in a most satisfactory manner to lawyers and litigants until his retirement in 1905.

Judge Bennett was always a " true blue " Democrat in politics, and was one of the idols of his party in the State. Possessing naturally a genial, joyful disposition, he was unusually popular with the masses, and in his campaigns for official recognition he never failed to secure a large following from opposing political organizations. He was defeated for the Democratic nomination by only a small margin in 1892, when a candidate for Governor of West Virginia. He was nominated by the Democratc party for Justice of the Supreme Court of Appeals in 1900, and at the general election received a thousand more votes than any other man on his ticket. In 1912 he was the nominee of his party for the same position, but was again defeated by a reduced majority.

Judge Bennett was a successful business man as well as an eminent lawyer. He was one of the promoters and organizers of the Clarksburg and Weston Narrow Gauge Railroad and one of its directors and attorneys for many years. He was also connected in a like manner with the Weston and Buckhannon Railroad. While yet a young lawyer he was on one of the State Boards of Hospitals for the Insane, and was appointed Commissioner to assess railroads for taxation in the State. He was probably the largest owner of farm lands in Lewis County. He owned six farms, comprising over six thousand acres of land, and his " Riverside Farm " is known throughout the entire country. He was an extensive breeder of fine blooded cattle and standard bred horses, and was a director of the American Association of Trotting Horse Breeders and director of the American Register Association. While he followed law practice his special delight was in horses of all kinds.

He was a prominent Mason and had been Grand Master of the Grand Lodge of West Virginia. William G. Bennett Lodge No. 46 of Ancient

Free and Accepted Masons, of Walkersville, was named in his honor. He was also a member of the Benevolent and Protective Order of Elks.

Judge Bennett was married in 1872 to Alice, daughter of the late Judge John Brannon, of Weston, and a member of one of the most prominent families in Lewis County and that section of the State.

## Harold W. Houston

Mr. Houston, son of Samuel W. and Emma A. Houston, was born at Freedom, Noble County, Ohio, March 10, 1872. When the son was young in years his parents moved to West Virginia and located for a time in Jackson County and finally settled in Kanawha, where he grew to manhood. He received his primary education in the public schools of Jackson and Kanawha Counties, which included the Charleston High School, that offers a pretty thorough academic course of study. His education in law was secured at the West Virginia University. Although his opportunities for schooling were somewhat meager, he is far from being without a rather liberal education. Even in boyhood he possessed the habits and the strong tendencies of a student. He has always been an earnest seeker after knowledge, always a reader of books and always an industrious toiler and worker. By these methods he has acquired more than an ordinary vocabulary, and we can justly say he is master of a clear, terse and vigorous style, both in writing and in speaking. He is fluent and forceful in speech, and has the reputation and standing, not only as a strong and well balanced trial lawyer, but has an unusually clear, logical mind, and is remarkably well read and well informed in the law and on general subjects also. He became a member of the Parkersburg Bar in 1901, and has been in continuous practice ever since, and has tried a large number of important cases in quite a number of the counties of West Virginia. For several years past his principal office has been at Charleston, the capital of the State, where he conducts a large business. His practice is general and extends into all the State and Federal Courts and the Circuit Court of Appeals of the Fourth U. S. Judicial Circuit. He has also appeared as counsel in several cases in the Supreme Court of the United States. He is a hard working attorney and is almost constantly engaged in important causes.

In politics Mr. Houston is a Socialist, and has been connected with that political organization for years, and is quite active in the management of its affairs. However, as to the question of a lawyer's politics we have nothing to say. This volume deals with lawyers not politicians. Mr. Houston for years has been, and is, chief attorney and counselor of practically all of the Labor Organizations of West Virginia, which includes the United Mine Workers of America, the most important as well as the largest distinctive labor organization of the State. It is, therefore, proper for us to say that the major part of Mr. Houston's extensive and varied practice comes through these various organizations.

As a lawyer Mr. Houston is not only strong and well balanced, but he is genial and companionable, and when interested in a case he considers no labor too great to devote to it. Hence he is a dangerous competitor in a court trial. His force of will, self-reliance and courage are more than common. In appearance he is commanding, being tall, prematurely white-headed, and extremely pleasant and sociable. What he believes he feels, and what he feels he speaks and acts promptly and vigorously, and with conscientious candor.

He married Miss Sophie Graff in May, 1899, at Parkersburg, West Virginia, and has two daughters. He is a member of the Benevolent and Protective Order of Elks.

He has never held a political office of any kind or character. All of his time is devoted exclusively to his profession. Much of his time, however, is devoted to the trial in the courts of the State and country of cases growing out of politics.

## Hon. John Thomas McGraw, LL.B.

Among the middle-aged, brilliant and successful members of the legal profession in central West Virginia is the subject of this sketch. He was born in the city of Grafton, Taylor County, Virginia, January 12, 1856. He was educated at St. Vincent's Academy at Wheeling in the prescribed classical course. Later he graduated from the law department of Yale University with the degree of Bachelor of Laws in the class of 1876. In the autumn of that year he was admitted as a member of the Grafton Bar and has since successfully practiced his profession in that city to the present time. Shortly after he opened his law office he was made one of the principal attorneys for the Baltimore and Ohio Railroad Company, and as such legal adviser and attorney he is still employed. In 1880 he was elected Prosecuting Attorney of Taylor County and served efficiently and popularly for the term of four years.

In 1882 he was appointed an Aide-de-Camp, with the rank of Colonel, on the staff of Hon. J. B. Jackson, Governor of West Virginia. In the spring of 1886, after his term of Prosecuting Attorney had expired, he was appointed by President Cleveland Collector of Internal Revenue for the State of West Virginia, which office he held for four years, and proved to be efficient and successful. In the meantime his general practice as an attorney had grown to larger proportions. While he was Internal Revenue Collector he was appointed Disbursing Agent for the new Government buildings at Wheeling, Charleston and Clarksburg, which was an additional responsibility, entirely independent of his duties of Revenue Collector. All of his public duties were discharged efficiently and to the entire satisfaction of all concerned therewith. All the while he never neglected to give attention to his large and rapidly increasing law business.

Colonel McGraw, from early manhood, has been an ardent Democrat. He was for years not only an active member of local Democratic committees, but for a score or more of years he has been the West Virginia member of the Democratic National Committee. He was, therefore, a powerful factor in local and national politics, as well as in the practice of the law. He has been a candidate for Congress, and because of the fact that he is one of the highest grade platform speakers in any political party in this or any other State, he is the idol of the Democratic party in West Virginia, and is admired by the people generally.

Colonel McGraw is not only an active laywer and politician, but he is one of the foremost public spirited citizens of the entire State. He is a developer and a pusher in bringing to public notice the great natural advantages and resources of his native State. No history of West Virginia can be truthfully written without giving Colonel McGraw prominent mention in almost every chapter. He is a brilliant lawyer, a prominent politician and a leading public spirited citizen.

In religion he is a Roman Catholic, and has never married.

## Levin Smith

Among the strong, reputable, progressive, conscientious members of the Wood County, West Virginia, Bar is the subject of this sketch. His parents were William Haimes and Sarah Rector Smith, well known and highly respected families of that historic county. Levin was born in the same county December 22, 1861, shortly after the storm-clouds of the Civil War had gathered above our hills and vales. He received his education in the country schools and the Parkersburg High School, which has always been noted for its high standard in its requirements. Having decided to become a member of the legal profession, he matriculated as a student in the law department of Harvard University, Cambridge, Massachusetts, and remained until he completed the required three years' course of study. After his return to Parkersburg he was, in 1884, admitted a member of the historic Wood County Bar, where he has successfully practiced his profession. He possesses strong natural qualifications which, coupled with almost boundless energy and integrity of the loftiest sort, have made for him an enviable record as a lawyer and has won to him a large and profitable clientele.

Mr. Smith is a lawyer of sound judgment, of a clear perception of right and wrong and of a deep sense of justice. His conclusions are never arbitrary nor sententious; naturally he falls on the moral side of all controversies. He practices law under all the rules of fairness and at all times adheres to the Golden Rule. His constant purpose is to carry above him the white flower of a blameless life. His personal character is as spotless as a maiden's and as unsullied as a ray of light. He is a profound student, a thorough lawyer, an untiring worker. He gives out advice carefully and conscientiously. He brings law suits not for revenue only, but that justice may prevail,— a rule all lawyers should follow.

Mr. Smith is a Democrat, but he never was an office-seeker, and never held but one public office, and that was Solicitor for the city of Parkersburg from 1891 to 1893. He is a member of the Methodist Episcopal Church, South, and is an active, useful worker, and has filled all the lay offices of his church, including the high honor of being chosen a Lay Delegate to its General Conference. He has also been active in all kinds of benevolent and eleemosynary kinds of work, and has spent practically all of his life in being helpful to, and considerate of, his fellow men, without parading it among the people. He is also active in the business affairs of his locality. He is Vice-President and a Director of the Central Bank and Trust Company of Parkersburg, and is also connected with a number of other business institutions in the community. He is a member of the County, State and American Bar Associations, and is also a member of the Independent Order of Odd Fellows and Benevolent Protective Order of Elks.

He married Miss Nellie Marshall Williams June 21, 1887. They have four children. Their home is in the beautiful residence city of Parkersburg.

## Edward Granderson Smith, A.B., LL.B.

E. G. Smith, son of Thomas Marion and Amy Minerva Smith, was born in Harrison County, West Virginia, April 8, 1868; was educated in the elementary branches in the local schools of his native county. Later, he graduated from the West Virginia University in the class of 1889. Subsequently he took a course in law at Washington and Lee University, Lexington, Virginia, receiving the degree of Bachelor of Laws in 1892. He returned to Clarksburg, the seat of justice of his native county, and was admitted to practice that year. He is the senior member of the firm of Smith and Jackson, a well-established and successful law firm of that flourishing city. Although he is yet comparatively a young man, his status as a lawyer is firmly fixed, as he ranks among the foremost lawyers of that historic Bar. He is, in his political affiliations, a Democrat, but never took an active part in politics. The only office he ever aspired to was to be a candidate for membership on the Supreme Court of Appeals of West Virginia in 1912, when he went down to defeat along with all the candidates of his party. He, however, received a larger vote than any other candidate on his party ticket, which showed that he was not short of popular support.

His diligence, energy and fidelity to the interests of his clients soon won deserved success and remunerative pecuniary rewards. Being thoroughly educated in the fundamental principles of the law, he prepares his cases with care, and in all court trials he is self-poised, forceful and effective. His prominent characteristics are a strong will, sound judgment, a keen knowledge of human nature, rigid devotion to what he believes to be right

HON. E. G. SMITH

and an integrity of character that cannot be attacked nor shaken. He is always careful and thoughtful in giving his opinions on questions of law before advising the bringing of a law suit. His custom, therefore, was not to practice his profession merely "for revenue only," but rather that justice should prevail in every court trial in which he engages. Distinguished in appearance, tall of stature, dignified, graceful, affable in manner, he is withal modest and unassuming, with ready sympathies and a cultured taste, and at all times shows marked legal attainments. Better than all, he is a man of upright and blameles personal character. In all relations, in his family, at the Bar, in his friendships and in the community where he resides, he is loyal, true and considerate. No one questions his ability to have made an able and satisfactory Appellate Court Judge, had he been chosen to fill that high position by the voters of the State.

He was elected in 1913 President of the West Virginia University Alumni Association, and was thrice consecutively re-elected to that position. He is a member of the Masonic Fraternity, is an Elk and a Woodman of the World, and a member of the Greek Letter Fraternity of *Phi Delta Theta*. He is the author of several able magazine articles, notably "Power Dams in Public Rivers," "Our Judiciary," "Needs of the West Virginia University," "The Plutocrat," etc. He was an attorney in the hydro-electric litigation in the courts of this State, in which he made an enviable record.

Mr. Smith is married, has two children, and is happy and contented in his home life. Among his friends he is always social, joyous and happy. No taint of any kind ever rested upon his private life, which is the crowning glory of any man's career.

## Walling Wallenson Van Winkle

Our subject, one of the nestors of the Wood County Bar, son of Adolph and Petina Van Winkle, of Lodi, New Jersey, was born in that town November 17, 1845. He received his primary education in the public schools of Jersey City, New Jersey, and later he attended the University of New York, where he was trained in the higher branches and also in law. Having relatives at Parkersburg, West Virginia, he migrated thither, and was admitted to the Wood County Bar, December 11, 1866. He soon opened a law office in that city, where he has continued to reside until the present, and has practiced in all the courts of WestVirginia, both State and Federal. He has also assisted in the trial of important cases in the Federal Courts of Maryland, Virginia and Illinois. At a Bar which counted among its members many men of distinction and more than ordinary ability, he early achieved success and became known as a skillful trier and manager of causes, a convincing advocate and a wise and conscientious counselor.

In him is united a keen sense of right and love of justice, a thorough knowledge of legal principles and a power of discrimination which make them easy of application. He has an acute, broad and penetrating mind,

W. W. VAN WINKLE

which cause him to be sought after as an attorney. Calm, dignified in manner, modest, but courageous in the expression of opinion, clean and pure of life, the soul of honor and integrity, the character of the man and his reputation for candor, uprightness and fairness, give to him, with court and jury, a power and influence which justly supplemented that produced by his learning and clean-cut presentation of the law and the facts. He is thorough in the preparation of his cases, has an accurate knowledge of all the details of pleading and practice and a coolness and imperturbability never shaken under circumstances the most adverse. He has not the gift of oratory, in the popular sense; he seeks to convince, not inflame or befog, but to cause others to see the points he is making as clearly as he, himself, sees them. Shortly after locating in Parkersburg he formed a partnership with B. Mason Ambler, an eminent lawyer of that city, which still exists and has a State-wide reputation, covering nearly a half century of time.

Mr. Van Winkle married Miss Hannah Cook, of Parkersburg, October 26, 1868. They have one child — a daughter. He is a Republican in politics, but never sought or held a public office. He is a lawyer *per se*. He is very prominent in all the branches of Freemasonry in the State and has ably filled many high offices in that great Fraternity. He is highly esteemed as a citizen by the people in the city where he has spent his professional life.

## Millard F. Snider, LL.B.

Among the high standing lawyers of the justly recognized high standard Clarksburg Bar, the subject of this sketch must be recognized. He is the son of Jehu and Virginia (Apsy) Snider and was born in Doddridge County, Virginia, September 24, 1860; was reared on a farm and inured to hard labor until he grew to manhood. It was by hard work, early and late, that young Snider had instilled into him the principle that best results are derived from diligent application and honest toil. This experience gave him a strong, and indeed, robust, physique, which has served him well all through life. He started out when a mere boy determined, somehow, to secure a thorough education, and although he never graduated from a college except in law, yet by the aid of the public schools and constant application to books, when he became twenty years of age, he was prepared to teach school, which he did for six years. While engaged in teaching every spare hour was given to systematic reading and study and the development of his mind, and it may be stated, therefore, that his education is equal to a regular college training, and in some respects superior. He went through the Junior year of the State Normal School at Fairmont, but did not complete the full course. He then read law under the direction of John Bassel, an able lawyer at Clarksburg, for a short time; he later matriculated as a student at the West Virginia University at Morgantown, where he took a complete law course, adding to it some important studies of the academic department, and graduating LL.B. in the class of 1887.

MILLARD F. SNIDER

After leaving college he located at West Union, the county seat of Doddridge County, opened a law office, and contrary to most young lawyers, he had a profitable clientele from the start. Although doing well in West Union, he saw the necessity of getting into a wider field of labor, presenting greater opportunities, so he decided to locate at Clarksburg, Harrison County, the commercial center of that prosperous section of the State, and he accordingly moved his residence and office to that city in the spring of 1898, where he still resides and is known and recognized as among the leading lawyers of that able Bar. His practice is general and extends into all the State and Federal Courts of West Virginia, the United States Appellate Court of the Fourth Judicial Circuit and the Supreme Court of the United States. He is unusually successful in the trial of his causes, especially in the Appellate Courts, as the records may be relied on to show that he, perhaps, never lost a single cause that he actually deserved to win. His rank, therefore, as a trial lawyer is very good. He is genial, companionable and eminently honorable in every respect. His business expands as the years go by. He is thoroughly grounded in the principles of the law, and in his office work and counsel he is careful and painstaking, in order that he may make fewer mistakes that might cause his clients trouble or loss by unconsidered advice. As an advocate he is resourceful, logical and forceful. Whilst he is a pronounced Democrat, he has never been a candidate for any office of a political character; twice, however, he was a candidate for Prosecuting Attorney of the two counties in which he has resided, which offices were strictly in the line of his profession, but was defeated along with all the other candidates upon the ticket, his party being in the minority in both of those counties. One of his leading desires has ever been to become an eminent lawyer, which he could never expect if he became a politician *per se*. Hence he stuck closely to his law office and used his time and energies with that end in view. The results show that in this he made no mistake. He is also a man of affairs, and devotes his spare time to the development of the community in which he lives. He is a factor and also a stockholder in several leading business enterprises in his adopted county of Harrison, and takes a vigorous hand in the development of the resources of that section of the State.

October 4, 1892, he was united in marriage with Miss Elizabeth Stuart, of Doddridge County, daughter of the late Judge C. J. Stuart, who, in his day was one of the most eminent lawyers and jurists of that part of West Virginia. They have one child — Virginia Ann — a classical graduate of Goucher Female College, Baltimore, Maryland, one of the highest grade female colleges of the entire country. Their home life is of the ideal sort on ''Quality Hill'' in the city of Clarksburg, where they are surrounded by hosts of admiring friends.

Mr. Snider is an active and useful member of the Methodist Episcopal Church, and is also a member of the West Virginia Bar Association and rarely misses a session. He is simple in his habits, admires plain and unpretentious people and has a specially high reagrd for those that are willing to do honest work in the world. He is one of the few men who never used intoxicating liquors or tobacco in any form at any period of his life. May we here add that he in this respect stands as a sentinel, almost solitary and alone, among the legal fraternity in this, or any other, country? May we further add that these virtues were harder to achieve than to be able to stand upon the top rungs of the legal ladder in any city or State?

## William Erskine, B.S., LL.B.

Our subject has long been classed among the leading lawyers of the Ohio County, West Virginia, Bar. He is a native of Washington County, Pennsylvania, is a son of Robert C. and Nancy B. Erskine, and was born March 18, 1845. He was graduated from Westminister College, New Wilmington, Pennsylvania, in 1868, with the degree of Bachelor of Science; and in 1870 he graduated in law from Albany Law School, Albany, New York, with the degree of Bachelor of Laws. The year of his graduation he was admitted to the Bar at Albany, but having decided to locate permanently for the practice of his profession in the city of Wheeling, West Virginia, he was admitted to the Bar of that city in June, 1870, and has there practiced, without intermission, until the present time. He is Lincolnian in appearance, is more than six feet tall, is erect, rather angular in build and is physically powerful, and possesses unusual powers of endurance and tenacity. He is high-minded, moral, clear-headed and has an abundance of practical, common sense. He is also a quiet, unassuming man and an industrious, well-grounded and efficient lawyer. His record as an attorney is without a blemish, and is worthy of emulation by any lawyer anywhere, in this or any other State. He is as tall in character as he is in inches and stands four-square before all men, and always has done so, since his location in Wheeling, nearly a half century ago.

Mr. Erskine has always been a Republican, but never sought a political office. The only office he ever held was City Solicitor of Wheeling, which he ably filled for two terms. Whilst thus serving he discovered an embezzlement by the City Collector, which resulted in a lengthy investigation, a law-suit and the recovery of $14,000. He practices in the West Virginia Courts and the United States Courts in West Virginia. He was a partner of Hon. William P. Hubbard, who is mentioned in another part of this volume, for two years, from 1875 to 1877, inclusive, and with the late Benjamin S. Allison for thirty-five years, under the firm name of Erskine and Allison. His present law firm is Erskine, Palmer and Curl. The junior member of the firm is, at this time, a Lieutenant in the United States Signal Service in France in the World War against the Germans and Huns.

Mr. Erskine was twice married. First, to Celeste S. Chase, in February, 1872, by whom he had four children, and second, to Miss Elizabeth Clohan, in 1902, both of whom were ladies of estimable character and highly respected by the citizens of Wheeling. In religious convictions he is a Presbyterian, and his influence is always on the side of good morals and honest government. He has never shown any tendency to sympathize with any movement that lowers instead of elevates the people. He is always affable and courteous in his manner, is a fair speaker, a close debater and stands high among his brothers of the profession.

## Edward Wallace Knight, A.M.

Our subject, the son of Edward B. and Hannah Elizabeth Knight, was born at Charleston, West Virginia, April 30, 1866; received his primary education in the public schools of Charleston; later entered Dartmouth College and graduated in the class of 1887 with the degree of Bachelor of Arts. He returned to Charleston and began to study law under the tutelage of his father, who was one of the leading attorneys of Kanawha County. After thoroughly familiarizing himself with legal principles laid down in the textbooks he passed a creditable examination and was admitted as a member of the Kanawha Bar in May, 1889, where he has practiced, without intermission, in all the State and United States Courts to the present time. In January, 1892, he became a member of the well-known and able law firm of Brown and Jackson, constituting the firm then as now of Brown, Jackson and Knight. The present members of the firm, in addition to those mentioned, are V. L. Black, John Wehrle, Angus W. McDonald, George S. Couch, Jr., and Oscar P. Fitzgerald, Jr. Whilst Mr. Knight is well posted in all branches of the law, he has specialized in corporation practice, in which he has become unusually familiar and successful. He has been general counsel of the Deepwater, Tidewater and Virginia Railways since 1892. He has but little taste for politics and has sought no political office. The only public position he ever held was a member of the Common Council of the city of Charleston from 1891 to '94, inclusive, but has held no other public office. His affiliations have always been with the Democratic party, but in no sense can he be classed as a pronounced partisan. He is a public spirited, progressive citizen and is a leader in the development and growth of the community in which he resides. His career, both as lawyer and citizen, has been able and exemplary. No stain of dishonor has ever been attached to his name. In physique and appearance he is almost the exact image of his distinguished father. Although he is stern in the maintenance of that which he believes to be right, and in the dictates of duty, his moderation is not less marked than his integrity. Whilst he is a man of earnest and intense convictions, his actions and expressions are always tempered with mildness and discretion. Consequently he is respected and esteemed by the members of the profession and also by the laymen with whom he transacts business. In the preparation of his cases he is profound, laborious, methodical and exact and is always well armed with precedent and authorities. In the trial of his cases he is, therefore, rarely

EDWARD W. KNIGHT

caught on any point unawares. This, doubtless, is largely the secret of his success.

January 25, 1893, Mr. Knight was united in marriage with Miss Catherine, daughter of Col. J. E. Dana, of Charleston. They have three children — one son and two daughters. Mr. Knight is a member of the Masonic Fraternity, and in his religious convictions is a Presbyterian. He is a forward-thinking man, broad and liberal in his views and thoroughly democratic in spirit. Although of a positive nature, he disagrees with his opponents without rancor. His home life is of the pleasantest character, and he enjoys associations with his friends. He is an upright citizen, keenly interested in the social welfare of the people.

## Col. George Selden Wallace, LL.B.

George S. Wallace, one of the best known attorneys of the Huntington, West Virginia, Bar, son of Charles Irving and Maria L. (Schlater) Wallace, was born at Greenwood, Virginia, September 6, 1871, and was educated in the public and private schools of his native section and later graduated from the Law Department of the West Virginia University, with a LL.B. diploma, in 1897. In June of that year he was admitted to practice in the local courts of Cabell County, and since that time he has engaged in continuous practice in all the State courts and Federal courts as well. He has, by close application to his work, managed to build up a lucrative legal business, and is acknowledged to be among the leading lawyers in the southern section of West Virginia. He is extremely courteous, is industrious and energetic and has the confidence of all the people with whom he associates. He is a safe and sane counselor and is genuinely upright and honorable in all his dealings as a lawyer and a citizen. Such an one will always have hosts of friends and followers in all of his private and public undertakings.

He has always been in politics a consistent Democrat, and the only political office he ever aspired to was that of Prosecuting Attorney of Cabell County, to which position he was elected by the people in 1904, which office he filled with great acceptability for the full term of four years.

Mr. Wallace was commissioned a Lieutenant in a company of the Second West Virginia regiment of United States volunteer soldiers, in 1898, in the Spanish-American War, and remained in that service until the close of hostilities, proving himself to be a high grade soldier and patriot. At the close of the short and decisive war with Spain he became a valuable officer in the National Guard of West Virginia, attaining to the rank of Lieutenant-Colonel, and was Acting Judge Advocate General of the military forces of the State during the pendency of the long strike of the coal miners in the southern portion of West Virginia, during the administration of Governor Glasscock.

COLONEL GEORGE S. WALLACE

Since the declaration of war between the United States and the Imperial Government of Germany, Colonel Wallace had charge of the enlistment of troops in West Virginia for the United States Army, under the recent Military Act of Congress, and has recently been assigned to active duty in the field in the office of Judge Advocate General of the United States Army, with the rank of Lieutenant-Colonel of Volunteers, a position he is admirably qualified to fill and is filling to the entire satisfaction of the War Department in the present war with the German Empire.

Colonel Wallace was united in marriage with Miss Frances B. Gibson, of Huntington. They have been blessed with five children as the result of this happy union.

## Hon. Eskridge H. Morton

Mr. Morton is one of the prominent members of the profession in the central portion of West Virginia and has been one of the successful practitioners of the Webster County Bar for a score or more years. He was born in Webster County June 18, 1866, and was educated in the common schools and at the West Virginia University, where he received his legal training and fitted himself for the practice of the law. His practice has extended into all the surrounding counties. He was licensed to practice shortly after graduating from the University, and has steadily grown into leadership among the strong attorneys of his section. He is a Democrat and has a strong liking for the political arena, in which he occupies a front rank in the entire State. He is, therefore, a success in both the law and in politics. He possesses many natural gifts, which have greatly aided him in both callings. He has also been square and upright in his dealings with his clients and the people generally, and has built up a reputation for probity and uprightness which have served him well in all of his undertakings.

His first political office was County Superintendent of Public Schools of his native county, which he filled satisfactorily from 1889 to 1891 inclusive. He was next Prosecuting Attorney of Webster County, from 1893 to 1897, in which he proved his ability and efficiency as a prosecutor. He was Assistant Prosecuting Attorney of the adjoining county of Nicholas for four years, from 1887 to 1901; was elected Sergeant-at-Arms of the lower branch of the West Virginia Legislature in 1903–4; was the candidate of his party for Attorney-General of the State in 1908 and was defeated with the other candidates of his party that year; was a Delegate to the National Democratic Convention in 1912; was elected a State Senator in 1916, where he is now serving with both tact and ability. He is a superior public speaker and debater, and is one of the leaders of his party on the floor of the Senate and takes a leading part in all of the discussions that come before that law-making body.

He is married and is rearing an interesting family. He resides at Webster Springs, the seat of justice of his native county, one of the best known summer resorts of West Virginia. He claims that it is one of the healthiest mineral springs in the United States, if not, indeed, in the entire world, and we surmise that his claims are well founded.

He is also deeply interested in the development and civic growth of his native county and the State at large. He is a tall, sun-crowned man and is full of energy and enterprise, and has won the confidence and respect of the people generally.

## Hon. William Alexander MacCorkle, LL.B., LL.D.

The subject of this brief sketch descended from a sturdy Scotch stock who settled in Virginia about the year 1730, being the son of William and Mary Morrison MacCorkle, of Rockbridge County, Virginia. He was born in that county, May 7, 1857, and was educated in the schools of that locality, and later matriculated as a student at Washington and Lee University, from which well-known institution he graduated as a Bachelor of Laws in the class of 1879. Shortly thereafter he came to West Virginia and located at Charleston, and entered upon the practice of his profession with that degree of vigor and determination peculiar to him since arriving at manhood, which has extended through his entire career and accounts for the success that has attended his efforts. When he was a very young man his parents moved to Missouri, where they remained but a few years, and returned to their former home in Virginia, so that practically the entire life of our subject has been spent in the two Virginias.

When he first came to Kanawha he had pretty rough sledding, but it was not long until business began to come his way, and he made himself known to the people of that section as a young attorney of ability and unusual force of character; consequently his practice rapidly broadened most satisfactorily.

Having a natural taste for politics, he did not hesitate to take a hand in public affairs. His first office was that of City Solicitor of Charleston, and he made a good one. His next public office was that of Governor, to which he was elected as a Democrat, and in that exalted position he introduced progressive ideas into State affairs which had not hitherto apparently been even thought of, and being a natural developer the State began to wake up and take on new life as it never had done before. His record as Governor can be pointed to with pride as showing wisdom, honesty and public efficiency. His leading purpose was to develop the great natural resources of the State, and no one can say that he did not labor early and late to accomplish this laudable and meritorious undertaking. In short, he made an excellent and able Chief Executive.

Governor MacCorkle was a member of the State Senate of West Virginia after his retirement as Governor, and his ability and aggressive earnestness made him one of the most influential members of that distinguished body of law makers. He is a member of the prominent and able law firm of

Chilton, MacCorkle and Chilton, which carries a vast and varied law business at the capital of the State and is a well-known law firm over the entire Commonwealth, and has a reputation beyond the limits of the State for ability, efficiency and integrity.

Governor MacCorkle, however, is not known as a lawyer only; he carries on vast business enterprises also. He is president of a bank and is an active member and stockholder of several large developing enterprises in the Kanawha Valley. It is, therefore, only fair to class him among the State's foremost developers.

He is a man of unusual physical strength, as well as mental faculties. He is a forceful speaker, and possesses literary attainments of a high order, being the author of several books of decided merit.

He married Miss Belle, daughter of William F. Goshorn, of Charleston, and has one son, William G. MacCorkle, who is a promising member of his father's law firm, and one daughter, Miss Isabelle, who resides with her father and mother at their palatial residence, on the south side of the Kanawha River, which overlooks, with a splendid view, the thriving city of Charleston.

Governor MacCorkle is a member of the Presbyterian Church, and is a Freemason of high rank. In recongition of his ability and scholarship, his *alma mater* conferred upon him the honorary degree of Doctor or Laws, a few years ago, an honor properly and worthily bestowed. He was the successful State manager of the five National Liberty Loans.

## Hon. Malcolm Jackson, LL.B.

Our subject is a member of the able and well-known law firm of Brown, Jackson and Knight, of the city of Charleston, which was organized more than thirty years ago and has more than a State-wide reputation in all of the varied branches of the profession. He is the son of Richard and Anna M. Jackson, of Richmond, Indiana, where he was born March 21, 1860. He attended the public schools of that city; later entered Earlham College, Indiana, and still later was an *alumnus* of the Naval Academy, Annapolis, Maryland. Having decided to enter the legal profession, he matriculated in the Law Department of the University of Virginia, and graduated therefrom in the class of 1881 with the degree of Bachelor of Laws. The following year he located in Charleston, this State, becoming a member of the law firm of Brown, Jackson and Knight, as stated above, where he has since practiced. In addition to the three principal partners already named, the following junior associates are connected with the firm: V. L. Black, John Wehrle, A. W. McDonald, George S. Couch, Jr., and O. P. Fitzgerald. Their offices occupy one entire floor of the large Kanawha Valley Bank building. Their practice includes all the branches of the law and extends into all the courts of the State and Federal Governments, from Justices of the Peace to the Supreme Court of the United States.

HON. MALCOLN JACKSON

Mr. Jackson is a man of large stature, is of commanding personality, is high-minded, moral, clear-headed and possesses a large supply of practical common sense. He has dignified the profession by exhibiting in the practice the highest type of integrity, fidelity, learning and wisdom. He thoroughly masters his cases and is particularly able in courthouse trials, rarely allowing himself to be surprised over any question that may arise or be thrust upon him. He throws his strong personality into the conduct of his causes, fears no antagonist and is never unfaithful to a client. As an advocate he is gifted with strong logical powers and a faculty of expression remarkably lucid and convincing. His proper rank is among the high grade lawyers of the State. He is proud of his profession and ambitious to excel in it. He is a warm-hearted man, a faithful friend and a generous foe. He is never impulsive, carries himself deliberately, and when he reaches a conclusion he adheres to it tenaciously. Firmness of purpose and unswerving integrity are his chief characteristics, and at all times he carries with him the confidence and respect of his fellows.

Mr. Jackson is a Republican, but never held but one political office — member of the State Legislature in 1901–2 from Kanawha County, wherein he was unusually efficient. He married Miss Louise Fontaine Broun, of Charleston, in 1891, by whom he had two children, a son and a daughter; his wife departed this life during the summer of 1917. He is a member of all the branches of the Masonic Fraternity and is a communicant of the Protestant Episcopal Church. During Governor Atkinson's administration he was the law officer of the State National Guard, with the rank of Brigadier-General on the Governor's personal staff.

## Albert Worth Reynolds

Mr. Reynolds was born in Virginia, June 25, 1856, and came to West Virginia with his parents in childhood and has been a resident of the State ever since. He is a son of Silas T. Reynolds and Araminta Walker Reynolds, now deceased. He attended public and private schools and finished his academic education at the West Virginia Concord State Normal School, and thereafter studied law in a law office and was admitted to the practice of law after passing the Bar examination in the year 1879. Though never having had a college or university degree conferred upon him, Mr. Reynolds is a man of broad information and splendid educational attainments. He has never held a county, State or Federal office and has never been an aspirant for office, although his name has been favorably mentioned by the press in connection with the judiciary, and especially for appointment as United States Judge for the Fourth Circuit; but he declined to allow his name to be presented for that position, preferring to continue in the practice of law. He has been recognized for many years as one of the best lawyers in the State and has had a law practice perhaps second to none in either

A. W. REYNOLDS

of the Virginias. He has appeared as counsel in many cases of local importance, a number of them involving property of the value of millions of dollars; and the decisions of the courts in his cases have established precedents that have settled many important questions, especially of the land laws of the State, in which he has specialized.

Mr. Reynolds married Miss Rhoda Haynes, a daughter of Col. William D. Haynes, a prominent lawyer of East Tennessee, by whom he has five sons and one daughter. Albert Worth Reynolds, Jr., the fourth son, is a graduate of Georgetown University and a lawyer.

Mr. Reynolds' second wife was Miss Edmonia Slaven, of Virginia, by whom he has no children.

One of Mr. Reynolds' most admirable traits of character is his courteous bearing and treatment of the courts and opposing members of the Bar, and especially his courtesies toward the younger members of the Bar.

At Princeton, where he resides, he has been a potent factor in the development of the industries and business interests of the southern part of the State, and although he has devoted his time mostly to the practice of law, he has accumulated a considerable estate and is interested in coal mining, banking, grazing cattle and other business enterprises.

## Hon. Edgar Parks Rucker, LL.B.

Mr. Rucker was born at Covington, Virginia, December 23, 1861, and died April 20, 1908, in Washington, D. C., where he had gone for medical treatment from his home in Welch, McDowell County, West Virginia. He was the youngest son of Dr. William P. and Margaret Rucker. At an early age he moved with his parents to Lewisburg, Greenbrier County, West Virginia, where he spent his youth and attended school at the Lewisburg Academy. In 1887 he received the degree of LL.B. from the West Virginia University and at once began the practice of law in partnership with his father at Lewisburg. A year later he moved to Princeton, Mercer County, where he practiced law for three years. When the county seat of McDowell County was established at Welch in 1892, Mr. Rucker located there, where he practiced law until the time of his death. He had as law partners at one time or another Benjamin F. Keller, James L. Hamil, Luther C. Anderson, William W. Hughes and Daniel J. F. Strother.

In 1896 Mr. Rucker was elected Attorney-General of the State of West Virginia and served with distinction the full term of four years. In this office he served with ability and distinction.

A Republican in politics, he was ever active in public affairs and was frequently honored by his party and by his fellow citizens.

He was an active member of the Methodist Episcopal Church, South, and was a Delegate to the General Conference of 1902.

General Rucker was an unusually brilliant and successful lawyer. Always intensely active, wholly devoted to the interests of his clients, ever resourceful, particularly in an emergency, a fine orator, a born leader of men, he was a good lawyer and a splendid gentleman.

He married Miss Maude Applegate, of Missouri, and his widow and their daughter, Margaret, now live in Cincinnati, Ohio.

## Hon. William Taylor George

The subject of this sketch, the son of John R. and Gay (Taylor) George, was born in the town of Belington, Barbour County, West Virginia, October 3, 1869. Although his opportunities for schooling were somewhat meager, he is far from being without education. For years he attended the public schools of his home section, where by close application to textbooks and a set purpose to procure a safe and solid foundation upon which to erect a fabric in the future, by a systematic course of reading and study that in some respects would answer as a substitute for the average college course. In this manner, by adhering to the plan he adopted in early life of reading and study reduced to system, and allowing none of his time to be wasted, he became master of a clear, terse and vigorous style, both in writing and in speaking, for which he became noted in his mature years.

He read law, not in a law college; he read the textbooks at home by his own fireside, where he read other books, in order to understand and digest and absorb their contents and their meaning. When he finished Blackstone, or Kent, or Stephen on Pleading, or Parsons on Contracts, or any other textbook for that matter, he knew what the authors were talking about, and consequently was able to pass a creditable examination for admission to the Bar. In the retreat of the rural sections, where the first lessons learned alike by members of both sexes is that of independence and self-reliance and where one straightway resists any one's interference with one's private affairs and belongings, there we find the basis of substantial and enduring character. He was admitted as a member of the Barbour County Bar in 1896, where he has since practiced with pronounced success. His practice is general and extends to all the courts of West Virginia, both State and Federal. He is an upright man, is careful and thoughtful giving his opinions to clients on questions of law and in his many years of successful practice he has demeaned himself as upright and trustworthy. He is also a careful pleader and a hard worker. He worked his way success, and better than all, he made his own way through life. He is absolutely self-made, and he made a good job of it.

He is a staunch Republican, but was never domineering nor "bossy." He was elected Prosecuting Attorney of Barbour County in 1900 and served four years faithfully. In 1912 he was elected to the West Virginia Legislature and was chosen Speaker of the House of Delegates during the session of 1913. In this exalted position he was able, just and universally fair in all of his rulings and decisions.

Mr. George married Miss Dara Howell, December 12, 1892. They have six children — five daughters, four of whom are living, and one son. He is a member of the Methodist Episcopal Church and the Orders of Elks and Knights of Pythias. He has recently added to his law business that of coal mining as a side issue. His home is at Philippi, the seat of justice of Barbour County, where he has a large circle of friends and admirers. He is a public spirited citizen and is active in the development of the resources of his county and State, and is frequently referred to in connection with higher honors at the hands of the voters of the State. He was a candidate in 1918 for a seat in the American Congress, but was defeated for the nomination in a primary election.

## Hon. Adam B. Littlepage

Mr. Littlepage was born in Charleston, April 14, 1859. His father, Adam Littlepage, for whom he was named, was a successful business man of prominence in his day and lost his life in the Civil War of 1861–5. Young Adam, from early boyhood, determined to become a lawyer of distinction, and his honorable ambition never waned until he reached the goal of his early desires. He is entitled to great credit for his success in life, because he had to open up the way by his own study, perseverance and untiring efforts. Nothing seemed to daunt him as he toiled, early and late, to make his life-work a success. To secure an education was his greatest drawback, because the means of a college education, which he deemed essential, were not at his command; but what he lacked in opportunity he made up in application, and received from the public schools of his native county the best they could offer. He subsequently added thereto information gathered from wide courses of systematic reading and study, which, coupled with an observing mind, and that knowledge which comes from experience, he pieced out a substantial education.

He took up the study of the law in Indiana, while a farm hand and superintendent, mastering textbooks, and after a few years of faithful toil was admitted to the Bar of that State. Shortly thereafter he returned to Charleston, opened an office and though clients came a little slow for a while, that faith in himself, which has always been one of his best assets, caused him "to stay on the job" until he had all the business he could attend to. He was not long in building up a reputation as one of the most successful and forceful lawyers of the Charleston Bar. He is one of the best illustrations of what grit and self-reliance will do for any young man who seeks to get on in life that the writer has thus far known.

Mr. Littlepage has always been a sterling Democrat, and has, in a number of campaigns, demonstrated his popularity before the people. In fact, he has never failed to receive many more votes than his party strength.

HON. ADAM B. LITTLEPAGE

He was four years a member of the State Senate, and is now serving his third term in Congress, although the district is largely Republican. The State being Republican, he was at one time defeated for the nomination for Governor. It is well understood among his party opponents that when Mr. Littlepage is a candidate against them they are almost sure of defeat, unless they have a big, round majority on their side of the political ledger. Mr. Littlepage, when his time allows it from his Congressional duties, to which he is always faithful, is still engaged in the practice of his profession along with his son Collett. The firm is conducting a successful and profitable law business in Charleston. He maintains a palatial residence at the western limit of the city and within sight of the spot where he was born. He always does his best in private and in public life.

## Hon. John Jacob Cornwell

Governor Cornwell, the fifteenth Governor of West Virginia, son of Jacob H. and Mary E. (Taylor) Cornwell, was born July 11, 1867, on a farm near Pennsboro, Ritchie County, West Virginia. His father moved, with his family, to Hampshire County, in the South Branch Valley in 1870, where his son, the future Governor of the State, was reared to manhood on a Hampshire County farm. He attended the public schools of that locality. Later he entered Shepherd College at Shepherdstown, Jefferson County, and remained there until he had received sufficient education to equip him for a public school teacher, and at the age of sixteen he received a teacher's certificate from the County Superintendent of Public Schools, which profession he followed for seven years. During this period he was principal of the graded schools of Romney, the seat of justice of Hampshire County. In the fall of 1890, with his brother, W. B. Cornwell, he bought the Hampshire Review, published at Romney, and has been the editor of that publication — the single newspaper published in Hampshire County — for a period of over twenty-five years, retiring as the active editor when he was sworn in as Governor of West Virginia. In connection with his newspaper work he studied law in the offices of his brother and was admitted to practice in 1894. He had a legal mind, and was, therefore, not long in impressing himself upon the community as one who would reach high standing as a member of the legal profession. He possessed a strong intellect and was gifted as a speaker. His mind was naturally analytical, and he could then, as now, state a legal proposition with unusual clearness and force. Had he devoted all of his time and energies to the profession he would easily have reached a high rank as a lawyer. As it is, he is far above the average of our West Virginia attorneys. He is conservative, deliberate and unusually clear in the preparation and presentation of his cases. Like the great Lincoln, he does not practice law for "revenue only," but rather that justice between man and man should be fairly administered by courts of law throughout the entire country. His purpose

HON JOHN J. CORNWELL

has always been to be fair to his clients and with the courts as well. He is pleasant in demeanor and is always courteous and fair with opposing counsel. He is an able advocate and never fails to make a strong impression upon both court and jury. He is honorable and upright in all of his dealings and has the confidence of all the people who have the pleasure of his acquaintance. He is a developer as well as a lawyer, and has been largely instrumental in the development of his section of the State. It was through his efforts that the railroad was constructed from Romney to Moorefield, tapping a rich territory and permitting development. He has been active for many years in the development of his section as a commercial fruit-growing country.

In 1896 Governor Cornwell made his entry into politics and was elected a delegate to the Democratic National Convention held at Chicago when William Jennings Bryan was nominated the first time for the Presidency. In 1898 he was elected to the State Senate from the Twelfth Senatorial District, which was composed of the counties of Hampshire, Hardy, Mineral, Grant, Pendleton and Tucker. In 1902 he was re-elected to the State Senate from the Fifteenth Senatorial District, the Legislature having re-districted the State, increasing the number of senatorial districts from thirteen to fifteen. While serving a second term as a member of the State Senate he was nominated by the Democratic party in State Convention at Parkersburg for Governor of West Virginia. In the campaign that followed he ran 25,000 votes ahead of his ticket, being defeated by 8,000 majority by the late Governor W. M. O. Dawson, when Theodore Roosevelt carried the State by 33,000 majority.

In 1912 Governor Cornwell was elected a Delegate to the Democratic National Convention at Baltimore and four years later was nominated in a general primary election to be the Democratic candidate for Governor of West Virginia. The vote in the 1916 election showed Governor Cornwell to have been the sole Democrat on the State ticket to be elected.

He was married in 1891 to Miss Edna Brady and they have one surviving child, Mrs. Eugene E. Ailes, of Washington, D. C.

Since his inauguration as Governor, March 4, 1917, Governor Cornwell called the State Legislature into extraordinary session May 14, 1917, and that body responded to his wishes in submitting to a vote of the people a constitutional amendment proposing a budget system, designed to place a check on ruthless expenditures from the State Treasury. The Legislature also enacted a number of war measures through the operation of which Governor Cornwell has been desirous of assisting the Federal Government in the prosecution of the war with Germany. He has been the "war Governor" in fact as well as in name, devoting his energies to the arousing of the people of the State to the causes which impelled America to enter the war against the Imperial Government of Germany. He has been a foremost figure in the Liberty Loans, Red Cross, Y. M. C. A. and other campaigns through which funds have been and are being raised to diligently and successfully prosecute the war.

## Harvey F. Smith, B.A., LL.B.

Our subject belongs in a class of successful, high grade lawyers of Central West Virginia, who have not only honored the Bar of that particular section, but of the entire State as well. He was born and reared on a farm on Big Buffalo Creek, Harrison County, West Virginia. He attended the public schools of his native county, and being an earnest and apt student, when not quite sixteen years of age, he had made sufficient advancement to obtain a No. 1 certificate, so he taught for two years in the public schools to secure funds to enable him to procure a college education. He accordingly entered the West Virginia University in 1892 and graduated B.A. in 1896. He then matriculated as a student of law in the Columbian University at Washington, D. C., and graduated in 1897 with the degree of Bachelor of Laws. He maintained a high rank in all of his classes in both of the universities he attended. While a student at the West Virginia University he was editor of the college paper published by the students, which is always regarded as a high honor among college students at all colleges and universities. He located at the City of Clarksburg and was admitted as a member of that able Bar September 10, 1897, where he has since unremittingly practiced with marked success.

In politics he is a Democrat, but in no sense can he be classed a politician. He was never a candidate for any political office, nor has he ever revealed any desires in that direction. His only ambition has been to make himself an able member of the legal profession. He has been admitted to all the courts, State and Federal, including the Supreme Court of the United States, and has practiced mostly in Harrison County, but his practice in special cases has extended to some ten to twelve counties in Central West Virginia. He began the practice of law with no means and borrowed money to sustain himself for a few months. He has by economical methods and close application acquired a fair competence. His diligence, energy, learning and fidelity to the interests of his clients won deserved success and remunerative pecuniary rewards. He handles his cases skilfully and successfully, and is genial and companionable and is popular among his associates at the Bar, as well as with the people generally. He was born July 20, 1873, and has not yet fully reached his prime. He is thoroughly grounded in the law and loves his profession dearly, which accounts for the success he has already attained, and portend still higher attainments for him in the future.

In December, 1917, he volunteered, unconditionally, tendering his services to the President and Secretary of War in the present European world war, and asked to be sent to France. He has pushed his case in every conceivable proper way, but the War Department declines to call him into active service at the age of 44 years, 40 being the age limit at that time. He is not only a patriotic citizen, but he is public-spirited also, and takes a vigorous part in the development of his city, county and State.

He married Miss Anita Collins, daughter of the late Hon. Creed Collins, of Ritchie County, West Virginia, June 17, 1903. Three children — Collins Haymond, Rachel Adelia and Thomas Harvey Smith — are the result of this union. He is a member of the Protestant Episcopal Church, and is a Freemason, having taken all the degrees of Symbolic Masonry and thirty-two of the Scottish Rite branch. He is also a member of the Mystic Shrine. He is a forward-thinking man, broad and liberal in his views and thoroughly democratic in spirit. Although of a positive nature and disposition he disagrees with his opponents with modesty, and never with rancor or hate. He enjoys his home and the associations of his friends.

His college fraternity was the Phi Sigma Kappa, and he belongs to the Sons of the American Revolution. He has one of the most extensive law libraries in West Virginia, and makes good use of it.

## Colonel Forrest W. Brown

Our subject is the son of Thomas Augustus and Annie S. C. (Washington) Brown, and is one of the able and distinguished lawyers of the "Eastern Panhandle" counties of West Virginia. He was born near Charlestown, Jefferson County, Virginia, October 15, 1855. His education was received in private schools in Missouri, Philadelphia and Charlestown. Later he attended the Charlestown Academy, a well known, high grade institution of Jefferson County, wherein he rounded out, what was in those days, an average college education. After leaving the Academy he read law in the office of White and Trapnell, a long established law firm of the eastern section of West Virginia. After thoroughly mastering the fundamental principles of the law as laid down in the required text books, he passed a creditable examination before the Judges of the Supreme Court of Appeals of the State, and was admitted, when only twenty-one years of age, to practice his chosen profession in all the courts of West Virginia. He opened a law office at Charlestown and has there practiced, without intermission, to the present time. His practice is general and includes all of the State and Federal Courts.

Col. Brown is a man of fine presence, of good stature, strong features, forceful as an advocate, possesses a logical mind, pleasant and agreeable in demeanor, and always makes a favorable impression upon courts and juries. In short he is an unusually successful trial lawyer. He is a close student, is well grounded in the fundamental principles of the law, and keeps abreast of the text books and court decisions. He is careful in the preparation of his cases, and is conscientious in advising his clients. He is a man of high personal character and has the confidence of all the people who know him personally. By upright living and fair dealing he has accumulated a large and profitable clientele, and has attained a high rank in the profession, not only in his section, but generally throughout

FORREST W. BROWN

the State. He is counsel for a large number of local corporations, and is thoroughly posted in corporation laws, to which he gives careful attention.

He was elected on the Democratic ticket Prosecuting Attorney of Jefferson County in 1885, and was thrice re-elected to the same office, making sixteen years of service in that capacity. This unusual term of service is positive proof of his superior qualifications as a prosecutor of violators of State statutes, and of his fairness in the discharge of his official duties. But few men in any State have been elected by the people to four consecutive terms as a Public Prosecutor.

He was a Colonel on the staff of Governor W. A. MacCorkle during his four years' term, from 1892 to 1896.

Col. Brown is not only a prominent and successful lawyer, but he has taken a leading rank in the public affairs of his locality, and stands among its leading developers. He is also a member of the Protestant Episcopal Church and a prominent member of the Masonic Fraternity. He is a member of the West Virginia Bar Association, and was its President in 1895–'96. June 15, 1885, he married Miss Emma Beverly Tucker, a member of the well known Tucker family of Virginia. They have one son, Forrest Augustus Brown, who is engaged with his father in the practice of law at Charlestown, and is a promising member of the profession.

## Hon. William Ellsworth Glasscock

William E. Glasscock, son of Daniel and Prudence Glasscock, was born in Monongalia County, Virginia, December 13, 1862, on a farm near Arnettsville, and received his early training in the public schools while living on his father's farm. At the age of eighteen he went to Iowa, and spent four years attending school and in teaching. He returned to West Virginia and taught school at Arnettsville. While engaged in teaching at that place he was elected County Superintendent of Public Schools, and after serving a term as such he was re-elected. While serving his second term in that office he was elected Clerk of the Circuit Court of Monongalia County, and was re-elected, without opposition, six years later. When serving as Circuit Clerk he decided to become a lawyer, and began a course of study of the necessary text books, and pursued the same with determination and vigor. After his term as Clerk expired he entered the Law Department of the West Virginia University, and after completing the course of study therein required he was admitted to the Morgantown Bar in January, 1903, and opened a law office in that city. In 1907, however, he was appointed by President Roosevelt Collector of United States Internal Revenue for the State of West Virginia, which office he satisfactorily filled until the summer of 1908, when he resigned, having been nominated by the Republican party as a candidate for Governor of West Virginia, and in November of that year he was elected to the highest office in the gift of the voters of his native State, and served therein for the full term of four years.

He made a creditable record as Governor of his native State, maintaining the best traditions of his party, administering the duties of his high office in a conscientious manner and with an intellgent understanding of the needs of the hour and all questions affecting the public welfare, so as to command the respect even of his political opponents. He is a man of integrity and of absolute honesty of purpose, and is just and square in all of his dealings, both in private and in public life. He was a little late in entering upon the duties of a practicing lawyer, but his service as Clerk of the Circuit Court was of great value to him in the preparation of pleadings and of framing orders, decrees, etc., the value of such practice and experience cannot easily be measured. By this long court room experience and by close attention to his duties, Governor Glasscock commands a paying and indeed a very satisfactory clientage, which is rapidly increasing.

Governor Glasscock married Miss Mary Alice Miller, of Monongalia County, August 15, 1888, and has one son, William Ellsworth, Jr., who is a volunteer in the United States Army in the war with the German Empire. They reside in the City of Morgantown, the seat of justice of Monongalia County.

The Governor is a member of the Methodist Episcopal Church, is a Mason, an Odd Fellow and also a Knight of Pythias.

## Col. Guy D. Goff, B.A., M.A., LL.B.

Among the legal fraternity of West Virginia the name Goff is a familiar one. The subject of this brief sketch, a son of Judge Nathan and Laura E. Goff, was born in Clarksburg, West Virginia, September 13, 1867; received his primary education in the public schools of his native city; later he took the classical course of study prescribed at Kenyon Miliatry College at Gambier, Ohio, one of the old and thorough educational institutions of the "Buckeye State," graduating therefrom with the degree of Bachelor of Arts, and later receiving the higher degree of Master of Arts *in cursu*. He then entered Harvard University Law School, and after taking the full law course prescribed by its curriculum, graduated in the class of 1892, receiving its diploma as a Bachelor of Laws. Before returning to his West Virginia home in June of that year he was received as a member of the Boston Bar, and in the summer of 1892 he was received as a member of the Clarksburg, West Virginia Bar. After maturely considering the matter he deemed it best to locate in some Western city, so he stopped in Chicago for a short time and was admitted as an attorney in all the courts of that great city. Not being fully satisfied he went still farther West, and located permanently in the City of Milwaukee, opened a law office and carried on a large and profitable law business until after the United States became involved in the present war with Germany, when he volunteered as a soldier in the defence of his country, and is now serving in the office of the Judge Advocate General of the United States Army at the City of Washington, with the rank of Colonel of Volunteers; and where it is said by those in position to know, " he is making good," and if the war lasts any considerable lengtn of time he is most likely " to go up higher."

We do not mention Colonel Goff in this volume simply because he is a worthy son of an illustrious sire, and was born and reared in West Virginia, but because of the high position he has attained in the profession, when at this hour his sun has just reached its meridian and he will, we are quite confident, before very many years, return to his native heath and spend the remnant of his years, which it is expected will be many, under the shadow of the trees where he reveled in the long gone by among the friends of his boyhood and early manhood " amid the West Virginia hills."

Colonel Goff inherited a natural tendency toward the law, and but few young men had the advantages for the thorough educational equipment that came his way, which, coupled with the more than ordinary gifts in oratory that he possesses, and being also an almost unexcelled worker and toiler, he could not fail to attain to a high rank in his chosen profession. His practice has been general and has extended into all the courts in which he has practiced from *nisi prius* up to the Supreme Court of the United States, and has been remarkably successful.

He was four years District Attorney for Milwaukee County, which includes the great City of Milwaukee, and filled the office ably and satisfactorily. Later he was United States District Attorney for the State of Wisconsin for five years, and we are assured by reliable men who know, that the State never had an abler one. This office he resigned when he volunteered in the United States Army in the war against Germany.

He is a broad, thorough, conscientious lawyer, devoted to his profession in which he early took a leading place, and his private life is without a blemish. He is a member of the Protestant Episcopal Church and has always been a Republican in politics. He married Miss Anita Baker, of Wheelng, West Virginia, and has one child. He is companionable and cheerful and possesses the happy faculty of drawing men to him. He is of medium stature and commanding appearance.

## Allebach, A.B., LL.B.

Our subject is a Pennsylvanian by birth and lineage, who located at Charleston as his permanent abiding place twelve years ago. His parents, Anson Milo and Clara Cornelia Allebach, are of " Pennsylvania Dutch " stock, who are known far and wide for their industry, intelligence and frugal habits. Leroy, the son, was born at New Bethlehem, Pennsylvania, July 25, 1880. He received his rudimentary education in the public schools of his native town. He possessed an inborn purpose to become some way and some how — for his parents were short of funds to aid him — to be more than an ordinary farm hand; so he got together, by teaching school and other means, funds enough to enter Grove City College, Pennsylvania, to meet immediate demands, and then secured different kinds of employment at Grove City, and during vacations to pay his way through college, graduating *cum laude*, in the classical course, with the degree of Bachelor of Arts, in the class of 1903. In his earlier years he formed the desire to become a lawyer, consequently after he had completed his academic course at Grove City he " packed his grip " for the University of Michigan, at Ann Arbor, and matriculated as a student in the Law Department of that widely celebrated institution, working as he did at Grove City to pay his way until he graduated, *magnum cum laude*, in the class of 1906; carrying with him the degree of Bachelor of Laws from this noted University, the best known Law School, and perhaps the very best in standing in the western portion of the Great Republic. In the manner we have stated he procured a thorough education and was now ready to enter upon a career of usefulness as a lawyer.

Looking about for a permanent location for a young lawyer he fell upon Charleston, West Virginia, as a place of unusual promise, and accordingly hung out his shingle as an Attorney and Counselor at Law in September, 1906, where it still hangs; and he has gathered around him a clientele large enough to keep him constantly occupied. He has specialized in corporation practice and represents a considerable number of concerns of that character, being regularly retained as one of the principal attorneys of the Kanawha and Michigan Railroad Company. His practice extends to all of the State and Federal Courts in West Virginia and Ohio, in which tribunals he often appears, and has been on several occasions heard in the Supreme Court of the United States. In these courts he has made an enviable record as a trial lawyer. He is a trained and forceful advocate and handles his cases with judgment and skill, and is invariably courteous to his opponents. He is a hard student of law and keeps up with the court decisions and modern text books. In college he was an all round athlete, is large and muscular and is pleasant and agreeable in his associations. He is careful, clear-minded and thorough in his work, and in all of his dealings, both in public and private life, nothing reproachful or dishonorable has ever marred the even tenor of his way. He is modest and retiring and at all times courteous to his associates and friends. Cool as an ocean breeze and entirely fearless, like an ancient Norseman, he never shunned an issue, but courted it.

He is a member of all the different branches of the Masonic Fraternity and is a Past Master of his lodge at Charleston, and has lived true to the high ideals of that institution. He is also a member of the Protestant Episcopal Church and the Benevolent Order of Elks. In all respects he is a forward-thinking man, broad and liberal in his views and thoroughly democratic in spirit. Though of a positive nature he disagrees with his opponents without rancor. Mr. Allebach was united in marriage with Miss Tella T. Thompson, February 19, 1917, and they have one child — Newton Webster. He is a Republican, but has never allowed politics to detract from his legal business. He is devoted to his home, and is keenly interested in the social welfare and the betterment of the people.

## Benjamin Beuhring Brown, A.M., LL.B.

Benjamin B. Brown, son of the late Judge James H. Brown, and brother of Hon. James F. Brown, was born at Charleston, West Virginia, December 7, 1863, and died at Nice, France, December 30, 1906. He was a graduate of both the University of West Virginia at Morgantown and the University of Virginia at Charlottesville, receiving from the former the degrees of Bachelor of Arts and Master of Arts, and from the later the degree of Bachelor of Laws, having completed his studies in law under the direction of that eminent instructor, the late Dr. John B. Minor. On his return home he entered upon the practice of his profession as partner of his father, and quickly demonstrated his ability and qualifications. But in 1888, because of ill health, upon the advice of his physicians that he should adopt an out of door life, he moved to Colorado Springs, and afterwards to Denver, Colorado, where, until his death, he made his home. It was the regret of his later years that he was inhibited from continuing in his profession for which he had remarkable gifts and in which he was developing at a rapid rate. The few years of his active practice gave him an enviable rank among the leading lawyers at the Kanawha Bar.

His strong and attractive personality and accomplishments soon made him a wide circle of friends, among whom were many of the prominent and influential men of the community, and debarred by his physicians from the confinement incident to his profession, he at once with the energy characteristic of him, joined in the active enterprises then bringing Colorado to the front in mining, industrial and financial standing.

Among other ventures he was one of the original syndicate first to recognize the merits of the "Porphyry Copper," and with his associates organized the "Utah Copper Company," now one of the largest, if not the largest, single producer of copper in the world. His mining interests extended to Creede, Cripple Creek, Leadville, Utah and Arizona, in all which his good judgment proved itself by bringing large returns. As he became more widely known he was brought to many positions of confidence and responsibility in connection with the strong institutions of his adopted city. Among others was the Colorado National Life Assurance Company, of which Mr. Brown was for a long time, and up to his death, the President.

Having been eminently successful in his undertakings and amassed a fortune, he spent as much of his later years as could be spared from his duties, in travel, several times crossing both the Atlantic and Pacific

BENJAMIN BEUHRING BROWN

Oceans and visiting most of the countries of the world, taking with him his wife and son, the latter then about twelve years of age, now an officer at the front in France. It was on one of these trips that he met his death at Nice.

Mr. Brown was a man of marked personality, force of character, exceptional judgment, kindly, but, nevertheless, firm and quick of decision. He married in 1888 Miss Anna L. Dickinson, of the pioneer family of that name in Kanawha, and left surviving him three children, Mary D., who married Charles L. Lowell, of Colorado Springs; Sallie L., who married Edward L. Whitaker, of St. Paul, and James F., who married Miss Lucile Ravenscraft, of St. Louis. Both of his sons-in-law and his son promptly responded to the Call of the Colors, and are now officers in the volunteer army against Germany.

## Captain Fleming Newman Alderson

Captain Alderson is the son of the late Hon. John D. and Eugenia Adeline (Rader) Alderson, of Nicholas County, West Virginia. The senior Alderson was an eminent lawyer, and for a number of terms represented the Third District of West Virginia in the Congress of the United States, a short biography of whom appears in another portion of this volume. Captain Alderson was born at Summersville, Nicholas County, January 8, 1884. He received a rudimentary education in the public schools of his native county. Later he attended St. Vincent's College at Wheeling, Ohio County, and graduated from the Law Department of the West Virginia University in the class of 1907. He became a member of the Nicholas County Bar October 8, 1907. He practiced in the Circuit Courts of that, and three or four adjoining counties, for several years, with offices at Summersville, the seat of justice of the county, associated with his father. He finally established a branch office in the City of Richwood in the same county, where he has since resided, and has conducted a very profitable business in that rapidly developing city. He, however, still maintains his original office at the county seat, and has a large volume of business at both places. He is tall, well proportioned and has a commanding appearance, and is also polite, courteous and is popular with the people.

In politics Captain Alderson is a Democrat, and like his father has always been a Democrat and a very active one. He was elected a member of the West Virginia Legislature from Nicholas County in 1910, and was active in framing legislation during the entire session. In 1913 he was appointed Assistant United States Attorney for the Southern District of West Virginia for the term of four years; but after serving two years he was made the nominee of his party as a candidate for Congress from the Fourth Congressional District, and was defeated by only a few hundred votes by his Republican opponent, the district being pronouncedly Republican. He, however, did not allow these public positions to materially

CAPTAIN FLEMING N. ALDERSON

interfere with his law practice. He was appointed Chief of the Division of Military Census and Enrollment, with the rank of Captain, in the United States Army, in June, 1918, which position he now holds in the war with the Imperial Government of Germany.

Captain Alderson is a member of the Masonic Fraternity and also the Greek letter " frats " of Phi Kappa Psi, Delta Chi and the law fraternity Theta Nu Epsilon. He has never married. He practices in all the State and Federal Courts and he has specialized in corporation practice, which has proved quite profitable and successful.

## Judge Isaiah C. Herndon, LL.B.

Judge Herndon is a native West Virginian, who was born near Princeton in the County of Mercer, March 9, 1868. He was liberally educated, having spent four years at Princeton Academy, two years at Emory and Henry College, Virginia, and graduated from the Law Department of the West Virginia University in the class of 1892, receiving the *pro merito* degree of Bachelor of Laws. The year of his graduation he was admitted to the Bar of his native county, and before the close of the year he located permanently at Welch, the seat of justice of McDowell County, where he entered upon the practice of his profession, throwing into it the enthusiasm of youth and that mental and physical vigor with which nature had liberally endowed him. Being gifted as a public speaker he ranked early among the best advocates and trial lawyers of that new and rapidly developing Bar. Business came to him rapidly, so that in a short space of time, by close attention to his business and the careful preparation of his cases, he was the possessor of a lucrative practice.

Like most young West Virginia and Virginia lawyers he possessed an inborn taste for the, to them, luxury of politics. So we find our young friend in 1896 a candidate on the Republican ticket for Prosecuting Attorney of McDowell County, to which office he was elected by a large majority for the term of four years. He handled the responsible duties of that important position so satisfactorily to the people that they nominated and elected him for a second term. By this time his reputation was established as one of the leading members of his county Bar. His practice had extended into the courts of the adjoining counties, and his reputation as a successful practitioner was firmly fixed.

In the fall campaign of 1904 he was nominated and elected a member of the Legislature of the State. He was attentive to his public duties and acquitted himself with credit and honor. In 1906 he was nominated and elected Judge of the Circuit Court to fill the unexpired term of Judge L. L. Chambers, deceased, in the Circuit composed of McDowell, Mercer and Monroe Counties. His services were so satisfactory to litigants and attorneys he was re-elected to a full eight years' term, which he is now serving ably and satisfactorily. He is careful, clear-headed and systematic in his work, and his history as a man, an attorney and as a judge is a record of manliness and courage complete in every detail. He is married, has a pleasant family and his home-life is ideal. Naturally hopeful and happy his hours with his friends are always social and joyous. He is, therefore, popular with all the people who know him personally.

## Hon. J. Luther Wolfe, LL.B.

Mr. Wolfe, son of G. B. and Laura Wolfe, was born at Given, Jackson County, West Virginia, February 14, 1875, and received his early education in the public schools of his native county. He has an inquiring mind and has always been an earnest seeker after knowledge. He reads much and digests what he reads. In this way he has pieced out a sound English education. To broaden his mind and increase his knowledge, while yet a young man, he engaged in the business, for several years, of teaching in the public schools of Jackson County, and proved efficient in that line of intellectual endeavor. While thus employed he decided to take up the profession of law, and with this object in view, he began the study of legal textbooks, applying all his spare time to this end. The more time he devoted to such investigation the greater became his interest, until, in 1898, he abandoned teaching entirely, entered the Law Department of the West Virginia University at Morgantown and completed the required course of law studies, graduating therefrom in the class of 1900. He returned to Ripley, the seat of justice of his native county, opened a law office in 1901 and became an active practicing attorney. By close application to business he has gathered about him a profitable clientele, which is steadily increasing. He is endowed with good morals, has maintained an upright life, is thoroughly trustworthy and by fair dealing has secured the confidence of his fellow citizens.

His practice is of a general character and extends into all the courts of West Virginia, both State and Federal, and also into the adjacent counties. The firm of Stone and Wolfe, of which he is a member, is firmly established and is carrying on a profitable and enlarging business.

Mr. Wolfe is a Republican in politics and in the campaign of 1916 was elected a member of the Legislature from Jackson County, and rendered efficient and satisfactory service as Chairman of the Committee on Railroads and also as a member of the Judiciary, Forfeited and Unappropriated Lands and Redistricting Committees. He, however, informs us that he has laid aside all side lines and for the future is devoting all his time to the legitimate practice of his profession.

February 23, 1902, he married Miss Ivy L. Guinn, by whom he has one child.

He is a member of the Methodist Episcopal Church, and holds membership in the Masonic, Odd Fellows and Knights of Pythias Fraternities.

He was re-elected to the West Virginia Legislature in 1918, and was chosen Speaker of the House of Delegates January 8, 1919.

## Coleman Cabell Higginbotham

Mr. Higginbotham is the son of William T. and Mary F. Higginbotham of Upshur County, Virginia, who was born December 19, 1850, and pieced out a creditable education, mostly by the reading and studying of such books as would develop his intellect and store his mind with knowledge that would be useful to him in a future career. He was always studious in his younger years, and since his admission to the Bar, in 1871, he has been one of the hardest workers in the profession to go to the bottom of every law question which arose in the many law cases he has handled in a professional career of almost a half century. He is known as an able and careful chancery lawyer and has the reputation of being one of the most judicious of lawyers in the preparation of his pleadings. He has never been noted for any particular gifts or attainments as an advocate or trial lawyer, but he stands high as one who is thoroughly posted in the fundamental principles of the profession, and never allows himself to enter a court trial without a full and clear understanding of his cases. He is, therefore, an office lawyer of a high standard, and knows beforehand what he must do or present before entering a courthouse contest; consequently it is difficult to disconcert him or throw him off his balance. The result is, he has had for years a profitable clientele and has maintained a high rank in the profession in the central section of the State. He practices in Upshur and surrounding counties, in the Circuit and Supreme Court of the State, and also in the United States District and Circuit Court of Appeals of the Fourth Judicial Circuit.

Mr. Higginbotham has always been a Democrat, but in no sense has he ever been a politician. He never was a candidate for any political office of any sort, but was once an aspirant for Circuit Judge, which was strictly in the line of his profession. All of his time and energies for nearly half a century have been devoted exclusively to the practice of the law.

He married Miss Mary Ida Day and they have a family of five children.

He is a member of the Masonic Fraternity and resides in the city of Buckhannon. He was admitted to practice in the Circuit Court of Upshur County in 1871, just after he had reached his majority, and has adhered faithfully to his calling, without loss of time, to the present. His personal life and character are above reproach.

---

## Walter Smith Sugden, LL.B.

Mr. Sugden, son of James T. and Elizabeth Smith Sugden, was born April 9, 1880, at Amsterdam, N. Y.; received his preliminary education in Amsterdam High School; was two years ('98 and '99) a student at Philips Andover Academy, Andover, Massachusetts; was four years ('99–'03) at Harvard University, and from 1903 to 1906 he took the full law course prescribed for the graduation of law students at that great seat of learning and was awarded the degree of Bachelor of Laws. But few lawyers have

C. C. HIGGINBOTHAM

entered upon the profession with an equipment and training equal to Mr. Sugden. He started with sharp tools, and has made good use of them. He came to West Virginia January 12, 1910, and on that day was admitted to the Tyler County Bar, where he has since practiced in that and the surrounding counties with marked success. He is the junior member of the able firm of Kimball and Sugden at Sistersville, West Virginia, where they maintain an extensive business in all the varied branches of the profession, but specialize in corporation practice. Their business extends into all of the State and Federal Courts, including the Supreme Court of the United States, and is steadily on the increase.

Like his partner, Mr. C. N. Kimball, he has adhered to the Republican party the greater part of his mature life, but both of them were "Progressives" in the political campaign of 1912, our subject that year being a Delegate to the National Convention that brought forth two Republican candidates for the Presidency. So this year he is at a loss to place himself politically; consequently he dubs himself a "Progressive." He, however, has not devoted much time to political controversies and never sought an office, and never held but one, viz., Solicitor for the city of Sistersville, one term. He is, therefore, a lawyer and not a politician, and that is one of the main reasons why he holds so high a rank in the legal profession of the State. Our observation, covering a period of many years, justifies the statement that, in most instances, those lawyers who intermeddle the least in political controversies, as a rule, are the most erudite members of the great profession.

Mr. Sugden is a man of simple habits; is courteous and dignified in his general deportment; attends to his duties promptly and faithfully; is a careful and thoughtful adviser, and is a strong, aggressive trial lawyer. He was a high grade athelete in his college days. He is also a member of the Masonic Fraternity, having connected himself with its different branches. He is an active member of the Protestant Episcopal Church, and belongs to a number of college fraternities and took a lively part in all of them. He is highly esteemed by the people in Sistersville, where he has spent the larger part of his thus far useful and successful life.

Mr. Sugden was united in marriage with Miss Rachel E. Hutchison, February 12, 1916, and one child is the result of this union.

## Judge Walter Hoyt O'Brien

We have in West Virginia, at this time, two Circuit Court Judges by the name of O'Brien. The one we are now considering is a native of Jackson County, Virginia, son of Thomas B. and Celia (McKown) O'Brien. He was born March 4, 1857, and attended the public schools until he was fifteen years of age, when he began to teach in the public schools. After teaching for a short time he attended select private schools at Lone Pine, Ravenswood and Ripley, both of them in Jackson County, where he availed himself of higher courses of study than were taught in the common schools; the object,

JUDGE W. H. O'BRIEN

at that time, being to attain higher grade scholarship in order to better equip himself for the profession of teaching, which he followed for seventeen years.

He was elected Assessor, in 1880, of the Second District of Jackson County, in which position he served from January 1, 1881, to December 31, 1884. He was next elected Clerk of the Circuit Court of Jackson County and served therein from January 1, 1891 to December 31, 1896. He studied law while Clerk of the Circuit Court and was admitted to the Bar March 4, 1897, when he was forty years of age. He was elected Prosecuting Attorney of Jackson County and served as such from January 1, 1901, to December 31, 1904. He was a Commissioner of the United States District Court from 1904 to 1912. While Clerk of the Circuit Court he became thoroughly familiar with all legal froms and pleadings, which were very helpful in his subsequent practice. He also necessarily absorbed the methods of successful lawyers in the trial of important causes, because of his constant presence being required in the courtroom during court sessions, all which aided greatly in making him a successful trial lawyer and helped to bring to him a profitable clientage. He was honorable and square in all of his dealings, and had the confidence of the people, which is the *sine qua non* to success in all callings.

In the fall of 1912 he was elected Judge of the Circuit Court of the Fifth Judicial Circuit for the term of eight years, and is now acceptably serving in that highly honorable position. His circuit is composed of Mason, Jackson, Roane and Calhoun counties. As a Judge his honor is unsullied and his integrity has never been questioned. As a matter of fact, in every office he ever held he was faithful, honorable and just.

He is a Republican "of the Old School," and being a good stump speaker, he has participated actively in a number of hotly contested political campaigns. He married Miss Dora Coe, June 16, 1877. They have six sons, four of whom are living, two of them are volunteers in the United States Army, in the war against Germany, and the two younger are subject to the last draft order. He is a member of the Masonic, Odd Fellows and Knights of Pythias Fraternities, and is an active member of the Methodist Episcopal Church, especially in its Sunday School department, being teacher of a Bible Class for nearly a score of years. He is always found on the moral side of every question that comes before the people. He is also an enterprising, progressive citizen, ever keeping his eyes to the front. He came to the Bar a little late in life, but he has been quite successful as a lawyer and jurist.

## Judge Neil Judson Fortney

The subject of this sketch was born near Independence, Preston County, Virginia, November 22, 1852 (in a former history stated as 1849, but the error was not discovered until too late for correction). He was the youngest son of a family of ten children of David H. and Angeline S. Fortney. Judge Fortney, who ranks among the leading lawyers of West Virginia, is

JUDGE NEIL J. FORTNEY

of French descent on the paternal side and of Irish and German on the maternal side. His grandfather, Daniel Fortney, who was a native of France, came to this country about the year 1780 and settled in Frederick County, Maryland, and from there removed to Preston County (then Monongalia County, Virginia), about the year 1796. His early education was received at Independence, Preston County, and he removed with his parents to Indianola, Iowa, in 1865, at which place he attended the public schools for two years. He then took a three years' course at Simpson Centenary College of that place. Leaving Iowa in 1872, he spent some time in traveling over Western and Northwestern States and Territories, and engaged in school teaching and other employments. Finally his native State and County appealed to him, so in 1873 he returned to Independence, near where he was born and had spent his early youth, and decided upon entering the profession of law. In 1877 he was appointed Deputy Clerk of the County Court of Preston, which place he filled for two years; then, in 1897, having passed an examination before the Supreme Court of Appeals of the State, he was admitted to the Bar of his native State as an attorney-at-law.

At the succeeding election, 1880, he was elected Prosecuting Attorney of Preston County, in which position he served well nigh continuously for twenty years. By display of great ability and the exercise of the most careful attention to the needs of the people of his county, coupled with absolute fairness in the discharge of his duties, he became and continued to be very popular as an officer, but voluntarily declined to offer himself for re-election to that office.

Combining the alert, constructive and compact reasoning powers peculiar to the races from which he sprang, endowed him with ready ability in digesting matters of law and fact and the true discernment of equity. His possession of these qualities, together with his untarnished record for impartiality and fairness in his long practice as an attorney, were so well known among the representative citizens of the judicial circuit now composed of Preston and Taylor counties, that it resulted in his selection in the year 1912, by the Republican party as its candidate, in his election to the office of Judge of the Circuit Court by next to the largest majority obtained by any of the Judges of the State. He is now in his sixth year of his service on the Bench, which service has proved most satisfactory both to litigants and attorneys.

Judge Fortney took up his residence in Kingwood in 1874, and on June 3, 1879, was married to Miss Alice Edna Godwin, daughter of Captain Joseph M. Godwin of Kingwood, and they have one son, E. Vernon, living, who is at this writing one of the two Republican nominees for member of the State Legislature from Preston County. Judge Fortney's personal and official character has, through all the years, been marked with probity and general uprightness, which has given him a wide influence in his native county and State. He is a member of the Elks, Odd Fellows, Knights of Pythias and L. O. O. M.

## Hon. William Gordon Mathews

"A man with noble ancestry," says Pauline, in Bulwer's Lady of Lyons, "is like a representative of the past." But like the supposed prince to whom this eulogy was applied, the subject of this sketch depreciates the idea of being "a pensioner on the dead," having sprung from the people and tracing his origin to an equally honorable and honest source. Being a scion of a noted Virginia family, all of whom were honorable, and some of whom were distinguished, yet this comparatively young man, while he duly respects his forebears, prefers to stand upon his own merits and rely upon his own achievements. His father, the late Hon. Henry Mason Mathews, a graduate of the University of Virginia, noted for his scholarship and distinguished as a lawyer, who was four years Attorney-General of West Virginia, and later served a like period as its Chief Executive, leaving behind him, in both offices, records which were highly appreciated by the citizens of the Commonwealth at large. He died all too soon, his sun only having fairly reached its noon. He was born in Greenbrier County, Virginia, in 1834 and died in 1884.

William Gordon Mathews is also a native of Greenbrier County, West Virginia; was born in 1877; after the usual period of public school attendance he became a student at the Lewisburg Military Academy and subsequently at the University of Virginia at Charlottesville, graduating therefrom when only twenty years of age, in the class of 1897. When he reached his majority he came to Charleston, Kanawha County, was admitted to the Bar and became a member of the well-known and able law firm of Mollohan, McClintic and Mathews, he being the junior member. After the death of Mr. Mollohan, a few years ago, the firm now is McClintic, Mathews and Campbell, and is conducting a large and profitable law business. They practice in all the State and Federal Courts and embrace all the different branches of the law.

Mr. Mathews belongs to the Democratic school of politics. He was the nominee of his party in 1908, being chosen by acclamation at the Wheeling Judicial Convention as a candidate for a seat on the Bench of the Supreme Court of Appeals of the State, but was defeated with his entire party ticket. Although he was quite young at the time of his candidacy, it was universally admitted that he possessed, in a pronounced degree, all the elements to become an able and successful jurist. He is thoroughly grounded in the law; is an industrious worker; is courteous and dignified in his general deportment; attends to his duties promptly; is more inclined to listen than to speak; is kind hearted, frank, straightforward and independent; is thoroughly honest and trustworthy, and is among the highly talented members of the entire State Bar. While he enjoys mixing in politics to a certain extent, yet he has never aspired to any office except strictly in the line of his profession. His one leading, single purpose in life seems to be to become a great lawyer, and he is rapidly heading in that direction.

The only public office Mr. Mathews has thus far held is Referee in Bankruptcy, which position he has filled acceptably for a number of years past. He is an active and efficient member of the West Virginia Bar Association; was its President in 1913, and was the youngest presiding officer the Association ever had. Its "Year Book" contains a number of timely papers on live subjects written by him. One of these, "Martial Law in West Virginia," created wide discussion both in and outside of the State, and was generally regarded as an able production, and exhibited deep research. It was ordered printed and distributed as a public document by the United States Senate.

January 28, 1903, Mr. Mathews married Miss Helen B. Davis, of Charleston, West Virginia, and they have an interesting family of three children. Mr. and Mrs. Mathews are prominent in the social and civic life of Charleston, and have the confidence and respect of all the people who know them.

Mr. Mathews was appointed by the President as the legal member of the District Board for the Southern District of West Virginia, under the Selective Service Act of May 18, 1917, and actively served as such since his appointment to the close of the war with Germany.

## Judge Henry Stuart Cato, LL.B.

Judge Cato, youngest child and only son of John Lane and Sarah Maury Lasley Cato, was born at Saint Albans, Kanawha County, West Virginia, February 26, 1878; was educated in the public schools of that place; entered the law office of Vinson and Thompson at Huntington, West Virginia, in August, 1897, and there served as stenographer and read law under their direction until September, 1899, when he entered the Law Department of the West Virginia University, graduating at the head of his class in June, 1900. In August of that year he began the practice of law at Charleston, West Virginia, and by close attention to his duties he drew attention to himself as a young attorney with far above the average attainments and possibilities, and gathered about him a rapidly increasing clientage. In 1902 he became the junior member of the firm of Linn, Byrne and Cato. In February, 1906, he formed a partnership with Hon. Adam B. Littlepage and Thomas A. Bledsoe, under the firm name of Littlepage, Cato and Bledsoe, which continued until February, 1911, when Mr. Littlepage withdrew, he having been elected a member of the American Congress, leaving the firm simply as Cato and Bledsoe, which continued until September 10, 1917, when Mr. Cato was appointed by Governor Cornwell, Judge of the Tenth Judicial Circuit, to fill the vacancy caused by the death of Honorable Samuel D. Littlepage, which office he filled with great acceptability.

As a lawyer Mr. Cato was careful, clear-headed, systematic, vigilant and thorough in his work. In argument he addressed the reason, the practical judgment, and was clear-sighted with respect of motives and ulterior influences. His history as a man and an attorney is a record of manliness

JUDGE HENRY S. CATO

complete. He is a hard student of law, and dignified it by exhibiting in the practice the highest types of integrity, fidelity and learning. His learning is varied and extensive. He is a most genial companion, deals fairly with his associates, is thorough and accurate, and as an advocate he is forceful and convincing. He acquired a large practice, because he possessed real knowledge of legal principles, which never fails to bring success. His strong forte was in trial practice.

As a Judge he measured up, in all respects, to the high standard fixed for him by his friends. He has the judicial temperament, is considerate, fair and just. His studious habits take him to the bottom of the cases that come before him, and he is honest and incorruptible. He is also kindly disposed in his make-up and has a charming personality. He is popular with both lawyers and suitors and made an excellent record as a *nisi prius* Judge.

Judge Cato has never married; is a member of the Protestant Episcopal Church; has always been a Democrat; is a member of the American, the West Virginia and Kanawha County Bar Associations and the Phi Kappa Psi Greek Letter Fraternity. His photograph shows him as possessing the bearing and appearance of a student and a Judge. He never was a candidate for any public office, and never held one until he was appointed a Circuit Judge. He was the candidate of the Democratic party for an election by the people for the position he filled by appointment of the Governor. His party being in the minority, he was defeated.

## Luther Colfax Anderson, A.M., LL.B.

Mr. Anderson was born in Lewis County, West Virginia, February 9, 1869; son of Lorenzo Dow and Rebecca Anderson; was educated in the public schools of his native county; later attended the Ohio Wesleyan University, Delaware, Ohio, from which he graduated in 1894, receiving the classical degree of Bachelor of Arts; in 1899 it conferred upon him the degree of Master of Arts. He then entered the Law Department of the West Virginia University, from which he graduated in 1896 with the degree of Bachelor of Laws. In June of that year he was admitted to practice in the Circuit Court of Lewis County. He, however, spent three or four years in public school work before entering regularly upon his profession. He was principal of Pennsboro, West Virginia, public schools in 1895; was Assistant State Superintendent of Public Schools of West Virginia from 1897 to 1899 inclusive; Assistant Editor "West Virginia School Journal" for two years; appointed Assistant Attorney-General of West Virginia in 1899 and served therein to and including 1900. In all of these public positions he acquitted himself most creditably.

While in college he was an associate editor of the "Ohio Wesleyan Transcript" and was editor-in-chief of "Monticola" at the West Vir-

HON. LUTHER C. ANDERSON

ginia University. He entered upon the practice of law at Welch, McDowell County, as a member of the large law firm of Rucker, Keller, Hamill and Anderson, which was dissolved by the death of General Rucker and the appointment of B. F. Keller to the position of United States Judge for the Southern District of West Virginia. The present firm is Anderson, Strother, Hughes and Curd. The firm practices in all of the State and Federal Courts, including the Supreme Court of the United States and the Federal and State Courts of West Virginia and Virginia. The record shows that Mr. Anderson himself has appeared in upwards of two hundred cases in the Supreme Court of Appeals of West Virginia, a record, perhaps, not surpassed by any other West Virginia lawyer. He is an upright man, honest in both thought and purpose. His life as a lawyer, whether judged with reference to labor performed or pecuniary gain, places him in the front rank of his profession. Rarely is there found among men one so systematic in mind and character, one so sound of judgment, so unswerving in moral perception, so faithful to duty and so loyal to the right as the subject of this sketch. His career is another evidence of the correctness of the proverb, "Work will never fail to win."

Mr. Anderson was united in marriage with Miss Frances Rummel, of Charleston, in 1902. They have three sons. They are all devoted to their home and enjoy the communion of the family circle. He is a member of the Methodist Episcopal Church and represented his State as a member of the General Conference of that Church in 1912. For years he has been active in Church and Young Men's Christian Association work. In 1910 he published a book entitled "The Trial of Christ, from a Lawyer's Standpoint." In 1907 he also published "The Negotiable Instruments Law," a textbook of value to the profession. He is a Republican in politics, but devotes his entire time to his profession. Among his friends he is always social, joyous and happy. He was elected a member of the West Virginia Legislature in the campaign of 1918.

## Hon. Wm. M. O. Dawson

The subject of this memorial was born May 21, 1853, on the strip of land which was in dispute between the States of Maryland and West Virginia, but which was afterwards determined to be a part of West Virginia. He was the son of Francis Ravenscraft Dawson and his mother's name was Leah Kite Dawson. He was twice married. His first wife was Miss Luda Neff, a daughter of John T. Neff, and by this union there was one son, Daniel Dawson, of the Huntington Bar. His second wife was Miss Maude Brown, of Kingwood, and by this union there were two children, Leah Jane and William Brown Dawson. His second wife and children are residents of the City of Charleston.

His life was a busy one. He was first a clerk in a store. He then taught school; then learned the printing trade; was next editor of the Preston

HON. WM. M. O. DAWSON

County Journal, which he made one of the strongest publications in the State, and by this means first attracted the attention of the public as a man of ability and absolute integrity. He later qualified as a practicing lawyer. His greatest successes, however, were in the political field and he entered on that work very early in life, and was Chairman of the Republican Executive Committee of Preston County at the age of twenty-one, which position he held for thirteen consecutive years.

In 1880, at the age of twenty-seven, he was elected to the State Senate, in which he served for eight years, declining a nomination for a third term. In this forum he demonstrated unparalleled ability as a legislative draftsman of important measures. In 1891 he was made State Chairman of the Republican organization, and it was during his term in that position that the first State-wide successes attended the Republican party. He served two terms as Secretary of State, and in 1904 he was elected Governor. During his term many important State reforms were introduced. After the expiration of that term he became an associate counsel in the controversy between the State of Virginia and the State of West Virginia, in which position he rendered efficient and satisfactory service. In 1913 he was appointed a member of the State Board of Control, and in 1915 he became a member of the Public Service Commission of the State. In all of these exalted positions he served the people with great acceptability.

The above are the main events of his career stated in their chronological order and they show an unbroken record of power and achievement, but such a listing of honors conveys but little real knowledge of the real man much as those of us now living knew him, and it is the despair of the biographer to daw a word picture of the man for coming generations.

For more than thirty years he was a power in the dominant political party of the State, and he is considered by many thinking men to have been the best adviser his party ever had and the most effective, and at the same time carrying himself as the most modest and the quietest man that ever took such a prominent part for so long a time in public life. He was a constructive statesman of far more than average attainments, and for nearly a generation left his impress upon the times in which he lived. His motives and purposes were often misconstrued. He, however, was honorable in all of his dealings and at all times stood four-square in all of his private and public acts. In due season his name will be properly placed among the most distinguished and ablest men the State has thus far produced. He was a good lawyer and a safe counselor.

Those of us who personally knew this reticent, retiring, powerful man, valued his friendship, admired his power of judgment, respected his sterling character for honor and uprightness and his lovable nature more than we have the ability to express. He was a faithful and consistent member of the Presbyterian Church and was also a member of the Masonic Fraternity, and devoted in later years much of his time to metaphysical and psychological research. He departed this life at Charleston while in the active discharge of his onerous official duties, March 12, 1916, and his remains were laid to rest at Kingwood, Preston County, the home of his earlier years, in the presence of a large concourse of sorrowing friends and relatives.

## Hon. Andrew J. Horan

Our subject is one of the able, all-round, well-known, firmly established lawyers of southern West Virginia. He was born at Malden, Kanawha County, Virginia, May 13, 1856, and is the son of P. D. Horan, a teacher of pronounced scholarship and ability in the Catholic Church. Andrew, or "Andy," as he has always been called, was educated in the public schools, also at Xaverian Brothers' Academy, Louisville, Kentucky, and was particularly and carefully taught by his father in the higher branches of learning. Whilst he never attended a college of any kind, it was generally understood that the private training he received at the hands of his father was, in all respects, equal to the average college course of that period. After completing his academic course of studies, he began to read law, mainly under his own direction, and pursued it with diligence and alacrity, until he was prepared to undergo a searching examination by Judges Adam C. Snyder, Homer A. Holt and Henry Brannon,— the last two being Circuit Judges at the time, but later all of them were members of the Supreme Court of Appeals of this State, and Judge Snyder, at the time he secured a license, was then a Judge of the Supreme Court. He was admitted to the Bar in April, 1888. During that year he and the late Hon. John D. Alderson formed a partnership under the firm name of Alderson and Horan, which continued with law offices at Summersville, West Virginia, until November, 1907, when he retired from the firm, and in November, 1908, formed a partnership with Hon. C. W. Osenton, at Fayetteville, West Virginia, under the firm name of Osenton and Horan, from which firm he recently retired and located in Charleston. Both of these firms were and are leaders of the Bar in their respective localities, and controlled large clientages. The firm at Summerville was employed on one side or the other of every important case in Nicholas and two or three adjoining counties; and the same is largely true of the firm of Osenten and Horan located in Fayette County. All three of the lawyers who composed these two firms ranked, in Mr. Alderson's life, among the ablest attorneys in southern West Virginia, and the firm of Osenten and Horan still maintains the same high standing.

Mr. Horan is an all-round lawyer, and is thorough in all the different branches of the profession. He is careful and thoughtful in his advice to clients, and is upright in thought and purpose. His personal character is without spot or blemish and he possesses, in a very large degree, that special essential to success in every profession — common sense. His judgment may not be unerring, but the writer knows him well enough to state that his conclusions are generally sound on all important subjects. Moreover, he is honorable and trustworthy in all of his dealings with his fellow men, which accounts for the success he has achieved as an attorney and counselor at law. With his modesty and urbanity, he never reveals any shadow of weakness or lack of decision. When satisfied that he is right he is unalterable, unchanging and unchangeable. With such equipment it is no wonder that he has succeeded in the law.

Mr. Horan, in his political affiliations, has always been a Republican. He was elected to membership in the State Senate of West Virginia in 1900 and served four years in that important legislative body. He was active, especially in committee work, being Chairman of the Judiciary Committee, the most important of all the committees of the body, and also a member of other committees. The Senatorial District he represented was composed of the counties of Nicholas, Braxton, Clay, Kanawha and Boone.

Senator Horan is married, but has had no children. He is an active member of the State Bar Association, and for many years has attended its annual meetings with marked regularity, and has prepared and read several valuable papers on different legal subjects before the Association.

## Hon. Charles Wesley Dillon

Mr. Dillon, son of John Wesley and Docia (Evans) Dillon — his mother being a cousin of "Fighting Bob Evans" of the United States Navy — was born in Bland County, Virginia, February 8, 1865, and grew up on the parental homestead in the country, enduring the hard knocks of a farmer boy. However he did not then know that he was building up a whip-cord muscle that would stay with him and serve him well through his entire life. He attended the district schools and received the best rudimentary education that class of schools could impart. Subsequently he attended the Virginia Polytechnic Institute at Blacksburg. After graduation he was employed as a grade hand for a short time on the construction work of the Norfolk and Western Railroad. He then moved to Fayette County, West Virginia, in 1886, and taught school for two years, during which period he was reading law under the direction of L. G. Gaines, a leading attorney of Fayetteville. In 1888 he was admitted to the Fayette County Bar, and immediately thereafter entered upon the practice of the profession, where his rise to prominence has been swift and sure. His practice has extended into the Supreme Court of Appeals of West Virginia, the Federal Courts within the State, and the Supreme Court of the United States. He is familiar with all branches of the law and is always apparently "at home," and sure of his position, in all his cases in whatever court he may be placed. He carries a distinguished personal appearance, is dignified and graceful in manners and withal is modest and unassuming. He is solidly grounded in the profession, is upright in character, and always

HON. CHARLES W. DILLON

shows marked legal ability in important causes. On the whole he has made a record to be envied.

Soon after entering upon the practice he associated himself with E. L. Nuckolls, a young man of about his own age, who was also able, reliable and industrious, and the firm of Dillon and Nuckolls is to-day one of the ablest and best known law firms in Southern West Virginia.

Mr. Dillon early allied himself with the Republican party, and for many years has been one of its active leaders in West Virginia. He filled the office of Prosecuting Attorney of Fayette County for two full terms of four years each, and it is but just for us to say he was one of the ablest and fairest prosecutors the entire State has ever had. Fayette is a large coal producing county and for many years past has been infested with all grades and characters of violators of the law, which requires a man of ability and courage as Prosecuting Attorney to enforce the law and thus keep crime reduced to the minimum. Mr. Dillon, therefore, was just the man for the place, because every man who committed a crime was taught to understand he would be punished for his wrong-doing. Hence the standard of citizenship was by him materially elevated in that county.

The tax laws of West Virginia had become antiquated, and it was found necessary to revise the entire tax system in order to assess the valuation of property on a more equitable basis. Mr. Dillon was a leader in that movement. The State Legislature enacted necessary laws in that direction; created the office of State Tax Commissioner, and in the fall of 1904 Mr. Dillon was appointed to that position by Governor A. B. White. He immediately entered upon his public duties, and at the end of three years, after he had thoroughly organized, in a most efficient manner the new tax system, resigned the office and resumed his law business in Fayetteville, which had necessarily materially suffered because of his three years absence.

In the spring of 1900 Mr. Dillon and his law partner, Mr. E. L. Nuckolls, compiled and published "The West Virginia Pocket Code," a compilation of the laws of the State, which proved to be a popular publication, and filled a long felt want by the legal fraternity of the State.

He was a candidate for the nomination for Governor under a State-wide primary law, but after a vigorously contested campaign, although he polled a large popular vote, he was defeated. Since that campaign he has devoted his undivided time to the practice of his profession. He, however, has a large following of strong political friends throughout the State and, therefore, need not feel discouraged over the failure of his first political adventure should he desire to "cast his hat in the ring" for future favors at the hands of his political friends.

Mr. Dillon is married and has one child. He is an active member of the Masonic Fraternity. In addition to his large legal business he is interested in the business of coal mining and banking in his adopted county, and is not only a successful lawyer, but maintains a high standing in business circles as well. He is a prominent State developer.

## Stephen Goodloe Jackson, B.S., LL.B.

Mr. Jackson is the son of J. Goodloe and Martha (Bassel) Jackson, of Jane Lew, Lewis County, West Virginia, well known and well to do citizens or one of the finest agricultural sections of the State. The Jackson's and Bassel's are both honored, historical families in West Virginia, several of whom have more than State-wide reputations. Young Stephen G. was born at Jane Lew, March 7, 1884, and after attending the public schools of his native town matriculated as a student at the West Virginia University and graduated therefrom with the degrees of Bachelor of Science and Bachelor of Laws. Subsequently he entered the Law Department of Yale University, and after taking the required course of law studies was awarded the diploma of Bachelor of Laws. In both of these great schools he was a popular and praiseworthy student. During his stay at the West Virginia University he enjoyed the honor of being class president, debater's league captain, cadet captain, and winner of a special gold prize for best all-round debater. He was also honored as being one of the three distinguished cadets for three years in the military department. He was a member of the Sigma Chi Fraternity at West Virginia University, and was one of the founders of the Phi Alpha Delta Law Fraternity at Yale, and has represented it in National Conventions and for several years as Trustee.

Shortly after leaving college in July, 1908, he was admitted as a member of the Weston, Lewis County Bar, in which profession he has ever since engaged with enthusiasm and brilliant success. Desirous of a wider field for display of his talents he located in the City of Clarksburg in an adjoining county, and is the junior member of the strong law firm of Smith and Jackson, is carrying on an extensive and profitable business (Mr. Smith is mentioned in another portion of this volume). The firm is engaged in all branches of the law in all the State and Federal Courts of West Virginia. Mr. Jackson is a fluent and forceful speaker and is regarded as a superior all-round trial lawyer. Although yet a comparatively young man in the profession he has made an enviable record as an attorney, and greater honors are yet in store for him.

He has been a member of the West Virginia University Athletic Board for several years past, and the present enviable position and tone of university athletics in football and base ball sports are largely due to his inspiring planning and leadership. He stands high not only in athletics and physical stature and prowess, but in everything that makes up the well rounded moral and upright useful citizen.

He belongs to the "Stonewall" Jackson stock. His outstanding personal characteristics are persistent energy, exceptional legal acumen and learning, fine integrity, and devoted loyalty to all worthy persons and purposes. He is married and has one child. Their home is in the rapidly developing, thrifty, enterprising City of Clarksburg, the seat of justice of Harrison County.

## George Perry Simpson

Mr. Simpson, son of Judge Nathan Simpson and Livia Nye, his wife, was born at Ruthland, Meigs County, Ohio, on the Josiah Simpson Revolutionary land grant, February 12, 1839. He was known throughout Southern Ohio as the "Young Simpson," as he was the only male representative of his generation representing the two Simpson brothers, Josiah and Robert, Revolutionary soldiers, who emigrated to Meigs County in 1817 from Corinth, Maine, settling upon lands granted them for services in the Revolution. Of these soldiers, Robert left daughters and one son, Robert, who died childless. Josiah Simpson and wife, Bethia Sweatt, left five daughters and son, Josiah who left daughters and one son, Nathan Simpson, born in Corinth, Maine, May 3, 1804, who married first Livia Nye, of Athens County, Ohio, daughter of George Nye and Lydia Gardner. George Nye was the son of Ebenezer Nye, Revolutionary soldier, and wife, Desire Sawyer. Lydia Gardner was the daughter of Benoni Gardner, Revolutionary soldier, and wife, Silence Grant, both families settling at Marietta, Ohio, with the colony from Connecticut.

The Simpsons descended from Andrew Simpson, a Scotch-Irish Presbyterian, who sailed from Colrain, Ireland, to Boston in 1725, thence to Nottingham, New Hampshire. His wife was Sarah Patton. Other ancestors of Mr. Simpson were sturdy New Englanders. Thus through thirty-two colonial officers he descended, beginning with his earliest ancestor in America, William Bassett, 1621; honored early emigrant ancestors being those of Hinckley, Lathrop, Porter, Hammond, Palmer, Stanton, Minor, Cook, Atwood, Place, Bourne, Prescott, Gardner, Howland, Sampson, Williams, Wheeler, Breed, Materson, Larned, Porter, Avery, Park, Dennison, Tupper, Burt, Nash, Hallet, Thompson, Greenslade, Borodell, Prentice, Lord, Ti den, et al., all sturdy, aggressive, resourceful pioneers. Men whose aristocracy was that of achievement as is testified by the pages of American History.

Judge Nathan Simpson was a pupil of the ante-bellum schools. Not until after his marriage with Livia Nye, and through her co-operation, was he enabled to attend Athens, Ohio, College; then Cincinnati, Ohio, College, where March 2, 1843, he received the degree of Bachelor of Laws. He became the law partner of Hon. Samuel Vinton, M.C. He served in many capacities of honor and trust. He resided during his long professional career at Pomeroy, Ohio, dying at Middleport, Ohio, April 11, 1875. His second wife, Ann Hendry, of Frederick County, Maryland, preceded him in 1868. His son, George Perry Simpson, was educated in the schools at Ruthland, Ohio; Pomeroy, Ohio, Academy, and at Athens, Ohio, College. In 1859 he entered the law office of his father, whose law partner and former pupil was the Hon. Charles H. Grosvenor, later for many years a Member of Congress. Upon Mr. Simpson's admission to the Bar this firm became Simpson, Grosvenor and Simpson. Judge Simpson's health failing he retired from practice in 1865.

GEORGE PERRY SIMPSON

In April, 1866, our subject migrated from Pomeroy, Ohio, to Mason City, West Virginia, where he held the office of Mayor of that (then) young town, thence to Point Pleasant in 1872. There he became the law partner of Hon. Henry J. Fisher, member of the Virginia Constitutional Convention of 1850, the most eminent lawyer in that part of the State. In his office were educated some of the most brilliant lawyers West Virginia has produced. Mr. Fisher retiring from practice because of advanced age, Mr. Simpson associated with him in the practice of the law Hon. Hiram R. Howard. This partnership continued until December 14, 1892, when occurred the death of Mr. Simpson at his home at Point Pleasant.

Mr. Simpson, at Gallipolis, Ohio, on May 28, 1861, was united in marriage with Phebe Almeda Kennedy, aged seventeen years, daughter of Mr. James Kennedy, of Pomeroy, Ohio (he a native of Pennsylvania and wife, Marie Marguerite Von Schriltz, a descendant of Louis Victor Von Schriltz, one of the French Five Hundred, who founded the City of Gallipolis, Ohio). This union resulted in the birth of children, Livia Nye (wife of Judge George Poffenbarger), Charles Kennedy, deceased, Mary Margaret (Mrs. N. L. Bryan), Dr. John Nathan Simpson and George Melvin Simpson.

Mr. Simpson was elected Prosecuting Attorney of Mason County in 1876. Those who sought his aid in misfortune and were acquitted because of his interest and never failing appeal, were now arraigned before the man who must prosecute offenders and no guilty one escaped. During his professional career he defended forty-eight men tried for their lives, one of whom served a year's imprisonment. The rest were cleared. Thus Mr. Simpson's record was unsurpassed in the State as the friend of the unfortunate. Judge Henry Brannon of the West Virginia Supreme Court, said of him, that while his reputation as a leading criminal lawyer was unchallenged, no man of the State at the time of his death had won more civil cases in the Supreme Court. While his professional record was a proud one his assurance of immortality laid in his devotion to his friends, his ideals and his unbounded charity. No client was ever turned aside because of his inability to pay.

Mr. Simpson's political affiliations were those of a Democrat. For many years he was the most magnetic man in State, Congressional or his own County Conventions. The alacrity with which he reached a conclusion made him invincible at such times. This with a vibrant ringing voice and splendid good humor, carried all as a whirlwind before him. He not only made the speech nominating Hon. John E. Kenna, resulting in each of his nominations for Congress, but when his election to the United States Senate was not assured, Mr. Simpson drove overland through ice and snow (there being no railroad connections) from Charleston to Wheeling, returning with sufficient petitions to give to Mr. Kenna the election by the West Virginia joint assembly of the Legislature, lacking one vote. Without rest Mr. Simpson turned his horses' heads toward Mason County again, and returning brought the pressure of petition that induced the casting of the vote of the Republican State Senator, Dr. J. M. Hensly for John E. Kenna.

Thus West Virginia was represented in the Upper House of Congress by a man whose statue is to-day in the Capitol at Washington among the most honored of the Nation.

Mr. Simpson was a Union man, but when hostilities of the Civil War had ceased and the terrible days of reconstruction followed (knowing the Southern people because he was reared by a Southern stepmother and loved her family as his own), he canvassed the entire State of West Virginia, advocating the first submission of the amendment that would enfranchise all men of voting age in the State, restoring to the Southerners the right of suffrage. While the first submission did not see the amendment carried, upon its second submission and final one no man in West Virginia did more for its passage than he. He not only canvassed West Virginia, but spoke in the States of Virginia, Maryland and Kentucky as well.

Whether his matchless magnetism and oratory was swaying a jury or a convention, or he was the center of conversation, or in his home, he was always the same leader. The broadest word in his vocabulary was Friend and for him it was all who knew him. He was a member of the A. F. and A. M. Lodge at Point Pleasant. His interment was at Point Pleasant (Lone Oak) Cemetery, December 18, 1892. A larger concourse followed him to his long resting place than any ever before or since known in that county. Services were conducted from the Presbyterian Church.

## Hon. Charles William Campbell

Mr. Campbell is one of the best known and best established attorneys in the southern portion of West Virginia, and at present is a member of the strong law firm of Campbell, Brown and Davis of Huntington, Cabell County, West Virginia. He is a son of Robert D. and Mary Campbell and was born in Monroe County, Virginia, September 29, 1856. He received his primary education in the public schools of his native county and later he attended the State Normal School at Athens, Mercer County; after leaving said school in June, 1877, he studied law, passed the required examination by three Circuit Judges and was admitted to the Bar at Hamlin, Lincoln County, in April, 1881. Shortly thereafter he removed his residence to the city of Huntington, where he has since resided and has conducted a very successful business, which has developed into large proportions, in all of the State and Federal Courts of West Virginia. His practice is general, although he has specialized in corporation business, in which he is well known as an able and successful attorney. He is studious, attentive to his duties, is an omnivorous reader and a constant student of valuable books, as well as those pertaining to his profession. His learning is extensive and varied. He is a genial companion, is of imposing appearance, is sociable and agreeable, and has the implicit confidence of all who come in contact with him. His character, in every respect, is above reproach, and his entire life has been devoted to raising the standard of the people to higher conceptions of life and duty. His life is an example of wisdom, learning, fidelity, a scrupulous attention to the best traditions of the profession and a stainless observance of its best methods.

In politics he is a Democrat, but in no sense is he a strenuous partisan. He has positive convictions, but always leans towards justice and right. He has never held but one political office and that was as a member of the West Virginia Legislature in 1911–12. Being a superior debater he was active in leadership, and was considerate and wise in the measures he supported as a law-maker.

He married Miss Jennie E. Ratliff, August 29, 1888, by whom he had five children. For many years he has been a very active and useful member of the Presbyterian Church at Huntington. He has also been an active leader in the civic development of his home city and delights in its growth and prosperity. He is President of the West Virginia National Bank of Huntington, and is interested in other business enterprises. He is always found on the moral side of every question that comes before the public. He is tall and commanding in appearance and in all respects is an ideal lawyer and citizen.

## Patrick J. Crogan

Our subject, the son of James and Rose (Doyle) Crogan, was born in Preston County, Virginia, June 17, 1856, and received his education in the common schools of his native county, and at a private school taught by Professor Painter, of Roanoke College, Virginia. He is a graduate of no college, but nevertheless he is a man of learning, and is also a lawyer of erudition and broad experience. He possessed an aspiration for knowledge which no circumstances of his youth could suppress, and an ambition to achieve a name and a place among men undaunted by any prospect which the future could present to his view. While a college education is always helpful to a young man starting out in a profession, yet many young men of energy and perseverance have demonstrated that it is not absolutely essential to one's success in life. Mr. Crogan possessed a vigor, perseverance and inquisitiveness of mind that permitted nothing to pass from his observation without his thorough comprehension of its character; and to these trained habits of sensation and perception was added a well regulated judgment. While these qualities will assert their superiority in whatever sphere they may be exercised, they are of all others the most important qualifications for success in the practice of the law.

Mr. Crogan after securing the best preliminary education at his command taught in the public schools of his native county for seven years and was measurably successful. He, however, had made up his mind in early life to become a lawyer, and whilst teaching school he read law under the direction of Judge John W. Mason, an able lawyer and an apt teacher.

PATRICK J. CROGAN

In this way he prepared himself for admission as an attorney of the Preston County Bar in 1881, where he has since practiced in that and the adjoining counties, embracing cases in all the State and Federal Courts. As a lawyer he is profound and exact. He is methodical and laborious in the preparation of his cases, and is always well armed with precedent and authority. He is cautious and deliberate in assuming his ground, and surveys with care every inch of the field before he makes an attack or plants his lines of defense; hence there is a fixed precision — an engaged certainty attending the positions he takes, which no skill of sophistry can shake. His judgment is intuitive and his logical powers spontaneous. He readily perceives the main points in a case and addresses himself to the gist of the controversy. Another feature which adds greatly to Mr. Crogan's success as a lawyer is his uniform placidity and good nature. While stern in his convictions and in the positions he assumes, his professional ethics are marked by a cultured suavity which preserves the most cordial relations between himself and the other members of the Bar, and in this way he often wields, with marked success, the club of a Hercules wreathed with roses, which leaves no scars in a court trial.

While he is a pronounced Democrat in politics he never sought office, preferring to give his entire time and energies to his profession. He has thus made himself a high-grade lawyer and one of the leaders of the profession in the State; and all the while he has lived a clean and upright life. Whilst he has been married for a number of years he nas never been blessed with even a single child. He resides in Kingwood, the seat of justice of his native county, where he has always lived and has the confidence and respect of all who know him.

## Judge Warren B. Kittle, LL.B.

The subject of this sketch was born December 23, 1872, at Belington, Barbour County, West Virginia. He is the son of George Monroe Kittle and Charity Ellen (Poling) Kittle, and is a descendant of Abraham Kittle, Sr., who was born in New Jersey in January, 1731, and who moved to Randolph County, Virginia, prior to 1781, where he died September 6, 1816, leaving numerous descendants.

Since 1875 Judge Kittle has resided at Philippi, West Virginia. He was educated in the public schools and the West Virginia University, where he received the degree of LL.B. in June, 1894. He was married June 30, 1897, to Zonie Wilson, and they have three children, Virginia, Nellie and George.

Judge Kittle was admitted to the Bar at Philippi, June 25, 1894, and has successfully practiced in the State and Federal Courts, participating in most of the important cases in his locality, where he is well and favorably known. He was elected Prosecuting Attorney of Barbour County in 1907

JUDGE WARREN B. KITTLE

and served satisfactorily until 1909. He was appointed by Governor William E. Glasscock Judge of the Nineteenth Judicial Circuit, May 24, 1911. His service being acceptable and satisfactory he was elected Judge of that Circuit by the people in 1912, and has served in that responsible position until this time. He has always been a hard student, owning one of the largest and best equipped law libraries in the State, and having a large and profitable clientage. He is the author of " The Law of Rule Days " and a recent treatise on " The Modern Law of Assumpsit," both of them being valuable books to the profession, and are in general use by attorneys.

Judge Kittle is a member of the American Bar Association, the Methodist Episcopal Church, the Independent Order of Odd Fellows and the Knights of Pythias. He is regarded as a just judge, a sound lawyer, a faithful husband and father and a man whose life and character are enriched with noble qualities of head and heart, and has acquitted himself well in both of the high public positions he has thus far held.

## Hon. Charles W. Osenton, LL.B., LL.M.

Senator Osenton is a native of Kentucky, and is a son of George N. and Daisy (Lansdowne) Osenton. He was born at Ashland, Boyd County, Kentucky, May 9, 1865, received several years instruction in the public schools of Carter County, Kentucky. Shortly after he was born his parents moved to Ceredo, Wayne County, West Virginia, where they resided until he was seven years old; then moved to Grayson, Carter County, Kentucky, to a farm; he lived and worked on a farm and went to the common schools until he was seventeen years old, then went to work on a railroad; followed railroading from the Construction to the Transportation Departments; worked as shipping clerk in a wholesale house in Portsmouth, Ohio, for one year and a half. In the fall of 1886 he came to Montgomery, West Virginia, and clerked in a hotel; studied law until 1893; was appointed Chief of a Division in the Treasury Department; moved to Washington; entered the Georgetown Law School; took a four years' course; graduated LL.B. in the year 1895, and later took a post-graduate course in 1896; and received the Degree of LL.M. from the same law school.

He was admitted to the Bar of Berkeley County, West Virginia, the year of his graduation from college. He, however, did not enter regularly upon active practice until 1897, when he located permanently at Fayetteville, Fayette County, West Virginia, opened a law office and entered upon what very shortly proved to be a remarkably successful career as a practicing attorney. He is gifted in an unusual degree in public speech, and because of that particular gift he, at an early period of his practice, took a leading place at the Fayette County Bar in the criminal side of the court, and in an unusually short time he had all the criminal practice he could attend to and thus assured his success as an attorney. His practice

HON. CHARLES W. OSENTON

extended into a dozen or more of the neighboring counties. In April, 1907, he formed a partnership with Gen. C. C. Watts, under the firm name of Osenton & Watts, in Fayette County; later General Watts retired from the firm; he then formed a partnership with Vernon C. Champe, now Judge of the Circuit Court of Fayette County, and A. D. Smith, Jr., under the firm name of Osenton, Smith & Champe, Mr. Smith and Mr. Champe retired from the firm in 1902; formed a partnership with the Hon. W. L. Ashby, of Charleston, under the firm name of Osenton & Ashby. In 1905 Mr. Ashby retired from the firm; formed a partnership with the late E. M. McPeak, which was dissolved by the death of Mr. McPeak in 1909; then formed a partnership with A. J. Horan, under the firm name of Osenton & Horan, which was dissolved, and Mr. Horan retired from the firm March 1, 1918; then formed the present partnership with Hon. W. L. Lee, former Judge of the Circuit Court of Fayette County, for the practice of law under the firm name of Osenton & Lee.

Mr. Osenton has always been an active adherent of the Democratic party, and being a high grade stump speaker his services are in great demand in every State and National campaign. His first public office was Chief of a Division in the Treasury Department at Washington from 1893 to 1897; elected to the State Senate from the Ninth Senatorial District, which was then composed of the counties of Fayette, Summers, Monroe, Greenbrier and Pocahontas. While holding office as State Senator in the year 1900 he was elected Prosecuting Attorney of Fayette County for four years, and served until January, 1905; was a delegate to the Democratic National Convention at St. Louis from the Third Congressional District in 1904, and also a delegate at large to the National Democratic Convention at Denver in 1908. However he never allowed office holding to materially interfere with his law business. In all the public positions he ever held he acquitted himself with honor, credit and ability. His practice for the first few years was mainly confined to the criminal side of the courts, but it has extended to all branches of the law in all the State and Federal Courts, including the United States Appellate Court of the Fourth Judicial Circuit and the Supreme Court of the United States. He is a thoroughly equipped lawyer, and handles his cases ably and generally successfully. He rarely loses a case that he ought to win.

He is a Presbyterian in his religious faith and is a member of the Masonic Fraternity. He is married and resides at Fayetteville, the seat of justice of Fayette County.

---

## Judge William L. Lee, LL.B.

Judge Lee's parents were Captain W. P. F. and Nannie S. Lee, of Crawford, Franklin County, Virginia, where the Judge was born May 10, 1879. He was educated in the public schools of that county, at Hampden-Sidney College, Virginia, Emory and Henry College also of Virginia, and took the law course at the University of Virginia, graduating with the Degree of

JUDGE W. L. LEE

Bachelor of Laws in June, 1902. In July of that year he was admitted to the Bar at Rocky Mount, the seat of justice of Franklin County. Immediately after his admission as an Attorney he formed a partnership with L. W. Anderson, which continued until September, 1904, when Mr. Lee desiring a better business location, decided to settle at Fayetteville, West Virginia, and the firm was accordingly dissolved. About two years after locating in West Virginia, Mr. Lee and Mr. R. T. Hubard, Jr., became partners in business at Fayetteville, which continued until January 1, 1913, when Mr. Lee, who had been elected a Circuit Judge, entered upon the duties of his office. He served most acceptably as a Circuit Judge from January 1, 1913, to March 1, 1918, when he resigned and became a member of the firm of Osenton & Lee at Fayetteville, Attorneys and Counsellors at Law, a strong combination of well known and successful lawyers.

While Judge Lee was a member of the Bar his energy, fidelity and integrity soon commanded an extensive and lucrative business, while his steady and vigorous application gathered a knowledge of law which equipped him admirably for the judiciary. He was married April 12, 1916, to Ann Montgomery Hawkins, by whom he has one child — William L. Lee, Jr. In politics he is a Democrat. He is also a member of the Masonic Fraternity.

Judge Lee's little more than five years' service as a jurist was both able and honorable and satisfactory to the people of all classes. It was marked by that degree of rectitude which finds its reward in the commendation of all good men, and in the smiles of heaven which mirror themselves upon the unruffled surface of a clear conscience. He, however, preferred the "saw dust" to the "wool sack," and was not entirely happy until he could mix in the causes as a partisan, rather than sit as an unbiased umpire from the throne of a jurist. In most cases the emoluments of a good practitioner are two or three times larger than the salary of a judge, and the labor is not as great. We do not mean to say that this influenced Judge Lee to return to the practice; and even if it did, we do not condemn him for so doing. Anyway, he was an upright and able Judge; but he is also an able and honorable counselor. Judge Lee has not yet attained his full stature as a lawyer, not yet being quite forty; he still has room to grow, and is growing.

Judge Lee has practiced in all of the State and Federal Courts in West Virginia and also in the Federal Circuit Court of Appeals of the Fourth Judicial Circuit at Richmond, Virginia. He is a well-known, able and honorable lawyer and jurist.

## John L. Hechmer

The subject of this sketch is one of the able and firmly established lawyers of the central part of West Virginia, where he has practiced almost continuously for more than forty years and has conducted a successful and profitable business. He was born at Baltimore, Maryland, in 1855, and is the son of Louis and Dorothea Hechmer. He was educated at St. Vincent's

College, Pennsylvania, and at Georgetown University, Washington, D. C., where he took its course of law studies. After leaving college he located at Grafton in Taylor County, West Virginia, was admitted to the Bar in 1877 and has since continuously practiced. Whilst he has always affiliated with the Republican party, he has never been active in politics, and cannot, therefore, be classed as an active partisan. He has never filled any political office, except a member of the City Council and Mayor of Grafton, the principal city of Taylor County. He has shown himself to possess a deep interest in the growth and progress of his county and State. His best efforts and energies, however, through a very active life, have been devoted to the practice of his profession. He is thoroughly grounded in the law, is a most industrious worker, is a careful pleader and tries his cases ably. His learning is varied and extensive. His force of will, self-reliance and courage are more than common. Into whatever duty he enters he throws his strong personality and he never fails when he deserves to succeed. He has a strong, logical mind and presents his cases clearly and forcefully, and generally successfully.

He was twice married and has fourteen children. He is a Roman Catholic in his religious convictions and is a member of the world-wide fraternity of Knights of Columbus.

Mr. Hechmer is a man of even temperament, sound judgment, never thrusts his opinions on others, is rather inclined to be reticent and reserved, is talked to more than he talks to others, and when he offers an opinion on any subject it is well worth careful consideration. When he prepares a law suit he rests it upon well-settled legal principles; does not allow himself to be flurried or frightened, nor can he be driven from what he believes to be sound, legal principles and conclusions. He knows the law and tenaciously adheres to it. He has achieved his high standing at the Bar of the State by strict application to his calling and constant watchfulness of the interests of his large clientage.

## Judge Ephraim F. Morgan

Our subject, the son of Marcus and Jennie Wymer Morgan, was born in Marion County, West Virginia, January 16, 1869, and received his education in the public schools of his native county, and at the Fairmont State Normal School. After nine years' experience teaching in the public schools of Marion County he entered the Law Department of the West Virginia University and graduated therefrom in the class of 1897. Immediately thereafter he was admitted to the Fairmont Bar and entered upon the vigorous practice of his profession. Being a young man of sound body and rugged intellect, and being known as a man of integrity and thorough reliability, he was not long in gathering about him a profitable clientele. His practice was of a general character in all of the State and Federal Courts. He very soon made a reputation or being more than an average trial lawyer. He is faithful to his clients, is a man of marked personal appearance, is of large stature, strong features, and possesses energy and force. He is also careful, clear-headed, systematic and thorough in his work, and is agreeable, kindly disposed and social in his makeup. Above all, his personal character has always been above reproach. It is not any wonder, therefore, that his life, thus far, has been a continuous success.

He began his official life as attorney for the city of Fairmont, in which office he rendered satisfactory service. He also served as President of the Board of Education of Palatine Independent School District. From 1907 to 1913, inclusive, he was Judge of the Intermediate Court of Marion County. In this capacity his public service was of a most satisfactory character, as he proved to be an able, just and upright Judge. At the expiration of this term of six years' service he returned to the practice with renewed energy and zeal, and his business was rapidly expanding when he was again called into the service by appointment from Governor H. D. Hatfield to a four years' term, from June 1, 1915, to May 31, 1919, as a member of the West Virginia Public Service Commission, a highly responsible and lucrative position. He has filled the same for nearly four years with credit and ability and to the satisfaction of all the parties concerned.

This Commission is a court of the people. The technical rules of pleading and procedure do not obtain. Any citizen feeling himself aggrieved by any act of a public service corporation, or of its failure to act when it is its duty so to do, can without cost to himself, make complaint to the Commission by simply writing a letter and stating the facts. The Commission holds daily sessions, except Saturdays and Sundays. It is in this line of work that the Commission is of the greatest benefit to the people. It is composed of three members — all of them lawyers, and their duties are semi-judicial. It is their business to prevent corporations from imposing excessive and unjust charges for services rendered or failure to render such service as the law requires. The Commission is bi-partisan, and is at present composed of two Republicans and one Democrat, Judge Morgan being one of the majority members.

Judge Morgan was a volunteer soldier in the Spanish-American War, serving until its close. He is married and has one child living and one dead. His home is in the city of Fairmont, but he is residing temporarily at Charleston, the Capital of the State.

## Hon. Ulysses Grant Young, LL.B.

Among the able, prominent West Virginia lawyers of the central portion of the State is the subject of this sketch. He is a native of Harrison County, West Virginia, where he was born January 22, 1865. He attended the public schools of his native county and then entered the National Normal University at Lebanon, Ohio, from which he graduated with the degree of Bachelor of Laws in 1888. Having chosen Buckhannon, in Upshur County, as his future residence, immediately after his graduation from

HON. U. G. YOUNG

college, he was received as a member of the Upshur County Bar and began life as a lawyer in that little city of great possibilities and of unusual promise, where he has since resided and has by industry and the strictest integrity won a high standing in his profession. Rarely is there found in the ranks of any calling one so symmetrical in mind and character, one so sound in judgment, so unerring in moral perception, so faithful to every duty and so loyal to the right, as is this man Young. He is, therefore, a broad, thorough, conscientious lawyer, who maintains a large general practice in all the State and Federal Courts of West Virginia and the United States Circuit Court of Appeals for the Fourth Judicial Circuit.

He has always adhered to the principles of the Republican party, and was its candidate for a seat in the State Senate in the campaign of 1894, was elected and served four years with ability, credit and honor. Later he was his party's nominee for Judge of the Circuit Court, but on account of some factional disturbance in the ranks of his circuit he was defeated. For a number of years past, he has given his undivided time to the practice of his profession, which steadily increases in volume and income.

Senator Young was a member of the Commission appointed to adjust the debt resulting from the Civil War, between Virginia and West Virginia, and served ably and efficiently for several years thereon. He is a useful member of the Methodist Episcopal Church, and for nearly a score of years he has been a member of the Board of Trustees of the West Virginia Wesleyan College at Buckhannon, and is also a member of its Executive Committee and attorney for the corporation. He is a Freemason and a Knight of Pythias.

He married Miss Lillie Cecelia Pifer, by whom he has four children — two girls and two boys. They live in an elegant mansion on Kanawha street in the city of Buckhannon.

## Hon. Riley A. Blessing, LL.B.

Senator Blessing, son of Calvin Thomas and Sarah Josephine (Board) Blessing, was born near Letart, Mason County, West Virginia, December 11, 1875, and received his education in the public schools of Mason County, at the Spencer Normal, at Spencer in Roane County, West Virginia, and at the Strayers Business College, Washington, D. C. Later he entered the Law Department of George Washington University, Washington, D. C., and graduated in the class of 1906 with the degree of Bachelor of Laws. Prior to his entering upon his law studies he taught in the public schools in Mason County from 1894 to 1901 on a No. 1 certificate, and made an enviable record as a teacher. He says that during this period he consumed no small quantity of midnight oil, not only on his work as a teacher, but in a systematic course of reading of valuable books in order to store his mind with knowledge, which he knew he must possess to get on in the world. From 1901 to 1911 he was an employee of the United States Senate, and while

HON. RILEY A. BLESSING

thus engaged he took the complete law course at George Washington University at the National Capital, and graduated as a Bachelor of Laws. After successfully passing the rigid examination required by the Washington Bar Association he was admitted as an attorney of the District Bar in 1906. He formed a partnership with David A. Butz and practiced with him in the city of Washington from 1906 to 1911 under the firm name of Butz and Blessing. Believing that there were better opportunities for a well-equipped young lawyer in West Virginia than any other place in the entire country, he returned to Point Pleasant, the seat of justice of his native county, formed a partnership with F. G. Musgrave, early in January, 1913, opened a law office and has made that his permanent abiding place. Mr. Musgrave is the present Prosecuting Attorney of Mason County, and the firm is carrying on a profitable and growing business.

Mr. Blessing is a Republican in politics and has been rather active since the campaign of 1896, having served as a member of the Mason County Executive Committee that year. He was nominated and elected to the State Senate in 1912 and was one of the leading members of that distinguished body for the full term of four years. He is a fluent and forceful public speaker, sees a point quickly, and readily took rank as a floor leader. He was also active in committee work and was at the forefront in shaping the legislation of that period. He ranked high as a debater, and his record was clean and honorable. His entire public career has been able and exemplary and his private life is without spot or blemish. He is methodical in the preparation of his cases, and is always well armed with precedent and authority. He is fluent and forceful in speech, and stands high as an advocate. In social life he is generous and kind, courteous and affable in his demeanor to all classes on all occasions and at all times.

Senator Blessing was appointed by the State Tax Commissioner July 1, 1917, to the position of Taxation Assistant for West Virginia, a very important legal office, where he is now serving with great acceptability.

He was united in marriage with Miss May Van Matre. He is a communicant of the Baptist Church, and is invariably found on the moral side of all important matters that come before him.

## Captain Samuel Brashear Avis, LL.B.

The subject of this brief biography is a native of Harrisonburg, Rockingham County, Virginia, where he was born February 19, 1872. His father was Braxton Davenport Avis and his mother was Hattie (Wilson) Avis. The father departed this life some three years ago at Washington, D. C. The mother still resides in that city. His father entered the military service of the Southern Confederacy, as a drummer boy, at the age of eleven years and remained until the close of the war. He was, perhaps, the youngest soldier in either of the armies during the late Civil War, and for that reason he was the subject of many flattering and deserved eulogies.

HON. S. B. AVIS

Our subject was educated in the public schools of his native county and at the well-known Military Academy at Staunton, Virginia. After the completion of an academic course of studies he matriculated as a student of law at Washington and Lee University of Lexington, Virginia, from which high grade institution he graduated a Bachelor of Laws in 1893. Shortly thereafter he opened a law office in Charleston, West Virginia, where he has since resided and where he has gathered about him a large and profitable clientage. He is now known and recognized as one of the very able lawyers of the southern portion of West Virginia, if not, indeed, in the entire State. He was twelve years Prosecuting Attorney of Kanawha County, which long experience enabled him to completely master every branch of criminal practice and to establish a reputation as, perhaps, among the foremost criminal lawyers in the entire State. His sincere, frank and aggressive disposition, coupled with unsurpassed industry and courage of convictions, render him a dangerous antagonist in any sort of a law-suit. He frequently devotes entire nights in order to go to the bottom of an important case. This fact, more than any other, has been the principal secret of his success. He has made good the old proverb that, in any calling, "Work Wins."

Since arriving at manhood, Mr. Avis has shown a strong liking for politics. He is a popular, and has always been an ardent, Republican, as was his father before him. He is an able and convincing "stump speaker" and an excellent organizer. He was employed for four years as the law clerk in the office of the United States District Attorney, and for a short time was Assistant United States Attorney for the Southern District of West Virginia; was elected in 1890 and twice re-elected Prosecuting Attorney of Kanawha County, which embraced a period of twelve consecutive years. In this important position he made an almost unparalleled record as a public prosecutor. In 1898 he served as Captain of Company A, Second West Virginia Volunteers in the War with Spain, and remained therein until the close of the war. He was elected a member of the Sixty-third Congress and made the reputation of an intelligent, attentive and able Representative. He was defeated for a second term and settled down to hard work in his law office, where much "midnight oil" is steadily consumed. For the past four years he has been employed as counsel and legal advisor of the West Virginia Public Service Commission, a position which requires both time and legal knowledge to properly fill, in which his services have been eminently satisfactory.

In December, 1899, Captain Avis was united in marriage with Miss Florence Miriam Atkinson, a daughter of Ex-Governor Atkinson, by whom he had two children — a boy and girl. They live in a neatly appointed home in the city of Charleston and make up a happy and affectionate household.

Captain Avis is a thoroughly grounded lawyer, and is a man of high integrity. He handles a large volume of civil business, and practices in all of the State and United States Courts within the State and in the United

States Court of Appeals for the Fourth Judicial Circuit, and also in the District Court of the Western District of Virginia. For a number of years his reputation as a lawyer was confined principally to the criminal side of the court, but for the past six or eight years he has devoted his time and energies almost exclusively to civil business, which is much more profitable in every respect. Of later years he has specialized in land laws and land-title litigations. In short, he is well equipped as an all-round lawyer and ranks among the able members of the profession in the entire State.

## Hon. William H. H. Flick

Mr. Flick is a native of the Western Reserve of Ohio, where he was born in 1841. He was educated in the public schools and at Hiram College, near Cleveland. In July, 1861, he volunteered as a private soldier in the Federal Army and was dangerously wounded in the left shoulder at the battle of Shiloh, Mississippi, but continued in the service until the fall of 1862, when he was honorably discharged on account of said wound. He returned to his home and taught school for three years. Having read law in the meantime, he was licensed to practice in September, 1865. In March, 1866, he moved to West Virginia, and began to practice law at Moorefield, the seat of justice of Hardy County, and in March, 1867, he changed his residence to Franklin, Pendleton County. He had a strong legal mind, was an able public speaker, and soon became recognized as a forceful and successful lawyer. He was elected Prosecuting Attorney of Pendleton County in 1867, also of the adjoining county of Grant in 1872, and he was re-elected to the same office in Pendleton County in 1873–4. In 1874 he resigned the office of Prosecuting Attorney and located at Martinsburg, Berkeley County, where he spent the remainder of his life.

In the fall of 1868 he entered the State Legislature from Pendleton and Grant Counties, and was re-elected in 1869. He took an active part in legislation. He was the author of what was known as "The Flick Amendment" to the State Constitution, which removed all restrictions from all persons who had engaged in the Rebellion of 1861–5, which gave him a State-wide reputation. In 1881 he was elected Prosecuting Attorney of Berkeley County, which he resigned in 1882 to accept the higher position of United States District Attorney for West Virginia. By this time he had become an unusually able lawyer, and one of the strongest and most successful prosecutors in the Commonwealth. We put it mildly when we state that he had but few equals, anywhere, as a trial lawyer. He was a very large man, and when he became aroused his reserve force was practically irresistible, because he apparently would break down all opposition and often sweep things before him.

In 1876 he was the Republican candidate for a seat on the Supreme Court of Appeals of the State, but was defeated along with his entire party ticket.

In 1886 and again in 1888 he was the Republican candidate for Congress in the Second Congressional District, and both times he was defeated by a very small majority. He was known as a man of unflinching loyalty to truth, justice and principle. He was conscientious and generous to a fault. He died of apoplexy at his home in Martinsburg, when but little more than fifty years of age.

## Hon. Wells Goodykoontz, LL.B.

Among the able lawyers of southern West Virginia is the subject of this sketch. He is a native of Pulaski County, Virginia, where he was born June 3, 1872. He was educated in the public schools of his native county and at Oxford Academy, Floyd County, Virginia. He received his legal education at Washington and Lee University, at Lexington, Virginia. Shortly after his graduation therefrom he came to West Virginia and located at Williamson, Mingo County, and entered upon the practice of the profession for which he had been thoroughly prepared. Being naturally of studious habits, he was not long in making himself known to the people as a coming man in the legal profession. He became the junior member of the firm of Sheppard and Goodykoontz, which continued until Mr. Sheppard became a member of the State Board of Control at the State Capital. In the meantime the firm grew to be one of the strongest and best known in the Norfolk and Western Railroad region of West Virginia, and had a large and profitable clientage.

For a number of years Mr. Goodykoontz took but little interest in politics, but in 1910 he was placed in nomination by the Republicans of Mingo County for a seat in the lower branch of the West Virginia Legislature and was elected thereto by the people. In that body he applied his industrious habits and made himself one of the most attentive and valuable members of the Legislature, serving on a number of important committees and being Chairman of the Finance Committee. At the expiration of two years' service the people elected him a member of the State Senate for a four years' term, of which body he was elected President, which made him *ex officio* Lieutenant-Governor of the Commonwealth.

Senator Goodykoontz is not only a man of high grade natural ability, but he is regarded among those who know him well as a lawyer of unusual erudition and an honor to the profession. For many years he has been active in the affairs of the West Virginia Bar Association and one of its most useful members. At its annual meeting in July, 1917, he was elected its President. He participates in all of its important discussions and has read papers on a number of valuable and interesting subjects, which have been published in the Year Book of its proceedings.

HON. WELLS GOODYKOONTZ

He is happily married, and, with his wife and her mother, lives in a splendid home in the city of Williamson, where they are well and favorably known and highly respected.

In the State-wide primary election held in June, 1918, he was the nominee of the Republican party in the Fifth District for a seat in the Congress of the United States, and was elected by a large majority.

## Judge Andrew S. Alexander, LL.B.

Andrew Sterrett Alexander, son of William A. and Leonora C. Alexander, was born in Putnam County, West Virginia, August 7, 1867, and was educated in the schools of his native county. On arriving at manhood he became a student at the West Virginia University, from which he was graduated with the degree of Bachelor of Laws. He was admitted as a member of the Kanawha County Bar in 1890, where he practiced until the close of 1891. He then located at Winfield, Putnam County, the next year, and was the junior member of the firm of Gunn and Alexander. Captain W. R. Gunn was an old and able practitioner, and the firm promptly commanded a large and profitable clientage. Captain Gunn died in 1904, and Lewis G. Barnhart became the new partner, under the firm name of Alexander and Barnhart, which partnership continued until 1914. Their practice embraced both the State and Federal Courts, and particularly the Supreme Court of Appeals of West Virginia, and their business grew to large proportions.

In 1892 Mr. Alexander, who had always been a Democrat in politics, was elected to the office of Prosecuting Attorney of Putnam County, which county was strongly Republican. He proved to be so efficient and fair in the enforcement of the laws during his four-year term that the people, without regard to politics, re-elected him in 1896. It is only just for us to state that it is questionable whether Putnam County ever had a more honorable or abler Prosecuting Attorney. After the close of his second four-year term as Prosecuting Attorney of Putnam County, our subject moved his residence to Charleston, where greater opportunities were open to able and energetic lawyers.

After locating in Charleston, Mr. Alexander associated Robert E. McCabe with him in the practice, under the firm name of Alexander and McCabe. Both of them being competent and able young men, who attended strictly to business, their practice soon grew to large proportions. In 1907 Mr. Alexander was chosen Solicitor of the city of Charleston, in which he served efficiently and satisfactorily for two years, and again in 1913 he was elected for another term of two years. He is of a modest, retiring disposition, and is so kind and courteous in his make-up that people are drawn to him. These are the principal reasons why the people always rally to his support when he is a candidate for public favor.

In the campaign of 1916 our subject was the nominee of the Democratic party for Judge of the Court of Common Pleas of Kanawha County, and notwithstanding the fact that the county has, for years, given a large Republican majority to its candidates, he was elected by a decisive majority, thus revealing again the fact that the people, as a rule, when it comes to the test, will stand by a man whom they believe to be square and upright in all of his acts. In this high judicial office Judge Alexander has measured up to the high expectations of the public.

Judge Alexander is a public spirited citizen, is an active worker in the Presbyterian Church, of which he has for years been a Ruling Elder. He is also a stanch member and supporter of the Young Men's Christian Association, and is always found on the moral side of every question that arises in the city, county or State. He is also an active member of the Masonic Fraternity, in which he ranks high and well. He has a wife and three children, and lives happily, as well as hopefully, in the city of Charleston, where he has a large following of true and abiding friends and followers.

## Staige Davis, LL.B.

This well-established attorney is a native of Albemarle County, Virginia, a son of the Reverend Dabney C. T. and Mary B. Davis, who was born in 1877, and was educated in the preparatory schools and at the University of Virginia, from which he graduated a Bachelor of Laws in the class of 1903. He was shortly thereafter admitted as an attorney in the State and Federal Courts of Virginia. In 1905 he and his brother, Dabney C. T. Davis, Jr., who is sketched on another page of this volume, located in Charleston, first under the firm name of Watts, Davis and Davis, and later as Davis, Davis and Hall, both of which proved profitable, and their present business is steadily increasing.

Mr. Davis is a man of more than ordinary natural gifts. His talents are brilliant and his energy indomitable, which have enabled him to advance to a high place in the profession, although he is yet comparatively a young man. He possesses an analytical mind and is versatile in expression. His perception is acute and vigilant, quick to seize upon the gist of a proposition and searching in its penetration. His judgment is balanced by caution in determining the real merits of a legal question, which makes him an unusually successful trial lawyer. His arguments are linked together with sound reason, and his briefs are well prepared and well argued. Supported by an ample store of precedent, strong powers of analogy and parity of reason, his positions, even amid the lurid merits of a doubtful case, are always well fortified and exercise a cogent bearing upon the convictions of a court and jury.

Mr. Davis' personal qualities are such as adorn the best minds and the best characters. He is a man of the highest sense of honor, stern and inflexible in the performance of duty, yet amiable and kind in his disposition, punctilious in gentlemanly amenities and professional ethics, and is highly esteemed by the Bar and the people. He is tall of stature, is naturally kind and courteous and has the confidence of the people who know him. In arguing a cause, he impresses his hearers, and especially the Courts, that he knows what he is discussing.

In politics he is a staunch Democrat, but never aspired to any public office. He is distinctly a lawyer, and devotes his entire time to the study and work of his profession. Whilst his personal appearance is much in his favor, it is rather strange that he has never joined the army of Benedicts.

In his Church relations he is a Protestant Episcopalian.

His firm is engaged in a general practice in all the State and Federal Courts of West Virginia.

## Judge Haymond Maxwell, B.A., LL.B.

Judge Haymond Maxwell, son of the late Judge Edwin Maxwell, was born in Clarksburg, West Virginia, October 24, 1879; received his primary education in the public schools of his native city; later attended the West Virginia University at Morgantown, and graduated therefrom in 1900 with the classical degree of Bachelor of Arts; later he was graduated in the Law Department of the same University in the class of 1901, as Bachelor of Laws. He was admitted to membership of the Clarksburg Bar, the year of his graduation, and entered into partnership with his father as an active practitioner of the law. His father had a large practice, and young Maxwell entered into a profitable clientele from the day his ''shingle'' was suspended over the front door of his law office. He was a clean, well-educated, sincere young attorney, and possessed the confidence and respect of the entire Clarksburg community, which, coupled with industrious habits and honorable methods of living, he was not long in forging to the front as a lawyer of both merit and ability. He is a Republican in politics, but has studiously avoided politics as a business, and preferred the law as a life-work; yet, yielding to entreaties of his friends, he was elected a member of the West Virginia Legislature of 1905, where he rendered efficient and valuable service as a maker of laws.

His father died in February, 1903, which left to him exclusively the control of the large volume of business of the firm of Maxwell and Maxwell, which he handled with ability, skill and judgment, until he was nominated and elected Judge of the Circuit Court composed of the large and populous counties of Harrison and Lewis, in 1914, where he is still serving, his term of office being for eight years. As a lawyer he had an active practice. He is well grounded in the fundamental principles of the law and was faithful to his clients, was eminently fair with his associates, and was thorough and accurate in the preparation of his cases. His practice extended into all the Federal and State Courts of West Virginia. Uprightness of character, firmness of purpose and unswerving integrity are his chief characteristics. As a Judge he is not impulsive, but is calm, deliberate and just. When once settled in his opinions and convictions he is decidedly fearless and frank in their expression. He is easily approached, and combines courtesy and affability with dignity and firmness.

Judge Maxwell is an ardent member of the Methodist Episcopal Church, and is a forward-moving citizen of the community in which he resides.

He was united in marriage with Miss Carrie Maxwell, a daughter of Mr. Porter Maxwell, of Harrison County, by whom he has two children. His residence is within gunshot distance of the spot where he was born. He has absolutely the confidence and respect of every citizen of Clarksburg who has the pleasure of his acquaintance.

## Judge Jake Fisher, LL.B.

Judge Fisher is a native of Flatwoods, Braxton County, West Virginia, where he was born May 26, 1871, and was there reared. He received the best education afforded by the public schools of that section. Having decided to become a lawyer, he early began the study of legal textbooks and later matriculated as a student in the National Normal University at Lebanon, Ohio, where he completed a thorough academic course of study. He then entered the Law Department of Washington and Lee University at Lexington, Virginia, where he took the prescribed course for students who contemplated entering the profession of the law. He possessed a bright mind, was an industrious student, and when he completed his textbook studies he had rounded out a very thorough education; far better than the average young man who contemplated entering the legal fraternity as a life work. He returned to his native county, was admitted to membership of the Braxton County Bar, "hung out his shingle" in Sutton, and in a very short time began to take in fees at a rate that was surprising to him as a young limb of the law. He was and is by nature kind and courteous and has the tact to draw men to him. He has legions of friends and has a broad acquaintanceship among the people. He has a wonderful gift in making friends and holding them. Being thoroughly grounded in the law, and being an industrious worker, and always acting fair and honorable, he was not long in building up a safe and profitable clientage. He is gifted in public speech, and is far above the average advocate. He is an excellent trial lawyer.

From boyhood he has been an adherent of the Democratic party, but never was a rigid partisan. The writer never knew him to act other than in the open in any of his political undertakings. Like most young lawyers, he took a lively interest in political campaigns, and generally got elected to any office he went after. He kept close to the people and almost invariably won out in all of his undertakings. He represented Braxton County two terms in the lower branch of the State Legislature, and was elected to the State Senate in 1904, serving four years. Being an able public speaker he was one of the floor leaders in both and was an active member of the Judiciary and several other important committees, and was liberal and just in all his legislative acts.

In the campaign of 1912 he was nominated and elected a Circuit Judge over several strong competitors, and has given eminent satisfaction to the people. Being well versed in the law, square, upright, industrious, painstaking and just, he has measured up to the high standard expected of him by the people when they elected him to that exalted position.

He is married, has an interesting family and resides at Sutton, the seat of justice of Braxton County, where he has spent practically his entire life. He is a member of the Masonic Fraternity and is personally known and respected by the people of the central portion of the State.

## General Thomas S. Riley

General Riley was born in Marshall County, West Virginia. His early life was spent on a farm; attended and taught public schools. His subsequent education was at Fairmont State Normal School, which he attended in 1875, and the West Liberty Normal School where he was a student in 1876 and 1877, graduating in the latter year. In July, 1877, he entered the law office of J. Dallas Ewing, Esquire, at Wheeling, where he read law, and was admitted to practice October 26, 1878. On April 1, 1879, he formed a partnership with Mr. Ewing, his instructor, and has been in active practice from the date of his admission to the Bar. November 21, 1891, Judge Thayer Melvin having resigned as Judge of the First Judicial District became a member of the firm, under the name of Ewing, Melvin & Riley. This firm continued until 1894 when he withdrew, and Mr. J. W. Ewing took his place in the firm. He was elected Chairman of the Democratic State Committee in 1887 and served as State Chairman for five years. He was appointed by Governor A. B. Fleming as a member of the Board of Regents of the State Normal Schools and served in that capacity for three years. He was elected City Solicitor of the City of Wheeling in February, 1891, and served two years. At the November election of 1892 he was elected to the office of Attorney-General of the State and served acceptably in that office for four years. In 1906 he was a candidate for Congress, being defeated, but succeeded in decreasing materially the normal majority of the opposition.

He was married November 11, 1891, to Miss Minnie B. Breinig, daughter of Michael and Elizabeth Breinig. They have three children, Thomas S., James B. and Robert J. He is a member of the Carroll Club, the Elks Club, the Fort Henry Club and the Country Club. The family are communicants of the Catholic Church and attend St. Joseph's Cathedral at Wheeling.

GENERAL T. S. RILEY

11

General Riley is a close student, a hard worker and has been remarkably successful in the practice of his profession. His standing is high at the Wheeling Bar, and also throughout the entire State, and his private and public character are above reproach. He is an active member of the State Bar Association, and is a regular attendant upon its annual sessions.

---

## Hon. William Edgar Haymond

Our subject was born at Falls Mills on the Little Kanawha River, Braxton County, Virginia, February 17, 1855. His parents were Eugenius and Mary J. Haymond, well-known residents of that locality. He attended the local schools of his neighborhood, and later became an earnest and faithful student of legal text books until he was twenty-four years of age, when, in 1879, he passed a creditable examination, and was admitted as a member of the Braxton County Bar at Sutton, where he has since resided, and where, by faithful application to his office duties, he has made the reputation of being one of the leading lawyers of Central West Virginia. He has given a large part of his time to a careful study of the land laws of the State, and has established a high reputation in that branch of the profession. He has never exhibited a taste or desire to intermeddle with politics, and has never held but one public office — that of Prosecuting Attorney of Braxton County, to which he was elected in 1885, and was re-elected in 1889. He proved to be a strong and successful prosecutor, showing neither fear of, nor favor to, any violator of the law. His eight years as attorney for the people marked him as a man of ability and of undaunted courage and integrity. His practice has extended to all State and Federal Courts, and embraces a large variety of civil causes. Wherever he is known he is regarded as a wise and safe counselor and a lawyer of erudition and of broad experience.

He is married and has two daughters. His home is one of the handsomest in the Town of Sutton, standing on the south bank of Elk River, one of the cleanest and most delightful streams of limpid water that can be found this side of Paradise itself.

His law firm (Haymond & Fox) is well and favorably known throughout Central West Virginia. His accompanying photograph shows him to be a man of medium stature, of firmness, and yet of modest and social disposition. Mr. Haymond is a member of one of the best known and most extensive families in the entire State of West Virginia, who live in Harrison and the near-by counties, and are universally recognized as honorable and prosperous citizens of the Commonwealth.

HON. WILLIAM E. HAYMOND

## Hon. Edward Arnold Brannon, A.B., LL.B.

Our subject, son of Judge Henry Brannon, West Virginia's most eminent jurist, was born in the City of Weston, Lewis County, West Virginia, April 4, 1870, and was educated at the West Virginia University, Princeton University, and the Law Departments of Maryland Law School, and Washington and Lee University, receiving their highest *in cursu* diplomas. But few young men have been favored with the thorough and liberal education that he received before entering upon a professional career. Possessing a strong and vigorous intellect, it is, therefore, not a question of wonderment that he was recognized as a thoroughly equipped lawyer from the time he was admitted to the Lewis County Bar in 1894. However, he has steadily, and we may add, rapidly grown, with practice and experience, until he has attained an enviable and gratifying rank as an attorney in all the courts of the State. His practice is in all the branches of the law in all the courts of the State and National Governments, including the Supreme Court of the United States.

Although he is a scion of a distinguished ancestry, he stands four-square upon his own attainments and his own merits. As we have already stated his father was an eminent jurist, having served eight years as a Circuit Court Judge and twenty-four years as a Justice of the Supreme Court of Appeals of West Virginia; his uncle, Judge John Brannon, was one of the State's distinguished lawyers and jurists, his cousin, the Hon. William W. Brannon, a distinguished attorney of the City of Weston; and on his mother's side he is descended from the distinguished Jackson family, which furnished to the State many able citizens and lawyers, notably Governor Jacob B. Jackson, Judge James Monroe Jackson and Judge John Jay Jackson, who was for forty-two years a Federal Judge and known as the "Iron Judge."

Mr. Brannon's personal character is without a blemish, and his record as a man and lawyer is of the highest possible character. He is also a man of marked personal appearance. He is of good stature, strong features, and in short, his whole aspect is full of force. Being a thoroughly equipped and highly educated lawyer, in the trial of a cause, he offers no apologies and fears no antagonist. In politics he is a Democrat. He, however, in no sense can be classed as an office-seeker. For a number of years he filled the position of Solicitor of the City of Weston, and filled it ably and satisfactorily. Much important litigation took place during his term, known as the street litigation cases, twenty-two in number, which went through the State Courts, the United States Circuit Court of Appeals, and two of them (the cases of James A. Tierney and Sallie E. Tierney against the Town of Weston) were finally appealed to the Supreme Court of the United States and were resolved in favor of the town. Mr. Brannon was the sole attorney for the town in these long drawn out legal contests. The only political office he ever held was as member of the West Virginia Legis-

HON. EDWARD A. BRANNON

lature from Lewis County. In that deliberative body he rendered intelligent and valuable service. Being a man of solid popularity he was vigorously urged by his friends for the office of Attorney-General of the State a few years ago, and since that time he was strongly pressed for a seat in the Congress of the United States, but he was not a seeker after political favors, and lent but little, if any, favor to the requests of his urgent friends, always preferring the law to politics. He was never a seeker after personal honors or self-aggrandizement; his tastes are consistent with his conservative mind in all things. His grasp of public questions, however, is firm and deliberative. Being a logical and forceful public speaker, a scholar and a thoroughly equipped lawyer, he would be an efficient and valued public official in the service of the public in any position worthy of a man of his capacity and high ideals.

Mr. Brannon married Miss Irma Cowey in 1909. They have three children and are residents of the city where Mr. Brannon was born and reared, and have the confidence and respect of all their fellow citizens.

## Abraham Burlew

Our subject is a son of James and Sophia Burlew, and was born near South Amboy, New Jersey, in 1840, and was liberally educated at the Old Shocara Academy and Charlottesville Seminary, New York. He was a law student in the office of Slosson, Hutchins & Platt, successors of Shell, Slosson & Hutchins, No. 40 Wall Street, New York City; passed the rigid examination required by the New York statute, and was admitted as a member of the Bar of that city in 1864. After spending about a year practicing in the New York Courts he was employed by the firm with whom he received his legal training, Scudder & Carter, of 66 Wall Street, New York, and was sent by them to West Virginia to look after the large land and other interests of John Holsted in West Virginia. Accordingly he came to West Virginia in 1865, opened a law office in Charleston, was admitted as a member of the Bar, and has constantly practiced his profession in this city since that time. He is now one of the oldest members of the Charleston Bar. The greater part of his professional life has been devoted to the settlement of the titles of lands owned by John Holsted in this State, which were in great confusion. Many law suits were brought by him for this purpose in the West Virginia Courts, several of which were carried to the Supreme Court of the United States for final adjustment. The titles were ultimately settled in Holsted's favor. At his death in 1899 Mr. Burlew was appointed trustee of his large estate in West Virginia by the Circuit Court of Fayette County, this State, and he subsequently settled the estate, which involved upwards of $300,000.

Mr. Burlew is a retiring, modest, unpretentious man; is well grounded in all the fundamental principles of the law in all of its branches, but has specialized for many years in the settlement of controverted land titles, ejectment suits, etc. He, however, is an all-round, well-read lawyer, who prepares his cases carefully, and is always ready for trial, because he prepares his cases thoughtfully and is, therefore, never taken by surprise. During the fifty odd years he has been a member of the West Virginia Bar he has borne an upright life, is thoroughly trustworthy, and has the confidence and respect of all the people with whom he has come in contact.

He is a Republican in politics; has never held an office of any sort, because he never desired one. He preferred the quietude of his law office. He has always possessed a lucrative practice; has settled a number of large estates, always to the satisfaction of all the parties.

He has never married, and has large property interests in and about Charleston. He is a member of no church, but says " he is a Methodist in belief." He is a member of the Benevolent Protective Order of Elks. He has recently retired from active practice. He never was rugged in health, but is quite active and vigorous for one of his advanced years. He, however, is still able for most any sort of work. He is an admirer of fine horses, and devotes considerable time horseback riding.

## General James William St. Clair

General St. Clair was born at what was then known as Big Lick, now Roanoke, Virginia, January 26, 1853, and completed his education in the College of Poughkeepsie, New York, after which he took up the study of law in the office of Judge D. S. Johnston, of Princeton, West Virginia.

He removed to Fayetteville in 1875, and in the following year established the first newspaper published in Fayette County, the Fayette Enterprise, which is still published as the Fayette Journal. Shortly after coming to Fayette County he formed a law partnership with the late Governor E. Willis Wilson, which continued until the election of the latter to the Governorship in 1884. He then formed a partnership with Hon. Joseph H. Gaines, which continued until 1888, when the final partnership of St. Clair, Walker & Summerfield was formed.

He always took an active part in politics, and was frequently selected by his party as their candidate for positions of honor, and serving as Prosecuting Attorney of Fayette County from 1881 to 1885, and as a member of the State Senate from 1891 to 1895.

He also served as West Virginia's Commissioner of the World's Fair at Chicago, where he was made one of the Board of Managers in control of the management of the Exposition, being associated in that work with Messrs. Geo. K. Massie, of New York, and L. O. Higginbotham and Charles Schwab, of Chicago.

General St. Clair was a Democrat in politics, and since coming to the age of maturity never missed attending a National convention of the party until the last one, which the condition of his health at that time precluded. He was a personal friend of William Jennings Bryan, whom he deeply admired, though not at all times wholly in accord with his doctrines.

He enjoyed an extensive and lucrative law practice, being retained by a number of the leading coal firms in that section, and was engaged in the trial of an important case in Charleston when stricken with his final illness. A man of powerful physique, unbounded energy, and apparently iron constitution, he withstood labors under which the majority of men would have utterly collapsed, until about five years prior to his death, when an affection of the heart became apparent, and after that time his health had been gradually declining until the final seizure came.

General St. Clair was twice married, his first wife being Miss Ella Mahood, of Pearisburg, Virginia, to whom he was united October 14, 1889, the offspring of the union being two sons, Will and Meador, both of whom were students at Culver Institute, and one daughter, Mrs. A. T. Wheeler, of Cincinnati. His second wife, who survives him, and to whom he was married on September 9, 1899, was Miss Cynthia McLaughlin, of New York.

Among the most notable suits in which he has appeared as counsel was the noted Goff-Fleming contest over the Governorship of this State, in which he represented Mr. Fleming, the successful contestant.

Mr. St. Clair received his title of General from Governor Fleming, who gave him a commission as General on his personal staff.

General St. Clair was unquestionably an eminent lawyer. He had a great mind, and very few men had a wider grasp of legal principles. He specialized in corporation matters and handled his cases masterfully. He was also able and strong on Constitutional questions. He could see a point clearly himself, and had the gift of making others see it also. He unquestionably possessed a marvelously discriminating mind. He was a great trial lawyer, and was widely employed in important causes. He was self-reliant, self-asserting and absolutely fearless. All who knew him well must admit that he possessed elements of greatness.

He died all too soon at his home in Fayetteville, November 4, 1900.

## Judge William Smith O'Brien, LL.B.

Judge O'Brien, son of Emmet J. and Martha A. (Hall) O'Brien, was born in Barbour County, West Virginia, January 8, 1862. Shortly after the close of the Rebellion his parents moved to Lewis County, where he grew to manhood. He was educated in the common and graded schools and took the law course at the West Virginia University, from which he graduated in the class of 1891. He taught school for several years before and after completing his law studies, and then was admitted as a member of the Circuit Court Bar at Weston, Lewis County. In 1892 he located permanently at Buckhannon, the county seat of Upshur County, where he opened a law office and began a successful career as a lawyer. In 1896 he

JUDGE WILLIAM S. O'BRIEN

married Miss Emma, the eldest daughter of A. Perry White, of Lewis County, by whom he has four children.

Judge O'Brien is naturally studious, and having read law in the office of Judge John Brannon, an eminent lawyer of West Virginia, for a considerable time before he entered the West Virginia University, he is well up in the technique of the profession; consequently the law course he completed in that institution thoroughly equipped him for a successful career at the Bar, and he made good from the start. He is a Democrat, and has a slight hankering after politics, although in no sense could he be classed as an office-seeker. He was nominated by his party at different times for membership in the House of Delegates and State Senate, but as Upshur County was overwhelmingly Republican, he was defeated with his colleagues on the same ticket; but it is only just for us to state that he invariably ran materially ahead of his ticket. He was later on nominated a second time for membership in the State Senate, but was compelled to decline on account of his rapidly growing law practice.

Judge O'Brien's history as a man and a lawyer, through his entire career, is a record of manliness, complete in every detail. His practice extended into all the branches of the profession, and he dignified it by exhibiting the highest types of integrity, fidelity, learning and wisdom. As an evidence of his personal popularity, he was nominated by the Democratic party of the Twelfth Judicial Circuit as a candidate for Circuit Judge in 1912, and although the Circuit contained a large Republican majority he was elected, with many votes to spare, and has served faithfully and well. He is an honest man and a just Judge. He gained strength rapidly by experience, and has the confidence of all the parties who have transacted business in his courts.

He has disposed of many important law and chancery suits during his term of office, but we will, however, mention but one, namely: what are known as "The West Virginia Bribery Cases," wherein five members of the Legislature were indicted, tried before him and convicted for bartering their votes for money in the election of a United States Senator. The trial was lengthy and tedious, and was conducted on both sides by some of the ablest lawyers in the State. Out of this great trial Judge O'Brien emerged and was universally commended for fairness and integrity. The cases went up to the Supreme Court of Appeals and Judge O'Brien's rulings were sustained.

## Hon. Frank C. Reynolds

Mr. Reynolds, son of Judge F. M. Reynolds, was born at Keyser, West Virginia, January 25, 1868. He attended the public schools of Keyser until he finished the courses, and then, at the age of seventeen years, he attended the University of West Virginia at Morgantown, from which institution he graduated in the year 1890. He was admitted to the Bar of West Virginia at Keyser, Mineral County, April 5, 1891; began the

HON. F. C. REYNOLDS

practice of law at his home town and practiced in most of the counties in that section of West Virginia, and a few in the States of Maryland and Pennsylvania. He was elected to the office of Prosecuting Attorney of Mineral County in the year 1891, and held that office for a term of four years, and was re-elected for another term of four years, making two terms of four years each. He was a thorough lawyer, a strong advocate and an able prosecutor.

He married Jessie R. Knight, November 7, 1894. Three children were born to them — all boys. The eldest, F. Marion Reynolds, Jr., is now in the United States Navy; Knight Reynolds, now at the University of West Virginia at Morgantown, is in the Students Army Training Camp, and Lester Reynolds is attending High School at Keyser.

He was a Master Mason, and belonged also to the Knights of Pythias, and was a member of the Phi Kappa Psi College Fraternity. He was a member of the Methodist Episcopal Church, Keyser, West Virginia; was a Republican in politics; took a very active part in politics and was Chairman for many years of the Republican County Committee of Mineral County.

He was general counsel for the Baltimore and Ohio Railroad Company for many years; attorney for the Central Railroad of New Jersey; Secretary of the McCullough Coal & Coke Company, and Secretary of the Blackwater & Potomac Railroad Company as well as their counsel; attorney for the Watson-Loy Coal Company; attorney for the Piedmont Grocery Company; attorney for the First National Bank of Keyser, West Virginia; attorney for the Keyser Electric Light Company; attorney for the Richardson Furniture Company, as well as many other important interests in that section. He was also attorney for the Union Tanning Company, and attorney for the Frederick Piano Company. Since the European war he was a member of the Legal Advisory Board of Mineral County, and gave his unlimited service and advice to the draftees and their families. He was attorney for the Abrams Creek Coal & Coke Company; also attorney for the Brydon Coal Company. He was attorney for so many large corporations that it is difficult to recall all of them. Whilst he was an able and successful all-round lawyer, he made a specialty of corporation practice, which explains why he was employed as counsel for such a large number of corporations. He was a superior trial lawyer, and ranked among the able stump speakers of the entire State. He departed this life in the midst of his usefulness during the summer of 1918.

## Judge Lewis N. Tavenner

The subject of this sketch ranks among the brilliant, successful lawyers of West Virginia. He is tall of stature, commanding in appearance, social and agreeable by nature, and possesses unusual popularity wherever he is personally known, and but few, if any, citizens of the State are better known or more highly esteemed. He is a son of Isaac Tavenner and was born at Elizabeth, the seat of justice of Wirt County, Virginia, February 17, 1855. His early educational training was in the common schools, but after he reached early manhood he attended Nash's Academy at Parkersburg, Wood County, taking the entire course in higher mathematics, English, literature, the sciences ana the Latin language. This was a noted Academy in its day. Its Principal — Professor John C. Nash — was highly educated, and like "Arnold of Rugby" was a master of the art of teaching. Many of our prominent West Virginia people were trained by him. Under his tutelage young Travenner received the equivalent or more than an average college education. He studied the necessary legal text books at home, passed a creditable examination, and was admitted to the Wood County Bar at Parkersburg in April, 1876, where he has since resided, and has become known as one of its able and well established attorneys and citizens.

He has always been a Democrat in his political associations, but in no respect can he be classed a politician. His leading purpose was to become a lawyer, and he confined his untiring energies in that direction. He is a hard worker, and gives his best efforts to his profession. He stands four-square as a man and lawyer and has always lived an upright life, and has the confidence of the people who know him. All the public offices he ever held were strictly in the line of his profession. His first official position was attorney for the city of Parkersburg. He was a Commissioner of the United States District Court for twelve years, and was Circuit Judge from April 25, 1896, to December 31, 1904. His strongest point as a practitioner is his fluent and forceful method of presenting a case to a court and jury. He has but few equals as a public speaker. His language is chaste, his utterances are rapid and pointed, and his arguments are convincing. In short, it is only fair to class him as a natural orator of unusual gifts. As a Judge his mind was bright and his analytical faculties were of a high order. He had an innate love of justice and his perception was keen and incisive. His leading desire was to be fair and just in all of his decisions. It can be truly said of him that he was a just and upright Judge. After his eight years' service on the Bench he returned to the Bar, and is conducting a profitable business at Parkersburg, where he has spent the greater part of his useful life.

Judge Tavenner and Miss Carrie Kraft were married October 27, 1886, and they have one son and one daughter. They are members of the Methodist Episcopal Church, South. The Judge is a member of all the different branches of Freemasonry. When comparatively a young man he filled the highest office in the Fraternity, that of Grand Master of the State. He is one of the most distinguished and best known Masons in West Virginia, and is highly esteemed by his fraters.

## Hon. William G. Barnhart, LL.B.

Mr. Barnhart, son of Lewis and Isabel Barnhart, was born at Buffalo, Putnam County, West Virginia, April 5, 1880; received a thorough primary training in the public schools of his native county; later he entered the West Virginia University and graduated from the Law Department in the class of 1902, receiving the degree of Bachelor of Laws. He was admitted to the Putnam County Bar the year of his graduation, and practiced his profession at Winfield, the county seat, with a marked degree of success, until April 1, 1907. Desiring a wider field in which to operate, and one which offered greater opportunities for an ambitious young lawyer, he moved his residence to Charleston, the Capital of the State, where he has since resided and is maintaining a profitable clientele. His practice, both in Putnam and Kanawha counties, covered all branches of the profession in State and Federal Courts.

Mr. Barnhart is a Democrat in his political affiliations, and, although his native county was strongly Republican, he was elected as a Democrat to the State Legislature, and served with efficiency and distinction during the session of 1903 and '04. In 1913 he was appointed United States District Attorney for the Southern District of West Virginia and served the full term of four years. It is conceded that he was an able and unusually successful prosecutor of all violators of the laws of the United States. He is an excellent trial lawyer. He prepares his cases carefully, and understands the art of applying facts to the law, and *vice versa*. He has a melodious voice and is attractive in public speech. As a campaigner in politics his rank is high. He is difficult to surpass in his ability to present a case to a jury, and he examines and cross-examines witnesses ingeniously. He understands legal principles thoroughly and cannot be easily camouflaged. He is thoughtful and self-poised, and is dangerous as an opponent in the trial of any sort of a cause. Since his retirement as United States Attorney he is conducting a profitable business in Charleston, where he has resided for many years and is a well-known personage in the community.

Mr. Barnhart married Miss Frankie Ellen Goodwin, January 1, 1908, by whom he has one child, Ruth Frances, born November 3, 1910. He is a member of the Knights of Pythias, the Elks, the Woodmen, the L. O. O. M. and the National Geographic Society. He has never united with any religious denomination.

## Samuel Tilden Spears, LL.B.

Our subject, son of Aaron N. and Rhodea E. Spears, was born in Wetzel County, West Virginia, October 7, 1877. During his younger years he attended the public schools; later he entered the State Normal School at Fairmont, Marion County, and graduated in the class of 1897; still later he became a student in the Law Department of the West Virginia University,

SAMUEL T. SPEARS

and graduated therefrom in 1903 as a Bachelor of Laws. Having decided upon the city of Elkins as one of the most promising locations for a young lawyer, at least, in the central part of West Virginia, he cast his lot there in the fall of 1903, hung out a sign with these words, painted in large letters thereon, "S. T. Spears, Attorney at Law"; and that conspicuous "Shingle" is hanging there yet, and is likely there to remain, it is to be hoped, for forty or fifty years to come. Samuel Tilden, the younger, and the city have developed in about the same proportion, and are still growing, and we hope and expect that they will keep on moving, hand in hand, until they attain full stature. "Elkins is some city," and it cannot be gainsaid that Brother Spears is "some lawyer" also. Nature endowed him with a strong and rugged intellect, and he has made good use of it. He early learned that application, promptness and fidelity are the qualities which insure professional success, and with these he brought to the Bar an honorable ambition and a zealous purpose in every sphere in which his professional services were employed. He possesses indefatigable industry, sound judgment, and is moral and upright in his conduct and dealings. For probity and fair dealing no man in his community stands above him. He is also a safe and sound lawyer, and ranks high in his profession. His practice is of a general character and extends into all the State and Federal Courts.

In politics Mr. Spears is a Democrat. He served for a number of years as a member of the Board of Managers of the State Reform School for Boys, and showed a deep interest in Reformatory work and did much to improve conditions in that institution. He was for six years solicitor of the City of Elkins, and all the while was an attentive and efficient officer. He is Chairman of the Local Draft Board, and has rendered patriotic service to his State and country in the European War. He is a prominent Freemason and is an active member of the Grand Lodge of the State. He is also an influential member of the Methodist Episcopal Church, and in 1916 was elected as a Delegate to the General Conference of that powerful religious organization of the United States and of the world.

Mr. Spears and Miss Stella Gail Ford were married September 21, 1900, and have one child — Marjorie Gail Ford, who was born at Fairmont, West Virginia, August 16, 1901.

Mr. Spears ranks among the splendid citizens of West Virginia, and has the confidence and respect of all the people who know him.

## Col. William Willey Arnett

In the front rank of criminal lawyers at the Wheeling Bar probably unequaled in his knowledge of criminal law, certainly unexcelled in its presentation to the jury, stands the subject of this sketch. This is manifested by his successful defense in some of the most noted *causa celebre* in West Virginia and at the St. Louis Bar. Not so much as an orator, not because of rhetorical finish or grandiloquent sentences, but in his deliberate, methodical presentation of the statutes, his singular power of explaining away damaging testimony, or handling the testifier, his convincing manner of arraying facts and law points as a general masses his heavy and light soldiery for a victorious charge — herein was his strength and the secret of his almost universal success.

Col. W. W. Arnett was the son of Ulysses N. and Elizabeth (nee Cunningham) Arnett, both natives of that part of Monongalia, which later became Marion, County, Virginia. In the latter county he was born October 23, 1843; prepared at Fairmont Academy for Allegheny College at Meadville, Pennsylvania, whence he graduated in 1860. He studied law, before and after his college term, under A. F. Haymond, Ex-Judge of the West Virginia Supreme Bench, and was admitted to practice in 1860 at Fairmont, but closed his office to enlist as a private in Company A, Thirty-first Virginia Infantry; directly after his enlistment he was appointed by Governor Letcher Lieutenant-Colonel of a battalion, which was afterwards merged into the Twenty-fifth Virginia. He resigned his commission, returned to the ranks of his old company and was soon elected its Captain, and so served until 1863, when he was elected Colonel of the Twentieth Virginia Cavalry, the command of which he continued until the close of the war. Twice during the war he was elected by the "refugees and camp voters" to represent Marion County in the Virginia Legislature.

In 1865, because of the "Test Oath" in West Virginia, he resumed practice in Berryville, Clarke County, Virginia; in 1868 he was nominated for the State Senate from that district, but declined, and was immediately after nominated and elected to the Legislature of Virginia from that county. In 1872 he removed to St. Louis, Missouri, and soon established himself in a remunerative and important practice, his reputation as a successful criminal lawyer having preceded him. One of his first cases there, the defense and acquittal of J. H. Fore on a charge of murder, was the subject of complimentary comment in public journals throughout the United States, the St. Louis papers describing his effort as "the most masterly in that Court since Blennerhassett's day." Like encomiums were passed upon his successful defense of Madame Julia Fortmeyer in the celebrated abortion case, and others.

In 1875 he returned to his native State and located at Wheeling, at once becoming one of the prominent attorneys of West Virginia. In the injunction case, Wheeling vs. Charleston, against the removal of the State archives from the latter to the former city, he succeeded before the Supreme Court in having the Capital removed to Wheeling. He was also employed to defend State Auditor E. L. Bennett and Treasurer John S. Burdett in their celebrated impeachment case. He was engaged in practice at Wheeling, as also in different counties throughout the State and before the Supreme Court of West Virginia until his death. After his resumption of practice in West Virginia he was retained on the defense or prosecution of almost every important criminal case before the courts in his section. It is universally conceded that Colonel Arnett was one of the greatest natural lawyers that West Virginia ever produced.

## Hon. Absalom M. Cunningham

The subject of this brief sketch, the son of Solomon and Mary J. (Lantz) Cunningham, of Upshur County, West Virginia, was born at Buckhannon, the seat of justice of that historic county, February 23, 1864, when the new State of West Virginia was not yet a ''yearling.'' For several years he attended the public schools of Buckhannon, and, being ambitious, and desiring to secure a thorough education, he, in early life, determined to prepare himself as a teacher, and when not yet sixteen years of age he secured a teacher's certificate and taught his first term of school. This profession he followed faithfully for twelve consecutive years. In the meantime, having decided to become a lawyer, he began the systematic study of legal textbooks, while he was teaching, and kept it up diligently. He entered one of the State Normal institutions, where he mastered a number of high academic studies. He, however, stuck to his law books with heroic tenacity in the meanwhile. Having acquired the necessary technical legal training, he passed a creditable examination before three Circuit Court Judges, and was by them granted a license to practice in the West Virginia Courts, and was admitted to the Bar in November, 1892, and since then has continuously practiced. His first location was in Tucker County, where he remained sixteen years and had a large clientele. He then, in 1909, moved his office to Elkins, Randolph County, where opportunities were much more advantageous, and is a resident of that thrifty city at this time. His practice is of a general character, and includes all State and Federal Courts and extends into the surrounding counties.

In his political affiliations Mr. Cunningham is an active member of the Republican party. He filled ably the office of Prosecuting Attorney of Tucker County from 1893 to 1897 and was a member of the State Legislature in 1903 and 1904. In both of these offices he acquitted himself with credit and honor. He is a superior public speaker, and, therefore, is an unusually successful trial lawyer; as a legislator he ranked high as a floor manager and debater, and was also useful in committee work. He is a man of large stature, of splendid address and of commanding personal appearance. He is naturally sociable and companionable, and attracts people to him. He is an orator of force and power, and will command attention in the discussion of any important subject. He is also clean and trustworthy, and is well grounded in legal principles.

Mr. Cunningham has been twice married. His first wife was Miss Maude Anvil, whom he married October 15, 1887, and by whom he had four children. His second wife was Miss Grace Isabel Keith, whom he married June 6, 1905, and by whom he had two children. His home life has ever been of the most desirable character.

While the most of Mr. Cunningham's energies are devoted to his profession, he has found time to take an interest in business ventures. He promoted and organized the Miners and Mechanics Bank at Thomas in Tucker County, an institution which pays large dividends. He takes a lively interest in every movement for the development of the internal affairs of his section of the State. His religious affiliations are with the Presbyterian denomination, to which his family has adhered for many generations. Mr. Cunningham is a determined man in character, wise in counsel, eminently practical and possesses the ability to concentrate his mind on one subject to the exclusion of all others, which largely accounts for his success in life.

## Hon. John Hanson Good, LL.B.

Mr. Good came on both sides of his family from early settlers in Ohio County, Virginia. His paternal grandfather, John Good, came to Virginia from Washington County, Maryland, about the beginning of the nineteenth century. Benoni S. Good, the father of the subject of this sketch, was born in Ohio County, Virginia, in 1816, and lived his entire life upon the farm on which he was born. He was a man of great industry and was noted for his hospitality and integrity. J. H. Good's mother was a McMechen, daughter of the pioneer Benjamin McMechen, and one of a numerous family of children. His descendants are plentiful in most every portion of the "Pan-Handle," and are reliable and enterprising citizens.

John Hanson Good was born in Ohio County, Virginia, in 1844. After attending the common schools for a few years he matriculated at the West Virginia University at Morgantown, where he remained about a year, and then entered Bethany College, Brooke County, from which he graduated in 1868. He afterwards attended law school at Louisville, Kentucky, and after finishing his studies, opened a law office in Wheeling. After practicing a short time he was elected Prosecuting Attorney of Ohio County. In this position he acquitted himself with the greatest credit, successfully defending and maintaining the peace and dignity of the State against all comers. He was not long in taking a leading rank as a jury lawyer. Indeed, he was for years regarded by far the most eloquent advocate at the Ohio County Bar. His career as an attorney was a great success.

In early manhood Mr. Good became interested in politics. His voice was heard in every campaign. He was both attractive and powerful on the hustings. West Virginia contained but few, if any, better platform speakers than J. H. Good. He was always an ardent Democrat, and was for years the idol of his party in Ohio County. He was elected a Delegate to the West Virginia Legislature, and in 1882 was the nominee of his party for a seat in the Congress of the United States. He made a brilliant campaign, but was defeated by General Nathan Goff. Exposures during that campaign led to ailments that would not yield to medical treatment, and the young and gifted lawyer was swept down within a few months after the close of the canvass. He had a large following of friends who were drawn close about him by his charming manners and genial nature. No West Virginian had the promise of a more successful future; but it was decreed that he should surrender his trust even before his sun had reached its noon.

Mr. Good was of medium stature, compactly built, of fair complexion, light hair, charming in conversation, and would be regarded everywhere as handsome. His brilliant attainments, coupled with his neat appearance, rendered him in any presence a commanding man.

## Hon. Frank Lively, LL.B.

Our subject, a son of Colonel Wilson and Elizabeth (Gwinn) Lively, was born in Monroe County, West Virginia, November 18, 1864, and was reared on a farm. He graduated from the Concord, Mercer County, State Normal School, at Athens, West Virginia, in the class of 1882. He promptly thereafter matriculated as a law student at the West Virginia University, and graduated therefrom in 1885, with the degree of LL.B. The following year he was admitted as a member of the Summers County Bar to be an attorney in the Circuit Courts of the State. Later on he was admitted to practice in the United States Courts and the Supreme Court of Appeals of West Virginia. In all of these tribunals he has had an extensive business and broad experience.

In 1900 he was elected Prosecuting Attorney of Summers County and proved to be an efficient prosecutor. Being a lover of "the rod and gun," and being desirous of the strict enforcement of the laws to protect the wild game and the fish of the Mountain State, he resigned the office of Prosecuting Attorney to accept, as he viewed it, the more important position of State Game and Fish Warden of West Virginia. In entering upon the duties of this office he devoted his entire time and his best energies to the protection of the game and fish of the State from total destruction by their thoughtless and ruthless persecutors and destroyers in almost every section of West Virginia. Under his administration those important laws were rigidly enforced and firmly established.

In April, 1905, he resigned as Game and Fish Warden to accept the office of Assistant Attorney-General of the State, which he filled with great acceptability until 1906, when he resigned to become Pardon Attorney during the administration of Governor Dawson. In 1909 he was again appointed to the office of Assistant Attorney-General, which position he is still holding. In this office he has made an enviable record as a lawyer of a strong, clear, safe and sane judicial mind. He is quick of perception, deliberate in judgment, and rarely, if ever, fails to catch on to the main points involved in a case. No lawyer in West Virginia is more familiar with all of the most important statutes of the State than he, and the natural result is his services are of almost untold value to the people at large in the office he is now ably filling.

HON. FRANK LIVELY

Mr. Lively has represented the State in the trial of a long list of important cases in the Federal, the Circuit and Supreme Courts of West Virginia, and has established a reputation as an able, successful and forceful trial lawyer. He is married, resides in Charleston, and has a wife and six children, and is a member of the Masonic Order. He is of tall, slender, sinewy build, and in his younger years was an athlete of considerable renown. He is yet, and perhaps will ever remain, a lover of the gun and rod, as well as an untiring student of the law. Mr. Lively has always been an earnest advocate of Republican principles and policies.

## Hon. Elam Dowden Talbott

Mr. Talbott is one of the strong, well known attorneys of the central counties of West Virginia. He is the son of William W. and Sarah Simms Talbott. He was born on a farm near Philippi in Barbour County, Virginia, November 8, 1857, and received his elementary education in the common schools of his neighborhood. Later he attended the Law Department of the West Virginia University, where he received a thorough training in the technique of the law, and was admitted to practice in the Circuit Court of Barbour County in 1882, where he remained for several years, and moved his residence to Elkins, in the adjoining County of Randolph, where he now resides, and is conducting a large and profitable legal business. As a lawyer he is profound and exact. He is methodical and laborious in the preparation of his cases, and is always well armed with precedent and authority. He is cautious in assuming his ground before entering upon the trial of a cause. His judgment is sound. He rarely enters upon the lofty strains of rhetoric and never in impassioned challenges of applause. But while his oratory is usually devoid of ornamentation, it is forceful, logical and laden with argument. He readily sees the main points in his case and addresses himself to the gist of the controversy. His life has been a commentary upon the value of amiability and gentlemanly traits of character, and impresses the lesson that a mild temper, a uniform decorum and moderation are virtues compatible with the greatest attainable success at the Bar. He is always calm, patient and practical, and has made the dictates of duty the rule of his conduct in public and private life, and is, therefore, highly regarded as a lawyer and citizen.

Mr. Talbott has always had a warm side for politics, although in no sense an office-seeker. The only political office he ever held was a member of the Legislature in 1913, wherein he proved able and efficient. He was sent as a Delegate to the National Democratic Convention in 1896, being an adherent of that political party.

He married Miss Lertie Lee Bosworth, June 15, 1886, and has five children. He is a member of the Baptist Church, also the Masonic and Odd Fellows Fraternities, and is in every respect an exemplary citizen.

HON. E. D. TALBOT

## Robert Emmet McCabe, A.B.

The subject of this sketch is the junior member of the strong and successful law firm of Blue & McCabe in the capital city of the State. He was born at Leesburg, Loudon County, Virginia, July 24, 1883, and is the son of Judge James B. McCabe, a well-known lawyer of the Mother Commonwealth. His preliminary education was obtained at the Episcopal High School, Alexandria, Virginia. Subsequently he graduated from Randolph-Macon College, Ashland, Virginia, and in 1904 graduated from the Law Department of the University of Virginia at Charlottesville. He, therefore, started out in the profession unusually well equipped, educationally speaking, to attain success in his high calling, and he is steadily marching toward the front.

He was admitted to the Leesburg, Virginia, Bar in 1904, where he practiced for a short time. From there he went to Norfolk, Virginia, but greater opportunities seemed to be opened to a young man in the legal profession in the new State of West Virginia, so he "packed his belongings," came to Charleston on the Kanawha, "hung out his shingle," and is now one of the best known young attorneys of that thriving city. He soon found out that he made no mistake in selecting a permanent abode, and is both happy and prosperous in his new home in a State where coal, oil, gas and timber abound more abundantly, perhaps, than in any other State of the Great Republic. A young, industrious, educated lawyer, in order to secure business, makes no mistake to locate where business is.

Mr. McCabe is a Democrat in politics, is married and has one child, and being of a genial, social, generous disposition is living happily among a host of warm, personal friends he has made in the capital of the expanding "Mountain State," with greater prospects of success ahead worthy of a lawyer much his superior in years and experience. His future is permanently secured.

## Judge James French Strother

Judge Strother was born in Pearisburg, Giles County, Virginia, and is the son of Judge Philip Williams Strother and Nannie (Pendleton) Strother. He attended the common schools, the Pearisburg Academy, the Virginia Agricultural and Mechanical College in 1887 to 1890, inclusive, and ended with a thorough law course at the University of Virginia from 1893 to 1894, inclusive, graduating with the degree of Bachelor of Laws. He was admitted to the Bar in Virginia in 1894 and located at Welch, West Virginia, in 1895, where he has since resided, and has successfully practiced in the State and Federal Courts of West Virginia and Virginia.

He has filled the following offices most successfully and satisfactorily: Deputy Collector and Cashier of the United States Internal Revenue Office, Sixth District of Virginia, from 1890 to 1893; United States Commissioner from 1897 to 1901; Judge of the Criminal Court of McDowell County since January 1, 1905, when he was appointed by Governor A. B. White Judge of that Court, to succeed Judge L. L. Chambers, who had been elected Circuit Judge, and resigned; elected in 1906 without opposition; nominated without opposition and re-elected in 1912, and unanimously renominated after having declined to stand for re-election August 15, 1918, to succeed himself for the term beginning January 1, 1919, and has no opposition in the present campaign. This shows what kind of a Judge he is and has been for the past dozen or more years. He is a thorough lawyer and is peerless and fearless as a Judge. Naturally he is kind and generous and has many admiring friends. No man in McDowell County is more popular with the people.

Judge Strother is a member of McDowell Lodge No. 112, F. and A. M., Welch, West Virginia; Lynchburg Chapter No. 10, Lynchburg, Virginia; Ivanhoe Commandery No. 10, Bramwell, West Virginia, and Beni Kedem Temple, Nobles of the Mystic Shrine, Charleston.

In politics Judge Strother is a Republican, and his residence is at Welch, the seat of justice of McDowell County.

## John Campbell Palmer, M.S., Ph.D.

Very few lawyers of his age in Northern West Virginia have had a wider and more varied experience in general practice than the subject of this sketch. His father was an erudite attorney, and his son has had many advantages in the way of fitting himself for the Bar. He was born in Brooke County, West Virginia, September 30, 1868. His primary education was received in the Wellsburg public schools, having graduated from the High School of that city in 1886; he graduated from Washington and Jefferson College, Pennsylvania, in 1890, receiving the degree of Bachelor of Science. In 1893 he received the degree of Master of Science from the same college. He later entered Wooster (Ohio) University, taking up the study of philosophy and psychology, and was awarded the degree of Doctor of Philosophy in 1902. He studied law under the tutelage of the late Judge John J. Jacob in Wheeling, West Virginia, and was admitted to practice in that city in 1891. He subsequently was admitted to the Supreme Courts of West Virginia and Ohio, and also to the Common Pleas Courts of Ohio and Pennsylvania and the United States District Courts in West Virginia and Maryland, and the Circuit Court of Appeals of the Fourth Circuit, also to the Supreme Court of the United States, in all of which he has appeared as counsel in the trial of important causes. He was Solicitor of the City of Wellsburg in 1899, which is the only public office he ever held.

Mr. Palmer is also an enterprising, public spirited citizen, and has been active in the development of the resources of his section of the State.

He is President of the Wellsburg National Bank and is counsel for the West Penn. Railway System in the Ohio Valley, including all the traction and power companies from Moundsville, West Virginia, and Belleaire, Ohio, to Charleston, West Virginia, and East Liverpool, Ohio. He has been since July, 1913, a member of the strong law firm of Erskine, Palmer and Curl of the City of Wheeling, that represents a number of corporations as their attorneys.

Mr. Palmer is a thorough lawyer, is an honorable and upright man, and is held in high esteem by members of both the Bench and the Bar, who personally know him. He is alert, patient and painstaking, and is sedulous in the preparation of his causes. As a man his character is symmetrical and elevated. He is faithful to his clients and deals fairly with his fellows. He is quiet and sedate, but always kind and agreeable. In private and social life he is somewhat reserved in his manners, but is courteous and kind-hearted and his personal qualities are staunchly subsidiary to his professional attainments. He married Miss Jeannette Ostrander, of Mt. Vernon, New York, August 1, 1902, and they are the parents of four children. He is a Democrat, but has never been active in politics. He is a member of the Presbyterian Church and the Order of Knights of Pythias, and is also an active member of the West Virginia and the American Bar Associations, and has prepared two or three papers of value to the profession, which have appeared in the Year Book of the Association and the American Law Journal. During the years of 1910 and 1911 Mr. Palmer was editor and manager of the Wellsburg Daily Leader and the Wellsburg Weekly Herald. He was one of the first to suggest the name of Woodrow Wilson for the Presidency. He has always taken a keen interest in educational matters, and was for a time Secretary of the Board of Education of the City of Wellsburg. He is a believer in technical education in the public schools, and advocates the continuous session of the schools.

---

## Joseph M. Crockett, B.A., LL.B.

The subject of this sketch, son of Samuel R. and Berta (Pendleton) Crockett, was born and brought up on a farm in Wythe County, Virginia, having first seen the light November 29, 1890, and was educated two years at Emory and Henry College at Emory, Virginia, and graduated in June, 1911, from Hampden-Sidney College, Virginia, with the classical degree of Bachelor of Arts, *cum laude*, after two years of hard study. The year of his graduation he won the Virginia State Oratorical Medal, which was contested for by the eight colleges and universities of Virginia, with courses and requirements leading to the first class Bachelor of Arts degree. After graduation in the college courses in Arts and Sciences he entered the Law Department of Washington and Lee University, Lexington, Virginia, graduating with the degree of Bachelor of Laws. He also attended the Law Department of the West Virginia University at Morgantown, and

JOSEPH M. CROCKETT

passed the required examination by the Law Faculty of that institution in January, 1913, and was immediately thereafter licensed to practice in the courts of this State. He located in the growing town of Welch, McDowell County, as a residence and entered upon what appears to be, and doubtless will be, a successful career as an attorney and counselor-at-law.

His father was one of the first slave owners of Virginia, who became a Republican, and cast his first vote as such for General Ulysses S. Grant for President of the United States. The son, following in his father's footsteps, adopted that faith and is, therefore, " a dyed-in-the-wool " member of that political organization. He was a United States Commissioner for the Southern District of West Virginia from October, 1913, to August 29, 1917, when he resigned to enter the military service of the United States. He entered that service September 5, 1917, and was assigned to Battery "A," 315th Regiment of Field Artillery. He entered the service as a private, and has been promoted to corporal, sergeant, sergeant-major, and was selected to attend the Third Officers' Training Camp, from which he graduated, and was recommended for commission as Lieutenant in field artillery.

He has received an excellent education for the profession he has entered, and was making rapid progress when he entered the service of his country. Being a natural orator he took high rank as an advocate and trial lawyer. His practice embraced all branches of the law, and extended into all State and Federal Courts which was not limited alone to McDowell County, but went out into several of the adjoining counties. The first two years of his practice he handled eleven different cases in the Supreme Court of Appeals of West Virginia, which is an unusual number for a lawyer just entering upon a general practice. He is a young man of ability and character, and we sincerely hope his life will be spared that he may return from the impending war with health and vigor and will, without reasonable doubt, reach the high position at the Bar for which he is so well equipped and which he was rapidly attaining when he answered "the call of the colors."

Mr. Crockett is unmarried; is a member of the Presbyterian Church, the Masonic Fraternity, the Odd Fellows, the Elks, the Loyal Order of Moose and also the Greek letter " Frat " of Pi Kappa Alpha. Furthermore he is a patriot of a lofty grade, and we wish him Godspeed and a safe and speedy return to his life business and his many friends in his adopted West Virginia home.

## Zachariah Witten Crockett

Mr. Crockett, son of Robert G. and Margaret E. Crockett, was born in Tazewell County, Virginia, July 21, 1875. He was educated at Emory and Henry College, Virginia, completing his college course in 1894. Shortly after leaving college he began to read law in the office of Judge Joseph M. Sanders, in the City of Bluefield, West Virginia. In 1897 he was licensed to

ZACHARIAH W. CROCKETT

practice and began the practice in the City of Bluefield, where he lived and practiced law for the balance of his life. In 1901 he and his brother, George P. Crockett, formed a partnership and practiced together, under the firm name of Crockett & Crockett, until October 1, 1907, at which time Judge Joseph M. Sanders, who had resigned from the Supreme Court of Appeals of West Virginia, Z. W. Crockett and George P. Crockett formed a partnership, under the firm name of Sanders & Crockett, with offices in the City of Bluefield. This partnership continued up to the time of the death of Z. W. Crockett, which occurred May 20, 1915, just as his sun had reached its noon and when the future was bright with promise.

Mr. Crockett was keen of intellect, learned in his profession, polished in his practice, and was in the legal arena a worthy antagonist and an associate to be desired; honest in mind and conduct, upright in principle and true to high ideals in his daily walk among men. He had every desirable attribute of a good citizen; gentle and true in his personal life, considerate toward others in word and deed, quick to respond to the demands of others for either aid or sympathy; he had no enemies and was loyal and faithful to his friends.

He was one of the most learned lawyers in Southern West Virginia, and manifested rare judgment in all exigencies arising in trials. He was scrupulously ethical in his practice; uniformly courteous to the court, to associates and to adversaries, and preserved the best ideals and traditions of the legal profession. He was not over contentious in the trial of a cause, but he had the correct idea of what a real lawyer should be. He believed and practiced that his province as a member of the profession was to contend only for those things which the higher law dictates to be right, and to establish them on a firm basis by sound reason; consequently the work of his life was no small contribution to that end. He discouraged strife and turmoil among litigants. He never provoked litigation, as some lawyers do, by whom discredit is brought upon the profession; but always sought to bring peace out of controversies, to bring people together who were at variance with one another, and cause them to compose their difficulties without law suits and litigations. He was not only an able lawyer and counselor, but he was in every respect an ideal citizen. He was a Christian. He was a gentle, manly man. Although he has passed away himself, he has left an influence that is not dead. His influence and example will continue in the minds and hearts of his friends, and be transmitted by them to others as examples in the future. It is the lives of such men as he that maintain the high standing of our noble profession, without which our civilization could not last; and while we have lost him, we have not lost the lessons of his manly life.

## Jacob Frank Cork, A.M., LL.B.

Our subject, the son of Captain John James Cork, was born in Clarksburg, Virginia, April 25, 1857. He received a liberal education in both public and private schools; graduated from the State Normal School at Glenville in the class of 1874; taught in the public schools for a few years to accrue funds to enable him to finish out a college course. He then spent parts of two years — 1878 and 1879 — in the State Normal School at Fairmont. In the fall of 1879 he matriculated as a student in the prescribed classical course at the West Virginia University, and in 1883 graduated, receiving the degree of Bachelor of Arts. In June of the following year, having in the meantime taken up the study of law, he graduated from the State University as a Bachelor of Laws. Later on, the degree of Master of Arts, *in cursu*, was conferred upon him by the West Virginia University. In 1884 he was licensed to practice law, and was admitted as a member of the Bar at Spencer, Roane County, West Virginia. About the time he was preparing to open a law office at Spencer he was tendered the position of Chief Clerk in the office of the State Superintendent of Public Schools, which he accepted, and remained there for eight consecutive years. At the expiration of this service, he located at the city of Charleston and entered upon a vigorous practice, which he has faithfully and successfully maintained to the present time.

Mr. Cork has specialized in land laws and chancery practice, and has made exhaustive researches into the subject of land titles, and has in process of compilation an exhaustive textbook upon this branch of the profession. He is an industrious worker, is thoroughly reliable, a safe counselor and is conscientious and upright. No lawyer, anywhere, has a cleaner or more honorable record. He is clear-headed and possesses a large amount of practical, common sense. He has a large clientele, and yet he is seldom seen in a court room. Like Abraham Lincoln, he discourages courthouse trials as far as he can do so without jeopardizing the interests and rights of his clients. It has been said, and we think aptly, that "it is only a wise and able lawyer who knows when to bring a law suit." We think Mr. Cork belongs to that class of counselors. At all events, he has accumulated much as proof that he has managed his business in a sound, financial way. His prominent characteristics, in addition to what we have already stated, are a strong will, clear judgment, a keen knowledge of human nature, rigid devotion to what he believes to be right, and a courteous and friendly manner in dealing with other members of the Bar. We believe that no one will dispute the statement that he is among the high minded, moral, common sense members of the Kanawha Bar.

## Judge James Damron

Judge James Damron, lawyer and jurist, residing at Williamson, Mingo County, West Virginia, was born in that county April 28, 1876. By close application and hard work in the short periods permitted him in the common schools and utilization of odd hours at home he acquired sufficient learning to enable him to obtain employment in the County Clerk's office of Mingo County in 1897, when he was but twenty years of age. He served as Deputy County Clerk for two years and then accepted employment with the Kirk-Christy Lumber Company, of Cleveland, Ohio, as bookkeeper and store manager, which position he held for one year, severing his connection to become a candidate for the office of County Clerk of Mingo County, to fill an unexpired term of two years, caused by the death of County Clerk Chafin. After a hard political fight he was elected to his first office by a small majority. In 1902 he was re-elected County Clerk for a full term of six years. In 1908 he was again re-elected to this office for a full term of six years, but resigning before his term of office expired to become a candidate for Judge of the Circuit Court of the Twenty-second Judicial Circuit of West Virginia, comprising the counties of Mingo and Wyoming.

Judge Damron, being reared by poor parents, did not have the advantage of a college education, but his experience as County Clerk of his own county for several years gave him an opportunity to read law for a number of years prior to his admission to the Bar under H. K. Shumate, who was one of the most prominent lawyers of the southern section of West Virginia during his lifetime.

In 1909 Judge Damron entered the Law Department of the West Virginia University at Morgantown, and in 1910 was licensed to practice law. As soon as he had procured his license he was admitted to practice in his home county and in the Supreme and Federal Courts of West Virginia. In the same year, 1910, he became associated with the well-known law firm of Sheppard, Goodykoontz and Scherr, of Williamson, under whose able preceptorship his progress was so rapid and his prominence so swift and sure that he was honored by his fellow citizens in the counties of Mingo and Wyoming by the election of Judge of the Circuit Court at the November election, 1912, by a majority of over one thousand votes. As Judge Damron is a Republican, this majority was quite surprising, as President Wilson carried the State by several thousand votes. His judicial record is an enviable one. He has a vigorous, analytical, discriminating mind and is independent, impartial and fearless in the rendition of decisions. He was not thirty-five years old when he was elected Circuit Judge, and was, perhaps, the youngest man who ever sat upon the Circuit Bench of West Virginia. Judge Damron has not only gained a State-wide reputation in administering the laws of his State and county, but he can point with pride to his judicial decisions rendered during the five years that he has

JUDGE JAMES DAMRON

been on the Bench, having been upheld by the Supreme Court of the State in all with the exception of three cases. He resides in Mingo County, one of the largest coal producing counties in the State. Prior to his election to the Bench, the records disclose that his county was third on the list in sending criminals to the West Virginia penitentiary, but by a strict administration of the law, Mingo County now sends fewer criminals to the penitentiary than any other coal producing county in the State. At the first term of court held by him he announced from the Bench that he believed in the strict enforcement of all laws, and that every officer, high or low, should measure up to the full responsibilities of his duties. He further announced that he would ask the officers of the law to see that all the laws were rigidly enforced, and that in all elections that the sanctity of the ballot should be upheld, and that corruptions in the elections should be made a thing of the past. From this standpoint he has not deviated in the least. It will be recalled that less than one year ago an attempted assassination was made upon his life, during a term of court being held in his home county, for the stand taken by him in the enforcement of the law.

Judge Damron is a member of the American Bar Association, as well as the West Virginia Bar Association. Besides his legal activities he has several business interests, being Vice-President and a Director of the First National Bank of Pineville, at Pineville, West Virginia. He is a member of the Baptist Church, a member of the Masonic Fraternity at Williamson, and of the Royal Arch and Knights Templar of Huntington, of the Mystic Shrine of Charleston, of the Elks of Huntington and has reached the thirty-second degree of the Scottish Rite branch of Masonry, belonging to the Rite at Wheeling, West Virginia.

## Judge John Camillus McWhorter, LL.B.

The McWhorters compose a numerous and noted family of citizens who are scattered over a large portion of West Virginia, who were among the early settlers of the western part of Virginia, many years before the mother Commonwealth was formed into two States. One of their peculiarities is, and always has been, a difficult matter to find "a black-sheep" among them. They are noted for integrity, sobriety and general uprightness of character. We can say, with positive assurance, that the subject of this sketch is not an exception to these noted characteristics.

John Camillus (commonly called "Jack"), a son of Dr. J. M. and Rosetta McWhorter, was born in Upshur County, West Virginia, July 5, 1866. He received his early training in the common schools of his native county. Later he took a four years' selective course at the West Virginia University, including the Department of Law, graduating with the degree of Bachelor of Laws. He was admitted as a member of the Buckhannon, Upshur County, Bar, in 1894 with all of its privileges and immunities. He

JUDGE J. C. McWHORTER

was later admitted in all of the courts of West Virginia, and the Federal Courts, as well. He went to California and was received as a member of the San Francisco Bar, but shortly thereafter he returned to West Virginia and began the practice of law at Buckhannon in his native county, and met with success from the start. In 1897 he formed a law partnership with Senator U. G. Young, under the firm name of Young and McWhorter, and their practice very quickly reached out into various parts of the State.

In 1904 he was elected Judge of the Twelfth Judicial Circuit of West Virginia, carrying each of the four counties composing that Circuit. The public estimate of his popularity and fitness for the office might be said to be attested by the fact that while the normal majority against him in the circuit was more than one thousand, he carried the circuit by about nine hundred majority, and while the normal majority in his own county was about one thousand and seven hundred against him, he carried the county by over one hundred majority the other way. In his official career his earnest aim was to be thoroughly impartial, fearless and energetic. After his eight-year term of office expired, he resumed partnership with Senator Young, and the firm is now, as then, Young and McWhorter, and is conducting an extensive and profitable law business in the city of Buckhannon. He has always been a Democrat in politics, but has never been classed as a vigorous partisan. For a number of years he has devoted much of his time, energy and means in the warfare against the liquor traffic. He was Chairman of the West Virginia Ratification Federation which conducted the State-wide prohibition amendment campaign, carrying it by over 92,000 majority, and was author, almost *in toto*, of the West Virginia Prohibition Law, generally known as the "Yost Law," now in force in the State.

Judge McWhorter and Miss Elizabeth Alkire were united in marriage August 26, 1895, and are the parents of three children. He is a member of the Presbyterian Church, and also is a member of the Masonic Order, and Phi Kappa Psi College Fraternity. He is a forward-thinking man, broad and liberal in his views and thoroughly democratic in spirit. Though of a positive nature, he disagrees with his opponents without rancor. He owns a beautiful residence in the city of Buckhannon, and his home-life is ideal. He is an upright citizen, keenly interested in the social welfare and the betterment of the human mass.

---

## Harrison Brooks Smith, A.B.

Son of Isaac N. Smith and Caroline Quarrier Smith; born September 7, 1886; attended public schools, Kanawha Military Institute, Washington and Lee University, Princeton University, from which he was graduated with the degree of Bachelor of Arts; also attended the University of Virginia Law School, but his course was interrupted before completion by an attack of typhoid fever. He subsequently studied law in the office of his uncle, William A. Quarrier, of the Kanawha Bar; was admitted to the Bar and practiced his profession for some years as the junior partner of the firm of Adams and Smith, his associate being W. W. Adams, Esq., since deceased.

In 1894 he became a member of the law firm of Couch, Flournoy and Price, and practiced his profession as a member of that firm and of its successor, Flournoy, Price and Smith and the present firm of Price, Smith, Spilman and Clay.

Since 1900 Mr. Smith's professional activities have consisted largely in acting as counsel for business interests and his active participation in the general practice has been curtailed. He is President of the George Washington Life Insurance Company and Elk Banking Company, and is largely interested in Kanawha Banking and Trust Company, all institutions with home offices in Charleston, West Virginia. He is also interested in many of the business enterprises of that city and vicinity. He is a member of the University Club, the Princeton Club of New York and other similar organizations.

Mr. Smith is a devotee of outdoor sports and has followed the traditions of his family in devoting a large part of his leisure time to the study of music.

In 1906 he married Katharine Dana Bowne of New York and has three children of this union. Mr. Smith is the fifth of his family in direct descent practicing the legal profession, his grandfather, Colonel Benjamin H. Smith, having been one of the widely known and respected lawyers of his period; his father, Isaac Noyes Smith, as senior member of the firm of Smith and Knight was one of the prominent members of the Kanawha Bar until his death in 1883.

His grandfather and father, who were eminent lawyers, are the subjects of sketches in this collection.

## Judge H. Delbert Rummel, LL.B.

Among the well-established, well-known, successful middle-aged lawyers of the Charleston Bar is the subject of this sketch. He is the son of Henry and Mary B. Rummel, and was born in Charleston, West Virginia, August 13, 1875. He attended the public schools of his native city, until 1892, when he entered St. Mary's College at Belmont, N. C. He took the law course of study at Maryland University at Baltimore, graduating with high honors with the degree of Bachelor of Laws, and later took advanced studies at Johns Hopkins University at Baltimore. He was admitted as a member of the Maryland Bar, where he remained for a short time. He then located permanently at Charleston, West Virginia, and was received as a member of the Kanawha County Bar in 1897, where he has since practiced with a pronounced degree of success in all the State and Federal Courts of West Virginia.

Judge Rummel is a man of striking and prepossessing appearance, tall, erect, graceful, with classical mold of features. He was, therefore, not long in finding his way into public life. He is an ardent Republican, and enjoys political associations, and possesses many elements of popularity. He is a splendid stump speaker, and in a court trial he is an able advocate. Possessing an acute discrimination he is generally successful in his undertakings. Self-assertion becomes easy when there is little to be apprehended from oppcsition. He, however, is never in the least daunted, nor is his masked power the least exposed. In the gage of the stress of conflict his thought flows without the slightest break in its coherency, and without the least disconcertedness, nor does his equable temper ever forsake him. He is sociable, agreeable and always easily approached, and is popular and enjoyable with his associates. He is well equipped in his profession, and always keeps about him a profitable clientele.

He filled the office of City Solicitor of Charleston two terms, from 1901 to 1905, and was Assistant United States District Attorney for the Southern District of West Virginia from 1905 to 1912, and filled both of these positions with pronounced fitness and success. His last official position was as Judge of the Common Pleas Court of Kanawha County, in which high office he made an enviable record as a just and able jurist.

He married Miss Ruth H. Millard, an estimable lady of Baltimore, June 25, 1900. They have no children, and have a delightful home in the Capital City of the State. He is a member of the Benevolent and Protective Order of Elks.

Judge Rummel was elected Judge of the Circuit Court of Kanawha and Clay counties in November, 1918, for a term of eight years and is ably fil ing that responsible position.

## Hon. Fleming C. Leftwich

Mr. Leftwich was born in Giles County, Virginia, April 17, 1866, and is the son of Tubal W. and Mary (Porterfield) Leftwich; attended the public schools three or four months in winter, and worked on his father's farm the remainder of the year, until he was eighteen years old, when he commenced teaching in the public schools, in winter, and still worked on the farm in summer; came to Boone County, West Virginia, in 1886, where he taught school and studied law until October, 1889, when he was admitted to the Bar at Madison, Boone County, and entered at once into active practice, forming a partnership with Col. Joel E. Stollings, who was then Prosecuting Attorney of Boone County; which partnership continued until the death of Colonel Stollings, in 1897. After the death of Colonel Stollings he formed a partnership with M. A. Byrnside, under the firm name of Leftwich and Byrnside, which continued until 1910, when Mr. Harry G. Shaffer became a member of the firm, and the name was changed to Leftwich, Byrnside and Shaffer, as it now stands.

HON. FLEMING C. LEFTWICH

Colonel Stollings had a large practice, which Mr. Leftwich took hold of as soon as he was admitted to the Bar, and held the same, and added to it, after Colonel Stollings' death, practicing, principally, in the Circuit Courts of Boone and Logan counties, in the Supreme Court of Appeals of the State and in the United States Court at Charleston.

At the time he was admitted to the Bar land titles were in a very unsettled condition in his section of the State, and, while he had a general practice, it was largely made up of cases involving the title to lands, many of which were very important, and would have been notable in any other State, or in the northern or eastern parts of this State. But, arising in this section, they were only considered routine business by a lawyer engaged in general practice.

Mr. Leftwich began to take an active part in politics before he was old enough to vote, and was Chairman of the Republican County Committee of Boone County almost continuously from 1888 to 1910. He was elected Prosecuting Attorney of Boone County in 1896, by a small margin, when the county was Democratic by a large majority; declined to stand for re-election, but was prevailed upon to accept the Republican nomination for Representative in the House of Delegates in 1900, and was defeated; was elected, on the Republican ticket, to the State Senate, from the Eighth Senatorial District, in 1906, to fill a vacancy caused by the death of Hon. J. A. Browning; was Chairman of the Senate Committee on Banks and Corporations, member of the Committee of the Judiciary, and of several other important committees; declined a renomination, and has never sought or held any other public office.

He aided in the organization of the Madison National Bank of Madison, the first bank organized in Boone County, and was its President until 1910, when he moved to Huntington, Cabell County, and took charge of the legal department of the Yawkey and Freeman land, coal and oil interests, in which he is still engaged. He was married, in 1893, to Miss Minnie, daughter of Col. Joel E. Stollings, and has one child, a daughter. He is a Past Master of Odell Lodge of Freemasons at Madison; member of Tyrean Royal Arch Chapter; Kanawha Commandery No. 4, Knights Templar; and Beni-Kedem Temple, Order of the Mystic Shrine, of Charleston; and of Huntington Lodge of Perfection No. 4, Scottish Rite Masonry; also member of Huntington Lodge No. 313, B. P. O. Elks.

Although Mr. Leftwich resides in the city of Huntington, he attends all of the sessions of the Circuit Court of Boone County.

## William E. R. Byrne

The legal profession requires of the men engaged in it mentality of the highest order. And yet it is not alone natural aptitude which makes for success in the practice of the law. If it is not combined with perseverance and capacity for severe brain work, no effective results can be achieved. We do not mean to say that the subject of this sketch does not possess the average natural gifts of the average lawyer, but we do mean to say that in the law, as in all of the learned professions, the man that toils hardest and longest is the one who succeeds best in the practice of the law. Mr. Byrne, by constant and unremittent toil, has made splendid headway in his chosen profession. He learned early in life that work wins, and by this sign he conquered.

William E. R. Byrne, of the Charleston Bar, son of the late Hon. Benjamin W. Byrne, who, in his day, was an eminent land lawyer in this State, was born at Fort Defiance, Virginia, October 26, 1862, and was educated in the common schools of Charleston and Wheeling, West Virginia, from 1873 to 1879. It is true that he did not have the advantages of a college training, but he acquired, by the careful reading of properly selected books, a varied and substantial learning and became master of a clear, terse and vigorous style, both in writing and speaking. He read law under the direction of his father, and kept "on the job," so to speak, until he became familiar with the elementary textbooks and was able to pass a creditable examination in his studies. He was admitted as a member of the Kanawha County Bar in 1884, a short time after he had reached his majority, and has kept constantly "at it" until the present time.

He first located at Sutton, in Braxton County, where he "hung out his shingle," and where he, in a short time, showed pronounced evidences that he had within him the elements of success as an attorney-at-law. His friends presented him as a suitable man for Prosecuting Attorney of Braxton County, and he was nominated and elected in 1892. In that important office, for the term of four years, he rendered efficient and satisfactory service, proving himself to be a vigorous and able prosecutor. Desiring a wider field of opportunity he moved his residence to Charleston some years ago, and formed a partnership with Robert G. Linn. Both being good lawyers, they have a large and profitable business in that city.

Mr. Byrne's practice includes all of the various branches of the profession in all of the State Courts and the Federal Courts, including the Supreme Court of the United States. He, however, has specialized, to a considerable extent, in land laws and land litigations, and maintains a high standing, particularly in that branch of the profession, although he is an able all-round lawyer.

Mr. Byrne, for many years, has had a strong penchant for politics, and for a number of years he has engaged in the management of political campaigns for the Democratic party, being a "dyed-in-the-wool" member of that organization. He has never been an office-seeker himself, but he takes special delight in helping his friends to political favors. He is an effective organizer and his backing and support are earnestly sought after by partisans of that political organization. In this line of endeavor he has been remarkably successful.

Mr. Byrne married Miss Amanda Austin, of Lewisburg, West Virginia, June 12, 1889, a lady of culture and refinement, and they have five children as the result of their marriage. He is a member of the Masonic and Elks Fraternities.

## Robert Thruston Hubard, Jr., A. B.

The subject of this brief sketch has not had a specially eventful career, and yet it has been in every respect successful. He started out with a well-rounded college education,which has been augmented by a continuous application to and an almost constant reading and study of such books as would be useful to him in fitting himself for the goal of his ambition, which was that of becoming a learned and accomplished member of the legal profession. Although but little over forty, he has, beyond question, more than "made good" in carrying out his early resolutions, being now known and recognized as one of the brightest and most successful practitioners of the southern portion of West Virginia.

He is not only learned in the law, but from the beginning, he has maintained a life of uprightness and probity, which marked him as an attorney who could be trusted in the handling of the many important cases, which have been trusted to his management. He, therefore, not only handles his cases skillfully in trial courts, but he is, at the same time, a careful and conscientious counselor. When he brings a suit, either in law or chancery, it is always with the belief that there is something in it, besides fees. And this is one of the prime secrets of his success as a lawyer. Another reason for his success in the law is the fact that he has eschewed politics, and has devoted all of his time and energies to the exclusive practice of his profession. He absolutely allows nothing to call his attention from the legitimate practice of the law. Being well informed and well grounded in legal principles, and devoting his energies and time exclusively to professional duties, he could not fall short of maintaining a profitable and large clientele in all the courts of his section. Indeed, his practice has extended into all the West Virginia courts, both State and Federal, and more especially in the State Supreme Court of Appeals.

Mr. Hubard was born June 2, 1876, at "Chellowe" in Buckingham county, Virginia, the home of his father's family. His mother was a Bolling and this was the old home of the Bollings in Virginia. He is the third in succession of the name, Robert Thruston Hubard, and his boy is the fourth.

Graduating from Hampden-Sidney College in 1897 with second honor and the A.B. and B.S. degrees, he taught one year in Locust Dale Academy, Virginia, one year as tutor for the Wilcox boys at "Flower de Hundred," the Wilcox home on James river, and two years as principal of the Smithfield Institute, Smithfield, Virginia. He then studied law at the University of the South, Sewanee, Tennessee, and at the University of Virginia that winter, completing the course there in 1902 and was admitted to practice in the Corporation Court in Lynchburg, Virginia, in the fall of 1902, having passed the examination and been licensed to practice by the Virginia Supreme Court, June 24, 1902.

R. T. HUBARD, JR.

He came to Fayette county, West Virginia, May 23, 1903, and has made that his home since. His practice is general, in State and Federal Courts; has been very successful and he has accumulated a competence. He married April 19, 1911, Miss Ruth Drewry Whittle, of Martinsville, Virginia, daughter of Judge S. G. Whittle, of the Virginia Supreme Court. They have four children. They are Episcopalians, but as there is no church of that denomination at Fayetteville they attend the local churches, in one of which he has been teaching the adult bible class for a number of years. He is a member of the Chi Phi Fraternity, and is a Mason in good standing, being a member of the Blue Lodge at Fayetteville, the Chapter at Thurmond, the Commandery at Mt. Hope and the Shrine at Charleston.

He is of a retiring disposition, fond of living, loves his friends, enjoys reading and "the out of doors," and has a nice home on a high hill overlooking Fayetteville and commanding a fine view of mountain scenery.

## Captain Samuel S. Green.

Captain Green, at one time one of the leading lawyers of the Kanawha Bar, was born in Culpeper county, Virginia, in 1840, and departed this life at Charleston, West Virginia, September 18, 1917. He was educated in the public and private schools of his native county, and at the University of Virginia. In April, 1861, he volunteered in the Confederate Army at the call of his state, and before the war ended he was promoted to the rank of Captain. He was a valient soldier, and remained in the service until the close of the war. After the close of hostilities he returned to his home, was admitted to the Bar, and for more than a half century was an honor to the profession.

In 1872 Captain Green located in Charleston, became a member of the law firm of Payne and Green, which continued for about twenty years, when it was dissolved by mutual consent, and he continued thereafter to practice alone until the time of his last illness and death. He was well grounded in the profession, and was a safe, sound and successful lawyer. His convictions, whether upon law, religion, politics or morals were granite like. Fidelity to duty and principle was his crowning virtue. He was affable, courteous and kindly disposed upon all occasions, and was highly esteemed by all of his associates in the profession. He practiced in all the State and Federal Courts, which embraced all branches of the profession, being well informed in all of them.

Captain Green was a Democrat in politics, a devout member of the Protestant Episcopal Church, and was a leader in every movement for the elevation of the morals of the people. He gave but little attention to politics, preferring to devote his entire time to the profession he adorned. His death was mourned by the people of Charleston, who respected him highly both as a lawyer and citizen.

He married Miss Goodwin, of Charleston, who died within a very short time of his own departure, with whom he lived in happy wedlock for a great many years. His home life was, indeed, beautiful. They left no children.

---

## Hon. William Sydney Laidley.

The subject of this brief biography, who for a half century was a prominent member of the Kanawha Bar, was born in Cabell county, Virginia, June 27, 1839, and died at his home in Charleston. He received his education at Marshall College, Virginia. In 1863 he moved to Charleston and read law in the office of his brother-in-law, the late Judge George W. Summers, of that town, and was admitted to the Bar in 1865, where he continued to practice until his fatal illness, as above stated. After his admission he became the partner of Judge Summers, and remained such until the Judge's death. He then formed a partnership with the late William H. Hogeman, which continued until the death of Colonel Hogeman. After this he practiced alone until his own demise. In addition to their general practice, the firm of Laidley & Hogeman was counsel of the Chesapeake and Ohio Railroad Company for many years. He followed his profession industriously, and maintained a high rank as a member of the Charleston Bar. He was thoroughly posted in every branch of the law, and was very successful in his extensive practice.

In politics Mr. Laidley was a Democrat. He was a member of the City Council for years and also was City Solicitor; was a member of the State Legislature in 1872–3, and was President of the Kanawha County Court for a term of four years. In all of these public positions he was intelligent, industrious, honest and useful. He was an active and useful member of the Episcopal Church for nearly a half century, and was a constant toiler for the advancement of his city, county and state. He had a special liking for the study of all historical subjects, and, with the exception of the late Virgil A. Lewis, he probably has written more historical articles, covering a larger field of Virginia and West Virginia events, than any other citizen of the present State of West Virginia. He was editor of a magazine for a number of years, which was published by the West Virginia Historical and Antiquarian Society, and his last work of this character was the publication of a History of Kanawha County and Its People, a royal octavo volume of more than one thousand pages, which is a living testimonial of his love of research, although his literary work was not allowed to interfere with the regular duties of his profession.

Mr. Laidley was an honored and highly esteemed lawyer, who enjoyed the affectionate esteem of all, in every station of life, who personally knew him. Gifted with a mind peculiarly legal, a student of his profession as well as of general literature for a half century, wielded a pen facile and interesting in his many publications, he always ranked among the ablest members of the Bar, and as one of the most prominent citizens of Charleston. With a sturdy honesty, and invariable candor, tempered with a genial courtesy and respect for all, he increased his friendship even in the heated conflicts at the Bar. Every one had confidence in his integrity and fair dealing. He aimed not at ornate diction or oratory, preferring the plain incisive speech of logic and studied analysis, and was a foeman well equipped for any contest in any court. Nature had endowed him with a kind, happy home circle. At the Bar or among friends or neighbors, his companionship was always welcomed as cheerful and entertaining, and was ofttimes mixed with rare wit and humor. He was in every respect an ideal citizen, and was universally loved by all who knew him. He had several daughters and a son, W. S. Laidley, Jr., who is a member of the Charleston Bar.

## Robert S. Spilman, B.S., LL.B.

Our subject is a member of the strong law firm of Price, Smith, Spilman & Clay, of the Charleston Bar, and is one of the able, rising young lawyers of West Virginia. His success has been marked and notable almost from his entrance into the legal profession. He possesses energy, a broad conception of important subjects, and is thoroughly trustworthy. He started in his life work with the dominant idea in his mind that one is sure to succeed, if he can steadily be found at his post of duty and stands four-square among his fellows; and those who know him well will admit that he has fully measured up to his early resolutions in the line of his high calling.

He was born March 22, 1876, at Warrenton, Virginia, one of the fertile and beautiful sections of the mother Commonwealth. In early life he became a student at the Virginia Military Institute, Lexington, Virginia, and graduated therefrom with the degree of Bachelor of Science. He then took the course in law at the University of Virginia, and with this splendid equipment in the technique of the law, he came to Charleston, West Virginia, and was admitted to that Bar in 1900, and has made this his permanent home. The practice of his firm embraces all of the State and Federal Courts, including the Supreme Court of the United States, and in some cases extends into surrounding States. He is married and is the father of four charming children.

For a number of years Mr. Spilman has been an active and valuable member of the West Virginia Bar Association, and has been a vigorous member of its Executive Council. He is affiliated with the Presbyterian Church, is a member of the Masonic Fraternity, and is a Democrat in politics. He is genial and kind in his disposition, and has a large and growing circle of personal friends. His life is a correct illustration of Lord Bacon's advice to professional young men: "I hold every man a debtor to his profession; from the which as men of course do seek to receive countenance and profit, so ought they of duty to endeavor themselves by way of amends to be a help and ornament thereunto.''

He has never filled, or even sought, a political office. His one and only aim has been to become a successful lawyer, and he is working out this single purpose grandly.

## Hon. Edward Theodore England, B.S., LL.B.

The present Attorney-General of West Virginia is a son of A. J. S. and Mary England, and was born in Jackson County, West Virginia, September 29, 1869. He prepared for college in the public schools of his native county and also of Mercer County. Later he entered the State Normal School at Athens, Mercer County, and graduated therefrom in the class of 1892. In 1898 he matriculated as a student in the Southern Normal University at Huntingdon, Tennessee, and in 1900 received the degrees of Bachelor of Science and Bachelor of Laws. The same year of his graduation he was admitted to the Bar of the Circuit Court of Wyoming County, and entered upon the practice of law at Oceana, the seat of justice of that county. The next year, however, he moved his residence to Logan, the county seat of Logan County, where he has since resided and continued his professional labors. He has by industry and application to his professional duties met with marked success, in that he has a large and profitable legal business. He is a man of unusual firmness of character, is fair and just in his dealings and has the confidence of the people who trust their business to his management and direction. He is known and esteemed as one of the able, enterprising, rapidly developing attorneys in the section of the State where he resides.

Mr. England has devoted some of his spare time to politics, and has been rewarded for his efforts in that line of endeavor. In 1903 and 1904 he served as Mayor of the thrifty, enterprising town of Logan and '' made good.'' In 1908 he was elected to the State Senate from the Eighth District for the term of four years, and was re-elected in 1912 to the same position. He took high rank in that law-making body and served actively and faithfully on a number of leading committees. In fact he was one of the floor leaders and did much in shaping the legislation of those sessions. During his last term he was President of the State Senate, and under our Constitution was *ex officio* Lieutenant-Governor of the Commonwealth. He made a fair, prompt and able presiding officer.

In the campaign of 1916 Senator England was nominated by the Republican party as its candidate for the highest legal office in the State — that of Attorney-General, and in the election that followed he was chosen to that responsible position by a majority of the voters of West Virginia, and is serving therein creditably and satisfactorily. He is a man of rugged frame and mind, and is capable of rendering hard and enduring work.

General England is a member of the Methodist Episcopal Church and the Masonic, Odd Fellows and Knights of Pythias Fraternities. In December, 1901, he married Miss Hulda Leona Lenburg, of Moulton, Iowa, and they are residing temporarily at the Capital of the State, where his official duties require him to stay.

## Hon. Louis Emory McWhorter

Our subject is a well-known member of the numerous McWhorter family distributed over a large part of West Virginia. He is a son of the late Judge J. M. McWhorter, of whom personal mention is made in another part of this volume. He was born at Spencer, Roane County, West Virginia, November 30, 1856. After his father had located at Lewisburg in Greenbrier County, Louis attended the public schools of that county, and subsequently became a student in the Lewisburg Academy, where he received a liberal academic education. After reading law for a year or more, under the instruction of his father and his uncle, the late Judge Henry C. McWhorter, who afterwards became an Associate Justice of the Supreme Court of Appeals of West Virginia, he matriculated as a student in the Law Department of the University of Virginia at Charlottesville, where he received a thorough training in the technique of the law. In 1882 he was licensed to practice, and in 1886 he became a partner with his uncle, Henry C. McWhorter, under the firm name of H. C. & L. E. McWhorter, at the City of Charleston, which continued until 1897, when the senior member became an Associate Justice of the Supreme Court of Appeals of the State, on account of which the law partnership was necessarily dissolved. Both being high grade lawyers their practice became large and profitable. Isaac Loewenstein took the place of Judge McWhorter and the firm was then McWhorter & Loewenstein, which continued for a number of years, when Mr. Loewenstein retired. In the meantime their business kept expanding until it reached large proportions. Although their practice was general in its character they, however, specialized in chancery and commercial law. Mr. McWhorter is known and recognized as one of the most active, able lawyers in the southern portion of the State, and has been connected with many important cases in the State and Federal Courts.

He is a Republican in politics, and although thoroughly wedded to his profession he has held several political offices, all of which he filled ably and well and acquitted himself with credit in all of them. He has been a member of the West Virginia Legislature, has been City Solicitor of Charleston and member and President of the Board of Education.

He has been an active, efficient member of the Methodist Episcopal Church practically all of his life, and for years he has been one of the leading official members of the First M. E. Church of Charleston, being for seven years its Sunday School Superintendent, and for a larger period a

HON. LOUIS E. McWHORTER

Trustee, Steward, etc. June 27, 1883, he married Miss Emma M. Champe, of Charleston, and they have reared an interesting family of children, all of whom are residents of the capital city of the State.

The firm name is now McWhorter & Carney, composed of L. E. McWhorter, H. L. Carney and L. E. McWhorter, Jr., the last named being now Lieutenant in the military service of the Government in the war with Germany.

## Hon. Joseph Allen Alderson

Mr. Alderson was a son of Col. George Alderson, one of the early settlers of Greenbrier County, Virginia, and Jeanette Creigh (McCreary) Alderson, his wife. He was born at Meadow Dale, Virginia, March 17, 1821; was educated in the common schools of his native county and took a course in law at the Ohio University, Athens, Ohio, and was promptly admitted to the Bar. He located at Summersville, Nicholas County, Virginia, and very soon worked himself into an active and successful practice. Lawyers were not as numerous then as now; but young Alderson had the character and grit to stick to his calling, and possessing a strong mind it did not take him long to establish himself as the leading lawyer of Nicholas and surrounding counties. The writer remembers when the people desired to institute a law suit they felt assured of success if they could secure the services of Joseph A. Alderson. He was a hard student, an inveterate worker, an honest man, was far superior to the average lawyer of his day, and handled his cases ably and successfully. He was employed on one side of practically all important cases that came before the courts of Nicholas County for more than a quarter of a century. Furthermore, he bore the reputation of an honest and just man, which added strength to his calling.

Mr. Alderson was a Democrat in politics. He was Prosecuting Attorney of Nicholas and Webster Counties for several terms prior to the Civil War, and was conscientious in the discharge of his official duties. He was elected a member of the Virginia State Senate at the beginning of the war, and was continued in that position until the formation of the new State of West Virginia.

He married Miss Mary S. Duffy, daughter of John Duffy, of Summersville, a man of large property and wide influence, January 13, 1852, and was the father of seven children — the eldest of whom was the Hon. John D. Alderson, who appears on another page of this volume. His grandson, Captain F. N. Alderson, son of J. D. Alderson, also appears in this volume. Thus we have three generations of successful lawyers, which is rather uncommon.

Senator Alderson was a member of the Baptist Church and the Masonic Fraternity. He lived at Summersville, the county seat of Nicholas County, from the early fifties until the time of his death, which occurred April 8, 1876, in the midst of his usefulness, greatly beloved by the people of the entire community.

## Hon. Armistead Abraham Lilly, LL.B.

The subject of this sketch was born in Summers County, West Virginia, March 25, 1878. His parents, however, moved to the County of Raleigh while he was young in years. There he attended the public schools for a number of years. Later he attended the High School at Bluefield; completing his work there he became a student at the Southern Normal University at Huntingdon, Tennessee, graduating from the Law Department with the degree of Bachelor of Laws. In 1900 he was admitted to the Raleigh County Bar. That year he was elected a member of the West Virginia Legislature and was the youngest member of that body. In 1904 he was elected to the office of Prosecuting Attorney of Raleigh County, and in 1908 was one of the Presidential Electors who cast the vote of the State for Hon. William H. Taft. In 1910 he sought the Republican nomination for Congress in the Fifth District, making a campaign which, while not successful in bringing him the honor he sought, gave him a State-wide reputation and made him a factor to be reckoned with in the future. In 1912 he was nominated without opposition for Attorney-General of West Virginia, and in the election of that year received the highest number of votes of any Republican State candidate.

As Attorney-General he had many questions of great importance to deal with, among them the Virginia debt case, the railroad rate cases, and the cases growing out of charges of bribery brought against members of the Legislature. In all these he showed marked ability and excellent legal generalship.

He is a man of large physique, and presents a commanding appearance. He is a natural orator and never fails to command the attention of an audience. He is not yet forty, and is one of the best known men in the State. He and Judge Ira E. Robinson were competitors for the Republican nomination for Governor in the campaign of 1916, and in this historic contest General Lilly delivered addresses in nearly every county in the State. It was by odds the most spirited contest ever known in West Virginia. After all the counts and recounts were made in the different counties Judge Robinson was declared the winner by a small majority.

Since Mr. Lilly's retirement from the Attorney-General's office he has located permanently in Charleston for the practice of his profession, and has erected a beautiful residence where he lives with his wife, *nee* Mary E. Glenn, of Arlington, Kentucky, a daughter and two young sons.

## Hannibal Forbes, A.B., LL.B.

For many years the subject of this sketch, now deceased, was one of the well-known attorneys of the Ohio County, West Virginia, Bar. He was the son of George and Eliza Echols Forbes and was born in the City of Wheeling, Virginia, June 1, 1837. He was prepared for college at the Linsly Institute, a high grade classical academy, now a little over one hundred years old, from which he went to Washington College, Pennsylvania, entering the junior class, and graduating therefrom with the degree of A.B. in the class of 1858 with fourth honors. He promptly entered the Cincinnati College of Law, and graduated in the class of 1859 as a Bachelor of Laws. He immediately returned to Wheeling and was admitted to practice in the autumn of that year, where he conducted a prosperous and profitable business up to two years previous to the time of his demise, which took place March 11, 1903, at Atlantic City, N. J. He was a man of pronounced integrity and was in all respects thoroughly reliable and trustworthy; hence he forged to the front as one of the leading and most successful lawyers and business men of the counties composing " the Pan Handle " of Virginia. There never was a time in Hannibal Forbes' mature life that his word, among the people who knew him, was not as good as his bond, and that too for any reasonable amount, because he was a man of large means and resources. In all of his relations, in his family, at the Bar, in his friendships in the community, he was loyal, true and upright, generous, charitable and considerate. He was also one of the most courteous and agreeable of men, always kindly disposed and full of wit and humor, and never was lacking for friends and followers. He was a safe and sane counselor, and could always be depended upon to do the wise and proper thing. He was a sound lawyer, an enterprising citizen and an upright man.

Mr. Forbes was a Democrat in his political convictions, but never was a candidate for political favors. He never was a candidate before the people for any office except City Councilman of Wheeling. He was elected and proved to be an able, safe member. He was Deputy Clerk of the United States District Court and also a Uinted States Commissioner at the City of Wheeling for about ten years, and always could be depended upon to discharge his official duties honorably and faithfully. He was twice happily married and had five children, only two of whom are now living. He was a member of the Masonic Fraternity and in college was a Phi Kappa Psi. He was a useful citizen of Wheeling and died all too soon.

## Hon. Harvey W. Harmer, LL.B.

Harvey W. Harmer, son of B. Tyson and Margaret J. Harmer, was born at Shinnston, Harrison County, West Virginia, July 25, 1865, and received his early educational training in the public schools of his native town, which has recently developed into a prosperous little city. Later he attended the State Normal School at Fairmont and graduated in the class of 1889, taking the complete academic course. Still later he attended the West Virginia University at Morgantown and graduated from the Law Department in the class of 1892, receiving the degree of Bachelor of Laws. The same year of his graduation he moved his residence to Clarksburg, was admitted to the Bar, hung out his " law shingle," began practice, and is carrying on a profitable business " at the old stand."

HON. HARVEY W. HARMER

Mr. Harmer is one of those men not uncommon in this country who pursue their course quietly through life, doing well and earnestly whatever they undertake; and at the same time living honest and upright lives, and are always found on the moral side of every question that comes before the people. His career has been that of a successful lawyer. Although he has for a number of years taken a deep interest and an active part in State and National politics, and has held a number of important public positions, he has never allowed this to materially interfere with his business as a practitioner of the law. He loves the law, sticks to it, and the result is he has achieved success. His practice embraces all branches of the law and extends into all State and Federal Courts. He has proved a safe and wise counselor, a conscientious adviser, and is deliberate in all of his acts; and better than all else he at all times seeks to be just and entirely fair with his fellow men.

He was a member of the lower branch of the West Virginia Legislature from Harrison County in the session of 1894–96, and being a strong and fluent public speaker, of sound judgment and honest purposes, ranked well among the members and was a valuable legislator. He was a member of the State Senate from 1900 to 1904, and was reckoned among its ablest and sanest members. He was a member of the Board of Regents of the State Normal Schools from 1895 to 1901, inclusive; was Secretary of the Board of Education of the Clarksburg Public Schools for nineteen years; was Mayor of the City of Clarksburg in 1896 and 1897; was Supervisor of United States Census of West Virginia for 1900, appointed by President McKinley, and reappointed in 1910 to the same responsible position by President Taft; was Referee in Bankruptcy from 1898 to 1901, inclusive, and was nominated in 1914 by the Progressive party as a candidate for Congress in the First West Virginia District, and was defeated along with all the other members of his ticket. In all of the public offices he ever held he proved efficient and faithful to every trust.

Senator Harmer married Miss Nellie B. Martin, July 18, 1901. They have no children. He is an active and influential member of the Methodist Episcopal Church; is a Trustee of the West Virginia Wesleyan College of Buckhannon; is a member of the Independent Order of Odd Fellows and is a Republican in politics. He is a man of good stature and of unusual firmness of character. He was again elected a member of the West Virginia State Senate in the campaign of 1918.

## Daniel James French Strother

Among the able and well-known lawyers of the Southern Division of West Virginia is the subject of this sketch. He is the son of James F. and Mary Botts Strother and was born in Washington, Virginia, June 29, 1872. His preliminary education was received in both private and public schools in his native section of Virginia, which was supplemented by

D. J. F. STROTHER

reading large numbers of valuable books, embracing all branches of important knowledge and information. In early life he determined to take up law as a profession, and accordingly began to devote his best energies to the careful and systematic study of legal text books. By this means and the unsparing use of the midnight oil lamp he became qualified for admission to the Bar, and after a critical examination was admitted to practice at Washington, Virginia, in 1893. Without the advantage of a collegiate education, but being a hard student and endowed by nature with a strong intellect, and by strict application and self-discipline in his chosen field of labor he became a good lawyer and in many ways a man of learning. In this way he developed into a successful attorney of high rank in the community in which he resides.

After his admission to the Bar he located for a short time at Williamson in Mingo County, when he decided to settle permanently in the growing town of Welch, the seat of justice of McDowell County, where he has since resided and where he has established a large and profitable business as a successful attorney. He is a Republican, but has never taken an active part in politics and never was a candidate for any office, but devotes his entire time to his profession in which he has made an enviable record. Only yet in middle age, possessing habits of industry and of unswerving integrity, there are yet even greater achievements in store for him both as a lawyer and a citizen. Mr. Strother is a member of the law firm of Anderson, Strother, Hughes & Curd, well-known throughout the entire Southern portion of West Virginia as one of the strongest aggregations of able attorneys in the entire State.

In November, 1902, Mr. Strother was united in marriage with Miss Elizabeth Garnett Grant, but has no children. They reside in a pleasant home in the City of Welch, where they enjoy the confidence and respect of all the people of that community.

## Judge John Thomas Simms

Judge Simms, son of Robert C. and Sarah Catherine Simms, was born in the Town of Ansted, Fayette County, West Virginia, May 10, 1875, and was educated in the public schools of that locality. Subsequently he attended the Normal School of Summersville, Nicholas County, and still later he received an additional academic training at the Academy at Fayettesville in Fayette County. In these high grade academies he received an education in many respects equal to an ordinary college course. Having decided upon the law for a profession he entered the West Virginia University, from which he graduated in the class of 1903, and was admitted to the Fayette County Bar in July of that year, and lost no time in entering upon an active practice. Being a young man of good address and of sound judgment and attentive to his duties as an attorney, he was not long in gathering around him a profitable clientage.

JUDGE JOHN T. SIMMS

In 1910 he was the nominee of the Republican party, of which he was an active member, as a candidate for Judge of the Criminal Court of Fayette County, and was elected by a large majority. In this important position he served the full term of four years, and acquitted himself in a creditable manner. Before his election as a criminal Judge his practice had extended into all the State and Federal Courts of the surrounding counties. His mind early became skilled in logical reasoning, which enabled him to solve intricate legal problems promptly and thoroughly, both as a lawyer and as a judge. As a trial lawyer he handles his cases with remarkable judgment and skill. He possesses self-reliance to an extent that he does not fear results in the trial of an important cause and a sufficiency of self-assertion to hold his own in any sort of a contest. Withal he is kindly disposed and is generous to a fault. He declined to be a candidate for re-election as Judge, and at the expiration of his term he returned to active practice.

For several years past he has been Chief Counsel for the State Tax Commissioner and Commissioner of Prohibition in all cases arising in both State and Federal Courts involving the interpretation and enforcement of the Tax and Prohibition Laws of West Virginia, a most difficult position to fill. Judge Simms has the unique distinction of never having been reversed by the Supreme Court of Appeals in a single case out of the large number of cases tried by him while Judge of the Criminal Court. This of itself is proof of the carefulness and exactness of Judge Simms as a *nisi prius* judge.

Judge Simms was united in marriage with Miss Eugenia A. Alderson, daughter of the late Hon. John D. Alderson, of Nicholas County, December 28, 1903, to whom four sons were born, viz.: John Alderson, Philip Robert, Frederick Eugene and Edward B. Simms, all of whom are strong, promising lads. The family are all members of the Presbyterian Church. The Judge is also a Mason and a Knight of Pythias and is a member of the West Virginia and American Bar Associations.

## Hon. William Wellington Hughes, LL.B.

Mr. Hughes is the son of Henry F. and Virginia (Hall) Hughes, and was born in Lewis County, West Virginia, April 8, 1873. He received his education at the West Virginia Conference Seminary at Buckhannon, Upshur County, and at the West Virginia University, from which latter institution he graduated with the degree of Bachelor of Laws. He engaged in teaching in the common schools for four years, one of which he was principal of the High School in the city of Weston. He began life as a lawyer in 1900 at Weston, in the county in which he was born and reared, where he remained ten months. Feeling that there were broader opportunities for a young lawyer in the extreme southern part of the State, he changed his residence to Welch, the capital of McDowell County, and shortly thereafter he became a member of the strong and well-established law firm of Rucker, Anderson and Hughes. Being a young man, strong and rugged in both body and mind, from the very beginning he was an acknowledged success as a lawyer. After the death of the senior member of the partnership, the firm was changed to Anderson, Strother, Hughes and Curd, one of the ablest and best known law firms of southern West Virginia. Their business covers all the branches of the profession in all the State and Federal Courts, and the cash receipts therefrom are known to be very large. All the members of the firm are high grade lawyers, and clients are constantly seeking their services.

Mr. Hughes is a hard student, and a diligent, energetic and reliable worker. He is a man of marked personal appearance, is of large stature, strong features, and his whole aspect is full of force.

He has dignified the profession by integrity, fidelity and learning, and interest in his work never lags until he has reached the bottom of his cases. He is a Republican in political affiliations, but has never sought political preferment, preferring to devote his entire time to his profession. He, however, served one term in the West Virginia Legislature as a representative from McDowell County, where he rendered faithful and efficient service. He is a member of the Methodist Episcopal Church, and has for a number of years been a Trustee of West Virginia Wesleyan College at Buckhannon. He is married and has two children. His home-life is ideal, and he is naturally hopeful and happy in his hours with his friends. He enjoys the confidence and respect of all those who know him personally.

## Clyde Beecher Johnson

The eldest son of James L. and Anna C. (Martin) Johnson, Clyde Johnson, was born June 17, 1871, on a farm in Pleasants County, West Virginia, near what was then Twiggs Post Office. His father, at the age of 74, is yet living at Ellenboro, Ritchie County, West Virginia, and has for many years been an active farmer and business man in that section of the State.

In conversation with the writer Mr. Johnson talked of little else than his mother, who died in 1909. He attributes to her any degree of success that has come to him, and among other things said:

"My mother was a queen among women. She was one of the early female graduates of Marietta College, and I yet believe she was the most thoroughly cultured and educated woman I have ever met. Her knowledge was encyclopedic, her memory marvelous, and her judgment of persons and situations unerring. After her graduation she taught in Mississippi, and later in Texas and during a portion of the war between the States she was principal of the Huntsville Female Academy, now, I believe, a Texas Normal

School. After the close of the war she came back north to care for her aged parents, and in 1866 opened " The Cedars," one of the first exclusive finishing schools for young ladies west of the Allegheny Mountains. In January, 1870, she married my father, and in addition to her duties as a wife and mother she found time to teach what was in fact a private college almost up to the time of her death in 1909. I have spoken thus at length of my mother because she deserves it. She is by far the most important part of this sketch, as whatever of success has come to me is almost wholly due to her example and teaching, and to such of her high ideals and splendid mind as I inherited."

Mr. Johnson was educated in the common schools of West Virginia, later spending some time both at Marietta and at West Virginia Wesleyan Colleges, but is not a graduate of either. He taught public schools for a number of years, in the meantime devoting himself to the study of law, being admitted to the Bar in 1895. He is proud of the fact that Arthur I. Boreman, the first Governor of West Virginia, and then Judge of the Third Circuit, was the first Judge to sign his law license. His first year of practice was at Sistersville in Tyler County, at the end of which he returned to Pleasants County and was the nominee of his party for Prosecuting Attorney in the election of 1896. He says that his defeat in that election at once curing him of running for office, and forcing him to settle down to hard professional work was a blessing in disguise.

He practiced in the town of St. Marys from 1896 until July 1, 1913, when he removed to Charleston and formed a partnership with Hon. William G. Conley, who had just finished his term as Attorney-General of the State. This firm represents The Baltimore & Ohio Railroad Company in many matters in West Virginia, and has a wide general practice in both State and Federal Courts.

In 1898 Mr. Johnson married Miss Anna Grace Hart, of Randolph County, West Virginia, and with their two children — Myra and Bosworth — they reside in a pleasant home in the City of Charleston. At this home with his family and in his modest home library Mr. Johnson finds his greatest pleasures. Amid pressing duties of a general law practice he has found a few spare hours to devote to literary pursuits, and in addition to some editorial work has written occasional bits of verse. Some of these were published in 1914 in a little volume entitled " Rhyme and Reason."

He is a member of the American Bar Association, the West Virginia Bar Association and the local Bar Association of the City of Charleston. His highest ambition is to be remembered when his life is finished as a lawyer worthy of fellowship in these associations, which include the great legal minds of America.

In politics Mr. Johnson is a life-long Democrat of the school, he says, that trusts the popular judgment and believes that no cause or party emergency is great enough to demand a sacrifice of candor. While never himself a candidate for public office since 1896, until the present year, being the nominee of his party as a candidate for State Senator, he has always taken an active interest in the affairs of his party, and has as wide an acquaintance throughout the State as perhaps any man of his age. He is a believer in Government by party, and it is never difficult to know where he stands on any public question. He is one of the ablest stump speakers in the entire State in all of the political parties.

Mr. Johnson confesses of having lived the quiet life of the country lawyer who must live by his work, and assures the biographer that there is little to tell about it that would seem of importance except to his family and intimate friends. He is an orator of high grade, and is a trial lawyer of pronounced ability and is a sound pleader as well.

## Andrew Price, LL.B.

Mr. Price is a son of the Rev. William T. Price, D.D., and Annie L. Price, his wife. He was born in Pocahontas County, West Virginia, January 29, 1871, and was educated in the public and private schools of the Greenbrier Valley, notably the Academy at Lewisburg, Greenbrier County, which offered a liberal education in the higher branches of studies, including the Latin language and the sciences; later he attended the West Virginia University at Morgantown, from which he graduated in 1892 with the degree of Bachelor of Laws. He was in the same year admitted to membership of the Pocahontas Bar, and has since practiced his profession uninterruptedly at Marlinton, the seat of justice of his native county. He married Miss Grace Leigh Clark, February 10, 1897. and has two daughters — Agnes and Margaret — who are graduates of the Lewisburg Seminary, and are now students at the West Virginia University. In his religious convictions he is a Presbyterian, having followed in the footsteps and teachings of his distinguished father.

In politics Mr. Price is an adherent of the Democratic party. and has always been liberal, reasonable and just. He is a man of strong convictions upon all subjects and allows, without reservation, the same privilege to others. He is by nature kind and generous, and enjoys the confidence and respect of the people who have personal and business relations with him, and but few men in the State have a wider acquaintance than he or who is more generally known. He is a man of staunch integrity, of conscientious purpose and ardent convictions, and his talents, energy and perseverance have gained him the reputation of a successful and able practitioner of the West Virginia Bar. He possesses mental traits peculiarly adapted to the requirements of his profession. He has an inquisitive and highly analytical mind and keen powers of perception, which penetrate every question of law or fact that engages his attention; consequently he is always prepared for any turn which a case may take and is, therefore, fortified against surprise or novel development.

Mr. Price's strong fort is that of an advocate — a public speaker. He is full of wit and humor, which are so natural and easy, and yet so quaint, they are peculiarly impressive. He apparently endeavors to suppress the humor in his make-up, but it will not down. It is too natural for that. It will leak out; and yet he can, at times, be as serious as if he were conducting a funeral. The distance between the sublime and the ridiculous with him is so close that they simply blend into one, and they are, therefore, entertaining, instructive and winning. He never speaks that every ear is not open and every mind is receptive.

He has never sought a political office except as a side issue. He has been Mayor of his town, President of the Board of Education, Postmaster and Notary Public. He is thoroughly public-spirited, and has a literary turn of mind; and when not engaged in professional work his leisure is devoted to the systematic reading of books, and we may add that he has written many valuable essays and a considerable number of real poems. To say the least he is a many-sided man. In a recent letter to the writer he closed with this sentence, which in no respect applies to himself: "After mature consideration he adventured the opinion that life is not what it is cracked up to be."

## D. Barger Evans

Among the well-known and successful lawyers of the Marshall County Bar is the subject of this sketch. His parents were Walter and Susanna (Francis) Evans, highly respected citizens of the "Northern Pan Handle" of Virginia. The son was born and reared in the splendid County of Marshall, beginning an honored career December 18, 1859. He was educated in private and public schools at Moundsville, the seat of justice of Marshall County. Later he spent two years (1881 and 1882) of hard and faithful study at Waynesburg College, one of the long established institutions of high grade in Western Pennsylvania. He says the reason he did not complete the entire college course was because money in those days was harder to get one's hands on than in these times of pushing and pulling, and we may add puffing also. We are inclined to the belief that he having decided to take up the law as a profession, was anxious to get back home and begin a course of study of legal textbooks. After all he was pretty well educated, and being as industrious a young fellow as the writer of these lines ever had the pleasure of knowing personally, and a natural born student, we are inclined to believe that he made no serious mistake to quit college and return to his home at the time he did. The fact is whilst a complete college education is important and always helpful, yet the real education must come from a life spent in reading, thinking, working and rubbing up against other men in a life of toil and digging. The truth is work is the only real winning card in this life. If one have the fundamentals upon which to base a fabric of learning, and will thereafter apply the necessary get-up-and-get, as our subject Evans has done, he is sure of success in any calling in life.

Mr. Evans while in college began the study of legal textbooks; but in the summer of 1882, after he left college, he returned to Moundsville, entered the law office of John Alexander Ewing, a number one lawyer, and began the reading of law in dead earnest. With Mr. Ewing's tutoring and his own systematic habits of study, Mr. Evans passed a very creditable examination before three of the Judges of the Supreme Court of Appeals of West Virginia, and was admitted to the Bar April 7, 1883, and promptly began to practice. At first it was " hard sledding," but he had the grit to stick to it and work, early and late, until his clients became more numerous and more profitable. Hence, it was not many years until the rule was reversed: instead of his hunting clients, clients began to hunt him; and that rule, to this day, is still working in his favor.

Mr. Evans is not only rated as a successful, able lawyer, but all through life he has stood forth as a clean, honorable, upright man. His practice has extended into all the branches of the profession in all the State and Federal Courts of West Virginia, and also in the Supreme Court of the United States. He is a careful pleader, and handles his cases well. He is naturally courteous and kind, and is a very successful trial lawyer. Being studious and industrious, he takes nothing for granted, but goes down to the bed-rocks both in thé law and the facts involved, before he enters upon the trial of his causes. Long years ago, he found out that the lawyer who wins is the one who is most familiar with his cases when he enters a court room for trial.

September 11, 1890, Mr. Evans was united in marriage with Miss Mary Estelle, daughter of the Rev. B. F. Myers. Two children are the result of this union. His home-life is ideal, and he enjoys associations with his friends, wherever he meets them. His standing among the people in the community in which he resides is that of a moral, upright, honorable gentleman, and an all-around successful lawyer. He is a member of the Benevolent Order of Elks.

## Hon. Carney M. Layne, LL.B.

Mr. Layne, son of William M. and Nancy E. Layne, was born at Crown City, Ohio, March 2, 1878. His primary education was received in the common schools in his early home town. Later he entered the Eastman National Business College at Poughkeepsie, New York, from which he graduated in 1898. Still later he entered the Law Department of George Washington University, Washington, D. C., from which he graduated, LL.B., in 1904. He successfully passed the Washington City Bar examination in 1905, which is known to be one of the severest in the entire country, and was admitted to the District Bar. He selected Huntington, West Virginia, as a permanent home, and in 1906 he became a member of the Cabell County Bar, where he is conducting a profitable and growing business. He is regarded, not only as a well-grounded lawyer in all branches of the profession, but he is known as a hard and faithful worker and a safe adviser and pleader. By fair dealing and manly conduct he has steadily built up a profitable clientele. He practices in all branches of the profession in all the courts, both State and Federal, within the limits of the State.

He is an adherent of the Democratic party and is one of its active managers in Cabell County, being at this time Chairman of the County Executive Committee. He was a member of the West Virginia Legislature, from Cabell County, in 1915–16, and took an active part in framing the laws of that period, and proved faithful to every public trust. He served on the Judiciary and several other important committees of the House of Delegates, and was an attentive and active member of all of them. He is an aggressive, enterprising, public spirited citizen, and takes a vigorous part in the growth and development of the unusually prosperous city in which he resides.

Mr. Layne married Miss Alice M. Lanahan, of Washington City, November 21, 1916. They have no children. He is a member of the Order of Freemasons and of the Delta Tau Delta College Fraternity.

## Thomas A. Bledsoe, A.B., LL.B.

The subject of this sketch is one of the very able young lawyers of the Charleston Bar. He is the son of Thomas A. Bledsoe, Sr., and Edmonia Page Bledsoe, and was born at Staunton, Virginia, May 5, 1882. He was educated in public and private schools of his native city. Later he matriculated as a student at Washington and Lee University, Lexington, Virginia, from which he graduated in 1901 with the degree of Bachelor of Arts. After teaching two years at Locust Dale Academy, having in mind in the meantime the law as a profession, he entered the Law Department of Washington and Lee University, from which he graduated in 1905 with the degree of Bachelor of Laws. The year of his graduation he was admitted to the Bar of the Supreme Court of Virginia. Later he located in Charleston, West Virginia, and became a member of the firm of Littlepage, Cato and Bledsoe, which handled a large volume of general court practice. This strong firm was dissolved by the election of Mr. Littlepage to Congress, but Cato and Bledsoe continued the practice until the fall of 1917, when Mr. Cato was appointed by the Governor to fill the vacancy created by the death of Judge Samuel D. Littlepage, as Judge of the Circuit Court of Kanawha and Clay counties, which leaves Mr. Bledsoe the sole survivor of the firm; but he is a strong lawyer and can sustain himself in any court, anywhere, and doubtless will be able to handle the large business of the former firm in a satisfactory manner.

Mr. Bledsoe in politics is a Democrat and was the candidate of that party in 1912 for Attorney-General of West Virginia, but was defeated along with the balance of his ticket.

Mr. Bledsoe is a man of marked personal appearance. He is of good stature, his features are strong, and his whole aspect is full of force. His personal character is above reproach, and his ability is beyond question. There is in store for him much more than he has already received, in the law as well as in politics. November 25, 1913, he was united in marriage with Miss Walker Bradford. They have one child — Thomas A. Bledsoe, 3d. Their home is in the Capital City, where they have many appreciative friends. In church relations Mr. Bledsoe is a Presbyterian. He is a splendid type of the thrifty, able and promising young members of the profession in West Virginia, and we opine there is a great future in store for him.

## Thayer Melvin McIntire, LL.B.

Our subject is a son of James W. McIntire, an old and able lawyer of Wetzel County, West Virginia. The son was born in that county June 22, 1881, and received his education in Magnolia High School of his native county. Later, in 1902, he graduated from the Law Department of the West Virginia University in the class of 1902, receiving the degree of Bachelor of Laws. Almost immediately after his graduation he was admitted to practice in the Circuit Courts of this State, and during the same year he was admitted to practice in the Supreme Court of Appeals of West Virginia and in the United States District Courts. He has had a large practice in Monroe County, Ohio, and has been engaged in extensive litigations in the Supreme Court of the State.

He was appointed Tax Commissioner of Wetzel County in 1905, and also served one term as a member of the Board of Equalization and Review of Wetzel County, and was twice elected a member of the City Council of the town of New Martinsville.

Our subject was practically reared in a law office, his father having been an active practitioner in the courts of this State since 1880. He has been active in politics and was always ready and willing to lend his aid to the Republican party and its candidates. He was a candidate for Prosecuting Attorney of his county in 1916, and although defeated, owing to the large Democratic majority in Wetzel County, he received the largest vote ever polled by a Republican candidate for that office in that county. He is a man of great energy and a hard worker at anything he undertakes. It is no wonder, therefore, that he has succeeded as an attorney-at-law. Such men rarely fail in their undertakings.

## Hon. G. G. Duff

Mr. Duff is a son of George W. and Henrietta Duff, and is a native of Doddridge County, West Virginia. He was born December 4, 1863, and was educated in the public schools of that county, West Virginia State College at Salem, and the State Normal at Fairmont, West Virginia. He taught in the public schools for seven years and was greatly benefited by the experience, as it fixed the habit of systematic reading and study after he had laid aside his textbooks. Whilst engaged in teaching he made up his mind to become a lawyer, and procured the necessary textbooks and began a course of study, which he pursued assiduously for several years. June 2, 1898, he was examined as to his proficiency by the Supreme Court of Appeals at Wheeling, West Virginia, and was licensed to practice law within the limits of the State. He located at Summersville, in Nicholas County, where he now resides and where he is conducting a satisfactory and profitable practice.

In politics Mr. Duff has always been an adherent of the Jeffersonian Democracy, but is rather of the conservative kind; nevertheless, he is "dyed in the wool." In 1902 he was elected Mayor of the town of Summersville, the seat of justice of Nicholas County, and served the people so satisfactorily that they re-elected him in 1904 for a second term. He was subsequently chosen for the office of Town Recorder, which he faithfully filled for six consecutive years. He takes a deep interest in the civic development of his town and county and spends much of his time and energies in forwarding its progress and development. Whilst Nicholas County has not forged to the front as rapidly as it might have done in the years agone, it, nevertheless, is rich in coal and timber, and in these later years it is having its inning, and much of this is due to the energy and enterprise of men of the makeup of the subject of this sketch.

Mr. Duff was elected a member of the West Virginia Legislature in 1912 and served efficiently for the full term of two years; and in 1916 he was elected Prosecuting Attorney of the county, and is now proving to the lawlessly inclined that they cannot violate the laws of the county and State without being vigorously prosecuted.

His practice covers all the branches of the law, in all the courts of the State — Federal as well as State — including the Supreme Court of Appeals, and affords satisfactory remunerative rewards.

Mr. Duff united in marriage with Miss Linda Chapman September 24, 1901, and they have one child — James H. Duff — now ten years of age. Their home is at Summersville, on the watershed between the valleys of Peters Creek and Muddlety Creek,— the latter being a beautiful stretch of country on the pike towards Sutton in Braxton County.

Mr. Duff is a member of the Baptist Church, and is also a Freemason, a Knight of Pythias and an Odd Fellow.

HON. G. G. DUFF

## Judge James W. Robinson

Judge Robinson was born on a farm near Clarksburg, West Virginia, on the 22d day of February, 1875. His parents are Joseph B. and Martha E. Robinson. He is one of a family of fourteen children; was educated in the public schools of Harrison County; graduated from the Fairmont State Normal School in 1900; took the law course at the West Virginia University, and was admitted to practice at the Clarksburg Bar in May, 1906. Before being admitted to the Bar, however, he taught school two terms, and was editor of a daily and weekly newspaper in Clarksburg for five years. After his admission to the Bar he participated in many of the important criminal and civil suits tried in the courts of the county, and frequently appeared in cases in the Federal District and Circuit Courts.

He was elected a member of the House of Delegates of the West Virginia Legislature and served in the sessions of 1910–12. In 1912 he was elected Judge of the Criminal Court of Harrison County, and again in 1916 he was re-elected to the same office. He discharged the duties of this responsible office to the entire satisfaction of the public. He is a good lawyer and a just judge, and a man of that makeup cannot fail to prove satisfactory in public office.

Judge Robinson is a Democrat in his political affiliations, and a Baptist in his religious convictions. He has always lived a conscientious, upright life and has the confidence and the utmost respect of the people of his county. As a Judge he is absolutely incorruptible, and is honest in both thought and purpose. He is a faithful husband, and a man whose life and character are enriched with noble qualities of both head and heart.

He was married May 19, 1913, to Mabel Lyon Stealy, and has no children.

He belongs to several fraternal organizations: Knights of Pythias and all of its co-ordinate branches, and at the present time is Grand Chancellor of the State, the Independent Order of Odd Fellows and all of its branches, and is a Mason and an Elk.

## J. Howard Holt

Mr. Holt is among the prominent lawyers of the northern portion of West Virginia, and he is largely a self-made man. He was born on Knawls Creek, Braxton County, Virginia, September 19, 1858, and is the son of Jonathan and Eve Ann (Mealy) Holt, and all the primary education he received was in the public schools of his native county and at West Milford in Harrison County; but he was all his life an omnivorous reader of valuable books, and in this manner he has pieced out a valuable, practical education, and is well informed on all important subjects, as well as the law. After all, what one makes of himself, and not what he is made by the aid and influence of friends and family, is the most patent and prom-

JUDGE JAMES W. ROBINSON

inent thought that arrests the attention and deepens the convictions of his fellow men. We must admit, however, that the value of collegiate education cannot be overestimated; nevertheless, many of the greatest lawyers and clergymen all along the history of our country never attended a college of any sort. Still they were gifted with extraordinary intellects, and are men of application and industry of an unusual sort. The fact, therefore, that a young man, for financial reasons, is barred from the privileges and advantages of a college education does not, by any means, prevent one from making a success in any of the learned professions, as the history of Mr. Holt and many of the other leading lawyers of the West Virginia Bar clearly prove. Still, our sincere advice to all young men who contemplate entering any of the learned professions, is to go through a college, if it is at all possible, and with most young men it is, or can be made possible. Grit, get and gumption are the only real essentials, and no man can succeed as a lawyer without these elements, college or no college; but the help of a college will aid one's chances amazingly. A large majority of the eminent lawyers, clergymen and physicians are college men. Then, go to college, if within one's reach, is our candid advice to one and all. The writer once heard Dr. John B. Minor, of the University of Virginia, one of the greatest law lecturers of this or any other country, say in one of his great lectures to a law class: "No man can be a great lawyer — a masterful lawyer — unless he is thoroughly posted in the technique of the law; and this he can never secure outside of a well equipped law school." This is putting it strong, but it is largely true.

Mr. Holt read law in his own home, was examined and admitted to practice by the Supreme Court of Appeals of West Virginia at Wheeling, November 8, 1884, and has since constantly practiced, without interruption, in the city of Moundsville, the county seat of Marshall, and also in the adjoining counties. He occasionally attends the courts of western Pennsylvania and eastern Ohio in important land litigation cases. He has given his entire time and attention, thus far, to the practice of his profession. For over thirty years he has been a Commissioner of both the Circuit and County Courts of Marshall County, which itself would give him a broad legal training.

He never held a political office of any kind. He was originally a Republican, but since 1886 he has been an active member of the Prohibition party, and has aided it in all of its campaigns. He is a member of the Methodist Episcopal Church and was twice married; his first wife was Miss J. Ella West, whom he married July 4, 1883, who died May 5, 1886. His second wife was Miss Annie P. Thatcher, to whom he was united in marriage June 22, 1887, and who still survives. They have had six children, two of whom are dead.

Mr. Holt is a man of high social and moral standing in the community in which he resides, and ranks high as a member of the legal fraternity of the State.

He has been a member of the Legal Advisory Board of Marshall County during the European War.

## Hon. Charles Powell

The subject of this brief sketch is one of the best known and really able lawyers of the northern portion of West Virginia. He was born March 12, 1865, in Marion County, West Virginia, and is the son of John W. and Lucy A. Powell. His early education was obtained from the common schools of his native locality, and was completed by a systematic reading of the best books at his command, covering all subjects which were necessary to store his mind with information useful and important in his future career. In early life he determined upon the law as a profession, and his reading and study were in that direction. He attended no college, but he possessed an aspiration for knowledge which no circumstance could suppress and an ambition which would not down. In this manner he procured an education that was of great practical value to him in later years, and enabled him to attain a high rank in the legal profession. He read law with great avidity and earnestness, and, being endowed by nature with an intellect singularly adapted to the discernment of truth, however veiled in the speciousness of reason, or enveloped in the delusion of circumstance. He early learned that application, promptness and fidelity were the qualities which insure professional success, and with these he brought to the Bar an earnest ambition and a zealous purpose which prompted him to the noblest exertion in every sphere in which his professional services have been employed.

Mr. Powell began his career as a lawyer in 1887 as a member of the Marion County Bar, and has since successfully practiced in that and the surrounding counties. He began early, and never allowed politics or anything else to distract his thoughts and purposes from the study and practice of the law. The only office he ever sought or held was Prosecuting Attorney of Marion County, which he ably filled from 1893 to 1897, and again from 1901 to 1905. Being a strong, firm lawyer, he was that sort of a prosecutor of all violators of the law. His practice is general, and extends to all the courts of West Virginia, both State and Federal. He has specialized in corporation practice, and particularly in coal, oil and natural gas cases, which are numerous in the courts of West Virginia.

He is married, but has no children, and his residence is at Fairmont, the seat of justice of his native county. In politics he has always been a Democrat. His career shows conclusively what grit and energy will accomplish in a young man's professional life.

---

## Hon. George R. C. Wiles

Mr. Wiles, son of J. T. and Mary C. Wiles, was born in Grayson County, Virginia, May 29, 1877, and received a thorough rudimentary education in the common schools of Virginia and West Virginia, and after establishing his residence in West Virginia he took the law course at the West Virginia University, which he completed in 1900, and was promptly thereafter admitted as a member of the Mingo County Bar at Williamson, the seat of justice of that county in the extreme southern portion of the State, which at that time was a small town, of great promise, and has since developed into a prosperous little city on the Norfolk and Western trunk railroad. As a lawyer he is sagacious and able and has succeeded well. He possesses a clear, strong, logical mind, and is liberal, though tenacious, in the maintenance of his own opinions, and never fails to express himself with exactness and force. Although not ambitious of political notoriety, he has been an active and influential factor in the Democratic politics of Mingo County. He was nominated and elected a member of the lower branch of the West Virginia Legislature in 1902, and served two years with honor to himself and credit to the county he ably represented. While he shows some taste for and tact in politics his prime purpose is to devote his best energies to the work of his profession, and it must be said he is making good this determination.

Mr. Wiles was appointed by Governor Cornwell, in 1917, to a six years' term on the Public Service Commission of the State of West Virginia, a position in influence and responsibility second only to the Chief Executive himself. This Commission is given supreme control over all the public service corporations within the State. Section 4 of the act creating the Commission requires every public service corporation to maintain adequate and suitable facilities, safety appliances or other suitable devices, and perform reasonable service in respect thereto safe and sufficient for the security and convenience of the public, and the safety and comfort of its employees, and in all respects just and fair and without any unjust discrimination or preference. All charges, tolls, etc., must be just and reasonable.

Every railroad company shall permit switch connections for intrastate business upon terms and conditions prescribed by the Commission, whenever the business offered by the connecting company shipper, in the judgment of the Commission, justifies it. The Commission may require railroad and other transportation companies to maintain such suitable public service facilities and conveniences as may be reasonable and just, to make reasonable connections with trains on branch lines of such railroads and other connecting railroads, to require passenger trains to stop at junctions with other railroads. The Commission may prescribe the number of men necessary to constitute safe crews for handling trains on steam railroads. No steam railroad shall discontinue any regular passenger train, or any other public service facility, or change any regular passenger train schedule, without authority of the Commission.

Sections 6 and 7 prohibit all unjust discriminations. No public service corporation shall by means of any special rate or rebate, or any other device or method, charge, collect or receive from any party a greater or less compensation for any service rendered or to be rendered than it charges, collects or receives from any other party for doing a like and contemporaneous service under the same or substantially similar circumstances and conditions. Nor shall any public service corporation give any undue or unreasonable preference or advantage to any person or locality, or any particular character of traffic or service, or subject any particular person or locality to any undue or unreasonable prejudice or disadvantage in any respect whatsoever.

The position is semi-judicial, and Mr. Wiles has held the office long enough to establish the conclusion that he is well equipped for the place, and is performing the duties thereof faithfully. His term of service will not expire until 1923.

Mr. Wiles married Miss Ethel Cole April 15, 1903, by whom he has three children. He is a man of medium size and is apparently the personification of good health. He is a good public speaker and a successful trial lawyer.

## Hon. Matthew M. Neely, A.B., LL.B.

Major M. M. Neely, son of Alfred and Mary Morris Neely, is a native of Doddridge County, West Virginia, where he was born November 9, 1874. He attended the public schools of his native county and also Salem College at Salem, West Virginia, during a part of which time he was engaged as a teacher in the public schools, which he followed for four years. In 1897 he matriculated as a student at the West Virginia University in the classical and military departments, and graduated, A.B., with high honors, in 1901. He then entered the Law Department of the University, graduating therefrom, LL.B., in 1902, and was admitted to the Marion County Bar in the autumn of that year. Being an industrious worker and a gifted public speaker, his practice rapidly increased. He joined the West Virginia National Guard in 1898, and filled the office of First Lieutenant, Captain and Major. He also served as a private volunteer soldier in the Spanish-American War. He was a military cadet during the several years he was at the State University, and, therefore, possesses a pretty thorough military education.

Like a great many young lawyers, Major Neely had an inclination to engage in politics. So he became the Democratic candidate for Mayor of the city of Fairmont, was elected, and proved to be an able and efficient official. Meantime his law practice was rapidly increasing, and, being an earnest worker, he did not neglect it, but it kept on growing, and he was often engaged in special cases in adjacent counties. Thus his reputation as a successful attorney rapidly spread throughout the northern portion of the State. He is careful, clear-headed, systematic, vigilant and thorough in the preparation of his cases. In argument he addresses the reason and the practical judgment of the courts and juries, and is clear-sighted and vigilant in respect of motives and ulterior influences. His public and private life as a lawyer and an individual have always been above reproach, which is the greatest of virtues. His character is determined, awakens confidence, and wins him popularity not infrequently among his opponents. Set over against every stern or strong quality is a check or balance that holds his character well in poise. He is a learned and incorruptible man, and a patriot of the highest mould. He moves among his peers with universal esteem, and amidst the temptations of public life he has preserved a reputation untarnished even by a breath of suspicion. He loves work equally from an instinctive energy and from a sense of duty.

Major Neely was elected Clerk of the House of Delegates of West Virginia in 1911, and served efficiently for two years. He was elected to the Sixty-third Congress October 14, 1913, to fill the unexpired term of Hon. John W. Davis, who was appointed Solicitor-General of the United States, and was re-elected to the Sixty-fourth and the Sixty-fifth Congresses. His record in this highest legislative body in the world has been brilliant and satisfactory to his many personal and political friends. He is a member of the Judiciary and other important committees of the House of Representatives.

Major Neely married Miss Alberta Claire Ramage of Fairmont October 21, 1903. They have two sons and one daughter. He is a member of the Fairmont Lodge of Ancient, Free and Accepted Masons, and stands among the highly respected and enterprising citizens of that section of his native State.

Major Neely was re-elected to Congress in the campaign of 1918.

## Col. Robert White

Not tall, but well proportioned and perfectly erect; with high forehead and top of head entirely bald; hair and mustache gray; eyes steel blue, bright and penetrating; voice clear and strong; movement quick and somewhat nervous; general appearance very much like that of a Prussian general, or a less portly reproduction of the Duke of Cambridge than like an American lawyer. Such is an off-hand portrait of Col. Robert White, one of the leading attorneys of the Wheeling Bar. He was a native of Romney, Hampshire County, Virginia. His great-grandfather, Robert White, was for years a surgeon in the British army, but adopting America as his home, he, at a very early day, located in Virginia. He had two sons, Robert, the grandfather of the subject of this sketch, and Alexander, a younger brother. The former became a distinguished Judge and President of the General Court of Virginia, and remained in office about forty years. The latter was elected to the first session of the American Congress, and was re-elected several succeeding terms. John Baker White, son of Judge Robert White, and father of the subject of this sketch, was Clerk of the County and Circuit Courts of Hampshire for upwards of fifty years. He died in 1862, at an advanced age, retaining till the end the respect and esteem of all who knew him. Colonel White's mother's maiden name was Streit, daughter of

COL. ROBERT WHITE

the Rev. Christian Streit, a native of Pennsylvania, and an able and prominent minister of the Lutheran Church. She died in 1868 at her home in Romney.

Colonel White was brought up at a time when educational facilities in Virginia were by no means advantageous. Public schools were indifferent, academies and colleges were scarce, and means of travel were slow, expensive and tiresome. In those days the few, and not the many, were thoroughly educated. Our subject was an ambitious young man, and by a resolute determination he succeeded in obtaining in public and private schools a thorough English training. He took up the study of law at his home, and after reading with care all the elementary books, attended the famous law school of the late Judge John W. Brockenbrough at Lexington, Virginia. Returning to Romney in 1854 he was admitted to the Bar, and began a legal career which uninterruptedly continued until his last fatal illness and death.

In 1861 he entered the Confederate army as a Captain, and served through the war in various capacities, retiring with the rank of Colonel of volunteers. At the close of hostilities he returned to Romney and formed a law partnership with John J. Jacob, who afterwards became Governor of West Virginia. This partnership was dissolved in 1871. Col. White continued the practice of his profession at Romney until his election as Attorney-General of the State in 1876, when he located in Wheeling, where he continued to reside. He was a successful lawyer, an eloquent public speaker and received a fair share of the legal patronage in that portion of the State. The Colonel was an enthusiastic Free Mason. For years he devoted a large measure of his spare time to the workings of that time-honored Fraternity. He filled nearly all the offices in both the subordinate and Grand Lodges, including the exalted position of Grand Master of the State. In faith he was a Calvinist, and for many years had been a ruling elder in the Presbyterian Church. He was an active member of the State Bar Association for many years and was its President in 1914. He was one of the most genial of men, and if he ever had an enemy the writer never heard of him. He was eighty-three at the time of his death.

## Hon. William Goshorn Caldwell, Ph.B., LL.B.

The law firm of Caldwell & Caldwell stands among the ablest and best known of the many successful practicing lawyers in the City of Wheeling in the northern portion of West Virginia. The subject of this sketch is the junior member of Caldwell & Caldwell, Attorneys and Counselors-at-Law. The senior member is the Honorable Alfred Caldwell, whose brief history appears in another portion of this volume.

William G. Caldwell, son of Alfred and Laura E. (Goshorn) Caldwell, was born in Wheeling, Ohio County, West Virginia, July 3, 1872. He graduated at Linsly Institute in 1890, a high grade academy of Wheeling, over one hundred years old; also graduated from Yale University in 1895;

HON. WILLIAM G. CALDWELL

graduated from West Virginia University in 1896, taking the degree of Bachelor of Philosophy, and graduated in the Law Department of the University of Virginia at Charlottesville in the class of 1897, receiving the degree of Bachelor of Laws. Very few young men, if indeed any, started in life with a better equipment, educationally speaking, than he received. Possessing a real knowledge of legal principles he started life with a sure guaranty of success. After receiving his diploma he returned to Wheeling, and in the fall of 1897 he was admitted to membership in the Ohio County Bar, and in partnership with his father, who had served eight years as Attorney-General of the State, a leading lawyer of Wheeling, who possessed a large and lucrative practice, young Caldwell started out as a most promising "limb of the law," and we are glad to state has made good. He has a keen, incisive mind, catches points quickly and tries cases ably and successfully. He, therefore, stands high as an advocate; is both witty and humorous and has a good all-round standing at the Wheeling Bar. He has not yet attained to his best, although he must be classed as a success and is rising all the while. His law firm does not specialize in any particular branch of the law but covers all the branches of the profession in all the State and Federal Courts; possesses a large profitable clientage and is busy from morn till night every working day in the week.

Mr. Caldwell is rather small of stature, has bright, sparkling eyes, strong features, and his whole aspect is full of force. He keeps up with both court decisions and textbook writers, and is at all times abreast of the rapid movements of the times. He is square in all of his acts, keeps his word sacredly and has the confidence of the people. He is a Republican in his political convictions, but devotes practically all of his time to his profession. His main purpose is to make himself an erudite lawyer, which he is doing splendidly. The only public offices he ever held were member of the City Council of Wheeling and a member of the House of Delegates of West Virginia, in both of which offices he rendered faithful and efficient service. He had views to express on all the important questions that arose in both the legislative bodies of which he was a member, and he never failed to assert himself and explain where he stood. "His banner was always hanging on the outer wall."

He has never married and, therefore, resides in the home of his father and mother in the City of Wheeling on the banks of the majestic Ohio River, which sweeps past his home in its meandering way to the sea. When he will join "The Benedicts" is still an open question among even those who know him best.

## Judge James William Ewing, LL.B.

Judge Ewing is one of the able, middle-aged, remarkably successful lawyers of the city of Wheeling. He followed in the foot-steps of his father, who was learned in the profession, from whom, no doubt, he inherited many of the habits and intuitions that guided him to success in the learned profession of the law. He was born at Moundsville, Marshall County,

West Virginia, October 25, 1869. His parents removed to Wheeling in 1879, where he attended the High School, and later graduated from Linsley Institute, a high grade classical academy in the city of Wheeling, in the class of 1887. He then attended the University of Virginia in 1893 and 1894, and graduated from the Law Department of that institution, in the class of 1894, with the degree of Bachelor of Laws. He, however, read law under a private tutor at Charleston, the Capital of the State, while he was Private Secretary to Governor Fleming in the early nineties, and before he attended the University of Virginia, and was admitted in 1893 as a member of the Wheeling Bar. After his graduation from the University of Virginia, in 1894, he returned to Wheeling and entered his father's law firm as the junior member, and has been engaged in almost constant practice since that time.

In 1915 he served six months as Postmaster of Wheeling to fill a temporary vacancy. In 1916 one of the Circuit Judges of the First Judicial Circuit suffered for several months with a serious illness and Mr. Ewing was elected by the Bar to serve in his stead. He filled the office ably and efficiently and to the entire satisfaction of both lawyers and litigants. In 1914 he was the nominee of the Democratic party for the seat of a Justice on the Supreme Court of Appeals of the State, a position, it is universally conceded, he was amply equipped to fill with honor to himself and credit to the State, and was defeated by his Republican opponent. There are but few, if any, more learned lawyers in West Virginia than he, and none are more upright, honorable and conscientious. Since his father's death he has practiced law exclusively on his own account, and has a large clientele, which is steadily on the increase.

Judge Ewing was united in marriage with Miss Elizabeth Rogers, of Wheeling, June 10, 1910. One son is the result of this union. He is a communicant of the Episcopal Church, a member of the Masonic Order, the West Virginia and American Bar Associations, the Wheeling Rotary Club, and the Phi Gamma Delta College Fraternity. He enjoys great popularity wherever he is known.

## Branty C. Eakle

Among the active attorneys of the Clay County Bar we find the name of the subject of this sketch the son of John E. and Nancy E. Eakle, who is a native of West Union, Doddridge County, West Virginia. He received his education in the public schools of Braxton County and at Shenandoah Collegiate Institute, Dayton, Virginia. He studied law, moved to Clay County and was admitted to the Bar in 1895, where he has established a profitable practice. He is a conscientious adviser, which measurably accounts for his success as a lawyer. He does not toil for "revenue only," but always seeks to do right and to see that substantial justice is meted out in the courts where he practices. Such attorneys are valuable in all communities and in the end never fail to be successful. Reward may be slow in coming, but it never fails in due course to reach one in the fullness of time. Mr. Eakle's practice is mainly in the Circuit Court of Clay and adjoining counties, but he frequently appears in the Federal Courts and in the Supreme Court of Appeals of the State.

He was united in marriage with Miss Mary B. Lough, October 27, 1897, and three children are the result of this happy union. Their dwelling place is beside the rippling waters of the beautiful Elk River as it sweeps past their home on its meandering way to the sea. No more delightful, picturesque spot can scarcely anywhere else be found.

Mr. Eakle is not only a safe counselor, and he is also a Christian gentleman, being an active member of the Missionary Baptist Church, where he resides. He is also a member of the Masonic Fraternity and is a faithful exponent of the principles and teachings of that honorable and ancient institution. He is a leader of the Clay County Bar and enjoys the confidence and respect of the citizens of the county. As a lawyer he is calm, patient and practical, and he makes the dictates of duty the rule of his conduct. He is unswerving in his integrity and devotion to principle, conscientiously faithful to the interests of his clients and engages all the powers of his mind and all the energies of his nature in the elimination of truth and the vindication of justice.

## Thomas P. Ryan

Mr. Ryan is the son of the Rev. Thomas P. Ryan, who was a prominent and influential Methodist preacher, for many years, in the West Virginia Annual Conference. The son was born October 15, 1869. He attended the common schools of his native section until he was qualified as a school teacher, which he zealously followed for several years. Whilst teaching in the public schools he read law, devoting all of his spare hours, day and night, to the careful study of legal textbooks, until he was able to pass the required examinations for license to practice, and was admitted to the Roane County Bar in 1896 at Spencer, the seat of justice of the county. He has since that time devoted his entire time to the practice of his profession, which has grown to large proportions and has extended into several surrounding counties. Whilst his practice is general, embracing all branches of the law in the State and Federal Courts, he has specialized in oil and gas, mines and minerals until he has attained a prominent rank in those classes of cases and is recognized as an authority in those lines of legal work. For years past he has been general counsel in West Virginia for several large producing oil and gas companies.

Mr. Ryan is a man of more than ordinary natural ability, is a well informed lawyer, and his professional career has been unusually successful. His management of his cases is methodical and practical. He possesses a correct judgment and an accurate comprehension. To his clients he is a faithful counselor and does not deceive them with apparitions of false

THOMAS P. RYAN

hopes or specious inducements to unjust or fruitless litigations; but on the contrary he is sincere in his dealings with them and they trust him with implicit faith. He is a strong trial lawyer; his mind is analytical and is, therefore, able to eliminate truth from the speciousness of circumstances. These qualifications, enhanced by habits of self-reliance and independence of thought, make him formidable in the trial of important causes. He has a large practice in the Supreme Court of Appeals of the State.

He married Miss Fannie Drennen, July 20, 1889; is a member of the different branches of Free Masons, the Odd Fellows and Knights of Pythias.

In politics he is a Republican, but has never held a political office.

## Harry Otis Hiteshew

Among the younger, successful and growing lawyers of the Wood County, West Virginia Bar, the subject of this sketch must be classed. His parents are Isaac W. and Columbia A. Hiteshew. He was born in the City of Parkersburg, West Virginia, November 12, 1882, and was educated in the public schools of that city, graduating from the High School. Later he entered the Law Department of the West Virginia University, where he received a thorough legal education. He was admitted to membership of the Monongalia County Bar in 1903 and practiced his profession in Morgantown for one year. He then changed his residence to Parkersburg, the place of his nativity, opened a law office and has there practiced uninterruptly until the present time. In politics he is a Republican, but he has never sought an office except that of Prosecuting Attorney of his native county, which is in the direct line of his profession. He was nominated and elected to that office during the fall of 1908 and served therein from January 1, 1909, to December 31, 1913, and was re-elected to the same office in 1912 for another four years' term. He was conscientious and energetic in the discharge of his official duties, and thus established a record as an able and fearless prosecutor of all violators of the laws of the State and county. By nature he is kindly disposed, but he saw to it that no guilty person was allowed to go unpunished or unwhipped of justice. During these eight years he established a record as an able and vigorous trial lawyer.

Mr. Hiteshew is a member of the firm of Kreps, Russell & Hiteshew, a well-established law firm of Parkersburg, whose practice embraces all branches of the profession in all the State and Federal Courts in West Virginia. As a lawyer Mr. Hiteshew is habitually calm, patient and practical and makes the dictates of duty the rule of his conduct. He is unswerving in his integrity and devotion to principle, conscientiously faithful to the interests of his clients, and engages all the powers of his mind and all the energies of his nature in the elimination of truth and the vindication of justice. These well-known features of his character engage confidence in him as a lawyer and respect for him as a man.

HARRY O. HITESHEW

He was united in marriage with Miss Ethel S. White, daughter of former Governor A. B. White, April 26, 1910. They have one child — Grace Talbott Hiteshew. Mr. Hiteshew is a member of the Protestant Episcopal Church, is also a Free Mason and an Elk and is a member of the Kappa Alpha Greek letter fraternity.

## Hon. George E. White, LL.B.

Senator White is the son of Clark and Katherine (Rohrbough) White, who was born at Freemansburg, Lewis County, West Virginia, November 4, 1884, and was educated at Broaddus Institute, Clarksburg, West Virginia, the West Virginia University, and the University of Virginia. He, therefore, possessed all the advantages that these long established schools of learning could give to an aspiring young man. The Law Department of the Virginia University at Charlottesville has long been recognized as a leading school to educate lawyers in the entire Southland, if not indeed in the entire country. So our subject started his professional life well equipped, educationally speaking, as one could obtain to make himself felt and appreciated in future years. After graduating he was promptly admitted to the Lewis County, West Virginia, Bar in 1909, where he began a successful legal career and where he has since practiced.

His force of will, self-reliance and courage are more than common. Upon whatever duty he entered he threw into it his resolute will and never failed when he should have succeeded. He had the courage of his convictions and never lowered his arm when he felt that duty urged him forward. He applied the law, as he had learned it at the feet of learned law teachers, in the preparation of his cases, and such a practitioner is rarely driven from a position that he takes in the trial of an important cause in any court of justice. Such are the ones who win and rarely fail. His practice is of a general character and extends into all the State and Federal Courts. He is yet comparatively young in years and his future is bright with promise.

In early life he showed a liking for politics. He was the candidate of the Republican party for a seat in the State Senate in 1912, was elected and served four faithful years therein and rendered efficient and satisfactory service. He proved himself a very useful legislator; was always in his seat and took an active interest in all bills that came up for action by the Senate. He has been editor of The Weston Independent, a Republican newspaper, since 1915, and is an apt and interesting writer.

In 1914 he was nominated for a seat in the American Congress from the old First Congressional District, but was defeated by a small majority. Since then he has devoted all of his time to his profession. He is a member of the Masonic, K. of P. and Elk Fraternities. Also the Greek letter "Frats" of Delta Chi, Sigma Chi and T. N. E. He is married, has two children and resides in the City of Weston.

HON. GEORGE E. WHITE

## John M. Baker, LL.B.

Our subject is a son of D. M. and Mary E. (Johnson) Baker, who was born in Jackson County, West Virginia, November 22, 1872, and received his preliminary education in the public schools of his native county. Later, in 1892, he was a student in the State Normal School at Fairmont, West Virginia, and in 1895 and 1896 he took the course in law at the West Virginia University at Morgantown and graduated therefrom with the degree of Bachelor of Laws. The year of his graduation he was admitted as a practitioner in the Circuit Court of his native county at Ripley, the county seat. Shortly thereafter he was admitted as an attorney in all the State and Federal Courts, his practice in the meanwhile grew rapidly until he has all the business he can attend to. He is an excellent trial lawyer and never fails to acquit himself creditably in the trial of his cases.

He is a Republican in politics and has been active in promulgating the principles of his party, but not in the sense of an office-seeker. He is public-spirited and shows an interest in the growth and development of his section of the State, and has been urged to accept official positions, but he prefers to devote his entire time to the practice of the law. The only office he has thus far held was Prosecuting Attorney of Jackson County, which he filled satisfactorily, industriously and ably for a four years' term, from 1905 to 1908, inclusive. For business reasons he moved his residence from Jackson to Roane County in 1909, where he now resides, and where his practice has materially increased and his field of labor has greatly widened. He has frequently presided as a Special Judge of the Circuit Court, and on one occasion he held the entire term in Calhoun County to the satisfaction of lawyers and suitors. This fact gave rise to general talk to induce him to become a candidate for Circuit Judge, which he has thus far declined to do. He is careful, clear-headed, systematic, vigilant and thorough in his work, and although he has made excellent headway in his profession there is still a broader field of usefulness and success before him.

Mr. Baker married Miss Jessie N. Riley, of Jackson County, in 1899, and as a result of this union a son — Clay Riley — and a daughter — Mary V.— were born to them. He is a member of the Masonic Fraternity and is also a Knight of Pythias. He has devoted much time to the cause of education and has served efficiently on Boards of Education. He also gives a large amount of thought and attention to civic matters generally. In short he is an enterprising, public-spirited, progressive citizen of the community where he resides.

JOHN M. BAKER

## Hon. George Jackson Arnold

George Jackson Arnold, one of the able and early advocates of the new State west of the Alleghenies, was born in Culpeper County, Virginia, March 16, 1816. He removed to Lewis County in 1830, where he resided until the time of his death. He read law late in life and was admitted to the Bar in 1848; was elected to the office of Prosecuting Attorney of Lewis County in 1852 and again in 1856 — serving eight years in a most satisfactory manner. In 1861 he was elected to the Legislature of Virginia. The war coming on, Mr. Arnold, being opposed to secession, went as a delegate to Wheeling in July, 1861, where the Legislature of the Restored Government of Virginia was in session. He was placed on the committee to prepare a bill for the formation of a new State, and gave the movement his hearty support. He was the draughtsman of the bill that gave us the new State of West Virginia. During that interesting session he participated in all of the debates with great fearlessness, and may be justly regarded as one of the old State's reorganizers in the dark days of war, having voted for the Union and taken that side of the question which made a new State an imperative necessity. His services to his country in those months when the flag needed friends and protectors were of great value and were highly appreciated. He retired to private life after West Virginia was made a State, and remained in the peaceful practice of his profession and in farming and stock-raising until 1878, when he was elected to the House of Delegates of West Virginia, and took an active part in the sessions of 1878 and 1879. On his return home he declined to be a candidate for re-election.

While engaged in the practice of his profession he made our land laws and land titles a specialty, and upon questions pertaining to them his opinions were entitled to great weight. Indeed he maintained a very high rank in that branch of the profession. Mr. Arnold was at one time an independent candidate for Judge of the Eighth Judicial Circuit, but was defeated. He held the opinion that a judge ought not to be elected as a partisan, but should be in all respects independent of party and party action. He issued a circular letter to the voters of the circuit, from which we excerpt one paragraph, which shows the true character of the man and reveals the fact that he was the right kind of material out of which to make a judge:

"My opinion always has been and is now, that a Judge, to be upright, impartial and just in his decisions, should divest himself of all prejudice, both personal and political, and mete out the law alike to all persons, whether of one party or another, whether rich or poor, exalted or humble — in other words, that in dispensing justice, he should 'know no man.' He should never suffer himself to lend his position in order to promote party ends, or use his office as an engine of oppression, or to gratify feelings of revenge."

Mr. Arnold quit the practice of law and removed to one of his large grazing farms on the upper West Fork of the Monongahela River. He was one of the largest landowners in West Virginia, and made stock-raising a special study. The farm on which he resided was a magnificent boundary of rich grazing land, which he kept under a high state of cultivation. Passing through it, it was not an uncommon sight to see his short-horned cattle grazing upon, not a thousand, but almost a hundred hills. He was in all respects a model farmer and grazier. He was perhaps by odds the largest stock-raiser in West Virginia and was classed among our wealthiest citizens.

Mr. Arnold was a man of large information and kept posted on the progress of affairs. He was practical in every respect and was charitable to the sick and the poor. His door was ever open to generous hospitality. He was more than an octogenerian at the time of his death.

## Joseph R. Curl

Our subject is a native of Washington City, District of Columbia, and was born December 29, 1886. He was graduated from the Business High School of that city in 1902. He then attended George Washington University of the same city, from which he graduated in the classical course in 1909, receiving the degree of Bachelor of Arts. Later he graduated from the Law Department of the same University in 1911, taking the degree of Bachelor of Laws. Shortly thereafter he located in the City of Wheeling, West Virginia, and became a member of the law firm of Erskine, Campbell & Curl, and entered upon a prosperous and promising career as a "limb of the law." He practices in all of the "Pan Handle" counties of Marshall, Ohio, Brooke and Hancock, in which his firm conducts a large volume of business, which give Mr. Curl constant employment. He was thoroughly educated and possesses energy and tact, and the result is unusual success in the trial of important causes as well as the preparation of pleadings. He possesses self-reliance and self-assertion in a large degree, which serve him well in court trials and prevent him from being thrown off his balance when confronted by opposing counsel with controverted questions of law. For one of his years as a practicing attorney he should be classed far above the average of lawyers and bespeak for him great possibilities in the years to come. He is a man of integrity and good morals and is courteous, generous and kind and maintains a high standing among friends and associates.

When war was declared by the United States against the German Empire he was among the first of our West Virginia lawyers to volunteer his service to the cause of liberty and the universal freedom of all the nations beneath the stars; and is now, as a First Lieutenant in the United States Army, in the trenches and on the fields of France and Belgium, backing the Stars and Stripes, which is the emblem of Liberty the wide world over, and is as sure to win at the wind-up as there is a "Got in himmel," and we firmly believe there is. "Justice moves with a leaden foot, but strikes at last with an iron hand." When this cruel war is over we shall hope to see our friend back among his friends, at his desk and in the courtrooms, all the better because of his experience in aiding to wipe the soulless Hun Rulers from the face of the earth.

Mr. Curl married Miss Lucie Hood, December 6, 1917. They have no children. He is a member of the West Virginia Bar Association and of the Sigma Phi Epsilon Greek letter Fraternity. In politics he is a Democrat and has never held a public office of any sort. His parents are Edward C. and Ella Fowler Curl.

## Jedediah Waldo Robinson, A.B., LL.B.

Jedediah Waldo Robinson, of Grafton, son of Frank P. Robinson, President of Taylor County Court, and Elizabeth C. (Hull) Robinson, deceased, was born near Grafton in 1881. He attended a country school, the Grafton High School and the West Virginia University, from which latter institution he received the degrees of A.B. in 1905 and LL.B. in 1906. While in college he was elected to the English Club and the Mountain, the only scholarship and honorary societies then at the University, and was editor of the college weekly and a member of the Sigma Nu Fraternity. He was admitted to the Bar of Taylor County in 1906, and later in other counties, and in the Supreme Court of Appeals of West Virginia, also the Federal District and Circuit Courts and Circuit Court of Appeals for the Fourth Circuit. He began to practice with Hon. Ira E. Robinson, who later became a Judge of the Supreme Court of Appeals, and is now associated with Hon. Hugh Warder, Ex-Member of the West Virginia House of Delegates, as the firm of Warder & Robinson, engaging in general practice. They are attorneys for the Baltimore & Ohio Railroad Company and other important clients.

Mr. Robinson was married in 1909 to Sarah C. Poe and has three sons, William, James and Charles. He has membership in the County, State and American Bar Associations, American Institute of Criminal Law and Criminology and American Judicature Society; is a member of the Interstate Executive Committee of the Young Men's Christian Association for Delaware, Maryland, West Virginia and the District of Columbia; an official member of the Methodist Episcopal Church and President of the Grafton Young Men's Christian Association and Grafton Business Men's Association. In war activities he is County Chairman of the Young Men's Christian Association War Fund Campaigns, a "Four Minute Man," a member of the County Council of Defense, a District Chairman in the War Savings and Liberty Bond Campaigns, a member of the Executive Committee of the local

JEDEDIAH W. ROBINSON

Red Cross and an associate member of the Legal Advisory Board. Mrs. Robinson is Chairman of the Taylor County Woman's Liberty Loan Committee. Masonically Mr. Robinson is a Past Master, former District Deputy Grand Master, Past High Priest, Commander of Knights Templar, Scottish Rite Mason and Shriner. He is also a Moose and Modern Woodman. He is a Republican in politics.

Mr. Robinson is a young man of clean character, and is honorable and upright in all his acts. He is a hard student and has kept abreast of textbooks and court decisions. He has dignified the profession by exhibiting in his practice the highest type of integrity, fidelity, learning and wisdom. His history as a man and attorney is a record of manliness complete in every detail. He belongs to a class of men that always succeed in all laudable undertakings. He already has a profitable clientage.

## William K. Cowden

Our subject, a well-known and successful member of the Huntington, West Virginia, Bar, is the son of William N. and Deborah (Laughlin) Cowden, and was born at Quaker City, Ohio, September 17, 1869. His younger years were spent on his father's farm in eastern Ohio, and in attending the public schools of that locality, where he received a fairly good rudimentary education. He then became a student at Wooster University, Wooster, Ohio, where he remained for some time, pursuing the higher branches of learning. He became interested in civil engineering and land surveying, and followed that occupation for some time. In the mean time he decided to take up law as a profession, and accordingly entered the law office of C. J. Howard, Esq., of Barnesville, Ohio, and began a systematic course of textbook studies. From there he went to Wheeling, West Virginia, and pursued his law studies under the tutelage of his cousin, the late William J. W. Cowden, and George W. Atkinson, who afterwards became Governor of West Virginia. He was an earnest, faithful student under their direction, until 1892, when he passed a satisfactory examination before three Judges, and was promptly received as a member of the Wheeling Bar. The next year (1893) he was admitted as an attorney in the State of Ohio. He then visited a number of cities and towns, with the view of selecting a permanent location. In 1894 he settled upon Huntington for his future home, where he opened a law office, and has been there ever since. He soon began to prosper, because he was industrious, attentive to business, thoroughly honest, reliable, conscientious and trustworthy. He has participated in many important litigations in the State and United States Courts, and controls a prominent and influential clientage. In addition to an extensive law practice, he is interested in a number of business enterprises in the growing city of Huntington, where he has gained recognition as a conscientious lawyer and a public spirited citizen. He is devoted to his profession, pleasant in his address and demeanor, is sociable and agreeable, and above all, he is an honorable Christian gentleman.

Although a Democrat, he takes but little interest in politics, has never held an office, and has never asked for one. He prefers to give his entire time and thought to his profession. He, however, enjoys supporting his friends who have a taste and desire for office seeking. The time he has to spare from his court and office work he devotes to the Presbyterian Church, of which he is a member, and the Masonic Fraternity, in which he holds high rank. He is Deputy Grand Master of the M. W. Grand Lodge of Masons, and in a year or so more, if he lives, he will reach the highest honor in the gift of that world-famed institution, Grand Master of the Grand Lodge of West Virginia. He has already been Grand High Priest of the Grand Royal Arch Chapter of the State.

In 1895 Mr. Cowden married Miss Mamie G. Riggle of Fairview, Ohio, and they have three children. Their home is in Huntington, where they are enjoying a happy and prosperous life.

## Burrell Kemp Littlepage, LL.B.

Among the strong, well equipped and promising young lawyers of the Charleston Bar must be mentioned the subject of this sketch. He is the son of the late Judge Samuel D. and Mollie Kemp Littlepage, and was born in Charleston, West Virginia, June 28, 1888. He was a student in the public schools of his native city during his earlier years. Later he attended St. John's Manlius Military Institute, Syracuse, New York, where he was taught the branches of study not available in the Charleston High School curriculum. Later he entered the Law Department of the West Virginia University, from which he graduated in the class of 1910, and in 1911 he was awarded the degree of Bachelor of Laws. The year of his graduation he was admitted as a member of the Kanawha County Bar, and also to membership of the Supreme Court of Appeals of West Virginia and the United States District Court for the Southern District of West Virginia. He promptly entered the law firm of Littlepage, Littlepage & Littlepage, composed of the Honorable Adam B. Littlepage, now a member of Congress from the Kanawha District, himself and Collett Littlepage, and has become a well-known, aggressive and successful member of the Charleston Bar.

President Eliot, of Harvard University, aptly said, in defining education: "Ability to earn, power to learn, and the faculty of looking forward are the three capacities requisite for success in any calling in life." Judging from the advancement Mr. Littlepage has made during the eight years he has been engaged in the practice of the law, we believe he possesses, in a marked degree, these three elements. At least, it is safe for us to state that he has, thus far, made a good showing in all of them. His diligence, energy and fidelity to the interests of his clients have won for him already remunerative pecuniary rewards. He has rapidly gained strength by experience. With his pleasant address and kindly disposition have gone no shadow of weakness or lack of decision; but, on the contrary, his self-reliance and proper self-assertion are a part of his nature, that are necessary to his own self-respect, which command the respect of others.

Mr. Littlepage is a member of the Democratic party, which is in line with the traditions of the Littlepage family to the third generation. He has exhibited an early liking for the game of politics. His first political office was that of Councilman for the city of Charleston, and he made a good one, because he attended to the duties of the position, and is fearless in demanding what he believes to be just and right. His next move was to become Prosecuting Attorney of Kanawha County. He sought the nomination for the same in 1916, and although his party was largely in the minority in the county, he was elected by a surprisingly large majority. He entered upon the duties of this highly important office January 1, 1917, and is proving himself to be an efficient and satisfactory incumbent of the office. He knows the law, and the art of prosecuting violators of the statutes, and is fearless and courageous enough to properly enforce them. He is doing, in a proper manner, what the people expected at his hands when they elected him.

In 1912 he was united in marriage with Miss Madge K. Robins, of Charleston, daughter of Dr. J. E. Robins, and they have two children. He is a Mason, an Elk, and is a member of the Sigma Chi Greek Letter College Fraternity.

## James D. Parriott

Our subject was born at New Martinsville, Wetzel County, West Virginia, June 16, 1880, and is the son of the Rev. George W. and Jane (Clark) Parriott. He received his education in the public schools of Marshall County and in the High School at Mannington, Marion County, of his native State. Later he entered the Law Department of the West Virginia University, from which he graduated in the class of 1909. He was admitted to the Moundsville, Marshall County, Bar in July, 1909, where he has since practiced with a marked degree of success. His office is at Moundsville, but his practice has extended into the adjoining counties and has become quite lucrative for a lawyer of his years.

Mr. Parriott is an industrious, well-equipped young lawyer, and is honest and upright in both thought and purpose, elements which are absolutely essential to permanent success in any business or calling in life. He has gained strength and standing by experience and associations, and in the same proportion his business has grown to satisfactory proportions for an attorney of his years. He has, therefore, it may be said, passed the experimental stage in his professional career.

JAMES D. PARRIOTT

Mr. Parriott is a Republican in politics, but his record shows that he prefers to be a lawyer instead of a politician, because he has never aspired to office except that of Prosecuting Attorney of Marshall County, which is strictly in the line of his profession, except one position, that of County Superintendent of Public Schools, which he held from 1903 to 1907, before he began to practice law. He was nominated and elected to the office of County Prosecutor in 1912, and filled that responsible legal office with such a degree of satisfaction that he was re-elected to the same office in 1916, and is now serving his second four years' term, ably and efficiently. He has shown himself to be a satisfactory officer for the people, who prosecutes all violators of the law, without fear or favor, and has seen to it that no guilty person has escaped. He has, therefore, made a clean record in that responsible position worthy of emulation by others in the same line of the public service.

Mr. Parriott married Miss Bessie Sadler, of Point Marion, Pennsylvania, in 1910, and is the father of two children. He is a member of the Methodist Episcopal Church, the Independent Order of Odd Fellows, the Knights of Pythias and of the Sigma Nu Greek Letter Fraternity. He resides at the city of Moundsville, where he is well known and is regarded as an honorable, upright Christian gentleman.

## Henry Bedinger Davenport, LL.B., C.E.

The subject of this sketch was born at Auvergne, near Paris, Kentucky, February 11, 1865. His father was Henry B. Davenport, son of Braxton Davenport, and Elizabeth Bedinger, the latter a daughter of Major Henry Bedinger of Revolutionary fame, and for many years a man of distinction in Berkeley County, this State. Braxton Davenport was Colonel of militia in Jefferson County, Virginia, for many years; was also a member of the House of Delegates in Virginia, and held numerous other offices of trust and responsibility; and was presiding magistrate of the court which committed John Brown of Harpers Ferry fame to jail.

Henry B. Davenport, the father of the subject of this sketch, was educated at the University of Virginia. He served as a Lieutenant of the Stonewall Brigade in the Confederate Army. He died in 1901 and is buried at Charles Town, this State. His epitaph, "A Soldier of the Stonewall Brigade," is at once a eulogy and a biography; he was born September 9, 1831. In 1860 he married Martha Clay, the mother of the subject of this sketch. She was a daughter of Brutus J. Clay of Bourbon County, Kentucky, who was a brother of General Cassius Marcellus Clay, some time Envoy Extraordinary and Minister Plenipotentiary to the court of Russia. Brutus J. Clay represented the Lexington District of Kentucky in the House of Representatives at Washington during two terms, 1861 to 1865, although a large slaveholder.

Our subject was educated at the Charles Town Academy; St. John's College at Annapolis, Maryland; Rensselaer Polytechnic Institute at Troy, New York, from which he graduated with the degree of Civil Engineer in 1886; University of Virginia, where he took a special course in applied mathematics; and the University of West Virginia, where he graduated in law in 1884. Upon graduating from the last mentioned University, he removed to Clay, West Virginia, where he practiced law for twenty years, his practice being in the Circuit Courts of this State, in the Supreme Court of Appeals, and in the United States District and Circuit Courts at Charleston. January 1, 1916, Mr. Davenport retired from the practice of the law to devote his entire time to his private business, being largely engaged in the development of the oil and gas resources of Clay County. He married Alma F. Stephenson, daughter of Thomas Benton Stephenson, January 22, 1902, to which union there has been born Benton Stephenson Davenport, aged 15 years, and Braxton Davenport, aged 9 years. Mr. Davenport lives at Clay C. H. with his family. In 1904 he was the nominee on the Democratic ticket for Member of Congress from the Third Congressional District, but was defeated by Hon. Joseph H. Gaines. Mr. Davenport has several times been Mayor of Clay C. H., and has been at various times member of executive committees of the Democratic party for senatorial, judicial and congressional districts.

He is a member of the Masonic Fraternity, being a Blue Lodge Mason, a Knight Templar and a Shriner. He has also taken fourteen degrees in Scottish Right Masonry. Mr. Davenport is at present Secretary of the Local Board for Clay County, and since May, 1917, has devoted almost his entire time, free of compensation, to the raising of an army for service abroad.

After his graduation as a civil engineer in 1886, Mr. Davenport followed that profession until 1893, when he entered the law school at Morgantown. As an engineer he saw service on the Norfolk & Western Railroad; the Cleveland, Akron & Columbus Railroad, and as an engineer in the construction of levees along the Mississippi River in Bolivar County, Mississippi. He also served two years as Professor of Civil Engineering in the University at Morgantown. As a lawyer he was engaged in most of the important cases before the Circuit Court of Clay County during the past twenty years. Without undue adulation it may be said that he has been a success as an engineer, a lawyer and a business man, having accumulated a comfortable fortune as the result of industry, perseverance and business acumen. He is a man of the strictest integrity, and has the confidence and respect of all the people with whom he associates, and stands high in the legal profession.

## John Marshall, M.A., LL.B.

One of our West Virginia young lawyers who has already "made good," and who is still rising rapidly in the ranks of his profession, is the subject of this sketch. His father, Hon. Oliver S. Marshall, is also a lawyer of prominence. Our subject was born in New Cumberland, Hancock County, West Virginia, July 28, 1881. He attended the public schools of his native town; graduated A.B. and A.M. at Bethany College; also graduated in the full classical course at Yale University, taking the degree of Bachelor of Arts. He then entered the Law Department of the West Virginia University, and graduated, *cum laude*, as an LL.B. But few young men of this, or any other State, started out in a profession with a higher grade education, and no young man of our acquaintance has made better use of it than this young man Marshall.

He was admitted as a member of the New Cumberland Bar in 1903, and the following year moved to Parkersburg, West Virginia, which offered a wider field of opportunity, where he still resides, and where he has established himself as one of its foremost barristers. His present law firm is composed of himself and former Judge Charles D. Forrer. His firm practices in all of the courts of the State, and in the Federal Courts as well, and embraces all important branches of litigation known to the law in West Virginia.

For a number of years Mr. Marshall held the office of Assistant United States Attorney for the Northern District of West Virginia, and demeaned himself as an able and erudite lawyer. Being a Republican, when the National administration changed he was succeeded in 1913 by a Democrat. He is a fluent and forceful public speaker, and is a refined, cultured gentleman, possessing all the elements of popularity before the people. Our candid opinion is, there is a distinguished future in store for him in the years to come. His portrait shows him to be a neat, clear-cut and handsome young man, with firmness and fairness clearly developed in every line of his countenance.

He married Miss Rebecca C. Paull, the accomplished granddaughter of the late Judge James Paull, of the West Virginia Supreme Court of Appeals, by whom he has two children — John Marshall, Jr., and Joseph Paull Marshall, who make up a pleasant, and, indeed, happy household.

JOHN MARSHALL

## Mason G. Ambler, LL.B.

Mr. Ambler is the junior member of the strong law firm of Van Winkle and Ambler, of Parkersburg, Wood County, at the confluence of the Little Kanawha River with the Ohio. He is a son of B. Mason Ambler, one of the noted, high grade lawyers of West Virginia, whose personal sketch appears on another page of this volume. The younger Ambler was born at Winchester, in the historic Valley of Virginia, August 27, 1876, and received his primary education in the public schools of Parkersburg, West Virginia. He then spent four years, from 1891 to 1895, as a student at the Episcopal Academy at Alexandria, Virginia, and ended up with a three years' law course at the University of Virginia at Charlottesville, graduating in the class of 1899, and being awarded the degree of Bachelor of Laws. After leaving that institution, he returned to his home at Parkersburg, and in November of that year was admitted as a member of the Wood County Bar, where he immediately entered upon a successful career as an attorney-at-law. For five years he practiced alone, asking help of no one, and was succeeding in building up a very satisfactory practice, and in 1905 he was invited to become the junior member of the long-established partnership of Van Winkle and Ambler, composed of W. W. Van Winkle and his father, B. M. Ambler, as stated at the outset of this short sketch. He thus showed that he was amply able to make his own way without depending upon the help of any one. He possessed the inherent grit to "paddle his own canoe," which he has succeeded in doing in a most satisfactory manner. It was, perhaps, best for him, at the beginning of his professional career, to be thrown upon his own resources, because what one makes of himself, and not what he is made by the aid and influence of friends or family, is the most patent and prominent thought that arrests the attention and deepens the conviction of one's fellow men.

Mr. Ambler, like his father, is a Democrat in his political convictions, and also like his father, it may be justly said, is entirely freed from the virulence of party and the malignancy of faction, which constitute for the upright lawyer a just claim to be a leader of his fellow-men. Neither of them ever held a public office, and better still, neither of them ever asked for one at the hands of his party or his friends. Both of them prefer law to politics, and both of them prefer to be known as *lawyers* instead of place-hunters; they preferred to be eminent in their profession than to be exalted to high official stations. However, not all gifted men are thus constituted. But it is true of most all the great lawyers in the history of the past in all Republics. Great lawyers, as a rule, never allow themselves to get plastered with office-holding tar. Nowadays men to become masters in any calling, must not allow their minds to become divided.

Mr. Ambler has been admitted as a practitioner in all the State and Federal Courts; also in the States of Ohio and Virginia. As a lawyer he is patient and practical, and makes the dictates of duty the rule of his conduct. He is unswerving in his integrity, and is ever faithful to the interests of his clients. His professional sun is just approaching its meridian, and although he has thus far run well, there is yet much of success awaiting him in the future.

He has never married, is a communicant of the Protestant Episcopal Church, and in college was a Delta Psi.

## John Cotton Donnally, LL.B.

Mr. Donnally is a native of Charleston, West Virginia, and is a son of William B. and Sallie Cotton Donnally, both of whom were also born and reared in the same city. The Donnallys were early settlers of the Kanawha Valley, and Dr. John T. Cotton, his grandfather, for whom our subject received his name, was one of the best known practicing physicians of Kanawha County for more than sixty years, and who departed this life at a little more than eighty years of age only a few years ago.

Young Mr. Donnally was born June 8, 1885, and received his early training in the Charleston schools, at Phillips Exeter Academy, Exeter, New Hampshire, where he took a thorough academic course, and in 1907 he was graduated from the Law Department of the University of Virginia, at Charlottesville, receiving the degree of Bachelor of Laws. He was admitted to the Kanawha County Bar the year of his graduation, and has since practiced in the State and Federal Courts. He is the junior member of the firm of Avis and Donnally, a well-known law firm in Charleston and the southern portion of West Virginia, the senior member being Captain S. B. Avis, who has been active in politics, as well as in the law, for a number of years past, and who at one time represented the Charleston District in the Congress of the United States. He is now acknowledged to be one of the strongest lawyers in the entire State.

Mr. Donnally is well educated and is trustworthy and ambitious. He is a hard worker, and delights to go to the bottom of all cases entrusted to his care. By perseverance, energy and application, although young in years, he has become a good lawyer, and his future, which is sure to be brighter, is already fixed. He is thoroughly grounded in the technique of the law, and is methodical and painstaking in the preparation of pleadings. He is also conscientious and honorable in all of his dealings, which are the *sine qua non* to success in any calling in life. He is still unmarried, is a Democrat in politics, but has never sought an office of any sort, preferring to devote his undivided efforts and energies to the study and practice of the law, in which he is admirably succeeding. He is of medium stature, and is well equipped in all branches of the law common to the courts of West Virginia.

Shortly after war was declared by the United States against the German Empire, Mr. Donnally volunteered in the United States Army, and has been promoted to the rank of First Lieutenant, and is now at the front in France defending the flag of his country. He was seriously wounded in one of his legs in Northern France and is still confined in a hospital.

## Bennett Randolph Bias

Mr. Bias was born in Lincoln County, West Virginia, in 1879, son of Rolan A. Bias and Lucy C. Bias; was educated in county schools, Guyandotte High School, Marshall College, and West Virginia University; was admitted to the Bar in 1910. He practices in the various local and State Courts, Federal District Courts, Supreme Court of West Virginia and of the United States; married in 1910 to Clotilde Gaujot; has three children; is a member of no lodge; member of Phi Kappa Sigma Fraternity; affiliates with the Protestant Episcopal Church and the Republican party.

His office and residence are at Williamson, Mingo County, where he has a large and rapidly increasing practice in all the State and Federal Courts of West Virginia, especially in the Supreme Court of Appeals. He is a safe and sane lawyer; is thoroughly reliable; is well and firmly grounded in the principles of the law; argues his cases with force and precision, and prepares them carefully; is a hard and constant worker, a superior pleader, and maintains a high rank as a trial lawyer. He in short is one of the best known and most successful lawyers in the southern section of the State.

He is also one of the most useful and attentive members of the State Bar Association. In his earlier years he was Post Master of the city of Williamson, and was an efficient officer.

## Dean Henry Craig Jones, A.B., LL.B.

Dean Jones of the Law Faculty of our West Virginia University at Morgantown, son of John B. and Jennie (Craig) Jones, was born at Central City, Iowa, June 18, 1879; graduated A.B. from Cornell College, Iowa, in 1900; also graduated A.B. from Harvard University, Boston, in 1903. In 1906 he also graduated LL.B. from that University; was admitted to the Illinois Bar in 1906, and practiced successfully to and including 1911 as a member of the law firm of Rubens, Fisher, Mosser and Rigby, of Chicago. At this time he reached the conclusion that it was preferable to be a law teacher than a practitioner, and accordingly accepted the position of membership in the law faculty of Georgetown University, Washington, D. C., where he remained until 1914, when he was chosen Dean of the Law Department of the West Virginia University, where he is now serving with great acceptability and usefulness. His splendid education in all branches of the law, coupled with many natural gifts as a teacher and executive qualities, specially equip him for the work in which he is now engaged. During his short period of service in our State University he has made a deep impression upon the young lawyers who have attended his lectures, and the older members of the profession who have given attention to the splendid work he has done and is doing in lifting to a higher plane the

DEAN HENRY CRAIG JONES

standard of the lawyers in this Commonwealth. He is a young man of unbounded energy, as well as a man of great learning for one of his years. His record as an attorney and teacher is one of manliness complete in every detail. He is a man of marked personal appearance; is of good stature; his features strong, and his whole aspect full of force. His face, as shown by his portrait, is proof that he is a hard student, and keeps full abreast of the present progressive times in the methods of turning out real lawyers, and not mountebanks. charlatans and sheisters. When a young man receives a diploma from his hands, one may feel assured that the graduate will be well equipped in all the branches of the law. We do not mean to convey the idea that our former West Virginia law graduates are charlatans, but we do mean to say that the standard is much higher now than it has ever been in the past. What Dean Jones believes, he feels, and what he feels he speaks, and acts promptly, vigorously, and with conscientious candor.

He is married, resides at Morgantown, the seat of the State University, and has the respect and confidence of the student body, the other members of the University faculty, as well as the community at large. He has been admitted to practice in all the courts of the State.

At the July, 1918, meeting of the West Virginia Bar Association he was elected its President. He is also the responsible editor of "The West Virginia Law Quarterly," the organ of the Association.

## George P. Crockett

Our subject is a son of R. G. Crockett, of Graham, Tazewell County, Virginia, and a younger brother of the late Z. W. Crockett, of Bluefield, West Virginia. He was born November 6, 1879. He graduated from the Graham High School, and later took the law course at the West Virginia University, graduating in the class of 1901, and in September of that year he was admitted to the Mercer County, West Virginia, Bar, where he has been in constant practice since that time. He formed a partnership in 1901 with his older brother, Z. W. Crockett, which continued until 1907, when Judge Joseph M. Sanders was taken into the firm, thus creating one of the strongest law firms in the southern section of West Virginia, and also one of the most successful. Although Z. W. Crockett departed this life in 1915, the firm now is Sanders and Crockett. Their practice extends through the Circuit Courts of southern West Virginia and southwest Virginia, the United States District Court of Southern West Virginia and the Supreme Court of Appeals of West Virginia, in all of these courts they have a very large and profitable business. As is true of all good lawyers, Mr. Crockett's diligence, energy and fidelity to the interests of his clients soon won for him deserved success and remunerative pecuniary rewards. He is yet young, and is growing rapidly in his well chosen profession, so that the better and larger part of his life is still before him.

GEORGE P. CROCKETT

Mr. Crockett is an active member of the West Virginia Bar Association, and, like his elder brother Zachariah, he has never married.

He resides in the thrifty and rapidly developing city of Bluefield.

Neither of the Crockett brothers ever held public office, and never sought one. Their undivided thoughts and time were given to the study and practice of the law. Generally speaking, these are the kind of men that develop into eminent lawyers.

## Hon. Raymond Dodson, A.B., LL.B.

Raymond Dodson, son of Dr. E. H. and Lucy B. (Fetty) Dodson, was born at Glenville, Gilmer County, West Virginia, October 28, 1880. After attending the public schools of his native county for several years he matriculated as a student at the State Normal School at Glenville and remained there until he mastered all the branches contained in its curriculum; graduated from the Department of Arts and Sciences of the West Virginia University in 1901, receiving its highest scholastic degree — that of Bachelor of Arts. He then read law and later attended the West Virginia University and took the complete law course of study, graduating with honor in 1903, receiving the degree of Bachelor of Laws. He located at Spencer in Roane County; was admitted as a member of the Circuit Court Bar of that county September 7, 1903, and has since practiced in that and the adjoining counties in all the State and Federal Courts, with greater than anticipated success. While he is familiar with all branches of the law, and has cases therein, he has specialized in oil and gas cases, representing as their attorney several oil and gas companies, and is himself largely engaged in the oil and gas business. He is, therefore, thoroughly familiar with all the State statutes and court decisions pertaining thereto. He has practiced in a number of important special cases in Ohio, Pennsylvania and Kentucky, because of his special knowledge of those difficult branches of the law. Mr. Dodson has succeeded in his practice in securing the confidence of the people of his own county and throughout that section of the State. He is proud of his profession and ambitious to excel in it, but like many young lawyers he has a liking for politics. Being a pronounced Republican he allowed his party to nominate him in 1916 for a seat in the State Senate, and was elected. Being a ready debater he took an active part in the discussions that arose on the floor of the Senate, and thus made himself an influential member of that body of the Legislature. He is firm and decided in his political opinions, and tenacious to party attachments, but he is courteous to his political adversaries, and tempers his zeal with such discretion as to never render himself personally obnoxious to his opponents. His Senatorial term is for four years, and the chances are that he will make a record before it ends, and thus add additional allurements to his political experiences.

When younger in years than he now is, he was Captain of a company of the West Virginia National Guard, and demonstrated many admirable

HON. RAYMOND DODSON

soldierly traits of character. October 27, 1910, he was united in marriage to Miss Nelle Rachel Smith, of Charleston, West Virginia. They have one child — Dorothy Annette, who was born October 25, 1912. He is a Ruling Elder of the Presbyterian Church; is a Mason, a Knight of Pythias and a member of the Delta Tau Delta Greek Letter College Fraternity. His home is in the city of Spencer, where he is well and favorably known. His portrait shows him to be of good stature and commanding presence.

He is not only a successful lawyer, but he is also an enterprising business citizen, deeply interested in the development of his section of the State.

---

## Henry Clay Duncan, Jr., LL.B.

Mr. Duncan, a member of the able law firm of Holt, Duncan and Holt, of Huntington, was born at Ceredo, Wayne County, West Virginia, November 1, 1875, and was educated in the public schools, the West Virginia University, and received the degree of Bachelor of Laws from the University of Virginia at Charlottesville. But few young men enter the legal profession educationally equipped as well as this young man. He began life as a lawyer at Ceredo, in 1896, and in 1898 he moved to Huntington and became a partner in the firm of Campbell, Holt and Duncan, which continued until 1904, when Mr. Campbell withdrew and the firm was changed to that prince of lawyers, Hon. John H. Holt, and the subject of this sketch. At present the firm stands as Holt, Duncan and Holt. It can be truthfully stated that it is one of the ablest law firms in this or any of the surrounding States. Their business extends to all of the State Courts, the United States Courts and the Supreme Court of the United States. They appear on one side or the other of nearly all the important causes in the southern part of West Virginia in both State and Federal Courts. While they carry on a general practice, they specialize in corporation litigations, and, therefore, maintain a high standing as corporation lawyers.

As a counselor Mr. Duncan is careful, clear-headed, systematic, vigilant and thorough in his work. In argument he addresses the reason and the practical judgment of the court and jury. He is a close and careful student of the law and keeps up with the decisions of the courts and textbook writers. He is a man of excellent personal appearance, as his portrait proves. His learning is varied and extensive, and his integrity is equal to his accuracy and his learning. His history as a man and an attorney is a record of manliness complete in every detail.

Mr. Duncan is a Democrat, but has never sought an office at the hands of the people. He is a member of the Masonic Fraternity, is married and has one son. His home-life is enjoyable, and his standing in the community is of the very best.

HENRY C. DUNCAN, JR.

## Arthur Spencer Dayton, A.B., LL.B.

One of the brilliant, able and most promising young men who has come to the Bar in West Virginia, in recent years, is Arthur S. Dayton, of Philippi, Barbour County, of this State. He is the son of Hon. Alston Gordon Dayton, who for ten years was a distinguished member of Congress from West Virginia and for a number of years past has been United States Judge of the Northern District of West Virginia. Our subject was born May 6, 1887, in Barbour County. He graduated from the classical department of the West Virginia University, receiving the degree of A.B., and later he graduated from its Law Department, receiving the *in cursu* degree of LL.B. He then went to Yale University, where he completed a post-graduate course and received the degree of A.M. It is quite apparent that but few young men have started out on a legal career as thoroughly equipped as did young Mr. Dayton. It is not surprising, therefore, that he commanded the attention of his associates from the trial of his first case, that he was sure to make good, which he has done in a most satisfactory manner. He has always been a hard student of the law, and has kept abreast of the court decisions and the textbooks, and has dignified the profession by exhibiting the highest types of integrity, fidelity and learning.

He was admitted to practice in the Circuit Court of Barbour County, June 3, 1908, and has since been licensed to appear in all the State and United States Courts in West Virginia. He has an unusually large clientele for a man of his years, and is steadily growing as the years roll on. He has written several articles for the "Standard Encyclopædia of Procedure," notably the ones on Certiorari, Dismissal, Discontinuance and Nonsuit, published by L. D. Powell & Co., which reveal knowledge and research on these important subjects. His practice extends into all the branches of the profession, with tendency to specialize in corporation directions. His learning, however, is varied and extensive, and his force of will, self-reliance and courage are more than common. As a lawyer he is thorough and accurate and has a firm grasp of legal principles, and those who know him best say his integrity is equal to his accuracy. That one statement contains a volume in itself, and lies at the bottom of all enduring success.

Mr. Dayton was married to Miss Ruth Woods, daughter of Hon. Samuel V. Woods, June 14, 1916.

## Robert Kemp Morton, B.A.

Mr. Morton's parents were William B. and Margaret (Crockett) Morton of Falls Mills, Tazewell County, Virginia, where Robert K. first saw the light, January 25, 1880, and where he received his preliminary education in the public schools of that locality. Subsequently, in 1898, he entered Randolph-Macon College, and graduated therefrom with the degree of Bachelor of Arts, in the class of 1903. Parts of 1903 and 1904 he spent in post-graduate work at Johns Hopkins University, Baltimore, Maryland, and in the autumn of 1904 he entered the Law Department of the University of Virginia and graduated in the class of 1906. He returned to his native county of Tazewell immediately after leaving the University, and was received as a member of the Circuit Court Bar of that county in the spring of 1906. Seeing better opportunities for success in another locality, he removed his residence to Graham in Tazewell County, on the main line of the Norfolk and Western Railroad, in the fall of that year, opened a law office, and entered upon an active practice. While he was getting on fairly well, he felt that he could do better by locating in a city where there was more work for a well-equipped young lawyer, so he located permanently in 1912 at Charleston, West Virginia, the Capital of the State, and the legal business center of the Commonwealth, and became a partner in the firm of Alexander and McCabe, where he remained four years. The firm conducted a large and profitable business. The partnership was dissolved in 1916, and since that time he has been engaged in business with Mr. D. N. Mohler — the firm being Morton and Mohler.

But few lawyers, anywhere, can boast of a better general and legal education than Mr. Morton. He is thoroughly posted in the fundamental principles of the law. He is also energetic and trustworthy, and is a tireless worker. He is a wise counselor, and a careful pleader; and when he comes into court he thoroughly understands his cases, and, consequently, is rarely taken by surprise. He is self-poised, and meets issues as they arise, without discomfiture or embarrassment. He is popular with other members of the profession and has never been charged with taking undue advantages of his brother members of the profession. He is a man of solid rather than of shining qualities, but impresses one as being utterly averse to a display of harshness, and able to control himself in meeting any sort of an emergency that might arise in the trial of an important cause. Mr. Morton's practice embraces all the branches of the profession, and extends to all the State and United States Courts in West Virginia and the United States Circuit Court of Appeals at Richmond, Virginia. He has appeared in special cases at Bluefield, Princeton, Union and Welch.

In politics he affiliates with the Democrats. He has never held a political office, because he prefers law practice to political office-holding, and therefore has never sought an office of any kind.

Mr. Morton married Miss Julia Ward Davidson, of Mercer County, West Virginia, October 7, 1909, and they have three children. He is a member of the Presbyterian Church, the Masonic Fraternity and the Order of Elks, and enjoys the confidence and respect of the people in the city in which he resides.

## Hon. Harry Hopkins Byrer

Mr. Byrer was born at Philippi, the seat of justice of Barbour County, West Virginia, April 20, 1877. His parents were Frederick S. and Isabella Woods Byrer, long time residents of said county. He was educated in the public schools of that section, and later graduated from West Virginia Wesleyan College, of Buckhannon, West Virginia, in the class of 1900. After a thorough course of studying of legal textbooks he passed the required examination and was admitted to practice in the courts at Philippi in February, 1902. Subsequently he became an attorney in the Federal Court, and also in the Supreme Court of Appeals of the State, wherein he has since practiced with gratifying results.

His first public office was Prosecuting Attorney of his native county, which he ably and industriously filled from 1909 to 1912, inclusive. This four-year term classed him as a vigorous, fearless prosecutor, who, although kind and merciful, yet at all times determined to enforce the laws, without the fear of results, or favor to any and all violators of the laws of the State. It can be truthfully said of him that he is a man who maintains in all of his private and public acts the highest ideals of honor and integrity. It is also true of him that when a question of moral principle is involved no one has to pause and ask where Harry Byrer stands. He is always found on the side of good morals and good government. Since April, 1914, he has been assistant United States District Attorney for the Northern District of West Virginia, which office he still holds and ably fills.

Mr. Byrer is an active and influential member of the Methodist Episcopal Church, and has been a Trustee of his *alma mater* (West Virginia Wesleyan College) since 1908, and has given much of his time and means for its support. He is a member of the Masonic Fraternity, Modern Woodmen of America, and Maccabees. He is married and has five children. There is a happy and successful future in store for a man of the makeup of Harry Hopkins Byrer.

---

## Hon. William Harrison Rardin, LL.B.

Among the well-known lawyers of the Raleigh County Bar is the subject of this sketch. He is the son of Thomas and Roena Rardin, and was born in Jackson County, Virginia, December 13, 1861. He was educated in the public schools and at the Southern Ohio Normal Institute at Hockingport, Ohio. Later he took the course in law at the Southern Normal University, Huntingdon, Tennessee, from which he graduated in 1902. He also took a course of study at the West Virginia University. He was admitted to the Tennessee Bar in 1902, and to all the West Virginia Courts in 1903. He located at Beckley, Raleigh County, opened a law office, and is now engaged in practice in the Federal and State Courts, including the Supreme Court of Appeals of West Virginia. Being careful, industrious, clear-headed and thorough in his work, he has succeeded in establishing a profitable clientage.

Before locating in Raleigh County, Mr. Rardin served one term as Superintendent of Public Schools of Jackson County, and proved to be a very efficient official. In 1905 he was elected a member of the Legislature from Jackson County, and rendered faithful service. In 1916 he had a large following of earnest backers who urged his candidacy for Member of Congress from the Fifth Congressional District. While he has somewhat of an interest in politics, his thoughts and energies are mainly directed in the line of his profession, in which he is admirably succeeding.

Mr. Rardin's history, both as a man and a lawyer, is a record of manliness complete in every detail. In argument he addresses the reason, the practical judgment, and is clear-sighted and vigilant in respect of motives and ulterior influences. He fears no antagonist, and is unfaithful to no client. He is optimistic and cheerful, and the effect of his society is reassuring. In all his dealings, in or outside of the profession, he stands unquestioned as an honorable, upright, straightforward man.

He is a member of the Methodist Episcopal Church, is also a Freemason, and is married but has no children. He resides in the thrifty little city of Beckley, where he maintains the respect of all the people who know him.

## Hon. Alexander Dulin

The subject of this sketch, son of A. H. and Rebecca (Burns) Dulin, was born in Wirt County, Virginia, February 22, 1854, and received his education in the common and high schools and a select school of that county; also by a careful reading of all the books on history and other subjects to which he had access. He possessed an inquiring mind, and he used every means possible to acquire knowledge. In this manner he managed to piece out a fairly good English education, and made good use of it in after years. In early life he decided to become a lawyer, and began the study of legal textbooks, which he kept up diligently until 1881, when he passed a creditable examination and was admitted to membership of the Braxton County Bar, where, at Sutton, the county seat, he has, without interruption, since carried on a successful career as an attorney and counselor-at-law in State and Federal Courts in Braxton and adjoining counties. He has always been a Republican in his political affiliations, but has devoted practically all of his time to his profession. Being an excellent stump speaker, however, he frequently engaged in campaigns to assist his friends who sought offices at the hands of the people. The only public office he ever held was Assistant Attorney-General of the State, under the administration of the late Hon. Romeo H. Freer, in 1900 and 1902 inclusive, wherein he acquitted himself with both ability and credit. When he retired from that responsible office he returned to Sutton and resumed his law practice.

His career as a lawyer has been able and exemplary and his demeanor as a man and an attorney has been exemplary and honorable. His force of will, self-reliance and courage are more than common. He is a persistent worker, and invariably goes to the bottom of his cases, and is always fair and just in all court trials. He is optimistic and generous to a fault and his social qualities are of a high order. He is a strong advocate and tries his cases well. He is not only devoted to the law, but he is always devoted to his friends. He is ever ready to even go out of his way to perform a friendly act towards a friend.

Mr. Dulin married Miss Cora B. Floyd, daughter of General W. H. Floyd, December 24, 1884, and they have a son and daughter living. Their home life has been of the pleasantest character. They are both active members of the Baptist Church. Mr. Dulin spent nine consecutive years as Moderator of the Elk Valley Baptist Association. He has frequently served as a special Judge of the Circuit Court, and always rendered satisfactory service. His entire life has been that of an exemplary citizen and Christian gentleman.

## Hon. Leonidas Hammon Kelly, LL.B.

Mr. Kelly is the son of John McHamilton and Alzira Hammon Kelly, who was born at Sutton, Braxton County, West Virginia, January 28, 1871. He received his education in the public schools of his native county and at Washington and Lee University, Lexington, Virginia, from which well-known institution he graduated in the class of 1893, receiving the degree of Bachelor of Laws, and in June of that year was enrolled as an attorney-at-law in the Circuit Court of his native county. Later he was admitted to the Bars of the Federal Courts of the State and in the Supreme Court of Appeals of West Virginia, where he has often appeared in important cases. The dear, old county of Braxton seems to be good enough for him as he has spent his life thus far within its limits, notwithstanding the fact, perhaps, that broader and more lucrative fields would have opened to one of his varied gifts and graces, had he sought a change of habitat.

He is a Democrat in politics, and has served as Mayor of Sutton, the seat of justice of Braxton County, and it is said of him that he saw to it that the laws were enforced to the letter. His next office was a four years' term as Prosecuting Attorney of his native county. He proved himself to be an active prosecutor of all violators of State statutes. He was not only a strong prosecutor, but he was fair and just in all the cases that came to his attention. In 1916 he was made Assistant United States Attorney for the Southern West Virginia District, which office he was filling with credit and honor when in 1917 a vacancy occurred in the District Attorney's office of his district. He was appointed to that highly responsible office, wherein he is now acceptably serving. His growth as a member of the Bar has been steady and of the substantial kind, which comes from merit and legitimate endeavor. He is careful, clear-headed, systematic, vigilant and thorough in his work, and his history as a man and lawyer is a record of manliness complete in every detail. His practice extends into all the branches of the

HON. L. H. KELLY

profession and in his own and the contiguous counties. He is thorough and accurate and has a firm grasp of legal principles, and his integrity is equal to his accuracy.

Mr. Kelly is married and has one son and two daughters. He is a member of the Presbyterian Church and never fails to be found on the moral side of every question that comes before him. He is genial and courteous in all of his acts and has a host of personal friends wherever he is known. The unanimous opinion of his many friends is that he will acquit himself as United States District Attorney with credit to himself and honor to the Government.

## Graham Sale, LL.B.

Our subject is the son of Andrew J. and Elizabeth Goodridge Wilson Sale, who was born in Wythe County, Virginia, May 21, 1881, and was educated in various private schools. Later he entered the Public High School at Lynchburg, Virginia, from which he graduated. Still later he matriculated as a student in the academic department and later in the School of Law at Washington and Lee University at Lexington, Virginia, from which well-known seat of learning he graduated in the class of 1902 as Bachelor of Laws. He was admitted as an attorney at Pikeville, Kentucky, the fall of the same year he left the university, and began the practice of his profession. He, however, saw greater opportunities for a young lawyer in the West Virginia coal fields, so he decided to change his location to Welch, the seat of justice of McDowell County, whither he moved in 1903, and opened a law office in that prosperous town, where he has since resided and is conducting a profitable and rapidly increasing business.

His practice embraces all branches of the law, with a tendency, however, towards specializing in corporation business, and he is now counsel for the Norfolk and Western Railway Company, the Southern Express Company, the Solvay Collieries Company and other coal companies of that section of the State. He is also attorney for several life insurance and trust companies who loan money and deal in mortgages, etc. His practice extends into all State and Federal Courts in McDowell and adjoining counties.

Mr. Sale is well grounded in the fundamental principles of the law, is attentive to his business, and although he is yet a young man, he has developed into a successful trial lawyer, and handles his cases with tact and earnestness. He has gained strength by experience, and being upright and just in carrying on his business, he not only gains clients continuously, but holds those that trust their business to his management. He is careful in counseling his clients, and has established a reputation in this regard. This is greatly to his credit. This would be a safe rule for all young lawyers to adopt when they enter upon the profession. No lawyer should ever advise the beginning of a lawsuit, unless the law has been infracted, and there is reasonable prospect of winning the suit. Some lawyers advise the bringing of lawsuits merely for the prospect of a fee. This is morally wrong, and no lawyer ever succeeds, except temporarily, who thus conducts his business. We are glad to state that Mr. Sale is not that sort of a counselor. His history as a man and attorney is a record of manliness complete in every detail. By these methods he has built up a large and profitable clientage, which is steadily increasing as the years go by.

Mr. Sale is married and has two children. He is a member of the Masonic Fraternity and Pi Kappa Alpha Greek letter "Frat."

## Harry Scherr, LL.B.

Mr. Scherr is the son of the late Hon. Arnold C. Scherr, deceased, who in his day was a man of great influence and power in West Virginia for many years. He was two terms of four years each Auditor of the State, and a few years ago had a strong following that vigorously favored his candidacy for Governor of the Commonwealth. The son was born at Maysville, Grant County, West Virginia, June 6, 1881, and received his education in the High School at Keyser, Mineral County, West Virginia, Alleghany County Academy at Cumberland, Maryland, Braden's School at Highland Falls, New York, and the West Virginia University, from which latter institution he was graduated from the Law Department, receiving a diploma as Bachelor of Laws. After his graduation in 1905 he located at Williamson, Mingo County, was admitted to the Bar in that county, and became the junior member of the law firm of Goodykoontz & Scherr, Mr. Goodykoontz being then as now known as one of the ablest lawyers of the southern part of the State. Mr. Scherr being at that time only a beginner, showed wonderful aptitude as an attorney, and was not long in taking rank as one of the coming lawyers of the State. Although modest and unassuming, yet he possessed self-reliance and self-assertion in sufficient degree to attract the attention not only of the older members of the profession, but the public as well, and throwing into his work the enthusiasm of youth and utilizing those legal principles in which he was thoroughly grounded, he was not long in establishing an enviable rank at the Mingo and surrounding county Bars. He rapidly gained strength by experience. With his modesty and urbanity went no shadow of weakness or lack of decision. He possesses an abundance of courage, and has superior judgment. He is a careful pleader and makes sure of his position before he acts. Although young in years, he is a good lawyer and a safe counselor. He is thoroughly accurate, and his integrity in all respects is on all fours with his accuracy. When one sums up the very promising younger lawyers in the State at large, Mr. Scherr must be taken into the account.

Mr. Scherr is also gifted with business tact in a very large degree. He is a director in the National Bank of Commerce of Williamson, and is also an officer and director in several industrial corporations. He is a member of the American Bar Association, West Virginia Bar Association, the American Academy of Political and Social Science, the American Political Science Association, and the American Historical Association.

In June, 1914, he married Miss Rosa L. Wall, and they have two children. He is a Republican in politics, but has never aspired to any public office. With unusual devotion and untiring vigor he sticks closely to his chosen profession. He resides in the city of Williamson.

## Major John Baker White

One of the well-known, successful members of the Kanawha Bar, who is classed with the younger members of the profession, is the subject of this sketch. He is a native of Romney, Hampshire County, in the beautiful, picturesque part of the South Branch Potomac region of West Virginia. He attended the schools of that locality and received a thorough preliminary English education, which he has supplemented with broadened courses of reading and private study, that make him largely a self-educated man.

Our subject, a son of Captain Christian Streit White, who was a lawyer of ability, and for many years Clerk of the County Court of Hampshire County, comes from a long line of able lawyers and distinguished citizens of Virginia. The father — Captain C. S. White — was a gallant Confederate soldier, having served under Jackson and Early during the entire war and was wounded three times while in action. Our subject's grandfather, John Baker White, was Clerk of both Courts in Hampshire County for over thirty years, and was a lawyer and a soldier in the War of 1812, and his great-grandfather, Judge Robert White, was one of the Judges of the General Court of Virginia, for many years, a leader of the Bar of Winchester, Virginia, and a gallant Revolutionary soldier, having been wounded several times during that war. He was an original member of the Order of the Cincinnati. Our subject now is a member of that Order, having succeeded to the rights of his great-grandfather in the same, and is also a member of the Sons of the Revolution through descent from Major Robert White and Rev. Christian Streit. Judge Robert White was a son of John White, one of the members of the first Bench of Magistrates of Frederick County, Virginia, and a son of Dr. Robert White, who along with his father-in-law, William Haige (Hoge), came to the valley of Virginia about 1734, and were formerly from Paisley, Scotland.

Our subject's mother was Bessie J. Schultze, a Scotch lassie, the daughter of Dr. Robert Schultze, Professor of Foreign Languages in the University of Edinboro, and Margaret Robb of the MacGregor Clan. Dr. Schultze was also, for a while, a member of the British diplomatic service.

Major White entered upon his public service career as Clerk for the Secretary of State in 1886, and remained in that capacity until he became the Private Secretary of Governor William A. MacCorkle, which high position he filled acceptably until the close of the Governor's administration. In the meantime he became interested in the National Guard of the State, in which service he remained for ten years, rising to the rank of Major. When the Spanish-American War came on he volunteered in the service of his country, and was commissioned by Governor Atkinson as Captain of Company B of the First Regiment West Virginia Infantry, United States Volunteers, and served faithfully and efficiently until the close of the war.

From early manhood Major White has taken a lively interest in the political affairs of his county and State. He has served as a Democrat in the City Council of Charleston; he also filled the responsible office as a member of the Board of Affairs of the city of Charleston, for the full term of four years, and on many occasions during that period he acted as Mayor, rendering most valuable and honorable service to the people of the city. His chief aim was to render a service that would advance the interests of the people, without showing favors to any class or classes of the citizens of Charleston. His service in that high office marked him as a man of high honor, firmness and probity.

He began the study of legal textbooks while employed in the Capitol building of the State, and was admitted to the Bar in 1897 when he opened a law office in the city of Charleston. His practice soon extended to all the Courts, both State and Federal, within the limits of West Virginia, which includes a considerable number of cases of State-wide importance.

Major White is one of the kindest-hearted gentlemen the writer has ever known. He never allows an opportunity to pass without extending a helping hand to any one who needs sympathy, friendship and help. Such men are rarely found in this or any other portion of this wide world which we inhabit.

Major White, somehow and for some reason best known to himself, has never married.

When the United States declared war against Germany he again tendered his services to his country, and is now serving in the Judge Advocate's Department at the front, and is a Major in the United States Army.

## Hon. Charles Wesley Good

Our subject, the son of John W. and Elizabeth Good, was born at Raymond City, Putnam County, West Virginia, September 8, 1874, and was educated in the common schools of Putnam and Jackson Counties. He did not have the advantages of a college education, but he was industrious and ambitious and possessed an inquiring mind, which by constant application to books of a proper kind he devoted his energies early and late to a systematic study and reading of such books as broadened his mind and thus enabled him to grasp the kind of knowledge that would be useful to him in a professional career; information absolutely essential to enable him to succeed in his professional undertakings. In this way he acquired correct methods of expression, logical methods of thinking and reasoning, and a terse and vigorous style both in writing and speaking.

To start with Mr. Good has an unusual amount of sound, common sense, and he is also thoroughly upright and honorable in all of his dealings with his clients, the courts and his brother attorneys. He is always open, frank, conscientious and sincere. When a man needs the services of a lawyer he will look for one who can be implicitly trusted and who will advise him honestly. Consequently when an attorney secures a reputation among the people based upon characteristics of this kind he will never want for clients. Mr. Good is this sort of an attorney; and being an untiring worker, one who prepares his cases carefully and tries them thoughtfully and honestly, has gathered about him a profitable and steadily increasing clientele, which no competition can take away from him.

Mr. Good is a warm-hearted, affectionate man; a faithful friend and a generous opponent, and is always friendly disposed. He is not impulsive, and when once settled in his convictions he is decidedly frank and fearless in their expression. He is easily approached and combines courtesy and affability with dignity and firmness. His efforts in the argument of a case are more remarkable for practical, common sense than for brilliancy of oratory or the flowers of rhetoric; his mind strictly practical in its scope and bearings is eminently utilitarian. Energy of character, firmness of purpose and an unswerving integrity are his chief characteristics. These characteristics, coupled with unswerving vigilance, have given him a solid standing as a member of the Kanawha Bar, to which he was admitted in October, 1901, where he has since successfully practiced.

He is a Republican and was elected a member of the lower branch of the State Legislature from Jackson County in 1901, and in 1908, after becoming a resident of Kanawha County, he was again elected to the same distinguished law-making body, serving honorably and efficiently throughout both terms of two years each.

He is a member of the Methodist Episcopal Church, the Knights of Pythias and National Union; is married, resides in Charleston, but has no children.

## Hon. E. Leslie Long

Mr. Long is a native of Tyler County, West Virginia, and is the son of L. H. and Martha A. Long. He was educated in the public schools of Tyler County, graduated from West Virginia Wesleyan College at Buckhannon in 1898, and from the Law Department of the West Virginia University in the class of 1901. He located at Welch, McDowell County, and was admitted to the Bar of that county in 1902, where he practiced his profession until he was elected State Treasurer of West Virginia, and after retiring from that office he remained at Charleston, the capital of the State, and resumed the practice of the law. His practice is general and extends into all the courts of West Virginia, both State and Federal. His diligence, energy and fidelity to the interests of his clients soon won deserved success and remunerative pecuniary rewards. He is well grounded in the fundamental principles of the law, and is a safe counselor and a conscientious adviser. He does not bring law suits for " revenue only " or for the glory of multiplying cases on a court docket. On the contrary when a party has legitimate ground upon which to build a law suit — when one has been wronged and justice and right have been trampled upon, then, and not before, will he advise a court procedure in order that justice may prevail. It is a sad thought, and is all too true, that many lawyers (not good ones) quite frequently advise the institution of court proceedings when they know that they could not make out a case, simply to increase their fees and to impress the public that their volume of business is large and is growing larger. Such men fail in the end. They are mountebanks and charlatans and the public never fails to find them out. The lawyer who succeeds must be sincere, honorable and trustworthy to win out in the long run. An old Scotch sailor once said: " Messmates, I tell you God Almighty has so arranged things in this world, that after all, it about pays all men to be honest." He was forever right! It can truthfully be said of the subject of this sketch that he is an honest, upright man and a conscientious practitioner of the law.

Mr. Long in his political convictions has always been a Republican. He, however, has only held two political offices. One of these was Postmaster of the City of Welch, which he held for a short time, and the other was Treasurer of the State of West Virginia, to which he was elected by the people, first in 1908 and again in 1912, making eight years of continuous service. In both of these public places he rendered faithful and efficient service.

He is a member of the Methodist Episcopal Church, the Masonic Fraternity and the Phi Kappa Psi Greek letter " frat." He has never married. " What do you think about that? " for one close on to forty?

## Herman Guy Kump, LL.B.

The Kump family is a well-known and somewhat historic name in the section of country bordering on the Valley of Virginia. Herman Guy is a son of Benjamin F. and Frances M. (Rudolph) Kump, who was born at Capon Springs, Hampshire County, West Virginia, October 31, 1879. He received his primary education in the public schools of his native county. Later he entered the University of Virginia, graduating in 1903; and in 1905 he was graduated from the Law Department of that historic institution with the degree of Bachelor of Laws. In October of that year he was admitted as a member of the Randolph County Bar at Elkins, where he has since continuously resided and practiced, and is a member of the West Virginia and American Bar Associations, and a regular attendant at their annual meetings. Being thoroughly educated in the fundamental principles of the law he was not long in reaching an enviable rank at the Elkins Bar, gaining admission to all the West Virginia Courts, both State and Federal, including the Supreme Court of the United States.

He is a member of the Democratic party, and is both politically and socially a very popular man. He was elected Prosecuting Attorney of Randolph County in 1908, and served so efficiently and with such general satisfaction that he was re-elected in 1912 for a second term, with an increased majority. In this important and exacting office he made a most enviable record. He is not only a safe, sound and successful lawyer, but he is honorable and upright in all of his dealings and acts, and stands four-square before the people, both as a citizen and an attorney. Governor Cornwell named him, along with Senator F. O. Blue, as Special Counsel for the State in the gas matters now pending before the Public Service Commission. He presided over the Congressional Convention at Keyser in April, 1916, which nominated a candidate to fill the vacancy caused by the death of Hon. W. G. Brown.

He married Miss Edna Scott, daughter of Hon. Cyrus H. Scott, a prominent attorney of Beverly, West Virginia, October 9, 1907. Five children resulted from this union. Mr. Kump is a member of the Evangelical Lutheran Church, the Odd Fellows, the Elks, the Sons of Confederate Veterans, and the Phi Delta Theta Greek letter society. He is an active, enterprising citizen, as well as a successful lawyer, and commands the respect of all the people who know him.

## Biagio Merendino, Ph.D., LL.B.

The subject of this brief sketch is a native of Italy, a son of Vincenzo and Francesca, and was born in Sicily (Corleon), May 5, 1876. He was educated at Seminoru Mt. Reale, Cumberland University, receiving the degrees of Doctor of Philosophy and Bachelor of Laws. He came to the United States as attorney for the Italian Consulate for West Virginia several years ago and located at Clarksburg. His duties are to look after the interests of Italian subjects who are either temporarily or permanently located in West Virginia, which he has done with great care and in a most satisfactory manner not only to his own Government, but to our West Virginia people as well. He is a man of great learning generally and is also an erudite lawyer. He was admitted as a member of the West Virginia Bar at Clarksburg in September, 1913, and his practice has extended into all of the State and Federal Courts, including the Supreme Court of the United States. He is a fluent and forceful public speaker, and argues his cases in an attractive and satisfactory manner. He, therefore, is regarded as an attor-

HON. BIAGIO MERENDINO

ney of high standing of the Clarksburg Bar, which has for many years been ranked among the ablest Bars in the State. He is also Vice-Consul for Spain in the State of West Virginia.

Dr. Merendino is a man of wide literary attainments. He has delivered a large number of literary addresses, and has written many magazine articles on a variety of subjects in this and his native country. He is a noted linguist and a stump speaker of renown. In politics he is a Republican, and is earnest and energetic in promulgating the principles of that organization. He holds membership in the Benevolent and Protective Order of Elks, and also belongs to the Independent Order of Odd Fellows. He is a man of high grade personal character and marked personal appearance, as his portrait on the accompanying page clearly shows. He is of good stature, his features are strong, and his whole aspect indicates a man of refinement, ability and force. He is a most genial companion and has a large circle of admiring friends. It is only just for us to say that his learning is varied and extensive. He married Miss Cora Binona, an accomplished musician, vocalist and linguist, and four children are the result of this union.

As a lawyer Mr. Merendino has been very active in the trial of cases, especially on the criminal side of the court. Since he began practicing in West Virginia he has been counsel in fifty-eight felony cases, in which he showed himself to be an able trial lawyer. He is now in partnership with Mr. H. Frank Stout, under the firm name of Stout & Merendino, at Clarksburg, where he is known and admired by a large circle of personal friends.

## Hon. Charles Edgar Carrigan, A.B.

Our subject, son of John and Amanda Ellen Carrigan, was born in the town of Sherrard, Marshall County, West Virginia, April 9, 1871. He received a preliminary education in the common schools of his native county, and later attended the West Virginia University, from which he graduated with degree of Bachelor of Arts in 1895. He taught in the public schools for a short time; read law, and was admitted to practice as a member of the Marshall County Bar, at the City of Moundsville, in 1902, where he has since practiced and has built up a profitable clientele. He has since been admitted as a member of all State and Federal Courts of West Virginia.

Mr. Carrigan is a man of striking and prepossessing appearance, tall, graceful, erect, with classical mould of features. He was, therefore, not long in finding his way into public life. He is a man of solid rather than of shining qualities, and his life is redolent of purity, and excels in a proper conception of duty. There is a delicacy of sentiment which characterizes his conduct, and an affableness and quietness of demeanor, an utter absence of display or harshness; a suavity and gentleness that no

HON. CHARLES E. CARRIGAN

action of his would even offend the humblest citizen, and withal his dominant characteristic is that of integrity.

He was elected a member of the State Senate from the Second Senatorial District of West Virginia, and served four years, with credit and ability, from 1903 to 1907; was Prosecuting Attorney of Marshall County for four years, from 1909 to 1913; in 1916 he was the nominee of his party for Presidential Elector from the First District and was elected; and was the nominee of the Republican party in 1910, and was defeated. Since that time, his undivided energies have been devoted to his profession, in which he has been very successful.

Mr. Carrigan married Miss Harriett Rebeca Davis, August 22, 1907, one child being the result of such union, a son — John Edgar — who is now nine years of age.

Mr. Carrigan maintains a high rank in the Masonic Fraternity, having filled its highest office, that of Grand Master of the State during 1916–'17. He is also a member of the Odd Fellows and Elks Fraternities, and the Phi Kappa Psi Greek letter "frat." He is a Presbyterian in his religious affiliations.

## Hon. Frank Cruise Haymond, A.B., LL.B.

Our subject is the third in line of noted lawyers in one Marion County family. His grandfather was an eminent Judge of the Supreme Court of Appeals of West Virginia. His father at this time is serving as a Circuit Court Judge in the State, and Frank C. is one of the rapidly growing lawyers of the same county of which all three of them are natives. The youngest of the trio was born at Fairmont, the county seat of Marion County, April 13, 1887. His early training was in the public schools of the City of Fairmont; he then graduated from the State Normal School in that city; next he entered Harvard University, Massachusetts, from which he graduated A.B. in the class of 1910; he then entered the Law Department of the same University and graduated in 1912. He returned to Fairmont, West Virginia, and was made a member of that Bar, December 6 of that year. Being thoroughly educated in the technique of all branches of the profession, he was not long in gathering about him a profitable clientele. He was thereafter admitted to practice in all the State and Federal Courts of West Virginia, also the United States Circuit Court of Appeals for the Fourth Judicial Circuit at Richmond, Virginia. Shortly after he began to practice he was appointed a Commissioner in Chancery of the Intermediate Court of Marion County, which position he creditably filled and still holds.

In politics he followed the footsteps of his father and grandfather and became a Democrat. In 1916 he was elected a member of the West Virginia Legislature from Marion County and proved to be an active and efficient legislator. He, however, kept up his law practice during the two years he was a member of the Legislature. In 1918 he answered the call of his country by volunteering as a soldier in the war between Germany and the allied nations that stand for liberty, civilization and progress. He is an upright young man, thoroughly honest in heart and purpose, and has, thus far, acquitted himself honorably in all of his undertakings. If his life be spared, which we sincerely hope it will be, we feel confident he will return to his home and greatly add to the achievements he has already made as a member of the West Virginia Bar.

## George Douglas Moore, LL.B.

The subject of this sketch, Mr. George D. Moore, son of the Hon. Cleon Moore, an eminent Virginia lawyer, of the old school was born at Charles Town, West Virginia, August 15, 1879, and has always resided in the city of his birth. He was liberally educated, having spent six years, from 1891 to 1897, at the Charles Town Male Academy; three years, from 1897 to 1900, as a student at Hampden-Sidney College, one of the oldest and best known educational institutions of the State of Virginia, and winding up with a two years' course in law at Washington and Lee University at Lexington, Virginia, graduating in the class of 1903, with the degree of Bachelor of Laws. After graduating he returned to his home at Charles Town. In the summer of that year he was admitted to the Bar, and entered upon a successful career as an attorney-at-law. His practice is general and extends into all of the Courts of West Virginia, both State and Federal, and of the United States Circuit Court of Appeals of the Fourth Judicial Circuit. He began practicing as a member of the firm of Cleon Moore & Son, his father being the senior member of the partnership, which continued until 1914, when the father departed this life, after a career of distinction and usefulness, both as a lawyer and a citizen.

Our subject has always adhered to Democratic principles, but has never been termed, in a strict sense, a politician. He has never held any political position outside of the line of his profession, and has never aspired to an office of any kind, except that of Prosecuting Attorney of his native county. He was elected to this important legal office in the campaign of 1908 and served four years. He discharged his official duties with such great satisfaction to the people of the county that they nominated and elected him for a second term. His public career has been able and exemplary. He is dignified in manner, and withal modest and unassuming. He is solidly grounded in his profession, is upright in character, and reveals pronounced legal ability in important causes. On the whole his record in the profession is worthy of emulation, as he is a broad, thorough, conscientious lawyer and has made a record worthy to be followed.

June 4, 1907, he was united in marriage with Miss Louise H. Blume. They have been honored with one child — Master John A. Moore. He is a member of the Presbyterian Church and is also a Mason and an Odd Fellow, and belongs also to the Chi Phi Greek letter fraternity.

Since the demise of his father he has practiced law alone, and has succeeded in holding a profitable clientele in the town where he was bred and born.

## Hon. J. O. Henson

Mr. Henson, son of John O. and Annie C. Henson, was born at Martinsburg, Berkeley County, West Virginia, September 4, 1887, and was educated in the public schools of his native county. Later he entered the Law Department of the West Virginia University at Morgantown, and was graduated in the class of 1908 and was admitted as a member of the Martinsburg Bar, September 4 of that year, and entered at once upon a successful career as an Attorney-at-Law in the city where he was born. He has reversed the Scriptural rule that "A prophet is not without honor, save in his own country," for "he has made good" among his home people. He has since his maturity been a hard worker, a close student, and is a careful, systematic and thorough toiler. He is not only thorough and thoughtful in the preparation of his cases, but he is a good advocate and a successful trial lawyer as well. In argument he addresses the reason and practical judgment of courts and juries, and invariably acquits himself as a self-poised, sincere, careful and judicious counselor. His practice has extended into all the State and Federal Courts in West Virginia, and embraces all branches of the profession, which he has dignified by exhibiting the highest types of integrity, fidelity, learning and wisdom.

Mr. Henson is a Republican in his political connections. He has, however, been thoroughly devoted to his profession, and consequently has never given much time to the study and practice of politics. He never held but one public office, and that was strictly in the line of his profession, namely: Assistant Attorney-General of West Virginia, in which he served two years and two months, from 1911 to 1913, with great acceptability, showing that he possesses many gifts and graces which give him high rank among his fellow members of the profession. He is a genial companion, and his force of will, self-reliance and courage are more than common. He is also an upright, honorable gentleman, and possesses the confidence and respect of all who know him.

He is a member of the Protestant Episcopal Church. He married Miss Fay D. Miller, November 1, 1913. They have no children.

He made quite a notable record in the trial of the Martial Law cases in West Virginia, during the administration of Governor William E. Glasscock.

HON. J. O. HENSON

## Tusca Morris, LL.B.

The subject of this sketch, son of William F. and Elizabeth C. Morris, was born at Metz, Marion County, West Virginia, October 17, 1873. He attended the neighborhood public schools for several years; graduated from the State Normal School at Fairmont, Marion County, in the class of 1899; also graduated in the Law Department of the West Virginia University in 1903, receiving the diploma of Bachelor of Laws, and was admitted to practice in the Circuit Court of Marion County at Fairmont, where he has since resided and has conducted a successful business. His practice extends over all branches of the law and into the adjoining counties. He was united in marriage with Miss Harriet B. Chesney, September 16, 1903, one child was the result of their marriage. He is a member of the Baptist Church, the Knights of Pythias, the Order of Elks, the American and West Virginia Bar Associations, and the Democratic party.

He has not been an office-seeker, and never held but one political office, that of Prosecuting Attorney of Marion County, to which he was twice elected. His first term was from 1909 to 1912, inclusive, and he was elected in 1913 to a second term, but resigned at the end of the third year to accept a legal position in the service of the Consolidation Coal Company, the largest coal mining corporation in West Virginia, and among the largest in the world, which position he still holds. He made an able and satisfactory Prosecutor, and is rendering valuable and satisfactory service where he is now engaged. He is a sound, safe lawyer and his record is established. Mr. Morris' standing not only as a lawyer is good, but he ranks high as a citizen among the people with whom he associates. His practice was rapidly increasing when he accepted the position on the legal staff of the Consolidation Coal Company.

## William Henry Bishop

Mr. Bishop, son of John and Sarah Roach Bishop, was born in Jackson County, Virginia, December 14, 1860, and received his primary education in the common schools of that county. Later he attended, 1885 and '86, the Peabody Normal College, Nashville, Tennessee, where he received careful training in the higher branches of learning. He was an earnest and faithful student and, at all times, used every opportunity to the best available advantage. In this way, he secured a well rounded English education. He read law at his home, passed a creditable examination, and was admitted to the Bar of Roane County, where he permanently located and has since resided at Spencer, the seat of justice of that county. He, however, has since been admitted to all the courts of the state, both State and Federal, and practices in all the adjacent counties. He possesses a strong intellect and a diction of unusual smoothness, which brought clients to him, which gave him a good rank as an attorney early in his career as a member of the Bar.

WILLIAM H. BISHOP

He has served three terms as Mayor of the City of Spencer; was Prosecuting Attorney of Roane County, four years, from 1904 to 1908 inclusive; was a member of a Municipal Code Commission provided by act of the State Legislature; is the author of a book entitled "Bishop's Cities, Towns and Villages," a book of real merit and of great advantage to the profession, and was a valuable public servant in all of these official trusts. He is well grounded in the law and is an incorruptible man and a patriot of the highest mould. He moves among his associates with universal esteem, and amid the temptations that surrounded him, preserved a reputation untarnished by even a breath of suspicion. He loves labor equally from an instinctive energy and from a sense of duty. His dominant characteristic is his integrity. He has never compromised a principle, always holding that principle is indivisable. To him, therefore, justice is a supreme principle, as it should be with every lawyer.

Mr. Bishop married Miss Gertrude M. Duling, July 7, 1892. They have two daughters — Monad A. and Sara C.— and the entire family are members of the Presbyterian Church. Mr. Bishop has always been a Republican in politics, and is a member of the Masonic Fraternity.

In the primary campaign of 1912 Mr. Bishop was a candidate for nomination for Judge of the Fifth Judicial Circuit, but was defeated by a small majority.

## Charles Nathaniel Kimball

The subject of this sketch, son of Chester Frayer and Sarah Margaret (Boydston) Kimball, was born at Parkville, Missouri, September 20, 1872, and was educated in the public schools of Portsmouth, New Hampshire, and at Wellsboro, Pennsylvania, also at Phillips Andover Academy, Andover, Massachusetts, and at Harvard University, Cambridge, Massachusetts. After leaving Harvard, having early in life decided upon the law as a profession, he entered the law firm of Elliott & Watrous at Wellsboro, Pennsylvania, was admitted to the Bar March 30, 1894, and immediately entered upon the active practice of his profession. Later he became a member of the firm of Elliott & Watrous. In 1902 Mr. Kimball located at Sistersville, West Virginia, and has since made his home in that city. He has been admitted to practice in the Federal Courts and Supreme Court as well, and most of the other courts throughout the State. He is the senior member of the able and well-established law firm of Kimball & Sugden at the City of Sistersville, Tyler County, where they have a large and profitable clientage, which steadily increases as the years roll by. While their practice is of a general character, they nevertheless specialize in corporation laws, in which they carry a large line of cases.

Mr. Kimball has always been a Republican in his political convictions, but has never been a candidate for political preferment. He, however, served one term as Mayor of the City of Sistersville, and was a high grade official. He is not only an active worker in his profession, but he takes a deep interest in the civic growth of his adopted city. He is a director of the oldest National Bank in Tyler County, and is also a director and stockholder of several other large, successful corporations, located within and outside of the State, which proves that he is a developer and is successful in his business undertakings and enterprises.

From boyhood Mr. Kimball has been a noted athlete. He gained prominence as a baseball and football player and also as a sprinter. His fame in this direction was more than local and among his prized possessions are medals and prizes won by him some years ago in athletic events.

In secret and fraternal organizations he occupies a place of prominence. He is a member of the Shrine and is a 32d degree Scottish Rite Mason. He is senior warden of St. Paul's Protestant Episcopal Church and is an active leader in church work.

From the time he was old enough to vote, Mr. Kimball, as we have already stated, has been an ardent follower and supporter of the Republican party. However, he has never but one time held public office, preferring to remain in the background on the political field. He is a firm believer in the " square deal " policy and he lives it every day of his life.

July 3, 1904, at St. Paul's P. E. Church, Boston, Massachusetts, Mr. Kimball and Miss Mary J. McGlinchey were united in marriage. They have three children, viz.: Chester Frayer, Mary Boydston and Walter Sugden Kimball. Their home is on the bank of the majestic Ohio River in the progressive City of Sistersville.

Mr. Kimball has always shown himself to be a man of a generous and joyful disposition. He is a safe and sane lawyer, and is an upright, honorable citizen.

## Judge William Wesley Wertz, LL.B.

Judge Wertz, senior member of the firm of Wertz and Atkinson, attorneys, is a well-known, successful practicing attorney of the city of Charleston. He was born on Elk River, at Pinchton, June 15, 1879, in Kanawha County, and was educated in the public schools of his native county and at Nash's Academy, at Graham's Mines, on Elk River, an academy, at that time, of high grade, which dispensed thorough academic instruction. Mr. Wertz, being unusually industrious, full of energy, and of an inquiring turn of mind, made quite an enviable advancement in his knowledge of the arts and sciences. After leaving the academy he taught school for a short time, and while teaching he read law, and then attended the West Virginia University, graduating from the Law Department with the degree of LL.B. in the class of 1899, and promptly thereafter he was admitted to the Kanawha County Bar and has since maintained an office in the city of Charleston, and has built up an active and successful practice. He is a natural orator and a superior advocate, which make him strong in a courthouse trial.

He is active on the side of the Republicans in politics, and has been elected to several important offices by the people in his native county. He has held the offices of City Recorder of Charleston, City Sergeant, Member of the City Council, Judge of the Charleston Police Court, Delegate to the State Legislature in 1912 and re-elected in 1914; and was unusually active in all of these positions, acquitting himself with credit in all of them. He is classed among the best campaign stump speakers in the southern section of the State; and withal, he never neglects his law office. His practice covers all the branches of the law, and embraces all the courts of West Virginia, both State and Federal. He is regarded as a very successful lawyer, especially in criminal cases, in which branch of the profession he transacts an extensive business.

He is literary in his tastes and is well posted in history and literature generally. A few years ago he published a novel based upon local scenes and local characters, which reveals a brilliant imagination, written in the choicest of English.

Judge Wertz married Miss Almeda K. Kieffer, of Charleston, by whom he has one child. They are active and useful members of the Methodist Episcopal Church.

About seventeen years ago Judge Wertz conceived the idea of having an annual reunion of Elk River people at Rockwood Glen, near Pinchton, ten miles from Charleston, which has developed into a popular and even more than prosperous institution, which lasts the greater part of three days every year, and is attended by more than a thousand of natives yearly. It is an incorporated institution, and has become noted for the addresses and historical papers that are delivered every August. They have erected an amphitheatre that will comfortably seat over a thousand people. It has become one of the Elk Valley fixtures, and Judge Wertz, more than any other one person, was and is its moving spirit, although practically all of the citizens of that section take a deep interest in promoting this annual home coming. The services begin Friday evening, Saturday is always the "big day," while Sunday is devoted exclusively to religious services, good preachers being selected by the program committee. These reunions have done very much toward elevating the standard of the citizenship of the people for many miles around the place of meeting.

## Ulysses Benjamin Atkinson

Mr. Atkinson is a son of the Reverend Benjamin Franklin and Nancy (Young) Atkinson, members of the Atkinson family, who were among the early settlers of Kanawha County, and, indeed, throughout the entire Kanawha Valley region. His great-grandfather, George Atkinson, settled in what was then known as "the Atkinson Bend" of Elk River, four miles from Charleston, who lived there the greater part of his life, and where his remains now repose. John Atkinson, son of George, and the grand-

ULYSSES B. ATKINSON

father of the subject of this sketch, was born in the Atkinson homestead and lived there a large portion of his long and useful life, having departed this life at the ripe, old age of seventy-six. He was a farmer and a miller, and he, and his younger brother James, were each Justices of the Peace for more than a quarter of a century. Benjamin Franklin Atkinson, one of the sons of 'Squire John, is a Baptist minister, who resides at Hunt in Kanawha County, and is the father of our subject, and a first cousin of Judge George Wesley Atkinson, a former Governor of West Virginia, and a retired United States Judge, whose residence is in Charleston.

U. B. Atkinson is also a native of Kanawha County, and was born July 23, 1879, and was educated in the public and private schools of his native county, and in early life began the business of a school teacher, which he followed faithfully for thirteen years and became widely known and esteemed in that profession. He taught in the graded high schools of Coalburg, Crown Hill and East Bank. For two years he was Chairman of the Cabin Creek, Kanawha County, Institute, and was Secretary of the Kanawha County Teachers' Institute for five consecutive years. He had from boyhood decided to become a lawyer, and began early to read legal textbooks with that object in view, which he systematically pursued a large part of the time he was engaged in teaching. He finally abandoned teaching, went to Morgantown, took the Bar examination, as prescribed by our West Virginia statute, and was admitted as a member of the Kanawha County Bar in 1910, and has since practiced in all the State and United States Courts of West Virginia.

In 1908 he was nominated by the Republican party, of which he has always been a member, as a candidate for Justice of the Peace for the city of Charleston, was elected, and served acceptably and satisfactorily for the full term of four years. Courts of this kind, under our State law, are of great influence in a city like Charleston, and are schools for young lawyers that fit them for usefulness and success when they regularly enter the practice of the law. During that four years' term Mr. Atkinson tried hundreds on hundreds of most every kind of cases known to the law, many of them involving intricate legal questions, which enable one to weigh testimony and also trees out one's mind so as to aid him greatly in arriving at just decisions in the cases that come before him. Mr. Atkinson proved to be a just and wise magistrate, and was popular with the suitors and attorneys who transacted business in his court. Since his admission to the Bar he has been a junior member of the law firm of Wertz and Atkinson, who are engaged in general practice in all State and United States Courts within the limits of West Virginia, and have a very satisfactory clientage which is steadily on the increase.

Mr. Atkinson is a member of the Methodist Episcopal Church, and has been a very active one for more than a score of years. He also holds membership in the Orders of Odd Fellows and Knights of Pythias. He married Miss Hannah Ada Flowers, February 17, 1877. They have had five children, one of whom is dead.

## Adrian Collins Nadenbousch

Among the well-known, successful lawyers of the "Eastern Panhandle" counties of West Virginia is the subject of this sketch. He is the son of Moses C. and Margaret A. Nadenbousch, of Berkeley County, West Virginia, and was born at Hedgesville, in that county, April 10, 1865. His early education was received in the public schools of his native county. Later he was a student at Randolph-Macon College, one of the well-known, high grade institutions of higher learning in the "Old Dominion," in 1882, '3 and '4, at Ashland, near Richmond. After leaving college he returned to his home and read law in the office at Martinsburg, of Faulkner and Ingles, one of the strongest law firms in the State, until they pronounced him well grounded in the technique of the law, when he passed a creditable examination before three Judges, and was admitted to the Martinsburg Bar, April 10, 1888, where he has since continuously practiced in all the State and Federal Courts in West Virginia. His practice has been general, embracing all branches of the profession. By industry, integrity and square dealing he has worked well to the front, and has built up a profitable clientele. He gained strength by experience, and with his modesty and urbanity with no shadow of weakness and no lack of decision, but on the contrary, the "*fortiter in re*" was an essential part of his nature, necessary to his own self-respect and commanding the respect of others.

In his political convictions he has always adhered to the Democratic party. He, however, has never been an aspirant for any political office, and has never filled any office, except that of Deputy Clerk of the United States District Court at Martinsburg, to which he was appointed in 1888. In this position, which is directly in the line of his profession, he has discharged the duties of the same in the most satisfactory manner to all parties who have business in that court.

Mr. Nadenbousch and Miss Margaret Wilen were united in marriage November 29, 1892, but they have not been blessed with any children. He is a member of the Methodist Episcopal Church, South, and is also a prominent and high official in all branches of the Order of Freemasons in West Virginia. His home is in the city of Martinsburg in the Valley of Virginia, claimed by many to be "the garden spot of the world." He is a courteous and popular lawyer and citizen and is respected by the people who have the pleasure of his acquaintance.

## Spurgeon F. Mitchell

The subject of this sketch, son of James and Caroline Mitchell, discovered America, so to speak, March 11, 1879, at Rock Camp, Monroe County, West Virginia. He was brought up on a farm and received his education in the public schools, including the high school of his native locality. He took his course in law at the West Virginia University at Morgantown, graduating in 1913. He was promptly admitted as a member of the Bar of Monongalia County, and has since practiced in that and the adjoining county of Preston, with offices at Terra Alta and Kingwood in the latter named county. He has never been a candidate for any public office, but has devoted his entire time and energies to the duties of his profession, in which he has met with much more than ordinary success. Indeed, he was successful from the day he opened an office and hung out his "shingle" as an attorney-at-law. His practice embraces all branches of the law in all the courts of West Virginia, both State and Federal. He is solidly grounded in the technique of the law, is upright in character, and shows marked legal ability in important cases. He is a broad, thorough, conscientious lawyer, and an honorable, enterprising citizen, and devotes much of his time and energy to the development of the county and section in which he resides. He is a hard student, and does not, at any time, neglect the interests of his clients. He tries his cases with ability and meets all the issues squarely, showing manly courage in all of his public and private acts. He maintains offices both at Terra Alta and at Kingwood, the county seat.

He married Miss Myrtle F. Lowe, March 27, 1906, by whom he has two sons, George and Harry. He is a member of the Methodist Episcopal Church, and the Odd Fellows and Knights of Pythias Fraternities. In politics he is a Republican. He has a large number of warm friends among the people with whom he is acquainted.

## Hon. J. A. Viquesney

Mr. Viquesney was born near Belington, Barbour County, West Virginia, April 7, 1869. His father emigrated to the United States from France when a boy, and his mother moved to Barbour County from Page County, Virginia, prior to the Civil War. He obtained his education from the common schools, the Commercial Department of the Methodist Episcopal Seminary at Buckhannon, West Virginia, and the law school of the West Virginia University.

Before he was twenty years old he was teaching in the common schools, and afterwards specialized in the teaching of penmanship. In the year 1893 he entered the employment of the Baltimore and Ohio and the West Virginia Central Railroad Companies, and worked as telegraph operator and assistant passenger and freight agent at Belington, West Virginia, for four years. Since that time he has been engaged in the buying and selling of real estate and the practice of law, becoming the junior member of the law firm of Ware and Viquesney, in the year 1905, with offices at Belington and Philippi.

February 23, 1909, he was appointed by Governor Wm. M. O. Dawson Game and Fish Warden of West Virginia for an unexpired term ending

HON. J. A. VIQUESNEY

July 1, 1909, and was appointed as State Forest, Game and Fish Warden by Governor Wm. E. Glasscock for a term of four years, and reappointed by Governor H. D. Hatfield for a like period.

Always taking an active part as a Republican in politics, he served a number of years as committeeman on both the County and Congressional committees. He was never a candidate for office, except he served four terms as Mayor of the town of Belington.

He is member of Grafton Lodge, B. P. O. E., and K. of P., W. O. W. and Modern Woodmen of America.

In a business capacity he is President of the Citizens' National Bank of Belington, officer and director of several corporations, engaged in horticulture and agriculture; and is President of the Allegheny and Cheat Mountain Clubs, two organizations controlling nearly one hundred thousand acres in Randolph and Pocahontas counties, on which is being demonstrated the possibilities of propagating all kinds of game and fish, and which he expects to develop into the most attractive club proposition in America.

While he has not devoted his entire time to the practice of his profession, he is, nevertheless, well grounded in the principles of the law, and has been very successful as a practitioner, and has built up a profitable clientele, which is rapidly increasing. He possesses a rugged intellect, and handles his cases with vigor and forcefulness. His many natural gifts are a sure guaranty of success in his calling as a lawyer and general practitioner. He is leading counsel in the prosecution of violators of the game and fish laws of the State, which, of itself, is enough to keep one lawyer quite busy.

## Thomas Henry Shelton Curd, A. B., LL. B.

Mr. Curd is a member of the strong firm of Anderson, Strother, Hughes & Curd, of Welch, McDowell County, West Virginia. He was born at Howardsville, Albemarle County, Virginia, December 19, 1882. His father was Joseph Howard Curd and his mother Elizabeth Julia Curd of that historic county.

He prepared for college at the Randolph-Macon Academy, Front Royal, Virginia, where he was a student for three years. Having completed the course at the Academy, he entered the University of Virginia, at Charlottesville, from which institution he was graduated with the degree of Bachelor of Arts in 1905. Continuing his studies at the University, he completed the law course, and received the degree of Bachelor of Laws in 1906 and, thereupon, he located, for the practice of his profession, in Wytheville, Virginia, but later removed to Welch, McDowell County, West Virginia, where he continued to practice his profession and where he has been a member of the leading law firm of Anderson, Strother, Hughes & Curd for the last several years. He has been admitted to all of the courts, both State and Federal, and has a wide and successful experience as a lawyer, particularly in Bankruptcy and Commercial law.

THOMAS H. S. CURD

Since the United States entered the present war, he has been active in war work and is now serving as Chairman for McDowell County of the Four Minute Men.

He was married February 28, 1910, to Miss Grace Harman. They have two children, Howard and Chandler.

Mr. Curd ranks high as a Mason, being a Knight Templar and a member of the order of the Mystic Shrine. He is an active member of the Protestant Episcopal Church.

In politics he is a Democrat and was the candidate of his party for the House of Delegates from McDowell County in 1918, but was defeated. He is a young man of high grade personal character, and of unusually flattering prospects in the profession he has thus far adorned.

## Hon. James Albert Toler

Mr. Toler, son of Henry P. and Darthula Toler, was born in Oceana, Wyoming County, West Virginia, November 28, 1882, and received a preliminary education in the public schools of his native county. Later he received an academic training at the Concord Normal Institute at Athens, West Virginia, and still later he took the law course at the Kentucky University at Lexington, Kentucky. These courses of training afforded him a thorough fitness for the legal profession. He was received as a member of the Wyoming County Bar, July 7, 1907, at Pineville, where he began a successful legal career. From 1910 to 1912, inclusive, he was Assistant Prosecuting Attorney of the county, and proved so efficient and successful that the people elected him, in 1912, Prosecuting Attorney, in which office he served with distinction for the full term of four years, ending December 31, 1916. He is a Republican in his political affiliations, but has sought no office except that of Prosecuting Attorney, which is in the line of his profession.

Mr. Toler is a thoroughly informed lawyer and maintains a leading rank at the Wyoming County Bar. He prepares his cases with care, and in the court room he exhibits confidence and proper self-assertion, although he is agreeable and kindly disposed. His diligence, energy and fidelity to the interests of his clients have enabled him to win deserved success and remunerative pecuniary rewards. His practice extends into all the branches of the profession in all the courts of the State. He is a hard student, and keeps abreast of the decisions and the textbooks, and when interested in a case he considers no labor too great to devote to it. Indeed, it may be truthfully said that application and industry never fail to win success in the law and in every other calling.

Mr. Toler is married, has five children, and resides at Pineville, the county seat of Wyoming, one of the rapidly developing counties of the southern part of the State.

J. A. TOLER

## Donald Orr Blagg

Mr. D. O. Blagg, the son of Benjamin H. and Luemma S. (Crawford) Blagg, was born in Mason County, West Virginia, July 31, 1886, and for several years had some experiences of farm life, which is an invaluable training for every young man. He was a student in the public schools of his native county; spent three summers in normal school training at one of our State Normal Schools; graduated from a business college, where he had a thorough training in the rules of business, and subsequently, in 1908 and 1909, he took the prescribed course in law at the West Virginia University, and was admitted to the practice of his profession on June 11, 1909. Soon thereafter he located in Charleston, where he has since resided, and engaged in the active practice of his profession, including all the State and Federal Courts in Kanawha and Mason counties, in which he has had very much more than ordinary success.

Shortly after locating in Charleston, in 1905, he was employed as Assistant to the Clerk of the Supreme Court of Appeals, in which he remained for seven years familiarizing himself with the rules of practice, drawing orders and decrees, etc., in which he became proficient, and which he has since found to be a training for him in the practice of the profession of incalculable value. While yet somewhat young in years, still in the six years of his practice it has been demonstrated that he is thoroughly posted in the technique of the law and is exact in the preparation of his pleadings. He is an industrious toiler, and is careful in giving his opinions on questions of law and is therefore a safe and sane adviser. He is upright in all of his dealings, and sincere and just in both thought and purpose. He has rapidly gained strength by experience, and has made a record for probity in all of his dealings at the Bar and in the community at large as a man who is upright, loyal, generous and considerate. Hence we hazard nothing in stating that there is before him a broader field of success and usefulness.

Mr. Blagg married Miss Annie Laurie Knopp, and they have been blessed with a daughter (Janet Annie) and a son (Joseph Arthur). He is a useful member of the Methodist Episcopal Church, and both he and his wife are held in high regard by the people of Charleston.

Since May 1, 1919, he has held the office of Solicitor of the City of Charleston.

## Marsh Watkins, LL.B.

Our subject was born at Wheeling, Ohio County, West Virginia, July 14, 1891; is a son of Charles H. Watkins, Jr., and Annie (Sadler) Watkins; was educated in the public schools and High School at Wheeling; was graduated from the West Virginia University with the degree of Bachelor of Laws; was admitted to practice at the Wheeling Bar, at the September term of the Circuit Court of Ohio County, in 1912, and has since practiced in the courts of Ohio County, the Common Pleas Court of Belmont, Ohio,

MARSH WATKINS

the Superior Court of Alleghany County, Pennsylvania, and in the United States District Courts for the Northern District of West Virginia, Western District of Pennsylvania, and Eastern District of Ohio. He has handled a large number of important cases, among which we mention Palace Furniture Company v. Clark, in Ohio County; Hawley's Administratrix v. Wellsburg Electric Company, Brooke County; and the receivership case involving the Ohio Valley General Hospital Association, which was finally settled by agreement of the parties involved.

Mr. Watkins was graduated from the Wheeling High School at the age of sixteen. He immediately entered the three-year law course at the West Virginia University, and had to take a fourth year's work, because in 1911 he could not have begun practice because of his minority. He received the degree of Bachelor of Laws at the age of twenty; commenced to practice law before Justice of the Peace Lee F. Dobbs, Wheeling, at that age.

He was elected Judge of the Police Court of the city of Wheeling at the age of twenty-five and still holds that position. He is a member of the Phi Kappa Sigma Fraternity; Wheeling Lodge No. 28, B. P. O. Elks; Baltimore Lodge No. 6, Knights of Pythias; Wheeling Lodge No. 5, A. F. and A. Masons; is a thirty-second degree Scottish Rite Mason, and is a member of Osiris Temple, A. & A. N. M. Shrine. As a side line he devotes some of his time to music, and has been identified with church choirs for seven years, and writes valuable short stories for magazines and newspapers. He is an attractive writer, as well as a musician of high standing.

He married Miss Ada Young May 7, 1917, and resides in Wheeling, the place of his birth. He is a many-sided young lawyer, and has a bright future ahead of him.

## Hon. B. F. Meighen, B.S.

The subject of this short memoir was born in Greene County, Pennsylvania, not far from the northern West Virginia border. His parents were Thomas H. and Louise (Morris) Meighen, who were intelligent, highly respected citizens of Pennsylvania, who afterwards settled in West Virginia and reared a large family. Thomas, the father, was a member of the "Bloody Seventh" West Virginia Regiment of Volunteers, and served nearly through the entire Civil War, before he was honorably discharged because of physical infirmities.

Benjamin F. was born October 31, 1847, and never ceased his efforts to secure a college education, until he, with persistent determination, won a college diploma from Waynesburg College, September 3, 1873. He attended public schools in the winter seasons, and worked on a farm during the summers in order to acquire the necessary funds to pay college expenses. After a term at the Southwestern Normal College at New California, Pennsylvania, he came to West Virginia, received a certificate of authority, and began to teach school. He revealed an aptitude for that sort of service,

B. F. MEIGHEN

and taught several schools in different localities, until he had laid by a sum of money large enough to pay his way through Waynesburg College (Pennsylvania). Being now able financially to gratify his early ambitions, he matriculated as a student in the Department of Arts and Sciences in the above-named college in the spring of 1868, and remained until September 3, 1873, as previously stated, when he graduated with the degree of Bachelor of Science. This shows the tenacity which dominated Mr. Meighen's entire career. Ordinary mishaps never daunted him in the least. If things miscarried, he went to it again, and kept on until he won out in the end.

After graduation from college in 1873, he entered the office of R. W. Downey, a prominent attorney of Waynesburg, as a law student, and threw into the work his strong, unflinching courage and energies until April 6, 1875, when he was able to pass a very creditable examination, and on that date he was admitted, in due form, as an attorney and counselor-at-law. October 6th of that year he located at Moundsville, where he conducted a profitable law business up to his last illness and death, August 29, 1906.

Mr. Meighen was not only a successful lawyer, he was clean, honorable and upright in all of his dealings. He stood four-square before all men in every public and private act. Men differed from him in politics, and perhaps in other things, but no man can truthfully say that he was not an honorable Christian gentleman. He was an intense Republican, and was an enthusiastic supporter of the principles of his party. He was, however, fair with his opponents, and was reliable in his statements. He never took an underhold on any man. He was a vigorous opponent, both in law cases and in politics, but he invariably did his fighting in the open. He held many positions of leadership in the Republican party, such as County and Congressional Committee Chairman, and for two years he was Chairman of the Republican State Committee. He was a superior organizer, and was rarely defeated in his political undertakings. When he was a friend to a man, he was a friend to the round up. He could be thoroughly trusted in all things, and therein we find the true elements of real manhood, which he carried to his grave.

In 1884 he was elected Prosecuting Attorney of Marshall County, and four years later he was re-elected to the same position. With due respect to all the other able men of Marshall County who have filled that responsible office, the county never had a more efficient and able prosecutor than B. F. Meighen. He was at one time a candidate for State Senator, but was defeated by a small margin.

By hard work and honest dealing he amassed an estate of considerable proportions. He was a good lawyer, a safe counselor and an all-round manly man.

January 3, 1882, Mr. Meighen married Miss Lydia F. Gans, of Moundsville, West Virginia. They had no children, but their home life was ideal. Kindness and gentleness dominated the lives of both of them.

When "Ben" Meighen passed into the "Great Unknown," West Virginia lost one of its best and wisest citizens.

## Hon. David Adam McKee

The subject of this sketch, son of David A. and Jennie McKee, was born in St. Clair County, Illinois, November 2, 1879. He received his primary education in the public schools of his native State, where he was a faithful student for a number of years. Although he did not have the advantages of a college education, he is by no means uneducated. He acquired by zealous application and systematic courses of reading and study of books that were available, knowledge which, added to his high school textbooks, furnished a substantial learning and made him master of a clear and vigorous style of expression, both in writing and in speaking. He is an excellent illustration of the fact that what one makes of himself, and not what he is made by the aid and influence of friends and family, is the most potent and prominent thought that arrests the attention and deepens the convictions of his fellow men. When one makes his own way in acquiring an education and the additional learning and knowledge to apply it, he will have graded a roadway, so to speak, over which he finds it not seriously difficult to travel. The men who make their law books their constant, everyday companions are the ones that make erudite lawyers, and winners in the end. College courses are helpful, very helpful, but they are not all of an education. We have observed that the everyday plodder and digger is the lawyer that wins the most law cases. Indeed, in all the learned professions, it has been plainly demonstrated that work, everyday work, is the *sine qua non* of success in any calling in life. Mr. McKee belongs to this class, and consequently is succeeding admirably.

When Mr. McKee was eleven years of age his parents moved to Missouri, and remained there until 1903, when they came to West Virginia and located in the city of Wheeling, where our subject has since resided. In early life he set his mind on law as a profession, and began to bend his energies in that direction. After locating in Wheeling he began a regular course of law textbook reading, and kept earnestly and zealously at the apparent herculean undertaking for three years, until he was prepared to stand the required examination, which he passed quite satisfactorily in 1906, and was promptly admitted as a member of the Wheeling Bar, where he has since practiced. His law business has had a steady, healthy growth, and he now has a representative, profitable clientage. From the first he established a reputation for candor and fair dealing, which to the present he has maintained with an unfaltering purpose, which has given him a standing in the community as a man of integrity and moral and social worth that are assets to a young lawyer of incalculable value. His practice has extended into all the courts, both State and Federal, throughout West Virginia, and has included a number of cases of more than usual importance, in all which he has shown skill and ability.

He is a Republican in politics. His first political office was Assistant Prosecuting Attorney of Ohio County, wherein he made a good record. He was next appointed to the office of Prosecuting Attorney of the County to fill a vacancy caused by the appointment of that officer to a Circuit Judgeship, and he again made good. Next, in 1916, he was elected Prosecuting Attorney of the county for the term of four years, in which he is now ably serving. In 1910 he was defeated, along with the rest of his party ticket, for a seat in the West Virginia Legislature. His office-holding, therefore, has been exclusively in the line of his profession. He is an active member of the United Presbyterian Church, is an Elk and a Knight of Pythias. He married Miss Katherine Poffenbarger of Mason County in 1910, and has no offspring.

## Hon. James Rogers Moreland, A.B., LL.B.

J. R. Moreland is a son of Joseph Moreland, a lawyer of prominence and ability for more than a generation, who departed this life in 1913. James was born in the city of Morgantown, West Virginia, December 9, 1879. He received his primary education in the Morgantown public schools; later he entered the West Virginia University, and was graduated, in the classical course, with the degree of Bachelor of Arts in 1901. Thereafter he entered the Law Department of the same university, and, after completing the entire legal course, received the diploma of Bachelor of Laws in 1902. The same year of his graduation he was admitted as a member of the Monongalia County Bar, and became a partner of his father, who had a large and profitable clientele, he being one of the leading lawyers of the Morgantown Bar. He remained the junior member of the firm until the death of his father as stated above.

Mr. Moreland, although a Democrat residing in a Republican city and county, has many Republican friends, as shown by his elevation to public office. In 1910, in a ward two to one Republican, he was chosen City Councilman, and in 1914 he was elected to the State Legislature with the distinction of being the first Democrat elected to a county office in Monongalia County since 1872. As a member of the Legislature he took an active part in advancing the interests of the West Virginia University, for which he obtained some $450,000 in appropriations and settled for all time the question of its removal from Morgantown. He married Miss Ethel B. Finnicum of Steubenville, Ohio, in 1904, and they have three fine boys.

In person he is tall, with strongly marked features, and exhibits a uniform habit of devoting himself earnestly and efficiently to the discharge of his professional and other duties. Although possessing enlarged and liberal views, he usually forms his own opinions, and adheres to them. As a lawyer he has many of the gifts of his father, among them he is sagacious and able, and never fails to express himself with plainness and force. He possesses a clear, strong, logical mind, and is liberal, though tenacious, in the maintenance of his opinions. He was never a seeker after office, always preferring to give his undivided energies to the work-a-day duties of his law

HON. JAMES R. MORELAND

office. In this way he has managed to retain the large business of the firm of Moreland and Moreland, and increase it. He is a man of courteous and affable demeanor, but frank in his manners and expressions. In political matters he is prompt, decided and inflexible. Whether he has been on the right or wrong side, it belongs not here to discuss; this much may be safely averred, however,— he has always been on the *same* side.

There is much less of success in life really dependent upon accident, or what is usually denominated *luck*, than is generally imagined. Much more depends upon the objects which a man proposes to himself; what accomplishments or attainments he aims at; what constitutes the circle of his vision and thoughts; what he chooses, not to be educated for, but to educate himself for; whether he looks beyond the present hour to the end and aim of the whole of life; or whether he listens to the appeals of indolence or pleasure, or to the stirring voice of his own soul, urging his ambition on to the higher and nobler objects of life. The man who toils on, day in and day out, and keeps himself "unspotted from the world," is the one who wins out grandly at the finish. Industry and character are the *sine qua non* of real success in any calling.

Mr. Moreland is an active member and worker in the Presbyterian Church at Morgantown, and is also a member of the Odd Fellows organization and Kappa Alpha Greek letter fraternity. He has been for some time past President of the West Virginia Society of the Sons of the American Revolution, and was recently re-elected to that honorable position, which stamps him indelibly as an American patriot.

## Hon. Samuel B. Montgomery

Our subject is the son of Adam and Susan (Digman) Montgomery, of Barbour County, West Virginia, who was born at Arden in that county, May 15, 1876. He attended the public schools of his native county for a number of years, and acquired a good common school education. In 1910 he entered the West Virginia University and took the full courses in law and economics, graduating in the class of 1911. In the meantime he had changed his residence from Barbour to Preston County, and in the autumn of 1911 he was admitted to the Preston County Bar at Kingwood, the seat of justice of that county, and the next year he was admitted to practice in the Supreme Court of Appeals. His home is at Tunnelton, in that county, where he served three terms as Mayor of the town. He was also a Justice of the Peace for a considerable period of time, and later he was appointed Postmaster of Tunnelton, which he held for a short time and resigned. All the while he was working up a law practice, and was doing well; but it was evident he was getting "too many irons in the fire." He, however, had carefully prepared himself for the practice of the law, and was succeeding admirably. He is a natural orator and is an excellent trial lawyer. He has been counsel for a number of labor organizations, and tries his cases ably and satisfactorily. He, therefore, maintains a high rank as a courthouse lawyer. He is always bright and cheerful; is a man of marked personal appearance, as his photograph shows; is of good stature, strong features, and his whole aspect reveals a man of character and force. In all relations, in his family, at the Bar, and in his friendships, he is loyal, true and generous, charitable and considerate. He naturally has a large following of friends.

He served as State Senator of West Virginia from 1905 to 1909, and took a deep interest in the legislation of that period, and was ranked high among the strong men of that body. He was Chief Special Agent of the Department of Commerce and Labor in 1909 and 1910; was Federal State Director United States Public Service Reserve, and is at this time Commissioner of Labor of the State of West Virginia, which office he is filling with great ability and usefulness.

He married Miss Grace K. Orr, of Kingwood, February 29, 1896; two children are the result of their marriage — Newton and Susan. Mr. Montgomery is a member of the Methodist Episcopal Church. He also holds membership in the I. O. O. F. and the Knights of Pythias, of which he is the Grand Keeper of Records and Seal of the Grand Lodge of West Virginia, and he is also a member of the National Geographic Society, American Academy of Political and Social Science, Southern Sociological Congress, etc.

## John H. Meek, LL.B.

Mr. Meek is a native of Kentucky, is the son of Ed and Amy Meek, and was born at Louisa, Boyd County, September 8, 1877. He received his education in the public schools and at Oakview Academy, at Wayne, West Virginia. Later he attended the West Virginia University at Morgantown, and graduated from the Law Department, in the class of 1899, with the degree of Bachelor of Laws. In the fall of that year he was admitted as a member of the Wayne County Bar, where he practiced faithfully for a number of years, when he moved his residence to the city of Huntington, Cabell County, where he has a large and profitable clientele. He has all along been an earnest student and attends strictly to his business, prepares his cases with unusual care, and when he goes before a court he is thoroughly prepared and knows definitely what he has to establish or defend. He is, therefore, clear-headed, systematic, vigilant and thorough in his work. He belongs to that class of attorneys who never fail to succeed. He has dignified the profession by exhibiting in the practice the highest types of integrity, fidelity, learning and wisdom.

He is a Republican in his political affiliations, but was elected Prosecuting Attorney of Wayne County, notwithstanding the fact that the county is strongly Democratic, and served faithfully in that important office for two years, during 1906 and 1907, when he resigned, and located in Huntington. He is a superior trial lawyer, and handles his cases with judgment, discretion and skill. He has never aspired to any office outside of his profession, and devotes his undivided time to legitimate law business.

His practice is of a general character and extends into all the State and Federal Courts of West Virginia. He is tall of stature, urbane in manners, and is popular, unassuming and courteous in his dealings with his brethren of the profession and with the people generally. He is devoted to his profession, and interest in his work never flags until he reaches the bottom of a case that has been intrusted to him. He, therefore, can be properly classed with the safe and sane counselors.

He married Miss Charlie Burgess in 1901, and has three children. Their home is in the charming city of Huntington.

## Thomas Coleman, A.M., LL.B.

Thomas Coleman, son of Thomas B. and Mary A. Coleman, was born at Muses Bottom, Jackson County, West Virginia, and was educated at Marietta College, Marietta, Ohio, graduating A.B. with special honors in Latin and Philosophy. He then took graduate work at Columbia University, New York City, receiving the degree of A.M. He was elected to the chair of Latin and English in Watson Seminary, at Ashley, Pike County, Missouri, where he taught two years. He accepted a position in one of the leading banks of New York City, and later was employed to gather data in the leading cities of this country and Canada relative to the history, methods and administration of the bank clearing-houses of both countries. He promptly gathered a wealth of data on this important subject. As a result of his investigations an exhaustive treatise on clearing-houses was published, which called forth the most flattering notices from the banking, financial and other business publications of of the country. Almost the entire work was written by Mr. Coleman. Having previously decided to become a lawyer, he went to Morgantown and took the law course in West Virginia University, remaining until his graduation in the class of 1900, receiving the degree of LL.B. He located at Parkersburg, and was admitted to the Bar of that city soon after leaving the University, where he has since practiced with gratifying success. He is the senior member of the law firm of Coleman, Light & Adams. Both of his partners, however, are volunteers in the great European War with Germany, leaving the entire business of the firm in the hands of Mr. Coleman, who also has been very active in all phases of war work and service in Wood County.

Mr. Coleman maintains a high rank. He was president of his class in the law school, and was chosen one of the four debaters to represent his class at Commencement in the public debate which was staged as one of the chief features of the Commencement exercises. He is a man of unusual

THOMAS COLEMAN

ability, and great erudition. But few lawyers of his age are as well grounded in the fundamental principles of the law as he, and but few who have enjoyed as thorough a training.

He has a large practice in the State and Federal Courts and in the Supreme Court of Appeals of West Virginia. He has been connected with a number of notable cases, and has had a full measure of success.

In politics, he is a Democrat. He was the nominee of his party for the State Senate in 1914 and was defeated by 429 votes in a district normally Republican, something like 2,000. He is a superior public speaker, which is very helpful in his practice. He, therefore, maintains a high rank as a courthouse trial lawyer. He is a genial gentleman and is popular with his brother attorneys, as well as the people at large. He is a member of the M. E. Church, South, and has always shown a keen and generous interest in all charitable and philanthropic work. In the upbuilding and reformation of the civic life of Parkersburg he has played a very prominent part. He is a member of the Phi Sigma Kappa fraternity and the local, State and American Bar Associations. In December, 1918, he removed to Charleston, where he is now practicing.

## James A. Meredith, A.B., LL.B.

Mr. Meredith, son of Absalom and Catharine (Riley) Meredith, was born at Alma, Tyler County, West Virginia, January 27, 1875, and was educated at the Normal and Classical Academy at Buckhannon, West Virginia, and at the West Virginia University at Morgantown. He completed the course at the Academy in 1895, and was a member of the graduating class of the State University of 1900, receiving the degree of Bachelor of Arts. Later he took the law course at the State University and was awarded the degree of Bachelor of Laws. He was admitted to practice at Middlebourne, Tyler County, the year he left the University. Desiring a wider field in which to use his talents and energy, he moved his residence to the city of Fairmont, in Marion County, where he is now conducting a large and profitable law business. His practice embraces all branches of the law. He is a hard student and works early and late in his profession, and is a safe counselor. He has thoroughly mastered the technique of the law, and ranks high as a trial lawyer. He prepares his cases thoroughly, and tries them in a masterful manner. He is an upright man, and is honest in thought and purpose. He never orders a law suit to be brought unless there has been an actual breach of the law which shows that there is just cause for a verdict. In other words, he is not engaged in the practice for revenue only. He is, therefore, careful and thoughtful in giving advice to persons seeking his opinion. With his modesty and urbanity go no shadow of weakness or lack of decision. On the contrary, he is firm and unchangeable in what he believes to be justice and right and his duty as a counselor to a client. He is solidly grounded in his profession, is upright in character, and shows marked legal ability in important causes in which he is often engaged. On the whole, although he is not yet at his best, he has made a record to be envied. He is particularly strong as a trial lawyer, being full of resources when he finds himself in a close place. His practice extends to all the courts of the State and to the general government also.

Mr. Meredith is a Republican in his political convictions, but has never sought or held an office of any kind. He is a member of the Methodist Episcopal Church, and is a Freemason and an Elk. He is a Phi Sigma Kappa, and is a member of the West Virginia and American Bar Associations.

He was united in marriage with Miss Gillian Jamison November 18, 1902. They have one child.

## Hon. Everett F. Moore, B.S.

Mr. Moore, son of F. T. and Eldora (Redd) Moore, of Marshall County, West Virginia, was born at Beeler Station in that county April 29, 1885; graduated from the High School at Moundsville, West Virginia, in 1903; later he attended the West Virginia University, from which he graduated B.S. in the class of 1905, and attended the Law School of the University of Virginia, at Charlottesville, one year. He was admitted to practice in May, 1906, at Wheeling, West Virginia, where he was a member of the firm of Handlan & Reymann for three years, he then located at Moundsville, the county seat of Marshall County, where he is engaged in active practice in all the branches of the law. He has since been admitted as a practitioner in all the courts of West Virginia, the United States District and Circuit Courts and the Supreme Court of the United States. By diligence and fair dealing with his clients and associates he has reached an enviable rank in his profession.

In his political convictions he has always adhered to the principles of the Republican party, although he has never been offensively partisan. He was elected a member of the West Virginia Legislature and served with unusual activity in the session of 1909 to 1911. He was counted one of its most valuable members. He was elected a second time a member of the Legislature in 1918, was Chairman of the Judiciary Committee, and was floor leader of his party. He was Solicitor of the City of Moundsville three terms of two years each, and served with great efficiency. While in public office, however, he never neglected his legal business, which from the first has steadily increased.

Mr. Moore married Miss Gertrude M. Redd at Denver, Colorado, April 15, 1914. They have no offspring. They are members of the Methodist Episcopal Church, and Mr. Moore is a member of the Order of Elks and also of the West Virginia and American Bar Associations. His residence is in Moundsville, where he has constantly resided since 1908, and is known and respected by all the people of that community.

## Waitman H. Conaway

Mr. Conaway, son of William S. and Mary A. (Arnett) Conaway, was born at Barracksville, Marion County, West Virginia, March 5, 1871, and was educated in the public schools of that section. He learned the trade of a brickmason in which he became proficient, and when he reached his majority he decided to become a lawyer. Indeed, for several years, while working at his trade, he devoted all of his spare time to the study of legal textbooks, in which he had already become quite proficient. He, therefore, through the school of experience and hard knocks made his own way and has reached more than an average standing in the greatest of all the learned professions. By years of diligent self-culture and hard work he has built up a large and profitable clientage, which is steadily increasing and becoming more and more profitable as the years go by. He is a broad, thorough, conscientious lawyer, devoted to his profession, in which he is now taking a leading part.

For many years he was the junior member of the law firm of Arnett & Conaway, of Fairmont, West Virginia, he having been admitted to practice in July, 1895. They represented the Baltimore and Ohio Railroad Company in Marion and Wetzel Counties, and the various branches of the Standard Oil Company throughout West Virginia. He is a superior trial lawyer, and has appeared as counsel in perhaps half of the Circuit Courts of West Virginia, the Supreme Court of Appeals of the State, and the Supreme Court of the United States. For several years he had a large number of important cases in the United States Court of Claims at Washington, D. C., against the United States, known as the Mississippi River Overflow Cases in the Southern States, and also damage suits against the Government for the construction of dams in the Monongahela River. Very few, if any, lawyers of his age, have appeared in as large a number of courts as he.

He was never a candidate for a public office of any sort, and never held an office of any kind. His great grandfather, John Span Conaway, and Rachel Willison, his wife, located on Buffalo Creek, Marion County, Virginia, in 1789, after the Revolutionary War, in which he was a Captain and connected with the Judge Advocate's Department, coming here from Somerset County, Maryland. He is buried on what is believed to be the Old Homestead, a photograph of which may be found in a County History entitled "Marion County in the Making," compiled and edited by the members of the James O. Watson, Jr., High School Class.

His grandfather, William Willison Conaway, lived and died on this farm. His wife (Waitman's grandmother), Rhoda Hendrix Conaway, and Waitman's father, William Sanford Conaway, and mother, Mary Arnett Conaway, are buried in the Barracksville Cemetery. His father was a member of the 6th W. Va. Volunteers in the Union Army. His grandmother being married the second time, was a widow pensioner of a soldier of the war of 1812, whose name was James Everly. Since 1789 his family has never

WAITMAN H. CONAWAY

lived outside of Fairmont Magisterial District, except Alpheus Conaway, a brother of his father, who moved up on Whetstone, near Mannington, in Mannington District, Marion County.

He is very proud of his ancestry, family record and loyalty to his native country. Some one of the family has been in every war since 1776.

He married Miss Mary Willa Cavender, December 26, 1898, and has one son, Harrison, fifteen years of age.

## Judge Thomas H. Cornett, LL.B.

The subject of this brief biography, son of Judge George W. Cornett, is a native of Independence, Virginia, where he was born September 15, 1862. He was educated at Elk Creek Academy, Virginia, Emory and Henry College, Virginia, and graduated from the Law Department of Columbian University (now George Washington University, Washington, D. C.) in the class of 1887, receiving the degree of LL.B.; was admitted to the Bar at Kearney, Nebraska, in September, 1887; remained there until 1893; in the meantime he was elected Probate Judge of Buffalo County; served one term, and was re-elected to the same office for a second term and served the full time. He returned to Independence, Virginia, his birthplace, where he formed a partnership with his father and brother, under the firm name of Cornett & Cornett, where he remained six years. In April, 1899, he located at New Martinsville, the county seat of Wetzel County, West Virginia, where he has since conducted a profitable and successful law business. His business is not confined to any particular branch of the law, but is general in its character, and is in the State and Federal Courts, including the Supreme Court of Appeals of West Virginia, where he has a large line of important cases. He has had a long and varied experience at the Bar and is thoroughly grounded in all branches of the profession, and has reached an enviable rank among his brother attorneys.

He married Miss Mary Louise Culver, of Washington, D. C., and they have two children, a son and daughter.

Judge Cornett is a Republican, is a member of the M. E. Church, also of all the branches of Freemasonry and the State Bar Association. He is a prominent member of the State Legal Advisory Board in the present World War; is Chairman of the Civilian Relief of Wetzel Chapter of the American Red Cross; is a member of the Fuel Committee, and is one of the popular Four Minute War Speakers in that section of the State.

## John Coleman Simpson

Our subject is the son of John Chidister and Ellen B. (Neff) Simpson, nd was born at Moundsville, Marshall County, West Virginia, October 3, 4. He received his education in the Moundsville public schools and several terms in a private school where the higher branches wer taught. He read law systematically under a private instructor (Robert McConnell, Esq.) and was admitted as a member of the Marshall County Bar, November 1, 1885, where he has since practiced with more than ordinary success. When he entered the profession he formed a partnership with Charles A. Showacre, and they practiced together for twenty-five years under the firm name of Simpson & Showacre. Both of them were hard workers and they in due time built up a successful and profitable business. For the past eight years, however, Mr. Simpson has been practicing alone and has all the business he can attend to. He practices in the Circuit Courts, and the Supreme Court of Appeals of the State, and the United States District Court for the Northern District of West Virginia, and in the Circuit Court of Appeals of the United States for the Fourth Judicial Circuit. His practice is of a general character and embraces all branches of the law.

Mr. Simpson is a forceful and graceful speaker and tries his cases well, He is a thorough lawyer and a good man and is devoted to his profession. He is known as responsible and upright, and has the confidence and respect of his brother attorneys and the people who know him. As a lawyer he is classed as a safe and sane counselor, and is thorough and accurate and has a firm grasp of legal principles. He is well and favorably known in his section of the State as a man of integrity and honor.

He married Miss Laura V. Purdy, of Moundsville, April 24, 1895. They have three daughters. He is a member of the Presbyterian Church, the Order of Elks, the Knights of Pythias and the West Virginia and American Bar Associations. Since our country has been involved in war with Germany he has been an active member of the Legal Advisory Board of Marshall County and has rendered valuable service to his State and Country.

Mr. Simpson served four years as Postmaster of the City of Moundsville, from 1893 to 1897, and gave entire satisfaction to the people.

## Col. Richard Randolph McMahon, A.M.

Robert Louis Stevenson aptly wrote, " Not only do our characters and talents lie upon the anvil and receive their temper during generations, but the very plat of our life's story unfolds itself on a scale of centuries, and the biography of a man is only an episode in the epic of the family.'' Our subject's grandfather, Thomas Bentley McMahon, was born in County Clare, Ireland, and came of the family that gave to France her Marshal President. His son, Sion Bentley McMahon, was a Canadian by birth, who came to Fauquier County, Virginia, in 1850, and there married Miss Mary Randolph. Ten children resulted from this marriage, the subject of this sketch being the second, who was born at Alexandria, Virginia, July 30, 1854. He was liberally educated at St. John's Academy, Alexandria, and

Georgetown University, District of Columbia. After completing his collegiate course he spent some time in Europe, and upon his return was associated with his *alma mater* as adjunct professor of Latin and English, but on account of ill-health he was forced to resign after three years of successful service in that capacity. In 1877 he removed to West Virginia, devoting the most of his time to journalism. In 1878 he was appointed by Governor Mathews an honorary Commissioner to represent the State at the Paris Exposition, but declined the appointment. The same Executive appointed him as a Colonel and Aide-de-Camp on his personal staff.

Later he began the study of law and pursued the same with his usual earnestness and vigor until he was qualified for admission to the Bar. In 1881 after passing an excellent examination he was appointed Law Clerk to the First Comptroller of the United States Treasury. He showed special aptness for this semi-judicial work, and four years later he was promoted by President Cleveland to the honorable and responsible position of Deputy Second Comptroller, whose duty it was to adjust and settle all accounts of the Army and Navy and the Indian Establishment. In this high and exalted office Colonel McMahon served most efficiently for four years, and the numerous important decisions he rendered were all imbued with the spirit of fairness and liberality. Distinguished in personal appearance, dignified, graceful and affable in manner, he is, withal, modest and unassuming, with ready sympathies, a keen sense of humor, and a refined and cultured taste in literature. He is solidly grounded in his profession, and shows marked ability in the preparation of his cases. After leaving the Comptroller's office he began practice in Washington, and was not long in securing a profitable clientage. He, however, never relinquished his residence at Harpers Ferry, where he has lived since 1885, spending a part of every week at that historic, picturesque town, where the Potomac River plowed its way through the Blue Ridge chain of mountains — a place of scenic grandeur and beauty.

In November, 1881, Colonel McMahon wedded Miss Emma Stringfellow Young, who several years ago, in the bloom of womanhood, passed on to "the summer land of song." They had no children. Their home-life at "Jefferson Place" was ideal. Colonel McMahon is naturally hopeful and happy. Among his friends he is always social, joyous and happy. He is devoted to his home and loved the evening communion of the family circle. He has ever been an upright citizen, keenly interested in the social welfare and in the betterment of the human mass.

Colonel McMahon was reared a Democrat, but when that party fathered the free and unlimited coinage of silver he joined the Republican party, and has since taken an active interest in its councils. He has never been a candidate for any elective office, but has filled several important appointive positions, such as Delegate to State, Congressional and National Conventions of the Republican party. He served a term as a Regent of the West Virginia University during the administration of Governor Atkinson. His learning and culture were most valuable to that great educational institution. In 1903 he was a Delegate to the American Bar Association. Since 1907 he has been a member of the Board of Directors of Columbia Hospital for Women, a Federal institution in the District of Columbia, serving without compensation. He was President of the Board from 1908 to 1914. He enjoys the respect and esteem of every person who knows him personally.

## Samuel Paris Bell

Mr. Bell is a son of Wm. E. and Rachel Rebecca (Ferrell) Bell, and was born at Grantsville, Calhoun County, West Virginia, July 23, 1870. In the English branches of the public schools he received the training necessary to enable him to become a teacher at the age of sixteen, which occupation he followed industriously for a few years; in the meantime he was storing his mind with additional knowledge by carefully reading and studying the best books that came within his reach. At the age of twenty-one he was elected County Surveyor of Lands of his native county, and later was re-elected to the same office, but he resigned before the second term expired. He then entered the law office of John M. Hamilton, who subsequently was elected a member of the Congress of the United States, and began the systematic reading of the legal textbooks under his direction. He, however, while teaching school, and while he was County Surveyor, had devoted all of his spare time to the study of the fundamental principles of the law. Under Mr. Hamilton's tutelage he remained until he was able to pass the required examination for admission to the Bar. He was duly licensed and was admitted a member of the Calhoun County Bar in 1896. He formed a partnership with A. G. Mathews at Grantsville, which continued until 1910, when Walter Pendleton, of Roane County, was taken into the firm, and offices were established at Spencer, Grantsville and Point Pleasant in Mason County, Mr. Bell taking charge of the Point Pleasant office, where he now resides. The firm is now conducting a profitable business at all three of the county seats named, and is known as an able, popular and aggressive team for the trial of causes in all the different courts.

Mr. Bell has had experience in the newspaper business as editor of the "Calhoun Chronicle," published at Grantsville, the "Mountain State Odd Fellow" and the "Methodist Laymen's Herald," the official organ of the Methodist Episcopal Church, South, of West Virginia. He, however, is not editing these papers at the present time, but is devoting all of his energies to the practice of his profession. His firm practices in all the State and Federal Courts in half a dozen or more counties in the State.

Mr. Bell holds membership in the Masonic, Knights of Pythias and Odd Fellows Orders, and was Grand Master in West Virginia of the latter in 1905 and 1906, and was its representative to the Supreme Grand Lodge in 1907 and 1908. He is also a member of the M. E. Church, South, in active service. He married Miss Ona Belle Stump, July 12, 1893, and is the father of eight children.

In politics Mr. Bell is a Democrat, and was the nominee of his party for Judge of the Circuit Court of the Fifth Circuit in 1912, but was defeated in the general election, along with the rest of his party ticket, although he ran more than 1,000 votes ahead of his ticket, which shows that he has a large popular following among the people who know him and with whom he associates. His private and public life are without a blemish.

## Frank A. O'Brien, LL.B.

The subject of this sketch, son of Honorable Thomas O'Brien, a former Treasurer of the State of West Virginia, now deceased, and in his day a man of State-wide influence and reputation, was born in the City of Wheeling, May 20, 1882; attended Mount St. Mary's College, Emmettsburg, Maryland, from 1896 to 1900, inclusive, taking the complete course of study, and from which institution the degree of LL.B. was afterward conferred upon him, and in 1901 he graduated from the Western University of Pennsylvania. Having decided to become a lawyer he immediately entered the Law Department of the West Virginia University at Morgantown, graduating in the class of 1903. He returned to his home in Wheeling and was admitted as a member of the Ohio County Bar May 20, 1913, where he has since practiced. He and his older brother, J. J. P. O'Brien, became partners, under the firm name of O'Brien & O'Brien, which still exists, and has become one of the well-known law firms in the City of Wheeling. Both of them possessing rugged intellects, being thoroughly trained in the technique of the profession, and both being gifted in the art of public speaking it was not long until they had a large criminal practice, which steadily grew later into a profitable law and chancery business, and is constantly growing as the years go by. It is a fact worthy of note that the senior brother is a strenuous Democrat, while the junior is just as determined and pronounced a Republican in his political convictions; and it is not a made up matter between them, because their father was a Democrat, and an elder deceased brother was a rather rabid Republican.

The Wheeling O'Briens are a noted family for native ability and integrity. They are men of the highest ideals of honor and uprightness. They have always stood forth as men whose personal characters are above reproach; and thus the subject of this sketch stands unchallenged today, which is the prime reason that he has won success in life. He is well grounded in the law, is an earnest student, a never ceasing toiler, and stands four-square before all men. He possesses a vigor and inquisitiveness of mind which cause him to study his cases thoroughly before entering upon trial. He is, therefore, known as a safe and successful trial lawyer.

He is naturally chivalrous and magnanimous in his disposition, and always treats his adversaries with proper consideration and respect. In social life he is a model of courtesy and amiability, and at the same time he is alert and sedulous in the preparation of his cases. He is a safe and sane practitioner and counselor. His practice embraces all branches of the law in all the State and Federal Courts.

Mr. O'Brien married Miss Estelle Schlandecker, June 12, 1909, and they have four children. In politics, as stated above, he is a Republican, and in religious convictions he is a Roman Catholic. He is a member of the Benevolent Order of Elks, the Knights of Columbus, and the Beta Theta Pi Greek letter fraternity and also the Delta Chi law fraternity.

The only political office he ever held was Assistant Prosecuting Attorney of Ohio County, which he ably filled from April, 1915, to December 10, 1916. He has never sought an office of any kind outside the strict line of his profession, his purpose being to devote all his time and energies to distinctive legal work.

## Judge Clarence Rand Burdette, LL.B.

Our subject, son of the late Hon. William T. Burdette. a brilliant lawyer of the Kanawha Bar, who departed this life while comparatively young in years, and Ellen (Rand) Burdette, is a native of Charleston, and was born September 8, 1874. He graduated in 1894 from the Charleston High School, and after deciding upon the law for a profession entered the West Virginia University at Morgantown, and graduated therefrom in the class of 1897, receiving the diploma of Bachelor of Laws. Soon after leaving the University he was admitted to membership of the Kanawha Bar, and has since practiced with considerable success. He has a strong legal mind, is thoroughly versed in legal principles, and possesses many natural gifts which are bringing him to the front. His practice has been mainly in the Circuit Court and the United States District Court for the Southern District of West Virginia. He has also tried several cases in the Supreme Court of Appeals of the State, where he has acquitted himself satisfactorily and successfully. He is one of the most urbane and courteous of men, and the light which illuminates his mind is kindled in his heart and shines with the brightest of lustre. He is also a man of an exceedingly amiable character, and while possessing firmness in his convictions, he is never overbearing or unjust to those who oppose him, but is kind and obliging in his disposition, polite and courteous in his professional ethics and social manners.

He has been Judge of the Police Court of the City of Charleston for nearly two years past, and has shown marked ability in the disposition of the many cases brought before him. He possesses the judicial temperament and an unusually sound judgment. Hence his record in that difficult position has been commended by the people generally. He disposes of cases with rapidity, firmness and fairness. His record in that position has marked him as an official of merit and ability.

He married Mrs. Pearl Bennett by whom he has two children.

In his religious convictions he is a Presbyterian, and in politics a Democrat.

He is also a member of the Loyal Order of Moose.

## James F. Shipman, A.M., LL.B.

Mr. Shipman is the son of Walter and Josephine (Coldren) Shipman, of Sunbury, Pennsylvania. His father and grandfather were prominent lawyers, and from them he inherited a desire, no doubt, to follow in their footsteps. He was born at Sunbury, Pennsylvania, October 29, 1884, and was thoroughly educated for the legal profession. He started in the public schools; was two years (1898 to 1900) in Bucknell Academy at Lewisburg, Pennsylvania; graduated A.B. from Lafayette College in the class of 1905 at Easton, Pennsylvania; graduated LL.B. from the Dickinson College School of Law in the class of 1909, at Carlisle, Pennsylvania. In the meantime he took post graduate studies at Dickinson College, and was awarded in 1909 the degree of A.M., *pro merito*. September 13, 1909, he was admitted to the Northumberland County, Pennsylvania, Bar. He practiced law with his father for about a year in Sunbury, Pennsylvania, when he decided to change his residence and located at Moundsville, West Virginia, and was admitted to the Bar of Marshall County, West Virginia, October 24, 1910, where he has since resided and is engaged in active practice. For a short time after locating at Moundsville he was associated in the practice with Martin Brown and E. F. Moore, but is now engaged in individual practice. His practice embraces all branches of the law in all the State and United States Courts of West Virginia, including the Supreme Court of Appeals, in all of which he has been more than successful. As a lawyer he is thorough and accurate, and has a firm grasp of legal principles. He is optimistic and cheerful, and possesses the knack of making friends and drawing them closely around him. Interest in his work never flags until he gets to the bottom of his cases. He is an energetic, trustworthy young lawyer, and possesses the necessary elements which promise abundant success. But few attorneys possess his knowledge of the technique of the learned profession.

He filled the office of Solicitor of the City of Moundsville for two years, from June, 1911, to May, 1913, and discharged the duties most satisfactorily. In politics he is a Democrat and in religion a Methodist. He is a Freemason and an Elk, and is a member of the Delta Chi Law Fraternity. He is also an active member of the West Virginia Bar Association.

He married Miss Mary E. Maxwell, September 20, 1911, by whom he has one child, a son. By nature he is extremely social and agreeable, and is a gentleman of solid and deserved popularity.

In addition to his other accomplishments, Mr. Shipman is a shorthand reporter of ability, and in that capacity has served all of the Courts of his District and has also reported the proceedings of the West Virginia Bar Association.

## Benjamin H. Blagg

The subject of this sketch is a native of West Virginia; is the son of B. H. and Sarah (Spicer) Blagg, and was born near Crawford, Lewis County, Virginia, February 4, 1860. The main part of his education was received in public schools of that county and the systematic reading and study of standard books on various educational subjects, and also in occasional teaching; of all which he made good use. He took much interest in educational subjects and was a faithful supporter of the free school system of the State. In this work he was quite successful. He located in Mason County many years ago, and in 1898 he was elected County Superintendent of the Public Schools of that county, and acquitted himself in that educational position most creditably to the satisfaction of the public, and particularly those interested in educational work. While engaged in public school work, he decided to become a lawyer, and began to turn his thoughts and energies in that direction. When his four years' term as County Superintendent expired he went to Morgantown and became a student in the Law Department of the West Virginia University, and remained there until he completed the prescribed course of studies. In 1902 he returned to his home in Mason County and was admitted to the Bar of that county, where he has since practiced.

Mr. Blagg is naturally industrious, and is conscientious and generous even to a fault. The people knew him and trusted him implicitly; consequently he was not long in bringing to himself a profitable clientage. His practice is not limited to any particular branch of the profession, but embraces all departments of the law, and has extended to immediate adjacent counties. In recent years he is handling a large number of cases in the Supreme Court of Appeals that go up from Mason County to that court of last resort. He has gained strength by experience, fair dealing, attentiveness to business and upright methods of living, which have made for him an extensive reputation as a safe counselor and a successful practitioner.

He was a Justice of the Peace from 1889 to 1897; that gave him unusual familiarity with the statutes of the State, which, coupled with his large common sense, rendered him specially qualified as a dispenser of real, genuine justice between man and man, which, by the way, should be not only the leading purpose of Justices of the Peace and the Judges of all our courts, but also of the lawyers as well. He was nominated by the Republicans, and was elected by the people, in 1908, to the responsible office of Prosecuting Attorney of Mason County, which he filled with great acceptability to the people for a full four years' term. In this position he performed his duties without fear of, or favor to, any litigant that came before him.

In or outside of his county, Mr. Blagg has always stood four-square before the world as a just and honest man.

Mr. Blagg is married and is the father of seven children, one of whom is a successful practicing lawyer in Charleston, the Capital City of the State, who is favorably mentioned in another part of this volume.

## Leo Loeb, LL.B.

Mr. Loeb, son of Charles and Hattie Loeb, of Charleston, West Virginia, was born in Charleston, Kanawha County, January 4, 1877, and was educated in the public schools of Charleston, graduating in the High School class of 1897. Later he attended the University of Virginia, and still later he graduated in 1902 from the Law Department of the West Virginia University with the degree of LL.B. In the autumn of that year he was admitted to practice in the Circuit Court of Kanawha County. Later on he was received as a practitioner in the Federal Courts of the State and the Supreme Court of Appeals of West Virginia. Before he entered upon his course of study at the University he spent five years in Charleston in newspaper work, mainly for the advantage it would be to him in his profession as a lawyer, which he had previously decided to take for his life work; and no doubt it was time well spent. Journalism is most helpful to "tree out" one's mind, to enable him to think properly, with exactness and precision, in any profession, and more especially the profession of the law.

Mr. Loeb is naturally industrious, and applies himself assiduously to anything he undertakes. As a lawyer, if not in attendance upon a court, he will be found, at any reasonable hour, at his office desk reading a law book or pondering over a case which he is preparing for trial. He is not only industrious, but he is a master of details. He goes after every feature of every case entrusted to him. He takes nothing for granted, but goes to the bottom of the facts and the law. If he has a specialty, we would say it is in the line of commercial practice. He, however, deals in all the branches of the law. He is thoroughly honorable in all transactions, and when he becomes an attorney for anyone in any kind of a case, one can be assured that no feature of it will be neglected. Although he is comparatively a young man, he has made a good record and has built up a profitable business, is living on "Easy Street" and is known as a thoroughly conscientious attorney and counselor.

He is a Democrat in his political convictions, but has never been a seeker after office. The only public office he has thus far held is a member of the City Council of Charleston, of which body he is President. As in his law business, he is always in attendance, and discharges his public duties faithfully and honorably. He can be justly classed as a reliable public servant. He is also an active and influential member of the Charleston Chamber of Commerce, and performs his duties in that body cheerfully, honorably and intelligently. He is courteous and kindly disposed in all his private and public acts.

Fraternally Mr. Loeb is a member of the Order of Elks, and in college he was a Delta Chi. In religious convictions he is a Jew, and in politics a Democrat, as stated above.

He married Miss Dora Bekenstein, of Charleston, and has three children. Their home is on the Southside high ground of the Capital City.

## Isaac Grant Lazzelle, A.M., LL.B.

Our subject is one of the leading attorneys of the Morgantown, West Virginia, Bar. He is the son of James and Eleanor (Courtney) Lazzelle, and was born in Monongalia County, Virginia, May 10, 1862. He received his scholastic training in the public schools of Monongalia County and at the West Virginia University, from which he graduated in the class of 1883, receiving the classical degree of Bachelor of Arts. In 1884 he was graduated from the Law Department, with the degree of Bachelor of Laws. In 1886 the University gave him the degree of Master of Arts, *in cursu*. He was admitted to the Monongalia County Bar at Morgantown in 1885. Before entering upon the regular practice of his profession he was principal of the public schools of Kingwood, Preston County, where he remained one year. He spent two years as principal of the public schools at La Grange, Arkansas. Having equipped himself for the practice of the law, he returned to Morgantown and opened a law office, and with Edgar B. Stewart as a partner, the firm of Lazzelle & Stewart entered the field as attorneys and counselors-at-law. This proved to be a fortunate association as the firm did a large and important business, gaining from the outset the good will and confidence of an influential clientele. It may be briefly stated that Mr. Lazzelle's entire career as a lawyer has been successful in every respect. For many years he has maintained a high rank among the able lawyers who compose the Morgantown Bar.

He is a Republican in politics, and in 1912 was the candidate of his party for membership in the State Senate of West Virginia.

He was Mayor of the city of Morgantown in 1894 and 1895, and in 1896 he was elected Prosecuting Attorney of Monongalia County and served faithfully and well. He proved to be a vigorous prosecutor of law violators, and during his four years' term he acquitted himself with both credit and honor. In addition to a large law practice, he has found time to engage in quite a number of outside business enterprises. He was President of the

Morgantown Bridge & Investment Company, of the Deckars Valley Lumber Company and of the Guardian Investment Company. He is also a director of a bank and a number of other local business institutions. He has shown himself to be one of the leading, progressive, enterprising, public spirited citizens of the rapidly developing city of Morgantown, where practically, thus far, his entire life has been spent.

He is a leading member of the Methodist Episcopal Church and is a Trustee of the local church at Morgantown. He has devoted considerable time to educational matters, and was President of the local School Board when the present handsome High School building was erected. In 1891 he was united in marriage with Miss Nora H. Jackson of Kingwood, West Virginia, by whom he has two children — Donald G., who graduated in the law course of the West Virginia University in 1917, and Eugene Lazzelle, deceased.

## Dabney Carr Terrell Davis, Jr.

Mr. Davis is a native of Virginia, and was born at Charlottesville, Albemarle County, March 7, 1867. He is the son of the Reverend Dabney C. T. Davis, Sr., and Mary B. Davis. He received his education in preparatory schools of his native county and in the University of Virginia, and was admitted to the Greenbrier County Bar at Lewisburg, West Virginia, in 1897, where he practiced his profession until a few years ago when he moved to Charleston and became a member of the well known law firm of Watts, Davis & Davis, who conducted a large and profitable business, covering all the branches of the profession, in all the courts of West Virginia, both State and Federal. He is a man of striking appearance, tall, erect and of rather serious mold, although he is kindly disposed and is very companionable. He is a man of solid rather than of shining qualities, and his life is redolent of uprightness and proper conceptions of duty, and an utter absence of display or harshness. He is dignified, forceful and affable in manner, and withal is modest and unassuming. He is solidly grounded in his profession, and shows marked legal ability in important trials of causes. He is also a man of upright and blameless personal character, and has the confidence and respect of the lawyers with whom he practices, as well as the laymen who know him in business and social relations.

Mr. Davis was twice married — first to Miss Mary Miller Mathews in 1897; second to Mrs. Mary R. Elliott in 1910. He has no children. He is a member of the Protestant Episcopal Church, and is a Democrat in his political convictions. He has never held a public office of any kind because he never had a desire in that direction. He is a lawyer and not a politician.

He is a member of the Phi Delta Theta College Fraternity. His home is in the city of Charleston, where he has many warm friends and social admirers.

## Clarence E. Copen

C. E. Copen, son of William A. and Alice Copen, was born in Wirt County, West Virginia, December 8, 1877, and was educated in the public schools and at the West Virginia University at Morgantown. After leaving the University he became a public school teacher for a few years, in which profession he was a pronounced success. During this period he decided to become a lawyer, and began the systematic reading of legal textbooks, which he kept up until 1904, when he was equipped to pass the rigid examination required by the West Virginia statute, and was, in that year, admitted to practice as a member of the Wirt County Bar, where he carried on a lucrative business in his native and adjoining counties. Being desirous to widen his field of labor, he moved to Huntington in Cabell County, where he became a member of the firm of Doolittle, Copen & Davis, which firm was dissolved by the death of Judge Doolittle. At this time, and for a few years past, he maintains an office at Winfield, Putnam County, where he spends a limited portion of his time each month. His present firm at Huntington is Copen & Darnell.

For the first few years his practice was mainly on the criminal side of the courts, because he was gifted as a public speaker, and, therefore, was a strong and successful advocate, especially before juries; but in later years he has given the most of his time and energies to civil practice, which he finds much more profitable and far more satisfactory. As a side issue he was connected with the publication of a weekly newspaper, which gave him an experience and knowledge that was very helpful to him as a trial lawyer, and added to his influence both as a lawyer and a citizen. He, however, did not allow this, in any way, to interfere with his business as a lawyer, as his practice steadily grew larger as the years passed by.

He was two years (1905 and 1906) Prosecuting Attorney of his native county, and, having had an extensive experience in criminal practice, he made an enviable record as a prosecutor of violators of the penal statutes of the State. This experience proved to be of large value to him in broadening his grasp of the fundamental principles of the law, thus fitting him for a wider field of usefulness in his chosen profession.

Mr. Copen is a Republican in his political convictions, but he has never been an extremist, nor has he ever allowed politics to interfere with his professional business. His one set purpose has been to make good as a lawyer, which he has succeeded in doing.

He is a member of the Baptist Church, and always takes the moral side of all questions that come before the people. He is also an active member of the Knights of Pythias, an institution which stands for good morals and good citizenship. September 24, 1898, he was united in marriage with Miss Rosa M. Mason. As a result of this union they have four children, all boys. Their home is at Huntington, the seat of justice of Cabell County, where they have many friends.

Mr. Copen's practice is of a general character, and extends into all the courts of West Virginia, both State and Federal. He handles his cases well, and is measurably successful. He is agreeable and courteous, and has a large following of friends both in and outside of his profession.

## Charles M. Alderson, B.L., LL.B.

Mr. Alderson is the son of S. I. and Martha J. Alderson, and was born in Greenbrier County, West Virginia, in 1867. The Aldersons were among the very early settlers of the Greenbrier Valley, and were an active factor in building the history of the southern portion of what now comprises the State of West Virginia. He was educated at the Concord Normal School at Athens, Mercer County, West Virginia, and at the University of Nashville, Nashville, Tennessee, from which latter institution he graduated in the class of 1891, with the degree of Bachelor of Letters. Having determined upon the law for a profession, he entered the Law Department of the West Virginia University, and graduated therefrom in the class of 1893, receiving the degree of Bachelor of Laws. In the fall of that year he was admitted to membership in the Greenbrier County Bar. Shortly thereafter he located at Charleston, Kanawha County, opened a law office, and has since practiced.

Mr. Alderson is a man of marked personal appearance; is a little more than six feet in height; is erect as an Indian, his features are strong, and he is genial and companionable. To know him personally is to be his friend and admirer. His personal habits are the very best, and he is industrious and honorable. For many years he served as one of the attorneys of the Chesapeake & Ohio Railway Company in West Virginia, and has handled much of that company's important legal business. He is of a quiet, reserved disposition, and is always found at his post of duty. As a lawyer he is thorough and accurate and has a firm grasp of legal principles, and is an educated, polished gentleman. He is also deeply interested in the development and growth of the community in which he resides, and is properly classed among the public-spirited men of the Great Kanawha Valley. He possesses a vigor, perseverance and an inquisitiveness of mind which permits nothing to pass from under his observation without his thorough comprehension of its character. His nature and disposition is to keep out of the limelight, and settle controversies outside of court forums as far as it is possible honorably and fairly so to do. In this respect he is particularly a safe and sane counselor. He considers his cases carefully and never acts upon impulses and half-baked conclusions. In social life he is generous and kind, courteous and affable in his demeanor to all classes, and consequently has no enemies.

His practice is of a general character and extends into nearly all the southern counties of West Virginia, in both State and Federal Courts.

In 1903 he married Miss Mary E. Comstock, of Charleston, a member of one of the oldest and best known families of the Great Kanawha Valley, by whom he has three children. They are all members of the Presbyterian Church, and maintain a high social standing where they are all well and favorably known and are highly esteemed. Mr. Alderson is also a Freemason of high rank in the city of his adoption. He is a Democrat in his political affiliations, but never allows politics to interfere with his business as a lawyer. He never held an office of any sort, because he never wanted to.

Mr. Alderson is devoted to his home, and loves the communion of the family circle. In this respect he is ideal, and no man of our acquaintance enjoys more fully the personal associations of his legions of friends.

## Hon. Benjamin H. Oxley

Mr. Oxley, youngest of eight children of Jenkins Madison and Elizabeth Miles Oxley, was born in Franklin County, Virginia, June 19, 1853. He and an only sister survive, two brothers having lost their lives in the cause of the South during the Civil War, the others, except one sister, having died young. His ancestors, on his father's side, came from England to Canada, early in the 17th century, afterwards moving to Virginia; his mother's ancestors were, on her father's side, also English, while on her mother's side they were Scotch-Irish, being among the earliest settlers in the Valley of Virginia.

At the age of six he began attending subscription or private schools in his native county, but when old enough to commence working on the farm went to school in winter only, until, at the age of fifteen, he came with his parents to Lincoln County, West Virginia, settling on a farm near Griffithsville, teaching in the public schools in winter and helping to run the farm the rest of the while.

When twenty-one he commenced attending local normal schools during the summer months continuing teaching in winter, and later on began reading law during his spare time, and in 1879 he was granted a license to practice law by the Supreme Court of Appeals, composed of Judges Greene, Haymond, Moore and Johnson. He then located at Hamlin, Lincoln County, attending regularly, for a number of years, the courts of that county as well as those of Boone and Logan. He was frequently, in the absence of Judges of Circuit Courts, chosen by the Bar, in these respective counties, to hold terms of courts. He has been also admitted to practice in both the Supreme Court of the State and in the United States Courts.

Mr. Oxley is the author of a law book, "Instructions to Juries, by West Virginia Courts," containing both the legal principles laid down by the Supreme Court relating to that subject, as well as numerous forms, having the approval of our Appellate Court. The work is considered, by the legal profession, as authority on Instructions.

In politics he has always been a Democrat, yet stands aloof from machine and ring rule. He is a Mason and a member of the Presbyterian Church.

He represented Lincoln County in the House of Delegates in the session of 1885, and was elected to the State Senate from the old Seventh District, composed of seven counties, in 1886, serving during the regular sessions of 1887 and 1889. During the latter year he made Charleston his home, where he still resides. For five years he was a bookkeeper in the State Auditor's office until in 1890, when he was appointed by Governor Fleming to the position of Adjutant-General and *ex officio* State Librarian, his term as such ending in March, 1893. Afterwards, for four years, he was Assistant Clerk of the Supreme Court of Appeals of the State. March 26, 1918, he was, by Governor Cornwell, appointed State Librarian.

May 6, 1889, he was united in marriage with Miss Fannie Burton, of Charleston, West Virginia. They have two living children, one a son, Edward, who, while engaged in Agricultural Extension work in Nevada, enlisted in the United States Navy, and afterwards, having been granted an honorable discharge, has resumed his former duties, being now located in Arizona, and a daughter, Frances, now a student in college.

## David Milton Easley, LL.B.

David M. Easley, son of John W. and Minerva B. Easley, was born at Pearisburg, Giles County, Virginia, March 10, 1875; was educated in the public schools of his native county, and at the Pearisburg Academy of Giles County in the ''Mother State.'' Later he entered the Legal Department of the West Virginia University at Morgantown, from which he graduated in the class of 1900, with the degree of Bachelor of Laws, which under the West Virginia statutes authorized him to practice law, without further examination. He was promptly received as a member of the Mercer County Bar at Princeton in August of that year. Having decided to locate in the city of Bluefield, he lost no time in opening a law office and entering upon the active practice of his chosen profession in that rapidly developing section of the State. Being well grounded in the fundamental principles of the law, and being industrious and attentive to his calling, he was measurably successful from the start; and with the experience which comes to one with active service, he has made good progress, which is steadily on the increase. He is a Democrat in politics, but has shown but little taste for that branch of public service which usually attracts the attention of young lawyers, and has devoted his time and his attention exclusively to the development of his profession, and the broadening and increasing his knowledge of the law, which he resolved, in early life, to make his life study. All good lawyers will say that he started wisely, and if he adheres faithfully to what he has thus far accomplished there can be no doubt as to his attaining the top rungs in the ladder of the great profession in his adopted

D. M. EASLEY

State. Thus far "he has run well," but there are still wider fields for him to conquer. His career has been able and exemplary and is more than gratifying to his many friends. We repeat that thus far, in Scripture language, "he has run well." He is accurate in the preparation of his pleadings, is courteous in his demeanor, fair and just to his clients, upright in his dealings with others, and tries his cases with energy and force. He is what is usually termed a successful trial lawyer. From what we have been able to learn of him, we are safe in classifying him with the able and successful lawyers of his age.

His practice is not confined to any particular branch of the profession, but is general in its character, and embraces all the State and Federal Courts in West Virginia.

Mr. Easley is married and has one child, and as we have already said, he has made his permanent home in the city of Bluefield, where his practice has grown to satisfactory proportions.

## Hon. Ellis Asby Yost

Mr. Yost is a native of Fairview, Marion County, West Virginia, son of R. W. and Elzena J. Yost, born December 12, 1872. Like some of the most illustrious examples of men who have made their influence widely felt in public affairs in State and nation, he was born and grew to manhood on a farm, and the foundation of his education was laid in the public schools of his native county. In those schools he developed a thirst for knowledge, which he, by pluck and perseverance, secured at the Ohio Northern University at Ada and the Ohio Wesleyan University at Delaware. In these well-known colleges he received a thorough, liberal education, which proved of incalculable value to him in his professional and business career. Like many another American young man, with proper ambition, he has made good in life. While engaged in the mercantile business for several years he decided to take law as a profession, and began the study of textbooks, which he kept up for a time, and completed his studies in the Law Department of the West Virginia University, and was admitted to membership of the Monongalia County Bar in 1908, where he has since conducted a successful business.

In early life he developed a liking for politics. His public service in a political way began at the age of 23 with his election as Mayor of the town of Fairview in his home county. Since 1904 he has been a resident of Morgantown and a member of the Monongalia County Bar, and he has twice represented the people of this county in the Legislature of the State. He is a man of high grade moral character, and is always found on the moral side of all questions that arise in politics and law as well. But he is very far from being a "re-former" of the one idea type. The Yost bill is not the only measure of great political and social interest in the shaping

HON. E. A. YOST

of which the subject of this sketch has had a hand during his two terms of legislative service. He worked hard for the enactment of the Public Service Commission Law, the Workmen's Compensation Act, the Hydro-electric Law, a Juvenile Court bill, a State-wide primary law and other measures promised in the platform of the Republican party upon which he was elected.

The Prohibition Law, for which Mr. Yost stood sponsor in the session of 1913, has now met the test of actual enforcement, and it is not too much to say that West Virginia to-day stands at the head of the growing list of States in which prohibition has been made to prohibit. The Yost bill was an attempt to put into definite legislative form the unmistakable mandate of the people of West Virginia, uttered in the election of 1912 by their vote on the adoption of the Prohibition Amendment.

In Charleston, during the legislative session of 1909, and later, in the session of 1913, Mr. Yost took a prominent part in the framing and championing of a number of constructive and progressive measures of the utmost importance, evincing in this work the qualifications that go with a high order of statesmanship. He proved to be alert and resourceful as a parliamentarian on the floor of the House and an indefatigable worker on the bills in which he was interested in their committee state of development.

In his business, professional and domestic life, Mr. Yost's career has been one of unquestioned integrity and fidelity to the highest ideals of good citizenship. He has been successful in business and in his professional work. Being a man of many gifts, he has proved an excellent advocate and a successful practitioner. In all his dealings he has been scrupulously honest, and consequently has a strong following of patrons and close friends.

He is happily married, has one son, and resides at Morgantown, the seat of justice of Monongalia County. His home life is ideal, and among his friends he is always social, joyful and happy. He is a member of the Methodist Episcopal Church.

## Hon. Charles Ritchie

Mr. Ritchie is the son of George W. and Phoebe Ritchie of Pendleton County, West Virginia, where Charles was born at the town of Macksville in said county, February 15, 1883. After attending the schools of his neighborhood, he taught in public schools of Pendleton and Randolph counties for four years, and later taught four years in Piedmont graded and high school in Mineral County, after which he took the academic course of stury required at the Keyser Preparatory School of the West Virginia University, completing the course in 1906; taught school two years, and then became a student in the Law Department of the State University at Morgantown. After completing the course of study required there, he located in the city of Keyser, Mineral County, and in 1912 was admitted to practice in the Circuit Court of that county. From the beginning he

HON. CHARLES RITCHIE

revealed marked and pronounced ability as a successful attorney, and has rapidly advanced in the way of securing a profitable clientage. He is studious and painstaking in the preparation of his cases, and has developed into a good trial lawyer and a safe pleader. He practices in all of the State Courts, as well as the Federal Courts of the State. He is a young man of good habits, of irreproachable personal character, dignified, graceful, affable in manner, and withal modest and unassuming. He has been, since March 4, 1917, one of the Assistant Attorneys-General of the State, and is making an excellent record for efficiency in that high and responsible department of State government.

December 20, 1909, Mr. Ritchie was united in marriage with Miss Eva Marie Tibbets, and as a result of this union they have one child. Their home is in the city of Keyser, but since Mr. Ritchie's appointment as a State official their residence is at the Capital of the State.

Mr. Ritchie is a member of the Independent Order of Odd Fellows and the Knights of Pythias. He also belongs to Kappa Alpha Greek letter college fraternity.

## Hartley Sanders, LL.B.

In the picturesque blue grass county of Greenbrier, West Virginia, the subject of this sketch, a son of the Reverend Wm. Henry and Margaret Hartley Sanders, first saw the light August 24, 1879. He received his rudimentary training in the public schools of his native county. Later, he became a student at Randolph-Macon Academy at Front Royal, Virginia. Still later he entered Randolph-Macon College at Ashland, Virginia, where he completed his academic education. Having decided to become a lawyer, he entered the Law Department of the University of Virginia, at Charlottesville, where he remained until he received his diploma as a Bachelor of Laws. After graduation, in July, 1907, he was admitted as a member of the Charlottesville, Virginia, Bar. Having concluded to locate in West Virginia, he came to Princeton, Mercer County, and in August, 1907, he became a member of the Bar of that county, where he has since practiced, and where he is carrying on a profitable business. His practice is in the Criminal and Circuit Courts of the Eighth Circuit, the Supreme Court of Appeals of West Virginia and the United States District Courts of West Virginia, and also in the Virginia courts near the West Virginia State line.

He was Solicitor of the city of Princeton for the year 1909, and again from July 1, 1915, to June 30, 1917, where he rendered satisfactory service. In June, 1916, he was nominated for the office of Prosecuting Attorney for Mercer County by the Democrats and was defeated at the election in a strong Republican County by about 150 votes in a total vote cast of about 12,000. He has appeared in many important felony cases, both as special counsel for the State in the prosecution and also for the defendants. He appeared as Associate Counsel for the city of Princeton in a celebrated

HARTLEY SANDERS

water rate case before the Public Service Commission; was also special counsel for the County Court in the case of White against the County Court, before the Supreme Court of Appeals of the State, involving the right of the County Court to change the location of public roads to be improved by bond issue after they have been voted on. He was also a special counsel for the State in the Snider murder case taken up before the Supreme Court of Appeals of West Virginia, which was a celebrated case from Mercer County.

Mr. Sanders has a high rank, especially as a criminal lawyer, in the southern part of West Virginia.

He is an active member of the West Virginia Bar Association, and has for several years past been Secretary-Treasurer of the Mercer County local Bar Association. He married Miss Ina Snow Hylton, February 14, 1915. Two children are the result of this marriage. His family are members of the Methodist Episcopal Church, South. His home is at Princeton, the seat of justice of Mercer County, one of the most prosperous cities of the entire State of West Virginia.

## Henry Simms, LL.B.

The subject of this sketch ranks among the prominent younger members of the Huntington Bar. He is a son of the late Henry Clay Simms, who was one of the noted members of the Bar in his day. The son is a native of the city of Huntington, Cabell County, West Virginia, where he was born May 7, 1885; was graduated from Marshall College, Huntington, in the class of 1901. In the autumn of 1901 he matriculated as a student of law in the Law Department of the West Virginia University at Morgantown, and was regularly graduated with the degree of Bachelor of Laws in 1905. After his return to his home at Huntington in October of that year, he was received as a member of the Cabell County Bar, and has since practiced, with satisfactory results, in all the State and Federal Courts of West Virginia. He has not, thus far, attempted to specialize in any particular branch of the law, but has included all the different branches of the profession. It may be, however, that later on he will follow in the footsteps of his distinguished father, and confine his attention exclusively to corporation business, in which his father became quite distinguished, having been for a number of years Chief Counsel of the Chesapeake & Ohio Railway Company for the State of West Virginia.

After thoroughly equipping himself in the technique of the law, the younger Simms settled down to hard work, and has admirably succeeded in building up a successful and profitable business. His father instilled into his mind, during his younger years, the truths that all young lawyers must first establish a character for integrity and probity, and then must work early and late, and deal squarely with the courts and his clients, if he may hope to win out of the legal profession anything more than a hand-to-mouth livelihood; but the lawyer who stands four-square to all the world and sticks to his calling will, sooner or later, reach the top rungs of the ladder upon which all may ascend, because the way is open and free to all practitioners in the great profession of the law. Some one has aptly said: "In all professions there is always room at the top." We are gratified to be able to say that Mr. Simms is working faithfully along the way blazed out for him.

In the campaign of 1913 Mr. Simms, as the nominee of the Democratic party, to which organization he belongs, was elected Prosecuting Attorney of his native county, which office he filled faithfully and efficiently for four years. He was not only a strong prosecutor, but he was eminently just and fair. When one had knowingly violated a statute he was vigorously prosecuted, and was made to suffer for his wrongdoing. This was the gauge of his conduct during the four years he served as attorney for the people of the State; and this rule he never varied from, which was greatly to his credit.

Mr. Simms married Miss Mary Mann, June 19, 1913. One daughter is the result of their union.

He is a member of the Order of Elks and of the Phi Sigma Kappa and the Delta Chi Greek letter "frats."

He is also a communicant in the Protestant Episcopal Church.

## Thaddeus Stevens Clark, B.S.

Mr. Clark is the son of Robert F. and Isabelle L. Clark of Carroll County, Ohio, where he was born December 30, 1867. His rudimentary education was received in the Ohio public schools. Later he entered Scio College, in eastern Ohio, where he took the scientific course, graduating with the degree of Bachelor of Science. Soon after graduating he began to read law, and pursued it faithfully until he was able to pass the required examination; changing his residence to West Virginia, locating at Charleston, and was admitted to the Kanawha County Bar in 1896. He was received as the junior member of the well-known law firm of Chilton, MacCorkle & Chilton, and has been a member of that strong legal aggregation up to the present time, now approximately a quarter of a century. He has practiced in all the courts, from the Kanawha County Criminal Court to the Supreme Court of the United States, and especially the Supreme Court of Appeals of West Virginia. His firm handles a large volume of business in all branches of the law, in all State and Federal Courts, and they specialize in large corporation practice, being general attorneys for no inconsiderable number of wealthy and influential public corporations.

Mr. Clark is thoroughly conversant with all the branches of the law; sticks close to his calling; works early and late; tries his cases well, and is a man of upright and blameless character. He is modest and urbane, is fair to courts and juries and to opposing counsel, and stands well in the community where he has thus far spent the greater portion of his mature life.

Mr. Clark is a Democrat, but has never sought or held an office of any kind. He married Miss Agnes Dooley, August 26, 1905, and has one child — a daugher, Miss Isabel. He is a Methodist, a Mason and an Elk. He is devoted to his home and loves the evening communion of the family circle. He has a warm side for his friends and enjoys associations with them. He, on the whole, is a man of enterprise, reliability and usefulness.

## William Burdette Mathews, M.A., LL.B., LL.M.

William Burdette Mathews, son of C. C. and Esther J. (Scott) Mathews, was born in Marshall County, West Virginia, August 27, 1866, and was educated in the public schools of his native county and at Waynesburg (Pa.) College, from which he graduated with the class of 1886. In 1889 he was given the *pro honore* degree of Master of Arts by his *alma mater*. He served a few years as a clerk in the Census office at Washington, D. C., and while a resident of that city he took the two years' law course of study at Columbian University, now George Washington University, of Washington, and received the *pro merito* degree of Bachelor of Laws. He added another year's study in the same university and was awarded the post-graduate degree of Master of Laws. Shortly after graduation, in 1892, he passed the critical examination of the District Bar and was admitted as a practitioner in the various Federal Courts of Washington. He, however, returned to his home at Moundsville, where he opened a law office, and was making good headway, when he was tendered, in 1897, the responsible position of Chief Clerk in the State Auditor's office at Charleston, which he accepted and filled with credit and ability, until he was made Assistant Attorney-General of the State, a position he was well equipped to fill, and in which he rendered satisfactory service, until he was elected to the responsible semi-legal office of Clerk of the Supreme Court of Appeals of West Virginia, which office he now holds and is filling with great acceptability to attorneys and litigants.

But few lawyers in West Virginia are better equipped in the technique of the law than Mr. Mathews. He possesses a trained mind, is quick and accurate in his movements, and is an untiring worker. No man can surpass him in keeping up with all sorts of details. Being an erudite lawyer, as well as the possessor of splendid clerical qualifications, and being also a Lord Chesterfield in urbanity and courtesy, it is no wonder that he is universally popular with all persons who have business in the highest body of our legal tribunals.

Mr. Mathews has a charming wife and two delightful daughters, who make up a happy household. He is an active and useful member of the Methodist Episcopal Church, and received its highest honors by being twice

HON. WILLIAM B. MATHEWS

elected a delegate to its General Conference, the law-making body of that religious denomination; is a Mason of high rank; a member of the Elks; and in all relations in the community where he resides he is loyal, true, charitable, generous and considerate. He is always at the forefront in every good word and work.

## John Wehrle, LL.B.

Our subject is the son of Ambrose and Mary Wehrle, and was born in Charleston, West Virginia, February 18, 1872. He is one of the junior members of the strong law firm of Brown, Jackson & Knight, of Charleston. His primary education was received in the public schools of his native city, including all the branches of the High School, from which he graduated in 1888. Later he attended the West Virginia University at Morgantown, and graduated from its Law Department in the class of 1907, being awarded the degree of Bachelor of Laws. He, however, was admitted as a member of the Charleston Bar upon the examination of three judges, who certified to his qualifications to practice law, in 1906, one year before he graduated from the State University. He subsequently pursued his law studies at the University until he mastered the entire course, and was admitted to practice in the Supreme Court of Appeals of the State and all the United States Courts within the State of West Virginia. Shortly after his graduation he became a member of the able law firm above stated, and has specialized particularly in the examination of Land Titles and the abstracting of the same, which is an important part of the business of the law firm to which he belongs. He is a zealous, careful worker, a hard student, and is thorough in his work. He goes to the bottom of every case he handles. He is conscientious, accurate and painstaking in all of his undertakings, and is fully trusted by the older members of his firm. When he completes a case it is understood that the work has been thoroughly accomplished. His experience as a trial lawyer has thus far been rather limited; but he is well read in the technique of the law, and doubtless will be heard from in all the different branches of the profession. He is the possessor of much more than an ordinary legal mind, which, coupled with his well-known industrious habits and his integrity of character, there is yet much in store for him as a member of the great profession.

He is a Republican in politics, but never held an office of any kind whatever, because he never had any ambitions in that direction. He prefers the duties and calling of a lawyer, and he sticks close to his law office and his books. In religion he is a Presbyterian, and is an honorable and upright citizen. He married Miss Sara G. Satterfield, of Greenwood, Delaware, February 27, 1901, and has no offspring. He is a member of all the branches of the Masonic Fraternity, including the Nobles of the Mystic Shrine.

JOHN WEHRLE

## John Miller Newton Downes

Mr. Downes is a son of John and Caroline Guest Downes; was born in Carroll County, Ohio, July 3, 1863, and was educated in the National Normal of Ohio and Glasgow Normal Schools, the latter of the State of Kentucky. He was admitted to the Bar of Pulaski County, Kentucky, in 1891, where he practiced for several years; united in marriage with Miss May Smith, of Glasgow, Kentucky, by whom he has had four children; moved his residence to Buckhannon, West Virginia, and became a permanent resident of that thrifty and enterprising city, where, by strict attention to his duties and by square and manly dealings with the people, he has built up and gathered around him a profitable clientele.

He is a Republican in his political affiliations, and ably and satisfactorily filled the office of Mayor of the City of Buckhannon in 1903–04, but has never aspired to any other political office, preferring to devote his entire time and energy to his professional duties. He is a wise and judicious counselor and is an excellent trial lawyer. His force of will, self-reliance and courage are more than common. His integrity is beyond question, and at all times he shows a deep interest in all religious and uplift movements. He is invariably found on the moral side of every important question that comes before the public, and is interested in the civic development of the community wherein he resides.

In his religious convictions he is a Presbyterian, and is a Mason and an Odd Fellow, and also belongs to the West Virginia and American Bar Associations. He is thoroughly devoted to the profession of the law and enjoys associations with his brothers of the Bar.

## H. Frank Stout, A.B., LL.B.

Mr. Stout is a son of Lemuel E. and Eleanor (Harter) Stout, and was born at Bridgeport, Harrison County, West Virginia, May 1, 1867, and received his primary education in the public schools of his native locality. Later he attended the State Normal School at Fairmont and graduated in the class of 1891. He then entered the West Virginia University at Morgantown, graduating in the class of 1897 with the degree of "Bachelor of Arts in Law," which carried with it the degree of Bachelor of Laws. He was admitted as a member of the Harrison County Bar immediately after graduating from the University, and has since practiced uninterruptedly in the City of Clarksburg, where he has built up a profitable business, which is steadily increasing. His practice is not confined to any particular branch of the law, but is general in its character and includes all State and Federal Courts. He has been a Referee in Bankruptcy since 1890 at Clarksburg, and is a specialist in bankruptcy matters. He prepared a book of forms for the use of Referees in Bankruptcy, which is in

H. FRANK STOUT

standard use by referees throughout the country, and has proved to be a book of rare value to the profession. As a referee it has been a rare instance to have his decisions reversed either by the United States District or Circuit Court of Appeals.

As an attorney Mr. Stout has been unusually successful. He is an excellent speaker and tries his cases with force and ease; besides he is careful in the preparation of his cases and argues them thoughtfully and systematically. He is thoroughly equipped in the technique of the law and is soundly educated in all fundamental legal principles. Moreover he is a man of high moral character, and has the confidence and respect of all the people with whom he has dealings, either as a lawyer or citizen. He is also a forward-moving citizen of Harrison County. He takes a vigorous part in every movement for the development of the community in which he resides.

He married Miss Ada V. Alexander, October 25, 1900, and resides in a palatial residence on an interurban car line, a few miles from Clarksburg, where he owns and operates a large farm, purely as a side issue to his law business. He is a member of the M. E. Church, the Masons, the Odd Fellows, the Elks and Knights of Pythias. In college he affiliated with the Kappa Alpha Greek letter fraternity. He is also a member of the Harrison County and West Virginia Bar Associations. For many years he has been active in Young Men's Christian Association and church work generally. In early life he pinned his faith to the Republican party, and has done much successful campaigning in its behalf. Taking him all in all he is one of the thorough-going, valuable citizens of Harrison County.

## Isaac D. Smith, LL.B.

Mr. Smith, son of Isaac D. and Mary L. Smith, is a native of Grant County, West Virginia, where he was born January 11, 1890, and was reared on his father's farm near Petersburg, the seat of justice of that county. After securing the best instruction obtainable, at the age of sixteen he secured authority to teach in the public schools of his native county, which occupation he assiduously followed for two years, with the sole purpose in view of procuring enough money to pay his way through college. In the fall of 1909 he became a student at the Preparatory Branch of the West Virginia University at Keyser, Mineral County, where he remained two years. In 1913 he entered the Law Department of Washington and Lee University, Lexington, Virginia, and graduated in the class of 1915, with the degree of Bachelor of Laws. In the fall of that year he entered Emerson College of Oratory, Boston, Massachusetts, where he took part in the ranks of classes from the Sophomore to the Senior and Post Graduate classes, specializing in all studies that pertained to the art of public speaking, which he has found of great value to him since entering

ISAAC D. SMITH

upon the practice of his profession. He returned to his native State and was admitted to the Grant County Bar in January, 1916, at Petersburg, and entered upon a most promising career as an attorney and counselor-at-law. He is industrious and honorable and is careful in the preparation of his cases; and being a trained public speaker he was not long in pressing his merits upon the minds of the people to an extent that his income has placed him on "Easy Street," and is still growing most encouragingly. His practice has extended into the adjoining counties of Hardy and Pendleton, which embrace the territory of the Upper South Branch Valley of the historic Potomac River, the really pictorial region of West Virginia.

Mr. Smith from early manhood has been an adherent of the Republican party, and was its nominee for the office of Prosecuting Attorney of Grant County in the campaign of 1916, and was elected for a four years' term, beginning January 1, 1917. In that important office he is even more than making good. Being a moral, Christian man he discharges his official duties conscientiously and "without fear or favor." He is a member of the Presbyterian Church and has always allied himself on the side of the moral element of the people of his county. He educated himself by his own efforts, has lived a clean and upright life, is industrious, is kind, generous and cheerful. He tells us he is still unmarried, but "Her glorious fancies come from far, beneath the silver evening star." Hence we conclude that the serious moment is not far off, and is liable any "old day" to break through the shadowy gloom that now hems him in.

Mr. Smith is a member of the Masonic and Odd Fellows fraternities, both of which are moral, patriotic, charitable organizations.

## E. M. Everly, A.B., LL.B., Ph.D.

Mr. Everly, son of Allen and Maria Brewer Everly, was born in Green County, Pennsylvania, in 1864; was educated at Waynesburg (Pennsylvania) College; graduated A.B. from the West Virginia University in 1892; took post-graduate course at same University and received the degree of Doctor of Philosophy in 1896. Afterwards he took the required law course at the West Virginia University and graduated LL.B. in the class of 1903. It is patent, therefore, that he procured a thorough education before he attempted to enter upon his career as a lawyer. He was admitted as a member of the Morgantown, Monongalia County, West Virginia Bar in 1903, and made that his permanent home, where he has since carried on a general practice in all the State and Federal Courts. He was reared on a farm, taught in the public schools and attended college alternately, covering a period of several years as stated above, until he succeeded in obtaining the best possible educational equipment within his reach. Since his admission to the Bar he has devoted all of his time and energies to his profession, and as a natural result he is reaping a just reward for the sacrifices he had to make in building up a remunerative clientage. He is careful, clear-headed, systematic and thorough in his work. He is a hard student and keeps up with court decisions and the latest textbook writers, deals fairly with clients, courts and juries, and has the confidence of the people who have dealings with him.

He devotes much of his thought and efforts to the advancement of the educational interests of the community where he lives, and to this end he spent five years as a member of the School Board of Morgantown Independent District, doing everything in his power to render the City Public Schools more efficient. He is, therefore, completely devoted to every effort which tends to advance and elevate the public school system of the City of Morgantown.

He married Miss Eva M. Keener in 1898. One daughter, Mary, is the result of this union. They are active members of the Baptist Church. In politics Mr. Everly classes himself as an Independent Democrat.

## Clinton Wellrose Flesher

The subject of this sketch is a son of Clayton and Harriett R. Flesher, and was born at Grape Island, West Virginia, September 10, 1870. He was a student in the public schools of the section of his nativity, and later matriculated at the Fairmont Normal School, from which he graduated in the class of 1894. Later he attended the West Virginia University as a student in the Law Department, taking the required course prescribed for an attorney-at-law. He located at Knoxville, Tennessee, and was admitted to the Bar of that State in September, 1901. Shortly thereafter he returned to his native State, located at the then new and growing town of Gassaway, Braxton County, where by ability, energy and close application to business he has succeeded in securing a large and profitable clientage. His practice includes State and Federal Courts, and extends into the adjoining counties of Nicholas and Webster. Mr. Flesher has a clear, strong mind and is an able advocate, and consequently is a successful practitioner.

Before entering upon the practice of his chosen profession he taught in the public schools of West Virginia for ten years; was principal of the public schools in Elkins for three years; helped to organize the Laymen's Association of the West Virginia Annual Conference of the Methodist Episcopal Church at Huntington in 1907, and was elected its first President, and has been its presiding officer ever since; was elected a lay delegate to the General Conference of the Methodist Episcopal Church in 1912 and 1916; is a member of the Board of Sunday Schools of the M. E. General Conference; was appointed Referee in Bankruptcy on September 16, 1916, by Honorable Benjamin F. Keller, United States District Judge for the Southern District of West Virginia, for the Counties of Braxton, Nicholas and Webster. His father was a soldier in the Civil War, and was born and reared in Lewis County. His father's ancestors took part in building the Block House at Weston, Lewis County, to protect the white settlers from the ravages of the Indians several generations in the past.

Mr. Flesher is one of the most active and best known lay members of the Methodist Episcopal Church in West Virginia, and devotes much time towards creating an interest in moral and religious work. He is married and resides in the Town of Gassaway, six miles below Sutton, on the historic Elk River, where he is known by and has the confidence of all the people.

## Michael Joseph Malamphy, Jr.

Mr. Malamphy, son of M. J. Malamphy, Sr., and Elizabeth Cecelia (Stanton) Malamphy, is a native of Cumberland, Maryland, where he first saw the light November 16, 1883, and there grew to manhood. In early life he was entered as a student at St. Patrick's High School at Cumberland, and continued therein until he was graduated from the academy, thus receiving a thorough training in all the branches of liberal arts and the sciences. He then entered the Mountain State Business College, where he received a business training, becoming an expert accountant, stenographer and typewriter. He next matriculated as a student in the Law Department of the West Virginia University and remained therein until he completed the required course. He chose Morgantown, a promising, thrifty city as a permanent residence, was admitted to the Monongalia County Bar, April 26, 1906, and has since practiced with much vigor and success. His business has increased with rapid strides the past five or six years. His practice has extended into all the branches of the profession and into all the State and Federal Courts. He is genial and companionable, is a hard worker, and when interested in a subject he considers no labor too great to devote to it. He is fluent in speech and tries his cases well. He possesses, in a large degree, the knack of attracting people to him and making them his friends.

Before entering upon the active practice, more for the experience than anything else, he served for a considerable time as shorthand reporter for the Circuit Court of Monongalia County, and it was time profitably spent. He also spent a short time as a shorthand clerk for the State Legislature and as Assistant Private Secretary to Governor William E. Glasscock, of West Virginia, all which broadened his experience and materially extended his acquaintance, thus equipping him for a more useful and successful future as a lawyer.

Mr. Malamphy is a Roman Catholic in his religious convictions; in politics he is a Republican; he belongs to no secret societies except the Pi Kappa Alpha Greek letter fraternity. He married Miss Phoebe Ann Turner, daughter of the late Dr. Eli Marsh Turner, former President of the West Virginia University, by whom he has two children — Richard Henry, age 8, and Elizabeth Cecelia, age 4.

## Charles Lee Estep

Mr. Estep is a native of Boone County, West Virginia. He is the son of Lewis and Louisa Estep, and was born April 9, 1884. He attended the public schools of his native county for several years until he obtained a fairly good English education. He then decided to become a teacher in the public schools, and worked earnestly and faithfully with that end in view. After acquiring sufficient knowledge he passed the required examination, received a certificate and entered upon the work of teaching in the common schools when yet a young man. This occupation he pursued vigilantly for six years. In the meantime he began the study of legal textbooks, and became deeply interested; so much so indeed that he gave up teaching, and in 1907 he matriculated as a student in the Law Department of the West Virginia University, where he remained two years, and received a certificate of graduation. In March, 1908, he was admitted to the Boone County Bar, and immediately thereafter entered upon the practice of what has proved to be a successful career as an attorney in his native county.

Being a Democrat in his political convictions he was nominated by that party as its candidate for the office of Prosecuting Attorney of Boone County, was elected and served four years faithfully in that important office from January 1, 1909, to December 31, 1912. It is universally conceded that he discharged his duties ably and efficiently and to the satisfaction of the people of the county. In 1912 he was the nominee of his party as a candidate for the State Senate from the Eighth Senatorial District, composed of the Counties of Boone, Logan and Kanawha, and on account of a fusion of the Republican and Progressive parties in that election he was defeated. Four years later he was urged again to be a candidate for the same office, but being desirous to devote all of his time and energies to his professional duties, he declined to enter the race. In the meantime his practice in all the State and Federal Courts had materially increased so as to occupy the entire time of his mental and physical energies. Like most young lawyers, however, he enjoys the excitement "of the political game"; but he has found out, as all others have done, that in the end sticking closely to the law pays far better. The writer, who, at times, has "played both games" vigorously, and with some degree of success in both, can testify to the correctness of this statement.

Mr. Estep has maintained an upright life; has been square in all of his dealings; has been fair with his clients, the courts and his fellow attorneys; has made an enviable record thus far, and is going on to further conquests in the future.

In 1911 he married Miss Lettie E. Miller and they are the parents of three comforting children. Their home is at Madison, the capital of Boone County, in one of the richest coal fields in this or any other State of the Great Republic.

He is a member of the Baptist Church and the Mason and Odd Fellow Fraternities.

## Angus W. McDonald, LL.B.

Mr. McDonald, one of the junior members of the strong law firm of Brown, Jackson & Knight, was born in Louisville, Kentucky, May 2, 1877; was educated in the public and private schools of his native city and at the West Virginia University. He graduated in the Law Department of the University of Kentucky in 1899, receiving the degree of Bachelor of Laws. He became a member of the Louisville Bar the year of his graduation, and practiced for two years in the courts of Kentucky; removed his residence to Charleston, West Virginia, where he has devoted practically all of his time to the practice of his profession, in which he has been very successful. In politics he is a Democrat, but in no sense is he a politician. The only political office he has ever held was member of the lower house of the State Legislature, to which he was elected by the people of Kanawha County in 1916, and in which office he rendered faithful and satisfactory service. He has been for a number of years President of the Provident Life and Casualty Company, whose home office is in Charleston, and which has done, and is still doing, a large, profitable business, because of its careful management, largely due to Mr. McDonald's business skill and acumen.

Our subject is a wise, safe counselor, and a skillful trial lawyer, and along with his associates has helped to build up a large and very profitable legal business in the southern portion of the State. In fact his law firm is known as one of the strongest and ablest in the entire State as well as one of the most successful. They are not only good lawyers, but they are all honorable, upright gentlemen who are thoroughly trustworthy and reliable.

In 1912 Mr. McDonald was united in marriage with Miss Elizabeth B. Brown, daughter of Hon. James F. Brown, of Charleston, West Virginia, where they still reside.

## C. Beverly Broun

Among the younger members of the legal fraternity of the City of Charleston, and one who has made good at the Bar, is the subject of this sketch. He was born December 9, 1878, and is a son of Roswell B. and Katherine Downing Broun, and is a native of Northumberland County, Virginia. He was educated at the University of Virginia, and shortly after his graduation from that noted institution he was admitted to the Bar of Middlesex County, Virginia, and immediately began to practice in the courts of that section of the "Mother State." In the meantime he served as Mayor of Urbanna, Virginia, for a short term of years. Upon learning of the rapid development of southern West Virginia, and desiring a wider field of opportunity and endeavor, he came to Charleston, opened a law office, and has by diligence, energy and fidelity to the interests of

HON. ANGUS W. McDONALD

his clients won deserved success and remunerative pecuniary rewards. His practice has embraced all branches of the law, and includes all of the courts of Virginia and West Virginia, and also the Supreme Court of the United States, in which he has had more than average success.

Mr. Broun possesses a strong mind and body, and is careful and thoughtful in giving opinions on questions of law; is social and companionable, and enjoys the companionship of his friends. His club life is most enjoyable, not only to himself, but to his friends also. He is a member of the Masonic Fraternity and the Benevolent and Protective Order of Elks. Although of marriageable age, he has never seen fit to take unto himself a life companion of the fairer sex.

## Hon. Wayne K. Pritt

The subject of this sketch was born in Randolph County, West Virginia, January 23, 1872, and is the son of George W. and Lucinda Pritt of said county. His education was obtained in the common schools of his native county and in the Law Department of the West Virginia University at Morgantown, Monongalia County. After graduation, he was admitted to the Bar of Tucker County at Parsons, September 19, 1911, where he has since practiced. He has been admitted as an attorney in the United States District Court in West Virginia and the Supreme Court of Appeals of the State. Before entering upon the practice he was elected Clerk of the Circuit Court of Tucker County in 1896 and served acceptably the full term of six years, and was re-elected in 1902 for a second term. This experience has been most valuable to him as an attorney, because he became thoroughly familiar with the rules of practice, the forms of pleadings, drawing orders and decrees, etc., etc. He was elected Prosecuting Attorney of Tucker County in 1912 and served four years. He proved a strong prosecutor, and enforced the law with vigor and fairness, and to the entire satisfaction of the people. From the first he showed remarkable tact in the trial of causes; is a strong advocate, and has the confidence of Judge and juries; prepares his cases with care and thoroughness; has confidence in the correctness of the positions he takes, and asserts himself with fervor and earnestness, but always with proper respect towards his opponents. He is upright and just, courteous and considerate in all of his dealings, and commands the respect and confidence of the people who know him.

He is a member of the Methodist Protestant Church, the Orders of Odd Fellows and Elks, and of the Beta Theta Pi Fraternity. He is an enthusiastic Republican, and takes a live interest in politics, but devotes practically all of his time and energy to the practice of his profession.

He has never married.

## Hon. James D. Morris

One of the old time, erudite, critical lawyers of the northern portion of this State is the subject of this sketch. He was born in Culpeper County, Virginia, January 26, 1806, and died at Moundsville, West Virginia, November 17, 1902, at the age of ninety-seven years. He grew to manhood in his native county, attending all the schools within his reach, and receiving the best education the schools of that section could impart. In the fall of 1826 he moved to Winchester, Virginia, and taught school for a year and a half. January 10, 1828, he moved to Clarksburg, in western Virginia, where he taught school for two years. While there he married Miss Mary A. Israel, sister of Capt. Jacob E. Israel, by whom two daughters were born. One of Mr. Morris' daughters married Alfred Tomlinson of Moundsville. He located in Moundsville in 1829 and taught school for a short period, during which time he became a student of the law and was admitted to the Bar and began to practice and was prospering. Marshall County was formed in 1835, and he was appointed Clerk of the Circuit Court by Judge Joseph L. Fry. All of the first records of the county appear in his very legible handwriting. The deed books and other writings having been written with a goose quill and remain as a sample of neatness and clearness rarely found in more recent records. He served as Clerk until 1859, at which time he resigned to accept a seat in the Legislature of Virginia at Richmond. He served during the regular term and was called to serve in the special session convened by Governor John Letcher, who called a special session of the Assembly, and it was during this extra session that some of the most turbulent and exciting times in the history of the State transpired. It was during this session that the convention assembled and passed the Ordinance of Secession.

His legal training was so thorough that he was of great value to the lawyers and the Judges; he was trusted by all of them to prepare the orders and decrees of the court in practically all the cases. The Judges frequently stated from the Bench, "If Mr. Morris drew the decrees, it was not necessary for them to read them," and they rarely did it, thus testifying to his integrity and ability. After retiring as Clerk he never returned to active practice.

Mr. Morris was a member of the M. E. Church until the beginning of the Civil War, when differences arose over sectional matters, which caused him to withdraw and become a member of the Episcopal Church. He was, however, active and useful in both Churches. His character was above reproach, and the people generally sought his counsel and advice on questions of law up to the time of his last illness. He was, in his political opinions and affiliations, always a Democrat. Although he was nearly a centenarian, his death was universally mourned by the people of Marshall County, where he spent the larger part of his long and useful life.

## Arthur Jay Valentine

Mr. Valentine is a son of Andrew and Rachel Valentine. He was born in Barbour County, West Virginia, March 8, 1866, and was educated in public schools, summer State normal schools and in private law offices. After having carefully studied all the required legal textbooks, he was examined by three Circuit Judges, who licensed him to become a practitioner, and he was admitted to the Beverly, Randolph County, Bar in 1887. He subsequently located at Parsons, the county seat of Tucker County, where he is engaged in active practice and has a large and profitable clientele. He is a Republican in politics, but has never sought an office of any kind, and devotes all of his time and energies to his legal business. Whilst he is well informed in all branches of the law, he specializes largely in corporation law, and as a result he represents practically all the corporate interests of his county, which, alone, keep him continuously employed. His practice, therefore, has been successful and profitable, and has extended into all the courts of West Virginia, both State and Federal.

He was united in marriage with Miss Lummie Kalar, December 2, 1891; they are the parents of six children, four of whom are living, and two have departed this life. Their daughter, Zillah, is a graduate of the Ithaca, New York, Conservatory of Music, and their sons Arthur J., Jr., and Mark Valentine, are students in the West Virginia University, preparing themselves for the practice of law. Their son Paul, who is nine years of age, is a student in the public schools of Parsons, where the family resides.

Mr. Valentine is a member of the Masonic and Odd Fellows Fraternities.

## Hon. William Sidney Wysong, LL.B.

Among the strong and successful attorneys of the central counties of West Virginia, the subject of this sketch must be recorded. He is a native of Hamlin, Lincoln County, West Virginia; is the son of William M. and Bettie Mayo Wysong; was born February 13, 1876; was educated at Hillboro Male and Female Academy, where he won the debater's medal for oratory and scholarship; at Hampden-Sidney College, Virginia, where he carried off medals for distinguished scholarship, public speaking, etc.; graduated in law from the West Virginia University in the class of 1896, with the degree of Bachelor of Laws. He was admitted to the Bar of Webster County in August, 1897, and later was received as a practitioner in the Circuit Courts of the adjoining counties of Nicholas, Braxton, Upshur, Harrison and Randolph, where he was employed in important controverted cases. He is a public speaker of prominence and an advocate and trial lawyer of unusual power and ability. He very soon took high rank, especially on the criminal side of the courts. He has a large and profitable clientage in the State and Federal Courts in civil as well as criminal cases,

A. JAY VALENTINE

especially in the Supreme Court of the State. He is tender in his sympathies, warm in his attachments, and is a man of refined social qualities. He is a lawyer of excellent attainments, and is thoroughly acquainted with the history and character of West Virginia jurisprudence. Whilst he is a man of earnest and intense convictions, his actions and expressions are always tempered with mildness and discretion. Hence he is respected and esteemed by men of all classes and politics.

Mr. Wysong is an adherent of the Democratic party, and is one of its most popular stump speakers. He enjoys mixing with the people as a sort of side issue, more for recreation than for political preferment. He filled the office of Mayor of the town of Webster Springs during 1907 and 1908, and was twice elected, in 1911 and 1913, by the people of Webster County to the Legislature of the State. Being a ready debater he took an active part in the legislation of those two sessions. He is a member of the Southern Methodist Church, is a Freemason and a member of the Greek Letter College Fraternity of Phi Gamma Delta.

He was married April 18, 1900, to Miss Mattie L. Wooddell, of Webster Springs, and has one son — William Prentiss Wysong, aged fifteen. Their home is at the famous summer resort of Webster Springs, which the citizens of that section claim is the Eldorado of the universe, and they are not far wrong in the arguments they set up for its medicinal properties. It is great medicinal water.

## Hon. Charles G. Coffman, B.S., LL.B.

Mr. Coffman is a native of Harrison County, West Virginia; is a son of John M. and Cornelia J. Coffman; was born August 30, 1875; attended Salem College, at Salem, West Virginia, from which he graduated with the degree of Bachelor of Science in the class of 1898; attended the West Virginia University and graduated from the Law Department in 1904, taking the degree of Bachelor of Laws. The year he left the University he was admitted to membership in the Harrison County Bar, where he has since practiced in all branches of the law, with more than ordinary success, in all the State and Federal Courts of West Virginia. He is a gifted advocate, and tries his cases with unusual fervor and earnestness. He is a man ot integrity and reliability, and is upright and just in all of his dealings both as a lawyer and a citizen. He takes unusual pride in the civic development of Clarksburg and Harrison County, and is a thrifty, progressive, enterprising citizen.

In politics Mr. Coffman is an enthusiastic Republican, and is always relied upon by his party friends for active service in all campaigns before the people. He was the Republican candidate for Mayor of the city of Clarksburg in 1906, and was elected to the West Virginia State Senate in 1908 and served for the full term of four years. Being a superior debater, he took an active part in the legislation of that period and was a member of several of the leading committees of the body. He was elected Secretary of the Republican State Executive Committee in 1916 and is efficiently filling that responsible position at the present time (1918). He was chosen Vice-President of the West Virginia Bar Association in 1914, and again in 1918.

Senator Coffman married Miss Alma E. Haymaker, of Clarksburg, October 14, 1909, by whom he has two sons and one daughter. He is a member of the Methodist Episcopal Church, the Masonic, Odd Fellows and Elks Fraternities, and the Delta Tau Delta College Frat. He has the confidence and respect of the people generally who have the honor of his acquaintance, and is warm-hearted and generous even to a fault.

## D. H. Hill Arnold, A.B., LL.B.

Mr. Arnold is the son of Thomas J. and Eugenia H. Arnold. He was born in the historic town of Beverly, Randolph County, West Virginia, January 18, 1879, and received his early training in the common schools of that rather ancient borough. Later he matriculated as a student at Washington and Lee University, Lexington, Virginia, and graduated in the classical course, in the class of 1900, with the degree of Bachelor of Arts. He then entered the Law Department of Michigan University at Ann Arbor, and graduated therefrom in its law class of 1902, with the degree of Bachelor of Laws, and was admitted to the membership of the Randolph County Bar at the city of Elkins, in the fall of the year he left the University of Michigan, where he has since practiced, with the exception of a short time spent at San Diego, California. He is the senior member of the firm of Arnold & Arnold, his brother, E. H. Arnold, being the junior member, who is now, however, Field Clerk, Intelligence Department of the United States Army service, and has been since 1913. The firm's practice is of a general character, and embraces all branches of the profession in all the State and Federal Courts within the limits of West Virginia.

Our subject, who entered the practice splendidly equipped, from an educational point of view, coupled with the facts that he is a man of high moral character and a hard worker, have given him a high standing as an attorney wherever he is known. He has never been a candidate for any political office, although he is a Democrat, and his county is largely of that political faith, and a nomination for any political office is equivalent to an election. This shows that he prefers the law to politics, and is further proof of the fact that he loves his profession and is in it to win. He is an earnest student of the law, and has established a reputation for carefulness in the handling of cases, and of answering "ready" when they are called for trial. He is also accurate in their preparation, and is both energetic and forceful in a courthouse controversy. Coupled with strict integrity, these qualifications invariably lead to ultimate success.

Mr. Arnold married Miss Rebecca R. Andrews, of Staunton, Virginia, August 4, 1914, and they are the parents of two children. He is a member of the Presbyterian Church, the Masons and Elks, the West Virginia Bar Association, the Rotary Club and the Kappa Alpha Fraternity.

---

## James R. W. Morris, Jr.

Mr. Morris was born in the city of Moundsville, West Virginia, June 11, 1887, and died in Charleston, West Virginia, October 9, 1918, of Spanish influenza, after only a few days' illness. He received his education in the Moundsville public schools, including a full course in the High School of that city, graduating in 1904. He also took the full course in Elliott's Business College, Wheeling, West Virginia, becoming an expert in stenography and typewriting, and in business matters generally. He entered the West Virginia University and after two years' close application, graduated from the Law Department of that institution in the class of 1909, and was admitted to the Moundsville Bar in the fall of that year, and entered upon the regular practice of his profession with flattering prospects. He, however, was tendered the position of Law Clerk by Judge W. N. Miller, of the Supreme Court of Appeals of West Virginia; he, therefore, closed his law office, came to Charleston, and remained in that position until his untimely death. He was attentive to his duties, and was an efficient Clerk. He was methodical and careful in his work, and was thoroughly reliable and trustworthy. All the while he was a close student of the law, and was fitting himself for regular practice in the future.

He was for nearly two years Secretary of the State Bar Association, and was well and favorably known by the members of the Association throughout the entire State, and to all of them his demise was a shock and a sorrow.

He was united in marriage with Miss Eva Woodruff, of Moundsville, in 1910, but they had no offspring. His charming, broken-hearted wife survives him. He was a member of the Masonic Fraternity, but was not a communicant of any religious organization. He was one of the publishers of this volume, and was its real business manager; for such work he was specially equipped. Now that he is gone, his associate fears that some errors will necessarily be found.

By nature he was kind and affectionate, and had many friends. His entire life was without a blemish or a flaw. Peace to his ashes, and rest to his soul. We knew no cleaner, upright man than was young Walter Morris.

## Henry A. Nolte, LL.B.

Our subject, son of Henry and Hannah (Carl) Nolte, was born in Benwood, Marshall County, West Virginia, October 7, 1876, and received a liberal education in the public schools of his native city and at Waynesburg College, Waynesburg, Pennsylvania. Later he was graduated from the Law Department of the West Virginia University with the degree of Bachelor of Laws. He was admitted to practice shortly after his graduation, in 1904, in the Circuit Court of Monongalia County, and has since practiced in the State and Federal Courts of West Virginia, principally in the city of Wheeling.

He later located in the city of Wheeling, where he now resides. His practice embraces all branches of the law common to the courts of West Virginia, and also the responsible position of Assistant Attorney-General of the State of West Virginia, an office especially requiring thorough familiarity with the statutes of the State, as he is required to appear on behalf of the State, in many important cases, as assistant to the Prosecuting Attorneys, when important questions arise, which often occurs, in which the State itself is concerned, wherein transcendent questions are frequently raised, and legal knowledge above the average is essential to protect the interests of the people at large. It is his duty also to assist the Attorney-General to construe the acts of the Legislature when called upon so to do by the subordinate law officers of the different counties. It is, therefore, not only an important, but it is also a most difficult position to fill. Mr. Nolte has been in his present responsible position since March 4, 1917, and is rendering faithful and satisfactory service.

Mr. Nolte married Miss Louisa Kunkle and has three children, and resides in the city of Wheeling. He, however, is required to reside at the Capital of the State during the tenure of his present office.

He is a member of the Orders of Elks and Moose, and is an active, thoroughgoing citizen of the Commonwealth.

## Buckner Clay, B.A., LL.B.

Mr. Clay, son of Ezekiel F. and Mary Woodford Clay, was born near Paris, Kentucky, December 31, 1877. He received his academic education at the Kentucky University, graduating in the class of 1897, and was awarded the classical degree of Bachelor of Arts, *in cursu*. Thereafter he entered the University of Virginia as a student of law, and in 1900 graduated therefrom with the degree of Bachelor of Laws. He was admitted as a member of the Paris, Kentucky, Bar the year of his graduation, and remained there until June, 1903, when he moved his residence to Charleston, West Virginia, and became a member of the able and well-known law firm of Price, Smith, Spilman & Clay, where he has since practiced with much more than ordinary success.

Mr. Clay is a young man of sound morals, high grade integrity, well educated and thoroughly grounded in legal principles. He is a zealous worker, a close student, of sound judgment and a careful pleader. He has thus far revealed no taste for politics, or any occupation that would, in the least, detract from his duties as a lawyer. He never held an office, and never sought one. His pride alone is in his profession, and thus far he has made unusual progress. This is a strong reason why his knowledge of the law is broad and exact. He is methodical and laborious in the preparation of his cases, and is always well armed with precedent and authority. Necessarily, therefore, he is a safe and successful trial lawyer. The firm of which Mr. Clay is the junior member covers all branches of the law in all the State and United States Courts, and yet it may be said that they specialize in corporation and commercial causes. All of the members of the firm are lawyers of ability, and can maintain themselves in any sort of a law or chancery cause, and therefore are well informed in any branch of the profession. The court dockets show that they are employed in a large number of important litigations, and that they are never short of a large and profitable clientele. All of them are not only known as thoroughly equipped lawyers, but they are also known as men of high grade personal characters and thoroughly reliable, trustworthy gentlemen.

Mr. Clay is a Democrat, is married and maintains a beautiful residence in the Capital City of West Virginia.

## Judge J. Frank Maynard, LL.B.

Our subject was born at Honaker, Virginia, January 26, 1875, and was educated at Tazewell College, Tazewell County, Virginia, and in the Law Department of the West Virginia University at Morgantown, graduating in the class of 1899 with the degree of Bachelor of Laws; located at Bluefield in Mercer County, and was admitted to the Mercer County Bar in 1900 and opened a law office in the city of Bluefield, where he conducted a successful and lucrative business until his election by the people as Judge of the Criminal Court of Mercer County in 1908, where he has since served with great acceptability, and is now serving his second term.

The first office he ever filled was Assistant Clerk of the House of Delegates of West Virginia from 1901 to 1903 inclusive; was City Attorney of Bluefield in 1903; was appointed United States Commissioner for the Southern District of West Virginia in 1902, and resigned in 1905; was elected Prosecuting Attorney of Mercer County in the campaign of 1904, and served four years with great efficiency. In the campaign of 1908 he was elected Judge of the Criminal Court of the county, as stated above. Before his elevation to the Bench, he had succeeded in building up a lucrative practice. He was attentive to his business; is an efficient advocate; tried his cases well, and was one of the popular attorneys of Mercer County. His personal character is above reproach, and he has the confidence and respect of all the people of his section of the State. He is a well-informed lawyer and is an industrious and faithful worker. In politics he has always been a stanch Republican. He is large of stature, commanding in appearance, is social and agreeable and has a large following of personal friends. His energy and integrity, his knowledge of law, his sound views of justice make him an excellent Judge. He is firm in his convictions, yet tolerant of the opinions of others, and never obtrudes or urges the reception of his views as a condition of his courtesy and regard.

As a lawyer he was habitually calm, abhorred the methods of artifice, and spurned a cause which he believed unjust. These features of his character engaged confidence in him as a lawyer and a Judge, and the highest respect for him as a man. He is unswerving in his integrity and devotion to principle and conscientiously faithful to the interests of his clients. He is comparatively a young man, and there is yet a bright future before him.

He is married and is a member of the Orders of the Elks and the Eagles. His residence is in the city of Bluefield.

## Captain Kemble White, A.B., LL.B.

Captain White, son of Hon. Henry S. and Lovia Fields White, was born at Bellton, Marshall County, West Virginia, April 5, 1873, and was educated in the public schools of his native county and at the West Virginia University, from which he was graduated A.B. in the class of 1894. Later he took the law course in the same institution, graduating LL.B. in the class of 1900. He was admitted to the Morgantown Bar in the fall of that year, and shortly thereafter located in the city of Fairmont, Marion County, where he has since successfully practiced. His practice embraced, for a time, all branches of the law, but of late years he has specialized in oil and gas litigations in which he has become quite an authority.

He was Captain of a company in the First West Virginia Infantry Regiment of Volunteers in the Spanish-American War; was a good soldier and served faithfully until the close of the war. He promptly returned to his law office, and devoted his time and his energies to the rehabilitation of his business which had scattered and largely disappeared during his absence in the field. He recouped rapidly and now has a large and profitable clientele.

He is a Republican in politics, but has never aspired to any public office, preferring to devote all of his time to his profession, in which he has been remarkably successful. His one predominating thought and purpose is to reach the highest possible standard as a lawyer, and his aspirations in this respect have been abundantly rewarded. He, therefore, as a lawyer, whether judged with reference to work performed or pecuniary gain, has reached an enviable position among his fellows. He has a superior analytical mind, and, therefore, is naturally as well as by education, fitted for the law. In his preparation for court trials he is thorough and tactful, and better than all, he can always be found at his post of duty. Such men rarely, if ever, fail to reach the goal of their ambition.

Captain White during the European War has rendered valuable service to the Government as Chairman of the Selective Draft Board of the city of Fairmont.

Captain White is married, has two children and resides at Fairmont. His home-life is ideal. Naturally hopeful and happy, his hours with his family and friends are always social and joyous.

## Felix Clarence Pifer, A.M.

Our subject is a native of Buckhannon, Upshur County, Virginia, where he was born January 28, 1856. His parents were Jacob B. and Cecilia Pifer, well known citizens of Upshur County. Our subject, after attending the public schools in rudimentary training, entered Allegheny College, at Meadville, Pennsylvania, from which historic institution he graduated in the classical course, in June, 1878, with the degree of Bachelor of Arts. Three years later he received the degree of Master of Arts *in cursu*. He read law, and was admitted to the Bar of Upshur County in 1880. While engaged in building up a law practice at Buckhannon he published the "Buckhannon Delta," a Republican newspaper, for several years. He was an active developer of the material interests and resources of Buckhannon and Upshur County, and vigorously aided in bringing the natural advantages of that section to the attention of the general public. He, along with other leading citizens, secured the location at Buckhannon of a large window glass factory and establishing a water and light plant for the city, which put it on the map as a progressive inland city.

With the object in view of seeking the larger advantages of an aspiring attorney, Mr. Pifer moved from Buckhannon to the city of Huntington in December, 1910, where he remained three years in the practice of his profession. He, however, saw, he thought, a better opportunity for an ambitious lawyer at the Capital of the State; moved to Charleston and formed a partnership with the Hon. Adam B. Littlepage, with whom he remained three years, and then opened an office on his own account, in the Charleston National Bank building, where he has since conducted a successful and profitable business.

Mr. Pifer is thoroughly grounded in the law, is an amiable and courteous gentleman, and is popular with his brother attorneys. He is a hard-working, painstaking attorney, prepares his cases with great care and has a good standing with his brother attorneys of the Charleston Bar. He has prac-

F. C. PIFER

ticed in the Circuit Courts of Upshur, Cabell and Kanawha counties, in the Supreme Court of Appeals of West Virginia, the Federal Courts within the State, and has tried several important cases in the Supreme Court of the United States. He is a safe and sane trial lawyer, states his cases clearly, and argues them with force. His practice extends into all the branches of the profession. He has always been a hard student and devotes his entire time to his office and court work. In politics he is a pronounced Republican and takes an interest in politics, but has never sought an office of any character, and has never been a candidate for any office whatever. He prefers the routine work of the plodding, work-a-day lawyer to the excitement and uncertainties of the professional politician and an ''in-and-out'' office-holder and office-seeker. Good lawyers, as a rule, only intermeddle with politics as a side issue.

He married Miss Sarah Ann Teece, June 4, 1885, and has three children — one daughter and two sons. He is a member of the Presbyterian Church, and has been a member of the Masonic Fraternity for about thirty-five years. He has, on a number of occasions, acted as Special Judge in holding different terms of Circuit Courts, and gave general satisfaction to lawyers and suitors.

## Captain Charles McCamic, LL.B.

Our subject ranks among the well-known younger members of the legal profession in West Virginia, and is actively engaged in the practice as a member of the firm of McCamic & Clarke in the City of Wheeling. He was born in the City of Wellsburg, Brooke County, West Virginia, December 4, 1874, and is a son of Nathan and Frances Dowden McCamic well-to-do citizens of the '' Northern Pan Handle '' of the State. He was educated in the schools of his native section, Linsly Institute (Wheeling), and at Yale University, from which nation-wide institution he graduated in the Law Department with the degree of LL.B.

After graduating from college Mr. McCamic located in the City of Moundsville, twelve miles below Wheeling on the Ohio River, and was admitted as a practitioner in the courts of Marshall and adjoining counties. Shortly thereafter he was admitted as an attorney in the United States District and Circuit Courts, and later on he became an attorney in the Supreme Court of the United States. He has practiced his profession with unabating ardor, and has won an enviable reputation and a profitable clientage. He is of medium height and of well-knit symmetrical figure; a vigorous and logical speaker and is potential on the platform of public assemblies, and enjoys the friendship and esteem of his fellow-citizen, irrespective of party politics He is married and lives in a palatial residence in the City of Moundsville, but his principal law office and place of business is in the City of Wheeling, where his well-known firm has a large and profitable clientage.

CAPTAIN CHARLES McCAMIC

From early manhood Mr. McCamic has had a rather strong liking for political life, although in no respect can he be termsd an office-seeker. The first and only political office he has ever held was a member of the West Virginia Legislature from Marshall County, to which he was elected as a Republican by the people of the county in 1903. Being a good judge of men, and always at his post of duty, he proved himself to be a valuable and influential representative.

For a number of years he has been a member of the State Bar Association, and from 1908 to 1916 he was the efficient Secretary of the Association, and is well and favorably known to all of the members of that able body of West Virginia attorneys. He is a member of the Masonic Fraternity and the Presbyterian Church.

He was among the very first young West Virginia lawyers to volunteer in the United States Army in the war against the German Empire and received a commission as Captain and saw active service with the 27th Division in said war.

He is a member of the National Art Club (New York City), the Edgewood Country Club (Charleston, West Virginia), Fort Henry Club, Wheeling, and the Country Club and University Club, also of Wheeling.

## Hon. Edgar Granville Rider

Mr. Rider, son of Benjamin E. and Teressa Rider, was born near Sutton, Braxton County, West Virginia, September 24, 1868. He received his preliminary training in the public schools of his native county. Later he matriculated as a student at the National Normal School, Lebanon, Ohio, where he remained two years (1888 and 1889) in the Academic Department. He then entered Washington and Lee University at Lexington, Virginia, from which he graduated in the Law Department in the class of 1893. He promptly returned to his native county of Braxton and began life as a lawyer by being admitted to the Bar of that county at Sutton, the seat of justice of the county, in June of that year. His life as a lawyer, whether judged with reference to labor performed or pecuniary gain, must be classed as honorable and successful. His career is an example of sound judgment, fidelity and painstaking preparation, and above all of absolute fairness and a scrupulous cultivation of the best traditions of the profession, and a stainless observance of its best methods. He is accurate in the preparation of his cases and in the giving of advice to litigants. His pronounced integrity has always been equal to his accuracy. Through his entire career he has always carried above him the white flower of a blameless life.

Mr. Rider in politics has always been a Republican. He, as the nominee of that party, was elected in 1904 Prosecuting Attorney of Braxton County, notwithstanding the fact the county, as a rule, returns large Democratic majorities. During his term of four years he proved to be a just and fear-

HON. EDGAR G. RIDER

less prosecutor. He never dealt in fears or favors, but saw to it that any violator of the law got exactly what was coming to him and no more nor less.

For quite a number of years he was a Referee in Bankruptcy for the Southern District of West Virginia. He resigned this office in September of 1916, when he was appointed by Governor H. D. Hatfield a member of the Public Service Commission of West Virginia to fill out the unexpired term of the late Gov. William M. O. Dawson, deceased, who was a member of said Commission. He was reappointed to the same office February 21, 1917, and is still serving on said Commission. This office in rank, influence and responsibility is, perhaps, in all respects, equal to that of the Governor, and even carries a larger salary. Mr. Rider has met the expectations of the public in measuring up to the requirements of this great office.

Mr. Rider married Miss Laura Morrison, of Braxton County, December 26, 1894, by whom he has three children. He is devoted to his home, and loves the evening communion of the family circle, and takes special delight in his associations with his friends and neighbors. He is a Freemason of high rank and is an active and useful member of the Methodist Episcopal Church.

## Russell S. Ritz

Mr. Ritz was born February 21, 1886, on the Ohio River, in Wayne County, West Virginia; attended public schools until the age of 14, during which time he lived and worked on his parents' farm. At the age of 14 he studied telegraphy, and after three months of this study he procured employment as a telegraph operator and worked as such for various railroads. After four years' service he was promoted to Train Dispatcher. He resigned in order to attend school at Marshall College. The following year he began the study of law at the West Virginia University and completed the course of studies in the Law Department at that institution in January, 1909. Immediately thereafter he engaged in the active practice of the law in Mercer County, locating at Bluefield, where he became a member of the law firm of Ritz & Ritz, which was composed of Harold A. Ritz, his older brother, now a Supreme Court Judge, and himself. He continued as a member of that firm until April, 1913, when the partnership was dissolved, and he began practice on his own account. His practice has been of an active character, being represented almost exclusively by litigations in the Circuit Courts of Virginia and West Virginia, and in the Supreme Courts of these two States, as well as in the Federal District Court for the Southern District of West Virginia and the Western District of Virginia, and of the Federal Circuit Court of Appeals for the Fourth Judicial Circuit. He has engaged in no outside business of any kind, but has given his entire time and efforts to the study and practice of his profession, in which he has been remarkably successful, and is ranked among

RUSSELL S. RITZ

the coming young men of the profession in the southern portion of the State.

He was married June 30, 1909, to Miss Cleon Boggess, as a result of which union two children have been born — Eleanor Cleon and Jean Elizabeth. In politics he is a Republican, and held the office of Assistant Prosecuting Attorney of Mercer County from 1912 to 1916. He is a member of the Masonic Fraternity and is also a member of the Presbyterian Church. He was nominated as a member of the West Virginia Legislature in 1918, but declined to accept the proffered honor.

## Ashton File, Jr.

Mr. File is a member of the able and well-established law firm of File & File at Beckley, the county seat of Raleigh County. He was born on a farm near Ransons, Buckingham County, Virginia, January 3, 1879. His parents were Ashton and Louisa (Tucker) File. He was educated in the public schools of Virginia and the Law Department of the West Virginia University, and was admitted to the Bar of Fayette County, West Virginia, in 1901. He remained a short time in that county and finally settled in the City of Beckley, in the adjoining County of Raleigh, where his firm has extended its business to large proportions, and is steadily increasing its already large clientele. He is a Democrat in his political faith, but has thus far shown but little interest in politics, and has not sought political promotion. The only office he has ever held was Mayor of the City of Beckley one term. He proved to be a faithful and progressive official. His practice has been general, and his learning embraces all branches of the law, and extends into all the courts of West Virginia, both State and Federal. His firm has a profitable practice in the Supreme Court of Appeals of the State.

His intuitive perception, close analysis and accurate judgment enable him promptly to resolve the gist of a legal proposition and to discriminate between the specious and the real, between truth and error, which enable him to impress his positions with a certainty difficult to assail or avoid. He has cultivated the habit of preparing his cases with unsparing pains and thorough research, and his powers of analogy and knowledge of precedent afford him abundant resources of parity of reasoning in the trial of his cases. He is a man of amiable qualities and courteous manners, and has been successful in his laudable undertakings, both as a lawyer and a citizen. He has demeaned himself uprightly, and stands with the moral element of the people of his city and county.

Mr. File was united in wedlock with Miss Frances Nancy Wiggin, June 14, 1911. They have two children — Dwight Ashton and Mary Frances File.

He is a member of the Masonic and Elks organizations, and as we have already stated, of the Democratic party, and is an enterprising, progressive citizen of his adopted State.

ASHTON FILE

## J. Bernard Handlan, LL.B.

Among the well-known, successful lawyers of the city of Wheeling is the subject of this sketch. He is a son of Hon. William C. Handlan, who, for a number of years, was one of the leading business men of Wheeling and wielded a large influence in that community. The son was born in Wheeling, November 29, 1868. He received his primary education in the Eighth Ward public schools. Later he entered St. Vincent's Academy at Wheeling, and took the complete course in the higher branches of education, including the Latin language and the sciences. After completing the course at St. Vincent's, in 1893, he matriculated in the Law Department of the University of Virginia at Charlottesville, and graduated with the degree of Bachelor of Laws in the class of 1894. He forthwith returned to Wheeling, was admitted to the Bar, and since then has practiced unremittingly in that city until the present time. As a rule, most young lawyers enjoy, and really delight to mix in politics. Mr. Handlan, while a pronounced Democrat in his convictions, has never sought to make a business out of politics; but on the contrary, has devoted his time and energies exclusively to the study and practice of the law. In this way he has made himself one of the leaders of the Wheeling Bar, and an attorney of force and usefulness in the profession. Consequently he has a large and profitable clientele. He has always been a hard student, and was never afraid of work. He is careful, clear-headed, systematic, vigilant and thorough in his work. These are essentials to any lawyer's success. He is also a cautious counselor. He does not advise the bringing of law suits for fees only. With him there must be some real, substantial hope of success before he orders the issuance of a *precipe*, which is a wise course for all lawyers to pursue. Because of special care in bringing suits, and attending to them after they are brought, Mr. Handlan can attribute his success at the Bar.

Mr. Handlan's practice is of a general character, and extends into all the State and Federal Courts. He specializes somewhat in corporation work, in which he has been measurably successful. He is public-spirited, and has devoted much valuable time, as a member of Council, to better the interests of the city of Wheeling. He was Prosecuting Attorney of Ohio County from 1908 to 1912, and saw to it that the State laws were vigorously enforced.

He has never married. In religion he is a Roman Catholic. In politics he is a loyal Democrat. He is a member of the West Virginia Bar Association and also holds membership in the Elks and the Knights of Columbus. He is patriotic and well-filled with civic pride and delights in the development and growth of his county and State. Any one who knows him will admit that "Bernie" Handlan is a good lawyer and a No. 1 citizen in every respect.

## Ole Everett Wyckoff

O. E. Wyckoff, son of Daniel B. and Susan Virginia Wyckoff, was born in Taylor County, West Virginia, September 6, 1878. This branch of the Wyckoff family came to America in 1637 and settled on Long Island, within a short distance of the end of the present Brooklyn, New York, Bridge, where the family remained for a term of years, and some of them moved to Western Virginia in what is now Taylor County, West Virginia, where our subject was born, as stated above. He received his education in the public schools of that section and in the well-known West Virginia College, a school of excellent standing, for many years, from which he graduated with an honorable record. He then became a student at the West Virginia University, receiving instruction in the higher branches of the University curriculum. He taught in the public schools of his native locality for four years, and having decided upon the law as a profession, he studied legal textbooks in the law office of Charles Preston Guard at Grafton, the seat of justice of Taylor County. He re-entered the West Virginia University for the purpose of ocmpleting his law studies in 1903, and in 1904 he successfully passed the required examination, and was admitted to practice at the City of Grafton in May, 1904, where he has since resided, and is conducting a successful and profitable law business. His reputation is that of a sound chancery lawyer, who gives close attention to his business in the State and Federal Courts, which has steadily increased since the day he "hung out his shingle." He is retained counsel for a number of corporations, among which are the Taylor County Bank at Grafton, the Flemington Bank, etc. He has also handled several estates of considerable proportions. He has served as Commissioner in Chancery, Commissioner of Accounts, Attorney for the City of Grafton, and is now and has been since 1907 Referee in Bankruptcy in the United States Court for the Northern District of West Virginia. His reputation all the while has been that of a conscientious, painstaking attorney, who deals justly and honorably with all men in all of his business transactions.

While he is a Republican in politics, and his resident county is stoutly of his political faith, he has never sought political favors, because he loves his profession, and adheres to it with tenacity and remarkable fidelity; consequently he is a sound and safe lawyer, and has a profitable clientele.

Mr. Wyckoff married Miss Mayme Bailey, of Flemington, West Virginia, July 12, 1905, and they have one son — Everett Bailey Wyckoff — who was born July 21, 1906. Among their friends they are social, joyful and happy. They are members of the First Baptist Church of the Ctiy of Grafton, and are reliable citizens of that community.

## Edmund Caskie Harrison

Born at Sewanee, Tennessee, May 8, 1882. He moved to Charleston, West Virginia, in the year 1907 and there became associated with the undersigned in the practice of law. His life was devoted to study and close association with his family. By inclination and heredity he was a student, and his scholarly attainments were manifest in all his professional and private activities. He had no military training and no aptitude for the strenuous, but he grasped the democratic idea of a national army, and with the quiet conviction so characteristic of all he did, determined to enter the ranks of a fighting regiment. On April 24, 1918, at Camp Lee, he enlisted as a private in Battery A, 313th Field Artillery. On May 26th, he sailed with his battery for France, there took part in the fierce fighting of the 80th division, and was killed by a German shell, November 1, 1918.

Mr. Harrison was a brilliant lawyer, a zealous advocate, a good citizen, an unselfish friend, a self-effacing associate. His answer to the call of his country, his voluntary service in duties foreign to all his training and inclinations, his death in action were in keeping with his life.

His quiet modesty, his cheerful courage, the loyal dedication of his conspicuous ability to the common interests, and above all his gentleness and nobility of soul made him more than our respected associate; we honor the memory of a faithful friend, a beloved comrade, a noble spirit.

NOTE.—The above brief memorial was prepared and signed by every member of the firm of Price, Smith, Spilman & Clay, of which firm Mr. Harrison was a member.—EDITOR.

## Judge George W. Atkinson, LL.B., LL.D.

A history of the Bench and Bar of West Virginia would be incomplete if no mention were made of the distinguished public services and especially of the honorable judicial record of Judge George W. Atkinson. Hence the publishers of this work insisted on a brief representation, in these pages, of the author, notwithstanding his objections thereto. Accordingly, they have prepared this sketch and in deference to Judge Atkinson's innate modesty have compressed it within very narrow limits.

Judge Atkinson was born on an Elk River farm in Kanawha County, June 29, 1845. After securing such advantages as could be obtained from the schools of that county, he attended Ohio Wesleyan University and was graduated therefrom in 1870. He took his law course at Howard University, Washington, D. C., and was admitted to the Bar in 1875.

From early life, Judge Atkinson has been active in civil and political affairs. West Virginia has no son whom the people have more delighted to

JUDGE GEORGE W. ATKINSON

honor with official preferment. In 1881 he was appointed United States marshal for the District of West Virginia, and held the position for four years, administering the office in a manner that won the special commendation of the Department of Justice. In 1888, while a resident of Wheeling, he was elected a member of Congress from the First Congressional District. Declining a re-election, he devoted himself to the practice of his profession in Wheeling until 1896, when he was elected to the governorship of West Virginia, the first Republican to hold the office since 1871.

The administration of Governor Atkinson was marked by a high degree of executive ability, and a continued strengthening of his party, which his retirement from office left free from factional differences and personal quarrels. This was largely due to his pleasant and agreeable personality, and the diplomatic methods which are natural with him. Possibly no other Governor of the State has ever left the executive office carrying with him in so great a degree the esteem of his party and the people generally.

Shortly after his retirement from the office of Governor, he was appointed United States District Attorney for the Southern District of West Virginia, and held that position until April 15, 1905, when President Roosevelt appointed him a member of the United States Court of Claims. After serving eleven years, he retired from the Bench, as he had earned the right to do, on April 17, 1916, and that occasion was marked by addresses by many men prominent in the life of the nation, eulogistic of his life and character and of his service upon the Bench.

Upon retirement from the Bench he did not cease the indefatigable industry which has characterized his whole life. The acceptable service he rendered as President of the West Virginia Bar Association and the valuable contribution he has made in preparing and preserving the history of the Bench and Bar of the State in this volume are incidents in his active life. His strong literary bent, aside from his legal, official and other work, is manifest in a number of books he has written on various subjects which were published at intervals in his busy career.

In addition to his other activities, Judge Atkinson has achieved high rank in fraternal circles. He became a member of the Masonic fraternity when a very young man. In 1876–7 he was Grand Master of the Grand Lodge of West Virginia, and was Grand Secretary from 1885 to 1905, a period of 20 years.

He has been a member of the Methodist Episcopal Church since his early youth, and his long church service and consistent life have given him wide influence with church people. He was a lay delegate to the general conference of the Church in 1876 and again in 1888. His religious views he has consistently adhered to and splendidly exemplified throughout his long and honorable business, political and professional career.

Judge Atkinson has long held a prominent place among public speakers in West Virginia, and his presence has been in demand at hundreds of meetings of many different kinds. Not only as a stumper of rare ability in political campaigns, but as a lecturer and platform speaker on a vast number of literary, religious and Masonic subjects he has made a reputation far wider than the limits of his native State.

In 1868 he was married to Miss Ellen Eagan, member of a well-known Kanawha County family. She died a number of years ago, leaving five children. In 1897 he was married again, this time to Mrs. Myra Horner Camden, widow of the late Judge G. D. Camden, of Clarksburg, and they reside in Charleston.

To his three daughters, two sons and a number of grandchildren he devotes such time as he may from the demands made upon him by the myriad friends of his boyhood and early manhood, and the time thus spent amid the scenes of his youth and his early triumphs is to him the happiest of the passing years. Kindly by nature, generous to a fault, true to his friends and his convictions, knowing no distinction in rank among men, except that marked by character, he is a fine type of the sturdy American boy grown to be a man of influence and power among his own people and of usefulness to the State and Nation.

THE PUBLISHERS